THE ESKIMOS

THE ESKIMOS

THEIR ENVIRONMENT AND FOLKWAYS

BY

Edward Moffat Weyer

ARCHON BOOKS
1969

Copyright 1932 by Yale University Press
Reprinted 1962, 1969 with permission
in an unaltered and unabridged edition

SBN: 208 00837 3
Library of Congress Catalog Card Number: 77-91393
Printed in the United States of America

TO MY FATHER

WITH

DEEPEST GRATITUDE AND RESPECT

PREFACE

THIS book is an endeavor to portray the life of the Eskimos as revealed through their customs and beliefs and to describe the environmental conditions under which they live. In order to include all the various tribes or groups in the study, the author has drawn information widely from other writers on the subject. To this variety of information the author has added the results of his own investigations in the region of Bering Straits.

The book had its inception in the Stoll-McCracken Arctic Expedition of 1928, and was completed, after various interruptions, just before the writer departed with the Peary Memorial Expedition to Smith Sound, Greenland. Approximately the first half of the manuscript was prepared as a dissertation for the degree of Doctor of Philosophy at Yale University.

The author wishes to express his deep gratitude to Vilhjalmur Stefansson and to William Thalbitzer for their very helpful criticisms. Similarly, he extends his thanks to Diamond Jenness of the National Museum of Canada; also to the Canada Department of Marine and Fisheries for supplying climatic data and other information. And to Clark Wissler and the American Museum of Natural History, he is especially grateful for the opportunity to carry on some of the observations contained in this volume.

E. M. W., Jr.

June, 1932

CONTENTS

CONTENTS

THE ESKIMOS

CHAPTER I

POSITION OF ESKIMOS AMONG PEOPLES OF THE WORLD

Distribution and Population

THE western limit of the Eskimos is in the region of Bering Strait, where Asia and North America lie closest to each other. On the Asiatic side of this narrow neck of water dwell some twelve hundred natives of Eskimo stock, the westernmost representatives of this people. Eastward to Labrador and to the east coast of Greenland, a distance of about thirty-four hundred miles, extends the province of the Eskimos. This belt embraces about 140 degrees of longitude, an actual distance longer than that from San Francisco to New York by about eight hundred miles. From north to south the greatest breadth of this realm is between northwestern Greenland, where dwell the northernmost inhabitants of the world, and the southern portion of the Atlantic coast of Labrador, a distance about the same as that from northern Maine to the southern tip of Florida.

An extensive domain is this of the Eskimos. Yet its total population is only 35,800, approximately. To comprehend these figures more easily, it might be said that the entire Eskimo population, adults and children, could be seated in the Yale Bowl and not half of the seats would be occupied.

Itemized according to localities, the Eskimo people are distributed, according to recent data, as follows:

Siberia[1]	1,200
Alaska[2]	13,698
Mackenzie region[3] . . .	400
Copper Eskimos[4] . . .	750
Barren Grounds[5] . . .	1,000 (of whom less than 500 are classed as Caribou Eskimos)
Baffin Island[6]	1,513
Labrador[7]	2,500
Polar Eskimos[8]	271
West Greenland[9] . . .	13,847
East Greenland[10] . . .	709
Total	35,888

Stage of Culture

THE Eskimos are, of course, purely a hunting people. Unlike certain peoples of Arctic Siberia who herd reindeer they have domesticated on their own initiative no animals save the dog.

They derive their sustenance from all the natural world of their environment: they hunt mammals both of the land and sea, obtain fish from fresh and salt water, and supplement these activities by securing birds and their eggs. In certain districts they even draw upon the scanty plant foods of their habitat by gathering berries and collecting roots and herbs. All these sources combined supply food enough for only a very sparse population. The Eskimos dwell at the arctic frontier of the habitable world.

Their sustenance is by necessity almost entirely meat; and being short of fuel some of them eat much of their food raw. The very name "Eskimo," indeed, means "eater of raw meat," being derived from an expression applied to the people by certain Indians.

The use of the appellation by a man named Biard in 1611 seems to be the earliest record of the word.[11] The Maskegon Cree south of Hudson Bay are observed to use the form *eskimau,* plural *eskimawok,* meaning literally "those who eat raw meat," which is undoubtedly the same as our "Eskimo"; and the Wabanaki (Abnaki or Abenaki) of Maine are said to have used the word *eskimantsik.*[12]

The Eskimos possess many fine qualities, and their reputation among explorers is far better than that of many other primitive peoples. Hospitable even in time of scarcity, open-hearted rather than sullen and scheming, they generally inspire confidence. They are not vicious in disposition or savage, but they are unrestrained by civilized conventionalities. One is willing to allow for any uncommendable traits on the grounds that their ways must harmonize with their harsh habitat, and that hardship is their heritage. It is noteworthy that even though they are ever at the mercy of severe, inexorable circumstances, their outward manner, at least, is characteristically one of good humor and joviality.[13]

Second only to the marvel of their perfect adjustment to their environment is their conformity to the broadly human traits of mankind.

"For they do, certainly, react to the suffering, the sacrifices, the hardships and the mysteries of evil which they face much as we do.

Their philosophy, even when untouched by any influences of civilization, has many curiously modern slants, including such ideas as autosuggestion, spirit seances, and catalepsy. Their poetry has many resemblances to ours, and their religion and folklore often resemble, even in phrasing, as well as in content, our earlier religious literature."[14]

The story of a flood, for instance, is included in the mythology of the Alaskan Eskimos, those of the central area, and of Greenland.[15] Also in their amusements they manifest similarities to civilized peoples. One of their favorite games, for example, closely resembles soccer football.[16] Like many other peoples of the world they make "cat's cradles" with string.[17] These features of their culture are perhaps trivial; but they are cited as representative of many which render the Eskimos not utterly foreign and ununderstandable to us. In spite of the fact that their mental horizon is astonishingly narrow and that the singularities of their habitat force them to lead a highly specialized life, they are above all very human.

Cultural Uniformity

THE Eskimos are among the most widely distributed of primitive peoples. Extending from East Cape, Siberia, to eastern Greenland, they are distributed over a distance about the same as that from southern Alaska to Guatemala. Yet cultural sameness is strikingly characteristic of them. All groups speak dialects of the same language.[18] Rasmussen's knowledge of the Greenlandic tongue enabled him to understand all the Eskimo tribes between Hudson Bay and Bering Strait.[19] Only south of the Yukon was he unable to converse on difficult matters of faith and ceremonial.[20] Even the language of the Aleutian Islanders, who physically are not Eskimos, is related to Eskimo.[21] "Even if one cannot call them sister-languages, they bear the impress of a more distant relationship in the many features which they evidently have inherited in common from a mother-tongue."[22] The dialects of the arctic Indians, on the contrary, are not thus associated with Eskimo.

In physical characteristics differences are observable, to be sure, among the various groups of Eskimos. Some resemble more closely the American Indian, while others show closer similarity to the more purely Mongoloid type; generally, however, the divergence is wide only where there has been recent racial intermixture. In view of their wide distribution and the fact that small groups have lived in relative isolation for many generations while others

have been influenced by contact with other peoples, it is not surprising that some physical variations have developed.

It is not the purpose here to inquire deeply into the physical attributes of the Eskimos; a few words might be said, however, regarding
their cephalic index and stature. Cephalic index, which is the ratio between the breadth and the length of the head, is one of the most widely
used criteria for distinguishing racial subtypes. Data determining this
figure among a fairly large number of groups of Eskimos reveal that
regionally the averages vary between a maximum of 81.6 and a minimum of 73.9 for males, and 78.8 and 72.2 for females.[23] As for adult
stature, the average of all groups on which data are available is 5 ft.
4 in. (163.3 cm.) in the case of men and 5 ft. 0 in. (153.1 cm.) in the
case of women.[24] The widest departure of the average of a group from
the general average is only 2.3 in. (5.9 cm.) for men and 3 in. (7.7
cm.) for women. These maximum departures from the average are not
extremely wide; and it is possible that they give an exaggerated impression of divergence from type since they are averages of very small
groups, of eight and ten individuals, respectively.

In the material culture of the Eskimos, as in language, but little variety is to be found. The similarity in the material equipment of life is widespread. From Alaska to Greenland they tailor
fur clothing after much the same style. Most groups use the dog
sledge and the kayak. Most, again, heat their dwellings or cook
their food over a shallow, open lamp of stone or pottery, burning
animal fat. Their distinctive weapon, the harpoon, is in universal
use. It differs from every other missile in that its penetrating head
remains imbedded in the flesh of the animal, enabling the hunter to
retain his quarry on the end of a line. Everywhere the religious
practices and beliefs of the Eskimos conform to a general scheme;
the powers and rites of the ubiquitous shaman vary only in minor
detail from place to place. Many myths are told without radical
alteration in Alaska and Greenland. Of fifty-two stories recorded
by Rasmussen among the Pâdlimiut, west of Hudson Bay, no
fewer than thirty were identical with ones he had already heard in
Greenland; this in spite of the fact that for centuries no intercourse had taken place between the two groups of people.[25]

The Eskimos present, therefore, a singular study. Distributed
thinly over a vast area, where peculiar environmental conditions
have necessitated a highly specialized mode of life, they have developed a culture at once broadly uniform in all its subdivisions and
distinct in a large measure from every other culture of the world.

Scope of the Present Study

THE purpose of the following chapters is to study, in so far as it is possible, the Eskimos in their natural condition, unaffected by influence from without. Contact with white people has modified their culture in some measure, transforming them from a nature people to a hybrid of the primitive and the civilized. Their reactions to this penetration of civilized influence lie beyond the present discussion. Here we are concerned simply with their adjustment in isolation to their original life-conditions.

This approach is somewhat difficult. The trader, the explorer, and the missionary have left their mark, especially in Labrador, Greenland, and Alaska, but even to some degree in the central area. Far back even in the history of white influence on the North American continent Europeans visited and lived among the Eskimos. Some were led to this borderland of the inhabited earth by missionary zeal. The appeal of proselytism was strong. God's frozen children required redemption. More recently the "black-robes" traveled into the white north, apostles to the benighted aborigines. Often with inflexible zealotry they attempted to graft their highly developed and specialized civilized social order onto the sturdy but primitive trunk of Eskimo culture. In some cases the operation extracted the life strength from the heart of the native social organization. At best the result must be regarded as an artificial hybridization.

Besides offering a field for the missionary the land of the Eskimos has lured men with promise of economic profit. The quest for fur and lately for gold has drawn adventurers northward.

Through these carriers of white civilization the time-honored ways of the Eskimo have here and there been transformed. The rifle and canned foods have partly superseded the harpoon and the meat cache. All these changes lie beyond the present subject. Full attention will be given to the influence of environment in shaping Eskimo culture; hence, it is understood at the outset that we refer to the environment before white men wrought changes in the distribution and abundance of game and introduced resources not native to the region.

Environmental Influences and the Science of Anthropology

THE earth is the arena in which men work out their destinies.[26] Whether they be Kirghiz herders on central Asian grasslands,

Papuans in jungly New Guinea, or Eskimos of the arctic tundra, men are earthborn, earth nourished. All food primarily comes from the earth.

Nourishment and bodily protection, the biological requisites for life, must be procured. If not, extinction results. Hence, the primary human activities are those which secure these necessaries from the natural world. Nature offers them in a variety of forms; the methods by which men appropriate them to their use are many and diverse.

In their struggle for self-maintenance people are forced to conform to their life-conditions. Among these must be included every element of the natural environment, whether it affects them favorably or unfavorably: all animals and plants, microscopic organisms; minerals; destructive storm and productive rain; wind and flowing water; snow and ice. Natural environment exerts an especially obvious control over primitive people who live close to nature and have but slight contact with other parts of the world. Where there is transportation and trade, regional differences are smoothed out; but a people who dwell in isolation are limited by the products and conditions of their own habitat. Their culture develops in specialized adjustment to the particular habitat. The natural environment serves, indeed, as a framework on which their most fundamental activities are shaped. It determines largely the sort of food they eat, the kind of clothing they wear, the type of dwellings they inhabit, and the materials and tools with which they work. Besides these material responses to life-conditions, a complex of customs and beliefs grows out of the self-maintenance activities. These, likewise, reflect the environmental background.

Taken in a broad sense, these responses directed toward the securing of the primary necessaries of life are the self-maintenance mores. They chiefly determine the character of a primitive culture. Just as the foundation of an architectural structure largely controls its height and breadth, so do the self-maintenance mores limit and shape the social structure.

About the self-maintenance mores is woven the cultural pattern. They determine the dominant figure in the design. Without a strong central complex of self-maintenance adjustments the pattern can have no unnecessary decorations and frills. The critical area in the social fabric centers here. It is the sphere of greatest wear and tear, where weak threads are soonest worn out.

It follows that the laws of evolution are most decisive in regard to self-maintenance adjustments. This applies in cultural evolution as in organic evolution. Adaptability means survival; lack of adaptability means death of the individuals and extinction of the group. Balanced adjustment between man and his habitat is basic; expediency is the test for survival.

Eskimos and Environment

THE world is the stage, its products the properties in the human drama; and as these properties differ from place to place, and to some extent from season to season, so do men act differently.

Thus it is that the natural environment conditions culture—as the nest, so the bird. This is particularly applicable to the Eskimos, because of the extreme character of their arctic habitat and their isolation. In order to survive there on the very fringe of the habitable earth, where climatic conditions are less favorable and material resources so limited, they have had to develop a very highly specialized culture. Indeed, many of the features that distinguish the Eskimos as a people are responses to their peculiar life-conditions, either directly or indirectly. Examples of this are the blubber lamp; the snow house of the central tribes and the Labrador and Polar Eskimos; the kayak; and the technique of harpooning seals through their breathing holes in the ice.

So powerful is the environmental control over life within the Eskimo region that civilized people even during a brief stay there are forced to adopt many of the Eskimo traits, such as fur clothing, the dog sledge as a means of travel and transportation during the winter, a diet that is preponderantly meat, and, to some extent, Eskimo hunting methods.

Such illustrations suggest that many phases of Eskimo culture, particularly their self-maintenance mores, are results of their natural environment. Even more striking is the utter inability of the Eskimo culture to fit life-conditions outside of the arctic and subarctic regions, a point which will be clearer after their culture has been considered more fully.

True enough, some of the characteristics of the Eskimos, on the contrary, are only slightly or not at all influenced by natural environment. Language, aspects of their religion and social organization, and certain prominent physical characteristics have little or no relation to the natural conditions around them. Nevertheless, a comprehensive understanding of the people can be got only through an acquaintance with the habitat in which they wage their struggle for existence. For this reason an analysis of their natural environment has been chosen for the first topic in the following discussion. While this procedure departs somewhat from the usual plan of exposition in anthropological subjects, it is selected as the method most adaptable to the present subject; and it is hoped that anything sacrificed through what may seem to be a roundabout approach will be offset by an ultimate gain in clarity.

NOTES

1. Rasmussen: 1927, 355.
2. Fourteenth Census of the United States, 1920, III, 1158.
3. Rasmussen: 1927, 300.
4. Jenness: 1922, 42.
5. Birket-Smith: 1929, I, 65 ff.
6. Kitto: 1930, 28.
7. Hawkes: 1916, 22.
8. Heinbecker and Irvine-Jones: 1928, 396.
9. Birket-Smith: 1928, 19.
10. Birket-Smith: 1928, 19.
11. Cadzow: 1929.
12. Birket-Smith: 1928, 202, footnote; Birket-Smith: 1929, I, 58–59; Hall: 1864, 311. Byhan mentions that the same meaning is implied in the name of Samojed or Syrojed. (Byhan: 1909, 18.)
13. See pp. 247 f. and 253 f.
14. Rasmussen: 1927, Introduction, xii.
15. Nelson: 1899, 452; Boas: 1888, 637; Kroeber: 1899, 319.
16. Nelson: 1899, 333–336 (Yukon to Kuskokwim); Stefansson: 1914,

169 (Mackenzie Delta); Birket-Smith: 1929, II, 119 (Copper Eskimos and Netsilingmiut). Birket-Smith: 1929, I, 272–274 (Caribou Eskimos); Turner: 1887, 107 (Ungava District, Labrador); Hawkes: 1916, 114 (Labrador); Birket-Smith: 1924, 393 (West Greenland).
17. Birket-Smith: 1929, II, 204–205, Table A106; Nelson: 1899, 332 (Cape Darby to Kuskokwim, Alaska); Jenness: 1924 (Copper Eskimos); Birket-Smith: 1929, I, 276 ff. (Caribou Eskimos); Mathiassen: 1928, I, 222 ff. (Iglulik Eskimos); Kroeber: 1899, 298–299 (Polar Eskimos); Birket-Smith: 1924, 399–400 (West Greenland).
18. Stefansson: 1930, 44.
19. Rasmussen: 1927, Introduction, x, and 64.
20. Rasmussen: 1927, 349.
21. Birket-Smith: 1929, II, 228.
22. Thalbitzer: 1923a, 57; see also Thalbitzer: 1913a, 96.

23. *CEPHALIC INDEX OF ESKIMOS*

Group	Males No.	Males Mean	Females No.	Females Mean
Alaska	114	79.2(1)	..	...
Seward Peninsula	40	77.96(2)	..	...
St. Lawrence Island	63	79.7(3)	..	...
Southwest Alaska	61	80.7(3)	..	...
Point Hope	13	78.3(4)	..	...
Noatak River	11	81.6(4)	5	78.8(4)
Mackenzie Delta (Stone)	12	73.9(4)	6	75.2(4)
Mackenzie Delta (Jenness)	4	76.1(4)	..	...
Coronation Gulf	82	77.6(4)	42	76.6(4)

Group	Males No.	Males Mean	Females No.	Females Mean
Southampton Island	35	77.2(5)	..	...
Labrador	11	77.0(4)	10	74.5(4)
Labrador	8	76.11(6)	..	...
Greenland	614	76.8(7)	..	...
Smith Sound	8	78.0(4)	10	77.4(4)
Upernivik District	..	74.9(8)	..	72.2(8)
Nordost Bay	..	77.2(8)	..	76.5(8)
Disko Bay	..	78.0(8)	..	76.8(8)
Agto-Holsteinborg	..	77.8(8)	..	77.0(8)
Sukkertoppen-Godthaab	..	77.0(8)	..	75.9(8)
Fiskenaes-Frederikshaab	..	76.8(8)	..	76.4(8)
Julianehaab Bay	..	78.1(8)	..	76.8(8)
East Greenland	..	76.9(8)	..	75.6(8)
Southeast Greenland	22	75.7(4)	23	75.0(4)
Northeast Greenland	31	77.8(4)	15	76.5(4)

(1) Shapiro: 1931, 364 (after Boas).
(2) Shapiro: 1931, 364 (after Weyer).
(3) Shapiro: 1931, 364 (after Hrdlička).
(4) From table compiled by Jenness: 1923, 55b.
(5) Shapiro: 1931, 364 (after Tocher).
(6) Shapiro: 1931, 364 (after Pittard).
(7) Shapiro: 1931, 364 (after Deniker).
(8) Sören Hansen's summary, in Birket-Smith: 1928, 49.

24. These averages, computed from the following compilation (exclusive of the items wherein the number of individuals measured is not specified), are weighted according to the number of individuals in each case.

STATURE OF ADULT ESKIMOS

Group	Males No.	Males Mean	Females No.	Females Mean
Alaska	34	165.8(1)	..	....
Alaska	85	163.0(2)	..	....
Southwest Alaska	61	162.4(3)	..	....
Seward Peninsula	39	165.4(4)	..	....
St. Lawrence Island	63	163.3(3)	..	....
Point Hope	13	166.5(5)	..	....
Noatak River	11	168.2(6)	5	155.5(6)
Nunatagmiut (Noatak River)	11	167.9(7)	..	....
Cape Smyth and Point Barrow	51	161.52(8)	..	....
Point Barrow	..	....	30	152.1(6)
Koukpagmiut (east of Mackenzie)	12	167.5(7)	..	....
Mackenzie Delta	..	....	6	151.5(6)
Mackenzie Delta (Jenness)	4	162.2(6)	..	....
Coronation Gulf	82	164.8(5)	42	156.4(5)
Iglulik	20	166.0(6)	20	153.7(6)
Cumberland Sound	9	162.0(7)	..	....
Southampton Island	35	162.0(9)	..	....
Melville Peninsula	20	165.9(10)	..	....
Labrador	11	157.7(11)	10	149.7(11)
Labrador	8	158.2(12)	..	....

Group	Males		Females	
	No.	Mean	No.	Mean
Labrador	26	157.5(1)	..	....
Labrador	5	159.6(13)	..	....
Greenland	614	162.1(2)	..	....
Smith Sound, Greenland	8	157.4(14)	..	....
Smith Sound, Greenland	..	....	10	145.4(6)
Greenland, southwest coast	21	157.6(15)	24	151.8(6)
Greenland, southeast coast	22	160.4(15)	23	152.9(6)
Greenland, northeast coast	31	164.7(15)	15	155.1(6)
Angmagsalik, East Greenland	..	163.1(16)	..	152.0(16)
Frederik VI Coast, East Greenland	..	160.4(16)	..	152.9(16)

(1) Boas: 1895.
(2) Deniker: 1900.
(3) Hrdlička: 1930.
(4) Shapiro: 1931, 360 (based on measurements by Weyer).
(5) Jenness: 1923.
(6) From table compiled by Jenness: 1923, 50b.
(7) Boas: 1901.
(8) Ray: 1885.
(9) Tocher: 1902.
(10) Parry: 1824.
(11) From table compiled by Jenness: 1923, 50b. Footnote: "The figures for Labrador are from Duckworth and Pain. Boas (*Zeitschrift für Ethnologie* [1905], 375) gives 1575 mm. for men and 1480 mm. for women."
(12) Pittard: 1901.
(13) Virchow: 1880.
(14) Steensby: 1910.
(15) Hansen: 1914.
(16) Birket-Smith: 1928, 44 (after Holm and Poulsen).

25. Rasmussen: 1927, 87 f.

26. Sumner and Keller: 1927, I, chap. i.

CHAPTER II

SURVEY OF ESKIMO HABITAT

§1. GEOGRAPHICAL CONDITIONS

THE Eskimos are essentially a coastal people. With exception of the tribes inhabiting the so-called Barren Grounds northwest of Hudson Bay and some inland dwellers in Alaska they live during the greater part of the year along coasts. Furthermore, these are arctic or subarctic coasts, characterized generally by sea ice during winter. Some groups of Eskimos, indeed, live mostly on the ice at this season.

A Treeless Region

MOST of the region inhabited by the Eskimos is treeless. This fact is illustrated in Figure 1 by a map showing the limits of forested land and the extent of the territory occupied since their appearance on the Arctic coast.[1] The tree line is not indicated on Greenland because of the difficulty of representing the condition on its narrow ice-free border. In the extreme south of Greenland there are trees which occasionally reach a height of four meters,[2] chiefly willow and birch. On the west coast as far north as Disko Island (70° N. Lat.) there are sturdy willow bushes sometimes as high as a man, and lungwort shrubs one or two meters high.[3] Along the east coast vegetation is stunted farther south. Even at Angmagsalik (about 66° N. Lat.) willows rarely reach a height of one meter.[4]

Certain Eskimos inhabit land that is characterized by the presence of trees, notably the natives living inland from Kotzebue Sound in northwestern Alaska and in the Mackenzie Delta.

Concerning the former region Rasmussen writes:
"At six in the morning we sailed across Hotham Inlet and entered the Kuvak . . . and we, who had been blockaded by ice throughout the summer, revelled in the sight of this new country, unlike any Eskimo territory we had ever seen. Here were wooded hills, fringing the fertile delta, rich grass land and soft warm breezes laden with the scent of trees and flowers. . . .
"In the course of the morning, we reached the Kuvak Delta, a big plain cut through by numerous channels, forming a maze which it

would be impossible to negotiate with safety were it not for the marks set up at intervals along the fairway. The landscape seems altogether tropical to us, after the desolation of the Arctic coast. Bushes, low trees and tall grass run right out into the water, and ducks, geese and other water fowl rise noisily as we near them. . . . The vegetation grows richer and taller as we advance, and a couple of hours after leaving the road house we have fir [spruce] trees on either side. Only a few at first, looking like forgotten Christmas trees, solitary strangers among the native birch and willow, but they soon grow bigger and more numerous as we go on, until there are whole woods, running down to the water's edge. Farther on again, the banks are tangled forest where axes would be needed to cut a way through."[5]

In the Mackenzie Delta the tree line lies only about a score of miles inland from the Arctic coast. Its position is defined by O'Neill as being about at the entrance to the Ministikug River and at Turnait. Very near this limit there are thirty-foot birches, eight- and ten-foot willows, and twenty-five-foot spruce, the latter species being the most abundant.[6] Well-developed willows are found even on the coastline at the mouth of the Mackenzie River (in latitude about 69° N.); ". . . and spruce, tamarack, and birch grow within 20 miles to the south. Many other forms of plant life are plentiful throughout the delta area."[7]

In the territory of the Copper Eskimos (roughly between 67° and 72° N. Lat., and 102° and 120° W. Long.) timber is found in only two places: in the valleys of the Tree and Coppermine rivers.[8] On the Coppermine, trees extend to within twenty miles of the mouth, but they are small. Forty miles from the mouth there is good timber for building or other purposes. "Big Stick island, about 35 miles east of Great Bear lake on the southeast branch of Dease river, is an area of several hundred acres covered by trees suitable for timber. It is surrounded by the Barren lands." In all this country the trees are confined to the immediate valleys of rivers and lakes.[9] "A willow eight feet in height has been noted in Victoria Island, but this is an exception."[10]

The tree line eventually reaches the western coast of Hudson Bay in latitude 58° N. (approximately) or eight hundred miles south of the Mackenzie Delta.

"The area lying between the northern limit of timber and the Arctic coast has frequently been referred to as the 'barren lands,' a name justified in some areas but not altogether descriptive of the country at large, as in many parts grasses, heather, and wild-flowers abound. The chief difference between the more fertile areas of the north and more southern prairies lies in the depth of fertile soil which in the south greatly exceeds that of the north.

"The shortage of plant life throughout the area at large is possibly due to several causes, the principal being: lack of moisture in summer; high winds which not only retard summer growth but during the winter concentrate the snow in the valleys, leaving much of the surface of the country unprotected; and the lack of animal life and, with it, absence of fertilization. It is noticeable that in areas where ground squirrels are plentiful the vegetation is more abundant and the depth of fertile soil greater.

"Within this treeless area local conditions greatly affect the development of plant life. At almost any point where the ground lying at not too great a height above sea level is protected from the winds and removed a few miles from a coastline visited by summer ice-floes, willows, grasses, and flowers are well developed. This point is well illustrated by the growth at the mouth of Burnside river, which enters Bathurst inlet from the west, where willows four inches in diameter are common and many other forms of plant life flourish, while two hundred miles directly to the south an area unsheltered by hills, and lying at an elevation of approximately 1,200 feet, is all but barren. The fact that this second area cannot be affected by the proximity of ice-floes would indicate that wind, altitude, and lack of moisture are the chief enemies of plant life in the north.

"Throughout the Arctic islands much of the country is but sparsely covered with vegetation. In the more sheltered areas rough grasses and hardy flowers are found. Willows are occasionally seen but they seldom exceed one inch in diameter and take the form of a creeping plant sheltered from the winds by the grasses and slight local elevations in the soil or rock."[11]

Turning to Southampton Island, situated in the northern part of Hudson Bay, we find that plant life is very sparse, great areas in the limestone section, for instance around Hansine Lake, being an absolute desert. Other portions are marshy or have the usual tundra vegetation; and along the Cleveland River there are willows.[12]

With regard to the region about Ungava Bay, Labrador, Turner asserts that on the west side of George River, which flows into the Bay, the trees are pushed back fifteen or twenty miles from the sea. "At the mouth of Whale river [which has its mouth at the southern tip of Ungava Bay], the trees attain a height of 30 to 50 feet on the eastern (right) bank and within two miles of the shore. On the left bank the trees do not approach to within 10 or 15 miles of the coast. . . . On the western side of False river the tree line extends in a southwesterly direction across the Koksoak and to the banks of the Leaf river nearly at its source from the large lake. From the south side of this lake the trees are very much scattered and attain inconsiderable size, scarcely fitted for other use than fuel." A line from the large lake in which

Leaf River has its source, southwest to the eastern shore of Hudson Bay forms the northern limit of trees for the northwestern portion of Labrador.[13]

"The actual Atlantic coast from the straits of Belle Isle northward is treeless from end to end. The inlets, however, extend into more sheltered regions where, except on cliffs or rocky summits, the surface is covered by the usual boreal Canadian forest."[14]

Driftwood

GROWING timber is not a feature of the Eskimo habitat, considering the region as a whole. Driftwood is an adequate substitute for trees among most Eskimos as material for implements, tent poles, boat frames, etc.[15] Often, however, it is too scarce to be used as fuel; and, besides, the Eskimos use other sorts of fuel, as will be explained later. There is a very serious lack of driftwood from Coronation Gulf[16] eastward along the western shore of Hudson Bay, locally, as far south as McConnell River.[17] The absence is most desperately felt in the region of Boothia Isthmus, King William Island, and Melville Peninsula,[18] where the natives have various ingenious methods of circumventing the difficulty, which will be discussed later. The so-called Polar Eskimos of Smith Sound, northwestern Greenland, also have suffered seriously through scarcity of driftwood.[19]

Plant Life

PLANT life on the Eskimo tundra is limited to bushes, mosses, lichens, flowering forms, grasses, and sedges. To be sure, plant life is rather varied and luxuriant in midsummer in parts of the Arctic. In Greenland there are three hundred and ninety species of flowering plants and ferns,[20] and in southern Greenland alone there are three hundred species of flowering plants.[21] One hundred and thirty species exist even in northwest Greenland; indeed, about the same number occur on Ellesmere Island, whose most northerly point lies but a little more than four hundred miles from the Pole.[22] In the whole of the Arctic Archipelago only a little more than two hundred vascular plants are known.[21]

Climate

ARCTIC climate is characteristic of all the Eskimo regions except southern Greenland, the lower Labrador coast, and the area occupied by the southern groups of Alaska. The climate in these latter sections, to disregard secondary distinctions, may be classed as subarctic. Speaking in conventionalized terms, however, more than half of the Eskimos live within the belt that is wrongly designated the temperate zone.

There has been much misunderstanding regarding the climate of the North. Early travelers writing on the climate in which the Eskimos live naturally emphasized the severe cold, because the long, hard winter is its outstanding feature. Consequently, a distorted conception became established in the minds of many, of a land of perpetual ice and snow. Undue emphasis upon the shorter warm season, on the other hand, can lead to an equally erroneous idea. First in importance in considering the climate of the Eskimo region is the fact that it is markedly seasonal.

In the following discussion of this aspect of the Eskimo habitat an effort is made to present an accurate, unbiased description of each of the seasonal phases. It is the aim to avoid the misapprehensions which are apt to result from disproportionate stress upon any one feature, from citing exclusively either average temperatures or extreme temperatures, and from comparing coastal conditions in the Arctic with inland conditions in lower latitudes and *vice versa*.

The series of maps reproduced on pages 21–26 giving the average monthly temperatures in Arctic America and Greenland will serve as a basis for the study of the climate.[23]

A glance at these maps will show that the temperature everywhere varies considerably with the seasons. To be sure, the summer and winter temperatures are held closer to a mean than they are in certain other parts of the world, especially in the interior of continents. With the exception of a few sections away from the coast, such as the Noatak region of Alaska and the arctic plains northwest of Hudson Bay, the province of the Eskimos, as has been said, is essentially coastal. Consequently, their habitat does not present as great extremes of heat and cold, by and large, as do certain other sections in the same latitude which lie inland, away from the moderating influence of the sea. Nevertheless, there are few regions in the entire world where the people are influenced to a greater degree by seasonal variations. The far-reaching effects of seasonal change are discussed at length in chapter v.

As a background, then, for this study, we shall consider the cycle of the seasons on the Eskimo tundra, together with some of the associated environmental conditions.

§2. THE CYCLE OF THE SEASONS

Seasonal Variation in Daylight and Darkness

AT the outset the reader is referred to the diagrams (Fig. 2) showing graphically the seasonal variation in the number of hours of sunlight daily.[24]

In temperate and tropical latitudes daylight and darkness alternate diurnally with relatively slight seasonal variation. In the Far North, however, daylight and darkness are largely seasonal, and at the Pole they are entirely seasonal. There the sun remains above the horizon for approximately six months (actually the center of the sun is visible for almost a week longer, because of atmospheric refraction), and then disappears for the remainder of the year. No Eskimos, of course, live under this extreme condition. The northernmost tribe experiences four months of continual sunlight during the summer, followed by two months of alternating sunlight and twilight ushering in the darkness of winter. For three and a half months they do not see the sun at all, though during this time the darkness is partly relieved by twilight, when the sun is not far below the horizon. The darkness of winter is superseded by a lingering dusk, with growing periods of sunlight until the sun once more circles the sky during all of the twenty-four hours.

Very slightly south of this region, in latitude 76° 56' N., Captain Osborn determined that the standard type of the *London Times* ". . . ceased to be legible after the 15th. December during any time in the day, and it was not until the 9th. of January, 1853, that it was again read during the brief space of 15 minutes."[25]

The Eskimo tribe mentioned above represents the extreme case throughout the inhabited world. Other groups of Eskimos to the south experience the seasonal variation of sunlight to less degree.

The chart in Figure 2 illustrates the seasonal variation in the number of hours of sunlight each day in various latitudes. Each graph includes the entire year in the latitude which it represents. The shaded and black portions indicate the periods during which the sun is below the horizon, the shaded bands being used to differentiate twilight from actual night. Using the accepted criterion, twilight is taken as the condition which exists whenever the sun is not more than 18 degrees below the horizon. Actually, it is virtually dark considerably before the sun sinks so far as 18 degrees below the horizon.

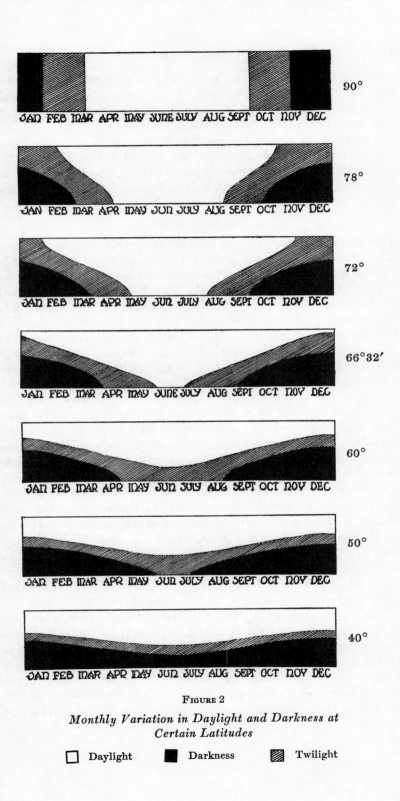

JAN FEB MAR APR MAY JUNE JULY AUG SEPT OCT NOV DEC — 90°

JAN FEB MAR APR MAY JUN JULY AUG SEPT OCT NOV DEC — 78°

JAN FEB MAR APR MAY JUN JULY AUG SEPT OCT NOV DEC — 72°

JAN FEB MAR APR MAY JUNE JULY AUG SEPT OCT NOV DEC — 66°32′

JAN FEB MAR APR MAY JUN JULY AUG SEPT OCT NOV DEC — 60°

JAN FEB MAR APR MAY JUN JULY AUG SEPT OCT NOV DEC — 50°

JAN FEB MAR APR MAY JUN JULY AUG SEPT OCT NOV DEC — 40°

FIGURE 2

*Monthly Variation in Daylight and Darkness at
Certain Latitudes*

☐ Daylight   ■ Darkness   ▨ Twilight

The arctic twilight is apt to be unusually bright for any given position of the sun, especially in clear weather, because the high refraction of the atmosphere and the reflecting power of the snow increase whatever light is available.

The moon, it should furthermore be mentioned, remains above the horizon for longer periods in high latitudes than it does in the temperate and tropical zones. Thus, in North Greenland it is visible for more than a week at a time, relieving the monotony of the winter darkness.

Sun and Climate

THE climate of the Arctic is influenced strongly by the seasonal distribution of sunlight and by the enfeebled effect of the sun in high latitudes. The *yearly total* number of hours of sunlight does not differ radically from the Equator toward the poles—what small change there is in high latitudes being a slight increase. But the *seasonal distribution* of sunlight does differ widely according to latitude. Wide variation in the length of days from season to season distinguishes the Arctic from the Tropics, and so, though less obviously, does the fact that in high latitudes the sun never rises very high in the heavens.

The height of the sun above the horizon influences the amount of its heat received at any point on the earth. When the sun's rays strike the earth at a low angle their effect is diminished. Striking the earth's outer atmosphere at an acute angle, the rays of the sun must, in the first place, pass through a greater thickness of air before reaching the surface of the globe. In other words, virtually a thicker blanket of air insulates the earth from the sun in high latitudes than in low. In the second place, each unit of heat from the sun, figuratively speaking, must distribute itself over a broader area. These two facts explain why the sun does not seem so warm when it is near the horizon. It should be noted, on the other hand, that *loss of heat* from the earth is not hindered any more in high latitudes than in low, for this takes place vertically upward through the atmosphere.

The temperature at any point on the earth at a particular time of the year is basically determined, therefore, by the daily duration of sunlight in conjunction with the angle at which the rays of the sun fall. In summer in high latitudes these two factors work toward opposite effects: the days are unusually long—even twenty-four hours when the midnight sun is visible—but at the same time the sun never rises high in the sky. The length of day makes for warm weather, while the low position of the sun has a counteracting effect. If the sun stood high in the heavens during the time that it is visible in the Arctic in summer, the weather would grow unbearably hot. Even with the sun remaining comparatively near the horizon, the long hours of sunlight cause it to become quite warm and even hot, especially inland away from the cooling influence of the sea. At Fort Macpherson, for instance, which is north of the Arctic Circle and about a hundred miles from the Arctic Sea, the average temperature of the warmest month is 58° F., only one degree less than that at San Francisco. And both to the east and west of this point the summer climate is even warmer, because of the absence of a prevailing wind which follows the valley of the Mackenzie River bringing the cooling influence of the Arctic Sea.[26]

Almost as much heat is received at the surface of the globe in the polar regions in summer as at the Equator. The ratio, as given by Angot, is 494 for the North Pole, to 517 for the Equator at the summer solstice. If we disregard the loss of heat in transmission to the earth through the atmosphere and consider the conditions at the upper surface of the air, it may even be said that in midsummer actually more heat is received within the polar regions than at the Equator.[27]

The dissipation of heat from the sun expended in melting the winter's accumulation of snow does not delay the advance of warmer weather as much as might be supposed, because the quantity of snow is slight over large areas. The cooling influence of the frozen ground, furthermore, is obstructed by the surface vegetation and the blanket of thawed earth, which even in the height of summer prevent thawing of the ground below a depth of about two feet. At Fort Yukon within seven feet of where a thermometer registered 100° F. in the shade there lay eternally frozen soil.

The lingering ice of the Arctic Sea, however, exerts somewhat more of a cooling influence upon the Far North in summer.

In winter, on the other hand, the shortness or total absence of sunlight combines with the narrowness of the angle at which the sun's rays strike the earth, to cause the polar regions to receive very much less heat than the equatorial.

Arctic Summer

SUMMER in the Arctic is not the summer of the temperate regions. It is short, and cool, especially near the sea. Inland, surprisingly hot temperatures are recorded. From Fort Yukon, on the Arctic

Circle, for instance, the United States Weather Bureau has reported 100° F. in the shade. On the other hand, at Smith Sound the highest temperature recorded by MacMillan in four years was 63° F.[28] There, the summer is very brief and for the most part cool; yet even so there is a complete disappearance of snow at sea level, a thawing of the surface soil, and a blossoming of plants.

Only a small proportion of the Eskimos live in what can be considered the high arctic belt, which includes northern Greenland and the Arctic Archipelago with the exception of the southern fringe of Victoria Island and the greater part of Baffin Island. In this belt the average temperature, even of the warmest month of summer, is within ten degrees (F.) above freezing, which is about the same as that during the coldest month of winter in Delaware. Thus, even on the extreme fringe of the inhabited world, the climate in midsummer is comparable with midwinter climate in a densely settled section of the temperate zone. Farther south in the Eskimo region the summer temperatures become increasingly milder; until at Dillingham, Alaska, near the southern limit of the Eskimos in the west, the average temperature of the warmest month (July) is 56° F., which is practically the same as the average temperature of the coldest month at San Diego, California. At Hopedale, Labrador, near the southern limit of the Eskimos in the east, the average temperature of the warmest month (51° F.) is comparable to that of the coldest month at Mobile, Alabama; and at Ivigtut, near the southern tip of Greenland, it is the same as the average of the coldest month at San Francisco. Farther north within the Eskimo province at Point Barrow on the northernmost point of Alaska; at Adelaide Peninsula, on the Arctic coast of Canada; and at Upernivik, in latitude 73° N. on the west coast of Greenland, the average temperature of the warmest month is approximately the same as the average temperature during the coldest month at Victoria, Canada; Portland, Oregon; Nantes, France; and Hankow, China.

In the series of temperature maps it will be noticed that the isotherm of 32° F. moves northward over the Eskimo region during April, May, and June, signifying that during these months the average temperature rises from below freezing to above freezing. This rise roughly marks the transition to the arctic summer. In any particular place the change is, as a rule, quite sudden. Everywhere within the Eskimo region it is complete, in that all the land at sea level is stripped of snow. Only north of the Eskimo lands

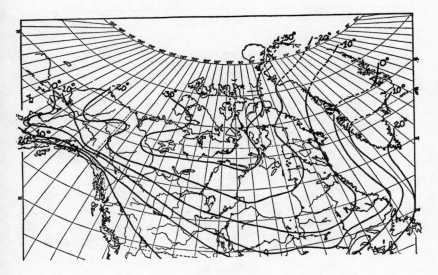

FIGURE 3A

Mean Temperatures—January

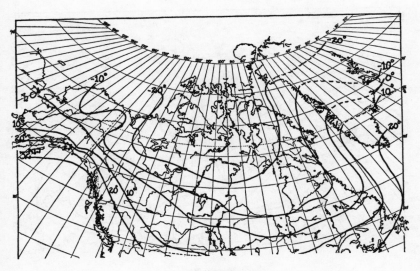

FIGURE 3B

Mean Temperatures—February

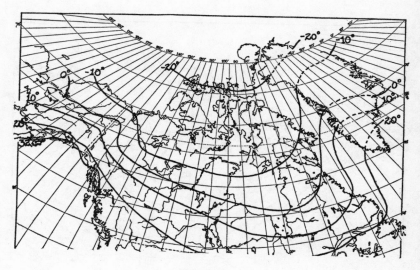

FIGURE 3C

Mean Temperatures—March

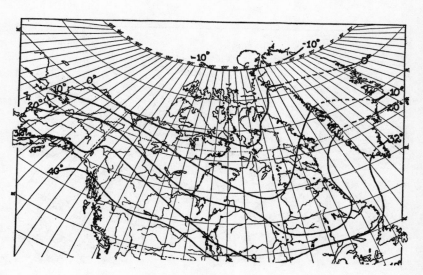

FIGURE 3D

Mean Temperatures—April

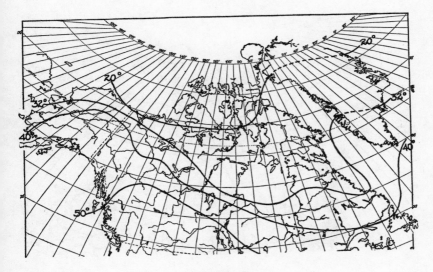

FIGURE 3E

Mean Temperatures—May

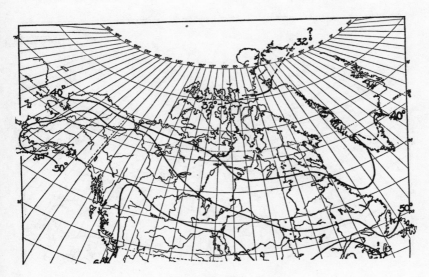

FIGURE 3F

Mean Temperatures—June

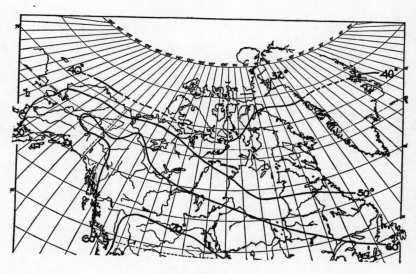

FIGURE 3G

Mean Temperatures—July

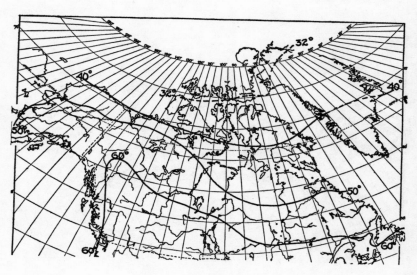

FIGURE 3H

Mean Temperatures—August

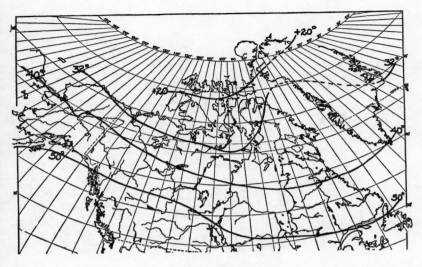

FIGURE 3I

Mean Temperatures—September

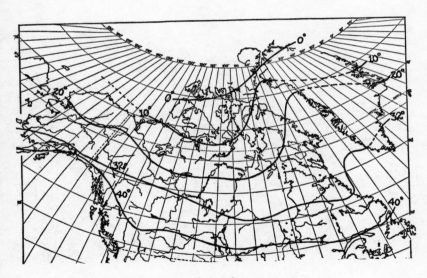

FIGURE 3J

Mean Temperatures—October

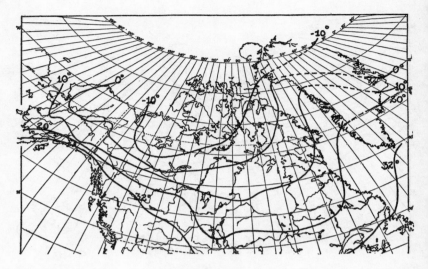

FIGURE 3K

Mean Temperatures—November

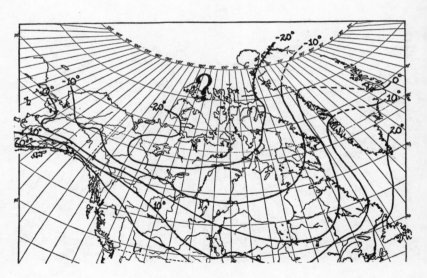

FIGURE 3L

Mean Temperatures—December

does snow lie on the ground through the summer, specifically near the northern extreme of Greenland in latitude about 82° 30'.[29] If it is true that the snow reported in this locality lay on open ground, not in ravines or other protected places, this is the only place of its kind known in the northern hemisphere.

Elsewhere permanent snow and land ice exist only on mountains and plateaus. The outstanding glaciated area within the region we are studying is Greenland. About 86 per cent of the island, the entire interior of it, is covered by a shield of ice.[30] In the Arctic Archipelago local areas are glaciated, such as in Grinnell Land and other parts of Ellesmere Island, in Devon Island, and Baffin Island.

With the approach of the warm period snow and ice at sea level melt. In general the ground becomes free of snow in June or July.[31] There are extensive areas where the snow is gone by about the tenth of May, and does not return till the first of October. On the other hand, there are areas where the ground is free of snow for only a month or six weeks.

River ice and lake ice break up about the same time that the snow disappears, or a little sooner.[32] The Yukon and Kuskokwim rivers of Alaska, for instance, break up about the latter half of May;[33] the Mackenzie River and the rivers of the Ungava District, Labrador, toward the end of May;[34] the rivers of Coronation Gulf, Queen Maud Gulf, and the Barren Grounds during June.[35] Jenness mentions a lake in the Colville Hills in the southwestern part of Victoria Island from which the ice seldom vanishes even during the warmest summers.[36] Likewise, the ice in the middle of Lake Yathkied rarely if ever thaws away completely. Appropriately, the Eskimos call this lake Hikoligjuaq, which means "the great water with ice that never melts."[37]

Snow flurries may occur, to be sure, in some sections during any month of the year. Thus, at Ungava, Labrador, snow falls every month.[38] And among the Iglulik Eskimos of the Melville Peninsula and northern Baffin Island none of the months is entirely free from snowstorms.[39] In southern Greenland, snow falls occasionally even in July and August. As far north as Godthaab it snows during these months on the average of once every two or three years.[40]

These cases of summer snowfall are not peculiar, however, to the arctic warm season. It could be asserted even of New York state that snow has been known to fall in every month of the year. The arctic summer is virtually a snow-free period. Further, the approach of summer is heralded by the breaking up of the sea ice.[41] This occurs as early as May in parts of Bering Sea and in the waters of southern Greenland, and even in April in some places. The break-up occurs in Coronation Gulf about the middle of May. In Hudson Bay and Smith Sound the critical period is about the middle of June. In Ungava Bay, Labrador, along the northwest coast of Hudson Bay, and in Ponds Inlet, the ice breaks up during July. Scattered sea ice remains through the summer in some waters within the Eskimo regions,[42] as, for example, in Foxe Basin, and the Gulf of Boothia.

On land the release from winter is remarkably sudden.[43] The earth is scarcely bare before the hardy flora burst into life. Most plants of the Arctic are perennials; the brevity of the growing season excludes annuals. Plant forms must hurry their life cycles to fit the short summer from June to August. Roots, liberated from their long frosty imprisonment, quickly absorb moisture from the spongy tundra. Flower buds are not infrequently open before the snow is off the ground. At the first suggestion of spring they are ready to bloom. Development is almost explosive. Turner[44] says concerning the Ungava District, Labrador, ". . . in the course of a few days, the plant-producing areas are clothed with verdure as if by magic."

With the same suddenness come the migratory birds. The Danish Expedition in northeastern Greenland remarked that the snow melted away in one day; the birds arrived almost the same day, most of them at the same hour.[45] It should be realized that a hundred species or more of birds nest largely or almost entirely north of the Arctic Circle.[46] Mosquitoes also appear, which make living on the tundra miserable. Caribou become much more numerous in the so-called Barren Grounds, along the coast of Labrador, and in the Arctic Archipelago, whither they migrate in herds.

At the height of the arctic summer only one or two feet of the surface soil is thawed. Beneath is a solid platform of frozen earth. Because of this rock-like subsoil, drainage of the abundant ground water from the flat tundra is slow. The earth is soggy. Small clumpy protuberances of mossy earth, "niggerheads," offer the only secure footing to the traveler. Elsewhere he sinks sometimes knee-deep into the sodden soil.

The warm season is brief in duration. In contrast with the sudden awakening of spring, autumn is a quiet dying away of nature. Winter arrives stealthily, almost imperceptibly.[47] In September some snow falls in most parts and small lakes and rivers freeze in the northern sections.[48] Inland water in the Barren Grounds freezes over in October.[49] By the end of this month the Yukon and Kuskokwim are ice-locked, and by early November the Mackenzie. It is said that the large lakes of southern Baffin Island do not freeze until the latter part of December.

Arctic Winter

THE Eskimo lands do not become buried deep in snow. Whatever falls is not likely to melt, but the annual snowfall is only moderate or light, particularly in the central and northern regions. Around Coronation Gulf the yearly snowfall does not aggregate more than two or three feet.[50] The total yearly precipitation in the Arctic Archipelago is less than eight inches, in many places probably only four inches.[51] In addition to the lightness of the snowfall, winds sweep much of the surface bare. Freuchen and Mathiassen noted this phenomenon on Rae Isthmus.[52] Mecking states that "more than three-fourths of the archipelago is almost entirely free of snow all year."[53] In the eastern and western portions of the Eskimo region snowfall is somewhat heavier than in the central area. Along the northwestern coast of Alaska and in the northern part of the Mackenzie Valley the yearly snowfall aggregates about five feet.[54]

Sea ice forms throughout most of the region during November, but this is a very variable phenomenon.[55] The Polar Sea, it should be remembered, never freezes very deep. Some waters are kept free of solid ice throughout the winter by ocean currents,[56] for instance in Smith Sound, Hudson Strait, and between southwestern Ellesmere Island and northwestern Devon Island.

During November the average temperature in the warmest Eskimo regions is but slightly below freezing; while in the central and northern sections it is as much as forty degrees (F.) below freezing. In January the divergence in temperature from south to north becomes even wider. Clearly, there is far less uniformity throughout the region with respect to winter temperatures than with respect to summer temperatures.

In comparing degrees of cold the well-known fact should be held in mind that humidity is an important factor in the physiological effect of cold, and that wind in combination with cold makes the weather far more severe.

The southerly parts of the Eskimo region have a winter comparatively mild in the arctic sense. The average temperature in southernmost Greenland in January, the coldest month, is the same as that in Albany during the same month. And the average temperature during the coldest month at Dillingham, at the southeastern corner of Bering Sea, is the same as that in the coldest month at Montreal.

The Arctic Archipelago and the extreme northern border of North America, on the other hand, are subject to average temperatures of −10°, −20°, and even −30° F. during the coldest period of winter. No averages comparable with these occur in the northern United States.

In the high arctic belt the winters are exceedingly cold; they are not, however, the coldest winters in the inhabited world. The coldest place where people dwell, or nearly the coldest place, is Verkhoyansk, in northeastern Siberia just north of the Arctic Circle. There the average temperature for the whole of January often is below −58° F. and occasionally the temperature drops as low as −94°. Such a winter climate is far colder than that among any Eskimos. In the summer, however, at Verkhoyansk it is warm even according to temperate-zone standards, and vegetation is consequently abundant. The wide extremes are due to inland position.

Daylight is, of course, greatly lessened during winter in high latitudes, and is completely absent during midwinter among the northern Eskimo groups. Figure 2 illustrates this circumstance better than words can portray it. Only with a thorough understanding of the seasonal character of sunlight in high latitudes can the arctic winter be comprehended.

At the approach of winter most of the birds of the Arctic and the greater part of the caribou, at least of Victoria and King William islands, migrate southward. The scarcity of living forms and the gloom of the protracted twilight give the wintry tundra an extremely dismal cast. Jenness gives a vivid description of the mainland near Coronation Gulf in the clutch of winter:

"The birds have migrated to warmer climes, except a few ptarmigan, an occasional raven, and the solitary snowy owl. Bears, squirrels, lemmings, and mice have denned themselves up in their holes; most of the caribou have retreated to the Barren Lands far to the south; and only the fox, the hare, and wolf contend with man against the winter storms. One may travel a hundred miles without finding a single track to break the monotonous surface of the snow."[57]

Birket-Smith describes the barren homeland of the Caribou Eskimo in a similar vein:

"As a rule the red ball of the sun is seen day after day describing its short path over a clear, pale blue sky. The country lies dazzling white, with blue shadows in the sun and some dark patches where steep rocky cliffs and wind-blown hill tops prevent the snow from settling."[58]

The Eskimos who inhabit this region see the sun during the height of winter for only a few hours each day.

§3. ANIMAL LIFE

Importance of the Seal

THE seal is the best all-round animal of the Arctic. Its skin furnishes material for boots and containers for oil. The meat and blubber are food for men and dogs. The blubber further provides light in winter and heat for house and for cooking. The intestines furnish waterproof clothing and translucent material for windows.[59] Three men and six dogs need about two seals per week.[60]

Ringed Seal

THIS species is otherwise known as the rough seal, the jar seal, *Phoca foetida*, *Phoca hispada*, and in Greenland as the fiord seal. It affords the choicest meat, light skins for clothing, and a good grade of oil.[61] It is found along practically all the coasts inhabited by Eskimos, but is most common in the truly arctic sections as distinguished from the subarctic.[62] It is, indeed, one of the most northerly seals, occurring even along northernmost Greenland where it is the only species found. In many places it is the most important seal to the Eskimos, as at Point Barrow,[63] along the arctic coast of Canada north of the Barren Grounds,[64] and in the northern settlements of Greenland.[65] It prefers the fiords that remain ice-covered the year round, where it lives under the ice, breathing at intervals of about fifteen minutes through an air hole which it scratches or thrusts through the ice.[66] It is only slightly migratory, if at all.[67]

Bearded Seal

THIS is the "square flipper" (*Erignathus barbatus*), and the *oogruk*, *oosook*, *ookjuk*, or *urksuk* of the Eskimos. It is found with varying frequency in all Eskimo waters,[68] and is only to a small extent migratory.[69] It is known that the Eskimos sometimes harpoon this species at breathing holes in the ice; but whether it actually makes the holes itself or merely appropriates the ones made by other seals, cannot be said with certainty.[70] Tougher of hide than the other seals, it is important to the Eskimos as a source of harpoon lines, dog harness, and boot soles.

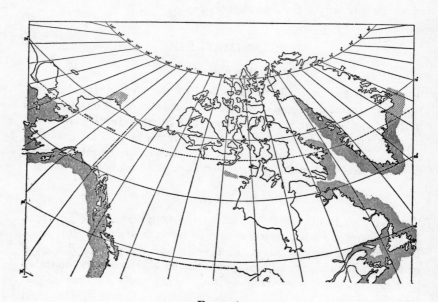

FIGURE 4

Habitat of Harbor Seal or Spotted Seal
(Phoca vitulina)—*shaded portions*

Harbor Seal[71]

THIS seal is somewhat similar to the ringed seal, described above, but is has a more southerly distribution. It is the spotted seal, the common small seal, *Phoca vitulina*, and is sometimes called, as is the ringed seal, the fiord seal. Since it is strictly nonmigratory[72] and shuns ice wherever possible, large areas in the heart of the Arctic are devoid of this species, as indicated on the map (Fig. 4).[73] It is confined entirely to coastal regions.

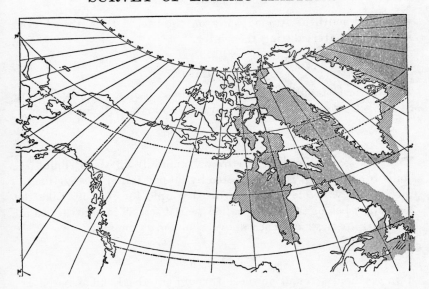

FIGURE 5

Habitat of Greenland Seal or Saddleback
(Phoca groenlandica)

▓ Usually found

▨ Occasionally found

Taken from Nansen:
Hunting and Adventure. . . .

Greenland Seal

Phoca groenlandica is the saddleback seal, or the harp seal. It makes no breathing holes in the ice[74] and avoids solid sea ice. Consequently, it is classed as a subarctic form. Its distribution in the Eskimo region is shown in Figure 5, taken from Nansen's *Hunting and Adventure in the Arctic*. This seal is migratory, moving, in general, southward in winter and northward in summer.[75]

Bladdernose Seal

THIS seal, otherwise known as the crested seal, the hooded seal, and *Cystophora cristata*, is peculiar for a sack on the top of its head, which it can inflate. It inhabits characteristically the North Atlantic rather than the Arctic, and visits no Eskimo waters except east and west of Greenland from Baffin Bay southward on the west, and south of Angmagsalik on the east.[76] It is absent even from these waters during the winter.[77]

Ribbon Seal

THIS form is familiar chiefly to Eskimos living south of Bering Strait.[78] Occasionally, one is seen as far north as Point Barrow.[79]

Fur Seal

THE fur seal[80] migrates northward annually to the Pribilof Islands for breeding. It is protected by international treaty. This is the species valuable among civilized people for its fur. Like the sea lion, it belongs to the so-called "eared seals," in contrast to all the other species mentioned above, which are true seals.

Sea Lion

THE sea lion is found nowhere throughout the Eskimo realm except in the Bering Sea region.[81]

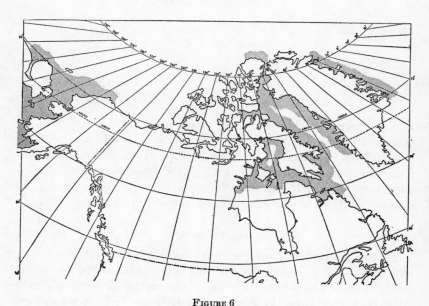

FIGURE 6

Habitat of Walrus—Shaded Portions

Walrus

THE distribution of walrus in the arctic waters of the western hemisphere is shown in Figure 6.[82] Formerly, they ranged as far south in the east as Nova Scotia. The walrus is of value to the Eskimos in that it furnishes meat and blubber, ivory for implements, and a tough hide used for boat covers, etc., and even for food.

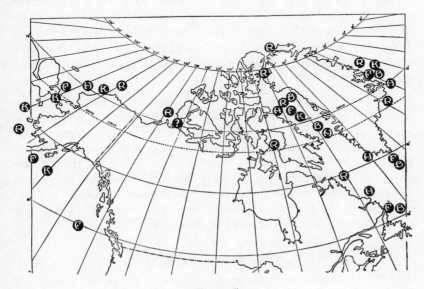

FIGURE 7

Habitat of Whales

R *Right Whales* (Balaena)
H *Hump-Backed Whales* (Megaptera)
F *Finners or Rorquals* (Balaenoptera)
K *Killer Whales* (Orca)
B *Bobble-nosed Whales* (Hyperoödon)

Whales

THE map in Figure 7 represents the distribution of the chief varieties of whales in the Eskimo region.[83] Of considerable importance to the Eskimos are the Greenland or arctic right whale (*Balaena mysticetus*), and the "bowhead" whale, a member of the same species, which inhabits the Okhotsk Sea, Bering Sea, and the adjacent Polar Sea. These seem to be truly "ice-whales," always dwelling among scattered floes or about the borders of ice fields or barriers and seen in summer only where winter ice fields occasionally occur.[84] In the waters off Point Barrow whales are present between the middle of April and the latter part of June, and they return again in autumn, appearing about the end of August.[85]

The Eskimos of Alaska and Greenland harpoon whales nowadays, though the wholesale killing of these animals by white hunters has greatly lessened their importance among Eskimos. Wherever whale hunting is practiced by Eskimos, whalebone (baleen) and whale oil are generally used to great advantage.

Narwhal

THIS curious sea mammal has a wide distribution in the Eskimo region, as seen from Figure 8,[86] but it is generally of rare occurrence except in parts of the eastern section. The peculiar characteristic of this animal is a single spirally twisted tusk, which sometimes exceeds half the length of the body. The narwhal belongs to the same family as the dolphins and porpoises. It is of minor importance to the Eskimos in comparison with seals and walrus. The Greenlanders make more use of it than other Eskimos.

White Whale (Beluga)

THE white whale also is grouped with the dolphins and porpoises. It is much smaller than the true whales, attaining a length of about ten feet. Its wide distribution in the Eskimo region is evident from the map (Fig. 9).[87] I do not find any mention of its occurrence, however, in the very center of the region. When the winter ice lies solid and without holes over wide expanses, it is not to be found.[88] Jensen mentions its migratory habits with regard to Greenland waters.[89] In summer it lives as far north as ice conditions permit, and in the autumn it migrates southward. Throughout the winter it keeps along the west coast round the Arctic Circle. The hide of the beluga is valuable partly because it is nearly waterproof.

Polar Bear

THE polar bear[90] is, in a sense, the most characteristically polar of all arctic animals. It lives in practically all arctic coastal re-

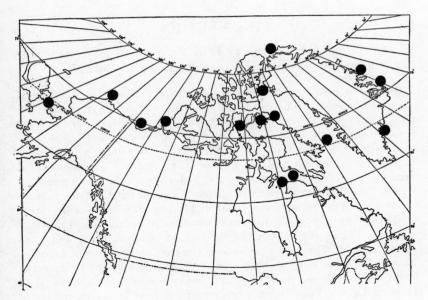

FIGURE 8

Habitat of Narwhal

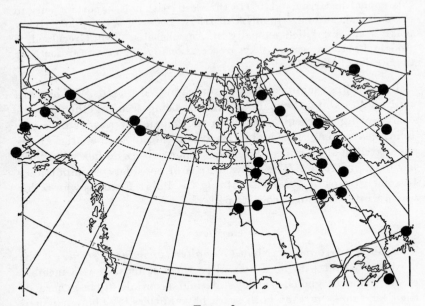

FIGURE 9

Habitat of Beluga (White Whale)

gions,[91] being seldom seen far from sea ice and most commonly near the edges of the pack where seals are more plentiful.

The polar bear is seen along the entire Arctic coast of Alaska and occasionally south of Bering Strait, especially about St. Lawrence Island.[92] It seldom appears in the region of Herschel Island or the Mackenzie Delta; but from Toker Point to Cape Parry it is more common.[93] On the southwest coast of Victoria Island it occurs commonly; in Dolphin and Union Strait, occasionally; and in Coronation Gulf, rarely, if ever.[94] Large numbers dwell during winter about southern Banks Island,[95] but among the islands to the north they are exceedingly rare.[96] On the southwest coast of Hudson Bay polar bears rarely land; but they are very numerous on Southampton Island and north of Baffin Island in Wellington Channel, Prince Regent Inlet, and Lancaster Sound.[97] They are also seen on the east coast of Baffin Island.[98] North of here the extreme limit of their distribution is said to lie at the north end of Eureka Sound and due westward from the south end of Heiberg Land.[99] Peary's observation of fresh bear tracks on the ice in 86°–88° is unusual.[100] Bears are numerous, however, in Kane Basin and along the Humboldt Glacier, as well as in Melville Bay.[101] This section and the northern part of the east coast are the chief resorts of this animal in Greenland.[102] On the west coast it is important only in the Julianehaab and Upernivik districts. Between seventy and eighty polar bears are killed annually at Angmagsalik, East Greenland.[103] And in Labrador waters they are occasionally found as far south as the Straits of Belle Isle.[104]

Polar bears weigh as much as nine hundred pounds.[105] They are solitary in habits, the male and female being seen together only in early spring. The cubs stay with the female for a year or more. Polar bears do not hibernate, but are on the move all winter. Holes excavated in snowdrifts while the mother is bearing her young are her only protection. The polar bear is of considerable importance to some groups of Eskimos, notably the Polar Eskimos who tailor warm winter clothing from its pelt.[106]

Caribou

THE Barren Grounds caribou (*Rangifer tarandus arcticus*) is the most important wild land animal to the Eskimos. It is a member of the reindeer genus, which is distinct from all other genera of the deer family in that both sexes have antlers.[107] The caribou is essentially the same animal as the reindeer of northern Europe and Asia.

The skin of the caribou is adaptable as clothing, particularly for winter use, while the sinew of the back and legs is highly satisfactory as thread. Marrow, meat, fat, blood, and, in rare cases, the partially digested contents of the intestinal tract furnish food for the Eskimos. The antlers provide material for bows and other implements. Further, some Eskimos, notably the Caribou Eskimos of the Barren Grounds, burn the tallow of this animal in their lamps; this is not so satisfactory for the purpose, however, as seal oil.

At the time of their discovery by white people, none of the Eskimo groups domesticated caribou. Northern peoples of the Old World, on the other hand, have long utilized the reindeer as a draft animal and a source of milk.

The caribou is found in practically all regions where Eskimos live. It is especially prominent in the central area, where its distribution extends northward among the islands of the Arctic Archipelago beyond the populated area.[108] In Alaska domesticated reindeer, originally introduced from Siberia toward the end of the nineteenth century, have largely taken the place of the indigenous caribou.

In Labrador large numbers of migrating herds of caribou are still killed at Fort Chimo, Ungava; and at Nachvak, Saglek, Davis Inlet, and Nain; and a few at the head of Hamilton Inlet and Sandwich Bay.[109] The interior is said to contain three immense herds,[110] two of which are hunted mainly by Eskimos. One spends the summer between Nachvak and Nain; and the other crosses the Koksoak near the west side of Ungava Bay. In Greenland caribou formerly were distributed over the whole coastal strip, with the possible exception of the northern section.[111] Though present in the region of Smith Sound, northwestern Greenland, at the time of its discovery, caribou were not being hunted by the Eskimos there. Since then hunting has greatly reduced their numbers as far south in this region as Rensselaer Bay (78° 40′ N.). The most southerly place in West Greenland where caribou now occur is near Narsalik, south of Frederikshaab. Formerly they existed all along the east coast and were hunted at Angmagsalik,[112] but they have disappeared entirely from this region.

The caribou feeds in summer on sedges, grasses, and the shoots and leaves of willow and birch; and in winter on lichens and mosses.[113] Approximately sixty acres of range are needed, on an average, to support one caribou the year round.[114] Crusting of the snow causes the death of considerable numbers of these animals due to their inability to reach buried forage, but they are known to paw through two feet of packed snow or three feet or more of loose snow.[115] In the Northern Plains northwest of Hudson Bay caribou calves are born at the end of June and the beginning of July.[116] The fatness of the animals changes seasonally, as Stefansson has pointed out.[117]

In some areas caribou migrate in response to seasonal changes, and their migration, especially on the tundra west of Hudson Bay, affects the life of the Eskimo. In general the movement of the animals is northward in spring into the Arctic Archipelago and southward in autumn, though they do not all follow this rule. Some remain on the arctic islands throughout the year. On Melville Island, for instance, the animals do not migrate according to any rule.[118] And on Banks Island, in so far as there is any migration, it is northward in winter and southward in summer, the reverse of what might be expected. In the islands north of Lancaster Sound there is no evidence of any migration.[119]

Along the southern belt of the Arctic Archipelago, however, summer brings a considerable accession of caribou from the mainland to the south. In August they are again wandering southward.[120] Some perhaps seek shelter in the forests to the south, but many do not leave the Barren Grounds at all.[121]

Rae Isthmus is a strategic point for the Eskimos in the migration route northward in spring to Melville Peninsula and Cockburn Land (Baffin Island) and southward in autumn.[122] In the vicinity of Chesterfield Inlet the caribou migration ". . . follows a line paralleling the coast and lying from fifty to one hundred miles inland."[123] On King William Island herds of hundreds from the mainland seek summer pasturage.[124] And in 1923 the herds passing Ellice River, which flows into Queen Maud Gulf, were so numerous that it took three days for the animals to cross the delta, though they were always on the move.[125] Farther west, about Coronation Gulf, the Copper Eskimos dwell in the route of a lively caribou migration. There the first herds reach the coast as early as the end of April; the main body moves across during May; and the migration continues well into June, when the ice ceases to be stable.[126] About the latter half of September and in October they begin to straggle back to the southern coast of Victoria Island to wait for the sea to freeze. They cross the straits between the end of October and early December. By Christmas they have disappeared from most places, though a few herds remain all winter, notably in the basin of the Coppermine River on the mainland. West of here, near the Mackenzie Delta, herds of caribou migrate into the region of the Eskimo Lakes for the warmer season; and in the Yukon, a herd passes near Dawson. The shooting of large numbers of the animals with rifles is causing them to change their migratory habits considerably throughout the area; and for this reason the facts set forth above do not represent exactly the conditions at the present day.

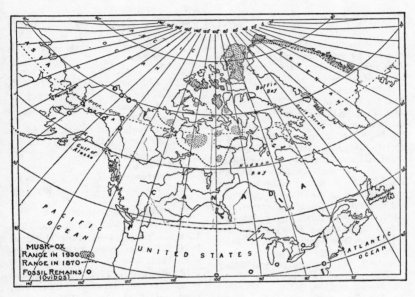

FIGURE 10

Habitat of the Musk Ox

Showing distribution in 1930 compared with that in 1870
By R. M. Anderson, 1930

Musk Ox

THIS animal, scientifically known as *Ovibos moschatus*, was formerly an important object of hunting among many Eskimo groups.[127] The ease with which it can be killed, however, simply by being lanced while held at bay by dogs, has led to a great reduction in its numbers, so that it can no longer be considered of foremost importance. Aside from the meat and the useful shaggy pelt, the horns of the musk ox have been utilized by the Eskimos in making ladles and other implements.[128]

The distribution of the musk ox is shown in the map in Figure 10;[129] the total number in Canadian territory and Greenland in 1930 was estimated to be 14,420.[130] The musk ox lives chiefly on grass,[131] is not a migratory animal, and never goes out on the sea ice; indeed, it never leaves the island on which it is born.[132]

NOTES

1. The map in Figure 1 is constructed by superimposing upon Wissler's map (Wissler: 1918, Map 1) the limits of forested land. The sources of information used in the construction of the tree line are: Brooks: 1906, Plate XII (a map showing the limits of sparsely timbered land in Alaska); Map of the Northwest Territories, 1929, Department of the Interior, Canada, showing the northern limit of wooded country; Birket-Smith: 1929, I, a map showing scattered timber in the Barren Grounds; and the following miscellaneous references: Mecking: 1928, 199 (Anderson River), 203 (a map showing tree line in Hudson Bay region); Byhan: 1909, 23 (a map showing tree line in Arctic America), 13 (general); and other sources referred to below.

2. Mecking: 1928, 241.

3. Mecking: 1928, 243.

4. Mecking: 1928, 256.

5. Rasmussen: 1927, 335 ff. See also Harrington: 1919, 212 f.

6. O'Neill: 1924, 15a.

7. Burwash: 1931, 101.

8. Jenness: 1922, 14, 20. Cf. Jenness: 1928, 70.

9. Chipman and Cox: 1924, 25b, 30b, 33b.

10. Brown: 1927, 115.

11. Burwash: 1931, 101 f.

12. Mathiassen: 1925, 560.

13. Turner: 1894, 173.

14. Coleman: 1921, 16 ff. Cf. Mecking: 1928, 209.

15. *Alaska*
　　Weyer: Field Notes.
　　Ray: 1885, 48.
　　Mackenzie River to Coronation Gulf

Stefansson: 1914, 14; 1921, 263.
Jenness: 1928, 9.
Chipman and Cox: 1924, 32b.
Labrador
　　Coleman: 1921, 14.
Greenland
　　Birket-Smith: 1924, 24, 83.
　　Birket-Smith: 1928, 68, 71 (Angmagsalik).
General
　　Brown: 1927, 125.

16. Stefansson: 1914, 14, 43; Jenness: 1928, 9.

17. Birket-Smith: 1929, I, 43.

18. Freuchen and Mathiassen: 1925, 558; Klutschak: 1881, 129; Mecking: 1928, 226; Rasmussen: 1927, 168; Jenness: 1922, 50.

19. Steensby: 1910, 277; Kane: 1856, II, 210; Kroeber: 1899, 272; Mecking: 1928, 267; Birket-Smith: 1928, 68.

20. Hutchison: 1930, 214; see also Ostenfeld: 1928.

21. Nordenskjöld: 1928.

22. Nordenskjöld: 1928; and Kitto: 1930, 16.

23. These climatic maps are compiled from the available data from the United States Weather Bureau and the Department of Marine and Fisheries of Canada, and also the records contained in *The Geography of the Polar Regions* by Mecking and Nordenskjöld (1928); and *Greenland*, I, a volume published by a commission composed of a number of authorities, as well as from miscellaneous other sources. Similar maps to show precipitation were not constructed, owing to the lesser impor-

tance of precipitation and the scantiness of the records in certain sections.

24. See also *Arktis:* 1930, 3 Jahrgang, Heft 1/2, 4–13; and Nansen: 1911, 133.

25. Osborn: 1858, 1 f.

26. Communication from Stefansson.

27. Stefansson: 1922, 267 f.

28. MacMillan: 1927, 274.

29. Mecking: 1928, 272.

30. Kayser: 1928, 357.

31. Harrington: 1919, 211 f.; Ray: 1885, 24; Birket-Smith: 1929, I, 53; Mathiassen: 1928, I, 10; Tarr: 1897, 134 f.; Hawkes: 1916, 25 f.; Coleman: 1921, 18; Turner: 1887a, 81; Turner: 1894, 172.

32. Murdoch: 1892, 31; Jenness: 1922, 123; O'Neill: 1924, 72a; Birket-Smith: 1929, I, 53; Storgaard: 1928, 565.

33. Day: 1921, sec. 3, 10; Harrington: 1919, 212.

34. O'Neill: 1924, 15a; Mecking: 1928, 197; Turner: 1894, 203.

35. O'Neill: 1924, 72a; Rasmussen: 1927, 213; Birket-Smith: 1929, I, 53.

36. Jenness: 1928, 127.

37. Rasmussen: 1927, 67. Stefansson translates the name as meaning "Great icy."

38. Turner: 1894, 172; Hawkes: 1916, 25 ff.

39. Mathiassen: 1928, I, 10.

40. Petersen: 1928, 260.

41. Brooks: 1906, 153; Weyer: Field Notes; Nelson: 1899; Day: 1921, sec. 3, 3, 10; Jenness: 1922, 121; Birket-Smith: 1929, I, 54; O'Neill: 1924, 72a; Birket-Smith: 1929, I, 130; Mathiassen: 1928, I, 10; Mecking: 1928, 206; Hawkes: 1916, 25–26; Coleman: 1921, 13; Mecking: 1928, 221; Steensby: 1910, 273; Birket-Smith: 1928a, 470–471; Thalbitzer: 1914, 20.

42. Freuchen and Mathiassen: 1925, 554, 558; Boas: 1887, 78; Burwash: 1931, 106.

43. Brown: 1927, 116.

44. Turner: 1887a, 81.

45. Mecking: 1928, 274.

46. Stefansson: 1922, 265. Concerning birds of the Canadian Arctic, see Kitto: 1930, 40 f.

47. Birket-Smith: 1929, I, 48.

48. Day: 1921, sec. 3; Harrington: 1919, 212; Murdoch: 1892, 31; Mecking: 1928, 197; Birket-Smith: 1929, I, 47–48; Mathiassen: 1928, 10; Boas: 1887, 78; Hawkes: 1916, 26; Coleman: 1921, 18; Turner: 1887a, 81; Turner: 1894, 172; Storgaard: 1928, 565.

49. Kitto: 1930, 20.

50. Chipman and Cox: 1924, 32b; O'Neill: 1924, 72a.

51. Mecking: 1928, 114.

52. Freuchen and Mathiassen: 1925, 357–358.

53. Mecking: 1928, 221.

54. Day: 1921, sec. e, 6; Department of Marine and Fisheries, Canada.

55. Day: 1921, sec. 3; Brooks: 1906, 153; Weyer: Field Notes; Nelson: 1899, 24; Jenness: 1922, 14, 247; Klutschak: 1881, 131; Mathiassen: 1928, I, 10; Mecking: 1928, 206; Rasmussen: 1929, I, 12; Hawkes: 1916, 25–26; Mecking: 1928, 221; Steensby: 1910, 273; Ekblaw: 1928; Mecking: 1928, 267; Birket-Smith: 1924, 23; Birket-Smith: 1928a, 470–471; Thalbitzer: 1914, 20.

56. Freuchen and Mathiassen: 1925, 557; Boas: 1888, 418; Ekblaw: 1928; Mecking: 1928, 222.

57. Jenness: 1928, 62.

58. Birket-Smith: 1929, I, 49.

59. Stefansson: 1921, 209.

60. Stefansson: 1921, 311.

61. Kitto: 1930, 39.

62. Allen: 1880, 614.

63. Murdoch: 1885, 95; Murdoch: 1892, 56.

64. Jenness: 1922, 15; Ross: 1835, app. xix.

65. Jensen: 1928, 328.

66. Allen: 1880, 448; *Encyclopaedia Britannica:* 1910, XXIV, 534.

67. Allen: 1880, 667 ff.; Jenness: 1928, 328.

68. Allen: 1880, 448, 667 ff.; Murdoch: 1885, 96–97; Stefansson: 1914, 144, 300 (Mackenzie Delta and Forsythe Bay); Jenness: 1922, 17 (Coronation Gulf); Burwash: 1931, 22 (Queen Maud Gulf); Birket-Smith: 1929, I, 44 (west coast of Hudson Bay); Mathiassen: 1928, I, 13 (Iglu-

lik Eskimos); Murdoch: 1892, 56 (Point Barrow); Rasmussen: 1921, 315 (Ellesmere Land, near Lady Franklin Bay and Hall Basin); Ekblaw: 1928 (Smith Sound); Jensen: 1928, 327 (Greenland); Birket-Smith: 1924, 29–30 (Greenland); Thalbitzer: 1914, 23 (East Greenland).

69. Allen: 1880, 448.

70. Stefansson: In a communication to the writer.

71. Jensen: 1928, 328–329; Allen: 1880, 589.

72. Allen: 1880, 488; Jensen: 1928, 328.

73. Murdoch: 1885, 95; Murdoch: 1892, 56 (Point Barrow); Birket-Smith: 1929, I, 44–45 (Baker Lake, Barren Grounds); Jensen: 1928, 328–329 (Greenland); Birket-Smith: 1924, 29–30 (Greenland); Thalbitzer: 1914, 23 (East Greenland).

74. Jensen: 1928, 328.

75. Nansen: 1925, chap. iii; Jensen: 1928, 327–328; Allen: 1880, 448.

76. Allen: 1880, 733.

77. Jensen: 1928, 326.

78. Allen: 1880, 681 ff.; Murdoch: 1885, 97.

79. Murdoch: 1892, 56.

80. *Bartholomew's Atlas:* 1911, 16; Weyer: Field Notes.

81. *Bartholomew's Atlas:* 1911, 16.

82. *Bartholomew's Atlas:* 1911, 15, and Plate 4, Map vi.

83. *Bartholomew's Atlas:* 1911, 23–24, and Plate 8; Jensen: 1928, 334; Jenness: 1922, 46; and communication from Jenness.

84. *Encyclopaedia Britannica:* 1910, XXVIII, 568 ff.

85. Murdoch: 1892, 56.

86. *Bartholomew's Atlas:* 1911, 23, and Plate 8, i; Murdoch: 1892, 56 (Point Barrow); Ray: 1885, 46 (northwestern Alaska); Murdoch: 1885, 100 (Point Barrow); Freuchen and Mathiassen: 1925, 558 (Melville Peninsula); Mathiassen: 1928, I, 13 (Ponds Inlet, Navy Board Inlet, and Admiralty Inlet); Mecking: 1928, 217 (Baffin Island); Turner: 1887a, 83 (Ungava District); Mecking: 1928, 232 (Ellesmere Island); Wissler: 1918, 113 (Wolstenholme Sound);

Jensen: 1928, 331–332 (Greenland); Thalbitzer: 1914, 23 (East Greenland).

87. *Bartholomew's Atlas:* 1911, 23; Brown: 1927, 134; Weyer: Field Notes; Petroff: 1900, 215 (Kuskokwim River to Kotzebue Sound); Murdoch: 1892, 56 (Point Barrow); Stefansson: 1914, 141 (Mackenzie Delta); Freuchen and Mathiassen: 1925, 558 (Melville Peninsula); Birket-Smith: 1929, I, 44 (Hudson Bay); Turner: 1894, 174 (Ungava Bay); Turner: 1887a, 83 (Ungava District); Coleman: 1921, 9 (Labrador); Mathiassen: 1928, I, 13 (Roes Welcome, Lyon Inlet, and Duke of York Bay); Jensen: 1928, 332–333 (Greenland); and Jenness, communication.

88. Jensen: 1928, 332.

89. Jensen: 1928, 332.

90. Brown: 1927, 129.

91. *Bartholomew's Atlas:* 1911, Plate 5, iii.

92. Nelson: 1899, 120; Petroff: 1884, map opposite p. 57; Weyer: Field Notes.

93. Stefansson: 1914, 145.

94. Jenness: 1922, 52–53.

95. Stefansson: 1914, 48.

96. Stefansson: 1921, 301, 333, 344; Mecking: 1928, 226.

97. Birket-Smith: 1929, I, 44; Freuchen and Mathiassen: 1925, 561; Mecking: 1928, 228; Mathiassen: 1928, 13.

98. Boas: 1888, 438; Mecking: 1928, 217.

99. Steensby: 1910, 397–398.

100. Mecking: 1928.

101. Mecking: 1928, 267–268.

102. Jensen: 1928, 325.

103. Thalbitzer: 1914, 404; Holm: 1914, 52.

104. Turner: 1894, 174.

105. Brown: 1927, 129.

106. Mecking: 1928, 268; Rasmussen: 1921, 18.

107. *Encyclopaedia Britannica:* 1910, V, 147d; VII, 922 ff.; XXIII, 56b; XXVII, 633.

108. Nordenskjöld: 1928, 82; Stefansson: 1921, 332, 344; Steensby: 1910, 393; Mecking: 1928, 223, 226 ff.

109. Hawkes: 1916, 32. See also Dugmore: 1913.

110. Low: 1895, 319.

111. Jensen: 1928, 319 ff.

112. Holm: 1914, 56 ff.

113. Brown: 1927, 127.

114. Anderson, R. M., in Hoare: 1930, 52.

115. Bilby: 1923, 40.

116. Birket-Smith: 1929, I, 56.

117. Stefansson: 1921, 246 ff.

118. Stefansson: 1922.

119. Stefansson: 1921, 350, 352; Mecking: 1928, 223.

120. Birket-Smith: 1929, I, 56 ff.

121. Birket-Smith: 1929, I, 48.

122. Freuchen and Mathiassen: 1925, 558.

123. Burwash: 1931, 52.

124. Mecking: 1928, 225.

125. Rasmussen: 1927, 246.

126. Jenness: 1922, 15, 17, 101, 187, and communication.

127. Steensby: 1917.

128. Boas: 1907, 100 ff.

129. Fig. 10 is taken from Anderson, R. M., in Hoare: 1930, 50. See also Nathorst: 1900; Allen: 1901; Allen: 1913; and Feilden: 1895.

130. Anderson, in Hoare: 1930, 51.

131. Mecking: 1928, 223.

132. Stefansson: 1921, 18.

CHAPTER III

BODILY ADJUSTMENTS OF ESKIMOS TO LIFE–CONDITIONS

§1. RESISTANCE TO COLD

HAS exposure to extreme cold through many generations fitted the Eskimos in a physical sense to survive the arctic cold better than peoples reared in warmer regions? The question is difficult to answer. Proper clothing and precautions against exposure are so effective both among Eskimos and outsiders from the temperate zone that it is hard to isolate the resistance to cold offered by the human body itself.

With regard to respiratory diseases such as colds, which must be considered indirectly in this connection, the Eskimos seem to be more susceptible than white people. As brought out later in the section on the responses of the Eskimo to the environment of microbiological organisms,[1] however, the bacteria causing these diseases cannot be considered in the main to have been originally a part of the Eskimo environment, inasmuch as they were brought by travelers from outside.

A distinction should be made between susceptibility to cold and capacity to endure cold. Apart from diseases associated with cold weather, the physical resistance of the Eskimo to low temperatures has never been evaluated. As a people they incline toward fatness, an advantage in withstanding cold; but so do many other groups who live in warm climates.

As for bodily hair, the Eskimos have decidedly less than Europeans.[2] Scantiness of facial hair is an advantage to the Eskimo in that it prevents the accumulation of frost.[3] The Polar Eskimo is known even to pluck his beard to prevent ice from forming on his face.[4]

That Eskimos sometimes suffer from frostbite is mentioned by many arctic travelers.[5] Whether their resistance to it is appreciably different from that of other people is open to question. Perhaps those who are not able to endure cold are, as a rule, eliminated fairly early in life. There may be a certain amount of unconscious selection in the killing of some of the children by their parents, a practice general among the Eskimos.[6] No instance appears of testing a child's endurance by exposing it to the cold, but the manner in which infants are exposed to the elements in the natural course of events must have some selective influence. Jenness remarks that he has seen a woman expose an infant to the weather with the thermometer at 30° F. below zero in a thirty-mile-an-hour blizzard while she leisurely changed its garment.[7] Mathiassen writes: "In —20° I have seen a woman bring her nine-months adoptive daughter out of the pouch and sit her on the sledge for a little while with her lower body bare."[8]

§2. CLIMATE AND MATURITY

BERTHELSEN determined that the average age at the time of the first menstruation was fifteen years and five months among 127 women in the Ũmánaq District, some of whom were of mixed parentage. Of the total, forty-two are put down as being of pure Eskimo race, and for them the average was fifteen years and six months.[9] Another determination of the age of Greenland girls at their first menstruation, based on one hundred individuals, is cited by Ploss[10] on the authority of von Haven as follows:

> 88 girls between the ages of 15 and 17
> 5 girls before the age of 15
> 7 girls after the age of 17

It is written of the Eskimos of Cumberland Sound that ". . . sexual maturity makes its appearance early, so far as can be learned of a people of whom no one knows his age, even at 13 or 14 years among females."[11] Lundberg asserts that among twenty-one Labrador Eskimo girls five who were not yet having their monthly periods were fourteen years old or less; of the sixteen others who were already menstruating, the function first appeared between the ages of fourteen and fifteen in four individuals, between sixteen and seventeen in three, and not until twenty in two cases. The average age thus amounts to about sixteen years.[12] According to MacDiarmid, who accompanied the arctic expedition under John Ross as its doctor, menstruation among the Eskimos often first begins at the age of twenty-three and even then occurs only during the summer months.[13] Again it is stated that Eskimo girls have their first menstruation when between the ages of thirteen and fifteen years.[14] Turner gives thirteen years for the approximate age in Labrador;[15] Kelly's estimate of the age of maturity in Eskimo girls is likewise thirteen years;[16] and according to Dr. Thompson, who has practiced for a number of years among the Eskimos of Alaska, the probable average age, not based upon statistics, is about fourteen years.[17]

Stefansson's attention was directed to the early age of maturity among Eskimo girls by Dr. H. R. Marsh, a medical missionary at Point Barrow, and he estimates the age among western Eskimo girls at from ten to fourteen years.[18] According to him the age at maturity is sufficiently young to seem at variance with the generally accepted relationship between coldness of climate and lateness of maturity, but he argues that the anomaly is only apparent. Stefansson explains the matter by the fact that the temperature inside the dwellings of the Western Eskimos, which are of stone, wood, and sod, is so warm that "for all intents and purposes the typical Eskimo . . . lives under tropical or subtropical conditions." Further, he explains an apparent increase in the age at maturity during recent years on the grounds of poorer clothing and less heated dwellings. It would be interesting to test this hypothesis with data from the Central Eskimos, who pass the winter in snow houses.

The question may fairly be asked, however, whether the age at maturity among Eskimos actually is early in comparison with other aboriginal peoples of North and South America. In answer to this the following data are cited:[19]

People	Region	Age of Girls at First Menstruation Years	Authority Quoted
Indians	Alaska	14–17	
500 Indians	Arctic	12.6	Engelmann after Mathews
Potawatomi	Lake Michigan	14	Keating
Ojibwa or Chippewa		14–16	Parker
Dakota, Algonquin, and Navajo		12–14	Comfort
Piute and Shoshone	Nebraska	13	Montezuma
Apache	Arizona	12	Parker
Mescalero-Apache Reservation	New Mexico	13	Marden
Omaha		12–13	Dougherty

		Number	Age	
Sioux (43 females)				Currier
Santee Agency	Nebraska	1	13	
Fort Peck Agency	Montana	14	14	
Fort Niobrara	Nebraska	13	15	
		5	16	
		5	17	
		3	18	
		1	19	
		1	23	

People	Region	Age of Girls at First Menstruation	Authority Quoted
		Years	
Grosventres, Arachara, and Mandan		15	Parker
Yankton and Crow Creek Indians		16	Wray
Dakota and Sioux		15–16	Keating
Indians	Surinam	12	Stedman
Payaguas	Paraguay	11	Rengger
Pampas Indians		10–12	Mantegazza
Campa and Anti	Amazon River	12	Grandidier
Creole Indians	Peru	9	
Mountain Indians	Peru	14	
Araucanians	Chile	11–12	Rollin
Indians	Tierra del Fuego	One girl at 18 had not yet menstruated; while 2 eleven-year-old girls were already menstruating. The authors conclude that menstruation generally begins later than among girls in Europe.	Deniker and Hyades

The data in the above table are not, of course, all equally accurate, but no effort can be made to weigh the separate items. Averaging the figures just as they stand, for all groups of Indians represented in the table with the exception of the Arctic Indians, the Alaskan Indians, the Tierra del Fuegians, and the Creole Indians of Peru, the figure is about 13.3 years. Thus obtained, the average age at the inception of menstruation among Indians of North and South America, exclusive of high-latitude regions, is doubtless far from exact, but a more accurate determination is impossible with the available data. Attempting by the same method to determine an average with the data previously cited pertaining to the Eskimos, 14.2 years is derived. It would seem, therefore, that the Eskimos do not differ very widely from other aboriginal peoples of the western hemisphere in more moderate latitudes regarding the age at which girls reach maturity,[20] but that the Eskimo girl is, if anything, slightly older when menstruation begins. This result is not greatly at variance with what might be expected in view of the relationship supposed to exist between climate and age at maturity. The uncertainty remains, however, as to the comparative influence exerted by climate, race, and artificial environmental effects produced by such means as clothing and dwellings. Diet, too, seems to be a factor. As George Maxwell Brown points out, overnutrition and excessive meat diet are among the factors which tend to accelerate the menstrual onset.[21] In view of the high percentage of meat in the diet of the Eskimo, perhaps here is an influence that should be given more consideration in this particular than has generally been accorded it.

It is suggested in addition that another matter which may have a bearing on this question is the apparent long delay after puberty before pregnancy and childbirth occur.

Thus, Dr. Simpson states that the women of Point Barrow (Alaska) do not commonly bear children before the age of twenty.[22] And Murdoch corroborates this testimony by asserting that his party "certainly saw no mothers who appeared younger than this."[23] Of the Copper Eskimos we read: "Girls . . . often marry before they reach puberty, though they bear no children until three or four years later."[24] Similarly, with reference to the Polar Eskimos, it is written that girls usually marry at the age of twelve, though they are unable to bear children before they are eighteen;[25] and it is stated by a different authority concerning the same group that "girls . . . never have children before three years after puberty."[26]

These statements suggest that productivity is delayed until some time after the Eskimo girl has attained puberty. This delay cannot be due to abstention from intercourse, since the Eskimos are notably lax in this respect. It is suggested here, therefore, that it may be inaccurate to say that Eskimo girls mature moderately early, for the inception of menstruation apparently may not imply full sexual potency.

§3. DISEASE AND THE ESKIMO

Jenness observed that among the Copper Eskimos measles, influenza, tuberculosis, and venereal diseases were unknown.[27] Among the Polar Eskimos (northwest Greenland) gastrointestinal lesions, such as appendicitis, are not known. Diarrhea ordinarily is caused only by the eating of too long-cached meat, especially bear meat. No incidence of diphtheria or of scarlet fever was obtained. Tuberculosis has been recently introduced from South Greenland.[28] In southwest Baffin Island, Heinbecker could obtain no histories of scarlet fever, diphtheria, or measles, and it seems quite unlikely that these illnesses have ever occurred in this region during the lifetime of the present population.[29] Rasmussen remarks concerning certain Eskimos living in the vicinity of King William Island: "They were not only cheerful, but healthy, knowing nothing of any disease beyond the 'colds' that come as a regular epidemic in spring and autumn."[30]

Thus, it can be said that many of the diseases known to white people were originally absent among Eskimos; but a full statement cannot be made as to their susceptibility or immunity to these diseases. Heinbecker's research shows that the Eskimos have a comparatively high susceptibility to colds and other upper respiratory infections, on contact with the outside world. "Such upper respiratory infections apparently never become endemic in the community. The epidemic subsides and no further case occurs until fresh contact is made with the outside world. Chronic carriers therefore do not play a part in the production of the disease nor does attack confer immunity."[31]

The Eskimos seem to be very susceptible to tuberculosis,[32] which has been introduced from the outside.

The above information is obviously very inadequate for drawing any generalizations on health and disease among the Eskimos in their natural state. Knowledge of this aspect of a primitive people is very slow to develop; it is one of the most intricate and difficult problems in an anthropological study. The information at hand suggests, however, that the Eskimo differs from other peoples in his susceptibility to some diseases, due chiefly to his not having been exposed to them through many generations.

§4. DIET

Meat Diet

THE salient fact regarding the food of the Eskimos is that they eat practically nothing but meat and fish. Considering the people as a whole, seal meat is the most important food, especially along the coast from Point Barrow to the west coast of Hudson Bay and among most of the Eskimos of Labrador and Greenland.[33] Polar bear is almost as important as seal in the diet of the Eskimos at Prince Albert Sound and Minto Inlet (Victoria Island).[34] Walrus meat is a staple food in some Eskimo sections, and among certain peoples, such as the Polar Eskimos, the walrus is the most valuable animal caught.[35] Seal and walrus combined form the chief foods along part of the west coast of Hudson Bay,[36] in the Ungava District, Labrador,[37] at St. Lawrence Island,[38] and in Bering Strait.[39]

Seal and walrus are used more during winter than summer. Caribou is hunted more extensively during summer than any other animal. Practically all Eskimo groups depend to some degree upon caribou. In some sections it is the staff of life the year round. This can be said of the inland Eskimos of the Barren Grounds, who are appropriately called the Caribou Eskimos.[40] In former times musk oxen supplied a large share of the food of these central tribes, but now these animals are scarce.[41] Whale meat was also used extensively by many groups before these animals were largely wiped out by white hunters.

Fishing is of importance among practically all Eskimos,[42] the Polar Eskimos by exception fishing but little.[43] Shellfish are rarely used as food. Birds and their eggs are important locally, as among the Polar Eskimos[44] and the Diomede Islanders.[45]

Vegetable Foods

THE proportion of vegetable food eaten by the Eskimos is nowhere very great, though it varies from group to group. This is due chiefly to the scarcity of edible plant food. However, it should be mentioned that the Eskimos do not always make full use of what vegetable food there is. Stefansson[46] mentions, for instance, that the Coronation Gulf Eskimos lived among an abundance of salmon berries (elsewhere known as cloudberries) without ever so much as thinking of tasting them.

Probably the Eskimos of certain parts of Alaska and Labrador eat proportionally more vegetable food than others. In Alaska during the fall they gather quantities of blueberries, heathberries, salmon berries, and cranberries.[47] They also collect a kind of wild sorrel; and young willow leaves are boiled and eaten. In the region of Bering Strait vegetable food cannot constitute more than about 5 per cent of the diet.[48] The stalks of a plant which is popularly known as "Eskimo rhubarb" are gathered, and, at least on the Diomede Islands, they are stored dry for winter use. This is true also of the small tuberous roots of a wild plant sometimes called "Eskimo potato."

Berries are used quite abundantly by the natives of Labrador, who distinguish by name nearly twenty edible varieties.[49] They also eat tuberous roots, and in time of need even caribou moss.[50]

The natives of the Diomede Islands[51] and St. Lawrence Island[52] eat kelp. At all hours of the day the Diomeders, especially the children, can be seen gathering and eating raw the rubbery stalks and ribbons of this seaweed. It can be collected only during the ice-free season; and the Eskimos at Cape Prince of Wales, only about twenty-five miles distant, do not have this form of food. Kelp is eaten by the Labrador Eskimos[53] in a medicinal way, and by the East Greenlanders in time of starvation, when, indeed, it may be quite a staple.[54] Coxe mentions sea wrack as a food among the Aleutian Islanders in time of scarcity.[55] Seaweed is never used by the Caribou Eskimos.[56]

In East Greenland crowberries, stonecrop and angelica are eaten, but the quantity is proportionally small compared with meat.[57] Regarding West Greenland, Birket-Smith states[58] that in point of quantity vegetable food is of practically no importance, but that it is important from a dietary point of view. There the chief vegetable food is the crowberry, or curlewberry.[59] In places in southern Greenland it is so plentiful as almost to blacken the ground.[60] The Eskimos consider these berries a luxury when mixed with blubber. The blue-black blaeberry, bilberry, or bog whortleberry is less common. In Greenland the Eskimos often think them unwholesome. The cloudberry or mountain raspberry (the salmon berry of Alaska) rarely produces ripe fruit in Greenland.[61]

In the foregoing discussion we have included some of the outstanding instances of vegetable food in the diet of Eskimos. It will be noticed that this information pertains chiefly to the extreme east and west of the Eskimo province, and especially the southern portions of these sections. In the central and northern parts, vegetable food is used in even lesser quantity. Murdoch[62] states that at Point Barrow his party never saw the natives eat any vegetable substances, though it was said that the buds of willows were sometimes eaten. Eastward from Alaska berries and roots are but a small item of diet, as, for instance, at Coronation Gulf.[63] Among the Caribou Eskimos of the Barren Grounds berry and root gathering are practiced, but not to any great extent.[64] The same applies to the Iglulik Eskimos.[65] Mathiassen says that the berries, leaves, and roots eaten by these people have not the slightest significance as food.[66] In the region of the Colville Hills (southwestern Victoria Island) the Eskimos knew no vegetable food save the semidigested moss in the stomachs of the caribou.[67] Similarly, the chief vegetable food of the Polar Eskimos is the contents of the paunch of the caribou and musk ox.[68] Aside from this the only plant food mentioned[69] among these northernmost people in the world is a small flower, which is eaten only by the women.

The half-digested contents of the caribou stomach is enjoyed as a luxury by most Eskimo groups.[70] This is sometimes frozen and kept for winter use.[71]

This survey of the Eskimo diet can be summarized by stating that meat, chiefly of seal, walrus, and caribou, forms the main food of the Eskimos. The quantity of vegetable food consumed is generally insignificant, except, perhaps, for its vitamin content.

Food Is Eaten Raw or Cooked

MEAT and fish are sometimes cooked, sometimes eaten raw. The eating of raw food is explained by circumstance rather than by choice, scarcity of fuel being largely accountable. In addition to the difficulty of securing fuel the awkwardness of Eskimo cooking gear restricts them in their methods of preparing food. The stone lamp,[72] burning animal fat, is the general instrument for cooking, especially in winter when vegetable fuels are less available. This implement is not adapted to roasting; boiling or stewing is the only common method of cooking.[73] And with only the stone cooking pot,[74] even the latter processes are difficult. A further deterrent to cooking lies in the fact that much of their meat is old and soft when eaten and consequently would be improved less than ordinarily by cooking.

The Eskimos use as fuel the fats and oils of various animals, burned in shallow lamps of stone or pottery. In open fires they burn different kinds of scrubby vegetation which are available chiefly during summer, as well as driftwood.[75] They have never learned to utilize coal as fuel, although there are outcroppings in a number of places in the region.

Whether cooking over the blubber lamp or with heather, willow, or peat as fuel, the process is slow. In winter, water has to be obtained by melting snow or ice, an operation requiring the expenditure of considerable heat in itself. And if the only utensil is a heavy stone pot, to bring the water to a boil further consumes time. As Jenness[76] points out, it takes one hour to boil meat in winter with the lamp and blubber, even after the snow has been melted. Still, the Copper Eskimos prefer to cook their food and generally do so except in summer, when fuel is often scarce. Rasmussen[77] writes that it took one of the King William Island Eskimos five hours to cook a potful of fish and boil a kettle of water using Dryas for fuel. As he remarks, "it is not surprising then that most prefer to eat their food raw."

Among the Koksoagmiut of Labrador food is invariably cooked when it conveniently can be.[78] The almost total absence of cooking among the

Eskimos of the Yukon-Kuskokwim region, Alaska, is accounted for by Jacobsen on the ground of scarcity of fuel.[79] Among the Caribou Eskimos fuel is apt to be scarce in winter, and much, perhaps most, of the meat is eaten frozen.[80] Indeed, apart from the Hauneqtôrmiut and a very few Qaernermiut, all Caribou Eskimos pass even the coldest winters without any artificial heat whatever.[81] Petroff[82] states that the Kaniags of Kodiak Island during summer generally cook fish, their chief sustenance, but that during winter they eat the air-dried fish more often raw than cooked. The same author[83] says that the Eskimos of the Yukon-Kuskokwim region do not eat raw fish or meat unless it is frozen or dried in the air. The Eskimos of Diomede Islands use only blubber lamps for cooking, and much of their meat is eaten raw, especially the cached meat.[84] While Stefansson was in the region of the Mackenzie Delta, there were months at a time when no cooked meat was eaten by anyone except those under taboo.[85] Stefansson says in addition that the Coronation Gulf Eskimos ate caribou meat more often raw than cooked.[86] They frequently ate fish raw, but seldom seal, and they usually had one cooked meal a day. Birket-Smith states[87] that among the Caribou Eskimos an entire meal of raw meat is unusual, unless it is frozen. According to Rasmussen[88] very little cooking is done among the inland Eskimos of Great Fish River (Backs River), most of the food, both meat and fish, being eaten raw. Raw and frozen meat is the common food among the Iglulik Eskimos.[89] The Eskimos of Labrador customarily ate the frozen meat of reindeer raw,[90] but fresh meat was ordinarily boiled. Crantz, the early authority on West Greenland, writes that meat is not eaten raw as much as fish.[91] Birket-Smith[92] adds, concerning West Greenland, that though much food is eaten raw, the usual thing is to cook it. Thalbitzer, commenting on the dietary customs of the Eskimos of East Greenland,[93] says that the hide of seal and shark is eaten raw, whale hide is sometimes boiled, but walrus hide is always boiled.

Summarizing, it can be said that probably about half of the food that the Eskimo eats has been cooked, generally parboiled.

Quantity Eaten

EXTRAVAGANT statements are made as to the amount of food that Eskimos eat. The appetite of the Eskimo, however, as Dr. Anderson has pointed out,[94] is no greater than that of the white man under the same conditions. Middleton Smith observed that thirty Eskimos at Point Barrow ate on the average eight and two-ninths pounds of meat a day per person over a period of two and a half months.[95] If this reckoning is accurate we have a case of very heavy eating. Mecking's[96] reference to the prodigious quantities of raw meat consumed by inhabitants of the Arctic (as much as fifteen pounds per person in a half day) is certainly exceptional. Heinbecker's[97] sober statement conveys a much more accurate impression. He testifies to the very large quantity eaten in times of plenty by adult Eskimos in the central region—four to eight pounds a day. He further states that in cold weather, especially when traveling, one half of their food may be fat.

Stimulants

THE fermentation of intoxicating beverages seems to have been unknown to Eskimos before they came in contact with civilized people. This appears strange in view of the fact that they are accustomed to storing berries for winter use and might be expected to have hit upon the discovery naturally. Possibly their apparent failure to do so is attributable to the cold, which is a hindrance to fermentation. Mr. H. B. Collins of the Smithsonian Institution informed me that the natives of St. Lawrence Island store a sort of wild spinach until it becomes sour, but whether it is intoxicating cannot be said. Petroff writes that, "Previous to their acquaintance with the Russians the Kaniags [Kodiak Island] undertook to make an intoxicating beverage by distilling alcohol from the fermented juice of raspberries and whortleberries, but this was prohibited by the Russian Company. Now they all know how to distill alcohol from flour, sugar, and molasses."[98] It is mentioned also that West Greenlanders sometimes make a drink from whortleberries which are left in water for a certain length of time.[99] It remains questionable whether this is intoxicating, and, indeed, whether it was an original process with them. Certainly, alcohol had no considerable influence upon the Eskimos as an aboriginal people; and it is doubtful whether they were acquainted with the process of fermentation at all.

§5. EFFECTS OF DIET

WHAT, then, are the effects on the Eskimo of this diet which is almost entirely meat and fish, largely raw, sometimes eaten irregularly according to fluctuations in the supply?

We might expect that rheumatism would be a common complaint among Eskimos, since it is thought to be unfavorably affected by a meat diet and by damp, cold weather. Information is so scanty and inconsistent that it is impossible to state conclusively whether rheumatism is commoner among Eskimos than it is among people living under other conditions.[100] The high percentage of fat in the Eskimo diet doubtless lessens the danger from kidney disorders which are aggravated by unbalanced protein consumption. Stefansson[101] comments on the generally accepted fact that a diet consisting almost entirely of protein leads to "protein poisoning" in the sense that illness results because the kidneys are overtaxed with the task of excreting the excess of nitrates. "This leads to nephritis or derangement of the kidneys, of which a common symptom is swelling of the body beginning usually at the ankles. . . . Having to live mainly on protein (lean meat) is an occasional experience of many Indian tribes in Canada and is referred to by them and the Hudson's Bay men as 'starvation,' no matter how much lean meat may be available."[102] The Eskimos, however, do not acutely experience the difficulty of conforming to an unbalanced protein diet, because the blubber-laden carcasses of the marine mammals supply an abundance of carbohydrates.

Metabolism

HEINBECKER determined certainly that the Eskimos of Baffin Land possess certain peculiarities in the digestive processes. Basal metabolism, for instance, is considerably higher than in persons living in temperate latitudes.[103] He proved that these Eskimos have a remarkable power to oxidize fats completely. In explanation of this he mentions as a possibility that the Eskimo actually does possess "an adaptation permitting complete combustion of fat without any intervention of carbohydrate and in this respect differs from other human subjects."

Scurvy

THIS disease is brought on by vitamin deficiency of a diet lacking in fresh foods.[104] There is some evidence that climate exercises a contributing influence. Thus, a cold, damp environment which depresses the various functions of the body, may exert an influence if the quota of antiscorbutic foodstuff is not quite adequate.[105] If this is true, the Eskimo habitat in most cases would be favorable for the occurrence of the disease even aside from the natural restrictions it imposes on diet. Various observers have stated that exposure to ultra-violet light seems to have a beneficial effect both in the healing and prevention of scurvy, similar to its effect upon rickets. If so, the diminished sunlight during the arctic winter would likewise be a contributing factor in the disease. An experiment on guinea-pig scurvy, however, shows that ultra-violet rays are entirely ineffectual in preventing or postponing scurvy, at least among those animals.[106] Scurvy is possibly more dangerous in arctic regions in that it seems to predispose to frostbite.[107] At any rate it is the most dreaded disease among arctic explorers.

Eskimos sometimes suffer from scurvy,[108] though apparently far less frequently than do white men in the Arctic. Possibly the Eskimo has a certain degree of natural immunity to the disease. Some writers claim that resistance to scurvy varies among different peoples.[109] Hess[110] states that if we admit that disposition and habits of life can play a rôle, it is quite possible for races to vary in their predisposition to the disorder. The chief explanation for the infrequency of scurvy among Eskimos, however, doubtless lies in their eating fresh meat sufficiently regularly. The skin of the white whale is mentioned as an excellent remedy against scurvy.[111] Raw meat, especially, is completely adequate in preventing the disorder, and explorers have discovered that white men can be entirely independent of fresh vegetables.[112] Therefore, scarcity of fuel has doubtless spared the Eskimos great suffering through forcing them to eat their meat raw or only partly cooked.

Anatomical Effects

ASIDE from physiological adjustments that may have developed in response to the diet of the Eskimos, certain anatomical modifications should be mentioned. These are purely superficial modifications, and not hereditary characteristics bred into the race through organic evolution.

A striking feature of the Eskimo is his teeth, which are characteristically worn down and look as though their edges had been rasped off with a file. This conspicuous condition is due, of course, to the chewing of tough materials, both as foods and in the form of thongs and hides which have to be softened by mastication. Often by middle age the crowns of the incisors and the cusps of the second and third molars are completely worn away.[113]

As a further consequence Virchow[114] suggests that the vigorous exercise of the jaw muscles may have produced certain cranial modifications. There is no question as to the hypertrophy of the masticatory muscles:[115] as Virchow states, they sometimes attain a size twice as large as in the average European, who eats a mixed diet of well-prepared food. The so-called *lineae semicirculares temporum*, the muscle above the ear, grows very high on the head of the Eskimo as it does on that of the large anthropoid apes. On some Eskimo skulls there remains only a narrow portion on the crest of the skull free from muscles. Virchow further suggests that the strength of this musculature might, from generation to generation through thousands of years, exert an influence on the form of the skull. Cameron[116] offers the same suggestion implying an evolutionary process, without definitely stating it. The crest-shaped form of the cranium which is certainly a very striking characteristic of some Eskimo skulls has been attributed to the influence of the highly developed musculature.[117] Hypotheses of this nature can scarcely be considered as likely, however, in view of the rather substantial evidence that acquired anatomical characteristics are not inherited.

In this connection should be mentioned also the fact that examination of skulls has revealed that the Eskimos are the most narrow-nosed people known.[118] In the western groups the nasal width approximates that of the Mongol, while toward the east it becomes gradually narrower, so that the nasal aperture of the Greenlanders is so markedly contracted as to place them in a class by themselves in this respect.[119]

The narrowness of the nose, like certain other cranial features mentioned above, has been connected by some with an exaggeration of the masticatory muscles.[120] Other investigators, however, including Cameron,[121] have explained it as an anatomical adjustment in response to the breathing of cold air. The antithesis is, of course, to be observed in the wide nose of the negro. Thompson and Buxton, who have carried out a broad study of this question, summarize their conclusions as follows:

". . . our evidence leads us to the belief that a platyrrhine nasal index is associated with a hot moist climate, and a leptorrhine nasal index with a cold dry climate. There is a positive correlation both on living males and on crania between the nasal index and the temperature. On living males there is also a positive correlation between the nasal index and relative humidity. On crania this correlation, although present, is small."[122]

The theory that racial differences in the nasal aperture appear in response to climatic conditions is interesting in that it does not absolutely presuppose the inheritance of acquired characteristics. Even though it is not conclusively proved, it is conceivable that a large nasal aperture in the arctic regions would be so inexpedient a characteristic as to cause death of the individuals possessing it and consequent elimination of the characteristic from the race.

NOTES

1. See pp. 51 f.
2. Birket-Smith: 1924, 213; Birket-Smith: 1928, 50; Stefansson: 1914, 187–188; Weyer: Field Notes (Dr. Thompson, a physician of many years' practice among the Eskimos of Alaska, testified that these people have very scanty genital hair); Holm: 1914, 27; Hansen: 1914, 178 (the Eskimos of East Greenland seem to have more bodily hair than other Eskimos).
3. Jenness: 1923, 41b (among the Copper Eskimos facial hair does not develop to any great extent before middle age); Weyer: Field Notes (among male Eskimos of Bering Strait facial hair generally does not appear to any extent before about the age of twenty-three; it does not reach maximum until about middle age, and even then it is sometimes rather scanty. Among these Eskimos facial hair is never very thick); Ray: 1885, 37 (the men of Point Barrow are beardless until they reach the age of 20–25).
4. Steensby: 1910, 385.
5. Smith: 1902, 115; Jenness: 1928, 177; Weyer: Field Notes (Dr. Thompson said that he had never known of an Eskimo suffering from actual frostbite. He further remarked that while he was subjecting Eskimos to a hot-air bath, using an alcohol lamp under a blanket, they often straightway fainted. His belief was that they were more easily affected by heat than white people); Nelson: 1899, 29 (this author gives some illustrations which suggest that Eskimos are better able to endure cold than

white people); Murdoch: 1892, 39–40 (Murdoch mentions frostbite among the Point Barrow Eskimos).
6. See pp. 132 ff.
7. Jenness: 1922, 118.
8. Mathiassen: 1928, I, 214.
9. Birket-Smith: 1928, 52.
10. Ploss: 1927, I, 686.
11. Schliephake, cited by Ploss: 1927, I, 686.
12. Lundberg, cited by Ploss: 1927, I, 686.
13. MacDiarmid, cited by Ploss: 1927, I, 686.
14. Engelmann after Mathews, cited by Ploss: 1927, I, 686–687.
15. Turner: 1894, 188.
16. Kelly: 1912, 83.
17. Weyer: Field Notes.
18. Stefansson: 1920; and 1921, 76 ff.
19. Ploss: 1927, I, 685 ff.
20. For that matter, the average age at maturity is almost the same as that of civilized girls of North America. M. Tolentino has pointed this out: ". . . the Esquimaux have their first menses at the age of 14.6, almost the same as the average age for American and Canadian girls, which is 14.5 years." (M. Tolentino: 1927, 373.)
21. Brown: 1924, 17.
22. Simpson: 1875, 254.
23. Murdoch: 1892, 39.
24. Jenness: 1922, 158.
25. MacMillan: 1918, 274.
26. Kroeber: 1899, 301.
27. Jenness: 1922, 42 f.
28. Heinbecker and Irvine-Jones: 1928, 404.
29. Heinbecker and Irvine-Jones: 1928, 397.

30. Rasmussen: 1927, 220.

31. Heinbecker and Irvine-Jones: 1928, 404.

32. Hrdlička: 1910, 223; Nelson: 1899, 29; Weyer: Field Notes; Heinbecker and Irvine-Jones: 1928, 404.

33. Ray: 1885, 40 f.; Smith: 1902, 114; Murdoch: 1899, 61; Jenness: 1922, 17; Mecking: 1928, 202; Ross: 1835, appendix xix; Hawkes: 1916, 29 f.; Stefansson: 1914, 288.

34. Jenness: 1922, 101.

35. Rasmussen: 1921, 23; Steensby: 1910, 272; Jensen: 1928, 330; Kroeber: 1899, 269 (Kroeber, citing Peary, ranks seal first).

36. Boas: 1907, 8 (Aivilik Eskimos); Mecking: 1928, 202. (Walrus is the chief animal between Cape Fullerton and Repulse Bay.)

37. Turner: 1887a, 83.

38. Moore: 1923, 352.

39. Weyer: Field Notes.

40. Birket-Smith: 1929, I, 137, 223; Boas: 1907, 465; Rasmussen: 1927, 57, etc.

41. Steensby: 1917.

42. Klutschak: 1881, 120 (Netsilik Eskimos); Jenness: 1922, 15 (Jenness estimates that fish constitute about one-third of the total food of the Copper Eskimos); Hawkes: 1916, 34 (Labrador); Birket-Smith: 1924, 33 (Greenland); Mathiassen: 1928, I, 13–14 (Iglulik Eskimos); Weyer: Field Notes (Port Clarence, Alaska).

43. Steensby: 1910, 304.

44. Ekblaw: 1928.

45. Weyer: Field Notes.

46. Stefansson: 1921, 63–64.

47. Nelson: 1899, 268.

48. Weyer: Field Notes.

49. Hawkes: 1916, 34; Turner: 1894, 233.

50. Hawkes: 1916, 34.

51. Weyer: Field Notes.

52. Moore: 1923, 354.

53. Hawkes: 1916, 371.

54. Thalbitzer: 1914, 23, 541.

55. Coxe: 1787, 228.

56. Birket-Smith: 1929, I, 133.

57. Thalbitzer: 1914, 22–23, 504.

58. Birket-Smith: 1924, 26, 74.

59. Birket-Smith: 1924, 371–372.

60. Brown: 1927, 117.

61. For further information concerning the diet of the Eskimos of southwestern Greenland see Krough and Krough: 1915.

62. Murdoch: 1892, 62.

63. Stefansson: 1914.

64. Birket-Smith: 1929, I, 55, 96.

65. Mathiassen: 1928, I, 12, 203, 207.

66. Mathiassen: 1928, I, 12.

67. Jenness: 1928, 148.

68. Brown: 1927, 118.

69. Kroeber: 1899, 269.

70. Turner: 1894, 232; Jenness: 1922, 97–98; Birket-Smith: 1924, 380; Bilby: 1923, 143; Mathiassen: 1928, I, 204–205; Steensby: 1910, 283.

71. Jenness: 1922, 97–98.

72. Birket-Smith: 1929, II, 189 ff. (general discussion of lamps); Hough: 1896; Hough: 1898; Mathiassen: 1927, 99 ff.; Petroff: 1900, 227, 233 (Kodiak Island); Holmberg: 1855, 102 (Kodiak Island); Sarycher: 1806–7, 72 (Unalaska); Weyer: Field Notes (Alaska); Moore: 1923, 349 (St. Lawrence Island); Jenness: 1929 (Wales, Alaska); Nelson: 1899, 63 ff. (Alaska); Murdoch: 1892, 105 ff. (Point Barrow); Jenness: 1922, 44, 53 ff., 61–62, 108, 123, 130, 133, 140–141, 184 (Copper Eskimos); Birket-Smith: 1929, I, 88 ff. (Barren Grounds); Mathiassen: 1928, I, 12, 145 ff. (Iglulik Eskimos); Hawkes: 1916, 89 (Labrador); Turner: 1894, 229–230 (Koksoagmyut, northern Labrador); Kroeber: 1899, 288–289 (Polar Eskimos); Birket-Smith: 1928, 86 ff. (Greenland); Birket-Smith: 1924, 161 ff. (Greenland, and other regions, citing references).

73. Birket-Smith: 1928, 202; Birket-Smith: 1924, 381; Bilby: 1923, 97–98; Turner: 1894, 231; Birket-Smith: 1929, I, 141 ff., II, 275, Table 71A (roasting on stones).

74. Turner: 1894, 231; Mathiassen: 1927, II, 103 ff.; Birket-Smith: 1929, II, 104–105 and 274–275 (Table 70A).

75. See pp. 102 ff.

76. Jenness: 1922, 98.

77. Rasmussen: 1927, 206 f.

78. Turner: 1894, 232.

79. Jacobsen: 1884, 330, 333.

80. Birket-Smith: 1929, I, 141 ff.
81. Birket-Smith: 1929, I, 92.
82. Petroff: 1900, 231.
83. Petroff: 1900, 216.
84. Weyer: Field Notes.
85. Stefansson: 1914, 133.
86. Stefansson: 1914, 57.
87. Birket-Smith: 1929, I, 141 ff.
88. Rasmussen: 1927, 193.
89. Mathiassen: 1928, I, 204.
90. Hawkes: 1916, 33.
91. Crantz: 1767, I, 142–143.
92. Birket-Smith: 1924, 381.
93. Thalbitzer: 1914, 540.
94. Jenness: 1922, 100; see also Birket-Smith: 1929, I, 138.
95. Smith: 1902, 116.
96. Mecking: 1928, 121.
97. Heinbecker: 1928a, 463.
98. Petroff: 1900, 232.
99. Birket-Smith: 1924, 389.
100. Birket-Smith: 1929, I, 299; Weyer: Field Notes (Dr. Thompson stated that these people seemed to be bothered only moderately with rheumatism); Murdoch: 1892, 39 (asserts that rheumatism is rather frequent at Point Barrow).
101. Stefansson: 1921, 718 f.
102. Stefansson: 1913, 140 ff.
103. Heinbecker: 1928a, 474 ff.
104. Hess: 1920, 62; see also Stefansson: 1918.
105. Hess: 1920, 54–55.
106. Clark, Janet: 1925, 45–47.
107. Hess: 1920, 180.
108. Birket-Smith: 1924, 423; Turner: 1894, 187; Acland: 1927, 31.
109. Hess: 1920, 56.
110. Hess: 1920, 56.
111. Jensen: 1928, 333.
112. Hess: 1920, 10.
113. Ritchie: 1923, 59c.
114. Virchow: 1880.
115. Cameron: 1923, 51c.
116. Cameron: 1923, 51–52c.
117. Birket-Smith: 1928, 47.
118. Birket-Smith: 1928, 48–49 (this writer gives the average nasal index as 42.99, which characterizes the skulls as leptorrhine, though the living Eskimos, as he states, should be described as mesorrhine); Cameron: 1923, 44c (Cameron indicates an average nasal index of about 43.7).
119. Cameron: 1930, 291 f.
120. Birket-Smith: 1928, 48.
121. Cameron: 1923, 44c, 51c.
122. Thompson and Buxton: 1923, 115 f.

CHAPTER IV

INFLUENCE OF GEOGRAPHICAL CONDITIONS ON MODE OF LIFE

§1. CULTURAL ADJUSTMENTS

IN the foregoing section I have attempted to analyze the relationships that might exist between the life-conditions of the Eskimo habitat and the man in a purely physical sense. It was learned that physiological and anatomical responses to life-conditions in the Arctic are, in general, only slight. Physically, the Eskimo is in all essential characteristics like other men.

Strip him of his clothing, deprive him of his tools and implements, his dwellings, and his ability to create these things essential to life, and he would be scarcely more fit to survive in his northern environment than a savage from the tropical jungle. Clearly, with no more than his natural physical attributes he would soon perish. He has neither the protective fur of the caribou, the polar bear, and the musk ox, nor the warmth-conserving fat of the seal, the walrus, and the whale. He cannot live on the scanty vegetation of the tundra as can the caribou, nor has he the migratory range of these browsers. He lacks the physical aids to hunting and fighting of the bear and the wolf.

The Eskimo cannot compete with the animals as an animal. He is not compelled to. What he lacks as a physical organism he acquires through ingenuity and invention. He survives, not chiefly through physical strength and endurance, as the animals do, but through mental capability. An ingenious hunting device can take the place of fleetness of foot or sharpness of tooth or talon; the use of fire and clothing can compensate for weak resistance against cold. In this manner, man's culture takes the place of physical adaptations among the lower animals. This is particularly true of his self-maintenance mores, his implements for securing food, and his clothes and dwellings.

The Eskimo culture is the growth of centuries. As with every culture, its evolution has been analogous to organic evolution among animals. Survival has been the criterion. The succession of variations, followed by the elimination of the inexpedient, and the selection and retention of the expedient, has perfected a harpoon head that will remain imbedded beneath the skin of the seal, walrus, or whale, and thereby prevent its sinking, a boot that is waterproof, and a method of glazing sledge runners that lessens friction on granular snow.

In some instances the evolution of culture traits can follow virtually the same laws as those which explain organic evolution. This is true of those which are so closely linked with man, the physical creature, that they might just as well be his physical attributes. A weapon, for instance, which fails a man in hand-to-hand conflict with a dangerous animal is, in its effect, the same as a weak set of claws. Its failure can mean death as surely as can physical incompetence. Similarly, a man who devises an unseaworthy craft may drown in rough water, and with him dies his inexpedient invention. Not necessarily, however, does cultural evolution or societal evolution follow the laws of organic evolution. Expediency or inexpediency in most culture traits is not a matter of immediate life or death. Yet selection continually goes on. Men can modify their culture, whereas animals cannot modify their bodily organisms appreciably. By repeated trial and error, unconscious for the most part yet rational in the final outcome, culture traits evolve.

This interpretation of cultural evolution applies in substance to all groups of people. Its application to the Eskimos, however, is uncommonly striking, partly because their adaptations are highly specialized and partly because they must struggle against an exceptionally severe natural environment.

The Eskimo is a cultural success. He survives farther north than any other people on earth, in exceedingly wretched and difficult conditions—an exemplification of man's cultural adaptability to nature in the raw.

Although in scattered sources one sees repeated instances of the Eskimo's astonishing ingenuity, no one seemingly has marshaled a mass of data which will give a fairly complete picture of this astounding attribute. To this task we shall proceed.

The habitat of the Eskimos is at once one of the coldest parts of the world and one of the poorest in available fuel. With wood scarce, the Eskimo burns animal oil in stone or pottery lamps. Thus the blubber that keeps the seal warm in the polar sea heats the igloo. All the Caribou Eskimos, however, inland dwellers of the Barren Grounds of Canada, with the exception of the Hauneqtôrmiut and a very few Qaernermiut, pass even the coldest winters without any artificial heat whatever.[1] Here the temperature falls sometimes as low as —50°, and the only way they can dry wet clothing is by their own bodily heat. Their only light during the long gloom of winter is a sort of tallow dip.[2]

The Eskimo strips the slain animal of his protective fur and makes clothing of it. The animal's coat becomes virtually the Eskimo's own skin, inferior only in that it will wear out. It likewise protects the newborn babe on its mother's back under her furs; thus the woman provides for the protection of her young much after the fashion of the kangaroo.

Reports which are not very convincing state that a baby Eskimo may sometimes be seen protruding from the top of the purposely large boot which its mother wears.[3]

Another assertion, incidentally, which is very frequently encountered in the literature and demands comment, is that the Eskimos customarily carry their infants *in the hoods of their jackets*. Stefansson, with his characteristic discernment, made an extensive inquiry into this question; and he has kindly offered for present use the testimony which he compiled with the assistance of his secretary, Mrs. O. R. Wilcox. Despite the fact that at least a score of authors, many of whom are recognized as authorities on the Arctic, would have their readers believe that the Eskimos carry their babies in their hoods,[4] the best evidence makes it questionable whether this practice has ever been actually followed.

The fact that in ten winters and thirteen summers passed among the Western Eskimos, Stefansson had never seen a woman carrying a baby in the hood of her coat, and the realization that such a method would involve practical difficulties, makes it probable that every report of the practice might have originated through faulty observation. Inquiry brought out testimony from various sections of the Arctic. Capt. George Comer, for instance, whose observations apply to Baffin Island, Hudson Bay, and North Greenland, stated in a letter to Stefansson that the idea of "Eskimo women carrying their babies in the hood of their garment is perfectly absurd. The child is always carried in the loosely made garment, while the strap which takes the weight of the child . . . [passes] across the front of the coat just above the breasts. . . ." The ". . . hood takes its bend at the level of the back of the neck and the mother would be choked by the garment being pulled up in front, if the child was placed there. . . ."[5]

A communication from Morten Porsild, who has lived in Greenland for many years, to Stefansson, reads, ". . . Of course, you and Kleinschmidt are right, babies were never carried in the 'hood.' . . ."[6]

And Knud Rasmussen expresses his opinion, together with Birket-

Smith's, with whom he conferred, as follows: "In the Hudson Bay district, as indeed along the arctic coast from the Netsilingmiut and further westwards, the child is likewise carried on the back in a small pouch in the coat and decidedly not in the hood, as that would simply choke the mother. . . .

". . . the women in Greenland have never in the past carried their children in their hoods, nor do they do so now."[7]

The conclusion to be drawn from the foregoing testimony, in conjunction with the numerous statements in the literature that are consistent with it,[8] is that the only credible practice is that of carrying the child inside the garment itself. It is customarily supported by a strap or cord on the outside which passes around the woman's body near the small of the back, close under the armpits, and high across the chest.

Human eyes cannot endure protracted exposure to the glare of sunlight on snow. The glare is especially difficult to withstand in the Eskimo region during springtime, the result being snow blindness, which is sometimes permanent. To avoid this, the Eskimo peers through snow goggles, made of wood, ivory, or bone, with a narrow slit for each eye.[9]

The throwing board which he uses to add impetus when hurling a weapon has the effect of lengthening his arm by a foot or so. Lacking the physical strength to handle the unwieldy carcass of the walrus, he has made use of the principle of the block and tackle.[10] The line is threaded through holes cut in the ice and in the hide of the animal, instead of being passed around pulleys. Aside from the greater friction the effect is the same: the Eskimo is able to raise a mass which he could not otherwise lift. The wheel as a mechanical device was unknown to the Eskimo before the advent of Europeans.

Often obliged to hunt seals and other creatures in the open sea, the Eskimo has fitted himself for that element. His kayak, about the size of a small canoe, is perhaps the most seaworthy small craft in the world. Inasmuch as its frame of driftwood or saplings is covered over entirely with water-tight skin save where the small circular manhole is left open, the paddler is able to propel his craft actually *through* waves that would swamp an undecked boat. Thus a kayak can be launched through surf that would preclude all except larger craft. An interesting method of launching kayaks is said to have been practiced on King Island, where surf breaking against the abrupt sides of the island renders the normal mode of embarking impossible.[11] The paddler seats himself in his kayak on the rocky shore, whereupon two of his comrades lift him, boat and all, and at a given signal *throw him entirely clear of the dangerous surf.*

When a kayaker secures his waterproof gut jacket about the hatch of the kayak at his waist and fastens the garment tightly around his wrists and face or neck, he makes the boat virtually part of his person. Nowhere can water enter the boat or even penetrate inside his clothing. Consequently, a skilful kayaker can capsize his boat and come up none the worse. The art of managing the kayak is perfected to the finest point in Greenland, particularly in southwestern Greenland, in Angmagsalik, and in the extreme island group of Vester Eyland.[12]

A very expert kayak-man can right himself even without his paddle "by help of his throwing-stick, or even without it, by means of one arm. The height of accomplishment is reached when he does not even need to use the flat of his hand, but can clench it; and to show that he really does so, I have seen a man take a stone in his clenched hand before capsizing, and come up with it still in his grasp."[13]

"The prettiest feat of seamanship I have ever heard of is that to which some fishers, I am told, have recourse among overwhelming rollers. As the sea curls down over them they voluntarily capsize, receive it on the bottom of the kayak, and when it has passed right themselves again. I think it would be difficult to name a more intrepid method of dealing with a heavy sea."[14]

The East Greenlanders as well as the West Greenlanders capsize their kayaks safely,[15] but not the Polar Eskimos,[16] who at the time of their discovery by white men were not even using kayaks.[17] Outside of Greenland the art of capsizing a kayak seems to have been practiced only in Baffin Island,[18] Alaska,[19] and possibly in Labrador.[20]

Even for the native unversed in the art of capsizing, the kayak is a remarkably effective craft. Few Eskimos can swim.[21] Their failure to learn is due chiefly, of course, to the coldness of the water, but the author can testify that Eskimo children sometimes bathe in the Arctic Sea in summer.

Aside from among the Eskimos, the kayak is used among tribes of northeastern Asia,[22] and "it has been shown that the Samoyeds on the North coast of Russia, and possibly also the Lapps in Norway have used *kayaks* in olden times, like the Eskimo."[23]

It should be mentioned in passing that the Eskimos may possibly have utilized sails before the coming of white people as an adjunct to the paddle and oar in propelling their larger boat, the umiak.[24] This is especially surprising in view of the fact that among other native peoples of the American continents only the Mayas of the Yucatan Peninsula and the inhabitants of the coast of Peru seem to have known the sail before the coming of Europeans.[25]

The Eskimo utilizes the strength and hardiness of the dog by harnessing him to a sledge;[26] and to protect his valuable animals' feet from sharp ice he makes little shoes for them. He also uses the dog in hunting. A keen sense of smell directs the animal to the breathing hole of the seal, and the Eskimo, following, benefits from his dog's faculty just as though his own nostrils possessed it.

§2. INGENIOUS UTILIZATION OF SCANTY RESOURCES

THE Eskimo shows remarkable ingenuity in making use of what simple resources his homeland offers, and, unlike the man with but one talent, makes the utmost of his scanty materials. His house of snow needs only to be mentioned in this connection. Knowing nothing of glass he fashions his window out of ice,[27] or from the translucent intestinal membrane of a sea mammal,[28] the gullet of the white whale or of birds,[29] or the pericardium of the caribou.[30] For thread he uses sinew, generally procured chiefly from the back and hind legs of the caribou but also from the white whale, and from the gullet, tail, back, and flippers of the seal.[31] Whalebone serves as cord for lashing implements; and the thin fiber stripped from the surface of bird quills is used for finer lashing.[32]

Only a small proportion of the Eskimos used metal before the coming of the white man. Two centers of metal working existed: one including the natives about Coronation Gulf, who are appropriately called the Copper Eskimos because of their utilization of native copper; the other in northwestern Greenland, where the Eskimos worked meteoric iron on a small scale.[33]

In the absence of metal the Eskimos used stone, of course, for blades and weapon points. They also used stone, commonly soapstone, for lamps and cooking pots. The importance of soapstone along the lower reaches of the Great Fish River is evident from the fact that the tribal name there, Utkuhikhalingmiut, means "Dwellers in the land of soapstone."[34] Iron pyrites, in addition, was of value in generating fire among practically all Eskimos.[35] Everywhere, however, the Eskimos were familiar with the process of generating fire with a drill.[36] Of course, they never employed such an intricate principle in kindling fire as that of a lens of ice.

Stone for implements and iron pyrites were in general available to all Eskimos, though in some cases they would have to travel to procure them.[37]

In natural resources, particularly in wood, the Eskimos of the central and northernmost regions are most poorly supplied. Their own resourcefulness is correspondingly conspicuous as under these circumstances they make their sledges of bone or ivory.[38] In Baffin Island if wood is scarce the natives make a strange shovel-shaped sledge by stitching together sheets of whalebone.[39] The height of ingenuity is displayed in the building of a sledge of frozen hide. Pieces of walrus skin or musk-ox skin are soaked in water, folded into the desired forms, and allowed to freeze solid. Thus the Eskimo fights the inexorable North with its own weapons; the extreme cold that makes his homeland a woodless country he utilizes in improvising this frozen sledge. This method is most common in the region of the Magnetic Pole, but is also practiced among the Iglulik and Copper Eskimos.[40] The frozen hide is used chiefly for runners, the crosspieces being commonly of bone. The Arviling-juarmiut (Pelly Bay) would roll up raw meat or fish in the hide that was to be frozen for sledge runners. After thawing, the skins were fed to the dogs that had drawn the sledge, while the contents were eaten by their masters.[41] Boas mentions[42] sledges of frozen salmon. Klutschak depicts a sledge of ice from Simpson Strait,[43] and Boas refers to the making of a sledge by freezing together slabs of ice.[44] Eskimos of the central regions are even known to make harpoon shafts by freezing walrus hide.[45] And the Arviling-juarmiut "made long slender harpoon shafts of horn, the pieces being straightened out laboriously in warm water and joined length to length. Tent poles were fashioned in the same way."[46]

§3. FOOD ECONOMY

GENERAL scarcity of food and seasonal variations in the quantity force the Eskimos to conserve and preserve their stores. They must hoard the products of the plentiful season as provision against want.[47] Naturally, this necessary economy in food influences the variety of the Eskimos' diet. Sometimes they are obliged to draw food from strange sources, and the Alaskan Eskimos, for instance, rob the nests of field mice and appropriate for their own consumption the titbits stored by these rodents.[48] Disciplined by famine, the Eskimo laughs at the fastidiousness of white men. When starvation threatens he may even eat the tough, leathery skin covering of his boat, or his boots,[49] though such things are more often devoured by the dogs than the people.

The very thought of some of the Eskimos' delicacies turns the civilized stomach. Every afternoon the hunters of Diomede Island would squat around their meal of long-cached walrus meat, which lay on bare ground strewn with the excreta of dogs and people.[50] The raw, rotten meat was reminiscent of highly ripe cheese. Strangely, these same Eskimos showed some reluctance about drinking water with a speck of dirt in it. Eggs they would eat in any stage of deterioration or incubation, discarding only the eyes of the embryo. The Eskimos of Bering Strait bury fish heads and allow them to decay until the bones become of the same consistency as the flesh. Then they knead the reeking mass into a paste and eat it.[51] A few other examples of Eskimo food will indicate his lack of squeamishness: raw intestines of birds[52] and fish,[53] swallowed like oysters; live fish, gulped down whole, head first;[54] slime scraped from a walrus hide together with some of the human urine used in the tanning process;[55] fatty soup thickened with the blood of seal or caribou (common among most Eskimos); fat, maggoty larvae of the caribou fly, served raw;[56] the contents of the caribou's paunch, left in the body so long that the whole mass has become tainted;[57] deer droppings, munched like berries,[58] or the feces taken from the rectum of this animal;[59] and marrow more than a year old, swarming with maggots.[60]

These examples are rather convincing evidence that hunger is the best sauce. It should be added, however, that even the Eskimo exercises some discrimination against what would be injurious to health;[61] also that he sometimes suffers from the folly of eating meat too long cached.[62] The wonder is that a diet containing such foods does not cause more widespread disaster.

§4. INGENIOUS HUNTING METHODS

THE foregoing examples taken from the industries and diet of the Eskimos show how they circumvent the privations of their ungenerous habitat. It is significant that in an environment affording a minimum of natural resources they catch and kill the largest animals in the world—whales. Groups having no metal for weapons and only enough wood for harpoon shafts, boat paddles, and the frame of the skin-covered umiak have waged successful battle against these monsters of the sea.

It is largely from the animals the Eskimo kills that he manufactures his hunting weapons. From the skin of the seal the Bering Strait native fashions a net with which to catch more seals.[63] To attract fish to his hook the Diomede Islander attaches the bright orange flap from the corner of the beak of the crested auklet.[64] From whalebone the Eskimo fashions "spring bait," one of the most ingenious of his hunting accessories. To make this he sharpens the ends of a strip of the baleen, doubles the springy material up under tension, and ties it in that position with sinew. He buries the mass in fat and allows it to freeze. When the wolf is enticed and swallows it, the warmth of his stomach and his digestive juices release the barbed baleen, which pierces the creature internally and kills it.[65]

Some central groups smear a knife with blood, and bury it in the snow with only the blade protruding. A hungry wolf licks the keen edge and cuts his tongue. Excited by the taste and smell he gormandizes, literally whetting his own appetite. Finally, he dies, bled to death and gorged with his own lifeblood.[66]

To catch birds an Eskimo sometimes builds a small snow hut with a hole in the roof around which he scatters bits of meat and blubber as bait. From inside he deftly snatches the feet of the attracted birds.[67] East Greenlanders, having poured train oil on the water so that swans alighting cannot easily take off, approach in a kayak and harpoon them.[68]

The Eskimo acknowledges no superior throughout the animal kingdom. Though sometimes dangerously challenged, he remains the master of his stern world. The largest animals, as has been pointed out, are his prey. Indeed, he outwits all forms from the whale down to the tiniest creature. He even tricks the lice which infest his body, by drawing a piece of bear fur on a string under his clothes and pulling it out filled with the vermin.[69]

Occasionally the Eskimos show an equally astonishing lack of resourcefulness, as, for instance, when Jenness observed that the Copper Eskimos obtained all their water throughout the winter from snow, being ignorant apparently of the fact that ordinary sea ice loses its salinity with age, and that an old cake of the previous winter will yield perfectly fresh water.[70]

But, in general, the Eskimo has achieved harmony with his

habitat. Generations of cultural evolution have developed a mode of living that fits his life-conditions. By mode of living we refer chiefly to his self-maintenance mores; and by life-conditions we mean the actual, physical, concrete, perceptible circumstances of his life. But here ends, in a large measure, the perfection of his judgment. Aside from his physical environment, the Eskimo faces another set of life-conditions, his spirit world. As with all peoples, though perhaps to a greater degree than among most groups, his imagination fills the world with ghosts, demons, and deities, to him just as exacting in their requirements as the forces of the natural world. And in his responses to this supernatural environment, in contrast with his responses to the physical environment, he often displays what, on the surface at least, might seem to be inefficiency and lack of economy. Fear crowds out rationality. To cite a specific example, the slip noose which the Alaskan Eskimo carefully sets at the doorway of his dwelling to frighten away the returning malicious spirit of a shaman recently deceased,[71] is, perhaps, a misdirected effort. The objects relinquished by all Eskimos for the use of the dead as grave deposits are a considerable economic sacrifice.[72] And the stern taboo that Rasmussen observed among the Netsilingmiut "which forbade them even to make themselves new clothes or warmer sleeping rugs until they had shivered their way through the first of the snow right on into November,"[73] does not seem conducive to their immediate well-being. The question raised by cases such as these, however, can be fairly discussed only in connection with the broad subject of the Eskimos' religion, which is dealt with in later chapters.[74]

NOTES

1. Birket-Smith: 1929, I, 92.
2. Rasmussen: 1927, 77–78.
3. The custom of carrying the baby in the woman's large boot is said to have been practiced over a broad belt at about 70° N. Lat. from Davis Strait westward across the islands north of Hudson Bay, through the straits up to Cape Bathurst. (Thalbitzer: 1914, 581, citing a number of references.) Birket-Smith (1929, I, 221) writes that the Caribou Eskimos do not carry babies in their boots; and a communication from Jenness states that the Copper Eskimos, while they wear wide-mouthed boots, do not practice this method of carrying infants.

4. Boas: 1907 (from notes collected by Capt. George Comer, Capt. James S. Mutch, and Rev. E. J. Peck), 104 (Aivilik Eskimos on the west coast of Hudson Bay between Repulse Bay and Chesterfield Inlet); Boas: 1888, 556 (Central Eskimos); Ellis: 1748, 136; Franklin: 1828, 118 (mouth of the Mackenzie River); Hall: 1865, 100, 180, 577 (Frobisher Bay and vicinity); Hall: 1879, 98 (Eskimos of mainland near Wager Bay); Han-

bury: 1904, 110; Hawkes: 1916, 112; Hayes: 1867a, 192 (Cape Parry, in North Greenland); Hayes: 1867, 226 (Cape Parry, in North Greenland); Hooper: 1884, 109 (Eskimos living between Bering Strait and the Colville River); Lewis: 1904, 53, 120 (Hudson Bay region); Light: 1835, 186 (Eskimos of Boothia Felix); Lyon: 1824, 315 (Central Eskimos), 20 (Hudson Strait); MacMillan: 1918, opposite p. 20, illustration with caption; Murdoch: 1892, 110, 118 (Point Barrow), 120 (eastern America), 415 (Point Barrow), 416 (Hecla and Fury Straits, after Parry; Labrador; Cumberland Gulf, after Kumlien; north shore of Hudson Strait, according to Ellis; and east of the Mackenzie River, after Franklin [Richardson]); Parry: 1824, 495, 496 (Melville Peninsula and the adjoining islands, more particularly Winter Island and Igloolik); Parry: 1821, 281 (Baffin Island); Peary: 1893, 43; Peary: 1901, 28; Rae: 1850, 39 (Melville Peninsula); Richardson: 1851, I, 252, 369 (north coast of Canada); Richardson: 1861, 306 (north coast of Canada); Richardson, in Franklin: 1828, 226 (east of the mouth of the Mackenzie); Seemann: 1853, II, 53 (probably Kotzebue Sound); Turner: 1894, 208, 210 (Ungava District); Coats: 1852, 73–74; Greely: 1886, 32 (southern Greenland); Rink: 1877, 183 (Greenland).

5. Further information from Captain Comer's letter dated East Haddam, Connecticut, May 22, 1930: "As for the hood. That is a continuation of the coat and its chief use is for a covering of the woman's head in storms or cold winds. . . .

"Often her sewing material or light work is placed in the hood but nothing of great weight.

"The position of the child would be like a frog, its knees being well up under the mother's armpits.

"Once when I spoke of the child being carried in the hood it made the women laugh. . . .

"To a person who has not wintered and summered with them, there might be times when a child standing up in the slack part of the coat might be thought to be in the hood proper."

6. Further information from Porsild's letter, dated Ottawa, Canada, May 23, 1930: "The amaut is always made of seal skin and has an extension of the back which gives room for the baby, and, its ample hood is trimmed with dog skin in order to protect the baby's head from the wind and is not to be used by the wearer. To prevent the baby from sliding down a leather strap is fastened on the inside of the garment above the small of the back. The loose ends of the strap pass over the hips and are adjusted in front or simply held by the woman who wears the amaut. To take the baby out she bends forward and takes hold of the baby with her hands. . . .

"In former times the amaut was carried on the naked body and the baby also was naked, except during extreme weather when a hooded garment was worn."

7. Further information from Rasmussen's letter, dated Hellerup, 12 Sigridsvej, Copenhagen, May 3, 1930: "Round Hudson Bay the child is carried in exactly the same manner as further west, i.e. in the coat and *not* in the hood. . . .

"The coat used by women with infants or by women who look after infants is in Greenland called amaut (means: 'that by means of which one carried something on the back'). The back of these coats consists of a continuous skin which is pouched, and in this sits the child. A Greenland amaut cannot be drawn up over the head at all, and therefore, for this coat there is a separate headdress. . . . I believe the position will be best understood by looking at the illustrations of skin dresses in 'Meddelser om Grønland,' Vol. XXXIX (Thalbitzer: Ethnogr. Collections from East Greenland) and Vol. LVI (Birket-Smith: Ethnography of the Egedesminde District). In the Hudson Bay district, as indeed along the arctic coast from the Netsilingmiut and further westwards, the child is likewise carried on the back in a small pouch in the coat and decidedly not in the hood, as that would simply choke the mother. In these districts, however, the hood, which is very large, is sewn on to the coat, and the mother can draw it over her own head if it is cold. Both among the Canadian Eskimos and in Greenland the child is held up by the mother's belt."

8. Kelly: 1890, 17, 18 (Alaska); Weyer: Field Notes (Bering Strait); Cantwell: 1889, 84 (Kowak River and Selawik Lake region); Brower, Charles D.: a letter to Stefansson (northern Alaska); Harrison: 1908, 93, 94 (Kogmolik and Nunatama Eskimos on the north coast of Alaska and Canada); Jenness, Diamond: a letter to Stefansson (Coronation Gulf); Simpson: 1843, 121; Hooper: 1853, 347–348 (Cape Bathurst, Maitland Island); Amundsen: 1908, I, 312 (King William Island); M'Clintock: 1859, 235 (Boothia Felix); Packard: 1891, illustration facing p. 200, 271 (Hopedale, Labrador); Nansen: 1893, 24 (South Greenland); Bellot: 1855, I, 186 (Upernivik, Greenland); Astrup: n.d., 87 (North Greenland); Mikkelsen: n.d., 327–328 (north coast of Alaska); Mikkelsen: 1913, illustration facing p. 16 (Greenland); Saabye: 1818, 13, 259 (Greenland); Egede, Hans: 1818, 132, 148 (Greenland); Crantz: 1767, I, 138, 162 (Greenland).

9. Birket-Smith: 1929, II, 96 and 188 (general discussion); Nelson: 1899, 167 (Yukon and Kuskokwim rivers and northward to Norton Sound); Murdoch: 1892, 260 ff. (Point Barrow); Ray: 1885, 37 (Point Barrow); Stefansson: 1914, 151 (Victoria Island); Mathiassen: 1927, II, 112–113 (Naujan); Birket-Smith: 1929, I, 213 (Caribou Eskimos); Boas: 1907, 108–109 (west coast of Hudson Bay); Boas: 1907, 76 (Southampton Island); Mathiassen: 1928, I, 196 (Iglulik Eskimos); Turner: 1894, 222–223 (Koksoagmyut, northern Labrador); Ekblaw: 1928 (Polar Eskimos); Kroeber: 1899, 289 (Polar

Eskimos); Birket-Smith: 1924, 191 ff. (Egedesminde); Trebitsch: 1910, 57 (Greenland); Holm: 1914, 31–32 (Angmagsalik); Thalbitzer: 1914, 592–597 (Greenland and Alaska); Thalbitzer: 1914, 597 (Greenland).

10. Birket-Smith: 1929, I, 129 (Qaernermiut, a group of the Caribou Eskimos); Mathiassen: 1928, I, 49 (Iglulik Eskimos); Steensby: 1910, 297 (Polar Eskimos); Astrup: "Blandt Nordpolens Naboer," 115 (Polar Eskimos); Ekblaw: 1928 (Polar Eskimos); Birket-Smith: 1924, 78 (West Greenland; uncertain).

11. Hooper: 1881, 15.

12. Birket-Smith: 1924, 271.

13. Nansen: 1893, 53.

14. Nansen: 1893, 53.

15. Thalbitzer: 1914, 382.

16. Kroeber: 1899, 300.

17. Kane: 1856, II, 210; Steensby: 1910, 402–403; Birket-Smith: 1929, II, 76–77; Thalbitzer: 1914, 385; Kroeber: 1899, 267, 269, 273 ff.

18. Bilby: 1923, 113. But not at Iglulik in Lyon's time (Lyon: 1824, 234).

19. Nelson: 1899, 222.

20. MacKeevor: 1819, 32; Cf. Rink: 1887, 6; Birket-Smith: 1929, I, 188.

21. Cadzow: 1929; Moore: 1923, 362; Jenness: 1922, 136; Stefansson: 1914, 317 f.

22. Bogoras: 1904, 135 (Chukchi); Sauer: 1802 (Chukchi); Birket-Smith: 1929, II, 172 (Yukagir); Thalbitzer: 1914, 717, footnote 2 (Chukchi and Koryaks).

23. Thalbitzer: 1924, 273, citing MacRitchie (in *Petermann's Mitteilungen* [1911], and in *Scottish Magazine* [1909]).

24. Birket-Smith: 1924, 258 f., citing a number of references; Bilby: 1923, 117 f. (Baffin Island); Lyon: 1824, 25 (Cape Dorset); Turner: 1894, 225 f. (Hudson Strait). The sail is not known to have been used at Angmagsalik (Thalbitzer: 1914, 379 f.; Holm: 1914, 42 f.)

25. Birket-Smith: 1924, 259.

26. See also pp. 99 ff.

27. Birket-Smith: 1929, II, 235 (Table 2A), 54. Additional refer-

ences: Murdoch: 1892, 80 (Point Barrow, an ice window in a wooden dancing house); Boas: 1907, 96 (west coast of Hudson Bay, ice window); Bilby: 1923, 75 ff. (Baffin Island, ice window); Turner: 1894, 225 (Koksoagmyut, northern Labrador, ice window).

28. Birket-Smith: 1929, II, 235 (Table 2A), 54. Additional references: Murdoch: 1892, 74 (Point Barrow, gut window); Ray: 1885, 40 (Point Barrow, walrus intestine); Stefansson: 1914, 145 (Mackenzie Delta, white-whale gullet); Mathiassen: 1928, I, 113 (Iglulik Eskimos, gut window); Comer: 1910, 86–87 (Southampton Island, seal-gut window); Hawkes: 1916, 61 (Labrador, seal-gut window); Steensby: 1910, 296 (Polar Eskimos, gut window for snow houses); Kroeber: 1899, 271 (Polar Eskimos, seal-intestine window for snow houses); Holm: 1914, 35 (Angmagsalik, gut windows).

29. Stefansson: 1914, 145, 273 (Mackenzie Delta).

30. Stefansson: 1914, 355 (near Cape Bathurst).

31. Nelson: 1899, 110; Weyer: Field Notes; Birket-Smith: 1929, I, 247; Turner: 1894, 206; Birket-Smith: 1924, 107; Holm: 1914, 35.

32. Weyer: Field Notes.

33. See pp. 104 f. for further discussion of metal working.

34. Rasmussen: 1927, 188.

35. Weyer: Field Notes (Bering Strait); Beechey: 1831, I, 252 (Kotzebue Sound); Beechey: 1831, I, 263 (Cape Thomson, just south of Point Hope); Ray: 1885, 46 (Point Barrow); Murdoch: 1892, 291 (Point Barrow); Nelson: 1899 (Alaska); Jenness: 1922, 108 (Copper Eskimos); O'Neill: 1924, 52 (southwestern Victoria Island); Jenness: 1928, 171 (southwestern Victoria Island); Rasmussen: 1927, 168 (west of Lord Mayor's Bay); Birket-Smith: 1929, I, 87 ff. (Barren Grounds); Parry: 1824, 504 (Iglulik and Boothia Eskimos); Lyon: 1824, 210 (Iglulik); Rasmussen: 1929, I, 28 (Iglulingmiut); Lyon: 1824, 210, 231 (Iglu-

lik); Hawkes: 1916, 97 (Labrador); Kroeber: 1899, 289 (Polar Eskimos); Bessels: 1884, 867 (Polar Eskimos); Birket-Smith: 1924, 160–161, citing a number of references concerning the Polar Eskimos. Junius Bird found pyrites in old house ruins which he excavated on Shannon Island, northeastern Greenland. Mathiassen: 1927, II, 109, citing a number of references; Birket-Smith: 1929, II, giving a table containing *many references concerning the entire region.*

36. Nelson: 1899, 75, 86 (illustration) (Alaska); Weyer: Field Notes (Bering Strait); Murdoch: 1892 (Point Barrow), citing a number of references from other sections, 289–290; Ray: 1885, 46 (Point Barrow); Jenness: 1922, 108 (Copper Eskimos); Birket-Smith: 1929, I, 87 ff. (Barren Grounds); Lyon: 1824, 210 (Iglulik); Bilby: 1923, 102 (Baffin Island); Hawkes: 1916, 97 (Labrador); Birket-Smith: 1924, 160–161 (all of Greenland, with a number of references); Crantz: 1767, I, 145 (Greenland); Thalbitzer: 1914, 530–531, 481, Plate XXXIX, Fig. 69 (East Greenland); Holm: 1914, 41 (East Greenland); Mathiassen: 1927, II, 109, citing a number of references; Birket-Smith: 1929, II, giving a table containing *many references concerning the entire region.*

37. Further information concerning resources in stone is to be found on pp. 105 f.

38. Kroeber: 1899, 274; Boas: 1907, 447.

39. Bilby: 1923, 133.

40. Birket-Smith: 1929, II, 72; Boas: 1907, 90; Mathiassen: 1928, I, 77; Lyon: 1824, 235 (Iglulik).

41. Rasmussen: 1927, 169.

42. Boas: 1888, 533 (Boothia).

43. Klutschak: 1881, 76.

44. Boas: 1888, 533.

45. Boas: 1907, 469.

46. Rasmussen: 1927, 168.

47. See also pp. 113 ff.

48. Nelson: 1899, 268.

49. Weyer: Field Notes; Markham: 1866, 131; Ray: 1885, 46; Hooper: 1881, 11; Jenness: 1922, 107.

50. Weyer: Field Notes.
51. Nelson: 1899, 267.
52. Turner: 1894, 232.
53. Jenness: 1922, 99.
54. Jenness: 1922, 1571.
55. Weyer: Field Notes.
56. Rasmussen: 1927, 65.
57. Jenness: 1922, 106.
58. Stefansson: 1914, 296; Jenness: 1922, 106.
59. Murdoch: 1892, 62.
60. Jenness: 1922, 106.
61. Birket-Smith: 1924, 380. Stefansson remarks that whenever the natives die from eating beluga, although it might appear that the cause was ptomaine, the disorder seems really more likely to be of the nature of trichinosis (Stefansson: 1914, 449, 196).
62. Jenness: 1922, 42 f.
63. Weyer: Field Notes.
64. Weyer: Field Notes.
65. Practiced all the way from the Chukchi in Siberia to Labrador. Bogoras: 1904, 141 (Chukchi); Nelson: 1899, 121 (Alaska); Petroff: 1900, 214 (Alaska); Murdoch: 1892, 259 (Point Barrow); Stefansson: 1914, 203 (Wainwright Inlet, Alaska); Stefansson: 1914, 203 (Mackenzie Delta); Klutschak: 1881, 192 ff. (Netchillak Eskimos); Mathiassen: 1928, I, 63 (Iglulik Eskimos); Hawkes: 1916, 85–86 (Labrador); Boas: 1907, 25 (Baffin Island); Bilby: 1923, 257 (Baffin Island); Birket-Smith: 1929, I, 113 (the Caribou Eskimos do not use "spring bait"); Mathiassen: 1927, II, 53; Schwatka: 1885, 133; Gilder: 1881, 225.
66. Klutschak: 1881, 192 (Netsilik Eskimos); Gilder: 1881, 224–225 (Netsilik Eskimos); Birket-Smith: 1929, I, 113, II, 71 (Caribou Eskimos); Mathiassen: 1928, I, 63 (Iglulik Eskimos); Boas: 1888, 510 (Baffin Island).
67. Mathiassen: 1928, I, 66 (Iglulik Eskimos); Bilby: 1923, 262 (Baffin Island); Thalbitzer: 1914, 406–407 (East Greenland).
68. Holm: 1914, 56.
69. Porsild: 1915, 230 (West Greenland); Mathiassen: 1928, I, 201–202 (Iglulik Eskimos).
70. Jenness: 1922, 107.
71. Nelson: 1899, 314.
72. See pp. 276 ff. and 454 f.
73. Rasmussen: 1927, 220.
74. See chapter xxvi.

CHAPTER V

INFLUENCE OF GEOGRAPHICAL CONDITIONS ON MODE OF LIFE (*Continued*)

§1. SEASONAL LIFE–CYCLE OF ESKIMOS

W E have already discussed the seasonal changes in the natural environment of the Eskimos. To this changing environment the Eskimos are forced to conform. The seasonal habits of the animals, the seasonal phases in the plant world, the variations in temperature and daylight, and the appearance and disappearance of snow and ice all bind them to a definite yearly program. There is hardly another people in the world whose self-maintenance mores are so strictly regulated by the changes in the seasons.[1]

The tables in Figure 11 illustrate in outline the seasonal differentiations in the mode of life of ten representative groups of Eskimos. This outline serves as a basis for the discussion that is to follow of the seasonal cycle of activities. It should be held in mind, however, that the tables are far from comprehensive, largely owing to incompleteness of data.

A broad fact to be noted at the outset is that practically all Eskimos, including those farthest north, live in tents during the summer, whereas in winter practically no Eskimos live without more adequate shelter than tents.[2] The dome-shaped snow house is by no means the commonest winter dwelling. Structures variously fashioned out of stone, wood, sod, and sometimes the bones of whales, form the regular winter abode of most Eskimos, notably those of Alaska and Greenland.

The type referred to in the outline as *qarmat* is a form of dwelling which commonly supersedes the snow hut when the approach of warm weather makes it impossible to use the dome-shaped roof. The walls of the *qarmat* are built of snow, but the roof is made of skins.

Seasonal Character of Hunting Activities

WHILE the sea is frozen over, the seals, being dependent upon air, are forced to make breathing holes through the ice. Where this condition exists the Eskimos are able to catch these animals only by harpooning them through these small breathing holes (*maupok* hunting).[3]

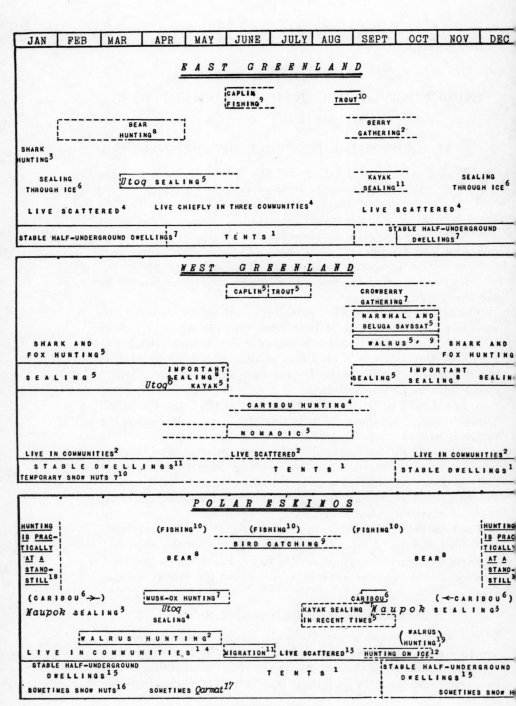

FIGURE 11 (i)

Seasonal Changes in Mode of Living and Hunting Activities of Major Eskimo Groups

JAN	FEB	MAR	APR	MAY	JUNE	JULY	AUG	SEPT	OCT.	NOV	DEC

UNGAVA DISTRICT, LABRADOR

BERRY GATHERING [12]

...TING OF CARIBOU, PTARMIGAN, ETC. [9]

CARIBOU HUNTING [8]   HUNTING OF CARIBOU PTARMIGAN, ETC. [9]

EGG GATHERING [7]

SALMON CATCHING [6]

WHITE WHALE [5]

WALRUS [3] AND SEAL [4] HUNTING

MIGRATE INLAND [13]

SNOW HOUSES [11] (OCCASIONALLY TENTS [2])   TENTS [1]   SNOW HOUSES [11] (OCCASIONALLY TENTS [2])

IGLULIK ESKIMOS,

OCCASIONAL SALMON FISHING [8]

CARIBOU HUNTING [10]   IMPORTANT ◄— CARIBOU — CARIBOU HUNTING [7] —   HUNTING [7]

WALRUS HUNTING [6]

Aupok SEALING [3]   *Utoq* SEALING [4]   SEALING IN KAYAKS [5]

...E ON POINTS OF LAND, ISLANDS, OR SEA ICE [9]   LIVE INLAND OR ACCESSIBLE TO HINTERLAND [9]

SNOW HOUSES [1]   *Qarmat* [2]   TENTS [1]   *Qarmat* [2] SNOW HOUSES [1]

CARIBOU ESKIMOS

1/3 OF GROUP HUNT SEAL AND WALRUS [9]

MUSK-OX HUNTING (FORMERLY) [10]   MUSK-OX HUNTING (FORMERLY) [10]

TROUT FISHING [7]

...RIBOU HUNTING [6]   IMPORTANT CARIBOU HUNTING [5]   MOST IMPORTANT CARIBOU HUNTING [4]   CARIBOU HUNTING [6]

LIVE-INLAND [8]   1/3 OF GROUP LIVE AT COAST [8]   LIVE INLAND [8] CAMPS MOST CONCENTRATED [10] ►►►

SNOW HOUSES [3]   *Qarmat* [2]   TENTS [1]   SNOW HOUSES [3]

FIGURE 11 (ii)

Seasonal Changes in Mode of Living and Hunting Activities of Major Eskimo Groups

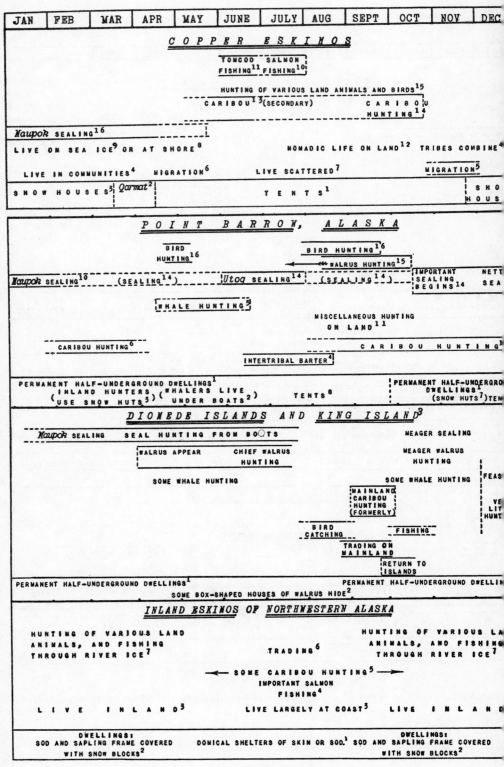

FIGURE 11 (iii)

Seasonal Changes in Mode of Living and Hunting Activities of Major Eskimo Group

FOOTNOTES TO FIGURE 11

East Greenland

[1] Holm: 1914, 42; Birket-Smith: 1928, 145.
[2] Thalbitzer: 1914, 504.
[3] Holm: 1914, 53.
[4] Thalbitzer: 1914, 346.
[5] Holm: 1914, 51; Birket-Smith: 1928, 145.
[6] Thalbitzer: 1914, 398–402.
[7] Holm: 1914, 35, 42.
[8] Birket-Smith: 1928, 145.
[9] Birket-Smith: 1928, 145.
[10] Birket-Smith: 1928, 145.
[11] Birket-Smith: 1928, 145.

West Greenland

[1] Birket-Smith: 1924, 142, 154; Nansen: 1893, 84; Jensen: 1928, 321–322.
[2] Mecking: 1928, 121.
[3] Birket-Smith: 1924, 235–236.
[4] Jensen: 1928, 321–322; Birket-Smith: 1928, 146.
[5] Birket-Smith: 1924, 375; Birket-Smith: 1928a, 470; Jensen: 1928, 333.
[6] Birket-Smith: 1924, 326.
[7] Birket-Smith: 1924, 371.
[8] Brown: 1927, 131.
[9] Birket-Smith: 1924, 322.
[10] Egede: 1741a, 16; Birket-Smith: 1924, 148; Thalbitzer: 1914, 377.
[11] Thalbitzer: 1914, 352–364; Birket-Smith: 1924, 148–152.

Polar Eskimos

[1] Steensby: 1910, 286; Birket-Smith: 1928, 142; Rasmussen: 1921, 20; Mecking: 1928, 267; Ekblaw: 1928; Kroeber: 1899, 270.
[2] Kroeber: 1899, 268–269; Ekblaw: 1928.
[3] Ekblaw: 1928; Steensby: 1910, 293 ff.; Kroeber: 1899, 269–270.
[4] Steensby: 1910, 293 ff.; Birket-Smith: 1928, 142; Kroeber: 1899, 269–270; Ekblaw: 1928.
[5] Kroeber: 1899, 269 ff., 282; Birket-Smith: 1928, 142.
[6] Ekblaw: 1928.
[7] Rasmussen: 1921, 17; Ekblaw: 1928.

[8] Ekblaw: 1928.
[9] Ekblaw: 1928; Steensby: 1910, 300; Birket-Smith: 1928, 142; Rasmussen: 1921, 22; Mecking: 1928, 268.
[10] Ekblaw: 1928.
[11] Ekblaw: 1928.
[12] Ekblaw: 1928.
[13] Kroeber: 1899, 269–270.
[14] Ekblaw: 1928.
[15] Steensby: 1910, 286, 312 ff.; Kroeber: 1899, 270; Rasmussen: 1921, 19, 24; Rasmussen: 1908, 198; Ekblaw: 1928; Mecking: 1928, 267.
[16] Steensby: 1910, 287; Rasmussen: 1921, 19–20; Rasmussen: 1908, 321; Mecking: 1928, 267; Ekblaw: 1928.
[17] Birket-Smith: 1924, 148.
[18] Birket-Smith: 1928, 141–142.
[19] Birket-Smith: 1928, 142.

Ungava District, Labrador

[1] Hawkes: 1916, 59, 63; Turner: 1887, 106.
[2] Hawkes: 1916, 63.
[3] Mecking: 1928, 209.
[4] Turner: 1894, 203; Turner: 1887, 105.
[5] Turner: 1894, 203; Turner: 1887, 105.
[6] Turner: 1894, 203; Turner: 1887, 105.
[7] Turner: 1894, 203.
[8] Turner: 1894, 203.
[9] Turner: 1887, 105.
[11] Hawkes: 1916, 58 ff.; Turner: 1887, 100, 106; Turner: 1894, 223 ff.; Mecking: 1928, 211.
[12] Hawkes: 1916, 28 ff.
[13] Hawkes: 1916, 28 ff.

Iglulik Eskimos

[1] Mathiassen: 1928, I, 119, 129–131.
[2] Mathiassen: 1928, I, 136.
[3] Mathiassen: 1928, I, 24, 30, 35.
[4] Mathiassen: 1928, I, 24, 30.
[5] Mathiassen: 1928, I, 24, 30.
[6] Mathiassen: 1928, I, 24, 30, 35; Mecking: 1928, 202.
[7] Rasmussen: 1929, I, 190–191; Ma-

thiassen: 1928, I, 24, 30, 35; Bartlett: 1928, 22; Mecking: 1928, 202.
8 Mathiassen: 1928, I, 24, 35.
9 Mathiassen: 1928, I, 35.
10 Freuchen and Mathiassen: 1925, 558.

Caribou Eskimos

1 Birket-Smith: 1929, I, 48; Rasmussen: 1927, 77 ff.
2 Birket-Smith: 1929, I, 84; Boas: 1907, 467.
8 Rasmussen: 1927, 77 ff.; Birket-Smith: 1929, I, 48, 76 ff.
4 Birket-Smith: 1929, I, 56–57, 110, 134.
5 Birket-Smith: 1929, I, 134.
6 Birket-Smith: 1929, I, 134.
7 Birket-Smith: 1929, I, 56 ff., 134.
8 Birket-Smith: 1929, I, 54, 125, 134.
9 Birket-Smith: 1929, I, 54, 125.
10 Birket-Smith: 1929, I, 71, 112.

Copper Eskimos

1 Jenness: 1922, 76 ff.; 125; Jenness: 1928, 90.
2 Jenness: 1922, 77 ff.; Stefansson: 1914, 237.
8 Jenness: 1922, 56, 77 ff., 125; Stefansson: 1914, 230; Rasmussen: 1927, 247.
4 Jenness: 1922, 110, 143 ff.; Jenness: 1928, 136 ff.
5 Jenness: 1922, 110.
6 Jenness: 1922, 116, 120 ff.
7 Jenness: 1922, 126 (map), 143 ff.; Jenness: 1928, 136 ff.
8 Jenness: 1922, 64.
9 Jenness: 1922, 110 ff.; Stefansson: 1921, 240.
10 Jenness: 1922, 123 ff.
11 Jenness: 1922, 123.
12 Jenness: 1922, 120 ff.; Jenness: 1928, 136 ff.
13 Jenness: 1922, 101, 120, 123.
14 Jenness: 1922, 123–125.
15 Jenness: 1922, 123 ff.
16 Jenness: 1922, 100, 101, 111, 112 ff., 119 ff., 123; Jenness: 1928, 229.

Point Barrow, Alaska

1 Hooper: 1881, 38; Petroff: 1900, 211.
2 Smith: 1902, 117.
8 Murdoch: 1885, 99; Smith: 1902, 115.
4 Ray: 1885, 38; Smith: 1902, 118.
5 Smith: 1902, 117 ff.; Ray: 1885, 38; Rasmussen: 1927, 310; Murdoch: 1892, 56, 264–265, 274.
6 Smith: 1902, 115; Ray: 1885, 38; Murdoch: 1892, 267.
7 Murdoch: 1885, 99; Murdoch: 1892, 267; Nelson: 1899, 242; Smith: 1902, 119; Jackson: 1880, 63, 67, 69.
8 Petroff: 1900, 211; Murdoch: 1892, 83 ff.
9 Nelson: 1899, 126; Ray: 1885, 40.
10 Ray: 1885, 40.
11 Ray: 1885, 38 ff.
12 Ray: 1885, 38.
13 Murdoch: 1892, 264.
14 Murdoch: 1892, 268–269.
15 Murdoch: 1892, 272.
16 Murdoch: 1892, 276–278.

Diomede Islands and King Island

1 Weyer: Field Notes; Nelson: 1899, 255 ff.; Jenness: 1929; Hooper: 1881, 15.
2 Nelson: 1899, 255 ff.; Muir: 1917, 218; Hooper: 1881, 15; Rasmussen: 1927, 344.
8 Rasmussen: 1927, 344; Weyer: Field Notes.

Inland Eskimos of Northwestern Alaska

1 Weyer: Field Notes; Rasmussen: 1927, 318; Leffingwell: 1919, Plate VII.
2 Rasmussen: 1927, 318; Weyer: Field Notes; Healy: 1887, 86.
8 Weyer: Field Notes; Rasmussen: 1927, 317 ff.; Healy: 1887, 75, 90.
4 Weyer: Field Notes; Healy: 1887, 75, 90; Rasmussen: 1927, 317–318.
5 Healy: 1887, 90; Rasmussen: 1927, 318.
6 Healy: 1887, 75; Weyer: Field Notes.
7 Weyer: Field Notes.

The release from winter inaugurates a new cycle of activities. The seals crawl out of the water onto the ice and bask in the sunlight, where they may be harpooned (*utoq* hunting).[4] Whales reappear in the opening waters of northwestern Alaska.[5] In the central area the northward migration of caribou to the Arctic Archipelago affords profitable hunting for the dwellers of the Barren Grounds.[6] The spawning of fish in summer is an event which determines the activities of many groups throughout the Eskimo region.

In northwestern Alaska, for instance, the salmon begin to spawn in late June, and the season continues through July and part of August.[7] To the east, in the region of the Copper Eskimos, the run of the salmon trout begins in July and is over by the end of the month.[8] In the Barren Grounds the only salt-water fish of any importance to the Eskimos is the trout, which ascend the rivers to spawn at the end of summer.[9] In the territory of the Koksoagmiut of northern Labrador the salmon season extends from the latter part of July to the first of September.[10] Similarly, the salmon ascend the rivers of Greenland to spawn in July and August.[11]

Bird life in Arctic America is likewise widely affected by the seasons. The catching of birds on a considerable scale can be practiced only during the warmer part of the year, while the migratory species are present. And, finally, berries can be gathered, of course, only when they are ripe, in late summer and early fall.

In the central regions the approach of winter dispossesses vast herds of caribou of their summer home in the Arctic Archipelago. As the herds migrate southward across the northern fringe of Canada, large numbers of the animals are killed by the Eskimos. It is during a short period at the end of summer and the beginning of fall that the hair of the caribou of the Barren Grounds and Alaska is best suited for clothing,[12] though the thick winter pelts are also used.[13]

At the approach of winter, Eskimos everywhere are busy preparing for the change in their mode of life. Sledges must be put in order, and winter clothing made ready.

In early winter a unique form of hunting is practiced in some parts, particularly in West Greenland. The blockading of bays and fiords by the early ice entraps herds of white whales, which the Eskimos kill by hundreds (*savssat* hunting).[14]

The Eskimo Calendar

IT is natural that these critical changes within the habitat of the
Eskimo serve as a basis for his calendar. The periods which correspond roughly to our months he designates generally by characteristic phases of climate, animal life, or plant life.[15] Typical of
this nomenclature is the calendar of the Eskimos of Ungava Bay,
Labrador:

January: "Coldest month for frost."
February: "Ground cracked by frost."
March: "The month of the young Jar seal."
April: "The month of the young Bearded seal."
May: "The month of fawning."
June: "The egg month."
July: "The mosquito month."
August: "The berry month."
September: "The fading-month" (leaves and mosses fade in color)
October: "The month when ice forms around the shore."
November: "The inland month" (they go inland to hunt caribou).
December: "The ice-forming month."[16]

These designations differ throughout the Eskimo region, naturally, as life-conditions vary from place to place. In addition, the
Eskimo commonly divides the year into seasons, of which the Copper Eskimo recognizes five,[17] and the Caribou Eskimo, the Iglulik
Eskimo, and the Baffin Island Eskimo, four.[18]

Seasonal Program Differs Regionally

JUST as environmental change undergoes different phases in different sections, so the cycle of activities differs among separate
groups of Eskimos. This lack of uniformity in the seasonal program is brought out in the tables (Fig. 11). Thus, during autumn,
we see the Copper Eskimos around Coronation Gulf forsaking
their inland hunting grounds and returning to the coast, later to
make their winter homes on the sea ice hunting seals through their
breathing holes. In some other sections, on the contrary, the
movement during autumn is in the opposite direction, from the
coast to inland winter quarters, as among the coast-visiting
groups of the Caribou Eskimos, the Eskimos about Ungava Bay
(Labrador), and the inland groups of Alaska.

In each region the inhabitants pursue their hunting in whatever
way they consider most productive at the particular season. Fur-

ther, cultural differences destroy the symmetry of the seasonal program. Each group of Eskimos manifests slightly characteristic cultural adjustments even in response to environmental conditions that are common to other groups. Possibly, such a cultural unconformity is seen among the inland Caribou Eskimos, whose traditional mode of life restricts them from hunting marine mammals along the nearby coasts.

The Eskimo mode of life, to sum up, everywhere changes with the seasons, differing moreover in character and degree from place to place. It should be stressed, however, that this statement applies chiefly to those activities which secure the material necessaries of life. Since it is the self-maintenance activities of any group that show the closest adjustment to their natural environment, these are the activities which vary most markedly with seasonal changes. Other aspects of the Eskimo culture, such as the social organization and religion, are influenced only indirectly. Here, the relationship is less obvious. It does depend partly upon the season, to be sure, whether the family or the village is the social unit.[19] And the religion of some groups includes a striking seasonal schedule of requirements and taboos. These various derivative effects of seasonal change, however, are so secondary to the main issues in each case that the discussion of them is withheld until the separate topics can be taken up fully. Exclusive of the self-maintenance activities, the differences between the Eskimos' environment in summer and winter do not radically affect the culture of the people and cannot be said to produce a dualism throughout the entire social order, as has sometimes been argued.[20]

§2. METHODS OF TRAVEL

Though omitted from the chart of seasonal activities, methods of travel undergo seasonal changes of far-reaching importance. It should be kept in mind that both sledges and skin-covered boats are used and that the presence or absence of snow and ice determines which of these means is possible. The crusting of the arctic waters with ice puts an end to hunting and traveling with umiaks and kayaks. It follows that throughout most of the Eskimo region in October or November dog-drawn sledges come into service as the vehicles of transportation. They are used until May or June, when the melting of the snow and the break-up of ice end their usefulness.

The Dog Sledge

WITH only minor exceptions the dog sledge is used throughout the entire Eskimo region. Where it is absent, along the west coast of Greenland south of the Arctic Circle and along the east coast south of about 62½° N., as well as in South Alaska and among the Aleutian Islands, climatic limitations are chiefly accountable for its absence.[21]

In Eurasia, also, dog sledges have been long in use; but, according to Birket-Smith, it is questionable whether the Indians in pre-Columbian times employed dogs as sledge drawers at all. Dogs for draft purposes are used much less in subarctic America than is often supposed.[22] On the other hand, dogs as pack animals, carrying burdens on their backs, were in general use in northwest America,[23] just as in some Eskimo groups.[24] Further information regarding the Eskimo dog is contained in chapter vi.

The Eskimo is very dependent upon facilities for travel and transportation during the period of snow and ice. The physical condition of his dog team is, therefore, a matter of deep concern. The accumulation of ice between his animals' toes, the laceration caused by crusted snow or sharp ice, and the irritation from slushy salt-water ice must be guarded against, or the animals will become useless. The sledge driver consequently does not wait until he sees a trail of blood-stained footprints behind his team to fit their paws with protective socks. The use of dog shoes is common among the Eskimos, and is also practiced by some other peoples.[25] At Bering Strait, furthermore, they make little shirts to protect their teams.[26]

As to the sort of food that is given dogs there is no uniformity. Naturally, they get what is less desirable to their masters, and they even supplement their rations by scavenging for human excreta.[27] They are often fed only every other day. Ekblaw[28] writes that fifteen to thirty pounds of meat every third day is the average meal for a North Greenland dog under forced traveling.

The dogs of Coronation Gulf are said to haul about one hundred pounds apiece, and sometimes as much as one hundred fifty pounds.[29] Drawing a sledge over the snow-free tundra a team of nine dogs can haul a load aggregating about two hundred pounds,[30] but in warm weather the dogs easily get overheated. As a pack load one dog generally carries between twenty and sixty-five pounds during a long day's march, according to its strength.[31]

It would be an exceedingly powerful dog, however, that could manage sixty-five pounds. A good general rule is that a dog can carry about one-third its own weight, which ranges between sixty and a hundred pounds.[32]

The customary number of dogs to a team differs regionally.[33] Even locally, along Hudson Strait, the number varies between one and twenty. Similarly, the length of sledges differs from place to place.[34] The sledges of the Angmagsalik Eskimos (East Greenland) average only 5¼ feet in length; whereas in the Barren Grounds sledges over thirty feet in length are used. Strangely, the teams that are harnessed to these longest sledges rarely number more than two dogs and never more than five.

There are two methods by which a dog team may be harnessed to a sledge: in one, the so-called tandem harness, they are attached on either side of a single line; and in the other they are arranged fan-shaped, each with his separate lead.[35]

"The *fan-shaped team* is present in the whole of the eastern area, but is also used occasionally towards the west, where the Asiatic Eskimos use it in their ceremonial races. In this Bogoras rightly sees a sign of the great age of this method. Otherwise the Western Eskimos use the tandem system, which gives a much greater effective power, because with it the dogs pull straight forward instead of more or less obliquely."[36]

The fan-shaped harness has an advantage, however, in that it allows the dogs to move freely among rough and hummocky ice without interfering with each other; but it also offers a difficulty in that each of the many traces is likely to catch around any projection of the ice.[37] It is also impractical, of course, in forested country.

The glazing of sledge runners with ice is an interesting expedient which the Eskimos resort to under difficult sledding conditions.[38] At extremely low temperatures snow is apt to be granular or powdery; it is almost as though the traveler were sledging over sand. The runners stick and the dogs soon become exhausted. A shoeing of ice on the runners greatly reduces friction. Ice will not adhere, however, to wood, bone, or steel. So the Eskimo first applies a shoeing to the runners. He makes a paste of earthy matter, pulverized and mixed with water—a moist muck containing turf, reindeer moss, or other vegetation, partly decayed. He plasters this onto the bottoms of the runners a few inches thick, shaping it smoothly before it freezes. Ice will adhere to this ground. Spraying tepid water on it from his mouth he hastily smears the liquid as it falls freezing to the runner, spreading it evenly with a bearskin pad or his ungloved hand. Sometimes urine mixed with melted snow is used in place of pure water. And instead of the turfy paste frozen solid as a background, seal's blood can be squirted on from the mouth and, when frozen, sprayed over with water to form a film of ice. The shoeing of frozen paste will last through the season, with patching, but the glazing of ice must be renewed every day or oftener. For emergency repairing the Eskimo sometimes carries a little pouch of water near his body.

Summer Traveling

DURING the summer, traveling involves a somewhat different set of problems. In place of cold and the brevity or absence of daylight, wetness is the vexing circumstance. Snow-free ground precludes the use of sledges, unless they are drawn with considerable exertion over the bare, spongy tundra. At this season dogs are more commonly used as pack animals.[39] The foot traveler, plodding with soaked boots over the uneven, marshy land, is soon wearied, and sometimes driving rain and raw wind add to his discomfort. Though less dangerous than traveling in winter, traveling in summer is often more trying. In the Barren Grounds, for instance, it is just at those seasons when traveling is most difficult—summer and autumn—that the caribou migrations take place, which the Caribou Eskimos must meet.

"The great stretches of tundra are a pathless waste, and the rivers are available only as their courses lie, often tending in the wrong direction for the pursuit of the caribou. It is not until late in the autumn, when the rivers and lakes are frozen over, and the country is covered with snow, that they are able to cover any distance; but under these conditions, they are splendid travellers, skilful and untiring."[40] The Togiagamiut (Bristol Bay, Alaska) wander restlessly, "having no shelter beyond that afforded by a kayak turned upon its side, supported by a paddle or two. This simple screen is shifted about as the wind changes, and whole families rest in the lee of this unsatisfactory shelter in pelting rainstorms, with only their heads enjoying the least protection. . . ."[41]

Though used extensively inland in summer, the kayak has limitations as a means of travel. Traveling between bodies of water, the Eskimo is obliged to portage his craft. Moreover, a kayak accommodates only one person conveniently, except those that are paddled by the Aleutian Islanders and the natives of neighboring parts of Alaska, who have built kayaks, since the discovery of the region by Russians, with two manholes, or even three.[42] Sometimes the Eskimos improvise a raft by lashing two kayaks together.[43] A tent can be carried conveniently during summer only when traveling in the larger, open boat, the umiak;[44] and this craft can generally be used only in the sea. With an umiak, however, a tent is not essential; for the boat itself can be inverted as a temporary shelter.[45] Jacobsen mentions an instance where this makeshift shelter sufficed a family throughout the winter.[46] The umiak is the common means of coastwise travel in summer among those groups who are acquainted with it; but it was unknown, at least at the time of their discovery, by the Eskimos from Coronation Gulf eastward to Hudson Bay, and northward from there among the Iglulik Eskimos and the Polar Eskimos.[47] Harnessed dogs sometimes track the boats along the shore.[48]

§3. WANDERING LIFE OF ESKIMOS

Life-Conditions Render Settled Existence Impossible

In a previous section it was emphasized that the Eskimos commonly change their hunting grounds seasonally. Aside from seasonal movements, often during a particular season they must shift hither and thither, scouring wide areas in pursuit of scattered animals. Thus the Utorqaq River natives (northern Alaska) are appropriately called "the Wolf People" because of their tracking the caribou like wolves throughout the winter.[49] The poverty of the country drives the Eskimo to wandering. Turner remarks[50] on the impossibility of the Itivimiut (western Labrador) procuring the necessary food and skins for garments, unless they are constantly scouring the plains and hills for reindeer, or the shore for seals and other marine mammals. The Smith Sound Eskimos make their settlements at certain places, but never form permanent villages.[51] Rasmussen states that ". . . one can scarcely find a people who lead a more nomadic life. . . . No Polar Eskimo will live for more than a year or two in one place. . . ."[52] They wander about in their territory exchanging hunting grounds and stone houses.[53]

The inland Eskimos of the Noatak River (northern Alaska) "lead a nomadic life, changing their base as often as is necessary to find fresh hunting and fishing grounds. . . . During the summer months they wander up and down the river, spending much of the time in fishing and providing for the needs of the coming winter."[54] Likewise, the Togiagamiut, on the tundra of Alaska inland from Bristol Bay, "lead a thoroughly nomadic life, wandering from place to place in search of game or fish. . . . Even the communities do not seem bound together in any way; families and groups of families constantly changing their abode, leaving one community and joining another, or perhaps forming one of their own."[55]

Aside from the hunting inducements, trading and the quest for wood and stone for implements lead the Eskimos into different regions. The Ahiarmiut (Queen Maud Gulf) are considered by Rasmussen[56] to be undoubtedly the most nomadic of the Eskimos and the most skilful and hardy travelers.

"They will sometimes spend the summer right over in Victoria Land at Albert Edward Bay, at other times penetrating far into the interior of the mainland, taking part in the great trading assemblies which, prior to the formation of the trading stores were regularly held in the Akilineq Hills, right up in the Barren Grounds. On these occasions they would even journey as far as the forest belt, to procure timber for kayaks and sledges."

Groups comparatively isolated, as the Diomede Islanders,[57] the King Islanders,[58] and the Tigiktagmiut of the eastern islands of Hudson Bay[59] are not self-sufficing. Caribou pelts for winter clothing, unobtainable on their native islands, can be secured only during summer trips to the mainland.

It should be pointed out, however, that most Eskimo settlements of any size are occupied throughout the year by at least some of the inhabitants. Thus, on Little Diomede Island (Bering Strait), and at Cape Prince of Wales opposite, as well as at other sites along the coast of Alaska we see permanent villages consisting of stable half-underground dwellings.[60] Here the people are not dislodged in a body at any time, as are many groups. But even so, the dwellings are not all occupied continuously. A truly settled existence is impossible; particularly, during the warmer season, hunting, berry-gathering, and trading lead contingents of travelers up and down the coast and into the hinterland.

Sometimes the Eskimo's journey is purely a pleasure jaunt to visit another settlement to see friends and perhaps to attend a festival. But generally such pastime is only incidental to a purpose in which he has but little choice. The scattered distribution of game, and the necessity for intertribal trading and for journeying in some cases far and wide to secure materials for implements and weapons all drive the people to a nomadic life. Antisedentary life-conditions constantly harass them.

Nomadism and Stage of Culture

ASIDE from the hardships imposed upon the individual by forced nomadism, the cultural progress of the people suffers. The quantity of their worldly goods is restricted, for instance, by the limitations of transportation. When traveling by dog sledge the important possessions are food, the heavy stone lamp together with fuel for it, the household and hunting implements, and the family furs. If there is room on the sledge the party breaking camp will cut out the thick ice window of the snow house and carry it to the new site.[61] To travel insufficiently provisioned is perilous. The travelers must carry enough food for themselves and their dogs lest they suffer starvation before they can again secure game. But provisions in excess of what they can carry must be cached, with some risk of losing the products of tedious hunting. The same control is exercised over material accouterments. Certain belongings demand primary consideration; beyond them it is a matter of sacrificing the least valuable in proportion to bulk. Thus, the expansion of material culture is cramped by the limits of portability.

Furthermore, the delays and inconveniences involved in the use of temporary dwellings are an added handicap. And in addition to the direct material limitations enforced by migration, the development and maintenance of the facilities for traveling require enterprise and industry which otherwise might be directed toward other arts and crafts. The energy that must be spent in making and repairing boats and sledges, and the trouble of training and caring for dogs, act in this way as a cultural check.

On the other hand, a nomadic life in some ways facilitates the expansion of culture. Intercourse with different tribes can cause cultural stimulation: a new technique may be learned, or a new tool secured through barter. Furthermore, a group wandering from one section to another is subjected to new environmental conditions which may lead to new adjustments. Thus, nomadism might permit the discovery of a natural resource which otherwise would remain unknown.

Though it is impossible to evaluate the advantages and the disadvantages to culture of nomadic life, in the case of the Eskimos restriction rather than stimulation seems the more pronounced.

NOTES

1. Birket-Smith: 1924, 375; Steensby: 1905, 36 ff.
2. The Slave Indians, it should be mentioned incidentally, who inhabit the south shore of Great Slave Lake and Mackenzie River as far down as Simpson, use tents in winter in a locality where the season is colder than among the Eskimos of the coast.
3. See Table, Fig. 11.
4. See Table, Fig. 11.
5. See Table, Fig 11, n. 5 (Point Barrow).
6. See Table, Fig. 11 (Caribou Eskimos).
7. Weyer: Field Notes; Nelson: 1899, 183; Healy: 1887, 90.
8. Jenness: 1922, 123.
9. Birket-Smith: 1929, I, 44, 57.
10. Turner: 1894, 203.
11. Jensen: 1928, 346.
12. Weyer: Field Notes; Jenness: 1922, 123; Birket-Smith: 1929, I, 191.
13. Murdoch: 1892, 109.
14. Birket-Smith: 1928a, 470; Jensen: 1928, 333; Porsild: 1918.
15. Rasmussen: 1927, 346 ff. (King Island, Bering Sea); Weyer: Field Notes (Selawik, Alaska); Nelson: 1899, 234 (Bering Sea Region); Petroff: 1900, 238 (Kadiak Island); Birket-Smith: 1929, I, 157 (Caribou Eskimos); Mathiassen: 1928, I, 232 (Iglulik Eskimos); Bilby: 1923, 46 (Baffin Island); Boas: 1907, 471 (Southampton Island); Hawkes: 1916, 28 ff. (Labrador); Turner: 1894, 202 (Labrador); Kroeber: 1899, 303 (Polar Eskimos); Crantz: 1767, I, 231 (West Greenland); Holm: 1914, 105 (East Greenland).

16. Hawkes: 1916, 28 ff.
17. Jenness: 1922, 13.
18. Birket-Smith: 1929, I, 157; Klutschak: 1881, 230; Mathiassen: 1928, I, 232; Bilby: 1923, 46.
19. See Table in Fig. 11: Copper Eskimos (nn. 4 and 7), Caribou Eskimos (n. 10), Polar Eskimos (nn. 13 and 14), West Greenland (n. 2), and East Greenland (n. 4).
20. Mauss and Beuchat: 1904–5, 110 ff., 124.
21. Birket-Smith: 1929, II, 72, and Table 42A; Thalbitzer: 1914, 722.
22. Birket-Smith: 1929, II, 169.
23. Birket-Smith: 1929, II, 171.
24. Birket-Smith: 1929, I, 184 ff.; Boas: 1907, 467; Jenness: 1922, 240.
25. Weyer: Field Notes; Birket-Smith: 1924, 248–249; Ekblaw: 1928; Birket-Smith: 1929, II, 170.
26. Weyer: Field Notes.
27. Weyer: Field Notes (Diomede Islands); Birket-Smith: 1929, I, 171; Trebitsch: 1910, 21.
28. Ekblaw: 1928.
29. Chipman and Cox: 1924, 34b. The same figures are given in *Natural Resources, Canada*, January, 1931.
30. Weyer: Field Notes: (Cape Prince of Wales, Alaska).
31. Jenness: 1922, 240; Chipman and Cox: 1924, 35b; Rasmussen: 1927, 204.
32. Communication from Fenley Hunter; and *Natural Resources, Canada*, January, 1931.
33. Nelson: 1899, 206 (5–9 in Alaska); Rasmussen: 1927, 77 (2–5 in the Barren Grounds); Bilby: 1923, 132 (5–18 in Baffin Island); Turner:

1894, 241 (1–20, but generally 7–9, in Hudson Strait); Hawkes: 1916, 68 (6–8 in Labrador); Birket-Smith: 1924, 251 (sometimes 16 among Polar Eskimos; 5–6 at Egedesminde; 8 at Disko Bay); Birket-Smith: 1928, 179 (Greenland); Thalbitzer: 1914, 370 (4–6 in East Greenland); Holm: 1914, 44 (3–8 in East Greenland); MacKeevor: 1819, 45 (Hudson Strait).

34. Petroff: 1900, 216 (8'–12' among coast tribes from Kuskokwim River to Kotzebue Sound); Nelson: 1899, 206 (9–10' in Bering Strait Region); Mecking: 1928, 200 (2 m., west of Coronation Gulf; 4–7 m. at Coronation Gulf); Rasmussen: 1927, 77 (as much as 10 m. in Barren Grounds); Birket-Smith: 1929, I, 173 (10 m. among the Pâdlimiut, Barren Grounds); Boas: 1907, 465–466 (few dogs and long sleds among the Sauniktumiut, south and west of Chesterfield Inlet); Turner: 1894, 241 (12'–16' at Hudson Strait); Birket-Smith: 1924, 242 ff. (242 cm. in Egedesminde District, West Greenland); Holm: 1914, 44 (5¼' at Angmagsalik).

35. *Dogs harnessed in Fan Shape:*
    Chukchi (rarely Nordenskiöld: 1880–81, II, 99 f.; Bogoras: 1904, 107 ff.
    Kamchadal, Ostyak, Samoyed: Birket-Smith: 1929, II, 170.
    Asiatic Eskimos: Sarytschew: 1806–7, II, 49.
    Diomede Islands: Weyer: Field Notes. Tandem harness is the only type used on the islands now, but a middle-aged native of Big Diomede asserted that he had seen the fan-shaped harness used; where, he did not state.
    Copper Eskimos: *Report of the Canadian Arctic Expedition:* 1913–18, XI, Plate XLII, Fig. 1; Stefansson: 1914, 206; Birket-Smith: 1929, II, 258.
    Netsilik Eskimos: Birket-Smith: 1929, II, 258.
    Caribou Eskimos: Birket-

Smith: 1929, I, 179 ff.; II, 258.
Iglulik Eskimos: Mathiassen: 1928, I, 78 f.; Parry: 1924, 516 f.
Baffin Island: Frobisher: 1867, 136; Boas: 1888, 531 f.; 1907, 38 f.; Bilby: 1923, 123–124.
Labrador: Low: 1906, 147 f.; Hawkes: 1916, 64 f.; Turner: 1894, 243; 1887, 101.
Polar Eskimos: Ekblaw: 1928; Birket-Smith: 1929, II, 258.
West Greenland: Birket-Smith: 1924, 247 ff.; Ekblaw: 1928.
East Greenland: Thalbitzer: 1914, 372 ff.; Holm: 1914, 45; Ekblaw: 1928.

Dogs harnessed in Tandem Form:
    Koryak: Jochelson: 1908, 504 ff.
    Chukchi: Nordenskiöld: 1880–81, II, 99 f.; Bogoras: 1904, 107 ff.
    Asiatic Eskimos: Bogoras: 1904, 99.
    Bering Strait: Nelson: 1899, 209; Weyer: Field Notes (Diomede Islands).
    Point Barrow: Murdoch: 1892, 358.
    Mackenzie Eskimos: Petitot, 1887, 11.

36. Birket-Smith: 1929, II, 74–75.

37. Ekblaw: 1928; Turner: 1894, 243.

38. Birket-Smith: 1929, II, 73–74; Table 43A; 168 (Siberia); Murdoch: 1892, 353–354 (an ice shoe applied without muck) (Point Barrow); Stefansson: 1921, 601 ff.; Stefansson: 1914, 226 (not even thinly iced; Kuwuk, Alaska); Stefansson: 1914, 175 (frozen muck smeared with water; Mackenzie Delta); Stefansson: 1914, 245 (moss and ice; Dolphin and Union Strait); Jenness: 1928, 186 (frozen turf coated with ice; Victoria Island); Jenness: 1922, 116 (mud and ice; Copper Eskimos); Birket-Smith: 1929, I, 176–178 (frozen peat glazed with ice; Caribou Eski-

mos); Rasmussen: 1927, 37 ff. (frozen peat glazed with ice; Barren Grounds); Boas: 1907, 466 (Sauniktumiut, south and west of Chesterfield Inlet); Mathiassen: 1928, I, 75 (frozen mud glazed with ice; Iglulik Eskimos); Bilby: 1923, 131 f. (frozen peat and seal's blood; Baffin Island); Boas: 1888, 534 (moss and ice; Central Eskimos); Boas: 1907, 90 (moss and ice; west coast of Hudson Bay); Hall: 1864, 331 (southeastern Baffin Island); Hall: 1866, 582 ff.; Turner: 1894, 242 (frozen peat; Hudson Strait); Hawkes: 1916, 65 (frozen moss glazed with ice; Labrador); Steensby: 1910, 352 (snow is mixed with urine; Polar Eskimos); Ekblaw: 1928 (Polar Eskimos); Birket-Smith: 1924, 245–247 (ice shoeing not known in Egedesminde District; ice shoeing very common in Upernivik District, but without the mud coating used among the Central Eskimos); and the following additional references from Birket-Smith: 1929, II, 258, Table 43A; Nordenskiöld: 1880–81, II, 99 (ice; Chukchi); Bogoras: 1904, 106 (ice; Chukchi); Richet: 1921–23, XXXXI, 198 (ice; Bering Strait); Petitot: 1876, xvii; 1887, 11 (Mackenzie Eskimos; peat and ice); Rasmussen: 1925–26, II, 34 (peat and ice; Netsilik Eskimos); Hanbury: 1904, 80 (peat and ice; Caribou Eskimos); Mathiassen: 1927, I, 275 (peat [?] and ice; Southampton Island); Parry: 1824, 514 f. (Iglulik Eskimos); Lyon: 1824, 324 (Iglulik Eskimos); Rae: 1850, 87 (Iglulik Eskimos); Klutschak: 1881, 43 f. (Iglulik Eskimos); Gilder: 1881, 66 (Iglulik Eskimos); Mutch: 1906, 493 (Iglulik Eskimos); from the foregoing references pertaining to the Iglulik Eskimos Birket-Smith concludes that this group use peat and ice in shoeing runners; Hall: 1864, II, 331 and Kumlien: 1879, 42 (peat and ice; Baffin Land); Low: 1906, 147 (Labrador); Wallace: 1907, 229 f. (Labrador); Waldmann: 1909–10, 434 (Labrador); Hutton: 1912, 117 (Labrador); Lindow: 1924, 25 (Labrador); upon the above references Birket-

Smith remarks that peat shoeing is lacking south of Cape Chidley; Peary: 1898, I, 228 (ice; Polar Eskimos).

39. Birket-Smith: 1929, II, 260, Table 49A.

40. Rasmussen: 1927, 75–76.

41. Petroff: 1900, 224.

42. Holmberg: 1855, 99; Petroff: 1900, 233; Hartmann, in Jackson: 1886–88; Birket-Smith: 1929, II, 77.

43. Stefansson: 1914, 81.

44. Turner: 1894, 228.

45. Weyer: Field Notes and photograph; Jacobsen: 1884, 339.

46. Jacobsen: 1884, 339.

47. Mathiassen: 1927, II, 64, citing other references; also Petroff: 1900, 233 (among the natives of Kodiak Island, etc.); Holmberg: 1855, 100 (Konjags of Alaska); Nelson: 1899, 216 ff. (Bering Sea); Weyer: Field Notes (Bering Strait); Petroff: 1884, 211 (north coast of Asia); Sarytschew: 1806–7, II, 49 (St. Lawrence Bay, just south of East Cape, Siberia); Murdoch: 1892, 335 ff. (Point Barrow); Stefansson: 1914, 141 (Mackenzie Delta; umiaks were formerly used); Jenness: 1928, 229 (Coronation Gulf Eskimos never possessed umiaks); Stefansson: 1914, 237 (neither the Haneragmiut nor the Akuliakallagmiut of Dolphin and Union Strait make umiaks); Birket-Smith: 1929, I, 151 (originally the kayak was the only vessel of the Caribou Eskimos); Birket-Smith: 1929, I, 189 (the Caribou Eskimos do not have umiaks and there is no tradition about their use in former times; however, Ellis: 1750, 244, 254 ff. mentions them in latitude about 62° N. and at Bibby Island); Mathiassen: 1928, I, 96 (among the Iglulik Eskimos the umiak seems never to have been known); Mathiassen: 1927, II, 64 (the Sadlermiut of Southampton Island did not use the umiak); Turner: 1887, 101 (the Itivimiut of eastern Hudson Bay used umiaks); MacKeevor: 1819, 35 (observed umiaks in Hudson Strait); Turner: 1894, 225–226, 237 (umiaks in Hudson Strait); Hawkes: 1916, 68–69 (Labrador);

Steensby: 1910, 289 (Polar Eskimos did not use umiaks at the time of their discovery); Ekblaw: 1928 (Polar Eskimos); Kroeber: 1899, 274 (Polar Eskimos); Birket-Smith: 1924, 256 ff. ("The umiak is more or less the same all along the West Coast and the inhabited part of the East Coast [citing Holm: 1914, 42 ff.; Thalbitzer: 1914, 377 ff.]. In the Thule District it is not used, but the name occurs in local names [citing Mylius-Erichsen and Moltke: 1906, 229]. On the northern part of the East Coast it seems to have been known, though no absolutely certain proofs are at hand [citing Nathorst, Ryder, Thostrup, Thomsen, and Mikkelsen].")

48. Weyer: Field Notes (Bering Strait); Nelson: 1899, 299 (Alaska); Turner: 1894, 237 (Labrador).

49. Rasmussen: 1927, 319.

50. Turner: 1894, 179.

51. Kroeber: 1899, 268, citing Peary.

52. Rasmussen: 1921, 25.

53. Mecking: 1928, 268.

54. Healy: 1887, 75 (by McLenegan).

55. Petroff: 1900, 224.

56. Rasmussen: 1927, 245.

57. Weyer: Field Notes.

58. Rasmussen: 1927, 348.

59. Turner: 1894, 180.

60. Weyer: Field Notes.

61. Jenness: 1922, 63 (footnote).

CHAPTER VI

ANIMALS, PLANTS, AND MINERALS
UTILIZED BY ESKIMOS

§1. A HUNTING PEOPLE

DUE to seasonal changes in the location of hunting grounds and to the necessity of scouring wide areas in the pursuit of scattered animals, the Eskimos must live a wandering life. Unlike pastoral peoples, who lead their domesticated animals in quest of grazing grounds and water, the Eskimos are themselves led hither and thither by the animals, which follow their natural instincts. Knowledge of their habits largely determines success in securing food. The Eskimo encounters the animals in their natural state.

It cannot be maintained, however, simply from the failure of the Eskimo to domesticate the caribou, for instance, that he is culturally inferior to all pastoral peoples. His indirect mastery over the animals in their wild condition displays a more highly developed cultural adaptation than do the simple adjustments of some herding peoples.

It is questionable whether the domestication of caribou would be an expedient adjustment among at least some Eskimo groups. Among tribes of Arctic Siberia, to be sure, it is successful. But with the Eskimos the attention necessary to hold such animals in domestication the year round would mean at some seasons the forfeiting of productive hunting activities. The experiment of introducing domesticated reindeer into the culture of the Alaskan Eskimo is apparently successful. It must be remembered, however, that the life-conditions are different from those in other regions and that the indigenous culture has been modified by the intervention of civilized people. Dogs, it should be added, which are so important an element in the Eskimo culture, are to some degree incompatible with the herding of reindeer. The impulse of the Eskimo dog, at least when he is untrained, is to fight a reindeer.[1]

§2. DOMESTICATION OF THE DOG

IT seems likely that the dog is the animal earliest domesticated by primitive man.[2] In the arctic regions his suitability as a sled hauler and an aid in hunting renders him often indispensable. The dog was the only animal domesticated by the Eskimos before the coming of Europeans, and he is one of their greatest single assets.

The utility of the dog in drawing a sledge and in packing a burden has already been discussed. He is of very great value also in the hunting of seals at their breathing holes, particularly in the central region, where this method of winter hunting[3] is very important and highly developed.

"When the ice first forms, the seal noses and scrapes a small hole through which to breathe; the site is indicated by a slight rise, or bell-shaped protuberance of the ice above the rest. It is a comparatively easy thing to harpoon a seal at this stage, but the matter becomes vastly more difficult when the ice has thickened to some two or three meters, with a further layer of snow above."[4]

The holes, which the seal keeps open by gnawing,[5] are two or three inches in diameter at the surface. Below, they widen to a maximum diameter of seven feet, in the shape of a cigar, to admit the body of the seal. No sign betrays the location of one of these breathing holes to the hunter when it is covered with snow, and as a rule only those that are covered over are used by the seal. In finding them, therefore, dogs render an invaluable assistance. The pack scatters over the ice, sniffing about for the invisible haunts of the seals.[6] The hunter watches them, he, too, searching about at the same time and probing every suspicious mound. Suddenly, a dog begins to scratch in the snow. The hunter hastens to the spot. Once having found a breathing hole he patiently awaits the return of the seal, whereupon he harpoons the creature through the hole in the ice.

Also in hunting polar bears and musk oxen the dog assists the Eskimo by holding the animals at bay while the men spear them with lances.[7]

Eskimo dogs do not conform closely to a physical type. The skull of the Greenland dog is said to bear the greatest resemblance to that of the North American wolf.[8] Though the Eskimo dog may not be so powerful an animal as the St. Bernard, for instance, he has the advantage over the latter in the soundness of his feet and the quality of his fur.[9]

Eskimo dogs suffer from some of the diseases common to dogs elsewhere. At Diomede Islands and Cape Prince of Wales dogs quite often go mad.[10] Murdoch saw no traces at Point Barrow, however, of any disease resembling hydrophobia.[11] In Greenland, hydrophobia occasionally appears and is carried by foxes.[12] In Baffin Island, on the contrary, it is said to be unknown.[13] The dogs of the mission stations of the Labrador coast in 1857 were attacked by a mysterious disease of the Arctic peculiar to canines, and many of them perished.[14]

The Eskimo is sometimes severe in his treatment of his dogs. It is perhaps largely through necessity, however, that he is brutal. Thus, to break up a dog fight, the Diomede Islander will unconcernedly jerk one of the participants out from the snarling mass by his tail and fling him against the rocks.[15] Though the dogs are vicious among themselves, they do not often bite the natives.

Some Eskimos force their dogs to fend for themselves during the summer, when they are of little use to the people. For example, certain Labrador Eskimos banish their dogs to an island, where, except for chance visits, they have to obtain their own food.[16] Similarly, in East Greenland "in summer, when they have no use for dogs, they leave them on a little desert island, whence one can hear at a very great distance their piercing howls."[17] The Polar Eskimos and the Angmagsalik Eskimos sometimes break off the teeth of their dogs so that they cannot eat their harness.[18]

Where the health and efficiency of the dogs are at stake, however, the Eskimos show great solicitude. And though at times obviously lacking in humaneness, their attitude is really one of gratitude and respect.[19] Coöperation between man and dog is essential.

The dog, beyond being esteemed for his practical utility, is elevated to the position of mythological progenitor of man. From the Aleutian Islands to Greenland this belief is common,[20] though other legends are also told in explanation of the origin of the human race.

"A caribou Eskimo may be a murderer, but it is with difficulty that he can be moved to kill a dog, even though it is sick"; neither will he touch a dogskin.[21] The taboos of this group regarding dogs are extreme, and of special interest since their customs sanction infanticide and the abandonment of the aged.[22]

As a rule Eskimos will not eat dog meat except in times of famine.[23] It is even stated that in the region dogs are never beaten for biting a person, for it is thought that the spirit of the dog would then become angry and prevent the wound from healing.[24]

And on the west coast of Hudson Bay a young angakok, or medicine man, must not whip his own dogs for a whole year after he has accepted the calling.[25]

The Eskimos attribute to the dog mysterious powers. At Ponds Bay a dog's head is given to a boy to eat when he is one year old, so that he will have a strong head.[26] The Greenlanders bury a dog's head with a child "so that that wise animal may show the little uninstructed soul the way to the happy land."[27] The Diomede Islanders kill a dead man's "best-friend-dog" and place it with his body.[28] Similarly, at Smith Sound a man's "favorite dogs, harnessed and attached to a sledge, are strangled to accompany him."[29] In case of a woman one dog is killed.[30] The St. Lawrence Islanders practiced a ceremonial greeting in which a dog was sacrificed.[31] "Three baydares, with ten men in each, approached us within ten paces, where they stopped, chanting in a pitiful voice; one of them, rising, spoke some words in an energetic manner, and while holding up a small black dog in his hand, drew forth a knife, with which he stabbed the animal, and then threw it into the sea."

§3. FUEL RESOURCES[32]

BLUBBER, burned in an open shallow lamp with a wick of moss or grass, is the characteristic fuel of the Eskimo. Also various forms of scrubby vegetation, and grass, moss, and peat are burned, in open fires, especially in the summer time. Another form of fuel is driftwood,[33] which, it will be remembered, is very scarce in the central area in the far north of Greenland. The Eskimos have never on their own initiative burned coal, so far as is known, though there are outcroppings of it in various places in their region.

Of the animal fuels, seal oil is the most commonly used. A seal weighing two hundred pounds will yield almost one hundred pounds of blubber; consequently, a seal-eating people will have enough fuel to use extravagantly in proportion to food.[34] Other marine mammals also yield fuel fat, of course; indeed, in the Cape York District narwhal and white-whale blubber is considered better than that of either the seal or the walrus.[35]

Fat of land animals is usable as fuel, but it is far less satisfactory than blubber. Tallow from the musk ox and caribou, for instance, is a miserable substitute. These animals are fat only during fall and early winter, and even then a very great number of them have to be secured to obtain enough fuel. A primitive tallow dip made of caribou fat and moss is the only source of light, however, which most of the Caribou Eskimos avail themselves of during the long, dark nights of winter.[36] Also the Saningaiyomiut, along the upper part of Great Fish or Backs River, burn tallow in their lamps.[37] All members of the Caribou group apart from the Hauneqtôrmiut and a very few Qaernermiut pass even the coldest winters without any artificial heat whatever.[38] This is due to the fact that with neither caribou fat nor plant fuel can a snow hut be heated, and these people, living inland, do not secure the blubber of marine mammals. Once an Eskimo has used the fuel of aquatic animals he is reluctant to substitute anything else.[39]

Fish also yield oil suitable for burning in lamps. Thus, in Greenland, fat extracted from the Norway haddock serves as an emergency fuel;[40] and oil allowed to ooze out of shark livers is considered in East Greenland better than seal oil for lamps.[41] Birket-Smith believes that fish oil, indeed, was the original fuel for the Eskimo lamp, whose origin he ascribes to the central regions.[42]

The Eskimos also use lichen, moss, heather, and scrub willow for cooking. Groups differ in their resourcefulness in utilizing these materials as fuel.[43]

Stefansson observed that the coast natives of northern Alaska, for instance, although they dug in the snow for willows, carried driftwood, seal oil, or whale oil when traveling inland. When their wood or oil gave out and there were no willows, they beat a hasty retreat to the coast without fire, in spite of the fact that they generally knew that there were other Eskimos in the interior—inland Oturkagmiut and their neighbors—who had the art of finding fuel other than willows in the open country wherever they went. The Mackenzie River Eskimos are completely ignorant of how to find any fuel but willows in the open country, even in summer. But the Eskimos of Coronation Gulf and the region to the east as far as Hudson Bay find plant fuel of various sorts, even though their country is very poor in such resources. The Coronation Gulf people use as fuel a sort of "heather" (*Cassiope tetragona*). Stefansson living in this region with three Western Eskimo companions was unable at first to convert the latter from the difficult use of willow to the easy heather. It seemed to them wrong or degraded to use "grass" as long as wood was available. This same conservatism had restricted their ancestors as long as they had lived in Alaska from learning the art of "grass" burning from the Oturkagmiut. No matter how soaked with water, Cassiope can easily be burned if one knows the method and if there is a strong breeze fanning the fire, and kindling enough to start the blaze.

Among the Copper Eskimos (Coronation Gulf) willow, where available, largely supplants heather as fuel; and in most places in their province by the time the snow has melted there is enough of one or the other of these fuels to allow them to cache away the seal-oil lamp.[44] In parts of the Colville Hills (Victoria Island), however, neither willow nor heather can be procured.[45]

At Amitsoq, King William Island, Cassiope is not found, and its nearest substitute, Dryas, is very difficult to keep lighted.[46] Melville Peninsula also is very poor in plant fuel; some Cassiope and willows that attain a height of about a half a meter in sheltered places in the extreme south are used for firewood.[47] The inland Eskimos of Great Fish River, who use tallow instead of blubber for lighting, utilize lichen, mosses, and a kind of heather in cooking and heating.[48] The Aivilik and Kinipetu Eskimos, who dwell to the north of Chesterfield Inlet, burn turf and moss.[49] The natives of the Egedesminde District, West Greenland, use peat, at least nowadays, and also heather.[50] Birch, willow, juniper, crowberry, and other shrubs also provide some fuel in Greenland.[51]

§4. USE OF METAL AND STONE

Copper

PURE copper is exposed in several localities about Coronation Gulf, chiefly along the Coppermine River, and also in Bathurst Inlet and in parts of Victoria Island, especially Prince Albert Sound.[52] The natives use it in making knives, ice picks, harpoon heads, etc.,[53] which are valuable trade objects.

Mathiassen found several pieces of copper while excavating at Naujan, Repulse Bay. He[54] says: "There is thus no doubt that the Eskimos of the Thule culture have had access to metal, presumably in very limited quantities. . . . The copper presumably came from the regions around Coronation Gulf and Bathurst Inlet. . . ." This discovery seems to prove that the use of metal was practiced by Eskimos fairly long ago. It is uncertain whether the Caribou Eskimos had become acquainted with metal; at any rate it had made no change in their technique.[55]

It is impossible to state whether among other groups than the Copper Eskimos resources were unavailable or simply not discovered. Mecking mentions the occurrence of copper in the Hudson Bay region south of Chesterfield Inlet,[56] but it cannot be stated how available it is for primitive use. We could scarcely expect the Eskimos to discover buried mineral resources, since the ground is

frozen solid except during summer, and they dig into it only in
building their semi-underground dwellings, an activity not engaged in everywhere.

Iron

AT the time of the arrival of the first whites in the Cape York District, northwestern Greenland, the Polar Eskimos there were fashioning composite knife blades from many small scales of iron
hacked from three large meteors in that vicinity.[57] The industry
was very small, however.[58] In South Greenland a knife of telluric
iron has been found at Fiskernaes.[59]

No telluric iron has been found in any ruin in the Egedesminde
District, but the fact does not prove that it never was in use.[60]
Thalbitzer states that it was not utilized in East Greenland so far
as is known.[61] Implements used by the only inhabitants ever seen
on Clavering Island (74° N. Lat.), however, were said to be tipped
with iron "which had all the appearance of being of meteoric
origin."[62]

It is uncertain from whom the Greenlanders learned the use of
metal. Frobisher, who rediscovered Greenland, found the Eskimos
of the west coast using iron.[63] Davis, his successor, saw them using
copper.[64] Steensby assumes that the knowledge came from elsewhere and not by independent acquisition.[65] Mathiassen gives his
opinion[66] that "the Greenland iron technique is of course undoubtedly connected with the knowledge of the more easily worked copper from the western regions." He found a little meteoric iron in
his excavations at Repulse Bay, which is just north of Hudson
Bay.

A noteworthy fact brought out by Thalbitzer[67] is that the
word *sawik* is used for "iron" practically everywhere within the
Eskimo region, except in East Greenland. At Cape Prince of
Wales, Bering Strait, *sow-eek'* means a man's knife with an iron
blade, and the word for iron itself is *soo-ik-mee'-nuk*.[68]

Stone

STEFANSSON mentions that the Eskimos of the Mackenzie region
journeyed two hundred miles above the head of the delta, into the
Indian country, to get stone for their weapons.[69] The Arvilingjuar-
miut, between Lord Mayor's Bay and Committee Bay, brought a
yellow flint some distance, from the neighborhood of Backs River,

and secured soapstone for lamps and cooking pots from the interior south of Pelly Bay. Iron pyrites they found near the sea west of Lord Mayor's Bay.[70] In the country of the Iglulik Eskimos there are not many minerals that can be utilized.[71] Soapstone is found around Wager Inlet and Repulse Bay; flint is abundant in the limestone regions, but only in small pieces except on Southampton Island; pyrites is plentiful in the limestone region; and slate is found all over. Steensby mentions that the Polar Eskimos are able to secure sulphur pyrites for making fire, and soapstone for lamps and pots.[72] The East Greenlanders go to Inigsalik and Pikiutdlek for potstone.[73]

Jade

JADE has commonly been used in the western regions for bladed and pointed implements and for ornaments. There is a vast deposit of this stone in northwestern Alaska. According to reports given the writer while in the region, this is on Jade Creek, a southward flowing tributary of the Kobuk River. An Eskimo from Diomede Island also stated, in a vague way, that there was a lot of jade inland somewhere from East Cape, Siberia.[74] Jenness says with regard to jade that no deposits of it are known to occur east of the Rocky Mountains, except on the Rae River in Coronation Gulf.[75] He had seen no jade implements from any district east of the Mackenzie River Delta except from Cape Dorset, southwestern Baffin Island.

NOTES

1. Weyer: Field Notes.
2. Sumner, Keller, and Davie: 1927, IV, 69 ff.
3. Rasmussen: 1927, 227 ff. (Netsilik Eskimos, King William Land); Stefansson: 1921, 301 ff.; Jenness: 1922, 112–113 (Copper Eskimos); Birket-Smith: 1929, I, 128 (Caribou Eskimos at Chesterfield Inlet); Boas: 1907, 39 (Cumberland Sound); Bilby: 1923, 87 ff. (Baffin Island).
4. Rasmussen: 1927, 227.
5. Stefansson: 1921, 301 ff.
6. Jenness: 1922, 112–113.
7. Birket-Smith: 1929, I, 112 (musk ox hunting by Caribou Eskimos); Boas: 1888, 509–510 (bear hunting among Central Eskimos); Hawkes: 1916, 83 (bear hunting in Labrador); Ekblaw: 1928 (musk ox and bear hunting by Polar Eskimos); Kroeber: 1899, 270 (bear hunting by Polar Eskimos); Steensby: 1910, 300 (bear hunting by Polar Eskimos); Jensen: 1928, 336 (Greenland); Thalbitzer: 1914, 404 (polar-bear hunting in East Greenland).
8. Birket-Smith: 1924, 250, citing Rikli and Heim.
9. Stefansson: 1921.
10. Weyer: Field Notes.
11. Murdoch: 1892, 358.
12. Birket-Smith: 1924, 250.
13. Bilby: 1923, 130–131.
14. Hawkes: 1916, 20.
15. Weyer: Field Notes.

16. Hawkes: 1916, 68.

17. Holm: 1887, 31.

18. Mylius-Erichsen and Moltke: 1906, 232; Birket-Smith: 1928, 183.

19. Stefansson: 1930, 47.

20. Boas: 1888, 641–643; Sauer: 1802, 272; Sarycher: 1806-7, II, 75 (Unalaska); Nelson: 1899, 446; Boas: 1907, 478; Rasmussen: 1908, 104–105.

21. Birket-Smith: 1929, I, 96, 171.

22. Birket-Smith: 1929, I, 98, 294–295, 258, 300.

23. Weyer: Field Notes (Diomede Islands); Moore: 1923, 353 (St. Lawrence Island); Ray: 1885, 46 (Point Barrow); Birket-Smith: 1929, I, 96; Steensby: 1910, 354; Birket-Smith: 1924, 252; Ross: 1819, 131; Holm: 1914, 45; Thalbitzer: 1914, 12.

24. Nelson: 1899, 435.

25. Boas: 1907, 510.

26. Boas: 1907, 514.

27. Fries: 1872, 121; Crantz: 1767, I, 237.

28. Weyer: Field Notes.

29. Peary: 1898, I, 506.

30. Rasmussen: 1908, 113.

31. Phillips: 1819, 41.

32. See also pp. 11 ff. and 66 f.

33. Murdoch: 1892, 63.

34. Stefansson: 1921.

35. Rasmussen: 1921, 24.

36. Rasmussen: 1927, 77–78.

37. Jenness: 1922, 248.

38. Birket-Smith: 1929, I, 92.

39. Rasmussen: 1921, 314; Steensby: 1910, 397; Jenness: 1928, 74; Brown: 1927, 149.

40. Jensen: 1928, 348.

41. Thalbitzer: 1914, 539.

42. Birket-Smith: 1929, II, 103–104.

43. Stefansson: 1921, 243.

44. Jenness: 1922, 14, 79.

45. Jenness: 1922, 98.

46. Rasmussen: 1927, 206.

47. Freuchen and Mathiassen: 1925, 558.

48. Rasmussen: 1927, 193.

49. Boas: 1907, 102, 446.

50. Birket-Smith: 1924, 74.

51. Brown: 1927, 118.

52. Jenness: 1922, 52; O'Neill: 1924, 53a–71a; Hanbury: 1903, 191; Rasmussen: 1927, 285; Burwash: 1931, 79–82, 84 ff.

53. Rasmussen: 1927, 285; Cadzow: 1920; also Jenness: 1923a.

54. Mathiassen: 1927, II, 127 ff.

55. Birket-Smith: 1929, I, 233.

56. Mecking: 1928, 202.

57. Ross: 1819, 98, 104, 121; Bessels: 1878, 362.

58. Kroeber: 1899, 285; Thalbitzer: 1914, 486; Wissler: 1918, especially 163 ff.

59. Birket-Smith: 1928, 166.

60. Birket-Smith: 1924, 75.

61. Thalbitzer: 1914, 486.

62. Clavering: 1830, 21.

63. Frobisher: 1867, 283, 285.

64. Davis: 1880, 20. For other references see Birket-Smith: 1924, 82–83.

65. Steensby: 1910, 275–276.

66. Mathiassen: 1927, II, 127 ff.

67. Thalbitzer: 1914, 486.

68. Weyer: Field Notes.

69. Stefansson: 1914, 12–13.

70. Rasmussen: 1927, 168.

71. Mathiassen: 1928, I, 9.

72. Steensby: 1910, 276.

73. Holm: 1914, 26.

74. See also Merril: 1885.

75. Jenness: 1925, 432.

CHAPTER VII

NATURAL RESOURCES AND POPULATION DENSITY

§1. SPARSITY OF POPULATION

IT must be remembered throughout this discussion that we are dealing with a borderland of the inhabited world. The Polar Eskimos are, indeed, the northernmost people on earth. The Eskimos as a whole, living as they do on the fringe of the habitable earth, naturally show a characteristic sparseness of population. In a table showing the comparative density of population among different groups of people, Ratzel cites the Eskimos as illustrative of the thinness of population in the outermost regions.[1] Their density of population as given by this authority, of one person to between sixty-six and two hundred square miles of land, conveys a forceful impression of the general sparseness. On no account to be overlooked is the fact that it is scarcity of food, primarily, that limits numbers.

The accompanying table (Fig. 12), compiled from various sources, gives a more detailed account of the density of population among the Eskimos. Clearly, the population is unevenly distributed.

TABLE SHOWING DENSITY OF POPULATION AMONG THE ESKIMOS

FIGURE 12

Region	Average Number of Square Miles per Inhabitant
Baffin Island[1] (about 1885)	198
(1927)	149
Netsiling Eskimos[2]	186
Caribou Eskimos[3]	142
Eskimos south of Hudson Strait[4]	120
Alaska[5]	
Arctic Division (including both Eskimos and Indians)	42.5
Yukon Division (total population exclusive of 37 whites and mixed breeds)	25.86
Kuskokwim Division (total population exclusive of 114 whites and mixed breeds)	12.9

Region	Average Number of Square Miles per Inhabitant
Greenland	
Entire island (including ice-covered portion)[6] . . .	56.8
Entire ice-free portion[7]	8.1
West Greenland (ice-free portion)[8]	3.25

	Average Length of Coast Line per Inhabitant Miles
Greenland[9]	
Thule	7.76
Upernivik	1.61
Umanaq	.81
Godhavn	.93
Ritenbenk	.52
Jacobshavn	.39
Christianshaab	.77
Egedesminde	.93
Holsteinsborg	1.18
Sukkertoppen	.93
Godthaab	1.12
Frederikshaab	1.06
Julianehaab	.69
Angmagsalik	1.62

[1] Kitto: 1930, 113 (area); Boas: 1888, 425 (population about 1885); Kitto: 1930, 28 (population 1927).

[2] Rasmussen: 1927, 218 f.

[3] Birket-Smith: 1929, I, 69.

[4] Sumner, Keller, and Davie: 1927, IV, 17.

[5] Petroff: 1884, 4 ff.

[6] Birket-Smith: 1928, 26 f.

[7] Birket-Smith: 1928, 26 f.

[8] Birket-Smith: 1929, I, 69.

[9] Birket-Smith: 1928, 27.

What, then, is the explanation for this wide variation in numbers? The fundamental cause is irregularity in the abundance of the resources necessary for life. Just as the general scarcity of these resources causes the population in general to be sparse, so do regional differences cause regional variations in density.

It is a principle, of course, that one factor influencing the density of population is the degree to which a people are able to avail themselves of the resources of their habitat. Thus, numbers depend partly on the perfection of adjustment of a people to their life-conditions. In the Eskimos, however, we have an example of a people who show fairly uniform cultural development among their various groups. Hence, differences in degree of skill in securing the necessaries of life are not an outstanding cause of regional variations in numbers. Furthermore, it can be said that differences in standard of living do not account for differences in density of population. The Eskimo standard of living, like the Eskimo cultural level, is fairly uniform. What differences there are in the standard of living are more conspicuously the effect of differences in life-conditions than the cause of differences in density of population.

Thus, general scarcity of the resources necessary for life limits the population to its characteristic sparsity, and differences in the abundance of resources account primarily for differences in the density of population. Settlements cluster thickest in areas richest in food resources.

§2. REGIONAL DIFFERENCES IN FOOD RESOURCES

WITH the foregoing principles in mind, let us inquire into the conditions that favor the development of population in the Eskimo region. Hunting of sea mammals, for instance, is of utmost importance to most Eskimos, especially during the winter, which is the critical period. And the productivity of this type of hunting depends largely upon the conditions with regard to sea ice. Stefansson points out that so far as seal life is concerned, there are certain deserts in the polar ocean. "They are caused by the sluggishness or absence of currents, just as deserts on land are caused by lack of rainfall and porousness of the soil." Seals can find food everywhere in the ocean, but in certain places they lack the easy opportunity to come up and breathe.[2] If seals, walrus, or white whales are present and have only scattered patches of open water in which to breathe, they are, of course, forced to remain in the vicinity of these openings, and the hunter can more narrowly localize his activities. On the other hand, a continuous expanse of sea ice excludes many forms. Only those seals that are able to scratch or thrust holes through the ice can remain in such regions. Hence, the variety of game is restricted.

The opposite extreme, marked scarcity of ice, is also a handicap; for it precludes the localization of hunting both by breathing holes and in open patches of water. Between South Ström Fiord and Julianehaab Bay, in southern Greenland, we are so far removed from arctic conditions that the ice, being of short duration and unsafe, is no longer an advantage but an obstacle in the way of sealing.[3]

By reason of this relation between sea ice and sea fauna, the hunting of marine mammals is, in general, most productive along coasts where there is considerable winter sea ice, but where currents prohibit the forming of a solid covering. And it follows that the coasts which are most favorably located in this respect generally accommodate the densest population. Birket-Smith has brought out this relationship along the west coast of Greenland.[4] Differences in the productivity of hunting account, at least in some measure, for the fact that the entire east coast of Greenland accommodates only about a fifteenth or a twentieth of the population of the whole island. On the east coast it is locally, at such places as Sermiligak, that rapid currents in the sounds between the islands prevent freezing over and cause the presence of excellent sealing grounds for the inhabitants.[5]

In the same manner, along the southern coast of Baffin Island, tidal currents coursing among the island-and-bay mazes keep open lanes of water and thereby increase the winter hunting grounds.[6] On the other hand, north of Cumberland Sound, where the tides are less strong, this effect is not noticed.

The northern Labrador Eskimos ". . . locate their villages where . . . the ice is kept moving by ocean currents during the winter, and there are open spots and blow holes for seal and walrus. There is only a month or so in midwinter when the ice is stationary."[7]

Where the sea is covered by continuous ice, as, for instance, in Prince of Wales Strait (Victoria Island), seals can be secured only through the tedious method of having dogs discover their breathing holes and waiting for the seals to come for air.[8] A similar condition of continuous ice exists in the Thule District of northern Greenland. There the sea is never entirely free from ice and the fiords are covered by permanent *sikûssaq* ice.[9] Some areas there are characterized by pressure ridges and hummocky ice, while others are smooth and unbroken. The latter offer the best hunting; for it is there that the seals have their breathing holes in winter and their basking places in spring. Furthermore, a smooth floe offers the best conditions for sledging. The result is that the Eskimos of the Thule District locally select sites for their settlements where the sea ice is smooth.[10]

Through these and other environmental influences, abundance of food resources differs throughout the Eskimo region. The Arctic Archipelago is, in general, poor in fauna. Westward from the barren Silurian limestone areas of Devon Island life increases, however, and attains a maximum on Melville Island.[11] "Similarly animal life becomes more and more abundant northward from Devon Island and develops to such an extent at Lady Franklin Bay that Peary was able to base on it the sustenance of his large number of Eskimos."[12]

Only the southern and the eastern sections of the Arctic Archipelago are inhabited. Rasmussen remarks on the poverty of the waters about King William Land, at the southern edge of the Archipelago, saying that at Malerualik the average catch per man between January and June would be about ten or fifteen seals, whereas a skilful hunter in Greenland would get two hundred in the same time.[13] Such discrepancies, taken in a body, explain the uneven distribution of population in the Eskimo region. Thus, the Netsilingmiut group numbers but 259 persons, though their hunting grounds include an area as large as all the ice-free portion of Greenland,[14] where the total population is about thirteen thousand.[15]

§3. SEASONAL FLUCTUATIONS IN RESOURCES

Winter the Period of Hardship

THE sparseness of game, the more severe weather conditions, and the scarcity of daylight combine to render winter in the Arctic the period of greatest hardship. The reader will recall the gloomy desolation which winter brings to the Eskimo habitat. The caribou thin out in the Barren Grounds; and even some of the seal emigrate from certain waters. Of the birds the migratory varieties, which constitute by far the greater proportion in numbers, fly southward. The land, in short, takes on a dismal, lifeless cast.

The absence of the sun, perhaps as forcefully as the diminution of game, makes it difficult to eke out subsistence during winter. Hunting activities are seriously handicapped by the continuous darkness which is characteristic of midwinter in the high Arctic. To be sure, land animals can be tracked more easily when there is snow; but even so, in caribou hunting, for instance, darkness is a severe handicap, even though it be relieved by moonlight.[16] Blizzards are an additional handicap in hunting; and, furthermore, caribou are apt to be more shy in winter than in summer.[17]

In hunting seals at their breathing holes, darkness is less of a drawback. An ingenious "indicator" placed in the breathing hole reveals the presence of a seal to the harpooner, even though the light be dim. Further, the netting of seals beneath the ice in winter, which is practiced by the Alaskan Eskimos, is exceptional in that it is possible *only* when it is dark. Moonlight or even bright aurora borealis is said to render this method fruitless.[18]

These sealing methods are exceptions, however, to the general rule that darkness is a hindrance in hunting. Everything considered, the lack of daylight presents serious difficulties.[19] In addition it increases the trouble and peril in traveling over ice. The Eskimos as a consequence are greatly restricted in their activities and at times are forced even to remain sedentary. Most severely handicapped by winter darkness are the Polar Eskimos, who dwell so far north that for two months in midwinter their hunting is almost at a standstill.[20]

It is quite understandable, therefore, that in general winter time is the period of greatest hardship. In the region of Bering Strait (Alaska) it is a season of possible famine, as history shows, and there is normally a slight feeling of uncertainty regarding the future. Summer time, on the other hand, is less exacting, with the result that the people are more cheerful, and inclined to give a heartier welcome to the stranger.[21] The Diomede Islander asserts that winter and spring mean hard work, sometimes with not much food; "summer is more better: just eat and sleep."[22] Similarly, at Selawik (Kotzebue Sound) starvation is more apt to occur in winter than in summer. On the contrary, however, the families who fish during the summer along the Tuksuk River (Port Clarence) look forward to winter, when they live inland, as an easy period of good times.

Among the Copper Eskimos the period of greatest hardship is from the middle of January till the middle of March.[23] Even from October to April these Eskimos, with the exception of the Kanghiryuarmiut, generally lead a hand-to-mouth existence. "Starvation may and does occur at any time, but generally the sunless days are most feared."[24] Farther east, among the Netsilingmiut of King William Land, there are periods during the winter when weeks pass without any possibility of procuring food; whereas during the great caribou hunting season, in autumn, and when the summer salmon fishing is particularly good, more game is killed than can be eaten at once.[25] The season of greatest privation among the Netsilik Eskimos is from the middle of January up to some time in February.[26] Among the Caribou Eskimos the hardest time is toward the end of winter. Almost every season one or two families die of hunger.[27]

The Angmagsalik Eskimos call one period in winter "time of famine." It is not literally, however, a time of general starvation, for during this period the people draw from their stored provisions.[28]

Food Must Be Stored

THE Eskimos are forced to lay aside provisions against the lean season. Preservation of food is fortunately favored by the coldness of the climate. Cached provisions represent a sort of insurance by smoothing out the seasonal inequalities in the productivity of hunting. Food resources strictly limit density of population in the Arctic; and if the Eskimos lived entirely a hand-to-mouth existence, the supporting power of the habitat would never exceed its supporting power at the poorest season. Some groups would be completely wiped out did they not cache supplies when they are abundant and draw from them in time of need. By this form of insurance the uttermost geographical limit of habitability is pressed northward beyond where it would otherwise lie.

A common method of caching supplies out of reach of dogs and wild animals is to place them on a scaffolding.[29] At Point Barrow meat is stored also in great subterranean digs, so deep that it remains frozen throughout the summer.[30] The King Islanders use as a storeroom a great cave, thirty meters deep, near the village but inaccessible during summer except by boat.[31] The Diomeders bury meat under the beach rocks. Sand, they say, is a poor caching ground.[32] In addition, tuberous roots and "Eskimo rhubarb" are stored in sealskin bags. They also keep eggs; but enterprising missionaries could not make them learn to keep them in seal oil, which preserves their freshness. Along the Alaskan coast as elsewhere in the Eskimo region fish are buried, and eaten after they are rotten.[33] The Eskimos of the Tuksuk River (Port Clarence) dry salmon on racks during the summer run.[34] Like the Copper Eskimos,[35] however, they do not smoke their fish as some in the western region do.

The Copper Eskimos commonly cache their stores on top of rock piles so that wild animals cannot plunder them.[36] These caches are deposited between spring and fall, when they are collected for consumption until the time of winter sealing.[37] The Netsilik Eskimos, likewise, count on their cached stores lasting until Christmas and a short time into the new year.[38] Birket-Smith[39] testifies that the Caribou Eskimos are improvident for the future. In Labrador reindeer meat is dried in the spring and frozen in the autumn.[40] On the west coast of Greenland caplin, dried, forms an excellent winter food.[41] In East Greenland meat is dried or frozen, seal blubber is stored in bags according to the general Eskimo custom, and berries and herbs are frozen in blubber for winter.[42] The Smith Sound Eskimos cache large numbers of eggs in late June and early July. Birds also are stored in May and June, being placed feathers and all in sealskin bags.[43] "The booty of the hunt, because of the difficulty of transporting, is laid down in depots far from the settlements, where it remains frozen until needed."[44] Seals, for instance, are cached in piles and frozen for winter use.[45] Among these so-called Polar Eskimos the meat caches must be filled in the spring for the following winter; for autumn with its gales and uncertain young ice is not a reliable season.[46]

§4. FAMINE AS A POPULATION CHECK

In spite of these various precautions against scarcity, famine occurs. Rasmussen reports the frequency of death through starvation in the region of King William Land:[47]

"Life is thus an almost uninterrupted struggle for bare existence, and periods of death and actual starvation are not infrequent. Three years before my visit, eighteen people died of starvation at Simpson Strait. The year before, seven died of hunger north of Cape Britannia. Twenty-five is not a great number perhaps, but out of a total of 259 it makes a terrible percentage for death by starvation alone. And yet this may happen any winter, when there are no caribou to be had."

Even though the people are farseeing, an exceptionally poor hunting season can bring destruction. Thus, genuine famine follows in Angmagsalik when the ice pack presses into the fiords early in winter and freezes tight.[48] And in the Barren Grounds when the surface snow melts and then crusts over, the caribou, being unable to scrape through for food, migrate elsewhere. Then the hunting of the Eskimos is interrupted and scarcity may result.[49] The Copper Eskimos suffer privation about one year in four, seriously once in fifteen or twenty years.[50]

"At Cape Bexley and to the east there is apparently hardly a winter when the people do not have to subsist for considerable periods on seal oil alone. . . . About fifteen years ago on a small island about three miles off shore from Cape Kendall, Coronation Gulf, about forty (?) people died in one winter of hunger."[51]

The Eskimos of parts of northwestern Alaska experienced severe famine between 1878 and 1880.[52] On St. Lawrence Island, where between one-third and two-thirds of the population died, the disaster has been attributed to excessive drinking by the natives of liquor bartered from traders; but a full consideration of the circumstances, including the testimony of the natives themselves, points to deeper causes. Stormy weather during the hunting season, and previous depredations of white hunters among the game animals upon which the Eskimos depend, must be regarded at least as probable contributory causes.[53]

During such periods of scarcity the Eskimos are forced to eat their dogs,[54] the tough skin coverings of their boats,[55] their sealskin boots and bow cases,[56] and even the bodies of their dead comrades.

§5. CANNIBALISM

AT Coronation Gulf "sometimes the natives would recall dreadful tales of years gone by, how, not a generation before, the Kanghiryuarmiut had chopped up the corpses of their dead and eaten the frozen flesh to save themselves from starvation." Again, it is stated that ". . . in one instance at least a boy was actually killed and eaten." "Away in the east, the Netsilingmiut had cut off a man's legs while he was still alive and tried to appease their hunger with his flesh."[57]

Boas writes of the Central Eskimos: "if the hunter . . . has tried in vain to procure food, if the storm does not subside, the terrors of famine visit the settlement. The dogs are the first to fall victims to the pressing hunger, and if the worst comes cannibalism is resorted to. But all these occurrences are spoken of with the utmost horror. In such cases children particularly are killed and eaten. Fortunately, however, such occurrences are very rare."[58]

"During the winter of 1890–91 in the neighborhood of Wager River no less than thirty-seven natives had died through starvation. . . . Among those who perished, one man (Toolooar) killed twelve people, and ate their bodies."[59] From the Iglulik group an instance is noted of a wife eating her dead husband and children to keep alive.[60]

The Itivimiut, on the east coast of Hudson Bay, ". . . are frequently reduced to the point of starvation. . . . Instances of cannibalism are frequent when parents are so reduced as to slay their children. . . . The wife may fall a victim to her husband if she is not able to escape."[61] And from the Koksoagmiut "instances are reported where, in times of great scarcity, families have been driven to cannibalism after eating their dogs and clothing and other articles made of skins."[62] Also the Polar Eskimos have been known to kill their own people to replenish their food supply.[63] And the East Greenlanders relate legends of the occurrence of cannibalism to avoid starvation.[64]

Although the Eskimos probably do not manifest as obstinate abhorrence of cannibalism as Europeans or Americans would in the same predicament, they do show a very decided aversion to the practice.

In the region of Bering Strait, for instance, the Unalit, while they resorted to it in time of famine, did so very unwillingly.[65] An Eskimo of Diomede Islands insinuated his definite revulsion of feeling when he told the author that two of the villagers had eaten human flesh by mistake. They had cached some reindeer meat brought from East Cape; and later, in the autumn, had found what they thought was part of their foodstores and ate it. Upon learning that they had consumed a part of a corpse which the dogs had dragged down from the exposed graveyard behind the village they were seized with great misgivings. Ever afterward they carefully observed a taboo against eating any meat that had not been cooked.[66] The natives of Point Barrow, according to Ray, look upon cannibalism with horror, and he could not find that a case had ever occurred there.[67]

In the region of King William Island, where famine presents a severe problem, cannibalism is by no means uncommon. "Many people have eaten human flesh," testifies a native there. "But never from any desire for it, only to save their lives, and that after so much suffering that in many cases they were not fully sensible of what they did. . . . One winter many years ago the hunting failed. And some starved to death and others died of cold, and the living lived on the dead. All at once Tuneq went out of his mind. He said the spirits had told him to eat his wife. He began by cutting bits from her clothing and eating them, then more bits, till he had bared her body in several places. Then suddenly he stabbed her to death with his knife and ate her as he needed and lived. But he placed the bones in their order as it is required to be done when anyone dies. . . . But we who have endured such things ourselves, we do not judge others who have acted in this way though we may find it hard, when fed and contented ourselves, to understand how they could do such things. But then again, how can one who is in good health and well fed, expect to understand the mad-ness of starvation? We only know that every one of us has the same desire to live."[68]

It is also mentioned that the natives of Ponds Bay, Baffin Island, in spite of an abhorrence of cannibalism, resort to it in case of starvation.[69] On the west coast of Hudson Bay the natives refrain from speaking of the practice in the hearing of women;[70] but at times starvation forces them to take recourse to it.[71]

Commonly it is held that one who has eaten human flesh must follow certain observances. In the region just mentioned, the person ". . . should never afterwards eat bear-meat, because it is believed that bear-meat resembles that of men, and that to eat it will keep alive the desire for human flesh."[72] A native of Cumberland Sound, Baffin Island, who has eaten human flesh must not eat bear or ground seal or raw seal.[73] Special observances after cannibalism also prevail among the Caribou Eskimos.[74]

Formalized observances of this nature indicate that one who eats human flesh breaks a taboo; and such observances are contributory evidence of the revulsion in the mind of the Eskimo. Other sorts of taboos may, it must be admitted, carry greater societal condemnation. We have the case of a girl from the Ungava District who was banished from her village in the dead of winter simply because she persisted in eating deer meat and seal meat together.[75] Many food taboos of the Eskimo are surrounded by more complex regulations than the taboo against eating human flesh; but this is rather due to their commanding more immediately the everyday concern of the people than to a deeper feeling of revulsion against their infraction. Unless we are misled by the phraseology of the investigators, the Eskimo's attitude toward cannibalism differs somewhat from his attitude toward other taboos.

A form of cannibalism distinct from that practiced under stress of circumstance occurs when a murderer ceremonially eats a small piece of the body of his victim, generally his liver or his heart, to render the spirit of the dead man harmless. So outstandingly ritualistic is this practice that a discussion of it is reserved for the chapter on religion.[76] It should be held in mind, nevertheless, that cannibalism is inseparably linked with the concept of the soul, and even though there is no obvious religious implication in the eating of human flesh in emergency, the attitude is bound to be colored by a realization that the offender eats not only his victim's body but also his soul. Viewed broadly, however, it seems that more than religious motives are needed to explain the aversion of the Eskimo to cannibalism.

Various peoples of the world hold widely different attitudes toward cannibalism, ranging from almost unparalleled revulsion to epicurean relish. The explanation is exceedingly difficult to fathom, for the practice is bound up with many phases of culture. Altogether, the question involves so many conflicting points that it is no wonder that primitive peoples have come to hold basically different ideas on the matter. One might fairly ask whether the anthropologist should presume rationally to explain a question that shows such intricate shades of implication. The subject demands attention, nevertheless, as a very important problem concerning which every social group must commit itself. Singular emphasis is attached to cannibalism for one reason because it bears upon the struggle for survival simultaneously in two opposite directions. When it involves murder under pressure of famine, it means the extinction of the victims and the self-preservation of those committing the atrocity. Unique as a custom, therefore, it influences both the food supply and the number of living people who must subsist on the available resources.

It should be remembered that the utilization of human flesh as food may occur in more ways than one. Killing a person in order to eat him must be distinguished from consuming the body of one who has died a natural death. Furthermore, to eat an enemy is one thing, and to eat a member of one's own group another. In the cases pertaining to the Eskimos, murder for cannibalism is comparatively common. And in every instance of its occurrence mentioned above, the victim was another Eskimo, indeed probably a member of the immediate in-group.

With these facts before us we are prompted to inquire whether mankind normally has an aversion to cannibalism which breaks down only under stress of famine. Authorities do not agree, however, on this question of an instinctive aversion. One can scarcely deny that when cannibalism entails the killing of a fellow tribesman, sympathy for the victim must be an ingredient in the complex of feelings. But some authorities do not follow the opinion of Westermarck that aversion to cannibalism of this sort is most likely an instinctive feeling akin to those feelings which regulate the diet of the various animal species. Westermarck writes:

"Although our knowledge of their habits in this respect is defective, there can be little doubt that carnivorous animals as a rule refuse to eat members of their own species; and this reluctance is easy to understand considering its race-preserving tendency."[77]

Sumner and Keller, on the contrary, state:

"There are enough facts at disposal to dispel the fancy of an instinctive revulsion against human flesh. . . . The conclusion seems inevitable . . . that the differentiation of human flesh from other meat by taboo was a product of societal evolution; that is to say that it was as likely to be used as food as was any other nutritious article prior to the imposition of a restriction that did not exist in nature."[78]

Inasmuch as the question of instinctive revulsion to cannibalism evokes opposite answers from separate authorities, each of whom has investigated the subject on an exhaustive, world-wide scale, it would, of course, be futile here to attempt to solve it with the single case of the Eskimos. But the subject as it affects this people peculiarly presents some interesting features that cannot be passed over. What may be the reason for aversion to cannibalism in a people among whom the occurrence of death through starvation from time to time might be expected to lend the practice an aspect of expediency? Since cannibalism is the habit of some peoples simply by choice of taste, why should the Eskimos, whom force of circumstance might be expected to render lenient to the practice, regard it as revolting? If there be no innate aversion to eating human flesh, why should not a people who are far more familiar with death through famine than some habitual cannibals, come to regard eating the bodies of those who have already starved to death as a reasonable solution to a very pressing emergency? Barring only food that is tabooed *under special circumstances*, the Eskimos put into their stomachs every conceivable substance that is of value as nourishment, including some things that the civilized person would consider not only inedible but injurious to health. It will be recalled that the dietary of the Eskimos does not exclude such things as deer droppings, maggoty larvae of the caribou fly, and raw intestines of birds. Revulsion against cannibalism stands out as strangely inconsistent among a people conspicuously free from every other gustatory qualm.

We cannot even know whether the ancient ancestors of the Eskimos practiced cannibalism more extensively and with less compunction. The position of the custom in the scale of cultural evolution is open to controversy. Sumner and Keller point out that ". . . traces of its former employment are very widespread, indicating a condition in the remote past verging upon the universality of the practice among all races."[79] Westermarck argues to the contrary, that since cannibalism is much less prevalent among the lowest savages than among races somewhat more advanced in culture, it is an illegitimate supposition to regard the cannibalism of modern savages as a survival from the first infancy of mankind, or more generally, from a stage through which the whole human race has passed. This author further points out that a cannibalistic people upon being exposed to white civilization generally drop the custom readily. Even among peoples who have been extremely addicted to it, cannibalism has disappeared with a rapidity to which there is scarcely any parallel in the history of morals. On the other hand, he cites cases from Egypt and Polynesia showing that the custom can, when once instigated by famine, suddenly become a respectable fashion.[80]

If the feeling about cannibalism is as unstable as this would indicate, it is to be surmised that whatever instinctive aversion there may be is fairly easily overcome if the folkways operate against it in a concerted manner. At least it can be said that the infant growing up in the society accepts the existing code almost without either reasoning or considering his own natural feelings. The Eskimo child early becomes aware that cannibalism is tabooed. The revulsion manifested by his elders in recounting tales wherein people were forced to eat human bodies readily molds the child's attitude. Cannibalism is tabooed even as a topic of conversation in the hearing of women on the west coast of Hudson Bay. The various funeral practices of the Eskimos revealing the concept that the corpse is unclean doubtless reinforce the aversion. Thus, the *persistence* of revulsion against eating human flesh can be accounted for. But simply an explanation of why the folkways persist along this line from generation to generation does not account for their assuming this aspect originally. We must search deeper if we are to learn why the Eskimos discountenance cannibalism, apparently having better reason to practice it than some peoples who are habitual cannibals.

To arrive at any definite understanding we must ask ourselves exactly what a favorable attitude toward cannibalism would imply in the Eskimo social organization. Would cannibalism occur more frequently, we first inquire, if the people felt no revulsion against it? The natural assumption is that it would. Aversion checks recourse to cannibalism, at least until circumstances become extreme. If the Eskimos had no such feeling, the practice would surely be more common, even if it were resorted to only in emergencies. Let it be supposed for the sake of argument that the Eskimos sanction cannibalism if not accompanied by murder. Although due to the smallness of Eskimo communities natural deaths are not very frequent, nevertheless from time to time occasion for this type of cannibalism would arise. But here we encounter a phase of the Eskimo folkways that is very important. Aside from those who die natural deaths, there are others who are put to death. It is a common practice to kill infants when hard times render the rearing of them difficult.[81] Children are relatively unproductive members of the group and if resources are scarce the society can carry along only a portion of the nonproducers. At the opposite end of the life span, old and infirm persons are also sometimes put to death.[82] The expedient of killing children and old persons to reduce numbers and lighten the burdens of the remaining group is firmly grounded in the Eskimo folkways. Therefore, aside from persons who die natural deaths, others who are purposely killed would become the subjects of cannibalism. But would it be possible longer to discriminate so sharply the act of murder from the practice of infanticide and killing the aged?

Under the existing code these two acts are clearly distinguished from murder. But if the Eskimos sanctioned cannibalism it would be hard to discriminate between merely killing unproductive members for the good of the group and murdering for the purpose of cannibalism.

Hence, with this difference removed it is possible to imagine a destructive course of events. Very little laxity in a code which countenances murder would entail fatal results upon the society; for the Eskimo population is already so sparse that in some sections a decrease of numbers would mean total extinction. The practices of infanticide and of killing the aged would offer an opening wedge for the detrimental practice of murdering with cannibalistic motive. The individual would feel little security from the treachery of his fellows. Thus, the aversion which the Eskimo actually expresses toward cannibalism may be mingled with the intention of fortifying individual safety against the very hazardous alternative. At any rate, aversion to cannibalism strengthens the social organization against self-extinction. Indeed, it can be imagined that groups in the past may have come to sanction cannibalism and may have perished as a direct consequence. Their cannibalistic proclivities would perish with them; on these considerations it is not surprising that the existing groups show no tendency toward habitual cannibalism.

§6. BIRTH RATE AND DEATH RATE

STARVATION, it is clear, acts as a very definite check against increase of population. As a result of fluctuations in the quantity of available sustenance, famine from time to time reduces numbers. On the other hand, during a series of fortunate years population may increase. The rapidity with which the population can swell if food is sufficient depends primarily upon the birth rate. And this factor is difficult to evaluate; for statements as to the fecundity of Eskimos are conspicuously contradictory.

Birth Rate among Eskimos

THE earlier observers who estimated the fecundity of the Eskimos, for the most part without statistical data, commonly comment on a characteristic fewness of children in the Eskimo family.

Typical is Armstrong's generalization that from all that he could learn the Eskimo race is not prolific.[83] Nelson writes with reference to Bering Strait that "families rarely have more than two or three children, and it is not uncommon for them to have none."[84] According to Petroff, "the females of the coast tribes (of Alaska) are not fruitful, and to see four children of one mother is quite a rare occurrence, one or two being the common number of children to a family."[85] We read of the Point Barrow Eskimos: "The women are not prolific. Although all the adults are or have been married, many of them are childless, and few have more than two children. One woman is known to have had at least four. . . . Dr. Simpson heard of a 'rare case' where one woman had borne seven children."[86] By another observer it is written of this group: "Large families are very rare, . . . they do not often bear children before twenty, and a couple is very seldom met with that has a family of more than three, though upon inquiry they may have some that 'nuna-mi-sinĭk,' sleep on the ground."[87]

In interpreting the remarks of casual observers account must be taken of the fact that infanticide, possibly augmented by a naturally high infant mortality, may cause the fecundity of the people to appear less than it actually is. Jenness, however, gives a definite statement:

". . . Among the Copper Eskimos from four to five children are born, on the average, to each woman, and three survive, while there are occasional instances of both lesser and greater fecundity. . . . I knew of two cases among the natives farther west where an unusually large number of children were born to one family. One was at Kittigaryuit in the delta of the Mackenzie river, where a woman bore five sons and five daughters. . . . A North Alaskan woman . . . had two boys and three girls, and was pregnant again in 1914. These were exceptional cases, however, for as far as I had means of judging the average in these regions too seemed to be from four to five."[88]

The average size of family at Cape Prince of Wales, Alaska, based on the thirty-one families comprising the village in 1928, is about 2.6 living children for each.[89] A few cases which Rasmussen cites[90] seem to indicate considerable fecundity among the Netsilingmiut. Two women had borne ten children each, two others eleven, and one twelve. One woman he met at Committee Bay had even had twenty children. In the Ungava District (Labrador) "the number of children born varies greatly, for, although these Eskimos are not a prolific race, a couple may occasionally claim parentage of as many as ten children. Two or three is the usual number."[91] Crantz writes: "The Greenlanders are not very prolific. A woman has commonly three or four children, but at most six; they generally bear one child in two or three years."[92] In agreement with this estimate is Nansen's statement: "On the average the pure breed Greenlanders are not prolific. Two, three, or four children to each marriage is the general rule, though there are instances of families of six or eight or even more."[93]

Many of the observers have not based their estimates on actual counts. Grave doubt, for instance, is cast upon these reports from Greenland, and slight uncertainty even upon reports from other sections, by accurate statistical investigations as to the fecundity of the West Greenland Eskimos. There the findings of Bertelsen have proved that the frequency of births is even very high, and that a birth rate that is exceptional in Europe is by no means uncommon in Greenland.[94] The average for West Greenland is approximately 37 per thousand, a figure which is about the same as that for countries like Roumania and Bulgaria, and considerably higher than that for the United States, which was 21.4 in 1925.[95] Furthermore, the birth rate in West Greenland is greater where the population is least mixed, which suggests that before intermarriage with whites the fecundity of the Eskimos was, if anything, greater than now.

Summarizing the information at hand, the birth rate of the Eskimos seems to be at least moderate.

Influences upon Birth Rate

As influences tending to lower the normal fecundity of the Eskimos we notice certain practices. Prolonged breast feeding, for instance, is supposed generally to inhibit menstruation.[96] It follows that the woman who nurses her young for three or four years is less apt to become pregnant during that period than the woman who nurses her child for only a year.[97] The Eskimo mother, therefore, who is forced to delay weaning due to the unavailability of proper solid food for her infant, may not be restored as soon to childbearing as otherwise she would be.

In a number of references it is stated that commonly three or four years pass before the Eskimo mother ceases feeding her child at the breast.[98]

Ray states that "it is no unusual sight to see a child nourished at the breast until it is four or five years of age. . . ."[99] Jenness writes that the Copper Eskimo mother "must suckle the infant up to three or four years, and sometimes even to five."[100] Bessels mentions a case from Smith Sound in which a child was suckled up to seven years of age;[101] and Nansen has "even heard of cases in which children of ten or over continue to take the breast."[102]

Perhaps the most accurate general impression is gained from the statement of Heinbecker: "Babies are wholly breast-fed until the end of the second year when meat is added to their diet. Children often nurse irregularly until the age of four or six."[103] Prolonged lactation, therefore, which is unavoidable largely because of the quality of food to which the Eskimos are restricted, may lower the birth rate below what it otherwise would be. The chief uncertainty in this connection seems to lie in the degree to which this factor may be an influence.

Possibly a second influence tending to reduce the fecundity of the Eskimos is sexual intercourse before puberty. Though the exact effect of early intercourse upon fecundity is not clear, it seems possible that the reproductive functions are adversely affected.[104] And among the Eskimos reference to this practice is found in several sources.[105]

Seasonal Fluctuation in Births

BERTELSEN has proved a curious seasonal fluctuation in the number of births, apparently attributable to environmental influences.[106] North of Disko Bay, or in the arctic regions proper, the number of births increases greatly during the first three months of the year; and the same phenomenon recurs in the two most southerly districts. The explanation given is that in these sections the second term of the year signifies a sudden transition from scarcity to superfluity which is naturally reflected in the sexual life.

Jenness remarks that although sexual intercourse takes place at all seasons among the Copper Eskimos it seemed that more children were born in the winter than at any other time. As he mentions, however, complete information of this nature is difficult to obtain.[107] The present author determined that out of thirty-five birthdays at Cape Prince of Wales, Bering Strait, thirteen fell within the first quarter of the year, and the next highest three-month period was that of May, June, and July, totaling ten. The remaining twelve were, of course, distributed throughout the remaining half year.[108]

Death Rate among Eskimos

THE table given below shows the death rate in Greenland over a period of fifty years.[109]

    1871–80: 36.9 per thousand (the west coast alone)
    1881–90: 32.2 per thousand (the west coast alone)
    1891–1901: 31.6 per thousand (the west coast alone)
    1902–11: 29.7 per thousand (the west coast and Angmagsalik)
    1912–21: 32.0 per thousand (the west coast and Angmagsalik)

These figures signify a very high rate of mortality. The rate for the United States, by contrast, was 11.8 per thousand in 1925.[110] In Greenland the death rate is high for both sexes and at all ages. "It is, however, doubtful whether racial peculiarities exercise any influence in this respect, or whether it is not rather the result of the hard struggle for life generally, and especially of the wretched hygienic conditions."[111] The death rate among young men is especially high; within the period dealt with by Bertelsen, proportionally four and a half times as many men of the age group thirty to thirty-five years died as did within the same age group in Denmark. This enormous rate of mortality among younger men is due primarily to the dangers of their hunting activities. Drowning in kayaks is the fate of many. In South Greenland in 1889 the death rate among males from this cause alone was 9.3 per thousand male population,[112] or almost as high as the death rate from all causes in the United States in recent years.

NOTES

1. Ratzel: 1882–91, II, 264 f.
2. Stefansson: 1921, 183 f.
3. Birket-Smith: 1928, 62.
4. Birket-Smith: 1928, 5.
5. Storgaard: 1928, 539.
6. Mecking: 1928, 216; and Millward: 1930, 51.
7. Hawkes: 1916, 26.
8. Stefansson: 1921, 288.
9. Birket-Smith: 1928, 8.
10. Birket-Smith: 1928, 60.
11. Mecking: 1928, 223.
12. Mecking: 1928, 223.
13. Rasmussen: 1927, 230.
14. Rasmussen: 1927, 218–219.
15. Rasmussen: 1927, 355.
16. Stefansson: 1921, 279.
17. Mathiassen: 1928, I, 53 ff.
18. Murdoch: 1885, 95; Murdoch: 1892, 270; Ray: 1885, 40; Stefansson: 1914, 350.
19. Stefansson: 1921, 218, 288.
20. Birket-Smith: 1928, 141–142.
21. Nelson: 1899, 298.
22. Weyer: Field Notes.
23. Jenness: 1922, 112.
24. Stefansson: 1914, 52.
25. Rasmussen: 1927, 223.
26. Jenness: 1922, 111, citing Amundsen: 1908, II, 22 ff.
27. Birket-Smith: 1929, I, 135.
28. Holm: 1914, 131.
29. Weyer: Field Notes (Cape Prince of Wales, Alaska); Murdoch: 1892, 75 (Point Barrow).
30. Rasmussen: 1927, 310.
31. Rasmussen: 1927, 346; Hooper: 1881, 16.
32. Weyer: Field Notes.
33. Weyer: Field Notes: Schwatka: 1900, 355; Stefansson: 1914, 160 (Kotzebue Sound).
34. Weyer: Field Notes.
35. Jenness: 1922, 103.
36. Jenness: 1922, 122.
37. Jenness: 1922, 110, 125.
38. Jenness: 1922 (citing Amundsen), 111.
39. Birket-Smith: 1929, I, 100–101.
40. Hawkes: 1916, 33.
41. Birket-Smith: 1924, 366.
42. Holm: 1914, 131; Thalbitzer: 1914, 504.
43. Ekblaw: 1928; Rasmussen: 1921, 22.
44. Mecking: 1928, 268.
45. Kroeber: 1899, 269.
46. Birket-Smith: 1928, 141–142.
47. Rasmussen: 1927, 223.
48. Holm: 1914, 131.
49. Bilby: 1923, 40.
50. Jenness: 1922, 107.
51. Stefansson: 1914, 131.
52. Nelson: 1899, 298; Hooper: 1881, 11; Ray: 1885, 46.
53. Weyer: Field Notes (H. B. Collins conveyed to the author the testimony given him by the natives themselves); Muir: 1917, 25, 107 ff.; Hooper: 1881, 11; Jackson: 1886–88; Petroff: 1884, 10.
54. See chap. vi, n. 23.
55. Weyer: Field Notes; Markham: 1866, 131; Ray: 1885, 46; Hooper: 1881, 11.
56. Jenness: 1922, 107.
57. Jenness: 1922, 108, 41 f.
58. Boas: 1888, 574.
59. Boas: 1907, 470.
60. Rasmussen: 1929, 1, 29 ff., 51; see also Lyon: 1824, 299.
61. Turner: 1887, 100.
62. Turner: 1894, 187.
63. Rasmussen: 1908, 33; see also Steensby: 1910, 368.
64. Holm: 1914, 131 ff.
65. Nelson: 1899, 270.
66. Weyer: Field Notes.

67. Ray: 1885, 46.
68. Rasmussen: 1927, 223 f.
69. Boas: 1907, 494.
70. Boas: 1907, 503.
71. Boas: 1907, 470.
72. Boas: 1907, 149; see also Rasmussen: 1929, 1, 189 (Iglulik Eskimos).
73. Boas: 1907, 489.
74. Birket-Smith: 1929, 1, 96, also 101.
75. Hawkes: 1916, 133.
76. See pp. 310 f.
77. Westermarck: 1906, II, 574.
78. Sumner and Keller: 1927, II, 1225 ff.
79. Sumner and Keller: 1927, II, 1227.
80. Westermarck: 1906, 578 ff., 572, and 577.
81. See pp. 132 ff.
82. See pp. 137 ff.
83. Armstrong: 1857, 195; also Hall: 1866, 568.
84. Nelson: 1899, 29.
85. Petroff: 1884, 127.
86. Murdoch: 1892, 38–39.
87. Ray: 1885, 44.
88. Jenness: 1922, 163–164.
89. Weyer: Field Notes.
90. Rasmussen: 1927, 226–227.
91. Turner: 1894, 189.
92. Crantz: 1767, I, 161.
93. Nansen: 1893, 150.

94. Birket-Smith: 1928, 23; Birket-Smith: 1924, 407.
95. *World Almanac:* 1927, 310.
96. Carr-Saunders: 1922, 102–103; Rasmussen: 1927, 226.
97. Sumner and Keller: 1927, I, 54.
98. Weyer: Field Notes (Bering Strait); Murdoch: 1892, 415 (Point Barrow); Jenness: 1928, 208 (Copper Eskimos); Mathiassen: 1928, I, 214 (Iglulik Eskimos); Nansen: 1893, 151 (Greenland); Crantz: 1767, I, 162 (West Greenland).
99. Ray: 1885, 46 (Point Barrow).
100. Jenness: 1922, 165.
101. Bessels: 1875, 113.
102. Nansen: 1893, 151.
103. Heinbecker: 1928a, 462.
104. Carr-Saunders: 1922, 103–104.
105. Murdoch: 1892, 419 (Point Barrow); Weyer: Field Notes (Diomede Islands); Jenness: 1922, 158 (Copper Eskimos); Turner: 1894, 188 (Ungava District, Labrador); Nansen: 1890, 320 (Greenland).
106. Birket-Smith: 1928, 24.
107. Jenness: 1922, 164.
108. Statistics recorded by S. David Mazen, stationed by the U.S. Government at Wales, Alaska.
109. Birket-Smith: 1928, 25.
110. *World Almanac:* 1927, 310.
111. Birket-Smith: 1928, 26.
112. Nansen: 1893, 55. Cf. Mauss and Beuchat: 1904–5, 58.

CHAPTER VIII

REACTIONS TO POPULATION PROBLEM

§1. ARTIFICIAL CHECKS AGAINST POPULATION INCREASE

EVIDENCE collected in the foregoing chapter indicates that the birth rate among the Eskimos is at least moderate. Manifestly, it is sufficient to insure the perpetuation of the race. The tendency is for the population to increase; but famine, as we have already learned, limits the numbers in proportion to the numbers in each section. Numbers cannot swell beyond the supporting power of the land; death through starvation is the natural check.

Food shortage implies maladjustment and suffering. Indeed, even before famine directly checks population a group is reduced to a lower standard of living. Thus, their well-being suffers when the density of population approaches the saturation point. Optimum density of population, therefore, lies safely within the supporting capacity of the environment. In view of this fact, it is of interest to know whether the Eskimos have used any expedients that have the effect of limiting their density of population. As a general proposition Carr-Saunders accepts the theory that "normally in every primitive race one or more . . . customs are in use [prolonged abstention from intercourse, abortion, and infanticide], and that the degree to which they are practised is such that there is an approach to the optimum number."[1] The answer to the question with regard to the Eskimos is emphatically that they do artificially limit population, chiefly through infanticide and killing the aged and infirm.

Unchecked, population will increase above the optimum. Artificial regulation alone can keep the density below the saturation point. Overcrowding inflicts hardship upon the group, and the killing of some of its members is the immediate remedy. Who, then, shall first suffer? Other things being equal, very young children and persons who are infirm either through age or physical defect are of least value to the society, and it is they who are eliminated.

Upon these principles rests the population policy of the Eskimos. Possibly it should not be called a policy, inasmuch as there is very little deliberate and purposeful group direction of group destiny.[2] If there is shown any approach toward a philosophy it is merely a blunt pragmatism.

Infanticide

OCCASIONAL killing of infants is a practice common to all groups of Eskimos.[3] Hardship entailed in rearing children under very severe conditions is the circumstance which chiefly moves the Eskimo mother to part with her offspring. Breast feeding continues until at least the end of the second year, as has been brought out, and sometimes even until the fourth or sixth year. Young children are a drag on the group. Especially during migration they are apt to become a handicap.[4]

If by chance the mother die within a short time after childbirth, the offspring is doomed also to perish.[5] The dominant reason is that there is no way to feed the baby, rather than a wish of the mother to have her child with her in the future life. Infanticide among the Eskimos does not carry a sacrificial implication. When twins are born, at least one of them is either killed or taken by another family, since it would be impossible for a mother to care for both.[6] Bessels reports that at Smith Sound after two children have been born, any others that may come are more often than not killed.[7]

In some cases deformed children and weaklings are killed.[8] Hall mentions the abandoning of an infant that was born freakishly spotted.[9]

There is mention of feticide at Cape Smyth (Alaska),[10] but among the Copper Eskimos it is said never to be practiced.[11] Abortion cannot be considered a common Eskimo practice.[12]

To the civilized person there is something heartless in the way in which an Alaskan family will take an infant girl out to the village graveyard naked, and fill her mouth with snow, so that she will freeze quickly.[13] Jenness mentions that a Copper Eskimo mother "laughed over a baby girl she had killed two or three years before, and said that it had provided the foxes with a good meal."[14] Though we find mention of the killing of girls between four and six years old, infanticide, when committed, generally occurs at birth or not long after.

Affection is certainly not lacking between parent and child. As Jenness states, once the danger of exposure is over, the child receives all the care and attention that the parents can lavish on it.[15]

The relationship is rather conspicuous for a touching devotion.[16] When food is scarce among the Netsilingmiut the children are the first to be fed.[17]

Attachment between Eskimo parent and child is reinforced by certain religious convictions. For example, a general custom is to name the child after some relative or tribe member who has recently died.[18] The name thus bestowed carries with it, in a sense, the soul of the deceased; because of this the child commands a singular respect. Thus, some Eskimos will not strike or even scold a child for fear of driving out the soul which is associated with the name.

The extent to which the concept of reincarnation, which sometimes at least vaguely attends the naming of children after deceased tribe members,[19] affects the population policy of the Eskimos is difficult to evaluate. For it seems never to be mentioned in the literature whether parents commit infanticide after the child has been given the name. The natural assumption, however, is that the characteristic naming custom contributes a restraining influence against the killing of children, through fear of the ghost.

The attitude toward children is further affected by a desire on the part of the parents to have someone who will care for them in their old age. This desire is even projected to include their life after death, since, among the Bering Strait Eskimos, the descendants are expected to make offerings to the shades of their departed ones.[20] With this idea in mind, childless persons generally adopt a child so that their spirits may not be forgotten at the memorial festivals.

Discrimination against Female Children

THROUGH infanticide the Eskimos generally discriminate against girl children.[21] When twins are born, for instance, if one of them is a girl, she is the more likely one to be killed.[22] A case was related in which an Alaskan family killed a two-year-old daughter when a son was born.[23] Among the Netsilingmiut of King William Land "girls are invariably killed at birth unless previously promised in marriage and thus provided for already."[24] Out of ninety-six births, thirty-eight girls were killed at once in accordance with this policy.

The Eskimo fully recognizes woman's indispensable part in life; but a girl is merely an unproductive consumer in the family up to the time when she can make herself useful, and then she is taken in marriage and her utility falls to the share of another household. Murdoch depicts a somewhat different attitude, however, at Point Barrow: ". . . a girl is almost as highly prized [as a boy], for not only will she help her mother with the cares of housekeeping when she grows up, but she is likely to obtain a good husband who may be induced to become a member of his father-in-law's family."[25]

Summarizing, however, there is a very general tendency among the Eskimos to discriminate against girl children. The result is a preponderance of male children. This fact is strikingly brought out by the table in Figure 13. The percentage column, indicating

FIGURE 13

POPULATION STATISTICS

PROPORTION ACCORDING TO SEX

CHILDREN

Location or Tribe	No. of Girls	No. of Boys	Girls per 100 Boys
Cape Prince of Wales, Alaska[1] .	46	50	92
Cape Smyth, Alaska[2] . . .	14	27	52
Bernard Harbor (Dolphin and Union Strait)[3]	18	21	86
Netsilik Eskimos (1902)[4] . .	66	138	48
Sinamiut (Boothia Peninsula) (1902)[4]	7	12	58
Sauniktumiut (south and west of Chesterfield Inlet) (1902)[4] . .	33	41	80
Qaernermiut (Barren Grounds)[5] .	11	24	46
Coast Pâdlimiut (Barren Grounds)[5]	26	31	84
Interior Pâdlimiut (Barren Grounds)[5]	20	28	71
Hauneqtôrmiut (Barren Grounds)[5]	10	13	77
Harvaqtôrmiut (Barren Grounds)[5]	15	23	65
Kinipetu (Qaernermiut) (Barren Grounds)[6]	27	38	71
Aivilik Eskimos (northwest coast of Hudson Bay)[6]	15	27	56
North Greenland exclusive of Thule (1921)[7]	773	803	96 (Age group 0–9 years)
South Greenland[7]	1,106	1,058	104 (Age group 0–9 years)
East Greenland[7]	117	118	99 (Age group 0–9 years)
East Greenland[8]	128	99	129

1 Weyer: Field Notes.
2 Smith: 1902, 114.
3 Jenness: 1922, 42.
4 Boas: 1907, 377.

5 Birket-Smith: 1929, I, 65 ff.
6 Boas: 1907, 6–7.
7 Birket-Smith: 1928, 22.
8 Hansen: 1914, 151 ff.

the average number of girl children for every hundred boy children, shows that in a wide collection of data there are only two exceptions to the generalization that boys outnumber girls. Both of these exceptions are in Greenland, where Christian influence practically excludes infanticide.

Among adults, on the contrary, there are almost always more females than males. Figure 14 shows this ratio. The preponder-

FIGURE 14

POPULATION STATISTICS

PROPORTION ACCORDING TO SEX

ADULTS

Location or Tribe	No. of Females	No. of Males	Females per 100 Males
Cape Prince of Wales, Alaska[1] . .	29	30	97
Cape Smyth, Alaska[2] . . .	52	45	116
Bernard Harbor (Dolphin and Union Strait)[3]	42	46	91
Cape Bexley (Dolphin and Union Strait)[4]	10	19	53
Netsilik Eskimos (Boothia Isthmus) (1902)[5]	123	119	103
Sinamiut (Boothia Isthmus) (1902)[5]	13	13	100
Sauniktumiut (south and west of Chesterfield Inlet) (1902)[5] . .	58	46	126
Qaernermiut (Barren Grounds)[6] .	30	25	120
Coast Pâdlimiut (Barren Grounds)[6] .	28	22	127
Interior Pâdlimiut (Barren Grounds)[6]	31	25	124
Hauneqtôrmiut (Barren Grounds)[6] .	18	13	129
Harvaqtôrmiut (Barren Grounds)[6] .	21	17	123
Kinipetu (Qaernermiut) (Chesterfield Inlet)[7]	46	35	131
Aivilik Eskimos (northwest coast of Hudson Bay)[7]	34	26	131
Iglulik Eskimos (north of Hudson Bay)[8]	161	146	110
Baffin Island[9]	119	111	107
North Greenland exclusive of Thule (1921)[10]	2,321	2,018	115 (10 years and over)
South Greenland (1921)[10] . . .	2,801	2,421	116 (10 years and over)
East Greenland (1921)[10] . . .	234	211	111 (10 years and over)
East Greenland[11]	175	146	120

[1] Weyer: Field Notes.
[2] Smith: 1902, 114.
[3] Jenness: 1922, 42.
[4] Stefansson: 1914, 131.
[5] Boas: 1907, 377.
[6] Birket-Smith: 1929, I, 65 ff.

[7] Boas: 1907, 6–7.
[8] Mathiassen: 1928, I, 15.
[9] Boas: 1888, 426.
[10] Birket-Smith: 1928, 22.
[11] Hansen: 1914, 151 ff.

ance of adult women is generally explained by the higher death
rate among men due to the natural hazards in hunting.[26]

Finally, Figure 15, giving the proportions between the sexes
(including all ages), shows but little uniformity, except for a general scarcity of females in the western regions, and a preponder-

FIGURE 15

POPULATION STATISTICS

PROPORTION ACCORDING TO SEX

ALL AGES

Location or Tribe	No. of Females	No. of Males	Females per 100 Males
Kodiak Island (1795)[1]	2,985	3,221	93
Cape Prince of Wales, Alaska[2]	75	80	94
Cape Smyth, Alaska[3]	66	72	92
Ahongahungarmiut (Dolphin and Union Strait)[4] .	37	46	80
Bernard Harbor (Dolphin and Union Strait)[5] .	60	67	90
Agiaq (Coronation Gulf)[6]	21	25	84
Kiluhigtormiut (Bathurst Inlet)[7] . . .	45	68	66
Umingmagtormiut (between Kent Peninsula and Bathurst Inlet)[7]	23	27	85
Eqalugtormiut (Cambridge Bay, Victoria Island)[7]	44	54	82
Ahiarmiut (Queen Maud Gulf)[7]	46	70	66
Netsilik Eskimos (Boothia Peninsula) (1902)[8] .	189	257	74
Sinamiut (Boothia Peninsula) (1902)[8] . . .	20	25	80
Sauniktumiut (south and west of Chesterfield Inlet) (1902)[8]	91	87	105
Qaernermiut (Barren Grounds)[9]	41	49	84
Coast Pâdlimiut (Barren Grounds)[9] . . .	54	53	102
Inland Pâdlimiut (Barren Grounds)[9] . . .	51	53	96
Hauneqtôrmiut (Barren Grounds)[9] . . .	28	26	108
Harvaqtôrmiut (Barren Grounds)[9] . . .	36	40	90
Kinipetu (Qaernermiut) (Chesterfield Inlet)[10] .	73	73	100
Aivilik Eskimos (northwest coast of Hudson Bay)[10]	49	53	92
Pond Inlet[11]	19	19	100
Polar Eskimos (northwestern Greenland) (1895)[12]	113	140	81
Polar Eskimos (northwestern Greenland) (1906)[12]	85	119	71
Polar Eskimos (1926)[13]	138	133	104
Greenland (1923)[14]			
Upernivik[14]	586	523	112
Umanak[14]	731	682	107
Godhavn[14]	188	170	111
Ritenbenk[14]	296	284	104
Jacobshavn[14]	324	271	120
Christianshaab[14]	284	271	105
Egedesminde[14]	807	772	105
Total North Greenland (west coast) . .	3,198	2,973	108

Location or Tribe	No. of Females	No. of Males	Females per 100 Males
Holstensborg[14]	401	413	97
Sukkertoppen[14]	696	580	120
Godthaab[14]	644	612	105
Frederikshaab[14]	493	417	118
Julianehaab[14]	1,837	1,583	116
Total South Greenland (west coast) . .	4,071	3,605	113
Total West Greenland	7,269	6,578	111
Angmagsalik[14]	366	343	107
East Greenland[15]	303	245	124

[1] Bancroft: 1886, XXXIII, 356.
[2] Weyer: Field Notes.
[3] Smith: 1902, 114.
[4] Rasmussen: 1927, 283.
[5] Jenness: 1922, 42.
[6] Rasmussen: 1927, 269.
[7] Rasmussen: 1927, 244–245.
[8] Boas: 1907, 377.

[9] Birket-Smith: 1929, I, 65 ff.
[10] Boas: 1907, 6–7.
[11] Acland: 1927, 40.
[12] Steensby: 1910, 255–256.
[13] Heinbecker and Pauli: 1928b, 280.
[14] Birket-Smith: 1928, 19.
[15] Hansen: 1914, 151 ff.

ance of them in Greenland. The preponderance in Greenland can be explained by the fact that there the rareness of infanticide, with its selective tendency, allows the survival of approximately equal numbers of males and females of youthful age, so that the risk of death to which the adult men are exposed in hunting causes a majority of females in the population at large.

Killing the Aged and the Infirm

INFANTICIDE, we have seen, is customary on occasion in all groups of Eskimos, with the effect of ameliorating the stress which accompanies scarcity of food. At the further end of the life span is the period of old age, when people have passed their productive years. Therefore, we may rightly expect to observe some similarity between the group attitude toward the aged and that toward infants. Like the newborn babe, the person who is infirm, either by reason of years or physical handicap, is likely to be eliminated under the stress of poverty.

Recourse to abandoning or killing outright such unproductive members of the group is a response to stringent, inexorable life-conditions. Such action, it should be understood, does not indicate a wholly heartless discrimination against the helpless. Devotion among friends and relatives comes into strong conflict with the deliberate elimination of members of a group. The disposing of one who is aged and infirm sometimes seems, indeed, to be more the will of the fated one than of those devoted to him who will live on.[27]

A hunter living on the Diomede Islands related to the writer how he killed his own father, at the latter's request. The old Eskimo was failing, he could no longer contribute what he thought should be his share as a member of the group; so he asked his son, then a lad about twelve years old, to sharpen the big hunting knife. Then he indicated the vulnerable spot over his heart where his son should stab him. The boy plunged the knife deep, but the stroke failed to take effect. The old father suggested with dignity and resignation, "Try it a little higher, my son." The second stab was effective, and the patriarch passed into the realm of the ancestral shades.

Women as well as men were sometimes killed. Strangling or hanging might take the place of stabbing. Always a member of the family would perform the act, in order to avoid any intimation of a blood feud.

From the region of Point Barrow we have mention of the abandoning of a crazy person.[28] Aside from such serious incapacity, however, old people were treated with the greatest respect and devotion.[29] Jenness writes that no doubt "the Copper Eskimos would abandon the old and infirm without much hesitation, but it has apparently never been a regular custom. . . ."[30] He mentions a case, however, among the Eqaluktormiut, wherein a man who had been stabbed and rendered an invalid unable to do any work was, after many years, left alone to starve to death.[31] Old folks of King William Land who are no longer able to provide for themselves generally hang themselves.[32] Likewise, among the Caribou Eskimos the aged sometimes commit suicide, commonly being assisted by children.[33] These Eskimos also leave the sick to die, either because they are a burden or through fear of being contaminated. Boas states that among the Central Eskimos a man may kill his aged parents.[34] The Iglulik group have a strong sentiment in favor of communalism of food and as a rule they treat their sick and aged with consideration; but in time of need the old and infirm are the first to suffer. Old women and worn-out folk are left behind on the road.[35] The Eskimos of Baffin Island have great respect for the aged and treat them well. But when a woman becomes so old that she is a burden, she may calmly resign herself to death, allowing herself to be walled into a snow hut and left to die. She thinks it is better; the tribe agrees.[36] A case is mentioned of a young man who was blind through repeated snow blindness. The tribe, considering him a burden, led him into a hole in the ice and capped it with a block.[36] The natives of Ungava Bay (Labrador) and the coast of Hudson Strait to the west often abandon or strangle helpless old persons who have no relatives upon whom they may depend for subsistence.[37] If a woman who has been abandoned succeeds in overtaking the party, a second escape is forestalled by binding her.[38] As elsewhere, however, when the Labrador Eskimos put an old person out of the way it is generally in accordance with the wishes of the one concerned, and is thought to be proof of devotion.[39] In West Greenland there is group action against invalids;[40] and in East Greenland an invalid will throw himself into the sea, often prompted by an admonition from his relatives that he has nothing to live for.[41] A Greenland woman is quoted as saying: "Once an old woman who was ill, but could not die, offered to pay me if I would lead her to the top of the steep cliff from which our people have always thrown themselves when they are tired of living; but I, having ever loved my neighbors led her thither without payment, and cast her over the cliff."[42]

§2. LACK OF LIMITATION THROUGH SEX MORES

In the foregoing section we have studied certain practices that limit numbers through the elimination of members of the group. By occasionally deliberately killing infants, invalids, and aged persons the Eskimos, either knowingly or unconsciously, control their numbers to conform to the supporting capacity of the land. Turning now to the sex mores, however, we observe no outstanding customs that have as a result the limiting of population. Indeed, it seems that the sex mores, in their most characteristic features, are perhaps conducive to the diametrically opposite result: the most rapid reproduction possible. This matter can be touched only lightly here; for to discuss fully the entire complex of customs built around the institution of marriage and the family would interrupt the immediate subject.

Limitation of numbers, either conscious or unconscious, is not effected by the Eskimos through abstention from sexual intercourse. They are remarkably free and unrestrained in this regard. Marriage occurs at a youthful age, especially in the case of girls.[43] Their fecundity is not limited, therefore, by celibacy during the early years of maturity. Before marriage, furthermore, there is far less societal disapproval of sexual intercourse than there is commonly among people of higher culture. Little or no disgrace is attached to childbirth outside of wedlock.[44]

Polygyny is sanctioned among all groups, but it is not the general practice.[45] Economic pressure, rather than any moral feeling, is the influence which restricts a man from keeping more than one wife. Polyandry is of very rare occurrence.[46]

Characteristic of the Eskimo sex mores is the singular custom of exchanging wives.[47] The trade may be for only a night or for a longer period, occasionally even becoming permanent. And the purpose may be purely practical or it may have a ceremonial significance. There are some instances of what seems to be temporary promiscuity within the group. Wife exchanging is mentioned in the present section because of its possible influence upon the fecundity of the Eskimos. In strict pair marriage, if either party is sterile the union remains unproductive; whereas if the exchanging of wives is practiced there is greater probability that every fertile person will have intercourse with a fertile mate. The influence, indeed, may reach further; incompatibility may exist between two parties each of whom, with the right partner, would be fertile; in which case wife exchanging would allow every fertile woman a greater chance of bearing offspring.

Such sex habits as have been mentioned certainly seem conducive to maximum propagation. Neither consciously nor unknowingly, therefore, do the Eskimos enforce a limitation of numbers through their sex mores. Women are under taboos on various occasions, to be sure, as for instance at Point Barrow during the whaling season.[48] And as a general rule the Eskimo woman observes restrictions during her menstrual period.[49] Since it is rarely specified, however, it is difficult to estimate how far the taboos applying particularly to women are extended to include abstention from intercourse.

The taboos on women seem to be very strict on the occasion of the Bladder Festival[50] in the region of the mouth of the Yukon. During this ceremonial ". . . the men and boys sleep apart and the men keep rigidly apart from the women. They avoid going to their own or any other house for fear of becoming unclean; and bathe twice a day. No females who have reached puberty are permitted near or under the bladders while they hang in the men's house. They say that if they fail in continence the shades will be offended." South and west of the Yukon the preparations for the annual ceremony for the ribbon seal begin in November and last a whole month. "During this time the men must live apart from the women, remaining in the dance house, while their wives are only allowed to enter when bringing their food. The women, who are regarded as unclean in connection with all animals hunted, must take a bath every morning before carrying food to their husbands, and when so visiting them must wear the waterproof garments used in stormy weather."[51]

It is stipulated with regard to the Iglulik Eskimos[52] and the natives of Cumberland Sound[53] that women must abstain from sexual intercourse during mourning. And on the west coast of Hudson Bay[54] and among the Iglulik Eskimos[55] a woman is under the same restriction for about three months after bearing a child.

Though the extent to which taboos of this nature among the Eskimos restrict sexual intercourse and ultimately fecundity cannot definitely be stated, the influence is probably not great.

§3. MINIMUM POPULATION FOR SURVIVAL

It has already been shown that scarcity of food sets a low maximum on the density of population in the Eskimo region. In the following paragraphs it is the aim to discuss the opposite limit: the minimum sparsity of population within which it is possible for the people to survive from generation to generation.

Obviously, this minimum sparsity can be no lower than that which obtains when the size of the association unit is restricted to the family in the narrow sense. Man, wife, and offspring comprise the lowest order of social unit capable of survival. When the resources of the land become so meager that there is no longer sufficient subsistence for the support of this unit extinction results. The individual might live for a time, but the society perishes. And here on the uttermost border of the inhabited world, as would be expected, the minimum of population density is frequently approached and sometimes actually reached.

It is stated that the Eskimos of Smith Sound (northwestern Greenland) "usually travel in groups of three or four families. Greater concentration of numbers would be dangerous on account of the scarcity of food."[56] The Point Barrow Eskimos during the winter caribou hunting at the rivers, similarly, "are scattered in small camps of four or five families, about a day's journey apart."[57] And the Eskimos who winter inland north of Nome at the village of Igloo disperse upon the advent of summer; so that along the Tuksuk River they are seen in a series of fishing camps, each composed of one or a few families.[58]

In some Eskimo groups at certain seasons the family becomes the social unit. Regarding the Koksoagmiut of northern Labrador Turner states that a family group consisting of grandfather, father, son, and the wives and their relatives, forms a sort of community, of which there may be only one in a locality.[59] The Copper Eskimos scatter during the warmer season in small bands; and in midsummer, when fish alone is the reliable food, the tribe no longer exists, the family is the unit.[60] Similarly, when the Caribou Eskimos are most widely dispersed their social unit is the family, but never, of course, the individual.[61]

The uninhabited areas to which the Eskimos have free access are for the most part regions where procurable subsistence is too scanty to allow the survival of even the smallest self-perpetuation unit. Eskimo stage of culture is assumed, of course, in this statement. One salient fact is indicated by the available information: that in no case does the family in the narrow sense live in isolation throughout all seasons and from year to year. One might argue that the pleasures of social intercourse naturally cause the people to congregate in groups and submit to the forfeiture of some personal rights which life in a group always entails. Obviously, this contention is at least a partial explanation; the association of numbers makes possible singing and dancing festivals, ceremonials, and other group phenomena which add enjoyment to the life of the primitive. It is suggested here, however, that there is another reason why we never see the Eskimo family persisting from generation to generation in complete isolation. May it not be due to the fact that the minimum size of the unit capable of surviving and perpetuating itself is larger than the family in the narrow sense? Children and women who are bearing children or caring for the very young cannot paddle their own weight, so to speak, in the self-maintenance organization. Yet the supporting of these less productive members is essential to the perpetuation of the group. Self-perpetuation, therefore, puts an added strain on the self-maintenance organization. Quite possibly, therefore, in the family in its smallest sense the combined efforts of the food-securing members, of whom there would be only one or at most a very few, would not produce sufficient subsistence continuously for all, including the nonproductive members. Wherefore, the question is raised as to whether the productivity of the individual is not increased through coöperative association. If so, the added increment resulting from coöperation must be a decisive factor in the size of the association unit at the arctic margin of the habitable world.

Sumner and Keller lucidly explain the advantages of association:[62]

"Association both augments and economizes power. Fifty men working in coöperation can do things that the same fifty men acting separately cannot; they can pull, one at a time, at a rope attached to a heavy weight, and the latter does not move; they pull no harder, at the same time, with someone to mark rhythm for them, and the shift is made. Herein lies the paradox that a society is greater than the sum of its parts. The extra power is due to organization; it is the superiority of a dozen policemen to a mob of hoodlums. Then there are the manifold economies attending on specialization, as in division of labor, by which men save time, effort, and materials, and yet get a better product. These can be realized only in association. The offensive against nature can be managed better under organization, and so can the defensive, against both nature and fellow-men."

Specifically, with regard to the Eskimos, the operation of the principle expounded in the above quotation is difficult to analyze, due to the fact that heretofore this phase of Eskimo life has scarcely been touched upon and the information is correspondingly very scanty. It can be said, however, that in the hunting of certain animals the yield per man is not so large when few as when many are engaged. In the commonly employed system of driving caribou between converging rows of stone or sod dummies, for example, which requires the coöperation of a number of men,[63] the average number of animals killed per participant is greater than if the animals be stalked by the men individually or in small teams. And the hunting of whales requires the coöperation of a complete umiak crew, composed usually of eight or ten men.[64]

The yield per person is not always greatest, therefore, when the number of people exploiting the available resources is least. Beyond a certain density the increasing of numbers naturally lowers the yield per person; but in each particular area there must be an optimum density of population. If this density occurs, either an increase above it or a decrease below it would diminish the average yield to the individual.

Of outstanding importance in the present discussion is the principle that, due to the advantages inherent in association, the greatest returns are not derived by the individual when numbers are smallest. Taken in combination with the fact that self-perpetuation requires a surplus of subsistence, it suggests that propagation can be successful only in an association unit larger than the family in the narrow sense.

In addition to the increased return resulting from the coöperation of numbers up to a certain point, in yet another way is survival insured through association. The group is better able to prevail against adversities of fortune than is the individual. To cite a single illustration, the Eskimo who is forced to hunt *alone* in his kayak because of scarcity of hunters is in greater danger of drowning than if he could be accompanied by a partner in a second kayak.[65] Likewise, when some of the members of a group experience temporary misfortune the others assist them in withstanding it. One of the conspicuous manifestations of this phase of coöperation among Eskimos is seen in their communalistic tendencies regarding food, a subject discussed fully in chapters x and xi. Unpredictable misfortunes visit the Eskimos from time to time and produce calamitous consequences. As Birket-Smith states:

"A trifling incident, a lengthy period of starvation, an epidemic, ptomaine poisoning due to the stranded carcass of a whale, may shift the balance, and a region which has formerly been inhabited may be laid waste. There is no doubt that the depopulation of the east coast [of Greenland] in many cases may be ascribed to such causes. No one is justified to draw lines across a map and to believe that it is possible, in this way, to make a permanent division between inhabited and uninhabited parts. Here, at the periphery, human life is in constant fluctuation, where one span of years may be characterized by an advance through inhabited regions and another by retreat."[66]

§4. MINIMUM POPULATION AND THE FOLKWAYS

In the foregoing paragraphs it has been indicated that there is a minimum size below which the association unit is incapable of successful propagation. This limit, it has been further shown, may require the unit to be larger than the family in the narrow sense, due to the weakness of the self-maintenance organization of such a small group and to the increased survival power inherent in numbers. If this be true, population in the Eskimo region lies even closer to the critical minimum than at first appears. This fact, perhaps, casts new light on the sex mores of the Eskimos, which, it will be remembered, seem conducive to maximum reproduction. Possibly the conspicuous lack of limitation through the sex mores is a necessary adjustment among a people whose density of population hovers so near the minimum for survival. Without the characteristic laxity in sexual relations, in other words, which on first sight seems to be so futilely opposite to the practice of infanticide, possibly the population would sooner or later fall below the minimum and the group would be exterminated.

It should be mentioned that one way in which the element of chance affects the small group more critically than the large is in the number of offspring that are born. Couples differ in fecundity; one pair may have too many children, while another has too few. And size of family, like size of association unit, is restricted by the man-land ratio within very narrow limits on the fringe of the habitable world. In the light of these facts, it is appropriate to consider the practice of adopting children which is so common among Eskimos. When a family already has as many children as it can support, an additional infant is often transferred to a less numerous family, instead of being killed.

If a father and mother among the Copper Eskimos, for instance, decide to cast out a child alive, another couple may recover it and rear it as their own, the parents having lost all claim; but in ordinary cases of adoption the parents must be compensated before they will relinquish their rights.[67] About Bering Strait adoption is common, one motive being, as previously mentioned, the desire that there be someone after the parents die who will make the proper memorial offerings to their shades.[68] "Where the people are poor it is not unusual for a mother to give away all but the first-born to some couple that have no children . . ."[69] (Point Barrow). Adoption is very common among the Caribou Eskimos and the Iglulik Eskimos.[70] Compensation of some sort is generally given to the parents relinquishing the child among these groups, as well as among the Copper Eskimos, the Mackenzie Delta Eskimos, and those of Kotzebue Sound.[71] Turner mentions the practice of adoption at Ungava Bay, Labrador.[72] Adopted children are usually treated just as though they were offspring of their adoptive parents.[73]

Adoption may be regarded, therefore, as an expedient for preventing numbers from falling below the minimum for survival. The natural desire for children must not be overlooked, of course, as a motive; but in the case of the Eskimos, among whom the practice is unusually prevalent, adoption achieves an additional end. In a sense it can be regarded as communalism in children, and as serving a purpose analogous to communalism in food by smoothing out the vicissitudes which normally visit so small a unit as the family.

It may seem in postulating these interpretations of the sex mores and the practice of adoption that the author is arbitrarily searching for a relationship where none can fairly be sought. It is not suggested, however; that the mores of the Eskimo in this connection manifest any rational deliberation. And the contention is maintained that the present subject merits serious consideration; for it involves a fundamental question in racial survival which is governed by laws closely analogous to those of organic evolution.

Summary

RANGE of population density in the case of the Eskimos is uncommonly restricted; for its maximum is determined by extreme scantiness of resources and its minimum by the size of the self-perpetuation unit. Infanticide is an indication that the rearing of children is already becoming impossible. Slightly more severe conditions would require that not some but all offspring die, which would mean the extinction of the group. A slight change in numbers in either direction has serious consequences. On the one hand there is the devil of overpopulation and on the other the deep sea of racial extinction. The Eskimos remedy overpopulation in the most direct, harsh, and rudimentary fashion; that is, by killing certain members who have little societal value. On the other hand, the apparent conduciveness of their self-perpetuation mores may represent a necessary safeguard against diminution of numbers below the survival limit.

NOTES

1. Carr-Saunders: 1922, 214.
2. Sumner and Keller: 1927, I, 69.
3. Simpson: 1875, 250 (Point Barrow); Stefansson: 1914, 173 (Point Barrow and the Mackenzie Delta); Jenness: 1928, 206 (Copper Eskimos); Schwatka: 1884, 544 (King William Land); Boas: 1888, 580 (the Central Eskimos); Birket-Smith: 1929, I, 98, 294–295 (Caribou Eskimos); Turner: 1887, 100 (east coast of Hudson Bay); and other references later cited in this section.
Regarding the Iglulik Eskimos,

Mathiassen's statement (Mathiassen: 1928, I, 212) that infanticide seems never to have occurred apparently is at variance with Rasmussen's testimony that orphan children were blocked up in snow huts and left there, buried alive (Rasmussen: 1929, I, 159).
4. Jenness: 1922, 165.
5. Boas: 1907, 117 (west coast of Hudson Bay); Lyon: 1824, 276 f. (Iglulik Eskimos); Rasmussen: 1929, I, 159 (Iglulik Eskimos); Hawkes: 1916, 139 (Labrador); Kroeber: 1899,

301 (Polar Eskimos); Peary: 1898, I, 506 (Smith Sound); Birket-Smith: 1924, 410 (West Greenland); Crantz: 1767, I, 238 (West Greenland); Holm: 1914, 62 (Angmagsalik).

6. Stefansson: 1914, 201 (Cape Smyth, Alaska); Jenness: 1922, 166 (Copper Eskimos); Rasmussen: 1929, I, 23 (Netsilingmiut and Iglulingmiut groups).

7. Bessels: 1875, 112.

8. Hooper: 1881, 57 (Alaska); Smith: 1868, 859; Boas: 1907, 117 (Repulse Bay); MacKeevor: 1919, 37 (Hudson Strait); Nansen: 1890, 330; Nansen: 1893, 151 (Greenland); Mecking: 1928, 249.

9. Hall: 1866, 330–331.

10. Stefansson: 1914, 201.

11. Jenness: 1922, 167.

12. Wells and Kelly: 1890, 19.

13. Nelson: 1899, 289.

14. Jenness: 1922, 166–167.

15. Jenness: 1922, 168–169.

16. Murdoch: 1892, 41–42; 417–418; MacKeevor: 1819, 35; Birket-Smith: 1928, 204.

17. Rasmussen: 1927, 231.

18. See pp. 291 ff.

19. Jenness, citing Stefansson (Stefansson: 1914, 363 ff.) and Crantz (Crantz: 1767, I, 201), states that contrary to the testimony of these authors writing on other sections he could not find among the Copper Eskimos any trace of the belief that the souls of the dead are reincarnated in their descendants or in the children of friends and relatives. (Jenness: 1922, 177.)

20. Nelson: 1899, 290, 364.

21. Jackson: 1880, 115 (Alaska); Nelson: 1899, 289 ff. (Alaska); Jenness: 1922, 42 (Copper Eskimos); Stefansson: 1914, 131 (Dolphin and Union Strait); Rasmussen: 1927, 225 ff. (Netsilingmiut).

22. Stefansson: 1914, 201; Jenness: 1922, 166 (Copper Eskimos).

23. Weyer: Field Notes.

24. Rasmussen: 1927, 225–226.

25. Murdoch: 1892, 419. Stefansson, on the contrary, states that at Point Barrow girl babies are more likely to be killed than boy babies (Stefansson: 1914, 173).

26. Birket-Smith: 1928, 23, 26 (Greenland); Bilby: 1923, 221 (Baffin Island).

27. See p. 248.

28. Stefansson: 1914, 382.

29. Ray: 1885, 45.

30. Jenness: 1922, 236.

31. Jenness: 1922, 95.

32. Rasmussen: 1927, 225.

33. Birket-Smith: 1929, I, 258, 300.

34. Boas: 1888, 165.

35. Mathiassen: 1928, I, 233; Rasmussen: 1929, I, 159; Boas: 1907, 117; and Lyon: 1824, 258 f.

36. Bilby: 1923, 149–150.

37. Turner: 1894, 178, 186.

38. Turner: 1887, 102.

39. Hawkes: 1916, 117.

40. Birket-Smith: 1924, 139–140.

41. Holm: 1914, 74.

42. Nansen: 1893, 170, after Niels Egede.

43. Ray: 1885, 43 (Point Barrow); Jenness: 1922, 158 (Copper Eskimos); Mathiassen: 1928, I, 210 (Iglulik Eskimos); Bilby: 1923, 155–156 (Baffin Island); Turner: 1894, 188 (northern Labrador); MacMillan: 1918, 274 (Polar Eskimos); Steensby: 1910, 369 (Polar Eskimos); Rasmussen: 1908, 63 (Polar Eskimos); Kroeber: 1899, 301 (Polar Eskimos); Crantz: 1767, I, 158 (West Greenland).

Bertelsen generalized on the marriage mores as revealed through his statistics on Greenland by giving the following features as characteristic: (1) extremely great frequency of marriages and the youthful age at which marriages are contracted by both sexes; (2) the short duration of marriages owing to early death, and the great tendency toward second and the comparatively still greater tendency toward third marriages; and (3) the fact that there are comparatively few unmarried adult persons, but a rather considerable number of widows. (Birket-Smith: 1928, 24.)

44. Nelson: 1899, 292 (Bering Strait Eskimos); Murdoch: 1892, 419 (Point

Barrow); Jenness: 1922, 158, 163, 239 (Copper Eskimos); Turner: 1894, 189 (northern Labrador); Holm: 1914, 67 (Angmagsalik); Nansen: 1893, 164 ff. (West Greenland); Egede: 1729, 78 (contrary evidence from West Greenland).

45. Holmberg: 1855, 118 (Kodiak Island); Petroff: 1900, 235 (Kodiak Island); Petroff: 1900, 213 (between the Kuskokwim River and Kotzebue Sound); Nelson: 1899, 292 (Bering Strait); Moore: 1923, 367 (St. Lawrence Island and Indian Point); Hooper: 1881, 58 (northwestern Alaska); Murdoch: 1892, 411 (Point Barrow); Ray: 1885, 44 (Point Barrow); Jenness: 1922, 158 (Copper Eskimos); Rasmussen: 1927, 232 (King William Land); Klutschak: 1881, 234 (between Chesterfield Inlet and King William Land); Birket-Smith: 1929, I, 294 (Caribou Eskimos); Boas: 1907, 115 (west coast of Hudson Bay); Boas: 1907, 466 (Chesterfield Inlet); Mathiassen: 1928, I, 210–211 (Iglulik Eskimos); Boas: 1907, 477 (Southampton Island); Bilby: 1923, 66 (Puisortak, Baffin Island); Turner: 1887, 102 (Tahagmyut, Labrador, along Hudson Strait); Turner: 1887, 100 (Itivimyut, east coast of Hudson Bay); Turner: 1894, 188–189 (Koksoagmyut, Ungava region, Labrador); Hawkes: 1916, 116 (Labrador and Greenland); Ross: 1819, 133 (Polar Eskimos); Kroeber: 1899, 301 (Polar Eskimos); Steensby: 1910, 369 (Polar Eskimos); Rasmussen: 1908, 65 (Polar Eskimos); Nansen: 1893, 171 ff. (Greenland); Birket-Smith: 1924, 406 (West Greenland); Crantz: 1767, I, 159 (West Greenland); Holm: 1914, 66 (Angmagsalik).

46. Coxe: 1787, 300 (Kodiak Island); Petroff: 1900, 227, quoting Shelikof (Kodiak Island); Jenness: 1922, 162 (Copper Eskimos); Birket-Smith: 1929, I, 294 (Netsilik Eskimos); Boas: 1907, 466 (Chesterfield Inlet); Boas: 1907, 115 (Iglulik, Ponds Bay, and Boothia Felix); Mathiassen: 1928, I, 211 (Iglulik Eski-

mos); Birket-Smith: 1924, 406 (Godthaab Fiord, West Greenland); Crantz: 1767, I, 159 (West Greenland).

47. Sauer: 1802, 177 (Kodiak Island); Nelson: 1899, 292 (Alaska); Weyer: Field Notes (Diomede Islands and Bering Strait region); Stefansson: 1914, 164 (Colville River, Alaska); Ray: 1885, 44 (Point Barrow); Murdoch: 1892, 413 (Point Barrow); Stefansson: 1914, 164 (Mackenzie Delta); Jenness: 1922, 53, 85–86, 238 (Copper Eskimos); Stefansson: 1914, 204 (Victoria Island); Rasmussen: 1927, 232 (King William Land); Birket-Smith: 1929, I, 152–153, 295 (Caribou Eskimos); Rasmussen: 1927, 148 ff. (Barren Grounds); Boas: 1907, 158 (west coast of Hudson Bay); Gilder: 1881, 197 (Repulse Bay); Murdoch: 1892, 413 (Repulse Bay); Mathiassen: 1928, I, 211, 227–228 (Iglulik Eskimos); Rasmussen: 1929, I, 241 ff. (Iglulik Eskimos); Boas: 1907, 139 (Cumberland Sound); Boas: 1888, 608 (Baffin Island); Turner: 1894, 189 (Koksoagmyut, northern Labrador); Bilby: 1923, 142, 157–158, 214 (Baffin Island); Hawkes: 1916, 115 (Labrador); Smith: 1894, 214 (Hamilton Inlet); Kroeber: 1899, 301 (Polar Eskimos); Rasmussen: 1908, 64 (Polar Eskimos); Steensby: 1910, 369 (Polar Eskimos); Birket-Smith: 1924, 406 (Greenland); Nansen: 1893, 169 (Greenland); Holm: 1886, 92 (East Greenland); Holm: 1914, 69 (Angmagsalik).

48. Ray: 1885, 39.

49. See pp. 372 f.

50. Nelson: 1899, 393. See also 440 and 286.

51. Rasmussen: 1927, 352.

52. Rasmussen: 1929, I, 199 f.

53. Boas: 1907, 145.

54. Boas: 1907, 160.

55. Rasmussen: 1929, I, 172 f.

56. Sumner, Keller and Davie: 1927, IV, 17–18.

57. Murdoch: 1892, 267.

58. Weyer: Field Notes.

59. Turner: 1894, 190.

60. Jenness: 1928, 136–137.

61. Birket-Smith: 1929, I, 98. For further information concerning the size of the social unit among Eskimos see pp. 204 ff.

62. Sumner and Keller: 1927, I, 14–15.

63. Birket-Smith: 1929, I, 108–109.

64. Weyer: Field Notes; Murdoch: 1892, 273.

65. Hooper: 1881, 6.

66. Birket-Smith: 1928, 17.

67. Jenness: 1922, 91.

68. Nelson: 1899, 290; Weyer: Field Notes.

69. Ray: 1885, 44; see also Murdoch: 1892, 419.

70. Birket-Smith: 1929, I, 295; Mathiassen: 1928, I, 212–213; Boas: 1907, 115; Lyon: 1824, 256.

71. Jenness: 1922, 91; Stefansson: 1914, 341.

72. Turner: 1887, 105.

73. Stefansson: 1914, 321; Birket-Smith: 1929, I, 295; Mathiassen: 1928, I, 212–213; Murdoch: 1892, 419.

CHAPTER IX

INTERTRIBAL RELATIONS

I N the foregoing sections the natural and artificial limitations on the density of population in the Eskimo region were discussed. Numbers tend to increase, it is understood, unless artificially checked, until starvation prevents. Furthermore, an approach toward the saturation point entails a lowering of the standard of living. Unrestrained growth of population, therefore, is not conducive to the well-being of the group. Infanticide, however, and the killing or abandoning of aged and infirm persons, as practiced by the Eskimo, have the effect artificially of forestalling distress.

Attention has been directed to the fact that these practices, while conspicuously effectual, are contrary to some deep-lying human sentiments. Parental affection in the case of infanticide, supplemented perhaps by certain religious concepts; and devotion to senior members of the kin-group in the case of killing the aged, conflict strongly with the deliberate elimination of members within the narrow societal unit. But there is an alternative which has the same effect in a broad sense as killing members of the in-group. We refer, of course, to warfare against another, contiguous group.

This brings us to the discussion of relations between groups. An understanding of the nature of them is possible only through a knowledge of the principles of the man-land ratio which have been set forth. To review, on the one hand there is an area of land relatively poor in resources of value to people on a primitive plane; on the other hand there exists on the land a population of such a density that though the resources are used to the limit some members starve. It is inherent in this very situation that there will be intergroup competition for the resources of the land. This competition may take a variety of forms, such as warfare, plundering, and barter.

In one way or another each group must contend with its nearest neighbors, unless, as sometimes happens, a group is so isolated as not to come into contact with others. Such isolation existed in the case of the Polar Eskimos, fewer than three hundred in number, who at the time of their discovery by white men knew of no other people in the world except through tradition. This is an exceptional case, however. Ordinarily, each group of Eskimos has contact with one or more contiguous groups either of Eskimos or Indians. The presence of competitors in the struggle for existence is one of their life-conditions. We may even regard the coexploiters of the resources of the land as a phase of their environment, in a broad sense. Thus, in addition to the natural environment in which a group of people live, there is an environment of fellow men, or, as it may be called, a societal environment.

Furthermore, the natural environment and the societal are closely interrelated in some ways. In proportion as the competing group is skilful in exploiting the common territory, for instance, the natural environment is impoverished. Out of this relationship grows animosity between contiguous peoples. But the presence of a neighboring people is not wholly disadvantageous. They may have resources at their exclusive command which, through barter, would become of great value. Where this is true, intergroup animosity may be laid aside and friendly trading relations pursued. And out of these relations other benefits are gained, through the interchange of ideas and the cross-fertilization of culture.

Let it be understood that the societal environment of the Eskimos is twofold. Generally, of most immediate concern to each group are the neighboring bands of their own kinsmen. These people speak the same language or an understandable dialect of it, and observe similar customs and beliefs. But aside from them there is a second element in the societal environment of many Eskimo groups. Inland from the fringe of coast land that represents the Eskimo territory on the mainland of Arctic America dwell Indians. As will be discussed below, there is intermittent contact at various places along the border line.

The native language of the Indian cannot be understood by an Eskimo, and there is no mutual sign language.[1] Furthermore, the Indian commonly differs from the Eskimo in culture, and to some degree in appearance. It is natural, therefore, that the Eskimos should regard the Indians as constituting an out-group. Characteristic of the spirit of ethnocentrism[2] prominent among primitive people, the Eskimos of Norton Sound, Alaska, derisively call the Indians *iñ-kǐ'lik*, or "Ingalik," which means "children of a louse's egg."[3] The implication is that their hair is filled with the eggs of these parasites. It seems that similar words used for designating Indians by the Eskimos of the Mackenzie region (*ik-kil-lin*), Fury and Hecla Strait (*eert-kai-lee*, or *it-kagh-lie*), and on the west coast of Hudson Bay (*ik-kil-lin*) show the same derivation as the Norton Sound word.[4]

The Norton Sound Eskimos call themselves, on the other hand, *Yu'pik*, meaning "fine" or "complete" people.[5] The usual word, however, which Eskimos use in referring to their own people is *Inuit*, which is simply the plural of *inuk*, meaning "person" or "man."[6] Seemingly of common derivation is the suffix *-miut*, generally applied to tribal names and meaning "people of" or "natives of."[7]

§1. ALASKA

THE southern territorial limit of the Alaskan Eskimos at present lies on the east coast of Bristol Bay and at Kodiak Island in the Pacific. Formerly, however, the Eskimos extended a few hundred miles farther to the eastward, along the Gulf of Alaska.[8]

Petroff[9] reports that: "The Chugachimute (Chugach of the Russians), or Chughchil-shvit (their tribal name), inhabit the shores of Prince William sound (or the gulf of Chugach). They are at present the easternmost tribe of purely Eskimo extraction, numbering less than 500 in all. . . . This tribe has always been in contact, both friendly and hostile, with its Athabaskan neighbors in the west and north, and with the Thlinket in the east, and this circumstance may have aided in making their character more warlike and repellent than that of other Eskimo tribes. . . . In their intercourse with their Athabaskan neighbors, before mentioned, the Tinnats of Cook's Inlet and the Atnahs of Copper river, this tribe does not seem to have indulged in intermarriage; but with the Thlinket, their eastern neighbors, such intermixture has been and is going on actively, forced, probably, by the latter strong and warlike tribe. Toward the end of the last century [the eighteenth century], when these natives first became known to us, another Eskimo tribe occupied the coast as far eastward as Mount St. Elias. These were the Oughalakhmute (Ougalentze of the Russians), Wallamute and Lakhamute of earliest visitors. This tribe, owing to its position, exposed to the constant attacks and encroachments of the Thlinket, has become mixed to such an extent that at the present day the Thlinket element predominates. . . . So complete has been the amalgamation that young men of the Oughalakhmute now employ an interpreter in dealing with their Chugachimute neighbors living at a distance of a few miles from them. The present custom among the Oughalakhmute and the Thlinket further to the eastward, of obtaining wives from their western Eskimo neighbors, shows clearly how this encroachment has been accomplished."

Around the base of the Alaska Peninsula the tribal patchwork is complex. Here dwells the buffer tribe of Aglemiut, comprising but a few hundreds.[10] They have lived from time immemorial upon the portage routes between Bering Sea and the North Pacific across the Alaska Peninsula. Only one of their villages, however, is actually located inland, that at the head of Lake Walker. This inland subdivision, according to Petroff's report, maintained a more constant communication with the Kaniagmiut of Katmai across the mountains than they did with their kinsmen on the coast of Bering Sea. Their coast villages to the west abutted on the Aleut territory on the Alaska Peninsula. Formerly, there existed among the Aglemiut a contingent of Aleut invaders, who for some time inhabited two settlements at the mouth of the Naknek River. As far as can be ascertained these Aleut retreated down the Alaska Peninsula to Oogashik at the beginning of the nineteenth century.

Throughout the entire Bering Sea region and northward to Point Barrow the Eskimos are in contact at intervals with inland Indians.

Inland from Bristol Bay, at the headwaters of the Nushegak River the natives, as Petroff[11] mentions, were in constant communication with the Athabaskan tribes. On the Yukon the demarcation between the Eskimo and Indian provinces seems to lie approximately three hundred miles upstream, somewhere between the villages of Anvik and Manki (or Makeymiut).[12] Along the Kuskokwim River, the Kowak, and the Noatak, likewise, the Eskimos penetrate the interior of the country to the forested region and come into direct contact with the Athabascan or Tinné tribes.[13]

Along this line of contact hostility characterizes the relations, especially in the region of Bering Strait and south of it.[14] The Malemiut of Kotzebue Sound and the Tinné inlanders, for instance, pursued a desultory feud in which each tribe sought vengeance upon any member of the opposing tribe.[15] From here southward to the Yukon the coast people have many stories of the destruction of villages by Tinné war parties.[16]

One such attack occurred upon the village of Shishmaref, just north of Bering Strait, in the days when the natives still hunted with bows and arrows.[17] The Eskimo women of the village were all assembled in a large dancing house, while the men were inland some ten miles where they customarily stored their fish. The dancing house, characteristic of these half-underground chambers, had but two exits, a small tunneled doorway, and a smoke hole in the roof. The attacking Indians stuffed the door with brush and wood and set fire to it. Entrapped, the Eskimo women were shot by the Indians from the smoke hole, and most of those who were not killed by arrows suffocated in the smoke. The men of the village, upon returning soon after and discovering the slaughter, vowed immediate vengeance. They circled craftily ahead of the returning Indian raiders, and lay in wait at the spot where they calculated the Indians would make their last camp before reaching their village. The Indians camped as anticipated and went to sleep. In the dead of night the Eskimos swooped upon them, and by cutting their throats and clubbing them killed them to the last man.

Nelson mentions that fighting of this sort took place even between various Eskimo groups.[18] Sometimes the victors took the women home with them; but "they killed all they could of the males of the opposing side, even including infants, to prevent them from growing up as enemies. The dead were thrown in heaps and left. The females were commonly spared from death, but were taken as slaves."[19] The Diomede Islanders showed the same spirit in giving no quarter to encroachers from either side of Bering Strait.[20]

The Malemiut are the largest and most warlike tribe of Alaskan Eskimos. Their early home was on Kotzebue Sound; but in following the wild caribou which formerly covered the interior of Alaska they spread across Seward Peninsula, crowding back the weaker tribes—the Kaviagmiut and the Unalit. The latter never resisted the encroachment of these powerful invaders, as they were continually harassed by the Magemiut of the lower Yukon, and in most encounters came off second best. Recently, the Malemiut and Unaligmiut have been on good terms, holding their great intertribal feasts together.[21]

As an assuagement to the usual murderous character of the fighting, an interesting form of truce is noted among the people of the Yukon Delta.

"If a fight lasted a long time, so that both parties became tired and hungry or sleepy, a fur coat would be waved on a stick by one side as a sign of truce, during which both parties would rest, eat and sleep, and then renew the conflict. During the truce both sides stationed guards who watched against surprise."[22] Furthermore, among these people and the Magemiut "when a man on either side had relatives in the opposing party, and for this reason did not wish to take part in the battle, he would blacken his face with charcoal and remain a non-combatant, both sides respecting his neutrality. In this event a man with his face blackened had the privilege of going without danger among the people of either side during a truce."[23]

Bering Strait seems to have been the center of the liveliest fighting in all Alaska, indeed, probably in all the Eskimo province. The young men of the region between Norton Sound and the Arctic Sea were

"regularly trained for war, hardening themselves in all manner of athletic exercises, dieting themselves, and often obliged to fast in order to habituate themselves to great hardships, or making journeys on foot for many days in succession as a test of endurance. Not only were the different tribes constantly at feud among themselves; they did not hesitate to enter upon combats with Indians or white men when these ventured into their territory. Fighting was carried on as a rule with bow and arrow, but they had also special inventions of their own; among the most notable were breastplates of walrus tusk, proof against arrows, or great saw-toothed clubs designed to crush the skull of an enemy."[24] "During the time that war was carried on between the tribes the best warrior planned the attack, and was known among the Unalit as *mû-gokh'-ch-tă*. He, however, had no fixed authority, as each one fought independently of the others, but all combined in the general onslaught. An enemy was termed *um'-i-kĭs'-tû-ga,* or 'one who is angry with me.' "[25] During conflict between the Magemiut and the Yukon men, "neither side had any recognized chief, but each fought as he pleased, with the exception that some of the older men had general supervision and control of the expedition."[26]

It is said that the Asiatic and Alaskan Eskimos of Bering Strait were constantly at war with each other in ancient times, and that it was customary for the people of the Siberian coast to kill at sight any Eskimo from the American shore who might have been driven by storm across the strait.[27] The two Diomede Islands, lying in the middle of this neck of water, naturally occupied a critical position. They are the stepping-stones, as it were, between two continents. The Diomede Eskimos, therefore, by virtue of their location, have been involved in the relations between their Alaskan and Asiatic kinsmen. Peaceful trading, for a large part, has characterized the intercourse; but on occasion armed conflict has raged. Once the inhabitants of Little Diomede became angry with those of Big Diomede, three miles distant, and united with the

people of Cape Prince of Wales against them, but were defeated.[28]
Sometimes the Diomeders would league with the Eskimos of the
Siberian shore against the combined forces of King Island and the
mainland between Kotzebue Sound and Port Clarence. Again, they
would maintain a haughty independence between both factions.[29]
The present-day Eskimos of these islands relate fascinating tales
of fierce fighting. It is told how at an early date the natives of Big
Diomede designed a clever ruse to save their island from the attack of superior numbers. They erected a sham army of man-sized,
stone dummies, which they clad in fur parkas. This harmless
battalion turned the tide by shattering the morale of the invaders. Surely, that was the cheapest standing army in the world,
and, what is more, it is still standing!

Some of the bands of Eskimos dwelling between Bering Strait
and Point Barrow are habitually inlanders, natives of the Noatak,
the Utorqaq, and the Colville river valleys. These groups were
constantly at war with the Indians farther inland, but with their
coast-dwelling kinsmen they were generally at peace.[30] Eskimos
from all parts of this section assembled annually at large trading
festivals.

"Cape Blossom and the mouth of Hotham Inlet are the principal
places of rendezvous for the natives of the surrounding country. The
coast natives, from Cape Prince of Wales to Point Hope, including the
Diomedes and King Island, assemble here about the last of July to
meet those of the interior, who came down the Koogarook, Sulawick,
Buckland, and another large river [Noatak?] which empties into Hotham Inlet on the north side."[31]

Farther north parties were made up in June to go to the mouth of
the Colville River. There the people of Point Barrow and Cape Smyth
met a band called *nu-na-tá'ñ-meum* ("inland people") with whom they
bartered oil and blubber for deer, fox, and wolverine skins. Here and
east of the Colville they sometimes met the "Itkû'dlĭñ," Indians speaking an understandable tongue, who peacefully bartered fox skins for
oil.[32]

This survey of the intertribal relations in Alaska depicts a
combination of war and barter. There is a striving on the part of
each group to get through plundering, in the case of war, otherwise by crafty trading, the resources which it cannot or will not
secure by direct appropriation from nature. In each case, the
well-being of the in-group is the primary aim; the felicity of the
out-group is of little concern, be they Indians or even other Eski-

mos. "Stealing from people of the same village or tribe is regarded as wrong. . . . To steal from a stranger or from a people
of another tribe is not considered wrong so long as it does not
bring trouble on the community."[33]

Warfare has as a result, furthermore, the reducing of the numbers of the opposing groups. The extent of the actual slaughter
in an Eskimo encounter, in distinction to lively, but for the most
part harmless, combat, cannot definitely be stated. While it cannot be said that the fatality is as great as in "civilized" warfare,
the spirit of antagonism is so pronounced that one would suppose
that during a fight the killing would be limited only by the implements and technique of warfare. The aim is the enfeebling of the
enemy as a fighting opponent. And the effect, which is the important matter in this connection, is the eliminating of a proportion
of the population which must subsist upon the given area. Warfare, therefore, must be included as an effectual factor in the
man-land ratio.

§2. MACKENZIE REGION

To the east of Alaska in the Mackenzie region, likewise, there has
been intertribal contact. Since very early times the Eskimos have
been drawn inland into the territory of the Indians on hunting
and fishing journeys.[34] The quest for stone for weapons was a
further incentive for their traveling upstream. To secure this they
would go two hundred miles above the head of the delta. The Indians feared them,[35] more especially for their habit of carrying off
their women folk as wives.[36] Though there were no organized war
campaigns,[37] there were murderous skirmishes.[38] The old Eskimo
stories represent the Indians as cruel, bloodthirsty, and treacherous.[39] It has not been very long since the last feud, but now the
two peoples are on friendly terms. At least, in fairly recent times
the Eskimos and the Indians used to convene for trading on Barter Island, at the mouth of the Hulahula River.[40]

§3. THE COPPER ESKIMOS AND THE BARREN
GROUNDS ESKIMOS

THE Copper Eskimos seem to have had but little contact with
Indians. Quoting Jenness:

"[They] had no intercourse with the Indians of Great Bear lake until Stefansson brought them together in 1910; since then they have regularly visited the lake each summer and traded their dogs for guns and ammunition. Up to 1910 they were afraid of the Indians, and apparently never reached quite as far as Bear lake, its north end at least.[2] They have a tradition that long ago some Indians came up from the south and massacred many of the Walliak natives, after which they went away west, carrying with them the Eskimos' pots. Possibly there is some reference in this to the massacre at Bloody fall. Higilak told me that the Eskimos never fought with the Indians, though the latter would steal their copper and pots. Once when the Indians were close to a party of Eskimos the latter kindled a great fire and threw ashes into the eyes of their enemies."[41]

"Probably half a century ago the Pallirmiut kept as a rule to the Rae river basin, and the Bathurst inlet natives to the country north of Backs river and east of the Coppermine, while the natives of the Coppermine basin itself kept for the most part to the lower reaches of the river, and only ascended as far as the Dismal lakes when they wanted to procure timber for making their sleds and tables. Fear of the Indians kept them away, and hence the early explorers, Franklin, Richardson, Dease, and Simpson, saw no traces of them south of Bloody fall."[42]

Intercourse between the Copper Eskimos and the Western Eskimos in the vicinity of Cape Bathurst seems to have been irregular.[43] Closer contact has been maintained with the Eskimos to the eastward. Though natives of Dolphin and Union Strait and the west side of Coronation Gulf seldom travel beyond Bathurst Inlet,[44] groups from the southern and eastern coast of Coronation Gulf and from Dease Strait journey southeastward and eastward to meet the Caribou Eskimos of the interior and the Netsilingmiut.[45] One great trading center for all the tribes west of Hudson Bay as far as Coronation Gulf was Akilinnik,[46] in the hill region of the Thelon River. In traveling thither the Copper Eskimos traversed an area in the Barren Grounds where no Indians were encountered, and generally no Eskimos either.[47] At Akilinnik they would meet other Eskimos, principally of the Caribou group, and would receive wood and the furs of caribou, musk ox, and fox, in exchange for sledges and weapons.[48]

"Sometimes they stayed with the Akilinnik people for a year or two, and went down to Chesterfield Inlet with them to meet and trade with white men; occasionally too, an Akilinnik native would return with them to Bathurst Inlet. These inland natives, however, being ignorant of the method of seal-hunting on the ice in winter, could never remain for any long period with their northern neighbors, but were compelled to hasten south again in quest of caribou and musk-oxen."

The friendliness between these two groups is expressed in the regular formula used by the inlanders in describing the Bathurst Inlet natives: "They are good people to meet, they are pleasant companions. They always have plenty of seal-meat. They are a friendly people. Whenever they go sealing they always secure plenty of seals."[49]

Eskimos from other groups, dwelling to the north along the Arctic shore also journeyed to the Akilinnik region.[50] Thither repaired members of the Arviligjuarmiut group from Pelly Bay, and the Ahiarmiut from Queen Maud Gulf, the latter being a nomadic and warlike people.[51] Wood for kayaks and sledges was their chief object, and in quest of it they would even penetrate the forest region, charily, however, by reason of a widespread belief that the trees are living beings, malicious toward humans.[52]

We see, therefore, that there is in general fairly regular contact among the Eskimos northwest of Hudson Bay. The Copper Eskimos sometimes met the Eskimos of Backs River, which lies only six days' journey to the eastward, and even the Netsilingmiut farther east.

"The country of the Netsilik is almost devoid of driftwood, consequently its people are eager for sleds and other objects of wood which the western natives possess, though the Netsilingmiut also purchase stone lamps and pots. In exchange they give the Copper natives articles of iron, such as knives and harpoon heads."[53]

"The Netsilingmiut, these Coronation gulf natives say, have a very peculiar manner of welcoming strangers; they give them a buffet on the head or shoulders with their fists. Their mittens deaden the force of the blow to some extent; nevertheless it is no mere tap, for in one case at least a visitor was 'killed for a time' (i.e., stunned) by a buffet behind the ear.[2]"[54]

The Copper Eskimos' customary salute upon meeting strangers is to hold the arms overhead to show that they carry no weapons. Stefansson describes their tactics when meeting strangers. They advance slowly in a line (not in a file) toward the newcomers, holding their hands above their heads and calling, "We are made glad by your coming."[55] Also a very different custom, of carrying a knife when going to meet strangers, has often been noticed.[56] As a Coronation Gulf native expressed it, "We carry knives in our hands when we go out to welcome strangers, just as the Netsilingmiut greet them with a buffet in the face. They have one custom, we have another." The presence of a woman in the party is a sure sign of peaceful intentions.

The Netsilik Eskimos, too, however, have been observed to carry knives when greeting visitors.

"We were welcomed in the true Netselingmeut manner," writes Major Burwash,[57] "the men first standing in a group at some little distance while the women of the settlement, who were mothers, each with a knife in her hand ran around our loaded sleds in a wide circle. According to their belief the track left by the women would encompass any evil spirits that had followed us across the ice, thus keeping them out of their settlement."

Especially characteristic of the Netsilingmiut is the custom of sending forward a woman as a herald of peace.[58] Klutschak describes this procedure[59] on the occasion of his approaching a native village:

". . . As she came nearer and nearer to our group the slower and shorter became her steps, and her facial expression betrayed a certain uneasiness. She had a small knife with her as a weapon, and however strange is this custom of sending a woman against the strangers, it is employed constantly by this tribe."

Between these Netsilingmiut and other Eskimo groups in former times there was continual war. Since the coming of the white men to the Hudson Bay District there has been peace with the tribes to the eastward, but relations with those on the west, especially in Victoria Land, are still somewhat strained.[60] Klutschak mentions that the Netsilingmiut through long war had conquered their neighbors the Ukusiksillik Eskimos after greatly depleting their numbers.[61] Similarly, for a long time the Netsilingmiut and the Eivillik Eskimos (Aivilingmiut) have been in a feud.[62] In more recent times, however, it is reported that these latter two groups trade with each other.[63] The Aiviliks and the Qaernermiut are reported to be peaceful toward each other generally, though one quarrel, arising through blood vengeance, assumed tribal proportions.[64] A custom observed among the Eskimos of Rae Strait illustrates the extent to which those people are distrustful and suspicious of strangers. "It is the custom on the coming of strangers, for all the women who have borne children, to step a circle round the sledge with its team; undesirable spirit entities are then 'bound' within the magic circle and can do no harm."[65] Thus, strangers are not alone to be feared as *people*, even the spirits associated with them must be placed under quarantine.

It is clear from the foregoing that relations among groups in this central region are not always harmonious. This is more striking in view of the fact that we have been considering only the attitude of Eskimos toward Eskimos and not toward Indians. It must not be supposed, however, that hostilities take the form of organized battles. The blood feud seems to be the basis of intertribal animosity where it exists, among these groups and also in Baffin Island.[66] Relations approach closest to war when the feud expands to include whole settlements. Organized fighting was never developed in the central area as it was in the Bering Strait region, and the general sparsity of population precludes war parties of considerable size. A further hindrance may lie in the fact that both factions are so poverty-stricken and harassed by the common hardships of their antagonistic and ungenerous habitat that intertribal fighting but poorly repays even the victor for the time and energy it consumes.

We have been considering in this area the relations between Eskimo groups only. Somewhat the same state of affairs exists between the Indians west of Hudson Bay and the Barren Grounds Eskimos adjacent to them on the north. The technique of war has never evolved here to the degree it has in the Bering Strait region. Certainly, the spirit is not lacking, however. We observe much the same animosity as is harbored between the Alaskan Eskimo and his Indian neighbor. Tradition supplements history in the assumption that the Caribou Eskimos have always been hostile toward the Indians.[67] In the first half of the eighteenth century the Eskimos often fought with the Cree. When, later, the Chipewyan came between these tribes the Eskimos were on no better terms with these new neighbors. Not a few of the Chipewyan speak broken Eskimo, but no Eskimo lowers himself to speak Chipewyan. They converse with each other politely and use the term *Arnaqătiga*, "my cousin," but no affection is observable. The Chipewyan used to make hunting trips up into the Barren Grounds north of the tree limit;[68] however, wars between them and the Eskimos were probably not a conscious protest against encroachment of the latter's hunting lands, but instead a series of blood feuds.[69] The Chipewyan and the Eskimos are hereditary enemies, therefore, and hostility has from time to time become active in the overlapping territory.[70]

Peaceful trading, nevertheless, also takes place between the two groups. The Chipewyan seem extremely eager to buy Eskimo dogs and caribou skins, and in former days soapstone for pipe bowls. In exchange the Eskimos receive pyrites, mittens, snowshoes, and moccasins.[71]

§4. LABRADOR

THE only remaining area where Eskimo territory is adjacent to Indian hunting grounds is in Labrador. When the Hudson's Bay post was established in the Ungava District about 1831 "a palisade was erected around the houses to prevent the intrusion of the natives, Indians and Eskimos, who were so lately at war with each other that the rancorous feeling had not subsided and might break out afresh at any moment without warning."[72] In more recent times, however, the utmost good will has prevailed generally.[73] Low, reporting in 1895,[74] states that the dividing line between these Indians, the Naskapi, and the Eskimos of northern Labrador is well respected: the Indians rarely cross it from the southward, and the Eskimos keep well north of the boundary when hunting deer inland. In this Ungava Bay region, "as elsewhere, they do not intermix, an Indian never taking an Innuit wife or the Innuit taking a squaw for a wife."[75] Intertribal marriage among the Eskimos, however, is quite common.[76] They are usually peaceful and mild-tempered. Among themselves affrays are of rare occurrence. In spite of the accepted custom of exchanging wives, jealousy arouses the worst passions, and murder of the offender is generally the result.[77]

On the Atlantic coast of Labrador the habitation of the Eskimos is broken only at Davis Inlet, where the eastern Naskapi come out yearly to the Hudson's Bay Company post to trade.[78]

§5. CROSS–FERTILIZATION OF CULTURE BETWEEN ESKIMOS AND INDIANS

PEACEFUL intercourse between groups of people whose cultures manifest dissimilarities results normally in interchange of ideas and assimilation by each of foreign culture traits. Cross-fertilization of culture between the Eskimos and the Indians is most marked, naturally, where the two peoples are in closest contact, namely, in Alaska, in Labrador, and in the region west of Hudson Bay. In this latter area Birket-Smith has clearly shown that the Caribou Eskimos have absorbed a number of culture traits from their neighbors the Chipewyan and the Cree.[79]

One element borrowed from the Indians, probably from the Cree, is the smoking pipe. The "monitor" form of pipe, which principally belongs to the northeasterly Algonkian tribes is displayed by the Eskimo pipes at Hudson Bay and in Labrador and has spread over the Barren Grounds to the Iglulik and Netsilik groups.[80] The Copper Eskimos, on the other hand, farther removed from pipe-smoking people, seem to have been ignorant of tobacco until recent years. Farther west, from the Mackenzie area to Bering Strait, a special form of pipe used by the Eskimos in early historical times was not adopted from the Indians, but from the Chukchi of northeastern Siberia, among whom the Russians introduced the practice of smoking.[81] Herein lies an astonishing example of the spread of a culture trait. The Western Eskimos had long remained unacquainted with tobacco by reason of the climatic barrier which prevents its growth, and when they first learned of tobacco it was not directly from the Indians to the south, who are the originators of the use of it, but from people to the west, who had adopted tobacco smoking only after it had been discovered by Europeans among the Indians and been carried completely around the globe.

But to return to the transfer of culture traits between the Indians and the Eskimos of the Barren Grounds, Birket-Smith mentions as coming under this category the conical tent, snowshoes, the two-handed scraper, the smoking and frying of meat, tongued bags, the woman's hair stick (?), ear ornaments of several strings of beads, the painting of skin with ocher, the whistle, double-curve, disk, triangle and zigzag ornamentation, and possibly the custom of setting up a pole by the grave.[82] The snowshoe presents an interesting study. This characteristically Indian device is of service to the Caribou Eskimos only during about two weeks in the spring; hence, they practically never make them themselves, but sometimes procure them from the Indians.[83] The snowshoe does not belong to the original Eskimo culture. "Whilst it is entirely absent in isolated Greenland, it now occurs all the way from Labrador to

Bering Strait and, of course, among the Chukchi and Koryak. In none of these cases, however, are they anything but more or less successful imitations of the snowshoes of the neighboring Indians. . . ."[84] The restricted use of snowshoes even among Eskimos who are acquainted with them is due largely to environmental reasons: the snow in the Eskimo region is not so soft and deep as that among some of the inland, Indian groups; consequently, the Eskimo has less need for snowshoes.

With regard to the dog sledge, common among practically all Eskimos, but among the Indians originally almost or entirely lacking, the same climatic influence operates but in the opposite manner. The sled has been adopted only to a limited degree by the northern Dené of the Mackenzie basin, for instance, because their toboggans are better adapted to travel over deep, soft snow.

§6. GREENLAND

Polar Eskimos Had No Relations with Other People

CARRYING the discussion of the societal environment of the Eskimos to Greenland, we find in the region of Smith Sound a band of about 250 people, the Polar Eskimos, who at the time of their discovery by white men believed themselves to be the only inhabitants of the universe.[85] Their reactions upon first meeting other men are consequently very interesting. This meeting occurred in 1818, when Ross, assisted by Parry, reached Cape York.[86] The explorers, standing on the sea ice, were separated from the Eskimos by a narrow lane of water. Speaking an Eskimo dialect differing only slightly from that of the natives, the visitors invited them to "Come on." To this the Eskimos replied, "No, no—go away." The boldest approached to the edge of the ice and drawing from his boot a knife said, "Go away; I can kill you." They regarded a string of beads and a checked shirt, thrown to them, with distrust and apprehension, still calling, "Go away, don't kill us." Thereupon the spokesman of the white men, Sacheuse, threw them a knife, saying, "Take that." The Eskimos approached with caution, picked up the knife, then shouted and pulled their noses, which actions Sacheuse imitated. The first man approached

"with every mark of fear and distrust, looking frequently behind to the other two, and beckoning them to come on, as if for support. They occasionally retreated, then advanced again, with cautious steps, in the attitude of listening, generally keeping one hand down by their knees, in readiness to pull out a knife which they had in their boots; in the other hand they held whips with the lash coiled up; their sledges remained at a little distance, the fourth man being apparently stationed to keep them in readiness for escape. Sometimes they drew back the covering they had on their heads, as if wishing to catch the most distant sounds; at which time I could discern their features, displaying extreme terror and amazement, while every limb appeared to tremble as they moved."[87]

They besought Sacheuse not to touch them, fearing that if he did they would certainly die. Sacheuse told them that he was a man, that he had had a father and mother like themselves; and pointing to the south said that he came from a distant country in that direction. To this they answered, "That cannot be, there is nothing but ice there."

It is not strange, therefore, that John Ross could not make clear to these Eskimos the idea of war.[88] According to Birket-Smith, however, legends prevailing among these people seem to suggest that an old trading communication with the Upernivik District, on the west coast, was interrupted by hostile encounters.[89] It seems probable that until not so very long ago communication was maintained between these Polar Eskimos and the West Greenlanders.[90]

Economic Relations among Greenland Groups

In Greenland as elsewhere in the Eskimo lands some natural products and resources are restricted to certain regions. It follows that

"on long journeys when the family came to regions yielding some natural product which was lacking in their own part of the country, they took care to provide themselves with it, and very often without the intervention of the local population, the latter only being necessary in certain circumstances, for instance in the case of baleen, the acquisition of which presupposes a knowledge of the difficult and dangerous whale hunting. Otherwise the middleman's profit—to make use of a modern expression—was saved. Soapstone was broken where this mineral occurred, driftwood was gathered where it was to be found in abundance, etc."[91]

Anyone was free to avail himself of such materials.

Some trading took place, but chiefly only incidental to the hunting trips. It was mere barter such as is natural when hunting parties meet at common grounds. From an economic point of view it was comparatively unimportant.[92] At Taseralik, however, on the west coast (about 67° 30' N. Lat.), natives met for trading no less than for hunting.[93]

"There Eskimos from Disko Bay and perhaps from still more northerly parts, met with their countrymen from as far south as the Julianehaab District. In his diary for 1766 the Rev. Glahn wrote: 'To this large gathering some travel in order to see their relations; some to look for a bride among so many beauties; some to settle their litigations before this solemn gathering; some to stand their trial in wrestling, slapping and being slapped on the back; some in order to be healed by a more noted physician, who is supposed to come here; some for the sake of buying and selling; some to be spectators, and some to find a hiding place in the large gathering when they intend to commit some foul deed.' (*Grönl. Selsk. Skrifter.* Bd. II, p. 42.)"[94]

Regional specialization in industry played some part in the relations along the west coast.[95] In the Godthaab District, for instance,

"which is distinguished by its soapstone, some families were occupied in the manufacture of lamps and pots, which were sold in the north and in the south. The Julianehaab Eskimos whose descendants are still considered economically farsighted and alive to everything new, made their long journeys to the above-mentioned Taseralik Island in order to trade seal thongs from their own regions as well as articles of soapstone, which they procured underway at Godthaab. In return they bought narwhal tusks and baleen from the North Greenlanders.

"Apart from the trade with these articles there was no doubt in the earliest times a very lively commerce in siliceous slate which was used for knife-blades and the heads of hunting weapons. It originates from the sediments underlying the basalt in North Greenland, but by means of barter it has been scattered far and wide. A knife of telluric iron occurring in the basalt has been found at Fiskernaes in South Greenland, and likewise cryolite from Ivigtût has been found in the Upernivik District."[96]

"At Aluk off the east coast of Greenland and close to Cape Farewell, similar meetings were held between the inhabitants of West and East Greenland, who assembled there for the hunting of bladdernose. The importance of Aluk as a trading place is, however, not particularly old, hardly more than about three hundred years. The East Greenlanders had nothing which the Julianehaab Eskimos could not as easily, or more easily, procure in the course of their extensive journeys along the west coast."[97]

Friendliness and Hostility between Settlements

THE relations among the Greenlanders have been for the most part peaceful.[98] War they regard as "incomprehensible and repulsive, a thing for which their language has no word; and soldiers and officers, brought up to the trade of killing, they regard as mere butchers." Their reluctance to fight has contributed largely to the general reputation of the Eskimos as a peaceable people. The attitude of the Greenlanders is strikingly expressed in a letter written by one of them in 1756, which Nansen quotes.[99] Commenting on the warfare in Europe at that time, the native cannot understand how it is that men of the same faith are hunting each other like seals and stealing from people they have never seen or known. He apostrophizes his own wretched land:

"How well it is that you are covered with ice and snow. How well it is that, if in your rocks there are gold and silver, for which the Christians are so greedy, it is covered with so much snow that they cannot get at it! Your unfruitfulness makes us happy and saves us from molestation!"

The writer was surprised that the Europeans had not learned better manners among the Eskimos and proposed to send medicine men as missionaries among them. Fighting about land seemed to him sheer greed, an attitude on his part which is understandable only in view of the principles held by these people with regard to property. Freedom in the exploitation of hunting grounds seems to characterize the mores of the Greenland Eskimos.[100]

Only rarely do we read of group assertion of rights, as for instance in the statement of Rink:[101]

". . . If a *new family wished to settle at an inhabited place*, the newcomers had to wait the consent of the people already settled there, which was given by means of certain signs of civility or welcome, the strangers having meanwhile put their boat ashore, but not yet begun bringing up their goods. If those signs were not given, they put off again and went to look for another place."

Restraint from active hostility, thus, may not mean absolute good will and harmony. We read that in East Greenland "the people of one settlement form, as it were, a society by themselves, which often is at enmity with the folk of another settlement" and a people on one side of a fiord will volunteer the information that those on the other side are bad men. "When we learned to know the natives better it appeared that it was very common for the one to disparage the other at the same time that he sought to place himself in the best light."[102]

NOTES

1. Among the Eskimos only the Pacific tribes are known to have a fully developed sign language. (Birket-Smith: 1929, I, 190, footnote, citing Hoffman: 1897, 947 ff.) In the Mackenzie region and on the west coast of Hudson Bay raising the eyebrows signifies "yes" and wrinkling the nose, "no" (Stefansson: 1914, 339, 456; Boas: 1907, 467). Also in the Bering Strait region wrinkling the nose signifies "no" (Weyer: Field Notes).

2. Sumner and Keller: 1927, I, 356 ff.

3. Nelson: 1899, 307. Other mention of the use of this name by Alaskan Eskimos: Dall: 1870, 28; Dall: 1877, I, 25; Jacobsen: 1884, 166 (Bering Sea); Schwatka: 1900, 248; Hawkes: 1913, 13 (Norton Sound). It is interesting that the Eskimos of Little Diomede Island, Bering Strait, call their island *Ing'-ahlī-lik*. The author learned no interpretation of the word; but if its similarity to the word applied to Indians implying an abundance of lice indicates its derivation, the appellation is indeed appropriate for the island. Compare *Igna-look*, the name given to this island on Beechey's map (Beechey: 1831), *Inalik* on Petroff's map (Petroff: 1884); and *Ima'lik*, as Bogoras gives it (Bogoras: 1913, 419).

4. Murdoch: 1892, 51. Petitot remarks that in the Mackenzie region the Eskimos derisively call the Indians *Irkrélêit, Ingalit* (Petitot: 1886, 5). Lyon gives the word *it-kăgh-līe* as the name used by the Iglulik Eskimos for "Indians" (Lyon: 1824, 250). And Rasmussen refers to a certain Netsilik Eskimo whose name *Itqilik* means "the Indian" (Rasmussen: 1927, 201). Further information concerning the Alaskan word *Ingalik* is given in the *Handbook of the American Indians,* I, 609.

The same origin apparently can be traced for the Greenland word *er-Kigdlit*, though it now refers to a fabulous inland people with faces like dogs (Schultz-Lorentzen: 1928, 231). See p. 394.

5. Nelson: 1899, 306–307.

6. Weyer: Field Notes (Bering Strait); Petroff: 1884, 124 (Alaska); Murdoch: 1892, 42–43 (Point Barrow) (*in'uin*); Birket-Smith: 1929, I, 58 (Barren Grounds); Bilby: 1923, 56 (Baffin Island); Birket-Smith: 1924, 37 (on the central part of the west coast of Greenland the word *kalâtdlit* is used exclusively, meaning the same as *inuit*); Thalbitzer: 1914, 331 and Holm: 1914, 25 (Angmagsalik Eskimos call themselves either *inik*, or *tâk* (singular) *taawin*, which in the singular form also signifies "a shade."

7. Birket-Smith: 1929, I, 58.

8. Rasmussen: 1927, 356. Rasmussen doubtless refers to Prince William Sound when he mentions Prince of Wales Sound in this connection.

9. Petroff: 1884, 145–146.

10. Petroff: 1884, 136.

11. Petroff: 1900, 225.

12. Schwatka: 1900, 248, 353; Schwatka: 1885a, 314; Nelson: 1899, 19.

13. Nelson: 1899, 23–24.

14. Nelson: 1899, 327; Bancroft: 1875, I, 120.

15. Nelson: 1899, 293, 301.

16. Nelson: 1899, 327.

17. Weyer: Field Notes.

18. Nelson: 1899, 327.

19. Nelson: 1899, 327–328.

20. Weyer: Field Notes.

21. Hawkes: 1913, 2.

22. Nelson: 1899, 329.
23. Nelson: 1899, 329.
24. Rasmussen: 1927, 306–307.
25. Nelson: 1899, 306.
26. Nelson: 1899, 329.
27. Nelson: 1899, 330.
28. Nelson: 1899, 330.
29. Weyer: Field Notes.
30. Rasmussen: 1927, 318–319.
31. Hooper: 1881, 26.
32. Ray: 1885; Murdoch: 1892, 44 ff.
33. Nelson: 1899, 293.
34. Rasmussen: 1927, 300.
35. Stefansson: 1914, 12–13.
36. Rasmussen: 1927, 301.
37. Stefansson: 1914, 12–13.
38. Rink: 1887, 31.
39. Rasmussen: 1927, 301.
40. Stefansson: 1921, 92 (footnote); further information from Fenley Hunter.
41. Jenness: 1922, 47, citing (2) Simpson: 1843, 347, and Stefansson: 1913, 216.
42. Jenness: 1922, 124.
43. Jenness: 1922, 44.
44. Jenness: 1922, 49.
45. Jenness: 1922, 48 ff.
46. It is due to a misunderstanding that this name has been applied to what is better known as the Thelon River. The word Akilinnik ". . . means 'that on the other side of something' and is used of the ridges on the south side of Thelon River, camp being pitched on the north side, but, according to Eskimo usage, cannot be used for the river itself" (Birket-Smith: 1929, I, 30).
47. Jenness: 1922, 48; Birket-Smith: 1929, I, 30.
48. Jenness: 1922, 48.
49. Jenness: 1922, 48.
50. Rasmussen: 1927, 76.
51. Rasmussen: 1927, 169, 245–246.
52. Rasmussen: 1927, 77; Birket-Smith: 1929, I, 29.
53. Jenness: 1922, 52.
54. Jenness: 1922, 50, citing Boas: 1888, 609; see also Mathiassen: 1928, I, 221 (Iglulik Eskimos); Boas: 1907, 116 (west coast of Hudson Bay); Birket-Smith: 1929, I, 161 ff.
55. Stefansson: 1914, 235 f.
56. Jenness: 1922, 55.

57. Burwash: 1931, 34.
58. Rasmussen: 1927, 233.
59. Klutschak: 1881, 76.
60. Rasmussen: 1927, 233.
61. Klutschak: 1881, 64.
62. Klutschak: 1881, 150; and Mathiassen: 1928, I, 101 ff.
63. Capt. Jos. F. Bernard in Jenness: 1922, Appendix, 245.
64. Mathiassen: 1928, I, 101 ff.; Klutschak: 1881, 227–228.
65. Rasmussen: 1927, 179.
66. Boas: 1888, 462 ff. For further discussion of the feud see pp. 220 ff.
67. Birket-Smith: 1929, I, 163 ff.; Rasmussen: 1927, 58.
68. Birket-Smith: 1929, I, 29.
69. Birket-Smith: 1929, I, 261–262.
70. Birket-Smith: 1929, I, 36.
71. Birket-Smith: 1929, I, 160 ff., 165.
72. Turner: 1894, 166–167.
73. Turner: 1887, 104.
74. Low: 1895, 42 ff.
75. Turner: 1894, 184.
76. Turner: 1894, 189.
77. Turner: 1894, 186.
78. Hawkes: 1916, 24.
79. Birket-Smith: 1929, II, 32 ff.
80. Birket-Smith: 1929, II, 32 ff.; Mathiassen: 1928, I, 207–208; Hawkes: 1916, 98–99.
81. Kroeber: 1923, 211 ff.; Murdoch: 1888, 325 ff.; Nelson: 1899, 271–285; Murdoch: 1892, 65 ff.
82. Birket-Smith: 1929, II, 33.
83. Birket-Smith: 1929, I, 151, 183–185.
84. Birket-Smith: 1929, II, 36; see also Boas: 1907, 40–41; Stefansson: 1914, 206, 174; Jenness: 1929; Murdoch: 1892, 334; Nelson 1899, 212 ff.
85. Ross: 1819, 123.
86. Ross: 1819, 83 ff.
87. Ross: 1819, 85.
88. Ross: 1819, 134–135.
89. Birket-Smith: 1928, 18, 162–163.
90. Birket-Smith: 1924, 238–239; Egede: 1741, 2; Rasmussen: 1919, 53 ff., 66 ff.; Stein: 1902, 196 ff.
91. Birket-Smith: 1928, 161.
92. Birket-Smith: 1924, 237; 1928, 165–166.
93. Birket-Smith: 1928, 162.

94. Birket-Smith: 1928, 162.

95. Birket-Smith: 1928, 161.

96. Birket-Smith: 1928, 166; see also Birket-Smith: 1924, 75.

97. Birket-Smith: 1928, 162.

98. Nansen: 1893, 162.

99. Nansen: 1893, 180 ff.

100. Birket-Smith: 1928, 161–162; Crantz: 1767, I, 180; Birket-Smith: 1924, 136; Thalbitzer: 1914, 525.

101. Rink: 1875, 31; also Nansen: 1893, 109–110, quoting Dalager: 1752, 15–16.

102. Holm: 1887, 45, 125.

CHAPTER X

TENDENCY TOWARD COMMUNALISM IN PROPERTY

I T was pointed out in a previous chapter that the natural resources available to the Eskimo are so scanty that he suffers severe privation. The occurrence of famine clearly shows that from time to time the products of hunting are not sufficient to support the existing population, and there is not enough food to go around.

The question naturally arises, therefore, as to who should be considered deserving of what resources there are. That is to say, upon what are the property rights based? Infanticide and the killing of the aged and infirm indicate that, at least under certain circumstances, property rights depend upon productivity and usefulness to society. Persons left to starve or to freeze to death, or killed outright, have no property rights at all. It is natural that the first to suffer should be those who are of least value to the group. Property rights must be earned. But the rule is not simple. As previously stated, there is not a heartless discrimination against the helpless. There is a decided tendency to support the weak, a tendency which comes into conflict with the inexorable demands of an impoverished habitat. And not only does the group assume responsibilities for the unfortunate individual; the individual has responsibilities to the group. He cannot selfishly appropriate all that he can secure. Such a policy would be fatal to society. Vicissitudes of fortune affecting different families of a community unequally at any one time necessitate the sharing of food. It is well to be aware of these principles involving the man-land ratio while analyzing the property mores of the Eskimos.

§1. THE PRIVILEGE OF EXPLOITING THE LAND

THE Eskimos have very little conception of ownership of land simply as land. Their interest, as is typical of hunting peoples, lies chiefly in the animals rather than in territories apart from their faunal life. Hence, their land laws are really game laws.

The Copper Eskimos consider that

"land is the property of the community which uses it as a hunting and fishing ground. Strangers have no rights there unless they are accepted as members of the tribe for the time being, and conform to its customs in such matters as the sharing of food. . . . Natives from the Copper-mine river basin and even from Bathurst inlet remained in Dolphin and Union strait throughout the spring of 1916 in order to be near the [Canadian Arctic] expedition; but they joined the local natives at their fishing weirs as soon as the salmon began to migrate, and merged themselves for the time being into the foreign community. The expedition refrained from using their weirs as long as the natives were there, but after they had left we caught a number of salmon in them, and no objection was raised; nor did the natives disapprove of our using nets in their rivers, or shooting the caribou, but only because it was obviously to their advantage that the expedition should remain in their country. Had food been scarce at the time they would have expected us to share our food with them, or at least to refrain from diminishing their own supplies by hunting and fishing in their territories."[1]

In Greenland a party of strange settlers must secure the welcome of any settlement already established before they can camp on its site.[2] The first and most important rule of the Caribou Eskimos with regard to the resources of the land is "that no one, either individual or community, may lay claim to any particular hunting territory. . . . Wood, soapstone, etc. occupy the same position as game: he who can take possession of it has the right to do it."[3] As Birket-Smith states, their attitude manifests "an essential difference from the division into certain hunting areas which is to be found among the Algonkian tribes, Californians and even much more primitive peoples such as the Veddah in Ceylon."[4]

Likewise in Labrador, the attitude of the Eskimos against any strict division of hunting territory may be contrasted with that of their near neighbors the Micmacs and Montagnais.[5] These Eskimos do most of their hunting on the sea,

"which is free to everyone. The same condition applies to the vast interior, where the Eskimo hunt for deer in the autumn and spring.

"The idea of restricting the pursuit of game is repugnant to the Eskimo, who hold that food belongs to everyone. This does not preclude them from having intricate laws for the division of game when in hunting parties.

"Under ordinary conditions, a family may occupy a fishing station in summer year after year undisputed, but it does not give them any special right to it. Anyone else is free to come and enjoy its benefits, and, according to Eskimo ethics, they would move away before they would start a dispute about it. Quite often a deserving but poor young hunter is invited by a more fortunate family to share their camping ground, and is thus enabled to get a start in life."

In West Greenland the hunting places are regarded as free to all,[6] although at least in some sections where "dams have been built in a salmon river to gather fish together, it is not regarded as the right thing if strangers come and interfere with the dams or fish with nets in the dammed-up waters. . . ."[7] A fundamental law of the Greenland community is that no one is able to acquire territorial dominion, including the presupposed products of the territory in the form of minerals, animal life, etc.[8]

Concerning East Greenland, salmon pounds in lakes and the mouths of rivers are specifically mentioned as being common property, though it is stated that the hunter owns his own seal breathing hole and has a potential right to seal caught in it.[9]

The property rights of the Alaskan Eskimos differ somewhat from those of the Eskimos elsewhere, being influenced by the folkways of the neighboring Indians. As will be discussed later, certain duties accompanying the accumulation of much property by a single person are peculiar to the Eskimos of Bering Sea. Furthermore, personal rights are more specifically defined here. Among the Unalit, thus, the most productive places for setting seal and salmon nets are sometimes regarded as being privately owned. "If anyone else puts a net in one of these places the original owner is permitted to take it out and put down his own. These net places are sometimes rented or given out on shares, when the man who allows another to use his place is entitled to half the catch."[10]

Somewhat the same attitude toward property rights, but with reference to the caribou hunting grounds inland from Point Barrow, is mentioned by Murdoch.[11] At the rivers the hunting parties were scattered in small camps of four or five families, about a day's journey apart.

"As well as we could learn these camps are in regularly established places, where the same people return every year if they hunt at all. It even seemed as if these localities were considered the property of certain influential families, who could allow any others they pleased to join their parties. [*Footnote*] Dr. Richardson believes that the hunting grounds of families are kept sacred among the Eskimos."[12]

Materials such as driftwood and stone usable for implements can be taken by whoever needs them.[13] Driftwood dragged above high tide thereafter belongs to the person who found it.[14] Similarly, it is written that in the region of Coronation Gulf articles picked up while traveling, like copper and pyrites, belong to the finder.[15] Sometimes besides carrying the wood above high water the owner marks it with an adze or places a stone on it.

§2. PROPERTY RIGHTS REGARDING ANIMALS HUNTED

THE observations cited above convey an impression of general freedom in the privilege of exploiting hunting grounds, with only occasionally a tendency toward the monopolizing of choice sites. The next question concerns ownership rights in animals killed. The apportioning of the products of the hunt is sometimes so wide as to include the entire settlement, sometimes so narrow as to be limited to the family or even the individual. The extent of the distribution depends to a great degree naturally upon the size of the animal.

Whale

WHALES, for instance, are commonly divided among all the members of the community.

The Diomede Islanders, for example, practice a sort of communalism in this regard, qualified by certain competitive features.[16] The crew who catch a whale apportion among themselves about half the animal, including the head and part of the back. The captain of the whaleboat is entitled to the longest pieces of the whalebone; but even nonparticipants sometimes receive shares of it. When an umiak of hunters catches a whale all the boats of the village are raced madly out to it. The first crew to reach the successful boat has a claim upon part of the back; the second crew gets the belly; the third, one side; and the fourth, the other side. In this way, generally every family in the village receives some of the animal.

It is stated that likewise at East Cape, Siberia, a communalistic attitude is held in regard to the ownership of a whale.[17] And essentially the same applies at Cape Prince of Wales.[18] Concerning the northwestern coast of Alaska, Hooper states that "the carcass . . . [of a whale] is the property of every man, woman, and child in the settlement; the bone, however, belongs to those who took part in the capture."[19] At Point Barrow the whalebone is divided equally among the crews of all the boats in sight at the time of the killing; but all comers are entitled to as much of the flesh and blubber as they can cut off in the general scramble.[20] Approximately the same communal rights were observed along the west coast of Greenland. Thus, ". . . if an animal of the largest size, more especially a whale, was captured, it was considered common property, and as indiscriminately belonging to every one who might come and assist in flensing it, whatever place he belonged to and whether he had any share in capturing the animal or not."[21]

White Whale

A WHITE whale, which is much smaller than a true whale, is divided among those who helped catch it, according to very definite rules, in West Greenland; unless there are many hunters and many of the animals secured as in the event of a *savssat*, when the apportioning is less systematic.[22] Stefansson mentions that in the Mackenzie region when a white whale is killed pieces of the skin are given to every family on the beach.[23]

Walrus

WHEN a walrus is caught at Point Barrow it is divided among the boat's crew, the owner of the boat apparently keeping the tusks and perhaps the skin.[24] Among the Pâdlimiut (Barren Grounds Eskimos) the hunter who kills a walrus has the claim, though it is not absolute, upon its head and tusks. Otherwise, all may supply themselves with meat and skin.[25] Gilder voices a similar observation with reference to the northwest shore of Hudson Bay, stating that all who arrive while a walrus is being cut up are entitled to a share, though the man who struck it has the first choice of pieces.[26]

Boas states in detail the principles upon which a walrus is apportioned on the west coast of Hudson Bay:[27] "The hunter who first strikes a walrus receives the tusks and one of the fore-quarters. The person who first comes to his assistance receives the other fore-quarter; the next man, the neck and head; the following, the belly; and each of the next two, one of the hind-quarters." Among the Iglulik Eskimos the hunter who first harpoons a walrus gets the forepart, and the remainder is divided among the other hunters.[28] The regular order for cutting up a walrus in southeastern Baffin Island is stated as follows: "The first man who arrives at the captured animal cuts off the right arm or flipper; the second, the left arm; the third, the right leg or flipper; the fourth the left leg; the fifth, the portion of the body, beginning at the neck, and so on till the whole is disposed of."[29] At Hamilton Inlet (Labrador): "The first one to spear the walrus has one of his 'ivories,' the second gets the other, and each one that spears it gets a special piece of meat, but all that go hunting get a part."[30]

Bearded Seal

LIKEWISE with regard to the bearded seal, or *ugruk*, the Eskimos tend toward a communalistic division of game. This seal, it should be remembered, is larger than the other varieties of seals, though it is, of course, smaller than a walrus.

In the Mackenzie region when a bearded seal is caught, pieces of the skin are given to every family on the beach.[31] When a Copper Eskimo spears one of these seals a great shout goes up and "all the hunters in the vicinity rush to his assistance. Everyone crowds round as the seal is drawn to the surface in order to obtain a share of the meat. Heedless of the value of the skin, heedless even of each other's hands, they hack away, not infrequently cutting each other as each man in his greed tries to hew off as large a portion as possible. The Rev. Mr. Girling, writing in 1918, said: 'There have been a great number of cases of maiming this winter arising from their ridiculous system of going temporarily mad when they strike an *ugyuk* (bearded seal) and all stabbing their knives in to get what they can grab; our surgical outfit has been kept busy.' Yet they know that when they return home both the raw meat and a portion of what is cooked must be distributed amongst the other families, so that all they gain for their exertions is a strip of the skin. Even that is often eaten, so that the only outcome of their folly is a number of severe wounds."[32] Also in West Greenland the larger seals are divided among the entire settlement.[33]

In the case of smaller seals, however, the same rules are not followed.[34]

Summarizing, it can be said that the property mores of the Eskimos imply a communalistic sharing of the products of sea hunting, at the same time maintaining certain preferential rights for whoever actually secures the game in any instance. Among the Copper Eskimos the rights of the hunter's family are obviously dominant:

"The family own all the food and skins that are acquired by any of its members, with this restriction, that all or some of the food must be shared with the neighbors. The amount that is kept by the family for itself depends upon the quantity of food in camp at the time. If ten seals, for example, are caught in one day, and there are only six families in the camp, it is obviously unnecessary to send more than a tiny portion of the meat to each household. On the other hand, if only one seal is caught, the whole of the meat must be distributed, otherwise some of the people would go hungry."[35]

It is written of the Caribou Eskimos that if there are two or three hunters together each gets a portion; but if there are more than three, there is no sharing. In return the hunter is obliged to provide the inhabitants of the camp with meat in the evening.[36] Sometimes all those who are present at a flensing get a share, as in the elaborate system of apportioning observed among the Qaernermiut, the Aivilingmiut, and other groups on the west shore of Hudson Bay.[37] Among the Polar Eskimos, if a solitary hunter cuts up and caches his kill alone it is all his.[38] When a party, however, secures a seal, all the members obtain a share; but the actual killer gets the head, and, of course, the skin.[39] The second share falls to him who first places his hand on the animal, and so on in order.[40] And in East Greenland whoever first harpoons a seal, walrus, or whale has the prior right to it.[41]

Sometimes it happens, of course, that the harpoon line breaks and a seal escapes with the harpoon head sticking in it. When this occurs in West Greenland the claim on the seal is forfeited to whoever can secure it permanently.

The rule is different, however, when the animal is struck with a bladder dart, a weapon which owes its efficacy not to a line but to an inflated bladder attached to the shaft which hinders the animal's escaping. When the seal struck with this implement makes away with it, the animal remains the property of the man who cast the dart, unless the creature is found afar, by different people.[42] Without designating the type of harpoon, Crantz mentions that when anyone finds a dead seal with the harpoon in it he keeps the animal but restores the implement to him who lost it.[43] In Hudson Bay, on the other hand, the finder of a harpooned animal can keep both the animal and the harpoon.[44] A Caribou Eskimo loses his claim on a seal or walrus which breaks the line and escapes; but when the animal is caught by another he will usually get his weapon again.[45]

Ownership Marks

AMONG some Eskimos, notably those in Alaska, it has been the practice to mark certain sorts of hunting implements with signs signifying ownership.[46] Typical examples of these marks are shown in Figure 16.[47] Such marks are perhaps the only instance wherein the Eskimos have developed a systematic symbolic representation of ideas; for it will be remembered that they have no written language.

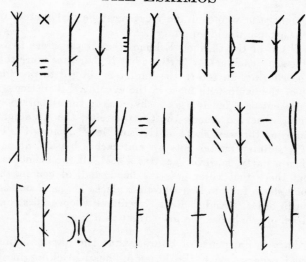

FIGURE 16

Ownership Marks on Darts from Point Barrow
Wissler, 1916

First in importance regarding these ownership marks is the fact that they imply ownership primarily of *the animal struck*, rather than simply ownership of the weapon as such. Hence, they represent a phase of the mores regarding property in game. A quotation from Petroff[48] will illustrate the application of the ownership mark in whale hunting among the natives of Kodiak Island:

"Upon the point of his spear each hunter carves his mark to enable him to claim his quarry. As soon as the whale is wounded he makes for the open sea, where, as the natives say, he 'goes to sleep' for three days. On the fourth or fifth day the carcass is cast upon the beach; but if the waves and currents are unfavorable this may occur in a locality remote from the killing place; and it is stated that on several occasions whales that have been killed at Kadiak were secured by the people of Oonalaska."

The people who find a whale that has been killed in this way first examine the wound in which is to be found the harpoon bearing the mark of the community who killed it. The latter are notified at once, and they divide the carcass with the finders.[49] That the dominant purpose of the ownership mark is to establish claim on animals secured in hunting is indicated by the fact that these marks occur almost exclusively on hunting weapons, of the sort that remain imbedded in the bodies of the animals they strike.

Aside from whale harpoons, walrus harpoons likewise are engraved with ownership marks, though less commonly.[50] Possibly this is due to the fact that in hunting walrus the harpooner is more likely to retain the animal on his harpoon line, rendering claim incontrovertible. Ownership marks are also found on the sealskin buoys which are attached to harpoons, on lance heads used for killing sea mammals, and on detachable arrowheads.[51]

It is known that the natives of Kodiak Island marked their arrows used in hunting sea otter. Only rarely was one of these animals killed by a single arrow; usually as many as four or five were required. The distinctive marks on the arrows of the various hunters determined the ownership of the valuable skin of the sea otter. It belongs to him whose arrow entered nearest the head.[52] In this latter instance, at least, individual ownership rather than group ownership seems to be implied in the property mark. In the case of the whale harpoons, however, the dominant implication is village or community ownership. Thus, many specimens of whale harpoons bear the same property mark.[53] The extent of the claim, however, which is inherent in property marks on the various hunting weapons, is impossible to determine exactly. Our knowledge of them comes largely from archaeological specimens, wherein differences of age render impossible any inference from the diversity of marks from the same village sites. Doubtless, the type of animal hunted determined largely whether the ownership mark should pertain to the individual, the boat's crew, the family, the house group, or the village. Boas considers that, in addition to the distinctive marks, the form and decorative designs of harpoon heads designated ownership.

The use of property marks among the Eskimos is restricted almost exclusively to Alaska.[54] This fact, taken in connection with the form and occurrence of such marks among the tribes of northeastern Siberia, suggests that the custom may have been adopted from Asiatic people. Distantly removed from the type locality are three examples of property marks found among archaeological specimens from King William Land. Mathiassen, their discoverer, believes that there is scarcely any doubt as to their being ownership marks and suggests that the Malerualik finds to which these three arrowheads belong may represent an earlier archaeological phase than the Naujan, which itself is of the Thule Culture.[55]

Far south of the Western Eskimos a property mark has been observed on a sealskin buoy from Vancouver Island.[56]

Caribou

IN caribou hunting the property mores seem to approach less closely to communalism than in the case of sea mammals, especially the larger varieties. Murdoch writing of Point Barrow, for example, classes caribou with the smaller animals and birds as belonging to the hunter himself rather than to the community in any sense.[57] And Birket-Smith testifies that the West Greenlanders do not observe so systematic a partitioning in the case of caribou as with the great seals.[58]

There are certain rules that apply when two or more men strike the same caribou, which quite commonly occurs.

Among the Copper Eskimos "the hunter who inflicts the first wound is entitled to the booty, but to prevent ill feeling, he generally gives some of the choicer parts of the meat, a whole saddle if he is generous, to his comrades. Avranna fired at a young caribou and grazed its leg. The animal was practically unhurt, and would have escaped us altogether had I not brought it down with a second shot. The deer nevertheless was Avranna's. If the caribou had made good its escape, though, and been brought down later, he would have had no claim," except on the arrow point that remained in the wound.[59] Both among the Caribou Eskimos and in West Greenland if two men shoot a caribou at the same time the animal belongs to the one whose missile has hit the most vital spot or lies nearest the heart.[60] In either place, however, if one man wounds a deer and another brings it down, it still belongs to the former.

Polar Bear

A PECULIAR claim is respected regarding polar bears in some sections, notably in East Greenland. At least the skin of the bear belongs to whoever first sighted the animal, regardless of who killed it.[61] The same rule is reported as being the time-honored custom among the inhabitants of southeastern Baffin Island.[62] It does not apply, however, generally among the other groups.

Among the Iglulik Eskimos, for instance, a bear belongs to the one who first wounds it.[63] Likewise, it is stated that among the Caribou Eskimos a bear becomes the property of the one who shoots it, without regard to who sighted it.[64] At Point Barrow the flesh and skin of a bear are divided equally among all who had any part in killing the animal.[65]

§3. SPECIAL CASES IN WHICH PERSONAL RIGHTS REGARDING GAME ARE FORFEITED

SOMETIMES, under special circumstances, greater emphasis than usual is placed upon the sharing of the products of the hunt. Thus, in some places in West Greenland the first walrus or white whale of the season is divided entirely.[66] And in East Greenland the first big bearded seal a man obtains in the season is plundered by all, and even persons not belonging to the village receive a share; whereas ordinarily seals are divided among the hunters present.[67]

Among the Unalit of Alaska if a net is set for any particular game and something else is caught, the latter likewise is divided among the villagers, it being said that if this is done additional animals of the same kind will in the future come to the net.

This is the practice when a white whale is caught in a seal net or a seal in a salmon net.[68] Another observance having a distinct religious significance is recorded from the region of Fury and Hecla Strait. When a man who is hunting alone has killed a caribou in a certain pond near Iglulik he must not eat of it until he finds some company.[69]

The communalistic spirit is stressed when a young man kills an animal for the first time in his life.

Among the Unalit, of Alaska, "the first deer, seal, white whale, or other kind of large game killed by a young man is brought to the village, and there one of the old men cuts it up and divides it among the villagers, without leaving a particle for the young hunter; this is done, they say, that the young man may be successful afterward in hunting."[70] On Little Diomede Island a young man can keep some of the first walrus he ever catches, but he must give the tusks to an old man, and at the same time he gives other presents such as rawhide, skins, and tobacco to the old people, for good luck.[71] On the Alaska shore opposite, a young man, upon catching his first *oogrook* (bearded seal), is forced to give away all but the head, even if he caught the animal all alone.[72] And at Point Barrow, "when a man had got his first whale, it was his duty, at the great whaling festival, to throw away all that he owned of furs and other things; his fellow-villagers had then to fight for a share, the costly furs being cut into fragments that as many as possible might have a part."[73] In the same connection it is written that among the Iglulik Eskimos a boy must not eat the flesh of any species the first time he kills it, and he must give away the skin.[74]

In Labrador, and on the west coast of Hudson Bay and in Cumberland Sound, a boy's first seal is divided completely.[75]

Though there probably are religious implications in these observances regarding a boy's first successful hunting, it is significant that at the outset of a young hunter's career as a food-producing member of society he is impressed through these observances with communalistic principles.

§4. PROPERTY RIGHTS IN FOOD STORES

So much for the property rights regarding the products of hunting. What ownership is observed, we next ask, concerning the meat that is put away to be eaten when necessary?

On King Island (Bering Sea) joints and carcasses are marked with their owner's mark, though one store chamber, a cave, serves as a caching place for all.[76] The Copper Eskimos observe strict differentiation in the food supplies according to families when they are traveling, as is evinced by an example from Jenness:[77]

"Kanneyuk generally remained with her mother, but not infrequently she accompanied her brother and his wife on short excursions that lasted only a few days. The implements and household utensils of the two families, even their stores of fish and meat, were kept strictly apart, just as if no bond of kinship had united them; each woman, for example, had her own blubber pokes and her own racks of drying fish." These natives consider that "surplus food is the property of the family, and can be stored away for future use. In summer innumerable caches of deer-meat and fish are strewn all over the country, each of which is the property of a single family. It is a serious crime to rob one of these caches, except under pressure of starvation."[78] In this regard it is stated that if natives of the Point Barrow region ". . . be away from home and run short of provisions they will help themselves of any meat cache which they may chance to find."[79]

Especially in time of stress or scarcity the Eskimos are apt to resort to communalism.

Among the Caribou Eskimos, for instance, though winter supplies ordinarily belong to the family, in time of famine anyone who is hungry may simply take from another's meat cache without making himself a thief.[80] Klutschak voices the same observation in the region between Chesterfield Inlet and King William Land. "So long as a piece of meat is procurable from their store, it belongs to all, and in its division everyone, especially the childless widows and the sick, will be regarded."[81] This statement indicates that not always do nonproductive members of society forfeit all property rights in time of scarcity.

When food is scarce among the Central Eskimos and "a seal is brought to the huts everybody is entitled to a share of the meat and blubber. . . . In time of plenty only the housemates receive a share of the animal."[82] The strength of the sentiment against the unequal sharing of food in time of dearth among the Koksoagmiut (northern Labrador) is expressed in an incident related by Turner.[83] A man discovered that his wife was hoarding food and eating it in secret. Thereupon he blocked up the snow hut with her inside. In reply to her inquiry as to why he had imprisoned her he replied that if she would come out she would learn. Knowing that if she ventured out she would be killed, she starved to death in the hut.

Especially in case of famine, in a Greenland village, whoever secures food must give a feast or share with the others so that each one is not at the hazard of each day's take.[84]

Stefansson's account of a meal in a dwelling among the Copper Eskimos exemplifies the communalistic attitude of these natives regarding food: "When this had been done, one extra piece was set aside in case I should want a second helping, and the rest of the boiled meat was divided into four portions, with the explanation to me that there were four families in the village who had no fresh seal meat. The little adopted daughter of the house, a girl of seven or eight, had not begun to eat with the rest of us, for it was her task to take a small wooden platter and carry the four pieces of meat to the families who had none of their own.

"I thought to myself that the pieces sent out were a good deal smaller than the portions we were eating, and that the recipients would not get quite a square meal; but I learned later that night from my two companions that four similar presents had been sent out from each of the houses where they were eating, and I know now that every house in the village in which any cooking was done had likewise sent four portions, so that the aggregate must have been a good deal more than the recipients could eat at one time.

"During our meal presents of food were also brought us from other houses; each housewife apparently knew exactly what the others had put in their pots, and whoever had anything to offer that was a little bit different would send some of it to the others, so that every minute or two a small girl messenger appeared at our door with a platter of contributions to our meal. Some of the gifts were especially designated for me—Mother had said that however they divided the rest of what she was sending, the boiled kidney was for me; or Mother had sent this small piece of boiled seal-flipper to me, with the message that if

I would take breakfast at their house tomorrow I should have a whole flipper, for one of my companions was over at their house now and had told them that I considered the flipper the best part of the seal."[85]

Among the Polar Eskimos "there is a community of food as of dwellings, only clothing and implements and utensils being personal property."[86] In West Greenland winter stores of food are classed by Birket-Smith as belonging to the family. When the catch exceeded a certain quantity, such as when a whale is secured, or was particularly rare, or in case of famine, it was always common property.[87] At Angmagsalik (East Greenland), where a number of families share the same dwelling (see *The Household*, under *The Association Unit*), all the housemates share the game and winter provisions of each member.[88]

§5. HOSPITALITY

DIRECTLY in accord with the Eskimos' ideas about property is their spirit of hospitality. Nelson states his observations among the Eskimos of Alaska as follows:

"Hospitality is regarded as a duty among the Eskimo, so far as concerns their own friends in the surrounding villages, and to strangers in certain cases, as well as to all guests visiting the villages during festivals. By exercise of hospitality to their friends and the people of neighboring villages their good will is retained and they are saved from any evil influence to which they might otherwise be subjected."[89]

The casual visitor in an Eskimo house is given food and is expected to eat as much as he wishes. Day after day he may be extended this hospitality, not begrudgingly. Taking food out of the house, however, certainly is not countenanced. The stored provisions obviously are the property of the inmates of the dwelling; sharing them with visitors is merely observing the customary etiquette.[90] A traveler is free to enter an Eskimo hut without being invited. A woman of the household dutifully turns his parka inside out, looks for rips to mend, dries the straw in his mucklucks. If his furs are wet she rubs snow into them to dry them. Such solicitude is taken for granted.

An incident was related to the author, however, which offers an interesting case of pretentious show in hospitality. The white man who recounts the incident stopped with his companions as a wayfarer in an Eskimo house at Shishmaref (northwestern Alaska). The usual formalities of hospitality were carried out with a kind and generous spirit on the part of the woman of the household. Then she turned her attention to brewing some tea for the visitors. She took out a dirty little sack containing about three teaspoonfuls of tea, and with obvious concern counted the large number of people present. The white man straightway gave her a pound of tea from his own stores. The next day the attitude of the Eskimo hostess in this little incident became obvious, when additional wayfarers stopped in her hut and she was observed to go through the same procedure, bringing forth the same little dirty bag of tea. In the same way on this second occasion she secured a second box of tea from the newcomers. In justice it should be said, however, that this incident wherein business seems to have been combined with hospitality is largely attributable to the fact that the visitors were white men and consequently were believed to have plenty of everything. The same fact should be taken into account also in interpreting such remarks as that of Nelson's: "During my sledge journeys among them I experienced a hospitable reception at most places, but on a few occasions the people were sullen and disobliging, apparently resenting my presence."[91]

White men are considered at first as belonging to an out-group, of course. Even Eskimos from another village may be so regarded in some degree. Failure to extend hospitality to fellow villagers, as Nelson[92] mentions, in the event of scarcity is very rare. As Murdoch states in his account of the Point Barrow natives,[93] hospitality is a universal virtue.

Among the Copper Eskimos, according to Jenness: "When a meal is in progress every stray visitor who looks in for a moment must be offered something, even if it be only a tiny morsel of meat or fat. The man may be exceedingly unwelcome, but in such cases the visitor himself will usually decline the food."[94] Klutschak writes of the kindness he received in the hands of the Ukusiksillik Eskimos near Cockburn Bay, as follows: "After the snow huts were built, the Ukusiksillik Eskimos summoned us to come into their huts and share a meal. It is certainly an evidence of their hospitality, when one realizes that the fifty pounds of muskoxen flesh, which they set before us, was their complete store of food [for seven families] and so long a time remained until the beginning of fishing would place further provisions in sight. In this communalistic meal, as well as in the mutual touching of the chest with the flat hand, accompanying which act the word *Ilaga* ('let us be friends') was spoken, lay the expression of hospitality of these aborigines."[95]

"Hospitality is a matter of course," writes Kroeber[96] of the Eskimos of Smith Sound, a people living under very severe conditions at the northernmost limit of the inhabited world. South of them on the west coast the spirit is no less pronounced.[97] And of the Angmagsalik Eskimos we read that "the mutual hospitality of the natives knows no bounds, it is not counted as a virtue by them, but as a stern duty."[98]

Since they consider hospitality as a duty, rather than a virtue, the Eskimos accept it without ostentation. It follows that civilized travelers, upon extending hospitality to them and having their generosity accepted as a matter of course, sometimes misjudge the natives, assuming them to be ungrateful. Their disposition in this regard can be appreciated only in the light of their mores defining property rights. It cannot be expected that an Eskimo will show gratitude for what he considers normally to be due him. Knowing this, one has only to be thrown upon the hospitality of the Eskimos to appreciate their simple and whole-hearted spirit.

§6. SUMMARY OF PROPERTY MORES REGARDING FOOD RESOURCES

THE cases cited so far elucidate the property mores regarding food, embracing the resources in their original state in nature and following them to the time when they are consumed. These mores are basic; for they govern the apportioning of the primary essential to life, sustenance. Naturally, they owe their distinctive character to the unusual life-conditions upon which they have developed.

Summarizing, the cases cited above seem to indicate that:

(1) Hunting grounds, or rather the privilege of hunting on them, is a communal right, except in rather rare instances.

(2) The hunter or hunters almost always have the preferential share in the game secured, but part of each catch is generally divided among the community or among those present at the apportioning.

(3) Stored provisions are normally the property of the family or household; but in time of scarcity there is a tendency toward communalism. Hospitality is stressed under all circumstances.

These generalizations signify that in the phases of the property mores so far discussed there is a definite communalistic tendency, accentuated through privation. This tendency has evolved as an expedient adjustment to irregularities in food supply. Food constitutes the most important capital of the Eskimo. In quantity it fluctuates within wide limits, according to seasonal phases and vicissitudes of fortune. The seasonal fluctuations are smoothed out, as already mentioned in another chapter, by the storing of provisions. But even aside from broad seasonal variations, from time to time the individual or the family suffers through misfortunes that do not affect the community as a whole and is hard pressed by privation. Under such circumstances the larger unit, wherein fluctuations are less extreme, serves as a stabilizing factor. Membership in the community confers, in a sense, insurance for the individual and for the family.[99] Through coöperation within the group, the ups and downs which would endanger the members if they were isolated are smoothed out. Frequent minor sacrifices on the part of the individual are substituted for less frequent, but more severe, misfortunes. Thus, communalistic customs are a cultural adjustment harmonizing these people with their environment. Through them the relationship between human needs and the natural resources is adjusted.

It must not be assumed, however, that this aspect of the property mores of the Eskimo manifests a deliberate group policy. The system grew by custom, without much reflection and without much foresight. Even in its present state, there is little implication that it is "just"; scarcely to any degree, if at all, has religion entered this phase of social life to sanction expedient mores.

Furthermore, individual interests rather than group interests are dominant. The group serves as an insurance organization, toward which there is little feeling of righteous responsibility, save in that kinship among its members makes the prosperity of one member the concern of another. Fundamentally, it is not solicitude toward the group as a group that prompts the individual to forfeit his premium; rather it is the conviction that unless he does so he will not derive the benefits when his personal or family interests are at stake.

Communalistic practices are expedient among the Eskimos; but they are not without their handicaps. Individual effort is stifled to some degree. Accumulation of property by the individual is thwarted; even the most industrious and skilful person cannot attain economic prestige through his superior qualities. The social organization enforces upon the individual a sort of slavery.[100] There is a premium on skill and industry, to be sure, as in the preferential rights enjoyed by hunters who secure game. But there is always the duty of sharing.

NOTES

1. Jenness: 1922, 91–92.
2. Rink: 1875, 31.
3. Birket-Smith: 1929, I, 261–262.
4. Birket-Smith: 1929, I, 260.
5. Hawkes: 1916, 25.
6. Crantz: 1767, I, 180; Birket-Smith: 1924, 136, citing Dalager: 1752, 12.
7. Nansen: 1893, 110.
8. Birket-Smith: 1928, 161–162.
9. Thalbitzer: 1914, 524–525.
10. Nelson: 1899, 307.
11. Murdoch: 1892, 267.
12. Murdoch: 1892, 267; footnote: Richardson: 1851, I, 244, 351; see also Richardson: 1852, 323.
13. Birket-Smith: 1928, 161–162.
14. Weyer: Field Notes (Cape Prince of Wales, Alaska); Murdoch: 1892, 428 (Point Barrow); Crantz: 1767, I, 180 (Greenland); Birket-Smith: 1924, 136 (West Greenland), citing Rink; Thalbitzer: 1914, 525 (East Greenland).
15. Jenness: 1922, 89.
16. Weyer: Field Notes.
17. Krause: 1882, 120.
18. Weyer: Field Notes.
19. Hooper: 1881, 60.
20. Murdoch: 1892, 273, 275, 428.
21. Rink: 1875, 29; Cf. Birket-Smith: 1924, 137, citing Glahn: 1784, 278; Birket-Smith: 1924, 138, citing Dalager: 1752, 18.
22. Birket-Smith: 1924, 281–282; also Birket-Smith: 1924, 138, citing Glahn: 1784, 284 (footnote).
23. Stefansson: 1914, 164.
24. Murdoch: 1892, 428.
25. Birket-Smith: 1929, I, 262.
26. Murdoch: 1892, 428 (footnote), citing Gilder: 1881, 190.
27. Boas: 1907, 116.
28. Mathiassen: 1928, I, 41.
29. Hall: 1864, 322.
30. Smith: 1894, 215.
31. Stefansson: 1914, 164.
32. Jenness: 1922, 113–114.
33. Birket-Smith: 1924, 279 ff.
34. Birket-Smith: 1924, 279 ff. (West Greenland); Stefansson: 1914, 164 (Mackenzie region).

35. Jenness: 1922, 90.
36. Birket-Smith: 1929, I, 262.
37. Birket-Smith: 1929, I, 262–263.
38. Ekblaw: 1928.
39. Kroeber: 1899, 270.
40. Steensby: 1910, 291.
41. Thalbitzer: 1914, 525.
42. Glahn: 1771, 291 ff.
43. Crantz: 1767, I, 181 (Greenland).
44. Boas: 1888, 582.
45. Birket-Smith: 1929, I, 262.
46. For general discussion of property marks throughout the world, see Sumner and Keller: 1927, I, 304 ff.
47. Taken from Wissler: 1916, 428.
48. Petroff: 1900, 234.
49. Boas: 1899, 601–602.
50. Boas: 1899, 608.
51. Boas: 1899, 601–602; Nelson: 1899, 147.
52. Petroff: 1900, 235.
53. Boas: 1899, 602 ff.
54. Boas: 1899; Wissler: 1916; Thalbitzer: 1914, 524.
55. Mathiassen: 1927, II, 125.
56. Andree: 1889, 84.
57. Murdoch: 1892, 428.
58. Birket-Smith: 1924, 349.
59. Jenness: 1922, 90.
60. Birket-Smith: 1929, I, 262 (Caribou Eskimos); Birket-Smith: 1924, 137, citing Glahn: 1771, 292 ff. (West Greenland).
61. Thalbitzer: 1914, 525 (East Greenland); Birket-Smith: 1924, 138, citing Fabricius: 1818, 267 (Cape Farewell).
62. Hall: 1864, 330 f.; also 1866, 582.
63. Mathiassen: 1928, I, 62.
64. Birket-Smith: 1929, I, 263.
65. Murdoch: 1892, 428.
66. Birket-Smith: 1924, 28.
67. Holm: 1914, 49; Holm: 1887, 35.
68. Nelson: 1899, 307.
69. Boas: 1907, 150.
70. Nelson: 1899, 307.
71. Weyer: Field Notes.
72. Weyer: Field Notes.
73. Rasmussen: 1927, 312–313.

74. Rasmussen: 1929, I, 179; Boas: 1907, 515 (Ponds Bay or west coast of Hudson Bay?).

75. Hawkes: 1916, 135; Boas: 1907, 161, 489.

76. Rasmussen: 1927, 346.

77. Jenness: 1922, 84–85.

78. Jenness: 1922, 90.

79. Smith: 1902, 128.

80. Birket-Smith: 1929, I, 263.

81. Klutschak: 1881, 233.

82. Boas: 1888, 582.

83. Turner: 1894, 187.

84. Nansen: 1893, 108.

85. Stefansson: 1930, 116.

86. Kroeber: 1899, 301.

87. Birket-Smith: 1924, 138, citing Dalager: 1752, 18.

88. Holm: 1914, 58.

89. Nelson: 1899, 295.

90. Weyer: Field Notes (Cape Prince of Wales, Alaska).

91. Nelson: 1899, 295.

92. Nelson: 1899, 297.

93. Murdoch: 1892, 42.

94. Jenness: 1922, 90.

95. Klutschak: 1881, 69–70. See also Lyon: 1824, 253 (Iglulik Eskimos).

96. Kroeber: 1899, 301.

97. Nansen: 1893, 116 ff. Also Saabye: 1818, 198.

98. Holm: 1914, 137.

99. Sumner and Keller: 1927, I, 326 ff.

100. Sumner and Keller: 1927, I, 328 ff.

CHAPTER XI

TENDENCY TOWARD COMMUNALISM IN PROPERTY (*Continued*)

§1. OWNERSHIP OF DWELLINGS

DWELLINGS are sometimes considered the property of several families, sometimes of a single family or the head of a family.

Among the West Greenlanders the house belongs to the household, but the tent is the property of the family.[1] Among the Copper Eskimos a tent is regarded as the property of the man whose family occupy it.[2] An exceptional case of communalistic ownership of dwellings is noted among the Polar Eskimos. There the stable stone houses accommodating one family at a time are regarded as the property of the group, in accordance with the shifting habits of the people.[3] In the Mackenzie region a dwelling is considered to belong to the occupants as long as they remain living there, but no longer unless enough of their goods are left in it to indicate that they intend to return.[4] In East Greenland an instance investigated by Thalbitzer[5] shows that the component parts of a dwelling which has been occupied successively by perhaps several families may remain the property of individuals who no longer live there. With certain roof-beams belonging to absent persons, and other structural members belonging to the present master of the house, it is impossible to designate whose property the house is.

§2. PRIVATE PROPERTY

FROM the emphasis that has been laid in the foregoing discussion on communalistic aspects of property it must not be supposed that the Eskimos do not recognize well-defined personal claims to possession in many matters.

It is stated with reference to West Greenland, for instance, that individual ownership is respected in clothes, hunting implements, the kayak, and the sledge.[6] In East Greenland the head of the family ". . . makes his hunting and working implements himself, this being the first condition for the right of possession. . . .

"The right of possession is however not absolutely bound to personal manufacture. Thus it is the men who make the knives, scraping-boards, bodkins (of bone) and combs possessed by the women and the women sew the men's as well as their own clothes, prepare all the skins and sew the harness for the sledge-dogs."[7]

Among the Caribou Eskimos the husband has personal claim upon his hunting implements and his kayak, while the wife owns her lamp, cooking pots, etc.[8] The Copper Eskimos consider that "personal property comprises everything that is employed by the individual in his daily life. Most of these articles have been made by their owner, or else acquired by barter. In the case of a man they include his tools and his weapons, the tent and the sled, together with some or all of the dogs that drag the sled. The wife's property similarly comprises her household utensils and implements, the pot and the lamp with the boards and poles that support them (but not the table, it would seem), her knives, her fire-making apparatus, her sewing-kit, her fishing rod, and her walking stick. Some of these things she has received from her kinsfolk before she was married, others she has made herself or obtained by barter, while a few articles may have been made for her by her husband. One or more of the dogs, too, may be her property. . . . Clothing is always the property of the wearer. Articles picked up while traveling, like copper and pyrites, belong to the finder. . . . The amount of property that may be accumulated in these ways by a single individual or family is considerable. . . . How nearly self-sufficing an Eskimo can be is shown by the popular remark that is often quoted:—

" 'The man needs nothing but the heavy skin of the bearded seal for his boot-soles, and the skin of the young rough seal for socks.'

"Formerly everything except the stores of food and blubber could be carried on a single sled."[9]

A discussion of private property would not be complete without mention of the fact that amulets and other religious "powers" are typically owned by individuals.[10] The value placed on such things is often exorbitantly high, due to the implicit confidence which the Eskimo has in their supernatural potency.

A Diomede Islander showed the author a blue bead, for instance, a charm supposed certainly to bring good fortune, which, according to its owner, had been traded at one time for a twenty- or thirty-foot skin boat.[11]

An actual amulet is not necessary for the possession of supernatural power: magic words and phrases[12] convey similar force. These sometimes also are prized as personal property, the possession of them as such depending upon secrecy. Among the Iglulik Eskimos "they can be bought, at a high price, or communicated as a legacy by one who is dying; but no other person save the one who is to use them may hear them, otherwise they would lose their force."[13] The value which these natives sometimes place on these *Erinatiu'tit,* as they call them, is evinced by the fact that one man agreed to provide a woman with food and clothing for the rest of her life in return for being told a few magic phrases. "The Greenlander has *serratit,* ritualistic formulae or charms to be used when in danger or under special circumstances. . . . Their force, among other things, depends upon the price he has paid in order to learn them."[14] Also in the category of intangible property is shaman-istic power. Among the Copper Eskimos this power can be bought, sold, and inherited.[15]

If a Copper Eskimo who has borrowed something "should lose or damage the article he makes no compensation of any kind; he merely expresses his regret at the loss and there the matter ends. Borrowed articles that have become damaged are usually not even mended before being returned to their owners."[16] The same atti-tude is observed among the Eskimos of Bering Strait, where

"if a man borrows from another and fails to return the article, he is not held to account for it. This is done under the general feeling that if a person had enough property to enable him to lend some of it, he has more than he needs. The one who makes the loan under these cir-cumstances does not even feel justified in asking a return of the article, and waits for it to be given back voluntarily."[17]

Similarly, among the Caribou Eskimos, if a man destroys a borrowed article he is not absolutely obliged to replace it; and if one finds a lost object he is not compelled to return it to its owner.[18] And on the west coast of Hudson Bay "a person who has unwittingly damaged the property of another regrets that he has been the cause of loss, par-ticularly if the owner should comfort him by minimizing the importance of the accident. If, on the other hand, the owner should express his an-noyance, the offender will take comfort, 'because it is sufficient for one person to feel annoyed.' "[19]

Also in Greenland the borrower of an article makes no reparation in case of injuring or losing it, unless he has borrowed it without the knowledge of the owner.[20] An isolated instance of this attitude toward personal property would scarcely be worth mentioning, but the fre-quency with which it has been observed lends significance to it.

The large skin boat, the umiak, capable of carrying twenty or even thirty persons, is sometimes owned by one man, sometimes shared by two or more families.

Among the Labrador Eskimos of Hudson Strait, brothers often live

together and own the umiak in common, the remainder of the household possessions, aside from the tent, being considered as individual
property not to be used by all without permission.[21] The importance
to these natives of owning one of these boats is considerable.[22] Men
who are too improvident to own an umiak, a kayak, or a tent "must
live with the others or dwell by themselves and pass a miserable existence, scarcely noticed by their fellows even during a season of abundance."[23]

§3. PROPERTY AND PRESTIGE

NOTABLY in Alaska, private ownership of an umiak carries decided
economic prestige. These craft are necessary in the hunting of
whale and walrus; and the owner of the boat is regarded as its
captain during a hunting campaign, even though there may be
more skilful harpooners among the crew. On the Diomede Islands
and at Cape Prince of Wales, Bering Strait, the captain receives
a double share in the catch in consideration of his owning the boat
that is used. By a sort of rotation of shares it is arranged so that
he will not always get the same parts of the animal.[24]

From Bering Strait northward a hunting captain becomes
known as an *u'-mĭ-a'-lik*, literally "the owner of an umiak."[25] It
is stated that at Point Barrow these men constitute "a regular
wealthy and aristocratic class, who, however, are not yet sufficiently differentiated from the poorer people to refuse to associate on any terms but those of social equality."[26] Sometimes these
wealthy persons seem to have no authority outside of their own
families.[27] But a more extensive influence is implied in Nelson's
statement of the situation among the Malemiut and among the
Eskimos of Bering Strait and the adjacent Arctic coast.[28]

"It is common for the shrewdest man in each village to accumulate
several hundreds of dollars worth of property and become a recognized leader among his fellows. . . . In every trading expedition
these men are usually the owners of the umiaks, and control the others,
even to the extent of doing their trading for them, but the authority
of the leader lasts only so long as he is looked upon as a public bene-
factor. Such men make a point of gathering an abundant supply of
food every summer in order that they may feed the needy and give
numerous festivals during the winter.

"The Eskimos are very jealous of anyone who accumulates much
property, and in consequence these rich men, in order to retain the
public good will, are forced to be very open-handed with the community

and thus create a body of dependents. They make little festivals at which are distributed food and other presents, so that the people appreciate the fact that it is to their interest to encourage a man in his efforts toward leadership, in order that they may be benefited thereby. . . . Whenever a successful trader among them accumulates property and food, and is known to work solely for his own welfare, and is careless of his fellow villagers, he becomes an object of envy and hatred which ends in one of two ways—the villagers compel him to make a feast and distribute his goods, or they may kill him and divide his property among themselves. When the first choice is given him he must give away all he possesses at the enforced festival and must then abandon the idea of accumulating more, under fear of being killed. If he is killed his property is distributed among the people, entirely regardless of the claims of his family, which is left destitute and dependent on the charity of others."

The tendency among these Eskimos of Bering Sea to restrict the individual from amassing an inordinate amount of property in his own hands reminds one of the custom practiced by the Indians of the North Pacific coast of distributing personal possessions on a large scale at a potlatch or festival held to gain prestige. In the region of Norton Sound, the "Inviting-in" Feast, for instance, resembles a potlatch in some ways, although it is primarily a religious ceremonial.[29] The giver saves for years, for he has to feed the entire tribe of visitors during the first day of the festival. He often beggars himself, but he gains great fame among the Eskimos and lays all his guests under lasting obligation to him. Nelson states that a trading festival, which in general plan suggests the "Inviting-in" Feast, is held at irregular intervals almost everywhere by the Eskimos of northern Bering Sea. It is given at the invitation of one man, an important trader, who sends a messenger around to the neighboring villages to get a forecast of the sort of trading desired and to set a date. The festival is characterized by a loosely defined giving and taking rather than by hard and fast bargaining, with the element of prestige through liberality figuring prominently.[30]

Widespread and obligatory exchanging of gifts is also the salient feature of the so-called "Asking Festival," which is held, with variations, from Bering Strait to the mouth of the Yukon.[31]

This formalized trading festival, *ai-yă'-g'ûk*, as the Eskimos call it, takes place, at least at St. Michael, each year after the middle of November, after the fish have left the shallow water along the coast and the people have gathered their winter stores. On the first night the festival consists in a sort of Hallowe'en visiting from family to family, and is known as *tu-tu'-ûk,* or "going around." The hunters and grown boys disguise their faces by blackening them and paint their bodies in stripes and dots. Then they make a round of the houses creating a great hubbub, and everywhere receive gifts of food. While in a house they turn their faces down so they cannot be recognized. Upon returning to the ceremonial room they wash off the paint, give some of the food to the old men, and have a great feast. On the second day a man chosen for the purpose makes a wand, which, like the festival, is called *ai-yă'-g'ûk.*[32] On the evening of this day the women are in their houses and the men are gathered in the ceremonial room. "The man who prepared the wand takes it in his hand and stands with it in the middle of the room; any man in the community has the privilege of telling him the name of any article he wishes, sometimes giving him the name of the woman from whom he desires to obtain it. The wand-bearer then goes to the house of the woman named and stands before her, swinging the hanging globes on the wand, at the same time telling her what he has come for, and then stands waiting. The woman thinks of something which she desires in return and tells the wand-bearer, whereupon he returns to the kashim [ceremonial room] and, swinging the globes before the one who sent him, tells what is desired in return for the object he demanded. In this way everyone in the village asks for something. When the messenger has completed his task, the men go to their houses and bring the objects for which they were asked, and when all have returned to the kashim a dance is performed. The women then come, bringing with them the things asked for, and the exchange is made through the messenger, who must have his face blackened and wear a fishskin coat, or some other poor dress, having a dogskin belt with the tail hanging on behind. If any article is desired which the person does not possess, he is bound by custom to obtain it as soon as possible. . . . The two exchanging presents in this way are considered to hold a certain temporary relationship, termed *i-lo'-g'ûk.* Formerly those once made *i-lo'-g'ûk* exchanged presents each succeeding year at this festival, but that custom is now less strictly observed." Sometimes the requests for gifts are made between persons of the same sex. It was shameful for anyone to decline requests, and a person refusing would be despised by all. Any man had the right to request the messenger to inform the woman he named, if she were unmarried, that he wished to share her bed that night.

There is an interesting connection between the sacred wand used in this *ai-yă'-g'ûk* festival and the gambling device known as the ring-and-pin game, well known to almost all groups of Eskimos and designated even so far distant as Greenland by the nearly identical word *ajagaq*. This common pastime follows everywhere the same principle: a pointed stick or bone staff, from which is suspended some object with perforations in it, is held in the hand, and the player endeavors to swing the object upward and catch it on the point of the stick by a thrusting movement. Porsild states:

"In Greenland the game is often a mere amusement or pastime for tedious hours, as for instance, during a journey, when weather-bound. But *ajagaq* is also used, or at any rate has been used, for playing games in earnest. I have not been able to ascertain the exact rules for these, either because they are really forgotten or because the Eskimo do not like to explain them to me, certain indecencies being also represented in the form of some of the specimens.

"The holes have different values; those which are most difficult to hit count the highest. Small stakes may be played for, e.g., matches, percussion caps, shot, etc. But when the passion for gambling seizes them, larger articles are staked, such as nets, lines, dogs, guns, kayaks, umiaqs, and even house and wife are said to be sometimes gambled away. . . ."[33]

Herein we perhaps see the rudiments of the rather complex *ai-yă'-g'ûk* festival of the Alaskan Eskimos. Whereas in the eastern province the *ajagaq* implement is used variously as a children's toy, an adjunct to the telling of a tale, and a gambling device,[34] in the western section the *ai-yă'-g'ûk* wand possesses cultic significance where it figures in a ceremonial involving the exchange of presents and favors.

A trading custom similar to the *ai-yă'-g'ûk* festival, which is called *pă-tukh'-tûk*, is practiced on the lower Yukon and southward.[35]

"When a person wishes to start one of these he takes some article into the kashim and gives it to the man with whom he wishes to trade, saying at the same time, 'It is *pă-tukh'-tûk*.' The other is bound to receive it and give in return some article of about equal value; the first man then brings something else, and so they alternate until, sometimes, two men will exchange nearly everything they originally possessed; the man who received the first present being bound to continue until the originator wishes to stop."

Among the Eskimos of Bering Sea, various events in family life also prompt the holding of feasts. Thus, at certain times in the lives of children, for instance when a boy's hair is trimmed for the first time, or when he first goes to sea alone in a kayak, or when he dons his first pair of snowshoes, or when the first incision in his lip is made to accommodate the labrets, a feast is given by the parents, if they are able. In cases of great poverty these ceremonies are frequently postponed until the young man himself is able to provide the necessary materials.[36] On Nunivak Island, at the birth of a child its father and mother hold a great feast and give away nearly all they possess.[37] The Kodiak Islanders had the rule that boys and girls could not attend festivals until they had been introduced by their father, who on this occasion cuts his best garment to pieces, giving away the fragments to the populace in memory of the event. In the absence of the father, the mother or other relative could take his place.[38]

It is chiefly the Eskimos of Bering Sea who lay stress on the giving away of property as a means of securing prestige. North and west of here this notion becomes less pronounced. Even at Point Barrow, on the northern tip of Alaska, Murdoch observed that there was apparently no limit to the amount of property that an individual, at least the head of a family, might accumulate; and he remarks that they never heard of any such elaborate donation parties there as are described at Norton Sound and in the Yukon region, where a man saves up his property for years to distribute it among his guests.[39]

It can be taken as a general rule among the Eskimos, however, that the communalistic tendencies already discussed discourage the amassing of property by the individual. The restriction is stronger or weaker depending upon the circumstances and folkways of the tribe, but unconditional toleration is never shown. Evidence from Greenland on this point is found in Rink's statement[40] that undue accumulation of property in the hands of an individual was jealously watched by the rest of the community and an adjustment brought about. Elsewhere among the Eskimos popular disapproval of economic inequality doubtless exists in much the same degree, though mention of it in the literature is rather rare, probably largely because the general poverty renders marked inequality impossible. It is stated concerning the Caribou Eskimos,[41] for instance, that the distribution of values does not give rise to any differentiation in society, because in their original state it has been almost impossible to accumulate capital. Their hunting life seldom yields more than a hand-to-mouth existence, and the constant journeying does not encourage the accumulation of much of the sort of property that deteriorates through lack of use. It is natural that Eskimo society should, in general, discountenance hoarding by the individual, since there is so little to go around.

§4. INHERITANCE

THE rules of the Eskimos governing inheritance of property are ordinarily very simple. Among the Unalit, of Alaska,

"when a man dies some of his implements and other articles are placed by his grave and the remainder are divided among his children and other relatives, the former usually receiving the larger share. The wife generally makes the distribution soon after her husband's death, often on the day of the funeral. In some cases, however, if a man's blood relatives are greedy, they make the division among themselves, leaving very little for the family. To the sons usually pass the hunting implements, and household articles go to the wife and daughters. If there are several sons the eldest get the least, the most valuable things being given to the youngest. Articles of particular value, such as heirlooms (*pai-tûk*), go to the youngest son, as does also the father's rifle, which, however is used by the eldest brother until the younger one is old enough to use it. . . ." The right to use the most productive places for setting seal and salmon nets "is regarded as personal property, and is handed down from father to son. After the death of the father the sons use these places in common until all of the brothers, save one, get new places at unoccupied points."[42]

On the Diomede Islands sometimes a man wills his property before he dies. Otherwise his wife and children receive his goods. Preference seems to be due to the one who did most in taking care of him, and perhaps also slightly to the eldest child.[43] It is stated that on Kodiak Island inheritance passes first to the brother and from him to the son of the deceased.[44] Ray writes that he "knew of a number of cases [at Point Barrow] where there was a general division of a dead man's effects on a basis of first come first served."[45]

Among the Copper Eskimos "a portion of the property is always laid on the owner's grave; the rest is divided among his kinsfolk, the children receiving most or all of it. The distribution is decided after a peaceful discussion, the elder children, as far as I am aware, having no priority of claim. Implements and utensils of value that may be left on the grave are often recovered in after years by one or other of the survivors, when time has effaced the memory of their misfortune."[46] Also among these people a person possessing shamanistic power can bequeath his knowledge of the art and what might be called his good will in the business.[47]

Among the Caribou Eskimos, the property that is not placed at the grave is divided among the family, but not by fixed rules.[48]

In West Greenland when the head of a family dies the widow keeps the lamp, cooking pots, and undressed skins. Inheritance follows the male line, and daughters receive nothing from the father.[49] In East Greenland "the weapons and implements made by the man himself are buried in his grave and are not inherited. The son inherits however his father's tent and umiak; also pots and lamps of soapstone may be inherited."[50] Considering that inheritance also involves obligations to provide for dependents, it is sometimes a burden rather than a gain.[51]

The foregoing cases give evidence of the extreme simplicity of the inheritance mores of the Eskimos. There is not a single instance in the cases at hand of inheritance through the wife's brother, a characteristic feature in the matrilineal order. Private property is generally very restricted in variety; and the differentiation between men's and women's property is so clear that there is seldom doubt as to what shall go to the sons and what to the daughters. Inheritance, on the whole, follows the simplest and most natural rules.

NOTES

1. Birket-Smith: 1924, 138; Nansen: 1893, 109.
2. Jenness: 1922, 88.
3. Steensby: 1910, 286; Kroeber: 1899, 271.
4. Communication from Stefansson.
5. Thalbitzer: 1914, 525 f.
6. Birket-Smith: 1924, 138; Nansen: 1893, 108 ff.
7. Thalbitzer: 1914, 524.
8. Birket-Smith: 1929, I, 263.
9. Jenness: 1922, 88 f.
10. See pp. 316 ff. and 425 ff.
11. Weyer: Field Notes.
12. See pp. 317 ff.
13. Rasmussen: 1929, I, 157.
14. Schultz-Lorentzen: 1928, 241.
15. Jenness: 1922, 92.
16. Jenness: 1922, 89.
17. Nelson: 1899, 294.
18. Birket-Smith: 1929, I, 264.
19. Boas:. 1907, 116.
20. Nansen: 1893, 111, citing Dalager.
21. Turner: 1894, 240.
22. Turner: 1887, 106.
23. Turner: 1894, 240.
24. Weyer: Field Notes.
25. Nelson: 1899, 306. Also Stefansson: 1914, 164.
26. Murdoch: 1892, 429 f.

27. Simpson: 1875, 273.
28. Nelson: 1899, 305.
29. See pp. 343 ff.
30. Nelson: 1899, 361 ff.
31. Nelson: 1899, 359 f.
32. Nelson gives an illustration of one of these curious wands, 1899, Fig. 139, p. 359.
33. Porsild: 1915, 227 f.
34. Thalbitzer: 1914, 663 (n. 7), cf. 655 ff.; Thalbitzer: 1925, 243 f.
35. Nelson: 1899, 309.
36. Petroff: 1900, 214.
37. Rasmussen: 1927, 350.
38. Petroff: 1900, 236.
39. Murdoch: 1892, 429, 374, citing Dall: 1870, 151.
40. Rink: 1875, 29.
41. Birket-Smith: 1929, I, 259.
42. Nelson: 1899, 307.
43. Weyer: Field Notes.
44. Holmberg: 1855, 119; Petroff: 1900, 235.
45. Ray: 1885, 43.
46. Jenness: 1922, 92.
47. Jenness: 1922, 92 f.
48. Birket-Smith: 1929, I, 264.
49. Birket-Smith: 1924, 138.
50. Thalbitzer: 1914, 524.
51. Rink: 1875, 25.

CHAPTER XII

STRUCTURE OF SOCIAL ORGANIZATION

§1. ASSOCIATION UNIT

Groups, or Tribes

THE designation "tribe" is not exactly applicable to the social organization of the Eskimos. The sparsity of their population and their shifting habits in pursuit of game preclude even an approach toward a unified tribal system. Furthermore, the culture of the Eskimos is so uniform over wide areas that it offers no basis for well-defined tribal divisions. Each group speaks a dialect of the same language, and the transition from one to another is so gradual that lines of demarcation cannot be established.[1]

Literal interpretation of the names applied to separate groups by the Eskimos themselves gives an insight into their own conception of population divisions. In these group names the suffix -*miut* is used generally, meaning simply "people" or "people of."

Representative examples are: Harvaqtôrmiut, "the people where rapids abound," a group of the Caribou Eskimos;[2] Arviligjuarmiut, "the people of the land of the great whales," a group related to the Netsilingmiut, or "seal people," of the region of King William Land;[3] Kitdlinermiut (of Queen Maud Gulf, Bathurst Inlet, and southeastern Victoria Island), "the frontier people," with the connotation of "the people farthest north."[4] In Labrador there are a number of designations, such as Kokso•ákmiut, "the big river people"; Nuvu′gmiut, "people at the point" (Cape Wolstenholme); Su•hi′nimiut, "those who dwell at or in the sun," i.e., the dwellers to the east, the Eskimos on the Atlantic coast and on the Ungava side as far south as Leaf River.[5]

Such group names refer, for the most part, to rather small divisions. The Eskimos do not think in terms of large population units. Thus, although the Eskimos of Queen Maud Gulf, Bathurst Inlet, and southeastern Victoria Island are called collectively Kitdlinermiut by the natives to the east, among themselves they comprise four subdivisions, the largest of which includes only 116 persons.[6]

Discussing the matter of divisions among the Copper Eskimos, Jenness writes that

"the term 'tribe,' if we use it at all, should be given a very broad interpretation, for the groups into which these natives divide themselves
have none of the permanence and stability that we are accustomed to
associate with tribes in other parts of the world. It is true that each
group has its local name, a name derived from the district it habitually
frequents in summer; but the individual members are constantly changing from one group to another, not merely temporarily for some special purpose, such as the acquisition of stone lamps and pots or the
obtaining of wood for sleds and tables, but permanently also, whenever
the new district offers greater advantages, especially in the matter of
game."[7]

"The inhabitants of a settlement are all, or nearly all, *nuatkattait,*
connected, that is, by blood or marriage. . . . The *nuatkattait* owe
special duties to one another. They must provide for each other in sickness, take care of the aged and infirm, the widows and the orphans, and
support each other in the blood feud. This gives the community its
solidarity. It has a corporate unity, and is called by a tribal name, the
suffix *miut* added to the name of the region it inhabits, or to a prominent place in that region, such as a lake or river."[8]

Thus the Kogluktomiut is the group that frequents the Kogluktok
or Coppermine River.

The Eskimo conception of population groups is based primarily
upon locality. The groups are generally comparatively small and
far apart. And since there is no rule of exogamy requiring marriage to be between members of separate groups, there is naturally
a strong bond of kinship in each settlement. Societal cohesion is
restricted to narrow spheres. This fact will be better understood in
the light of the extremely rudimentary character of the regulative mores, which will be discussed later.

The Village

THE nature of the hunting activities of any group of Eskimos
largely determines whether they live in congested settlements comprising many families or in small scattered bands of a few families
or even single families. Furthermore, hunting activities change
with the succession of the seasons, as outlined in chapter v. Therefore, the size of the social unit changes even in a single group. A
settlement may be a cluster of snow huts, a group of stable, half-
underground, stone, wood, or bone dwellings, or a tented camp.

Favorable hunting opportunities attract families of Eskimos to
certain sites, where nodes of population are formed. An Eskimo

village of two hundred persons is a fairly large settlement. Indeed, in some areas, notably in the central regions, settlements even of this size do not exist. Rasmussen remarks[9] that a population of eighty-three natives comprising a settlement near the small island of Ahongahungaoq (Dolphin and Union Strait) is considerable for one village in these regions. Typical of the larger villages of Alaska are Point Barrow, with 250 Eskimos,[10] Cape Prince of Wales, with 156,[11] and the village on Little Diomede Island, with 126.[12] Thirty-four villages on Bristol Bay (Alaska) were found to have a total population of 4,340,[13] showing an average of 122. Kotzebue Sound (northwestern Alaska), with its camp of about a thousand Eskimos,[14] is an uncommonly large center of population even in Alaska.

An idea of the size of the Eskimo villages of Labrador may be gained from the following figures giving the populations of some of the settlements in the vicinity of the Moravian Missions:[15]

	1840	1890
Nain	298	263
Hopedale	205	331
Okkak	352	350
Rammah	...	59
Zoar	...	89

In West Greenland the average number of inhabitants per settlement (exclusive of Danes) is 76.5. If, however, only the chief settlements of this region are averaged the figure rises to 275 persons, the maximum being represented by Sukkertoppen (335 individuals) and the minimum by Christianshaab (128 individuals). Of the two hundred and seven dwelling places which were to be found on the west coast and in Angmagsalik District in 1921, more than half had under fifty inhabitants, and nearly a fourth only 25.[16] Three settlements are tabulated as follows according to their populations in 1884–85:[17]

Sermilik	132
Angmagsalik	225
Sermiligak	14

The Household

THE foregoing statistics indicate that the Eskimo village or camp generally numbers only a few hundred persons or less. Furthermore, the appearance of a settlement is generally dwarfed due to the fact that the natives customarily live in very crowded quarters. The average number of occupants to each dwelling in the region of Norton Sound[18] is twelve, in the region of the Yukon Delta eighteen, and around the Kuskokwim Delta twenty. The average in these three sections combined is seventeen. The emphasis of these figures is strong in view of the fact that the dwellings referred to are generally quite small and contain only one room for sleeping, cooking, and eating. On Diomede Island the author found four or five families comprising sixteen adults and children living in a single dwelling-room about twelve by eighteen feet in size.[19] Nelson mentions an instance of twenty-five persons sleeping in a room only fifteen by twenty feet,[20] and another of sixteen persons sleeping in a small hut ten by twelve feet, where the air was so foul that a candle, upon being lighted, would flare up and immediately become extinguished as though dipped in water! Though from one to three families may occupy the platforms in a single room of the Bering Strait house, each will be quite separate and independent in all of its domestic affairs.[21] The usual arrangement at Point Barrow is for two families to occupy one house.[22]

Copper Eskimo families will sometimes share the same snow hut, or build huts so that they are connected. Convenience is the usual motive, and the association of two particular families usually lasts only until the settlement is moved.[23] In summer each family has its own tent, but even so, additional members, visitors, sometimes share their shelter.[24]

There is no uniformity among the Caribou Eskimos as to the number of families living together. Sometimes two families live in one snow hut, sometimes more; generally they are related.[25] In the Ungava District "several families may dwell under the same shelter. . . ."[26]

The little pear-shaped stone huts of the Polar Eskimos (Smith Sound), by exception, are regularly built to house only one family.[27] The opposite extreme is observed on the east coast of Greenland, where the people live in large communal winter houses, about sixteen feet in width and twenty-six feet or more in length.[28] One instance in that section is mentioned of fifty-eight inmates to one dwelling.[29] Twenty-two is the average number of persons living in each of thirty-two dwellings comprising the East Greenland settlements in 1923.[30] On the west coast, on the other hand, the average to the house is between six and nine,[31] though in former times large communal winter houses were also used here, at least in the south.

To summarize, the size of the Eskimo household varies widely, but in its typical form consists of two or more families.

Seasonal Changes in the Size of the Association Unit

As intimated earlier in this chapter, the size of the social unit varies sometimes in response to seasonal phases which necessitate different modes of life. According as the game is scattered or localized, the Eskimos disperse or congregate. Naturally, some groups undergo seasonal changes in the size of the social unit more than others.

Almost the entire tribe of Smith Sound Eskimos (the Polar Eskimos), numbering about 271, congregate at one center (Pituarvik) for the period from the middle of February, when the sun reappears, until late May, when the ice begins to break away from the outlying capes and islands. There they live in snow huts and devote themselves to hunting walrus, which are especially plentiful.[32]

The East Greenlanders are less scattered in summer than in winter. Their winter houses lie apart from one another; whereas their summer settlements group themselves into three nuclei.[33]

Among the Copper Eskimos in the dead of winter tribe combines with tribe to wrest a precarious living from the frozen sea by united effort.[34] During the warmer season, on the other hand, they scatter in small bands;[35] so that in midsummer, when fish alone is the reliable food, the tribe no longer exists; the family is the unit.[36] The habitations of the Caribou Eskimos of the Barren Grounds of Canada are most concentrated in autumn, when their camps lie near the crossing places of the caribou, and in winter, when they center chiefly near the lakes for fishing.[37] When they are most widely dispersed the family becomes the social unit, but never, of course, the individual.[38]

It is stated that the Eskimos of Smith Sound ". . . usually travel in groups of three or four families. Greater concentration of numbers would be dangerous on account of the scarcity of food."[39] And the Point Barrow Eskimos during the winter caribou hunting at the rivers "are scattered in small camps of four or five families, about a day's journey apart."[40] The Eskimos who winter inland north of Nome at the village of Igloo disperse upon the advent of summer. Along the Tuksuk River they may be seen in a series of fishing camps, each composed of one or a few families.[41]

§2. RIGHTS AND AUTHORITY

Classes

THE social organization of the Eskimos is so simple, as has been seen, that there are no strictly defined tribal groups. Likewise, class distinctions are almost nonexistent. Among the Caribou Eskimos, for instance,

"there are no chiefs, nobility nor slaves. No clan system and no secret society lay bonds upon the initiative of the individual, . . .[42] They know no government. Here, for once, is a society which is entirely built upon that voluntary agreement of which Kropotkin dreamt. Subject to personal liability towards the inherited laws everyone enjoys full individual freedom."[43]

It is stated that among the Central Eskimos sometimes men who may almost be considered servants are adopted—particularly bachelors without any relatives, cripples who are not able to provide for themselves, or men who have lost their sledges and dogs.[44] Similarly, class distinction attending poverty is implied in a statement concerning the Eskimos of Hudson Strait. There men who have been too improvident to provide themselves with the essential property "must live with the others or dwell by themselves and pass a miserable existence, scarcely being noticed by their fellows even during a season of abundance."[45] Nelson mentions that in the region of Bering Strait female captives taken in wars, unlike other captives, were commonly spared from death and taken as slaves.[46]

Actual slavery, however, is observed only among the southernmost Eskimos of Alaska. Thus, the natives of Kodiak Island, who are certainly not typical Eskimos in many respects,

"held slaves, but their number was small, and the wealth of individuals did not depend upon slaves entirely, as among the Thlinkets. The sacrifice of slaves was unknown; they were looked upon only as laborers or servants, and their lot was a happier one than that of their Thlinket neighbors. . . . The principal mode of obtaining slaves was by barter with other tribes; but no slaves have existed in the Kodiak group for at least a generation."[47]

These people, the Kaniags, sometimes tortured prisoners of war, sometimes took them as slaves.[48]

Within the *kaz'-gee*, of the Bering Strait Eskimos, which is their ceremonial chamber and meeting-room, certain social distinctions were observed.

"The sleeping place, near the oil lamp which burns at the back of the room opposite the summer entrance, is the place of honor, where the wise old men sit with the shamans and best hunters. The place near the entrance on the front side of the room is allotted to worthless men who are poor and contribute nothing to the general welfare of the community, also to orphan boys and friendless persons. . . . All guests whom it is desired to honor are given seats on the side of the kashim [*kaz'-gee*] where the old men of the village sit. If that side of the kashim chances to be fully occupied, some of the men make room for their guests."[49]

Chieftainship

THE Eskimo is unacquainted with the office of chieftain in its ordinary sense. Leadership exists only in a very elementary and restricted form.

The Diomede Islanders assert that they have never had a headman with authority which extended throughout their little village.[50] The most influential persons among this clan are the *angutkut* (medicine men), skilful or venerable hunters, and successful traders who have managed to gain some measure of economic prestige. Their authority does not, however, unite the people into a unified body. Whatever unity there is, is the result rather of coöperative mores, the enforcement of which does not require an executive head. The Alaskan Eskimos, so far as Nelson observed, "have no recognized chiefs except such as gain certain influence over their fellow-villagers through superior shrewdness, wisdom, age, wealth, or shamanism. The old men are listened to with respect, and there are usually one or more in each village who by their extended acquaintance with the traditions, customs and rites connected with the festivals, as well as being possessed of an unusual degree of common sense, are deferred to and act as chief advisors of the community.

"On the lower Yukon and beyond to Kuskokwim river such leaders are termed näs-kuk, meaning literally 'the head.' Among the Unalit Eskimos they are called äñ-ai'-yu-kŏk, 'the one to which all listen.'

"These terms are also applied to men who gain leadership by means of their greater shrewdness, whereby they become possessed of more property than their fellows, and by a judicious distribution of food and their superior force of character obtain a higher standing and a certain following among the people.

"The man who has accumulated much property, but is without

ability to guide his fellows, is referred to merely as a rich man or tu'-gu.

"All Eskimo villages have a headman, whose influence is obtained through the general belief of his fellow-villagers in his superior ability and good judgment. These men possess no fixed authority, but are respected, and their directions as to the movements and occupations of the villagers are generally heeded. . . . Sometimes they obtain a stronger influence over the people by combining the offices of shaman with those of headman."[51]

On the Arctic coast of Alaska the captain of a whaleboat has unrestricted authority over his crew and even holds the position of a chieftain in his own community.[52] His title, *umialik*, literally means "owner of a boat," but its connotation is wider. The captain of an umiak often strengthens his prestige by accumulating wealth, within limits imposed by public opinion.[53]

"It was not uncommon among the Eskimos, particularly about the shores of Bering Strait and northward, for some man of great courage and superior ability to gather about him a certain following and then rule the people through fear; such men usually confirmed their power by killing anyone who opposed them. In order to keep their followers in a friendly mood, they made particular effort to supply them with an abundance of food in time of scarcity, or to give them presents of clothing at festivals; they also try to secure the good will of white men whenever they think it to their interests to do so."[54]

"Sometimes a head man may be succeeded by his son when the latter has the necessary qualities."[55]

"During the time that war was carried on between the tribes the best warrior planned the attack, and was known among the Unalik as mû-gokh'-ch-tă. He, however, had no fixed authority, as each one fought independently of the others, but all combined in the general onslaught."[56] Neither the Magemiut nor the Yukon men "had any recognized chief, but each fought as he pleased, with the exception that some of the older men had general supervision and control of the expedition."[57]

Among the Alaskan Eskimos the office of chieftain is possibly developed to a higher degree than in any other group. This is not strange among the Eskimos of Bering Strait and the adjacent coast of Alaska, where the natives are outstanding for their war-like tendencies.

Elsewhere among the Eskimos, even in other parts of Alaska, there is less centralization of authority.

Even at Point Barrow, for instance, where an *umialik* commands some recognition, the "people have no established form of government nor any chiefs in the ordinary sense of the word, but appear to be ruled by a strong public opinion, combined with a certain amount of respect for the opinions of the elder people, both men and women. . . ."[58] Likewise, the natives at the headwaters of the Noatak River "have no tribal organization; there is usually one man in a village who is known as the oomélik, or chief, but he has none of the authority usually implied by the name, and practically has no power over the others. Shamanism, or the rule of superstition, seems to be the only governing spirit among them."[59] The Eskimos in the region of the Yukon Delta "have no chiefs in the strict sense of the term, although there are individuals among them who exercise more or less influence through accumulated wealth or otherwise without necessarily being endowed with the spiritual powers which the shamans are supposed to possess."[60]

Petroff, who seems to have been the first white man to visit the Togiagamiut and the Kassianmiut groups in the region of Bristol Bay, Alaska, reports that there is scarcely any social cohesion beyond the family. He writes: "Among the Eskimo tribes heretofore described the traveler generally finds someone in each village who acts as spokesman, though not possessing any real authority, but the Togiagamutes seem to live in the most perfect state of independence of each other."[61]

The Eskimos of the Mackenzie Delta believe through tradition that long ago there were chiefs who had great powers.[62] The natives of Coronation Gulf and Victoria Island present no exception to the striking absence of chiefs from Eskimo society. "A man acquires influence by his force of character, his energy and success in hunting, or his skill in magic. As long as these last him age but increases his influence, but when they fail his prestige and authority vanish. Although there were at least half a dozen shamans in Dolphin and Union strait, and Ikpakhuak himself professed no shamanistic powers, yet his personal dignity, his sagacity, and his prowess as a hunter won him the most prominent place among the natives of this region. He had no delegated powers, no established authority, but his counsels always carried the greatest weight and his advice was constantly sought in all matters of importance. . . . The Eskimo is intolerant of anything like restraint. Every man in his eyes has the same rights and the same privileges as every other man in the community. One may be a better hunter, or a more skilful dancer, or have greater control over the spiritual world, but this does not make him more than one member of a group in which all are free and theoretically equal."[63] Rasmussen writes with reference to the natives of Dolphin and Union Strait, that "the Eskimos of these regions, like those farther east, have no regular chiefs, but each settlement has one man who acts as a sort of general advisor and leader in common undertakings."[64]

Among the Caribou Eskimos "an elderly, skilful hunter with great experience always enjoys great esteem as *primus inter pares*. When a number of families are gathered in a camp, there is often an elderly *pater familias* who is tacitly looked upon as [ihumatAk], i.e.: he who thinks, implying: for the others. His advice is often taken, but voluntarily; he has no legal authority at all and cannot be called a chief in the ordinary sense. Ordinarily, only the shamans have stood out from among the mass, but, be it noticed, without actually enjoying any great respect for that reason. A clever shaman may possess great power because he is clever and feared, not actually because he is a shaman. And a poor shaman never attains the same level as regards respect as an ordinary skilful hunter."[65]

Essentially the same condition is observed among the Iglulik Eskimos: "Within each settlement, which as a rule comprises a few families, often connected by kinship, there is as a rule an older man who enjoys the respect of the others and who decides when a move is to be made to another hunting centre, when a hunt is to be started, how the spoils are to be divided, when the dogs are to be fed, etc. He is called isumaitoq, 'he who thinks.' It is not always the oldest man, but as a rule an elderly man who is a clever hunter or, as head of a large family, exercises great authority. He cannot be called a chief; there is no obligation to follow his counsel; but they do so in most cases, partly because they rely upon his experience, partly because it pays to be on good terms with this man."[66] "It would seem that among the Aivilik a man may attain considerable influence, more so than is the case nowadays in Cumberland Sound. Captain Comer mentions one man, by the name of *Coo-nic Char-ley* (Kunuk ?, Kunuksialuk ?), who was a leader of this tribe. . . . One of his sons, called Albert by the whalers, was also considered a leader of the tribe. When he [Albert] died, his nephew, on account of his ability, became his successor, as a leader of the tribe." This latter person, at his birth, "was blessed by his grandfather with much ceremony, that he might become a great hunter and whaleman. All skins taken by him should be prepared only by the very best workers. His guardian spirit would become angry at the woman who had done work on his skins carelessly, and cause her death."[67] At the same time we learn that each tribe in Baffin Island has its leader, especially during their wanderings.[68] Hall writes that ". . . in every community, with them as with all the rest of the world, there is some one who, in consideration of his age, shrewdness, or personal prowess is looked up to, and whose opinions are received with more than usual deference; but he has no authority whatever, and an Innuit is subject to no man's control." "Though in olden times there were chiefs among the

Innuits, there are none now. There is absolutely no political organization among them."[69]

It is written that among the Koksoagmiut, of northern Labrador, "there is no such person as a chief; yet there is a recognized leader who is influenced by another, and this last is the conjurer or medicine man. These two persons determine among themselves what shall be done."[70] The natives of the east coast of Hudson Bay "have no chief, and the authority acknowledged by the community is that of the elders and wealthier individuals, aided at all times, by the decrees of the shaman; the authority of the latter is, however, often set at naught."[71]

The Labrador Eskimos sometimes have leaders called *angajorkak,* whose authority seems to be confined to localities, each bay or fiord having one of its own. These men must always be first-rate hunters. When one dies, his son has the first claim to be his successor if he possesses the required qualities. If not, another is appointed who probably has already been elected during the father's life.[72] Hawkes, writing on the Labrador Eskimos, states that "the Eskimos have never had any 'chiefs' in the Indian sense of the word. They have had leaders, great hunters or enterprising shamans, who have been accorded position by general appreciation of their worth. But the office has never carried any particular authority with it."[73] Again we read that "the recognized authorities among all the Innuit are the older or wealthier men of the community . . .";[74] and that the Tahagmiut, of Labrador, "have no chiefs; the decisions and desires of the elders and wealthier men are carried out by the remainder of the people."[75]

The Polar Eskimos, upon first meeting white men, did not understand the word *nullikab,*[76] which, according to Ross, signifies among the Eskimos to the south of them a person in authority. They responded to the word *pisarsuak,* however, used as a title of a chief, and said that his name was *Tulloowak.*[77] "They all acknowledged Tuloowah as their king, represented him as a strong man, as very good, and very much beloved; the name of his residence was Petowack, which they described to be near a large island, which could be no other than Wolstenholme island. He had a large house built of stone, which they described to be nearly as large as the ship: that there were many houses near it, and that the mass of the natives lived there; that they paid him a portion of all they caught or found, and returned to this place whenever the sun went away, with the fruits of their labours."[78] Kane writes[79] that among the Smith Sound Eskimos "the angekok of the tribe . . . directs the policy and movements of the little state, and though not the titular chief, is really the power behind the throne." The tenor of the latter two quotations, it scarcely needs be remarked, is dissonant with what is now known of the social organization of the Eskimos and must be considered as being colored by preconceived notions based on the systems of more advanced peoples. According to Kroeber,[80] the Smith Sound Eskimos "apply the term 'naligaq' to leaders of Arctic expeditions; but if used in reference to any of themselves, it means merely a good hunter. Nalegak is the most skilful hunter, but he has no authority, states Hayes."

In the Egedesminde District, West Greenland, the old men in a household were respected and consulted, but a chief with hereditary powers was unknown.[81] In East Greenland the angakok is not the headman. He plays no important part in the social life. Only the skilful hunters are respected;[82] ". . . each larger household comprising several families has a chief, as conscientiously venerated and obeyed as heads of communities or magistrates elsewhere."[83] The head of the household gives orders when to move into summer habitations, etc.; ". . . the position as chief of the house has no relation to that of 'angakok,' though both dignities may occasionally be united."[84]

NOTES

1. See Mauss and Beuchat: 1904–5, 50 ff.
2. Birket-Smith: 1929, I, 60–61.
3. Rasmussen: 1927, 167.
4. Rasmussen: 1927, 244–245.
5. Hawkes: 1916, 22–23.
6. Rasmussen: 1927, 244–245.
7. Jenness: 1922, 32.
8. Jenness: 1922, 86.
9. Rasmussen: 1927, 283.
10. Rasmussen: 1927, 304–305.
11. Weyer: Field Notes.
12. Weyer: Field Notes.
13. Jackson: 1886, 13. For tables giving the Eskimo population of Alaska itemized according to villages, the reader is referred to Petroff: 1884.
14. Rasmussen: 1927, 335. It is estimated that at one time, however, the village at Point Hope (Alaska) and its immediate neighborhood had a population of something like two thousand, or as many inhabitants as are now found throughout the whole of the Northwest Passage between the Magnetic Pole and Herschel Island. Likewise, evidence from various other regions seems to suggest that formerly the Eskimo population was greater than it is now; but early records are inaccurate and in some cases conflicting. The opposite trend is observed on the west coast of Greenland, where it appears that the population has more than doubled in the course of the last century. (Birket-Smith: 1928, 20.)
15. Hawkes: 1916, 19 ff.
16. Birket-Smith: 1928, 64.
17. Holm: 1914, 26.
18. Averages obtained from Zagoskin's data contained in Petroff's report, 1884, 37.
19. Weyer: Field Notes.
20. Nelson: 1899, 298.
21. Nelson: 1899, 288.
22. Murdoch: 1892, 75.
23. Jenness: 1922, 65 ff.
24. Jenness: 1922, 81.
25. Birket-Smith: 1929, I, 76.
26. Turner: 1887, 106.
27. Rasmussen: 1921, 19; Steensby: 1910, 311 ff.; also König: 1927, 699.
28. Holm: 1914, 35; Birket-Smith: 1928, 71.
29. Rink: 1887, 25; see also Holm: 1914, 57; Hansen: 1914a, 185; Thalbitzer: 1914, 356 f.
30. Birket-Smith: 1928, 79.
31. Birket-Smith: 1928, 78.
32. Ekblaw: 1928; Kroeber: 1899, 268–269.
33. Thalbitzer: 1914, 346.

34. Jenness: 1928, 136–137.

35. Jenness: 1928, 136–137; Jenness: 1922, 143–144.

36. Jenness: 1928, 136–137.

37. Birket-Smith: 1929, I, 71.

38. Birket-Smith: 1929, I, 98.

39. Sumner, Keller, and Davie: 1927, IV, 17–18.

40. Murdoch: 1892, 267.

41. Weyer: Field Notes.

42. Birket-Smith: 1929, I, 259.

43. Birket-Smith: 1929, I, 260.

44. Boas: 1888, 581.

45. Turner: 1894, 240.

46. Nelson: 1899, 327.

47. Petroff: 1900, 228.

48. Petroff: 1900, 237.

49. Nelson: 1899, 286–287. See also Hawkes: 1913, 4 f.

50. Weyer: Field Notes.

51. Nelson: 1899, 304–305.

52. Rasmussen: 1927, 312; also Stefansson: 1914, 164.

53. The question of economic prestige is further discussed on pp. 196–200.

54. Nelson: 1899, 303.

55. Nelson: 1899, 304.

56. Nelson: 1899, 306.

57. Nelson: 1899, 329.

58. Murdoch: 1892, 427.

59. McLenegan, in Healy: 1887, 75.

60. Schwatka, in Ray: 1900, 356.

61. Petroff: 1900, 224.

62. Stefansson: 1914, 168.

63. Jenness: 1922, 93–94.

64. Rasmussen: 1927, 283.

65. Birket-Smith: 1929, I, 259.

66. Mathiassen: 1928, I, 209.

67. Boas: 1907, 115.

68. Rink: 1887, 27.

69. Hall: 1864, 316.

70. Turner: 1894, 193.

71. Turner: 1887, 101.

72. Rink: 1887, 27.

73. Hawkes: 1916, 110.

74. Turner: 1887, 105.

75. Turner: 1887, 102.

76. Thalbitzer, in a communication to the author, states, "The form is no doubt misunderstood instead of 'nallegal' or rather 'nâlagkap.'"

77. Ross: 1819, 121.

78. Ross: 1819, 134.

79. Kane: 1856, II, 118.

80. Kroeber: 1899, 300; citing Hayes: 1867, 256.

81. Birket-Smith: 1924, 153.

82. Holm: 1914, 58.

83. Rink: 1887, 24.

84. Rink: 1887, 26.

CHAPTER XIII

FOLKWAYS OF LAW AND ORDER

§1. CODE RESTRICTED CHIEFLY TO IN–GROUP

A CODE of justice embraces all the customs and rules that define the rights and duties of the individual and maintain law and order in the community. The discussion of this aspect of the regulative mores is the purpose of the present chapter. Let it be understood at the outset that the scope of the mores pertaining to justice is limited to the in-group, often in a narrow sense. Relations between in-group and out-group, on the other hand, have already been discussed under the subject of the societal environment. That discussion treated of the relations between the Eskimos and the Indians and also between contiguous groups of Eskimos. Now, however, we are concerned with relations *within the association unit*. In a sense this is a phase of the same study, the adjustment of people to one of their life-conditions, namely, their environment of fellow creatures. But it is a very different phase of the study; for people react quite differently to their community associates or to their own kinsmen than to outsiders, especially those of a different race. That there is a sharp distinction in attitude will be recalled by Nelson's[1] statement concerning the region of Bering Strait:

"Stealing from people of the same village or tribe is regarded as wrong. . . . To steal from a stranger or from people of another tribe is not considered wrong so long as it does not bring trouble on the community. . . . The only feeling of conscience or moral duty that I noted among the Eskimo seemed to be an instinctive desire to do that which was most conducive to the general good of the community, as looked at from their point of view."

"In general the Eskimos are extremely honest among themselves; but all consider it not only allowable, but even very praiseworthy to rob strangers. A clever robber of foreigners is an object of admiration, provided he does not let himself be caught."[2] Jenness[3] writes with reference to the Copper Eskimos: "The absolute lack of privacy in their lives, however, makes concealment very difficult, and partly for this reason, and partly because the average native is naturally inclined to be honest and upright, theft is comparatively rare among themselves. Their morality being based on purely social sanctions that hardly operate outside the community, the same restraint is not always observed towards strangers, as we found to our cost. Not only did they steal many articles from our station, but they even robbed one of our caches along the coast, a far more serious offense in the Arctic."

The first people that the Polar Eskimos had ever seen, either Eskimo or civilized, were John Ross and his men. No sooner had they met the white men than they started trying to steal various articles from them.[4]

To be sure, travelers among the Eskimos have often extolled their fairness even in dealing with white men. Nevertheless, the attitude of an Eskimo toward other men differs according to whether he feels that they belong to his in-group or not. In his dealings with people who seem strange to him, white men, for instance, or Indians, his sense of justice is weakest. In his relations with other Eskimos, particularly if they are from a tribe known to him, he generally displays more openness, fairness, and willingness to coöperate. But only between members of the same village or camp do the mores governing justice attain their full development. In a study of these mores, therefore, their scope must generally be considered to be limited by the in-group in a rather narrow sense.

§2. THEFT

The Caribou Eskimo regards theft rather lightly, murder and witchcraft being the only serious crimes.[5] Among the Copper Eskimos "until recently, when firearms and steel knives and other articles of civilization were introduced, there was little inducement to steal, for practically all their possessions could be made or acquired without much labour."[6] Among the Utkuhikhalingmiut (Backs River) when Rasmussen announced that he would leave his property unguarded in his tent taking it for granted that it would be safe, one of the elders answered proudly: "Among our people, it is only dogs that steal."[7] Murdoch's observation at Point Barrow seems to indicate less security there regarding property. "Before starting for the deer hunt the hunters generally take the movable property which they do not mean to carry with them out of the house and bury it in the snow for safe keeping, apparently thinking that while a dishonest person might help himself to small articles left around the house, he could hardly go to work and dig up a cache without attracting the attention of neighbors."[8] In Greenland, Eskimos let their goods and chattels "lie open to everyone without fear of anyone stealing or taking away the least part of them. . . . This misdemeanour is so repulsive to them that if a girl is found stealing, she loses all chance of making a good marriage."[9]

§3. ENFORCEMENT OF JUSTICE BY THE INDIVIDUAL

No pronounced group action operates in the execution of justice in the case of many crimes, particularly minor ones. Among the Copper Eskimos, for instance, recourse to community enforcement of justice

"can rarely be taken, because there is no common council wherein the will of the people can find voice, no spokesman to give it public expression, and no leader to translate it into action. The shamans, who might be expected under certain circumstances to take the initiative, are rivals of one another. Moreover, they are frequently men and women of little credit or standing even among their own people; they themselves are the victims of injustice quite as often as the rest. For minor offenses, therefore, such as theft and abduction, there is no remedy unless the victim takes the matter into his own hands and exacts compensation or vengeance. . . . Feuds may be settled occasionally by single combat."[10]

Jenness states that although he has no record among the Copper Eskimos of the regular stand-up fight such as occurs among the Netsilik Eskimos farther east, they are acquainted with the practice. One dispute between two men was settled by their pelting each other with dog excreta. "As a rule, however, the quarrel is either dropped or settled in a more deadly manner."

The boxing duel is practiced among various central groups. Thus, among the Aivilingmiut, the Netsilingmiut, and the Iglulingmiut, disputes between two persons are settled by fisticuffs, in which each party in turn delivers a blow against the other. The one who holds out the longer is the winner. These contests were held both with the aim of settling grudges and simply to demonstrate control in spite of pain.[11] The Caribou Eskimos never fight duels nowadays except, perhaps, over women.[12] Among the Netsilingmiut when a wife yields to the advances of a man other than her husband, it is the woman, as a rule, who will be punished; but occasionally the corespondent will be called to account. In the latter event the matter is settled by a boxing bout between the two men.[13] Similarly, it is said in the region of Bering Strait that in olden times when the husband and an interloper quarreled about a woman they were disarmed by the neighbors, whereupon they settled the trouble with their fists or by wrestling, the victor in the struggle taking the woman.[14] And among the Tahagmiut of northwestern Labrador incontinence on the part of wives "is certain to be more or less severely punished. The male offender, if notoriously persistent in his efforts to obtain forbidden favors, is usually killed by the injured lover."[15]

§4. MURDER AND BLOOD VENGEANCE

MURDER is fairly common among the Eskimos. Life has not the sacredness which is generally attributed to it among highly civilized peoples. One circumstance which must influence the attitude toward human life is apparent: the Eskimo passes his life killing animals; the flowing of blood is commonplace to him, the death throes of the wounded animal merely the promise of a square meal. Is it not natural then that his sensibilities regarding human life should be somewhat blunted? In Rasmussen's words, ". . . life in these inhospitable regions, exposed to the cruelest conditions and ever on the verge of extermination is not conducive to excessive gentleness."[16]

The foregoing statement was in comment on an imposing list of atrocious crimes recorded by Rasmussen in a single settlement called Kunajuk, on the Ellice River, which enters Queen Maud Gulf. It is illuminating to quote regarding his findings there: ". . . I questioned each of the men as to whether they had taken part in or been subject to acts of violence. The results are set out as follows: and it should be noted that in nearly every case the victims were of the same tribe; the motive was invariably some quarrel about a woman.

"Angulalik had taken part in a murderous affray but had not himself killed anyone.

"Uakauq had killed Kutdlaq in revenge for the latter's killing of Qaitsaq.

"Angnernaq had two wives. One had been stolen away from him, but he had not yet taken vengeance.

"Portoq had carried off the wife of a man who had not yet taken vengeance.

"Kivggaluk had lost his father and brother—both murdered.

"Ingoreq had attempted to murder two men, but failed.

"Erfana had killed Kununassuaq, and taken part in the killing of Kutdlaq.

"Kingmerut had killed Maggararaq and had also taken part in a murderous attack upon another man.

"Erqulik stated that two attempts had been made to carry off his wife, both without success.

"Pangnaq, a boy of twelve, had shot his father for ill-treating his mother.

"Maneraitsiaq had shot a man in a duel (with bow and arrow) but had not killed him.

"Tumaujoq had killed Ailanaluk in revenge for the murder of Mahik."[17]

Writing of conditions among the Netsilingmiut the same author states: "Natural desire and economic necessity, combined with the fact that there are not enough women to go round, give rise inevitably to keen competition among the men, as well as to quarrels, not infrequently with a fatal termination."[18]

Regarding the Copper Eskimos it is similarly stated that "murder . . . with its corollary, the blood-feud, has always been frequent, and nothing but external influence can prevent it."[19] "In the winter of 1914–15 a Kanghiryuak woman taunted another woman of the same tribe with childlessness, and the latter stabbed her in the stomach with a knife and killed her. In the following year a man of the same people was sitting in his hut sharpening a knife that he had just made, when a neighbor entered and began to jeer at him, saying that he did not know how to make a knife. The owner quietly continued to sharpen his weapon until its edge was keen enough, then he drove it into the jester's stomach with the remark, 'Now see if I can't make a knife.' "[20]

The Malemiut of Alaska ". . . had the reputation of being extremely treacherous among themselves, not hesitating to kill one another, even of their own tribe, when opportunity offered while hunting in the mountains—a gun or a few skins being sufficient incentive. As a consequence, hunters among this tribe would not go into the mountains with each other, unless they chanced to be relatives or had become companions by a sort of formal adoption.

"One intelligent Malemute, who was a fine hunter told me it was very hard work to hunt reindeer in the mountains, as a man could only sleep a little, having to watch that other men did not surprise and kill him."[21]

Murder is reported to have been rare among the Iglulik Eskimos[22] and the Baffin Islanders;[23] and it seems to have been uncommon in Greenland,[24] although occurring more frequently on the east coast than the west.[25]

The life of the Eskimo is not safeguarded by the concept of a divine right to life; nor is he governed by any heaven-sent decree that he shall not kill. His conduct in this regard is controlled chiefly by a simple and practical code: *If he kills another person he will probably himself be killed by a relative of his victim.* Among all Eskimos this duty of blood vengeance is strong.[26]

The tribe or community is not consulted in the enforcement of blood vengeance; it devolves upon the family or the kin-group. In the Bering Sea region the duty of avenging murder fell upon the nearest relative of the murdered person. There

". . . it is not an uncommon thing to find men who dare not visit certain villages because of a blood feud existing, owing to their having killed someone whose near relatives live in the place. . . . The duty of blood revenge belongs to the nearest male relative, so that if the son is an infant, and too young to avenge his father at the time, it rests with him to seek revenge as soon as he attains puberty. . . . If a man has no son, then his brother, father, uncle, or whosoever is nearest of kin must avenge him."[27]

The Caribou Eskimos likewise regard blood vengeance as a sacred duty, and money would not be taken as a substitute for it. A man who has taken blood vengeance is not himself exposed to vengeance in turn, at least in theory.[28] Lyon writes that among the Iglulik Eskimos, to the contrary, blood revenge seemed to be unknown and that he never heard of an instance ". . . of any one man having ever killed another, or of a son imbibing from his father any dislike towards particular persons. At the distant northern settlements, however, of which we know nothing but by report, murders are said to be frequently committed."[29] "If a murder is committed," states Hall concerning southeastern Baffin Island,[30] "it appears, from what the Innuit say, that the nearest relative or most intimate friend of the slain has a right to kill the murderer."

The Koksoagmiut, of northern Labrador, take a murderer by surprise and kill him, usually by stoning. They consider that "in a case of a premeditated murder, it is the duty of the next of kin to avenge the deed, though years may pass, while the murderer pursues his usual occupations undisturbed, before an opportunity occurs to the relative for taking him by surprise."[31] Similarly, the Tahagmiut, of Labrador, "will wait a long time for their revenge, which is certain to result in the death of the offender"; and the next of kin may not be related through blood to the murdered person.[32] Females of this group are exempt from participation in feuds, although they may be the inciting cause and may prompt the taking of revenge.

In none of three murders among the Copper Eskimos mentioned by

Jenness was blood vengeance executed, so far as he was aware.[33] Another instance he cites, however, shows the primitive code in full play. "About 1908, at Asiak, east of Kent peninsula, a woman named Mittik was accused of causing a man's death by sorcery. At once a quarrel arose, for this was a straight charge of murder, and a man was stabbed with a knife. He ran outside to get his rifle, but fell dead in the snow before he reached it. Another man stabbed his murderer, then three men were shot, but none fatally. The feud seems to have ended at this stage, no one being willing to carry it further. An even more serious affray had occurred in the same region a few years earlier. There had come to the settlement from Netsilik an elderly couple with three sons, the eldest of whom brought his wife with him. An Asiak native wanted to share the woman, but the young man objected to her having two husbands, and, when he could not prevent it, stabbed his wife with a spear as she was stooping down to enter her hut. The woman staggered outside and fell dead in the snow. Her father then came up, and with the help of some of the other natives seized the murderer and stabbed him to death. The second brother crept up behind them and stabbed the father in the back, but the other natives pursued him and stabbed him also. They now decided to put an end to the vendetta by destroying the whole family, so they killed the old father and wounded the third son. This boy, however, managed to escape, while the second son, who had been stabbed with a knife, recovered through the care of his mother. Altogether four people were killed and two wounded in this affair."[34] Stefansson asserts that the Copper Eskimos who live at Prince Albert Sound apparently had the idea, of which he had never heard before, that property payment might take the place of the ordinary payment of a life for a life.[35]

The Eskimo requires no complicated judicial proceedings. In striking contrast with the rash revenge wrought in the above-mentioned quarrel is the administration of justice through white officials in a killing which took place also near Kent Peninsula, in 1922.[36] Five persons had been murdered, "the original cause of the trouble being that one of the attacking party wanted to steal another's wife, who, however, was killed in the struggle, together with her husband." Among the assailants were two young men. These were captured by the police, but only after one of them had managed to shoot the corporal who arrested him, together with a trader living near. "Judges, advocates, and witnesses had to be brought from a long distance. . . . The trial with its ceremonial made no great impression on them; they seemed to have an easy conscience in the matter. Both men were condemned to death; but the sentence had first to be confirmed by the supreme authority in Canada. . . . Just before going to execution, they gave the Police Inspector's wife some little carvings of walrus tusk, as souvenirs, to show they bore no ill will against the police. Both met their death calmly and without signs of fear." It is said that the execution cost Canada something like $100,000, "among other expense items being the cost of the executioner, who had to be brought up and kept there all winter, as none of the Police themselves would have any hand in this part of the work." The *New York Times* comments on the Eskimo's reactions to white man's justice:[37] "The Eskimo, especially when he or one of his fellows has admitted killing a white man, finds it extremely difficult to understand why the red-coated mounted policeman, representative of the white man's law, should not shoot him on sight, but instead should bring him out to civilization where a big white chief, dressed like a woman, sits on a bench and hears another white chief say, on the Eskimo's behalf, that though he killed the white man in question he should not be punished. Several natives having been brought out to civilization for trial, given good treatment and then returned to their own people fatter than when they left, the Eskimo mind has been unable to understand this situation when all the murderers' friends had given them up for dead, in some cases the men having confessed to the murder of whites."

§5. ENFORCEMENT OF JUSTICE BY THE GROUP

COURTS of law are beyond the ken of the Eskimo. Punishing a murderer devolves generally upon the immediate relatives of the man killed. Sometimes, however, the community takes a hand in the enforcement of justice. For instance, in Greenland, as a variation from the usual execution of blood vengeance, in cases of extreme atrocity the men of the village have been known to make common cause against a murderer, and kill him.[38]

There, furthermore, blood vengeance might be executed even upon another person than the murderer: upon a relative of his, or even upon simply a member of the same dwelling place.[39] The offense of one, therefore, exposes others to punishment; and the good behavior of the individual consequently is the concern of the kin-group or the household.

Among the Koksoagmiut (northern Labrador) the censure of the community falls upon a murderer who, upon being attacked by an avenging relative of his victim, turns upon his assailant and kills him also. Thus guilty of two murders, he is suffered to live only at the pleasure of the people, who soon decree his death.[40]

A murderer, by his act, places himself in the out-group. He is an offender against society, and the mores governing his punishment are so molded that the responsibility of avenging devolves upon other members of the victim's in-group.

Whether the duty of vengeance devolves simply upon the narrow kin-group or upon the household, or upon the whole village or community, depends partly upon the status of the murderer. If he belonged originally to an outside people he is more apt to be considered a common enemy of the community. In this connection the cases cited in a previous chapter suggesting that intertribal quarrels arise through an expansion of the blood feud to include whole settlements may be recalled.

What is a menace to all must be opposed by the concerted action of all. Group solidarity in the Eskimo village unit is essential to its survival. One aspect of this was seen in the communalistic tendencies in the sharing of food, a provision against the common danger of famine. In many ways the societal organization exerts a united effort against common perils. Jenness' statement regarding group solidarity among the Copper Eskimos is relevant:

"The inhabitants of a settlement are all, or nearly all, *nuatkattait,* connected, that is, either by blood or by marriage.[2] Since no one person has any recognized authority over the rest, it is this bond of relationship that keeps the people united and maintains peace and harmony in the community. The vicissitudes of life, too, in these regions tend to prevent any discord, for there are many occasions, both in summer and in winter, when sickness or ill-luck in hunting will make a family dependent for a time on its neighbors. The *nuatkattait* owe special duties to one another. They must provide for each other in sickness, take care of the aged and infirm, the widows and the orphans, and support each other in the blood-feud.[3] This gives the community its solidarity."[41]

"To the Copper Eskimo goodness means social goodness, that and no more. Whatever directly affects the welfare of the community as a whole is morally good or bad, while whatever relates to the individual alone, or affects the community so remotely that its influence is barely perceptible to their short-sighted view, is neither good nor bad."[42]

Group enforcement of justice is clearly embodied in the code of the Greenland community as enunciated by Rink:[43] no one was exempt from the dangerous sea hunting except through bodily incapacitation; subsistence was divided among the inhabitants according to certain rules; and the community retained the right to decide whether a newcomer should be permitted to settle among them.

The use of black magic, especially with intent to kill, is generally considered punishable by death.[44]

In the Egedesminde District, West Greenland, all persons of mean and dangerous character were punished by group action; and the killing of the infirm is further evidence of group solidarity.[45] It is asserted that on the west coast of Hudson Bay "people who have made themselves obnoxious are disposed of by common consent." An angakok had wished that a great many of the Eskimos would die. "This matter was talked over, and it was decided that the hostile angakok should be disposed of. One day, when he had made a hole in the ice of a pond, and was reaching down to clean out the broken pieces of ice, he was stabbed in the back by an old man, who received the thanks of the others for his feat."[46] The Koksoagmiut (northern Labrador) forbid a bad character to enter the huts, partake of food, or hold any intercourse with the rest.[47]

In the Bering Strait region a thief "is made ashamed by being talked to in the kashim when all the people are present, and in this way is frequently forced to restore the articles he has taken."[48]

The mode of group enforcement suggested in the last quotation—popular disgrace—is characteristic of many groups of Eskimos, especially those of Greenland. There the so-called *nith*-songs are a well-known method of punishing offenders against society.[49] Two parties in a dispute or quarrel confront each other before the assembled community, and voice their contentions through the medium of songs and dances improvised for the occasion. According to Elisha Kent Kane's quaint account from Upernivik, the accuser

". . . pours out in long paragraphic words all the abuse and ridicule to which his outrageous vernacular can give expression. The accused meanwhile is silent; but, as the orator pauses after a signal hit or to flourish a cadence on his musical instrument [drum], the whole audience, friends, neutrals, and opponents, signalize their approval by outcries as harmonious as those which we sometimes hear in our town-meetings at home. Stimulated by the applause, and warming with his own fires, the accuser renews the attack; his eloquence becoming more and more licentious and vituperative, until it has exhausted either his strength or his vocabulary of invective."[50]

After this lyric accusation the accused person is given a hearing. Besides defending himself eloquently before the gathering, he often scathes his opponent in a surpassingly caustic tirade. One scurrilous lampoon follows another.

So humiliating were these *nith*-song contests at Angmagsalik that an offender against society might be turned out of his house in midwinter.[51] Only by such a drum match could public opinion be brought to bear on murder and theft. The same grievance might be contested repeatedly for years in a series of *nith*-songs. Sometimes fierce invective was supplemented by actual blows. But, strangely in contrast to the spirit of the contests, between matches the opponents seemed to be good friends.[52]

The wide, though not continuous, distribution of the song contest as a means of adjusting personal grievances is evinced by the performance reported from the Aleutian Islands, outside the province of the Eskimos, by Weniaminow, a pioneer Russian missionary in that locality:

"Among the Atchinzen there was a peculiar performance or evening palaver, a seeking for revenge, in which only the actors were personal enemies. To put on such a performance the opponents made preparations which consisted in the composing and putting together of songs and dances, which contained abusive and scornful reproaches. When both sides were ready the accused arranged a meeting and invited his opponent with his helpers in song and dance, and neighbors. The reception of the opponent and all the people was friendly, and there took place the usual entertainment. After the entertainment the evening performance began with the customary songs. Thereupon the defamations and insults gradually began to be voiced and the villainy of the adversaries to show itself in the songs and dances prepared by them in advance, in which they endeavored each to out-strip the other in their expressions. And in consequence such performances ended not infrequently in public insults, blows, and even death."[53]

The Iglulik Eskimos also sing songs similar to the *nith*-songs with the purpose of settling old grudges, but in a more humorous vein.[54] And the practice is mentioned as occurring likewise among the Bering Sea Eskimos.[55] The Caribou Eskimos, too, compose libelous ditties, but the singing of them does not constitute an institution as it does in Greenland.[56] From an incident mentioned by Rasmussen we may gather that personal criticism is a thing of extremely great consequence among this group. The man Utahania upbraided his foster son by saying, "I wish you were dead! You are not worth the food you eat." And the young man took the words so deeply that he declared he would never eat again. To make his sufferings as brief as possible he lay down the same night in the snow stark naked and was frozen to death.[57]

It has been seen that the Eskimo code of justice sometimes operates through the individual, sometimes through the community. In matters involving the security of the group there is concerted action. Strong sentiment requires that in many cases the interests of the individual be sacrificed for the welfare of the community; when an individual member acts against the interests of the group and produces discord, he must be punished.

The interests of each person, on the other hand, must in some measure be the concern of the group. An injustice wrought against one member by another receives the condemnation of the community; and even if the actual executing of justice is left to the individual, the sentiment of the community is with him.

Only on the foregoing principles can there rest a sense of private security and group coöperation. A settlement that is closely knit by a spirit of coöperation is better able to endure the vicissitudes of the Arctic than one divided against itself. Group solidarity, in other words, has decided survival value.

§6. INFLUENCE OF RELIGION ON SOCIAL CONDUCT

In the foregoing section it has been seen that crime is punished either by the individual or by the community, depending upon the scope of the injustice. The transgressor of the mores is exposed to the danger of retribution at the hands of the person offended and to the condemnation of the group.

There is, however, another regulative influence: religion.[58] Among the Eskimos, as among other peoples of the world, religion sanctions what is "good" and condemns what is "bad." But the sphere of its influence is decidedly different from that in civilized society. Strictly social crimes scarcely come within the scope of the Eskimo religion. Its regulative influence operates chiefly through an elaborate system of taboos concerned with the propitiation of the spirits, especially the spirits believed to control the food supply. Far removed for the most part from the immediate, mundane relations among members of society, the religion of the Eskimos enforces the mores pertaining to the invisible world.

Its sphere is chiefly the relations of persons with their supernatural environment.

Only to lesser degree does it control conduct in matters which, according to the civilized code, involve morality—such offenses as theft, adultery, falsehood, and murder. Of these, perhaps murder is the crime wherein religious beliefs come into play most obviously. The Eskimo religion owes its force to the power attributed to the spirits. The Eskimo believes that spirits control all the phenomena of the natural world that he cannot explain on rational grounds. Since his knowledge is narrowly circumscribed, the power attributed to the spirits for working evil is conversely great. The ghost of a dead man becomes an effective entity in the supernatural world. An incensed ghost is an especially dangerous power; and what sort of ghost would be more incensed than the ghost of a murdered man against his slayer? Ghost fear, therefore, deters men from murder.

To conciliate the ghost of his victim, a murderer is required to observe various practices in addition to the regular customs regarding the dead. On Big Diomede Island the observances to propitiate the ghost of a murdered angakok take a peculiar form. The person who killed him cuts off the fingers and toes of the dead angakok and puts them into the latter's mouth. In addition he cuts out the murdered man's bladder and makes a bonnet of it for the corpse.[59]

A custom common among practically all Eskimo tribes, apparently with the purpose of rendering the spirit of a murdered person innocuous, is eating some of his liver.[60] This practice, which is at variance with the general abhorrence of cannibalism, is strictly ceremonial.

It was carried out in the murder of two missionaries at Dismal Lakes in 1913;[61] and the custom is mentioned in several references pertaining to Greenland.[62] We read that at Upernivik, after an evil magician was put to death "small portions of his heart were eaten, so as to make it secure that he could not come back to earth unchanged. All this in accordance with venerated custom."[63]

These cases suggest that it is when the man who has been murdered is believed to have religious powers, rather than when he is an ordinary person, that the conciliatory measures are observed most seriously. This would be natural, since exceptional potency is attached to the ghost of a medicine man.

Determining Guilt or Innocence

A COMMON way among primitive peoples of the world of ascertaining guilt or innocence is by observing supernatural signs.[64] The Eskimos employ methods of this sort to discover what specific religious regulations a person has violated, but rarely, if ever, it seems, to establish guilt in strictly social affairs. The outstanding means of divination used by the Eskimos is a process which we may term "head-weighing." A thong is passed around the head of a recumbent person, by means of which a second person lifts the head up and down. Whether it feels light or heavy determines the answer to whatever question is asked. Sometimes instead of the head, the foot or a bundle of clothing is used.

By this method the Eskimos sometimes seek to determine guilt or innocence in the matter of breaking taboos,[65] often with the aim of determining the cause of illness.[66] "Head-weighing" is not limited to these purposes, however, but is applicable for other sorts of divination.[67]

It is to be noticed that this method of deciding a case by magic is used apparently only when the offense involves the spirit world. A case of mundane crime is settled differently. At Cape Prince of Wales, for instance, when a criminal is to be discovered, the persons interested sometimes pay the angakok, or medicine man, to find out, but he uses no magical means.[68] The detection of crime, indeed, is not one of the regular duties of the Eskimo angakok.

The Concept of Reward or Punishment after Death

RELIGIONS of more advanced peoples commonly regulate social relations by sanctioning the code of laws. Not so with the Eskimo religion. The requirements which it imposes constitute a distinct system of duties and taboos, quite separate from the code of justice.[69] The morality of the Eskimos in purely mundane matters, on the other hand, is influenced by religion only in one way: by the fear that the spirits of the ancestors might be offended if the traditional code of justice were not adhered to.

Whether the soul of a person after death will go to a happy or unhappy place depends scarcely at all upon whether he has been law-abiding according to the civilized code. Actions involving worldly morality are rarely specified as entailing punishment in the after world.[70] Only in isolated instances are theft and homicide, for instance, taken into account in this connection; and it seems that adultery never is. Thus, the regulative force of religion operates chiefly in a different way among the Eskimos than among civilized peoples. The greatest importance is attached to the manner in which a person dies and to the extent to which he has observed the religious taboos. Strict compliance with these taboos is regarded as a moral duty, however; for the violation of them will anger the spirits and bring calamity upon *the whole group*. Confession in the event of breaking them is required. But they seem to a civilized person, at least on first sight, largely arbitrary and extraneous to the well-being of the group or of the individual in his after life. Hence, it must be concluded that the folkways of the Eskimos do not appear to embrace in any broad sense enforcement of worldly morality through religion.

NOTES

1. Nelson: 1899, 293–294.

2. Sumner and Keller: 1927, I, 117, quoting Letourneau: 1892, 53–54.

3. Jenness: 1922, 236.

4. Ross: 1819, 91–92, 107.

5. Birket-Smith: 1929, I, 265.

6. Jenness: 1922, 96.

7. Rasmussen: 1927, 191–192. See also Lyon: 1824, 251 f. (Iglulik Eskimos).

8. Murdoch: 1892, 267.

9. Nansen: 1893, 158, quoting Egede.

10. Jenness: 1922, 94.

11. Rasmussen: 1929, I, 232; Mathiassen: 1928, I, 221; Birket-Smith: 1929, I, 226, citing Richardson: 1851, I, 367 and Franklin: 1828, 197 ff.

12. Birket-Smith: 1929, I, 266, citing Turquetil: 1926, 424.

13. Rasmussen: 1927, 232–233.

14. Nelson: 1899, 292.

15. Turner: 1894, 178.

16. Rasmussen: 1927, 236.

17. Rasmussen: 1927, 235.

18. Rasmussen: 1927, 233.

19. Jenness: 1922, 96.

20. Jenness: 1922, 94–95.

21. Nelson: 1899, 301.

22. Lyon: 1824, 254.

23. Hall: 1864, 317.

24. Nansen: 1893, 162.

25. Birket-Smith: 1924, 139; Holm: 1914, 59.

26. Nelson: 1899, 292–293; Cadzow: 1929; Lyon: 1824, 299; Saabye: 1818, 225 ff. (West Greenland). See also Sumner and Keller: 1927, 454 ff., 643 ff., for comparative cases from other peoples.

27. Nelson: 1899, 292–293.

28. Birket-Smith: 1929, I, 265, citing Klutschak: 1881, 227 ff., and Gilder: 1881, 242.

29. Lyon: 1824, 254, 299.

30. Hall: 1864, 317.

31. Turner: 1894, 186; see also Hawkes: 1916, 109.

32. Turner: 1887, 102.

33. Jenness: 1922, 94–95.

34. Jenness: 1922, 95.

35. Stefansson: 1921, 566 f.

36. Rasmussen: 1927, 279–280.

37. *New York Times:* 1922, October 8.

38. Nansen: 1893, 162.

39. Birket-Smith: 1924, 140, citing Crantz: 1765, I, 249 ff., and Glahn: 1771, 330.

40. Turner: 1894, 186.

41. Jenness: 1922, 235, and footnote (2) "Another word that is sometimes heard, *tuakattait,* appears to be synonymous with *nuatkattait*"; footnote (3) "Aksiatak sprained his ankle in the early spring of 1915, and Ikpakhuak was ill for a week or more

during the following winter. In both cases the invalids and their families were supported by the rest of the community."

42. Jenness: 1922, 235.

43. Rink: 1862, 99 ff.

44. See pp. 442 f. and 451 ff.

45. Birket-Smith: 1924, 139–140.

46. Boas: 1907, 117–118.

47. Turner: 1894, 186.

48. Nelson: 1899, 293.

49. Nansen: 1893, 186 ff.; Crantz: 1767, I, 178–179; Birket-Smith: 1924, 140, citing H. Egede: 1741, 85 ff., Dalager: 1752, 40 ff., Crantz: 1765, 231 ff., Holm and Garde: 1887, 179, 308 ff., Kruuse: 1912, 35 ff., Kruuse: 1902, 214 ff., Rüttel: 1816, 70 ff.; Thalbitzer: 1923, 318 ff.

50. Kane: 1856, II, 128–129.

51. Rink: 1887, 26.

52. Holm: 1914, 127.

53. Taken from König's German translation of Weniaminow (Teil III, S. 14/15). The reader is referred to König (1925) for a comprehensive study of the juridical song contest.

54. Rasmussen: 1929, I, 231 f.

55. Nelson: 1899, 347.

56. Birket-Smith: 1929, I, 266, citing Rasmussen: 1925–26, I, 205; Rasmussen: 1927, 95.

57. Rasmussen: 1927, 96.

58. Sumner and Keller: 1927, I, 303 f.

59. Weyer: Field Notes.

60. See pp. 310 f.

61. Jenness: 1928, 79.

62. Rink: 1875, 45; Birket-Smith: 1924, 139, citing Dalager: 1752, 49, Rink: 1868, 213, and Saabye: 1816, 109.

63. Kane: 1856, II, 127.

64. Sumner and Keller: 1927, I, 697 ff.

65. Rasmussen: 1929, I, 141 (Iglulik Eskimos); Bilby: 1923, 232–233 (Baffin Island).

66. Jenness: 1922, 212–215 (Copper Eskimos); Boas: 1907, 158–159 (west coast of Hudson Bay); Boas: 1907, 495 (Ponds Bay, Baffin Island); Hawkes: 1916, 119, 138 (Labrador); Thalbitzer: 1924, 285 f.

67. See pp. 443 f.

68. Weyer: Field Notes.

69. See pp. 367 ff. also 333 ff.

70. See pp. 247 ff.

CHAPTER XIV

BASIS OF ESKIMO RELIGION

D ISCUSSION of the religion of the Eskimos here will be confined, in so far as possible, to the original native concepts, unmodified by Christian influences. Throughout much of the region missionizing has, to a greater or less extent, masked or stifled the original cult. Since this hybridization of the Eskimo religion is not to be considered here, the picture presented will not portray exactly the present-day spiritual concepts of all groups. We are concerned rather with the primitive, self-taught religion of the Eskimos as it was before the dawn of civilization broke upon them.

Before embarking upon this broad subject, which is of profound importance to these people, it is well to determine from what point of view it is to be surveyed. A religion can assume a chameleon-like changeability due to a shifting point of view. Inherently, it remains what it is to the people who embrace it; but from without it will appear now one way and now another, depending upon the frame of mind of the observer. The missionary, for instance, often has but little sympathy toward anything in the primitive cult that does not correspond exactly to the tenets of his own faith: the outlook of the zealot is tinged by the tinted glasses of his preconceived ideas. The scientist, on the other hand, is apt to protect himself against the faults of a biased or narrow mind by the armor of cold reason. He will tear the primitive religion limb from limb as though he were dissecting a specimen in a biological laboratory. Under his critical scrutiny it becomes a study in comparative anatomy; and as such, to be sure, yields interesting revelations. Like the skeleton of a prehistoric animal, the structure of the primitive cult reveals features that are interesting because of their rudimentary form or their naked, unadorned simplicity.

Nevertheless, the cold, calculating rationality, which the investigator is apt to assume in order to escape the influence of his own preconceived ideas, too readily resolves into an attitude inwardly unsympathetic and cynical. This frame of mind does not permit full understanding of the primitive man's religious beliefs.

He who leans backward in his broadmindedness in order to pick apart his subject with lofty detachment, simply betrays his own smallness in the face of a tremendous force. Neither the scientific observer who casts off sympathy along with emotional prejudice nor the biased zealot of the more highly developed religion will grasp the significance hidden in the primitive ritual. Pedantry or bigotry only muddles the interpretation. It is nature-man himself, in short, who best knows the meaning of his religion. To him it is vital, compelling, and true.

§1. RELIGION IS VITAL TO THE ESKIMO

A Diomede Islander showed the author a blue bead about the size of a marble, which would not be valued at more than a fraction of a cent among us; yet because of its imputed power as an amulet it had been traded for a large skin boat, which is about the equivalent of an automobile in our own country. The word "superstition" is too weak. Primitive spiritual beliefs are not to be thought of in terms of black cats and the number thirteen. An Eskimo of the Iglulik group purchased a few magic phrases, which had been handed down for generations, for the promise that he would supply the former owner with food and clothing for the rest of her life.[1] We may pity the purchaser, if we will, for his extravagant gullibility; or condemn him for clinging to a false faith; or, if it suit our mood, merely marvel how deep must be the ignorance that can create such a distorted standard of values. Yet our sentiment will be foreign to the issue and we shall remain remote from an understanding. Let us endeavor to sense the impulse of the native and we shall approach the heart of the matter. I am simply making a plea for the Eskimo, and begging that in all fairness we try to view his religion through *his* eyes.

A native of the Mackenzie River is willing to pay the equivalent of $150 or $200 for a familiar spirit.[2] A large price, it cannot be denied, for an intangible "power"! But this evaluation has been determined only after careful deliberation. It rests upon generations of deliberation, in a sense. It fits into the general scheme of life, and the people accept it implicitly. In short, here is something *real*, something powerfully genuine.

§2. EMOTION IN RELIGION

IT might be asserted that the value of $200 placed upon a familiar spirit cannot have been determined through logical reasoning. But to study the Eskimo religion with the aim of finding everywhere an underlying foundation of rationality and consistency is to lose one's self in an empty maze and again to miss the salient significance. For the religion is based not so much upon reason as upon emotion. Spiritual beliefs which by the very nature of the mystery surrounding them cannot be tested through reason are supported by powerful emotional convictions. Their truth in the mind of the Eskimo depends upon emotion. His religion is so much a part of his inner person that without sensing his feelings about it we cannot see rhyme or reason in it. If a religious cult is stripped of all emotion it is no more possible to understand its full significance than it is to discover life by analyzing the lifeless elements composing an organic body.

What, then, is the elemental emotional basis of the Eskimo's unquestioning faith? It is the same emotion that moves other primitive people throughout the world to shrink from the menace of invisible, evil powers and to cling with tenacious confidence to a faith that gives a defense against these dangers. Even in civilized people this same emotion lurks behind the veneer of knowledge and enlightenment. Here its force is generally impoverished, however, and is exposed only where the shadow of ignorance creates a quandary of doubtful apprehension or where unreasonable superstition crops out in defiance of fact. The mind of the Eskimo, since it is narrowly circumscribed, attributes relatively a great deal more to the agency of terrible, unpredictable spiritual forces. And since the savage tests his complex preventive measures against misfortune only imperfectly by experience and knowledge, his religious convictions bear a conspicuous emotional quality. The emotion is compelling; it is vital. It is fear. Very real dangers are its source; hence, it ought not to be slurred as unnatural or unworthy. Seeking to fathom the mysteries of life, the Eskimo attributes whatever is otherwise inexplicable to the agency of spiritual powers. The evil spirits, which are instrumental in the misfortunes of life, command the Eskimo's most serious consideration. He seeks an escape from his blank fear of these spirits, and he finds support in the blind hope that he may be able to forestall their designs, at least partially, by conciliation and exorcism.

This philosophy lies at the root of the whole religious cult of the Eskimos.

A conversation between Knud Rasmussen and an Eskimo northwest of Hudson Bay reveals the inner spiritual thoughts of the primitive.

"Tell me something about your religion," said the explorer. "What do you believe?" "We do not believe," replied the Eskimo. "We only fear. And most of all we fear Nuliajuk. . . . Nuliajuk is the name we give to the Mother of Beasts. All the game we hunt comes from her; from her come all the caribou, all the foxes, the birds and fishes. . . . We fear those things which are about us and of which we have no sure knowledge; as, the dead, and malevolent ghosts, and the secret misdoings of the heedless ones among ourselves." "Is there anything else you fear?" asked Rasmussen. "Yes, the spirits of earth and air. Some are as small as bees and midges, others great and terrible as mountains."[3]

So impressive to a certain angakok, or medicine man, were the fantastic spirit creatures that haunted him both while asleep and awake that when he was asked to draw pictures of them he lapsed into deep thought under the influence of strong emotion, and trembled from time to time to such a degree that he could scarcely draw.[4]

With convincing earnestness a hardy hunter of Diomede Island assured the author that he and everyone else of the village had seen the ghosts of those who had recently died. In the gloom of winter, when the moon or the northern lights add an eerie, pallid glow, the dead man returns to life and flits in and out among the houses with menacing manner. Is this phantom the hallucination of a temporarily disordered mind? or has the wily angakok disguised himself as the dead person to pass threateningly among the gloomy shadows and instil dread into the hearts of his fellow villagers? Either interpretation may be correct; or, perhaps, the true interpretation lies simply in a fallacy of vision, enhanced in the imaginative mind and elaborated through mistaken memory. More vital to the immediate issue than the actual explanation is an appreciation of the subjective reality of the Eskimo's spiritual ideas. The Central Eskimos believe that the visible spirit of a dead person is a harbinger of bad luck, and that to be touched by the spirit means instant death.[5] Implicit belief in the dreadful potency of the supernatural is a tremendous force. It can cause death where there is no natural ailment or accident.[6] "I command you to die," charges an angakok of Baffin Island; the man against whom he has directed his fatal influence is in the prime of life, strong, and healthy, yet his eating and drinking become sparing, and within four days he is dead. He has been killed by suggestion.[7]

Let us acknowledge, therefore, the force of the Eskimo's spiritual convictions; for the host of spirit entities that compose the imaginary, supernatural environment are more awesome in their fickle maliciousness and more dreadful in their incomprehensible designs than the known physical dangers of the natural environment. Let us accept his religion for what it is *to him:* a vital, stirring, exacting factor.

§3. LUCK, OR CHANCE

INSUFFICIENT knowledge prevents the Eskimo gaining from a scientific understanding of many natural phenomena. Comprehending no well-defined concept of natural law, he resorts simply to fanciful speculation regarding much that comes under his experience. Thus, the extent of the unknowable or unpredictable is comparatively wide. Luck, or chance, takes on a mysterious quality of spiritual volition. Supernatural design is inferred where natural causation is not apparent.

Under the shadow of his ignorance there gropes a searching curiosity and a vague cognizance of the relation between agency and effect, so that to whatever he cannot assign natural causes he imputes hidden purpose. Inquisitive even when his restricted knowledge precludes a logical answer to a question, the Eskimo tries to comprehend nature. Why must there be bad luck? he wonders. What causes famine, sickness, and other sufferings? He seeks an understanding so that he may effect a remedy.

Rasmussen[8] tells how a certain Eskimo, Aua, of the Iglulik group, philosophized on the mystery of life:

"Aua pointed out over the ice, where the snow swept this way and that in whirling clouds. 'Look,' he said impressively, 'snow and storm; ill weather for hunting. And yet we must hunt for our daily food; why? Why must there be storms to hinder us when we are seeking meat for ourselves and those we love?

"'Why?'

"Two of the hunters were just coming in after a hard day's watching on the ice; they walked wearily, stopping or stooping every now and then in the wind and the snow. Neither had made any catch that day; their watching had been in vain.

" 'Why?'

"I could only shake my head. Aua led me again, this time to the house of Kuvdlo, next to our own. The lamp burned with the tiniest glow, giving out no heat at all; a couple of children cowered shivering in a corner, huddled together under a skin rug. And Aua renewed his merciless interrogation: 'Why should all be chill and comfortless in this little home? Kuvdlo has been out hunting since early morning; if he had caught a seal, as he surely deserved, for his pains, the lamp would be burning bright and warm, his wife would be sitting smiling beside it, without fear of scarcity for the morrow; the children would be playing merrily in the warmth and light, glad to be alive. Why should it not be so?

" 'Why?'

"Again I could make no answer. And Aua took me to a little hut apart, where his aged sister, Natseq, who was ill, lay all alone. She looked thin and worn, and too weak even to brighten up at our coming. For days past she had suffered from a painful cough that seemed to come from deep down in the lungs; it was evident she had not long to live.

"And for the third time Aua looked me in the face and said: 'Why should it be so? Why should we human beings suffer pain and sickness? All fear it, all would avoid it if they could. Here is this old sister of mine, she has done no wrong that we can see, but lived her many years and given birth to good strong children, yet now she must suffer pain at the ending of her days.

" 'Why? Why?'

"After this striking object lesson, we returned to the hut, and renewed our interrupted conversation with the others.

" 'You see,' observed Aua, 'even you cannot answer when we ask you why life is as it is. And so it must be. Our customs all come from life and are directed toward life; we cannot explain, we do not believe in this or that; but the answer lies in what I have just told you.

" 'We *fear!*

" 'We fear the elements with which we have to fight in their fury to wrest out food from land and sea.

" 'We fear cold and famine in our snow huts.

" 'We fear the sickness that is daily to be seen among us. Not death, but the suffering.

" 'We fear the souls of the dead, of human and animal alike.

" 'We fear the spirits of earth and air.

" 'And therefore our fathers taught by their fathers before them, guarded themselves about with all these old rules and customs, which are built upon the experience and knowledge of generations. We do not know how or why, but we obey them that we may be suffered to live in peace. And for all our angakoqs and their knowledge of hidden things, we yet know so little that we fear everything else.' "

The mental scope of the Eskimo is relatively so narrow that a large measure of what he experiences in the workings of nature would remain inexplicable, were it not for the ever ready answer to be found in spirit forces. The curiosity which leads him to assign an agency for every occurrence is the same that impels the scientist to search for understanding through experimentation and observation. The Eskimo's theories are not always verified by actual experience; but, as pointed out above, his convictions have an emotional support. Inescapable fear and blind hope form the framework of his religion. A dreadful apprehension of unpredictable misfortunes drives him to cling to his belief that they are caused by evil spirits and to nurture the slender hope that by discovering the desires of the spirits he may forestall their designs.

§4. THE REASONING OF THE ESKIMO

NAÏVE simplicity characterizes many explanations which the Eskimo propounds for complex natural phenomena. Simplicity, indeed, forms one bulwark of his beliefs. He never needs to pursue an inquiry further than one step: his mind accepts the all-sufficient instrumentality of spirit agencies and so requires no other explanation. The belief is common among Eskimos, for instance, that the aurora borealis is produced by the spirits playing ball; the wavering lights are evidence of the struggles of the contending players.[9] Contrast with this simple explanation the modern scientific discussion of the aurora borealis in *The Encyclopaedia Britannica:* "Two theories have been advanced. One is that the cause lies in negative particles shot off by that body [the sun] and caught in the magnetic field of the earth. The second is that alpha-particles, with a plus charge, come to us from radioactive substances in the sun."[10] Not until very recently has science approached a reasonable theory, and even now the matter is subject to some speculation. Can it not be fairly asked, therefore, whether centuries of scientific progress, providing one theory after another, have made any real advance over the naïve explanation for this natural phenomenon that the Eskimos accept implicitly?

"Science explains nothing. It cannot answer the question of a child of six. It can only reduce to simpler and more concise terms our crude description of phenomena which, in the last analysis, are perhaps inexplicable."[11]

Let us not ridicule the Eskimo, therefore, for holding different ideas regarding final causes. He has no complex background of scientific knowledge which would form a basis for abstruse reasoning. The simplicity of his reasoning is to be attributed to restricted knowledge rather than to a different mental process. The Eskimo's logic is not to be condemned.

An instance will illustrate the manner in which a causal relationship is sought. Once in mid-February on the lower Yukon there was an eclipse of the moon and soon afterward a throat disease caused the death of about a dozen persons. Both events were unpredictable and striking. The epidemic was a serious calamity, to which a single cause might well be assigned. The only other outstanding manifestation at the time was the eclipse, which preceded the epidemic by a short time. We cannot be sure that this particular happening was the first occasion on which disease was associated with an eclipse, but in any case we may infer the reasoning of the Eskimo. The eclipse was an unusual phenomenon which the native would naturally suppose to be an omen, and this suspicion was corroborated by the epidemic that followed. Spirits, as any Eskimo knows, cause disease; therefore the Moon-Spirit must have sent the epidemic. Hence the belief on the lower Yukon that during an eclipse a subtle malignant essence descends upon the earth, which may lodge in any utensils lying about. Immediately upon the commencement of an eclipse, every woman turns her pots, wooden buckets, and dishes bottom side up.[12] This train of reasoning is, of course, a clear case of *post hoc ergo propter hoc* which constitutes the foundation of many beliefs in omens.[13] The same logical process, when executed with thoroughness and discrimination, yields also sound scientific knowledge.

Even the Eskimo arrives at very creditable conclusions through observation, as in the realization by the Angmagsalik Eskimos that the moon causes tides.[14] The Eskimos of southeastern Baffin Island, like many of the other groups,[15] have a tradition of a deluge; and they attribute it to an unusually high tide. A native woman of this region, when asked by Captain Hall why her people thought that the earth was once covered with water, replied: "Did you never see little stones, like clams and such things as live in the sea, away up on the mountains?"[16] Our admiration is commanded by this inference coming from a lowly savage, wholly untutored in science. About twenty-five hundred years ago the same basic principle of paleontology was derived by the Greek philosopher Xenophanes and recorded perhaps for the first time. Twenty-five hundred years is not long in comparison with the thousands of years of cultural development that separate civilization from the stone-age Eskimo who answered Captain Hall's question so shrewdly.

Again, when the Eskimo is confronted with a complex riddle he is seen to flounder about in a sea of inadequate factual knowledge. Mylius-Erichsen asked an angakok why not a single bear had yet appeared in the neighborhood of Agpat late in the year; and the reply was: "No bears have come because there is no ice, and there is no ice because there is too much wind, and there is too much wind because we mortals have offended the powers."[17] The first part of his explanation shows the unerring perspicacity of the clever hunter: he knows that the wind affects the distribution of the ice and that the bears follow the ice. But he is not satisfied without a prime cause, and this he finds in the supernatural forces.

Abundant instances might be cited of the Eskimo's conspicuous astuteness in cases where his knowledge has been derived through objective experience. Brought face to face with actual conditions and facts of the natural world, he often distinguishes himself as a clever thinker in solving the problems of his daily activities. We must not set him down, therefore, as a person who will favor the fanciful guidance of his imagination when concrete enlightenment is offered. But the purpose of the present discussion is to reveal his characteristic approach toward the solution of problems that lie beyond his grasp.

In his theories for explaining the origins of things and for fathoming the mysteries of the heavens he, like other peoples, gives full play to phantasy, customarily imparting to the things beyond his perception a likeness to the world which he knows. A complete presentation of the cosmogony of the Eskimos is beyond the scope of the present study, for it would entail a compendium of mythology. A few examples must suffice to illustrate the point.

A very common legend among the Eskimos traces the origin of the sun and moon to a sister and brother who at one time lived on the earth. The boy was prompted to chase the girl, and both of them soared off into the sky, where ever afterward the boy in the form of the moon has pursued his sister the sun.[18] Similar myths are widely known among Indian tribes.[19]

Thunder is sometimes said to be caused by spirits rubbing hides together.[20] Rain is occasioned, according to the West Greenlanders, by a lake in heaven overflowing; and snow is the blood of the dead, or chips of narwhal tusk carved by the man in the moon.[21] The Malemiut of Kotzebue Sound (Alaska) say that the north wind is the breath of a giant, and when he builds himself a snow house the snow flies off his shovel and comes to earth as a snowstorm. The natives of Selawik account for snowfall in a different way: the sky is a land like the earth but hanging upside down, with the grass growing downward; and when the wind blows the grass is stirred and the snow is sifted to the earth. Furthermore, there are a myriad of lakes in the sky and at night these shine and appear as stars.[22] In northwestern Alaska and Coronation Gulf shooting stars are thought to be star dung.[23]

A variety of stories are told in explanation of the constellations.[24] The Great Bear is personified as one or more caribou, in Alaska, Coronation Gulf, the central regions, Labrador, at Smith Sound, and elsewhere in Greenland with the exception of Angmagsalik.[25] There is not always uniformity in the interpretations given the constellations. Thus, the Pleiades are described by the Eskimos of northwestern Alaska as a litter of fox cubs,[26] by the Caribou Eskimos as "branches of antlers,"[27] and by the Polar Eskimos as a number of dogs pursuing a bear on the ice.[28] And Orion's Belt is referred to in northwestern Alaska as posts on which rawhide lines are being stretched,[29] in the region of Coronation Gulf and Greenland as some sealers who never returned,[30] and in Smith Sound as steps cut in a steep snowbank.[31]

Often critical in matters where observation can check inference, but credulous of the fanciful philosophy contained in his traditions, the Eskimo presents a combination of opposites. The all-sufficient explanation to be found in spirit agency provides a ready answer to any puzzling question. Consequent upon the restricted nature of the Eskimo's knowledge regarding things that lie beyond the immediate range of his senses, much is relegated to the sphere of the supernatural.

Sometimes the Eskimo contemplates the spirits complacently, merely as beings remote from human affairs and therefore not to be pondered over seriously. Again, he broods over them with the deepest perturbation. They command an awe that is inescapable. Ever and anon the native is prompted to give heed to the overwhelming power of the supernatural. He cannot disregard the embodiment of all that is terrible; the spirits are linked with his very life.

NOTES

1. Rasmussen: 1929, I, 165 f.
2. Stefansson: 1914, 368.
3. Rasmussen: 1927, 195 f.; also Rasmussen: 1929, I, 56 f.
4. Rasmussen: 1927, 122.
5. Boas: 1887, 36.
6. Sumner and Keller: 1927, 1105 ff.
7. Bilby: 1923, 228 ff.
8. Rasmussen: 1927, 129 ff.; Rasmussen: 1929, I, 55 ff.
9. The belief that the northern lights represent the struggles of the spirits as they play football with a walrus skull is held by the Eskimos of Alaska (Nelson: 1899, 336, 449; Weyer: Field Notes [Diomede Islands]); by those of the Iglulik group (Rasmussen: 1929, I, 95; Rasmussen: 1927, 28); by the natives on the west coast of Hudson Bay (Boas: 1907, 146); and in West Greenland (Birket-Smith: 1924, 435; Crantz: 1767, 202, 233; see also Rink: 1875, 37). At Angmagsalik the belief differs in that the aurora is supposed to be caused by children who were stillborn or were put to death, and they are believed to be playing ball with their afterbirths (Holm: 1914, 82). In Hudson Strait the aurora is supposed to be caused by torches held in the hands of spirits searching for those who have recently died (Turner: 1894, 266). It is stated that the Eskimos of Smith Sound have no myth regarding the northern lights (Kroeber: 1899, 319). The Copper Eskimos call the aurora *ahanik*, and believe it to be a manifestation of the spirits that bring fine weather (Jenness: 1922, 180). In Alaska and among the Iglulik Eskimos the belief is held that if one whistles while the northern lights are playing they will come closer (Bering Strait—Weyer: Field Notes; Iglulik Eskimos—Rasmussen: 1929, I, 95). The Point Barrow (Alaska) Eskimos are very much afraid of the northern lights. Going about at night they carry a knife as protection against them, or throw dogs' excrement and urine at them (Murdoch: 1892, 432; Ray: 1885, 42).

10. *Encyclopaedia Britannica:* 1929, II, 697.
11. Russel Gordon Smith: 1930, 5 f.
12. Nelson: 1899, 430 f.
13. Concerning miscellaneous omens see Birket-Smith: 1924, 448 f.
14. Holm: 1914, 106; see also Crantz: 1767, 231 (West Greenland).
15. Mackenzie River and Greenland, exclusive of the Polar Eskimos —Kroeber: 1899, 319; Central Eskimos—Boas: 1888, 637; Cumberland Sound—Boas: 1907, 173; Bering Sea —Nelson: 1899, 452; and Kodiak Island—Petroff: 1900, 238.
16. Hall: 1864, 318; also Boas: 1888, 637 f.
17. Steensby: 1910, 363 f.
18. See pp. 381 ff.
19. Boas: 1904, 3, n. 3. James Mooney: 1900, 256, 441.
20. Holm: 1914, 106 f. (Angmagsalik); Birket-Smith: 1929, I, 157 (Caribou Eskimos); see also Boas: 1907, 497 f.; Boas: 1887, 37 (Baffin Island); Boas: 1888, 600 (Central Eskimos); Crantz: 1767, I, 233, and Thalbitzer: 1928, 408, citing H. Egede and P. Egede. At Smith Sound thunder is unknown and there is no myth concerning it (Kroeber: 1899, 319).
21. Birket-Smith: 1924, 435.
22. Nelson: 1899, 515.
23. Nelson: 1899, 449; and Jenness: 1922, 179.
24. Jenness: 1922, 179 (Copper Eskimos); Birket-Smith: 1929, I, 157 (Caribou Eskimos); Rasmussen: 1908, 176 ff. (Polar Eskimos); Birket-Smith: 1924, 436, and Crantz: 1767, I, 232 (West Greenland); Holm: 1914, 106 f. (Angmagsalik).

25. Kroeber: 1899, 319; Jenness: 1922, 179 (Coronation Gulf); Birket-Smith: 1929, I, 157 (Caribou Eskimos); Hawkes: 1916, 29 (Labrador); Crantz: 1767, I, 232 (West Greenland).

26. Nelson: 1899, 449.
27. Birket-Smith: 1929, I, 157.
28. Kroeber: 1899, 319.
29. Nelson: 1899, 449.
30. Jenness: 1922, 179.
31. Kroeber: 1899, 319.

CHAPTER XV

THE GHOST CULT

WHAT sort of spirits, we next ask, stands in closest relation to the Eskimo and furnishes the most direct and convincing manifestation of their reality? The answer is: The ghosts of dead relatives and associates. The phenomenon of death, with its suggestion of the flight of some invisible spirit entity, life, into another sphere, offers a ready answer as to how the spirit world becomes peopled. The departing soul enters a sphere where it can take part in the governing of unpredictable and inexplicable events of worldly life. The soul carries with it the needs and desires of its earthly owner and experiences the human fretfulness that is evoked by deprivation. When an Eskimo of West Greenland hears a buzzing in his ears he invites the spirits: "Take as much food as you like"; for then he knows that the dead are hungry and unless appeased will send punishment.[1]

§1. GHOSTS OF THE DEAD ARE FEARED

Dreams about the Dead

ONE Eskimo voices the belief of the Iglulik group: "We believe that men live on after death here on earth, for we often see the dead in our dreams fully alive."[2] The state of sleep closely resembles death, and the dream of the ghost is a very obvious manifestation of the reality of the supernatural sphere. Peary asserts that when one of the Eskimos of Smith Sound dreamed of seeing a deceased woman, all were in terror the next day.[3] Even among the Christianized Eskimos of southern Labrador, when someone dreams about a grave they put food on it to cause the hunting to be successful.[4] A confabulation between a Smith Sound Eskimo and his recently deceased wife is illustrative of the intimate bond that the dream creates between the living and the dead. With the corpse before him he enjoined her spirit that if there were anything she desired she should appear to him at night in his dreams, and he would carry out her wishes. But he was emphatic in discouraging her from coming near him at other times. After passing his right hand over her body from her head to her heart, he took her by the shoulder and shook her hard, telling her to remain where she was. He also spat on her forehead three times, instructing her to wash herself. A number of times he repeated the injunction to remain where she was buried, to trouble no one, and to refrain from following him when he was in his kayak.[5]

Evil Powers Are Ascribed to the Dead

"As soon as death is certain," writes Hawkes concerning the Labrador Eskimos, "the household sets up an unearthly wailing, the women tearing their hair and beating their breasts, otherwise giving vent to excessive grief. The virtues of the deceased are magnified and his faults forgotten. The villagers crowd in and add their lamentations to the general woe."[6] Dread of the power of the ghost to send disaster upon the living adds decided fervor to the mourning of the Eskimos. The native is capable of genuine grief for a vanished friend, but his immediate misfortune in the loss is easily overshadowed by his belief in the capacity of the ghost to inflict far-reaching adversity.

The Copper Eskimo knows only one cause for those forerunners of death, accident and sickness: the malignant activities of evil spirits or the shades of the dead. ". . . Aksiatak, for example, dislocated his ankle while wrestling in the dance-house. . . . A year later his son Nakitok fell from the roof and broke his thigh. . . . Both accidents were ascribed to the machinations of evil spirits, and the shamans were asked to appease them. . . . In most cases he discovers that some taboo has been broken, or that the patient has committed some action which offended a certain dead person's shade."[7] Almost any form of mischance may be attributed to the incensed spirits of the dead, and the attitude toward them ranges widely from mild inquietude to desperate, gripping fear. "The Copper Eskimo hardly knows the comforting doctrine that the souls or shades of the dead hover around their living kinsfolk like guardian spirits and protect them from every harm. The shade to them is a malignant being, at least potentially; and its activities know no bounds of time and space. . . . Unseen, save when of their own accord they render themselves visible or are revealed to a shaman through his familiar spirit, they haunt the hapless natives night and day, ever ready to seize a favorable opportunity to work them harm; the shade of a man who died in one place may cause the death of another man a thousand miles away. In some vague manner too these shades control the weather and the supply of game."[8] Relentlessly malicious and continuing so as long as they remain in the memory of the living, the ghosts of the dead wander over the face of the earth, making their wants known by signs and manifestations readily interpreted by the shaman,[9] or revealing their presence by a kind of whispering.[10]

The sending of bad luck rather than good is the will of the ghosts. When fortune favors the Eskimo he inclines to attribute it to his own foresight and skill, and even if he acknowledges the agency of spirits he is apt soon to forget the good luck. Rather than being intent upon improving his condition he seems apprehensive lest he be reduced by spirits to a more arduous, dangerous, and painful life. The evil influences must be reckoned with; the good ones will take care of themselves. In short, the Eskimo is more deeply moved by fear of misfortune from the supernatural powers than by a feeling of gratitude toward them for good luck.

§2. ATTITUDE TOWARD DEATH AND THE FUTURE LIFE

THE Eskimo believes implicitly that upon dying his soul[11] will continue conscious in another world. The nature of this other world varies in the concepts of the different groups; but the conditions of life after death are generally thought of, for better or worse, in terms of earthly existence. Without much idealization the familiar circumstances of living are projected into the world beyond. Boas relates how a young Eskimo girl once sent for him a few hours before her death and asked for some tobacco and bread to give her mother who had died a few weeks before.[12]

The Eskimo's concept of the future life provides more than one possible destiny for the soul, as will be shown later. In advance of our detailed discussion of this point, let it be said that this concept does not correspond entirely to the Christian belief in a future realm of happiness as a reward for moral living, alternative to one of punishment for sinning. What differentiation there is in the after world of the Eskimos does not depend on what we would consider moral conduct. While a distinction generally is made between hardship and well-being in the after life, the happier region being characterized, quite understandably, by the absence of snow and cold, even this differentiation is sometimes very vague.

"Death," according to the belief of the Copper Eskimos, "rolls back the gate, not of a happy hunting ground, or of a heaven of peace where friends and lovers may unite once more, but of some vague and gloomy

realm where, even if want and misery are not found (and of this they
are not certain) joy and gladness at least must surely be unknown."[13]

"Melancholy thoughts of death seem to be always hovering in the
penumbra of the Eskimos' minds. Especially is this true of the older
people, for the young, here as elsewhere, are little troubled by its im-
minence. During the summer of 1915, when the natives were formu-
lating their plans for the future, even though it might be for but a
month ahead, Ikpakuak or Higilak would often say 'Granting that we
are still alive' and added 'Evil shades are constantly assailing us.' Not
infrequently too, some such expression as 'People are constantly dying
here' would fall from their lips. Yet in their minds there seemed to be
no anxious clinging to life, only a profound resignation and melancholy
calmness in the face of the inevitable issue."[14]

In the pursuance of his hunting activities the Eskimo is constantly brought face to face with death, and he grows to regard
life as a thing of little account. Life sometimes seems harder than
death, and so is regarded as a little thing to give.[15] Like the Stoic
who argues, metaphorically, that if the chimney smokes one should
get out of the house, the Eskimo justifies suicide, especially if age
or infirmity renders one useless and a burden.[16]

On King William Island, old folks no longer able to provide for
themselves generally hang themselves.[17] Among the Iglulik Eskimos
suicide by hanging or drowning is rather common.[18] The act must be
performed while the hut is empty and a lamp must be left burning so
that one entering will see the body.[19] Suicide is stated to be fairly
common among the Koksoagmiut, south of Hudson Strait; remorse and
disappointed love are the only causes, death being sought either by
strangulation, by pitching one's self over a cliff, or by shooting.[20] Also
the Tahagmiut to the west not infrequently commit suicide, strangulation and shooting being the common methods.[21] A native of Angmagsalik will throw himself into the sea, often prompted by the admonition from his relatives that he has nothing to live for.[22] The Copper
Eskimos, however, resort to suicide but rarely, according to Jenness.
This observer remembers hearing of only one case and that was due not
to any morbid weariness of life, but to terror of the revenge that
might be expected for a crime that the man had committed.[23]

The Eskimo has an abiding confidence that at death he will go
to live in another sphere, which, although it may not be a happy
hunting ground, may easily be fraught with less hardship than his
earthly home. So when he commits suicide he has the composure
and assurance of a civilized man who purchases a railroad ticket

to another city. He meets death with sober resignation. When a crew of Diomede Islanders in a skin boat are confronted with death by drowning, the captain goes around and slashes all the men's throats with his knife and finishes the job by cutting his own.[24] The author, upon questioning an Eskimo hunter who was sick as to whether he wanted to die, received the reply, "Um? . . . Not just now; no wood in village for make coffin." Dr. Thompson, who for a number of years has rendered medical service to the Eskimos of Alaska, asserted his conviction that when a native makes up his mind that he is going to perish, death is almost inevitable. The influenza epidemic among the Alaskan Eskimos so terrorized them that many seemed simply to lie down and die.

It is fear of the dead, more than fear of dying, that is at the root of the ghost cult.[25] Fear of the hardships that the spirits can mysteriously cause, rather than fear of punishment after death for moral transgressions, forms the emotional background. The immediate ills of everyday life require more urgent consideration than the trials to be encountered after death. The Eskimos generally find ample punishment for their breaches of custom simply in their earthly misfortunes. Failure to comply with the taboos and other observances may bring calamity upon the whole village. Fear of punishment in the after life is only a secondary check upon conduct. The destiny of the soul seems, indeed, to depend as much upon the manner of death as upon earthly behavior. And it is to be noticed that punishment after death does not follow chiefly moral transgression in the form of social, mundane misdoing, and depends less than might be expected even upon compliance with the elaborate, and often seemingly arbitrary, taboos and compulsions.[26]

The Eskimos of Bering Strait believe that the shades of shamans and of such as die by accident, violence, or starvation, go to a land of plenty in the sky, where there is light, food, and water in abundance; while the shades of people who die from normal causes go to the underground land of the dead, where they depend entirely upon the offerings of food, water, and clothing made to them by the relatives. Even in the land of plenty, shades can be made happier by being remembered with presents. "Some few persons are supposed to be uncomfortable after death. These are mainly thieves who steal from their fellow villagers, sorcerers or bad shamans, witches, and the people who practise certain forbidden customs."[27]

Stefansson writes, chiefly with reference to the Mackenzie region,

that the Eskimo ". . . has nothing which corresponds to either heaven
or hell. For four or five days after death the spirit remains in the
house where death occurred; from then on it remains by the grave
until it is summoned to enter a new-born child; and from that time
until the death of the child the soul remains with it, unless it is compelled to abandon it earlier, as would happen if the child were habitually punished. It is not known to the Mackenzie Eskimo what would
happen to a soul in case it abandoned the person it was guarding."[28]
There seems to be no other idea of a pleasant abode for the soul than
in the child who is named after the dead person, and the character of
this abode in no way depends upon the dead person's merits in life, but
only on the accident of how the child, his *saunñra,* is treated. It is the
duty of the relatives to provide the souls of the dead with *saunirks.*[29]

The Iglulik Eskimos believe that the dead suffer no hardship no
matter where they go. Even so, most prefer to go to the land of the
moon spirit rather than to the other realm of spirits under the sea, a
purgatory where some (or all?) dead persons are believed to stay for
a period up to several years according to the magnitude of their taboo
breaking.[30] "There are two places appointed to receive the souls of
the good," as Lyon states it. "One of these is in the centre of the
earth, the other in kāyl-yak or heaven. To the latter place, such as
are drowned at sea, starved to death, murdered, or killed by walruses
or bears, are instantly wafted, and dwell in a charming country. . . .
The place of souls in the world below is called Aād-lĕe generally; but
there are, properly, four distinct states of blessedness, and each rank
has a world of itself, the lowest land being the last and best, which all
hope to reach. . . . The three first are bad uncomfortable places. . . .
In the lowest Aād-lĕe a perpetual and delightful summer prevails; the
sun never sets, but performs one unceasing round; ice and snow are
unknown; . . ." etc.[31]

It is stated that on the west coast of Hudson Bay people are afraid
of going to the sea spirit, and that the period of penance there is
escaped by all who perish by drowning, or who are killed by others, or
who take their own lives, and by all women dying in childbirth.[32]

The abodes of the souls of dead Eskimos are again described in
Boas' report on the Central Eskimos[33] as follows: Some souls dwell
above (Qudliparmiut), where there is no snow, ice, or storms, and all
are always happy. Thither journey all who have been good and happy,
or were killed by accident or by their own hand. Below is another abode
for spirits of the dead (Adliparmiut), where it is always dark, snowy,
and stormy. To this region go all who have been bad, unhappy, or wil-
ful murderers, and there they must always remain. In northeastern
Baffin Island it is believed that those who have disobeyed the commands of Sedna, their principal deity, journey after death to her

abode, where they must live for one year.[34] Then they go to live in Adlivium, where they hunt whale and walrus. Those, however, who have obeyed Sedna's commands, and all who die by violence or by drowning or in childbed, go to a heaven that is called "Qudlivun." No ice or snow exists there, and herds of deer roam on the hills and are easily obtained. The Cumberland Sound natives are reported to believe that "there are three heavens, one above another, of which the highest is the brightest and best. Those who die by violence go to the lowest heaven. Those who die by disease go to Sedna's house first, where they stay for a year. Sedna restores their souls to full health, then she sends them up to the second heaven. They become *omiktū'miut*, or inhabitants of *Omiktu*, in which place there are many whales. It is not quite certain that the second heaven and Omiktu are not the same, as it is also stated that only the lighter souls that leave Sedna's house ascend to the second heaven. Those who die by drowning go to the third heaven. Their souls are very strong and healthy. People who commit suicide go to a place in which it is always dark, called 'Kumetoon' and where they go about with their tongues lolling. Women who have premature births go to Sedna's abode, and stay in *Alipā'q,* the lowest world, which is under the sea, and not far from Sedna's house. It is said that some souls go to *Tukeychwen,* a place of which no full description is given."[35] Captain Hall[36] reports that in southeastern Baffin Island it was believed that "All Innuits who have been good go to Koodleparmiung, that is, all who have been kind to the poor and hungry—all who have been happy while living on this earth. Any one who has been killed by accident, or who has committed suicide, certainly goes to the happy place.

"All Innuits who have been bad—that is, unkind to one another— all who have been unhappy while on this earth, will go to Adleparmeun. If an Innuit kill another because he is mad at him, he will certainly go to Adleparmeun."

Again it is stated regarding the future life of the Baffin Islanders that those who die on the hunt go to a blissful heaven, as do those who die a violent death by any sort of accident and women in childbirth. Quarrelsomeness and ungenerosity are thought to be punished. When a sick person, having confessed, dies regardless, it is believed that he had some mental reservation. These bad folk go to the Eskimo hell, to the awful realms of Sedna. But there is a third idea, of a sort of purgatory, a place to which the damned can escape before they are finally admitted to bliss. The spirit of the angakok or medicine man is able to go below and fight the evil one, and liberate the soul in question; but the undertaking is generally a rather expensive one for the relatives of the deceased.[37]

The Koksoagmiut (Ungava Bay, Hudson Strait) believe that souls after death, go either up to the sky, *keluk,* where they are called *Ke-lugmiut,* or down into the earth, *nuna,* where they are called *Nunamiut.* "The place to which the soul goes depends on the conduct of the person on earth and especially on the manner of his death. Those who have died by violence or starvation and women who die in childbirth are supposed to go to the region above, where, though not absolutely in want, they still lack many of the luxuries enjoyed by the Nunamyut. All desire to go to the lower region and afterwards enjoy the pleasure of communicating with the living, which privilege is denied to those who go above. If death result from natural causes the spirit is supposed to dwell on the earth after having undergone a probation of four years rest in the grave."[38] Similarly it is stated that according to the belief of the Labrador Eskimos, "the place to which the spirit finally takes departure depends more on the mode of death of the deceased than the manner of his life. Those who have been murdered or have committed voluntary suicide and women who die in childbirth are recompensed with the highest heaven, located in the Aurora Borealis, where they enjoy themselves playing football with a walrus head. Those who die an ordinary death descend to the world below, where they carry on a monotonous existence, which is free, however, from the cold and hardships of their earthly home."[39]

The Polar Eskimos have no definite ideas of punishment or reward after death.[40] There are three possible destinations of the spirit: the moon, under the sea, and the atmosphere; but it is not clear who goes to which place, except that women who die in childbirth go beneath the sea.

In East Greenland it is thought that "after a man's death the soul comes to life again, either below the sea or up in the sky. . . . It is good to be in either place, but the sea is to be preferred."[41]

Commenting on the beliefs of the West Greenlanders the early authority Crantz remarks that inasmuch as they acquire most of their sustenance from the bosom of the sea, "many or most of them place their *elysium* in the abysses of the ocean, or the bowels of the earth, and think the deep cavities in the rocks are the avenues leading to it. There dwells Tornarsuk and his mother; there a joyous summer is perpetual, and a shining sun is obscured by no night. . . . But to these seats none must approach, but those who have been dexterous and diligent at their work (for this is their grand idea of virtue), that have performed great exploits, have mastered many whales and seals, have undergone great hardships, have been drowned in the sea, or died in childbed.

"Hence it is obvious, that they had formerly a tradition that good would be rewarded."[42] The "hell" imagined by these Eskimos exists in the upper regions, where it is desolate and cold. In Julianehaab District there is the belief that the soul of a dying person can be sent to the good or bad realm by lifting the person from the platform onto the floor or *vice versa.*[43]

Broadly speaking, the Eskimos generally believe that the destination of the soul after death depends partly upon how the person dies: whether by starvation, drowning, or murder, in childbirth, or from sickness. Thus, the lot of the soul in the after world is determined by circumstances that are largely beyond human control. Other religions of the world sometimes teach that moral conduct is the chief or the only factor determining the fate of the soul. But according to the Eskimo conception the matter depends to a great extent upon events that are properly to be set down as "accidental," though, to be sure, the word has a slightly different connotation in the primitive mind.

It may very well be that this notion of accidental determinants is linked with the rather conspicuous fatalism often observed in the disposition of Eskimos.

"Life would be hard enough if they had none but natural forces to contend with, forces that they could see and estimate. But the mysterious and hostile powers, invisible and incalculable, and therefore potentially all the more dangerous, hem them in, as they believe, on every side, so that they never know from day to day whether a fatal sickness will not strike them down or a sudden misfortune overwhelm them and their families—from no apparent cause, it may be, and for no conceivable reason, save the ill-will of these unseen foes. Young and old, the good and the bad, all alike are involved in the same dangers, and all alike share the same fate. . . . It is little wonder therefore if the mind of the average Eskimo is deeply tinged with fatalism. Life would be unbearable indeed with this religion did he not possess a superabundant stock of natural gaiety and derive joy from the mere fact of living itself. The future holds out no golden promise, not even the hope of a life as cheerful as the present one; so the native banishes as far as possible all thoughts of a distant tomorrow, and drains the pleasures of each fleeting hour before they pass away forever."[44]

Perhaps as a reaction against the soberness of a philosophy so unconsoling, outwardly the Eskimo usually shows a highly buoyant nature. His good humor is a conspicuous characteristic. The simplest joke tickles him into volatile laughter; and he is very prone to remain apparently optimistic through the temporary adversities of everyday life. But sound the depths of his mind, and this joviality and good nature appear as but a defensive veneer. At bottom his thoughts revolve about the misfortunes that are unpredictable and inescapable; and he accepts these ills with fatalistic, melancholy complacence.

Thus, there are two opposite sides to the Eskimo's nature: one a deep, sober, fearful reverence for the awesome mysteries of life, the other a mobile light-heartedness, which is a sustaining balance. An exemplification of this chameleon temperament is perceived in the attitude of an Eskimo woman of Smith Sound visiting the grave of her husband. Very solemnly the bereaved widow trudges through the snow to the lonely spot. She is quaking with strong emotion as she lifts the stone at the head of the grave and places some food beneath it for the spirit of her husband. After complying with the time-honored ritual she retreats from the haunted scene; her recent frightful intimacy with the ghostly realm has stirred her with an awful perturbation. She is wailing and whimpering as she withdraws, walking backward and covering her footprints with snow in order that her contact with the dead be severed and that she may escape irrevocably from the shadow of death. But as soon as her solemn duty is completed her mood brightens abruptly. A few minutes later she is laughing and joking again, fortified by her characteristic cheer against the inevitable trials she must face.[45]

§3. AVOIDANCE OF THE GHOST

Fear of Contamination by Corpse

ACCORDING to the Eskimo belief, one cause of sickness is possession by an evil spirit.[46] If efforts fail to placate the whims of the spirit or to exorcise it from the body, the patient grows weaker and approaches death. It is then obvious that the cause of the disease is more powerful than human expedients, and that the malicious spirit is a dangerous force, not to be thwarted. It is risky even for a healthy person to come in contact with the dying or the dead lest he become contaminated by the evil influence. Out of this belief follow a variety of avoidance measures, practiced among practically all groups of Eskimos in one form or another, such as preparing the body for the grave before death has actually occurred, abandoning a dwelling wherein someone has died, and discarding the possessions of the deceased. These precautions are not to be mistaken, however, for preventives of contagion in the medical sense. The rarity of contagious diseases among the Eskimos in their native state renders such an explanation implausible. The Eskimo may fear that death can be transmitted from the dead, but his ideas can scarcely have arisen through actual observation. And aside from a specific fear, a dead body is thought to be surrounded by an evil influence that may attach itself to the living and cause them misfortune in almost any way imaginable.[47]

Petroff[48] writes of the Eskimos of Bering Sea: "Like all Eskimos these tribes are superstitious and afraid of the dead and dying; and sometimes a sick person at the point of death is carried into an abandoned hut and left there alone to die of hunger and neglect." The people below Ikogmut on the lower Yukon ". . . are very averse to having a dead body in the house, and the corpse is placed in the grave box at the earliest possible moment. This is so marked that the relatives frequently dress the person in the new burial clothing while he is dying in order that he may be removed immediately after death."[49] At St. Michael "when a person dies during the day his relatives, amid loud wailing, proceed at once to dress him in the best clothing they possess, using, if possible, garments that have never been worn. Should death take place at night, the body is not dressed until just at sunrise the following morning."[50] In Kotzebue Sound when a man was supposed to be about to die, all bedding was carried out of the house except what the invalid was using.[51] Among the Nogatogmiut (inland in northwestern Alaska), burials often took place before a man was dead. One of the natives had seen one man hauled out who sat up in the sled on the way; and there were said to be frequent cases of men who had been bundled up corpse-fashion who kept the hungry dogs at bay for a while by saying "goh" at them.[52] At Point Barrow "the sled used to carry the body out on the tundra is not brought back to the village at once, but left on the tundra not less than two moons. . . ."[53] No great fear seems to have been caused by the dead there, however, for the people would eat food part of which the dying had eaten just before and they would wear his good clothes.[54] On the contrary some of the Nunatama (inland Eskimos of northwestern Alaska) were afraid to use clothes, etc., that belonged to the deceased and were afraid to stay in the tent with a dead man.[55]

The Kittegaryumiut, of the Mackenzie Delta, contrary to most other Eskimos, do not avoid or abandon the house where death has occurred except occasionally when epidemic has killed the entire family in the house, in which event the house is allowed to cave in upon them.[56] In summer the Copper Eskimos leave the body inside the tent and move on to another camp; in winter they remove it from the hut and build a windbreak of snow blocks to protect it.[57] Klutschak writes that when an Eskimo woman of the Aivilik group, near Chesterfield Inlet, was apparently soon to die, "immediately the inmates of the hut in which she lay took all their belongings and went to find another sleeping place, the hut was closed and the dying stayed there alone. . . . Next morning she was a corpse."[58] When a member of the Saglernmiut group, of Southampton Island, was dying he was taken into the open; for the occurrence of death in any house necessitated its abandonment.[59] Boas writes of the Central Eskimo that if someone dies in a dwelling all the stuff, even including tools, must be thrown away; consequently when death is imminent a snow house or a hut is built, according to the season, and the dying person is left there alone.[60] "A sick woman is frequently built or blocked up in a snow-hut," writes Lyon concerning the Iglulik Eskimos, "and not a soul goes near to look in and ascertain whether she be alive or dead."[61] Again it is reported of this group that everything can remain in the house where a person is dying except the rugs belonging to him,[62] and that at the termination of the mourning the snow house is abandoned.[63] The Qaernermiut, of the Barren Grounds, require that everything that was in the house of the dead person lie in the open air during mourning.[64] At Cumberland Sound a dead person's tent, the clothes he wore when he died, and the skins he had obtained must all be discarded;[65] it seems possible to avoid this waste, however, if the dying person is removed from the tent.[66] From the region of Frobisher Bay, Hall reports the practice of abandoning the dying in the tent.[67] Similarly, in Labrador, a dying person is removed from the dwelling lest everything be contaminated.[68] Sometimes the body is clothed in fine funeral garments before the breath has left the body; and if the patient recovers they must be given away.[69] Among the Polar Eskimos "when a person is dying, he is removed from the house when possible. . . . Sometimes also, if the person was disliked, the corpse is left [in the house]. In that case, the house in which he died is demolished, the best stones being used for a new house."[70] "If death took place in a tent, the poles are removed, allowing it to settle down over the site, and it is never used again; if in a house, it is vacated, and not used for a long time."[71] On the death of a woman at Narksami (Naqsaq), the natives all removed to Netiulumi (Natilivik).[72] Again it is related that a certain woman among the Polar Eskimos was carried out of the house when she was dying, and that after she was dead her husband prepared to see her by putting on fresh underclothes and dressing fully, and tying a cord below his hips inside his trousers.[73] When someone has died the Polar Eskimos remove all articles, not simply the property of the dead person, and leave them on the ice, pointing seaward.[74] On one occasion, in the process of destroying all the property of a dead woman a part of her dress accidentally was left in the room where she had been, and her husband never entered that room.[75] The West Greenlanders, as soon as a person is dead, ". . . throw out his things, that they may not make themselves unclean and unfortunate. All the people in the house must also carry out their things till the evening, that the smell of the corpse may evaporate."[76] Burial alive might even occur, through fear of being contaminated by the dead.[77] For the same reason the natives of Angmagsalik shrink from rescuing a drowning man.[78] It might be mentioned in passing that the seamen of Orkney and Shetland also deem it unlucky to rescue persons from drowning, in the belief that the sea is entitled to certain victims and if deprived of them would avenge itself on those who interfered.[79] If a Diomede Islander fell among the rocks and was killed his fellows left him where he lay, taking care to put moss on his eyes and to deposit offerings, but omitting the custom of washing the body.[80]

Sometimes there are certain stipulations as to who shall perform the funeral duties. On Diomede Island these rites are incumbent upon some relative of the deceased, unless he has been murdered, in which case the murderer washes the body, etc.[81] In Labrador "all except the relatives are forbidden to touch a dead body";[82] whereas on the lower Yukon, none of the relatives touch the body, this work being done by others.[83] The Qaernermiut require that only old women and young girls touch a corpse; whoever enshrouds it must wear mittens, and all the mourners must leave their mittens at the grave. If a man touch a corpse he must not hunt for a whole year.[84] In an Iglulik funeral all who have taken part in setting stones around the grave or have been in the death house throw away their clothes and leave the snow house.[85] The Polar Eskimos are careful for five days not to cross the footprints of those who dragged the body of a dead person.[86]

Striking by reason of its variance from typical Eskimo custom is the statement[87] that the Koksoagmiut (Ungava District), when they start for another locality, sometimes carry with them a beloved child that has just died. And Lyon's statement applying to the Iglulik group, although it does not harmonize with other known mores of these people, might be cited: "The presence of the dead body does not at all distress them; and I once saw them place their plate of meat on a little dead child, which lay wrapped within a blanket in my cabin."[88]

The Aleutian Islanders, contrary to the Eskimos, seem to have held an attitude of affectionate devotion toward a deceased relative.

A mother would keep the body of her infant, mummified after a fashion, near her for weeks or even months after it had died.[89] At

variance with the Eskimo practice of abandoning a house of death, the
Aleutian Islanders sometimes buried their dead actually within the
dwelling.[90] And there seems to be no mention that the Aleut, in the
event of removing a dead body from the hut, carried it out through a
false door, with the aim of bewildering the ghost and preventing its
return.[91] In view of these facts it is questionable whether the Aleutian
custom of lashing the corpse in a doubled-up posture[92] should be interpreted as an effort to curb the activities of the ghost, although among
some groups of Eskimos and in other parts of the world, this motive
undoubtedly lies behind the practice.[93] On Kodiak Island, likewise,
there seems to be less dread of the corpse and the ghost. The body of a
great whale hunter may be cut up and pieces of it distributed as amulets;[94] and when a ghost reveals himself to his earthly relatives it is regarded as a sign of good luck.[95] Nevertheless, it is stated that the
house wherein a man has died cannot longer be occupied and is torn
down.[96]

Measures Taken to Avoid the Ghost

THE Iglulik Eskimos always cover the face of a corpse when taking it
to the "grave."[97] The Eskimos of Little Diomede Island would leave
the corpse on the rocks behind the village, sometimes naked, but they
were careful to close its eyes and put a piece of moss over each of them
and likewise over the navel and genital regions. Previous to disposing
of the corpse it was washed in urine. Special safeguards were employed
against the return of the ghost to the home where he had lived. Urine
was painted all around the door; similarly, brass was rubbed on like a
pencil; and a walrus penis bone was laid at the doorsill.[98] After a death
at St. Michael ". . . when the people prepared to retire, each man in
the village took his urine tub and poured a little of its contents upon
the ground before the door, saying, 'This is our water; drink;' . . .
believing that should the shade return during the night and try to enter,
it would taste this water, and finding it bad, would go away. . . . On
the evening of the second day the men in every house in the village
took their urine buckets and, turning them bottom upward, went about
the house, thrusting the bottom into every corner and into the smoke
hole and the doorway. This, it was said, was done to drive out the
shade if it should be in the house. . . ."[99] When the deceased had been
an angakok, furthermore, every man improvised a sham snare out of a
stem of grass at the entrance to his home in order that the returning
ghost would be frightened away for fear of being entrapped.[100] On the
Lower Yukon below Ikogmut, as soon as a dead person has been
taken out of the house, his sleeping place must be swept clean and piled
full of bags and other things, in order to leave no room for the shade
to return and reoccupy it. At the same time the two persons who slept

with him upon each side must not, upon any account, leave their places. If they were to do so the shade might return and, by occupying the vacant place, bring sickness or death to its original owner or to the inmates of the house.[101] On the northern shore of Norton Sound it was observed that for ". . . three months after the death of a son the father must not drink from an uncovered vessel, for if he does he may swallow some impurity from the shade that may be present, and die."[102]

The Qaernermiut (Barren Grounds)[103] and the inhabitants of Sentry Island (latitude about 61° N., Hudson Bay)[104] for a few days after a death always keep a knife under their heads while they sleep. And the Eskimos of Baffin Island have been observed to leave a knife with its edge facing outward at the entrance of the igloo during the three days following a death.[105]

The grave is regarded as a dangerous spot by reason of the abiding evil spirit of the dead. Thus the Qaernermiut of the Barren Grounds require that a sledge be set on end at the grave as a warning to those passing. Anyone approaching it will stop his sled some distance off and walk up to it with a knife in his hand.[106] Again it is stated that on Sentry Island a sledge was stood on end in front of a house where anyone had died.[107] Klutschak mentions a superstition among certain Eskimos of the Barren Grounds that it is not wise to linger long on the salt-water ice near the graves of the ancestors.[108] When an Eskimo visits a grave it is a common ritual to walk around it one or more times in a prescribed direction.[109]

A singular custom practiced by some groups of Eskimos as a protection against the evil exhalations from the dead person, is the plugging of one or both nostrils with fur, moss, or other substance. These nose stoppers are commonly worn for a few days after death. The distribution of the practice is essentially central,[110] though a similar custom is observed on St. Lawrence Island, in the extreme western section of the Eskimo region, where sprigs of mint are bound under the nose by two stems of grass passed under the ears and tied behind the head.[111]

Frequently, when a dead person is removed from the dwelling a special door is made, or the body is passed out through a window or other unusual exit. The practice rests upon the belief that taking the corpse out through a special opening will so bewilder the ghost that it will not be able to find its way back. There may also be the notion that a soul which is about to go on a journey to the realm of the dead ought to be given a fittingly fantastic send-off. Widely distributed peoples have observed this practice of using "doors of the dead," including the Norsemen, Hottentots, Bechuanas, Samoyeds, Chukchis, Ojibways, Algonquins, Laosians, Hindus, Tibetans, Siamese, Chinese, Balinese, Fijians, and Europeans in former times.[112]

On the lower Yukon below Ikogmut the corpse is "drawn up through

the smoke hole in the roof and carried to the graveyard. . . ."[113] Also
at St. Michael, Alaska, "by means of cords the body is usually raised
through the smoke hole in the roof, but is never taken out by the doorway. Should the smoke hole be too small, an opening is made in the
rear side of the house and then closed again."[114] At Cape Prince of
Wales and on the Diomede Islands the smoke hole (*canook*) was similarly used. At the latter place, at least, the body was removed feet
first.[115] In Kotzebue Sound the corpse was lifted through the window—
". . . for the hole in the floor was unhandy for such things"—and
taken to the burial place.[116] The Kittegaryumiut of the Mackenzie
Delta region removed the body through an opening made in the house
wall, generally on one side of the real door.[117] The Iglulik Eskimos
dragged the body through a hole cut in the back wall in the case of a
snow house, and in the case of a tent beneath the skin behind the sleeping place,[118] or through a hole in the back wall of the tent.[119] It seems,
however, that among the Iglulik Eskimos the custom is followed regularly only in the case of women, men being removed through the ordinary passage of the snow hut.[120] Again, it is mentioned that doors of
the dead are employed by the natives living on Sentry Island, off the
west coast of Hudson Bay in latitude about 61° N.[121] Regarding the
Koksoagmiut (Ungava Bay) it is written that if one ". . . should die
within he should not be carried out of the door but through a hole cut
in the side wall, and it must be carefully closed to prevent the spirit of
the person from returning."[122] Writing likewise of Labrador, Hawkes
states that the body "is never taken out by the doorway, as the ghost
might find its way back."[123] At Smith Sound a man's corpse is removed through the door, a woman's through the window.[124] And in
West Greenland the window of the house or a back flap of the tent
serves as a door for the dead. When the body is conveyed out a woman
behind waves a lighted chip backward and forward and says, "There is
nothing more to be had here."[125] In East Greenland "a rawhide thong
is fastened round the legs, and the dead body is then quite unceremoni-
ously dragged out through the passage, or, in order to save trouble,
through the window."[126]

Certain customs observed by some Eskimos that are analogous to the
use of doors of the dead might be mentioned here. On the western
shore of Hudson Bay, when a woman who has had a child is permitted,
after a few days of seclusion, to reënter the hut, she must pass in by a
separate entrance cut through the snow wall.[127] On Southampton Island a woman during menstruation must not use the doorway but must
lift the bottom of the tent and crawl in and out.[128] And among the Iglulik Eskimos a couple with children must bring their sleeping skins into
a new snow hut only through a hole cut in the wall.[129]

The custom of binding the corpse is frequently practiced by the Eskimos with the idea that the ghost will thereby be prevented from returning. This avoidance measure is discussed in connection with other details of the funeral in the ensuing chapter.

NOTES

1. Birket-Smith: 1924, 444, citing Rink: 1868, 213, and Rink: 1871, 187.

2. Rasmussen: 1929, I, 93.

3. Kroeber: 1899, 311.

4. Kroeber: 1899, 311.

5. Related to Boas in New York by an Eskimo of Smith Sound. Kroeber: 1899, 314.

6. Hawkes: 1916, 119.

7. Jenness: 1922, 171.

8. Jenness: 1922, 178.

9. Turner: 1887, 101 (Itivimyut, Labrador).

10. Turner: 1887, 108 (Ungava District, Labrador). Regarding the aborigines of Kodiak Island, whose folkways differ further in other ways from those of the Eskimos proper, Petroff states (1900, 235) that they consider it a sign of good fortune if a spirit reveals himself to his relatives.

11. See pp. 289 ff.

12. Boas: 1888, 613.

13. Jenness: 1922, 190.

14. Jenness: 1922, 171.

15. Birket-Smith: 1924, 39.

16. See pp. 137 ff.

17. Rasmussen: 1927, 225.

18. Rasmussen: 1929, I, 95 f.

19. Rasmussen: 1927, 135.

20. Turner: 1894, 186 f.

21. Turner: 1887, 102.

22. Holm: 1914, 74.

23. Jenness: 1922, 233.

24. Weyer: Field Notes.

25. Hawkes: 1916, 118; Boas: 1888, 612 f.; Rasmussen: 1929, I, 94; Schultz-Lorentzen: 1928, 244.

26. See pp. 378 f.

27. Nelson: 1899, 423.

28. Stefansson: 1913, 402.

29. Stefansson: 1914, 364.

30. Rasmussen: 1929, I, 94 ff.

31. Lyon: 1824, 270 f.

32. Rasmussen: 1929, I, 73 f.

33. Boas: 1888, 589; Hall: 1866, 572.

34. Boas: 1887, 36.

35. Boas: 1907, 130.

36. Hall: 1864, 317 f.

37. Bilby: 1923, 206 ff.

38. Turner: 1894, 192.

39. Hawkes: 1916, 137.

40. Kroeber: 1899, 310.

41. Holm: 1914, 80.

42. Crantz: 1767, I, 201 ff.; see also Fries: 1872, 144; and Birket-Smith: 1924, 434 ff., citing several authorities.

43. Birket-Smith: 1924, 435, 428, citing several authorities.

44. Jenness: 1922, 190.

45. Recounted to the author by Billy Pritchard, who served under Peary.

46. See pp. 323 ff.

47. See pp. 245 ff.

48. Petroff: 1900, 214.

49. Nelson: 1899, 314.

50. Nelson: 1899, 310.

51. Stefansson: 1914, 316.

52. Stefansson: 1914, 341.

53. Ray: 1885, 43.

54. Stefansson: 1914, 190.

55. Stefansson: 1914, 162.

56. Stefansson: 1914, 316.

57. Jenness: 1922, 174.

58. Klutschak: 1881, 207.

59. Comer: 1910, 87.

60. Boas: 1888, 612.

61. Lyon: 1824, 259.

62. Rasmussen: 1929, I, 197.

63. Rasmussen: 1929, I, 97; Lyon: 1824, 268.

64. Birket-Smith: 1929, I, 300.

65. Boas: 1907, 125, 144.

66. Boas: 1907, 485; also Bilby: 1923, 165 (Baffin Island).

67. Hall: 1864, 192 f.

68. Hawkes: 1916, 119; Turner: 1894, 191.

69. Hawkes: 1916, 119, 138.

70. Kroeber: 1899, 311.

71. Peary: 1898, I, 227; see also Steensby: 1910, 308.

72. Peary: 1898, I, 227.
73. Kroeber: 1899, 314.
74. Rasmussen: 1908, 113 f.
75. Kroeber: 1899, 316.
76. Crantz: 1767, I, 237.
77. Birket-Smith: 1924, 428.
78. Holm: 1914, 75; and Nansen: 1893, 137.
79. Sumner and Keller: 1927, II, 1074.
80. Weyer: Field Notes.
81. Weyer: Field Notes.
82. Hawkes: 1916, 138.
83. Nelson: 1899, 315.
84. Birket-Smith: 1929, I, 300 f.
85. Rasmussen: 1929, I, 200.
86. Rasmussen: 1908, 113 f.
87. Turner: 1894, 192.
88. Lyon: 1824, 267 f.
89. Weyer: 1929; also Dall: 1878, 6; Sauer: 1802, 161; Sarychev: 1806–7, II, 77.
90. Dall: 1878, 6 f.
91. See pp. 259 f.
92. Coxe: 1787, 230; Sarychev: 1806–7, II, 77; Dall: 1878, 6 f.
93. See pp. 268 ff.
94. Petroff: 1900, 234, citing Lieutenant Davidof.
95. Petroff: 1900, 235.
96. Holmberg: 1855, 122.
97. Rasmussen: 1929, I, 198 f.
98. Weyer: Field Notes.
99. Nelson: 1899, 313 f. Klutschak mentions that after a funeral among the Aivilik Eskimos, near Chesterfield Inlet, the inner circumference of each snow house was treated with a substance which he does not deem appropriate to name, the same being fastened over the door during the entire mourning (Klutschak: 1881, 210).
100. Nelson: 1899, 314.
101. Nelson: 1899, 315.
102. Nelson: 1899, 422.

103. Birket-Smith: 1929, I, 300.
104. Rasmussen: 1929, I, 202.
105. Bilby: 1923, 168 f.
106. Birket-Smith: 1929, I, 300.
107. Rasmussen: 1929, I, 202.
108. Klutschak: 1881, 154.
109. Boas: 1907, 516; Rasmussen: 1929, I, 201 (Iglulik); Rasmussen: 1908, 113 f. (Polar Eskimos).
110. Boas: 1888, 614 (the Central Eskimos); Boas: 1907, 516 (West coast of Hudson Bay?); Birket-Smith: 1929, I, 301 (Qaernermiut); Rasmussen: 1929, I, 197; Lyon: 1824, 268 (Iglulik Eskimos); Boas: 1907, 144 (Cumberland Sound); Hawkes: 1916, 120, 134, 138 (Labrador); Rasmussen: 1908, 114; Kroeber: 1899, 314; Bessels: 1884, 877.
111. Moore: 1923, 369.
112. Sumner and Keller: 1927, II, 861.
113. Nelson: 1899, 314.
114. Nelson: 1899, 311.
115. Weyer: Field Notes.
116. Stefansson: 1914, 316.
117. Stefansson: 1914, 315 f.
118. Rasmussen: 1929, I, 94; also Lyon: 1824, 268.
119. Mathiassen: 1928, I, 229.
120. Rasmussen: 1929, I, 197 f.
121. Rasmussen: 1929, I, 202.
122. Turner: 1894, 191.
123. Hawkes: 1916, 119.
124. Kroeber: 1899, 311.
125. Crantz: 1767, I, 237; Birket-Smith: 1924, 428.
126. Holm: 1914, 74; cf. Kroeber: 1899, 312.
127. Boas: 1888, 611; see Sumner, Keller, and Davie: 1927, IV, 1067, regarding a similar practice in northern Asia.
128. Boas: 1907, 478.
129. Rasmussen: 1929, I, 182.

CHAPTER XVI

THE GHOST CULT (*Continued*)

§1. METHODS OF DISPOSING OF THE DEAD

INASMUCH as the ground is frozen solid in the Eskimo region except during the summer months, when it thaws to a depth of only a foot or two, it is only with great difficulty that a body can be buried, especially by a people not possessing effective digging tools. Practically no Eskimos inter their dead actually underground. Cremation, to mention another conceivable method of disposal, is a wasteful process where fuel is scarce. It is practiced by none of the American Eskimos, although it is employed by the Asiatic Eskimos, as well as by the Chukchi,[1] the Koryak, and the Kenaige (or Kenaitze) of Cook's Inlet in the Gulf of Alaska.[2] Other methods of disposing of the dead to be considered are: the depositing of the body on the surface of the ground, either covered in some way or exposed; interment in caves; and burial in the sea. Surface burials, which constitute by far the commonest mode of disposal, will be discussed below. Interring corpses in caves was a practice elaborately developed by the Aleutian and Kodiak islanders,[3] but otherwise the utilization of caves is so rare that we need not even consider it in the present study. The custom of casting corpses into the sea is common only in East Greenland. There, if an ancestor of the deceased has perished in a kayak, as is doubtless always the case, the descendant's body is thrown into the ocean. Quite possibly this practice arose through the fear that otherwise evil magicians might utilize the flesh of corpses for dark purposes.[4]

Among some other Eskimos the body is sometimes placed on the sea ice, where it will eventually sink.[5]

The Alaskan Eskimo Grave Box

THE Eskimos of Bering Sea deposit the dead in wooden boxes which are secured in position above the ground by stakes. Somewhat similar to these boxes are the more massive driftwood sarcophagi of the Aleutian Islanders, which, however, are sometimes heaped over with earth or actually sunk in the ground.[6]

The Kwikpagmiut of the Lower Yukon and all the tundra people between them and the Kuskokwim River inter the dead in boxes erected on four posts, with sometimes a center stake underneath, after much the same fashion as the Indians of the same region. The boxes were sometimes lying on the ground covered with stone or wood to keep the lids from coming off.[7] At St. Michael the coffin is constructed by some of the male relatives or friends of the deceased, out of drift logs or planks. The dead person is laid in the box doubled up on his side, wrapped in his own bedding. Certain decorations on the coffin are interpreted by Nelson as totem marks.[8] Near Ishingachmiut on the Kuskokwim River, "it is customary to bury the dead above the ground. The dead body is laid in a rude box made of logs or driftwood, raised by other logs to a height of two or three feet above the ground, and covered with the same material to protect the remains from the dogs."[9]

Even north of Bering Strait the box burial has been used. Beechey observed at Cape Espenberg in 1826 that the corpse was "deposited in a sort of coffin formed of loose planks, placed upon a platform of driftwood, and covered over by a board and several spars, kept in their places by poles driven into the ground in a slanting direction, with their ends crossing each other over the pile.[10] At Point Hope, ". . . the bodies were placed in rude boxes built of driftwood, above the ground, and surrounded by implements."[11]

Platform burials have been employed in parts of northwestern Alaska, one purpose being probably the protection of the body from animals.[12]

Stone Graves

VARIOUS types of graves wherein the body is more or less protected simply by stones have been used extensively from northeast Asia to Greenland and doubtless represent an old form of burial.[13] The most highly developed form of the stone grave takes the shape of a rectangular erection covered over with large flat stones, upon which smaller ones are piled. This variety was employed by the ancient Eskimos belonging to what is known as the Thule Culture.[14] Stone graves constructed by recent Eskimos show all gradations down to the most rudimentary circle of stones.

On St. Lawrence Island and at Plover Bay, Siberia, bodies have simply been laid out on the ground inside an oval formation of separate stones, from the edge of which at the foot end there extended outward and upward a section of driftwood. Sometimes in these locations and also on Sledge Island and at Cape Lisburne the stones which were removed to leave a shallow depression were laid around in the form of a low wall and gave support to a roofing of slabs or pieces of drift-wood.[15]

From the region east of the Mackenzie even to Labrador and East Greenland there are abundant references to the custom of covering the body with stones.[16] In fact among Central and Eastern Eskimos this practice constitutes the only common method of disposal, aside from plain abandonment or exposure of the corpse. Although the present Copper Eskimos seem never to cover their dead with stones, cairn graves have been observed in their country. These are probably the relics of an earlier tribe that peopled the coast from Baillie Island to Dolphin and Union Strait.[17] The Caribou Eskimos are known to construct coffins of stone and inclosures of stone.[18] On the west coast of Hudson Bay graves are generally made of stone but sometimes the body is only wrapped in caribou skins.[19] When a death occurs in summer among the Iglulik Eskimos they pile an irregular heap of stones over the body[20] or simply lay a crude circle of stones.[21] At Cumberland Sound graves were built of stones with a vaulted covering.[22] Crude cairn graves are used widely also among the Eskimos of the Labrador Peninsula.[23] We read of Labrador that "most old graves present the appearance of a cluttered heap of stones, but in a newly-made grave, the method of building an enclosing wall can be distinguished. . . . Having fixed upon a place of burial, stones are piled up in an oval or oblong wall 2 or 3 feet high, leaving just space enough for the body. The bottom of the space is lined with moss, and the body, wrapped in heavy deerskins, is placed on this soft bed. Large flat stones and, at a later date, pieces of wood, form a covering over the enclosure. The grave box is then covered with rocks to keep the body from wild beasts and birds."[24]

The Polar Eskimos also sometimes bury their dead under stones.[25] Sod and stone were used to cover the dead in West Greenland;[26] and at Angmagsalik, at least in recent days, the body is occasionally covered with loose stones.[27]

Exposure of Corpses

THE cairn type of grave described above is in its most rudimentary form but slightly removed from out-and-out exposure. Indeed, the availability of stones sometimes determines how well the body shall be covered. Or custom, founded upon precedent and rationalization, determines the manner of disposing of the dead.

An old Eskimo of St. Michael, Alaska, informed Nelson that the Unalit of that vicinity in ancient times, before the custom of using grave boxes had been acquired from the people to the south, simply threw all their dead out on the tundra back of the village. The informant spoke of the effectiveness of the grave box in preventing the shades from wandering about as they formerly had done. The Malemiut Eskimos to the north were still simply throwing many of their dead out upon the tundra.[28] Likewise, the Point Barrow people laid their dead upon the tundra, usually wrapped in deerskins.[29] The Diomede Islanders either buried the body under the stones or simply stretched it out on the individual's *panasee'tok* (a rack in a dwelling for bedding) placed on top of the rocks just behind the village; the dogs devoured the corpse.[30]

The present-day Copper Eskimos never cover their dead with stones, so far as Jenness could learn. "The natives of Bathurst Inlet and farther east leave the corpse inside the hut or tent and abandon camp immediately. . . . In the Coppermine region and in Dolphin and Union Strait the Eskimos also leave the body inside the tent in summer and move on to another camping ground. In winter, however, they lay the corpse out in the snow, and build a wind-break of snow blocks around it to protect it from the weather. Usually it is conveyed to the land a few days later and deposited on the beach above highwater mark, though sometimes it is simply left neglected on the ice."[31] Among the Iglulik Eskimos a stone grave is the exception; snow may be piled over the body.[32] The Tahagmiut, at the western end of Hudson Strait, treat the dead with little ceremony. "They simply lash the limbs of the deceased to the body and expose the corpse to the elements, removing it, however, from the immediate sight of the camp."[33]

When a body is exposed it naturally becomes a prey to animals, commonly to the dogs belonging to the people themselves. The Diomede Islanders seem to think nothing of the dead being devoured by the dogs.[34] Nelson[35] reports that at East Cape, Siberia, "the enclosures were so roughly and lightly made that the village dogs had robbed many of their contents. . . . I found a dog devouring the remains of a boy ten or twelve years of age. Some village children who had followed me did not pay the slightest attention to this, although but a few days before the dead boy must have been their playmate." At Point Barrow, "the bodies are usually eaten by the dogs, especially in winter, and it is no uncommon sight to see them gnawing the bones on the roofs of the iglus."[36] Likewise, among the Iglulik Eskimos, a corpse is usually torn to pieces by the dogs or other animals.[37]

Some Eskimos, however, are offended by the thought of a corpse being devoured by dogs. Klutschak reports from near Chesterfield Inlet (Aivilik Eskimos), that dogs were not used in drawing the funeral sled for fear that when hungry they would visit the grave.[38] The Baffin Islanders are said not to like to have dogs eat them;[39] and among the Koksoagmiut, of Ungava Bay, it is considered a great offense if a dog is seen eating the flesh from a body.[40]

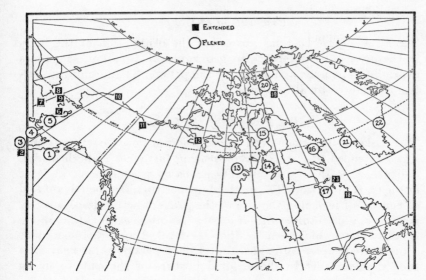

FIGURE 17

Map Showing Distribution of Burial Postures

1 Dall: 1878, 27 f. (Kodiak Island; flexed or some natural attitude).

2 Dall: 1878, 5 f. (Aleutian Islands; poor people are buried extended).

3 Dall: 1878, 6 f. (Aleutian Islands; flexed). Sarychev: 1806–7, II, 77; Coxe: 1787, 230 (Aleutian Islands; flexed).

4 Nelson: 1899, 317 (Kushunuk, near Cape Vancouver; flexed).

5 Nelson: 1899, 314 (Lower Yukon; flexed). Dall: 1870, 19, 145, 227 (Yukon; flexed). Nelson: 1899, 311 (St. Michael; flexed). Petroff: 1900, 214 (general region; flexed).

6 Nelson: 1899, 312 (St. Michael; extended in ancient times).

7 Moore: 1923, 368 f. (St. Lawrence Island; extended). Nelson: 1899, 321 (St. Lawrence Island; extended).

8 Nelson: 1899, 321 f. (East Cape and Plover Bay; extended).

9 Weyer: Field Notes (Diomede Islands; extended).

10 Murdoch: 1892, 424 (Point Barrow; extended).

11 Stefansson: 1914, 317 (Mackenzie Delta; extended).

12 Jenness: 1922, 174 ff. (Copper Eskimos; extended?).

13 Birket-Smith: 1929, I, 300 (Qaernermiut, Caribou Eskimos; flexed).

14 Boas: 1907, 61 (Southampton Island; flexed; bodies that apparently had been long buried).

15 Rasmussen: 1929, I, 94 (Iglulik Eskimos; flexed).

16 Boas: 1888, 613 (Cumberland Sound; flexed).

17 Turner: 1894, 191 (Koksoagmyut, northern Labrador; flexed).

18 Junius Bird: Communication (near Nain, Labrador; extended; apparently a very old grave).

19 Kane: 1856, II, 118; Peary: 1898, I, 506 (Polar Eskimos; extended burial is the commoner).

20 Kane: 1856, I, 51 (Polar Eskimos; flexed).

21 Crantz: 1767, I, 237; Egede: 1745, 149 (West Greenland; flexed).

22 Holm: 1914, 75 (East Greenland; sometimes flexed).

23 Hantzsch: 1930, 180 (northeastern Labrador; always extended).

Orientation of Corpse

THERE are local customs governing the orientation of the body in the grave with reference to geographical direction, sometimes depending upon the age or sex of the person, but no uniform system is followed by all groups.[41]

The Posture of the Corpse

THE Eskimos lay their dead sometimes in a flexed posture, sometimes extended. Figure 17, representing instances of both modes, indicates that the flexed burial is probably predominant, at least in the eastern section. The doubled-up position has the advantage, of course, of lessening the size of the grave, whether it be a pit, a coffin, or a structure built of stones. Another explanation sometimes offered, which seems rather far-fetched when attributed to a primitive people, is the idea that a dead person in his final attitude should revert to the original posture of the embryo in its mother's womb.

Binding the Corpse

ACCOUNTS given suggest that this practice of placing the corpse in a flexed position is intimately associated with binding the body. This process, which the Eskimos, like many other peoples of the world,[42] commonly perform soon after death has occurred, is generally interpreted as a preventive against activity on the part of the ghost. If the body is to be left in a doubled-up position it is very natural that bindings or lashings should be employed, at least until it has become set. Hence, we may fairly ask the question whether the practice of binding the body has grown up merely accidentally because of the advantage inherent in the decreased size of a flexed body, or whether there lies behind it the idea of restraining the ghost. Jochelson, for instance, acknowledges that among some peoples of the world fear of the dead presents a real cause for the binding of corpses. "The Aleut," however, according to the statement of this authority, "lashed the body with thongs only to keep the bent bones together, while the squatting position corresponds to the posture of which the living Aleut are so fond."[43]

Since authors reporting on the practice rarely give the Eskimos' reason for binding the body, it is very difficult to analyze the question as it applies to them.

Separate authorities describing the custom in West Greenland, indeed, take opposite views: Crantz explains the doubling-up of the corpse as a means of decreasing the length of the grave;[44] while Saabye asserts that the feet are drawn under the body to prevent the ghost from walking.[45] The Eskimos at St. Michael, Alaska, tie the deceased hand and foot to prevent evil spirits from wandering and taking possession of dead bodies and from thus giving them a fictitious animation for evil purposes. They have a myth which serves as an explanation of the origin of this precaution. They believe that the man who was the father of the moon and sun became seized with the desire to kill and eat people. Finally, the shamans combined to tie him up. In memory of the binding of this evil one, the dead are no longer thrown out, as they had been, to satisfy the man's hunger, but are lashed in the position in which this demon was bound, and placed in the grave box.[46] Hawkes writes in *The Labrador Eskimo* that the dead are bound to restrain the malicious spirit during the three days that it is supposed to remain on earth before taking its departure to the spirit world.[47] The reasonable assumption is that even where this motive is not specifically mentioned it exists in the minds of the natives. While flexing the body affords a practical advantage in itself, shortening the length of the grave, there exists a belief that a corpse bound insures a fettered ghost. In the Bering Sea region, "in ancient times the sinews in the arms and legs of a dead person who had been of evil repute during life were cut in order to prevent the shade from returning to the body and causing it to walk at night as a ghoul."[48] Possibly, the Aleut custom of fracturing the bones[49] has a basis in this purpose, aside from the imputed one of facilitating the consolidation of the remains, although it is to be noticed that these people seem not to harbor a very deep fear of corpses.[50] The aim toward curbing the activity of the ghost may even be present in the common Eskimo practice of covering the body with stones.[51]

Light is shed upon the question of corpse binding by the custom among some Eskimos of cutting the lashings when the body is fully deposited.

Thus, the inhabitants of St. Lawrence Island wrap the extended corpse in skins and tie it up with a series of half hitches from head to foot; but at the grave the ropes are severed, and the body is left entirely nude.[52] And on the lower Yukon below Ikogmut: "Just before the body is placed in the box the cords that bind it are cut, in order, they say, that the shade may return and occupy the body and move about if necessary."[53] Similarly, the Iglulik Eskimos and those of Cumberland Sound cut the lashings at the grave.[54]

The lack of uniformity shown in the practice of sometimes loosening the cords and sometimes leaving them fast is merely an instance of seeming inconsistency often to be noted in a primitive cult. The primary concept holds good in both modes, like the law of gravity that makes a stone drop and a balloon rise. Whether the people leave the body bound or free, they act with an ulterior motive: in the first case the policy is forceful restriction, in the latter it is lenient conciliation.

§2. MOURNING OBSERVANCES

A RIGID system of taboos and requirements controls the activities of the Eskimo during the period of mourning. Customarily three, four, or five days are devoted to the observance of these restrictions, but even months may pass before the mourner puts aside every taboo. In practically all of these customs of mourning one perceives an attempt to forestall the evil powers of the ghost by coercion or conciliation. One means toward this end is simply a continuance of the avoidance policy observed with regard to the corpse. Since the ghost is apt to return to familiar scenes, the mourner must guard against exposing himself to its baleful influence.

Thus, the Eskimos, like many other peoples of the world, observe the custom of remaining indoors during mourning.[55] On Little Diomede Island, violation of this restriction is supposed to bring deafness.[56] Another measure to protect a person from the shade of the dead is a restriction against uncovering the head by slipping back the parka hood. This taboo is reported as occurring among the Bering Sea Eskimos;[57] also in the Mackenzie Delta;[58] and again in far-distant Greenland among the Polar Eskimos[59] and south of them on the west coast.[60] The St. Lawrence Islanders[61] and the Diomede Islanders[62] require in addition that mourners turn their parkas inside out for four or five days. On Diomede they must also wear gloves.

Cutting off some of the hair is practiced on the southern Bering Sea coast,[63] and in West Greenland,[64] and among the Iglulik Eskimos.[65] This custom may be interpreted either as an attempt to disguise the person against the ghost, or simply as a form of self-defacement, with possibly a connotation of survivalistic sacrifice. Also, with the implication of disguise and self-defacement, Eskimos of the central region observe a mourning taboo against combing the hair, cutting the nails, and washing.[66] Similarly, at Qeqertarssuatsiaq in Greenland, a widow must not comb her hair toward the window.[67]

Taboo on Name of Dead

THE fear that uttering the name of a deceased person will summon his ghost, or somehow offend it, has given rise to a restriction, observed in various parts of the world, against speaking the name. This custom is known as *hlonipa*, from the African taboo term.[68] This practice among the Eskimos should be viewed in the light of a belief sometimes held that the name is one of the souls that the person possesses,[69] and of the custom generally practiced by Eskimos of naming children after persons who have recently died.[70]

It is chiefly the Greenland Eskimos who practice the taboo on the name of a deceased person. At Angmagsalik if two persons have the same name, when one of them dies the other changes his. If a person whose name was that of an animal or an object dies, the language itself undergoes alterations. In this manner the word *kaiak* was changed to *sarkit*. In time, however, the old terms crop up again.[71] When a man by the name of Angmagsalik died, the natives of Angmagsalik ceased calling the place by that name.[72] *Hlonipa* is observed in the same way by the natives of Smith Sound;[73] while the natives of West Greenland,[74] and the Iglulik group as well,[75] are simply reluctant to mention the name of a dead person, at least until it is bestowed upon someone else. It is stated, on the other hand, that among the Copper Eskimos there is no taboo against mentioning the name of the dead.[76]

Mourning Taboos on Various Kinds of Work

TYPICAL of the mourning customs of the Eskimos is a taboo against working with sharp instruments, such as knives, picks, and, particularly, needles.[77]

On the lower Yukon during four days after death had occurred none of the relatives were permitted to use any sharp-edged or pointed instrument for fear of injuring the shade and causing it to bring misfortune upon them, or, as one man explained it, for fear of injuring their own shades.[78] Similarly, at St. Michael, when a death has occurred ". . . relatives must perform no labor during the three following days. It is especially forbidden during this period to cut with any edged instrument, such as a knife or an ax; and the use of pointed instruments, like needles or bodkins, is also forbidden. This is done to avoid cutting or injuring the shade, which may be present at any time during this period, and if accidentally injured by any of these things it would become very angry and bring sickness or death to the people."[79] Again at the time of the feast for the dead in Norton Sound

there is a taboo against working with sharp-edged or pointed tools.[80]
On Little Diomede Island no work must be performed by the members of the family wherein death has occurred for four days if the deceased was a man, five days if a woman. The taboo is especially strict with regard to the use of pointed instruments, such as the pick with which they dig roots; violation, they believe, will cause sickness.[81]
When someone dies at Point Barrow the women are not allowed to do any sewing, except in the most urgent cases; and then they circumscribe a circle on the ground with the point of a knife and remain inside this safety zone.[82] And the relatives of the dead must refrain from working on wood with an ax or hammer, probably for four or five days.[83] For one year after a death among the Qaernermiut (Barren Ground Eskimos) housemates may not cut bone or wood with a knife;[84] and in Labrador there is a taboo against working with sharp instruments for three days, in the belief that during this period the ghost is especially irritable.[85] Certain Eskimos of the central region observe a taboo against working on skins.[86] The mourning taboo against needlework for a widow is also mentioned as occuring at Qeqertarssuatsiaq, Greenland.[87] And among the Kittegaryumiut, of the Mackenzie Delta, there must be no sewing of new garments for five days after a death.[88] Among the Polar Eskimos, blackening the eyebrows offers the only escape from a five-day taboo against sewing.[89]

The explanation of these taboos against the use of sharp instruments for fear of injuring the spirit is not derived through baseless theorizing on the part of the anthropologist; it is the ungarnished assertion of the natives themselves. In many other parts of the world, though sometimes, at least superficially, with a different implication, similar taboos are observed against the use of sharp instruments, especially needles. It is scarcely necessary to point out that on the Christian Sunday a taboo against sewing is observed by some.

During the Eskimo period of mourning any sort of loud noise (unless it be wailing) is likely to be discountenanced.[90]

Hunting and Eating Taboos

WHEN a person dies his soul is believed to retain a human need for bodily nourishment. It follows that provision should be made to satisfy this need, lest the spirit become angered. This motive is obviously present in the practice of making offerings of food either at the grave or at the festival for the dead.[91] Various abstention taboos might also be classed as a negative aspect of the same measure, the idea behind such taboos being that whatever the living leave unused will accrue to the dead. In addition, it is hoped that obvious self-denial will demonstrate reverence for the dead and thereby effect conciliation.

Among the Qaernermiut (Barren Grounds), for five days after a man loses his wife he must not go hunting and he must sink the skin and half the meat of the first caribou or seal he catches.[92] At Chesterfield Inlet a taboo against all hunting lasted for five days after a death.[93] Among the Iglulik Eskimos the duration of the taboo on hunting was six days after a man's death, ten after a woman's;[94] or it might even last all season.[95] A death among the Polar Eskimos put an end to hunting and fishing by the villagers or the housemates for five days.[96] There "the bereaved husband may be required even to abstain from the seal- or walrus-hunt for a whole year, from Okiakut to Okiakut—from winter to winter. More generally he is denied the luxury of some article of food, as the rabbit or a favorite part of the walrus. . . ."[97] Again it is stated with regard to these Eskimos of Smith Sound that "certain kinds of meat—bear, fox, and especially ground seal—may not be eaten."[98] The taboo against hunting during mourning is so rigid among the Central Eskimos that it renders famine inevitable if the death has been preceded by a long spell of bad weather occasioning privation.[99] The Kittegaryumiut (Mackenzie Delta) believe that every family wherein a death has occurred must refrain from eating the head of any animal for one year.[100] And it is stated that sometimes at a festival held by the Alaskan Eskimos in honor of the ancestors one person, desiring to show special reverence, would sit naked for three days on a mat in the corner of the ceremonial room without eating or drinking, chanting a song of praise for his dead relative.[101]

The above examples are representative of many mourning taboos against securing and consuming food. One motive in these practices, already mentioned, is to prove through self-denial one's esteem and veneration for the departed and thereby to forestall the vengeance that might be taken for disrespect. The same motive probably influences the Iglulik Eskimos[102] and the natives of Cumberland Sound[103] in refraining from sexual intercourse during mourning. Other taboos following a death simply stipulate how and by whom food shall be prepared. Taboos of this nature, which sometimes seem arbitrary, are very common. Some of them, it will be noticed, prohibit the cutting of meat and therefore come under the category of restrictions against using sharp instruments.

Natives of the Iglulik group observe a taboo against cutting one's own meat for cooking. It lasts for three days after a man has died and four after a woman.[104] Among the Polar Eskimos those who have had to do with a corpse must not prepare their own food or cut up cooked meat for five days.[105] During this period the widower had his eggs broken for him and his meat cut, and would eat it only raw or rare.[106] An Iglulik widow, on the contrary, would not eat raw flesh for six months after the death of her husband.[107] Certain Bering Sea Eskimos believe that a widow must refrain from fresh food for twenty days after the death of her husband; and they frequently observe the same custom in the case of a widower.[108]

It is sometimes believed that those who have been closely associated with a person who has died, somehow are a hazard to the success of hunting.

Thus, at Point Barrow, "a woman who during the winter has lost a child by death is not allowed to go on the ocean ice during the Eskimo whaling season, for if she were to go, the whales would either not come at all or would pass in their run to the north and east far from the shore ice."[109] Caribou Eskimo "widows and women who have lost small children must not look at any game or mention it by name for a whole year, but only by circumlocution."[110]

Miscellaneous Mourning Taboos

In addition to the taboos classified above there are many miscellaneous ones, which differ widely from place to place.

The Qaernermiut[111] and the Iglulik Eskimos[112] refrain from driving sleds during mourning; and the natives of Cumberland Sound do not feed their dogs until after the fourth night after a death.[113] In Greenland "those who have clothed the dead man must refrain from working iron. This precaution, it seems, must be obeyed for several years, lest there come upon the family some ill luck. When they begin again, a spell must first be employed."[114] Taboos against working and using iron are also commonly held among the Eskimos, apart from mourning.[115]

It is difficult to account for some mourning observances, such as the Baffin Island custom of biting the third finger of the left hand of a dead child, and singeing a piece of hair on its left temple.[116] But most of the various local observances fall naturally under the broad headings laid down above and are motivated by the same aim of preventing the ghost from causing misfortune.

Termination of Mourning

WHEN the mourning observances are completed a cleansing ceremony is sometimes performed.

The Polar Eskimos wash their hands and bodies, and throw away the clothes they have been wearing.[117] Among the Unalit of St. Michael, Alaska, on the third morning after a death every man, woman, and child, before eating, bathed in urine, in order to be cleansed of every evil that might have gathered about their persons and to render their flesh hardy and able to withstand the ordinary influence of the shade.[118] Klutschak mentions that in the neighborhood of Chesterfield Inlet at the termination of mourning all the housemates faced in different directions in the hut and spoke the word *taba* meaning "enough," and then, to finish the ceremony, they washed their faces and hands.[119]

Duration of Mourning

As indicated in the cases cited above, the strict observances of mourning commonly hold for three, four,[120] or five days. The duration is commonly longer in the event of a woman's death, a fact that is to be associated with the belief that a woman is supposed to have an especially dangerous capacity to cause contamination, as evinced by the taboo enforced during menstruation.[121]

Sometimes certain of the mourning taboos must be observed for longer periods.

At the upper end of the Yukon Delta an old man ". . . was prohibited from doing any work for three moons following the death of his son."[122] Klutschak states with reference to certain Eskimos of the Barren Grounds that the angakok stipulates a period of time from eight days to a month, according to the nearness of the relationship, during which those concerned must remain in their dwellings.[123] At Cumberland Sound a mother remains in mourning for her child for a year;[124] and at Angmagsalik a mother or a wife must mourn for a month.[125]

The duration of mourning depends somewhat upon the length of time that the soul is believed to sojourn in the body or on this earth, or in some other particular sphere. For this reason we shall consider briefly the ideas held by the Eskimos regarding the stay of the soul in the body after death.

The Iglulirmiut believe that the soul leaves the body immediately after death and descends to Adli.[126] Again, it is stated that the Eskimo believes that one soul, exemplified by the breath and warmth of the body, leaves the man at death, but that another spirit which everyone possesses lingers around the village for three days before taking its final departure.[127] At Cumberland Sound it is believed that the dead body harbors the soul for three days.[128] Similarly, a polar bear's spirit is supposed to linger for three days near where the animal died.[129] Again, it is reported that the Baffin Island native believes that the spirit of a dead person is earth-bound for three days.[130] "On the lower Kuskokwim river the Eskimo believe that the shade of a male stays with the body until the fifth day after his death; the shade of a female remains with the body for four days. On the Yukon and among the Eskimo to the north the shades of men and women alike are believed to remain with the body four days after death. . . . None of the relatives of the deceased must do any work during the entire time in which the shade is believed to remain with the body."[131]

Among the Unalit of St. Michael, Alaska, during the first day after the death everyone near the village was said to be soft and nerveless, with very slight power of resistance to injury by the evil power; but the next day the people said they were a little harder than before and on the third day the body was becoming frozen and they were approaching hardiness again.[132] Among the Koksoagmiut (Ungava Bay, Hudson Strait), "if death result from natural causes the spirit is supposed to dwell on earth after having undergone a probation of four years' rest in the grave. During this time the grave may be visited and food offered and songs sung, and the offering . . . is consumed by the living at the grave."[133] Regarding the Eskimos of West Greenland it is said that the soul is believed to stay five days by the grave where the body lies, whereupon the person rises again and seeks his maintenance in the other world;[134] and again it is stated that five days were thought necessary for the soul to travel to the future world.[135]

§3. SACRIFICES AND OFFERINGS TO THE DEAD

Grave Deposits

ONE of the most obvious manifestations of spiritual belief among a primitive people is the practice of depositing food, clothing, or implements at graves. Grave deposits are *prima facie* evidence of the belief that the soul persists after death and that it retains its human needs and desires. The practice of depositing offerings for the dead at the grave is observed by the Eskimos almost without exception.

At St. Michael, Alaska, the graves of both men and women receive implements and food, and water is poured on the ground near by. Even at the grave box of a bad man food and water were deposited, but no weapons or other marks were placed and no feast was made to his memory.[136] When the corpse of a Diomede Islander was deposited behind the village, implements and food were left with it just as though the man were going on a hunting trip. There was a separate, sham graveyard for those who were lost at sea, where grave offerings were deposited.[137] In the Yukon-Kuskokwim region, in memory of those who are drowned or otherwise lost so that their bodies cannot be recovered, posts are erected and offerings made from time to time.[138] On Queen Maud Gulf, among a people who do not even bury their dead, but lay them out on the bare ground, Rasmussen discovered a row of stone cairns which had been erected as monuments to the memory of dead persons lost at sea.[139] Eskimos at Cape Chidley, Labrador, likewise, informed Bernhard Hantzsch that they occasionally erected stone graves for people whose bodies were lost through drowning or otherwise.[140] At Selawik (Kotzebue Sound, Alaska) food was laid at the grave so that the dead would not send sickness.[141] On the Mackenzie Delta the Eskimos made grave deposits,[142] including food, which was replenished sometimes two or three years later.[143] The Netsilik Eskimos were observed to bury pieces of old clothing under large stones preparatory to leaving the place where their ancestors had been born and died.[144] The Qaernermiut and coast Pâdlimiut, Barren Grounds Eskimos, deposit offerings and sometimes renew them.[145] Among the Iglulik natives, offerings are taken to the grave by a childless woman.[146] An Eskimo of Southampton Island who requested his body to be placed on the ice so that it would fall into the sea promised to send aid to the living if they would throw a piece of meat into the water when they went sea hunting.[147] Mention is made of grave deposits at Ponds Bay, Baffin Island,[148] among the Itivimiut on the east coast of Hudson Bay,[149] and in West Greenland.[150] The grave offerings of the Labrador Eskimos are inviolate and are renewed regularly.[151] The Angmagsalik natives always leave the principal implements at the grave; but when burial at sea occurs only the kayak is sunk.[152]

Sometimes miniature implements serve as grave offerings, as for instance on Kodiak Island,[153] on the Diomede Islands,[154] among the Copper Eskimos,[155] the Iglulik Eskimos,[156] the Eskimos of Cumberland Sound,[157] and the Polar Eskimos.[158]

Nonobservance of the practice of leaving grave offerings is extremely rare. The only negative cases in a wide compilation of positive evidence are of the Harvaqtôrmiut (near Chesterfield Inlet), who assert that they never give grave goods, and the Arviligjuarmiut (Pelly Bay), who refrain from leaving grave deposits for the reason that the dead might use them to do harm.[159] Therefore, no wide application can be attached to a statement such as Hanbury's[160] regarding certain

Eskimos that, so far as he could discover, they had no idea of a future state. The remark made in his hearing, "Husky die. No more Husky," cannot be considered typical of the Eskimo.

"Killing" Grave Offerings

THE practice of destroying the utility of the objects placed at the graves by breaking them or drilling holes through them, which is observed by many peoples throughout the world,[161] is followed by many Eskimos. The most obvious reason for mutilating grave deposits is to prevent their being stolen. The articles appropriated for the use of the dead must remain inviolate and must not fall into the hands of others. Thus, the property of a person who is passing into the other world is rendered useless, much in the same way as the guns of a fort which is being abandoned are "spiked."

At Plover Bay a musket, numerous spears, and other implements which were scattered about were all broken, so as to render them useless.[162] On St. Lawrence Island "part of the personal effects of the dead are broken at the home or at the village limits while part are carried to the grave and left there."[163] At Point Barrow a sled was broken at the grave.[164] Kayaks and sleds used as grave deposits on the Mackenzie Delta were almost invariably broken.[165]

Another motive, however, also prompts the "killing" of objects left as grave deposits. Perhaps even more basic than the first-mentioned motive is the belief that breaking these objects or drilling holes in them will liberate their spiritual essence to serve their ghostly owner in the shadowy realm.

Thus, among the Eskimos of Labrador, "all the effects of the deceased are broken to liberate the spirit residing there, so that it may be useful to the shade of the owner. The clothes are torn; the dishes split; and holes bored in the soapstone lamps and kettles."[166] The Copper Eskimos explain their custom of breaking grave deposits by saying that the man is dead and will want dead implements.[167]

Grave Escort

THE custom of sacrificing servants or slaves to attend the soul departing to the future world is practiced by the Aleut[168] and the natives of Kodiak Island;[169] but it is not characteristic of the Eskimos. They often kill a young infant at the death of its mother, to be sure, but this is due rather to inability to rear the child than to the hope that the soul of the child will add to the happiness of the mother in the future world.[170]

The practice of sacrificing one or more dogs at the grave has been observed on Little Diomede Island[171] and at Smith Sound, Greenland.[172] The West Greenlanders followed a custom of burying a dog's head with a child so that the wise animal might show the little uninstructed soul the way to the happy land.[173]

Masks and the Dead

ALTHOUGH masks are used by many groups of Eskimos for ceremonial purposes,[174] they are only very rarely employed in the funeral rites.

It is stated[175] that in East Greenland when a person died the mask was thrown into the sea with the body. Another method of using masks in burials is reported from Big Lake Village, between the Yukon and Kuskokwim rivers: "In front of many of the graves at this place were large headboards, made from hewn planks about four feet long, placed across the tops of two upright posts. To the middle of these were pinned from two to three wooden maskoids, representing human faces with inlaid ivory eyes and mouths, from holes or pegs at the ears were hung small strings of beads, such as the villagers wear, and below the masks were bead necklaces, some of the latter being very valuable from the Eskimo point of view."[176] The Aleutian Islanders, however, seem to have employed masks typically as appurtenances of the dead; a deceased person had one of them placed over the face for requisite protection beyond the grave.[177]

Festival for the Dead

WHEN a person's earthly existence ends and he enters the spirit world he remains subject to his original human appetites and susceptible to the same vanities. Hence, it is well to feed and flatter the ghost of the departed in order that he be induced to lessen the asperities in the life of mortals. Grave offerings most obviously manifest intention to conciliate the ghost. Another expression of deference and solicitude for the departed ones is witnessed in certain festivals to which the participants invite the company of the dead.

On Nunivak Island (Bering Sea) "feasts are held for the dead, with a view to preparing the way for them and making them happy in the world beyond. The ceremonies here last a week, with various rites each day, and costly gifts to all present. As a rule several families combine in the festival for their respective dead, but even then the proceedings may be so expensive that several years of saving may be required to defray the cost of a feast worthy of the standing of the deceased."[178] After a death among the Iglulik Eskimos, those who carried the corpse, on returning to the dwelling, must each drink water from the dead person's cup, so that he may have a drink.[179]

When a feast constitutes a regular part of the mourning program it is characterized by that attitude of fear and subservience which attends all ceremonies designed to placate a recently departed ghost. The spirit is still lurking within the corpse or in the company of the recent earthly associates of the deceased. Animosities and grudges that the deceased may have held toward living persons are fresh in the memory. Now endowed with supernatural powers for evil the dead person is able to inflict terrible vengeance. Therefore, lest the ghost may exert its baleful influence, its whims must be pandered to and its every want satisfied.

The festival for the dead, however, may occur months or even years after the funeral and partake of the nature of a memorial ceremonial. Time may have ameliorated the dread that is held for an earth-bound ghost; nevertheless, the motivation remains the same. "Drink, our dead kinsman," invites the native of Norton Sound, as he sprinkles a few drops of water on the floor from his wetted fingers; and as he scatters a few morsels of food he prays: "Take this, our dead kinsman, from our stores, and help us to obtain more during the coming year."[180] To be sure, the invitation to the dead to join once again the family circle may ring with a note of yearning attachment, yet behind it there remains a wheedling cajolery. An attitude of "I sacrifice my worldly goods, you reciprocate with supernatural assistance" forms the ulterior bond between living and dead.

The festival to the dead has achieved its highest development in Alaska, where the ceremonial lasts sometimes five days and manifests some of the features of a potlatch. At Norton Sound ordinary festivals are held three times yearly: on the last of November and the first of December, again around New Year, and a third time just before the opening of the fishing season in spring. Besides, at intervals up to ten or fifteen years, a Great Feast to the Dead is held, its occurrence depending upon the ability of the surviving relatives to accumulate sufficient property.[181] A description of the ordinary feast is omitted,[182] because it is essentially a small replica of the Great Festival which is here described in detail.

Great Feast to the Dead (Norton Sound, Alaska)

A YEAR or more after a man's death the nearest blood relatives begin to save skins, clothing, and other valuables, which they accumulate for four, six, or even more years. The shades are notified of the approaching festival a year ahead by a slender stake four to six feet high placed at the grave and surmounted by a small painted wooden image of an animal with which the deceased is identified. On the appointed day natives from surrounding villages stream in, sometimes from as far as two hundred miles. On the second day, before the shades are summoned, there is a preliminary ceremony. In groups of five the feast givers dance until all have performed. They are dressed in fine new clothing, and some of the women wear men's clothing to indicate the sex of the person whom they are honoring. This feast is built around the concept that the shades of the dead may be honored vicariously through those living persons who are named after them. At Ikogmut, on the Yukon, a festival is held during which the namesakes of dead men are paired with the namesakes of their dead wives, without regard to age, and during this period the men or boys bring their temporary partners firewood, and the latter prepare food for them, thus symbolizing the former union of the dead.[183]

On the third day the shades are summoned. The feast givers, clad in their poorest and oldest clothing, file into the ceremonial room, and with their heads bowed in apologetic humility creep to their places. The invitation to the shades to return to earth and attend the festival takes the form of a melodic invocation. Drummers chant to the broken throbbing of their instruments, and at intervals the others severally break forth in a song of invitation to the particular deceased relative whom he or she is honoring. Throughout the festival the participants keep a number of seal-oil lamps burning night and day in their ceremonial chamber, that the shades may have their road lighted coming and going. In order to encourage them to undertake the journey the feast givers, both male and female, do imitative dances suggesting paddling a kayak or walking on snowshoes. The dancer pursues a winding course about the chamber symbolic of a circuitous route through dale and over barren hillock. His hands, palms down, shuffle along before him in imitation of the shambling gait of the shade wearing snowshoes, and he alternately inclines his body obliquely to the right and left to indicate the slopes of the hills.

When at last the spirits have answered the call, offerings are given. Each feast giver is eager to make the greatest sacrifice in property, and is humble before his fellow men and the shades lest his gift prove to be less than expected and he lose credit. The feast givers bring buckets of frozen fish and drop fragments of them beside each of the lamps. Then a bucket of water is given to each person who bears the same name as one of the honored dead, and he dips his hands into it twice and sprinkles some of the liquid on the floor. After this each feast giver presents the remainder of the fish to the namesake of his dead; and, finally, the fish is distributed among the guests, the greatest share being given to him who has come the longest distance.

On the fourth day there is an almost identical repetition of the offerings of the third day. As much as three or four thousand pounds of fish are thus distributed at the festival. There is also much dancing on the fourth day in the ceremonial chamber and beside the grave boxes in the cemetery and by the frozen Yukon, this rite being a commemoration performed by those who have lost relatives by drowning. In addition, women feast givers bring in various articles and their husbands or nearest male relatives make deprecatory remarks concerning them; whereupon, the women give away all these things to persons present. Next a line with many other articles tied to it is let down through the smoke hole in the roof of the ceremonial room. Each of the women feast givers in turn sits below and hauls in the line and takes off the gifts, at the same time singing an invitation to her dead relative to come. All the while that the articles are being piled up many derogatory remarks are made about the poverty of the gifts. Then they are all distributed among those present, and the fourth day is finished.

On the fifth day there is a repetition of the last-mentioned ceremony. As each feast giver finishes taking the things out of the bag he or she calls out, "Come to me, my best beloved relative," at which the namesake of the deceased relative comes forward and accepts the gift. It is believed that the honored ghost will profit by receiving the essence of the gift. If it be clothing, the namesake is undressed by the donor and clad in his new attire. As the namesake turns away, the feast giver cries out in a loud voice bidding the shade of his relative to return to the grave where his bones lie.

The festival ends with dancing on the fifth day. Then no one is allowed to leave the village for fear of offending the shades; for it is supposed that they do not completely disperse until the following morning. Finally, to cleanse themselves of any evil contamination, the men all take a sweat bath.

With the observance of this great festival a person is thought to have done his entire duty to the dead. The shade is supposed to be supplied with sufficient food and property to exist thenceforth without fear of want.[184]

Memorial Observances Elsewhere among Eskimos

NOT all groups of Eskimos, however, perform memorial ceremonials for the dead, at least in so elaborate a style.

Even slightly outside of the Bering Sea culture area, at Point Barrow, it is said that "as a rule the dead (Nu'nami-sinik, on the ground asleep) are soon forgotten, and the names of the noted whalemen or hunters only live in legend."[185] The people of Hudson Strait at times hold a ceremony at the grave, but it does not attain the magnitude of that of the Bering Sea Eskimos; instead they merely sing at the grave and eat food in communion with the dead sometime during the four years while the spirit is supposed to rest in the grave, before it returns to live on earth.[186] The natives of southeastern Baffin Island are known to hold a memorial feast at the grave, and some of the food is put under a stone.[187] Near Frobisher Bay a native was observed to deposit some meat and caribou fur, exclaiming, "Here, Nukertou, is something to eat and something to keep you warm." "They never visit the grave of a departed friend until some months after death, and even then only when all surviving members of the family have removed to another place. Whenever they return to the vicinity of their kindred's grave, a visit is made to it with the *best* of food as presents to the departed one." Neither seal nor walrus, however, is taken.[188] After a burial at Cumberland Sound the relatives visit the grave and converse as if the dead were still among them. They tell one another how good he was and that when a child is born it shall be named after him. They promise to come again and bring something to their friend, as they have a great desire to please him. After catching game, they take part of it, eat it at the grave, and leave a portion for the dead one.[189] Not far distant, in northeastern Labrador, the natives often placed food near the graves.[190]

The Kittegaryumiut (Mackenzie Delta) observe a celebration a year after death, singing and dancing, not necessarily at the grave.[191] One of Stefansson's Eskimos describes how in the region of Kotzebue Sound two parents made a pilgrimage each year to the grave of their ten-year-old daughter. They would dress the body in new clothes and set the grave to rights. So long as they were about the grave a fire was kept burning. They ate their food raw, not cooking over this fire until their work was done. As they commenced eating some of the food of which the dead had been especially fond, a piece would be cut off and put in the fire. It was said that this was food for the dead. And at the termination of the memorial, all of the remaining food that had been brought near the grave was burned.[192]

NOTES

1. Birket-Smith: 1929, II, 121 f., 379, Table 111A.

2. Petroff: 1900, 227.

3. Dall: 1878, 6 f., 27 f.

4. Holm: 1914, 75, 101. In the Ungava District (Hudson Strait) it is stated that the dead are never placed in the water (Turner: 1887, 107). Regarding the distribution of the custom of disposing of the dead by drowning the body, the world over, see Birket-Smith: 1929, II, 206 ff., and Table 73B.

5. Jenness: 1922, 174 (Copper Eskimos); Comer: 1910, 89 (Southampton Island); Rasmussen: 1929, I, 95 (Iglulik Eskimos).

6. Weyer: 1929. See also Sauer: 1802, 161, and 247 (illustration); Sarychev: 1806–7, II, 77.

7. Jacobsen: 1884, 208; Nelson: 1899, 315.

8. Nelson: 1899, 310 f. See also pp. 302 ff.

9. Hartmann, in Jackson: 1886, 60.

10. Beechey: 1831, I, 328, 333 (illustration).

11. Nelson: 1899, 322.

12. Weyer: Field Notes (Port Clarence); Murdoch: 1892, 425 (Point Barrow); Stefansson: 1914, 316 (Kotzebue Sound); Hooper: 1853, 88 (Chukchi).

13. Birket-Smith: 1929, II, 121 f.

14. See Mathiassen: 1927, II, 130 f., citing many references.

15. Nelson: 1899, 320 ff. See also Dall: 1870, 382.

16. Murdoch: 1892, 426.

17. Jenness: 1922, 29, 50, 174 f.

18. Birket-Smith: 1929, I, 301 f.

19. Boas: 1907, 161.

20. Mathiassen: 1927, I, 130–131.

21. Rasmussen: 1929, I, 199; Rasmussen: 1927, 134.

22. Boas: 1888, 613; see also Bilby: 1923, 165 f.

23. Turner: 1887, 101 (Itivimyut, east coast of Hudson Bay), 103 (Tahagmyut, western end of Hudson Strait); Turner: 1894, 191 f. (Koksoagmyut, Ungava District); and

Hantzsch: 1930, 180 (Northeastern Labrador).

24. Hawkes: 1916, 119 f.

25. Rasmussen: 1908, 113; Kane: 1856, II, 118; Markham: 1866, 134; Kroeber: 1899, 311.

26. Crantz: 1767, I, 237.

27. Holm: 1914, 75.

28. Nelson: 1899, 312.

29. Ray: 1885, 43.

30. Weyer: Field Notes.

31. Jenness: 1922, 174.

32. Mathiassen: 1928, I, 229.

33. Turner: 1894, 178.

34. Weyer: Field Notes.

35. Nelson: 1899, 321.

36. Ray: 1885, 43.

37. Mathiassen: 1927, II, 130; Lyon: 1824, 259; and Mathiassen: 1928, I, 229 (Repulse Bay).

38. Klutschak: 1881, 208.

39. Bilby: 1923, 168.

40. Turner: 1894, 192.

41. Stefansson: 1914, 187 (Point Barrow); Murdoch: 1892, 424 (Point Barrow); Birket-Smith: 1929, I, 301 f. (Caribou Eskimos and Iglulik Eskimos); Lyon: 1824, 371 ff., 1824 (Boston), 269 (Iglulik Eskimos); Boas: 1888, 613 (Iglulik and Caribou Eskimos); Rasmussen: 1929, I, 49 (Iglulik Eskimos of Hudson Bay); Rasmussen: 1929, I, 94 (Iglulik Eskimos); Rasmussen: 1908, 113 (Polar Eskimos).

42. Sumner and Keller: 1927, II, 879 ff.

43. Jochelson: 1925, 43.

44. Crantz: 1767, I, 237.

45. Saabye: 1816, 34.

46. Nelson: 1899, 481.

47. Hawkes: 1916, 128.

48. Nelson: 1899, 423.

49. Dall: 1878, 6.

50. See pp. 257 f.

51. See pp. 264 f.

52. Moore: 1923, 368 ff.

53. Nelson: 1899, 315.

54. Rasmussen: 1929, I, 198; and Boas: 1907, 144, 468.

55. Nelson: 1899, 315 (Lower Yukon); Moore: 1923, 370 (St. Law-

rence Island); Stefansson: 1914, 315 (Kittegaryumiut of the Mackenzie Delta); Rasmussen: 1929, I, 202 (Sentry Island, about 61° N. Lat. in Hudson Bay); Rasmussen: 1929, I, 97 (Chesterfield Inlet); Rasmussen: 1929, I, 94 (Iglulik Eskimos); Lyon: 1824, 368 (Iglulik Eskimos); Rasmussen: 1908, 113 f. (Polar Eskimos); Rasmussen: 1921, 30 (Polar Eskimos); Kroeber: 1899, 312, 315 (Polar Eskimos). The duration of the seclusion is specified variously in each of these instances as three, four, or five days.

56. Weyer: Field Notes.

57. On the lower Yukon, uncovering the head is forbidden for four days, to prevent the shade from entering the head and killing the person (Nelson: 1899, 315). On St. Lawrence Island the taboo holds, except while the person is inside the ogrut, for ten days (Moore: 1923, 370).

58. Stefansson: 1914, 315.

59. For five days. Rasmussen: 1908, 113 f.; Rasmussen: 1921, 30. See also Kane: 1856, II, 118; Kroeber: 1899, 313; Boas: 1888, 614.

60. Crantz: 1767, I, 240.

61. Moore: 1923, 369.

62. Weyer: Field Notes.

63. Nelson: 1899, 315; Petroff: 1900, 214. The Kodiak Islanders, in addition to cutting their hair, blacken their faces (Holmberg: 1855, 122).

64. Crantz: 1767, I, 240.

65. Lyon: 1824, 267.

66. Among the Iglulik Eskimos, for three days if the deceased is a man, four if a woman (Rasmussen: 1929, I, 199 f.; Rasmussen: 1927, 134); for three days at Cumberland Sound (Boas: 1907, 144, 486 ff.); for three days in Baffin Island (Bilby: 1923, 168 f.). A woman of the Qaernermiut group (Barren Grounds) must wear her hair loose for three days when a man dies, and for four when a woman dies (Birket-Smith: 1929, I, 300).

67. Birket-Smith: 1924, 428.

68. Sumner and Keller: 1927, II, 865 f., 1099; III, 1815, 2018, 2020; IV, 368 ff.

69. See pp. 289 ff.

70. See pp. 291 ff.

71. Holm: 1914, 79 f.; also Thalbitzer: 1923a, 50.

72. Holm: 1914, 24.

73. Kroeber: 1899, 309; Rasmussen: 1908, 116.

74. Birket-Smith: 1924, 413.

75. Rasmussen: 1929, I, 106.

76. Jenness: 1922, 168.

77. Boas: 1907, 364 f.

78. Nelson: 1899, 312, 315.

79. Nelson: 1899, 312. See also Dall: 1870, 146.

80. Nelson: 1899, 364.

81. Weyer: Field Notes.

82. Ray: 1885, 42. Ray implies here that the taboo lasts until the body is carried out of the village; while M. Smith (in Kersting: 1902; 120) states that the taboo is in effect between sunset and sunrise, a period of varying length, it should be remarked, in this latitude.

83. Murdoch: 1892, 424.

84. Birket-Smith: 1929, I, 300.

85. Hawkes: 1916, 136 f.

86. Rasmussen: 1927, 134; Bilby: 1923, 168 f.

87. Birket-Smith: 1924, 428.

88. Stefansson: 1914, 315.

89. Rasmussen: 1908, 113 f.

90. Nelson: 1899, 312 (St. Michael, Alaska); Stefansson: 1914, 315 (Mackenzie Delta); Hawkes: 1916, 137 (Labrador); Rasmussen: 1921, 30 (Polar Eskimos).

91. See pp. 276 ff. and 279 ff.

92. Birket-Smith: 1929, I, 300.

93. Rasmussen: 1929, I, 97.

94. Mathiassen: 1928, I, 228.

95. Lyon: 1824, 368.

96. Rasmussen: 1908, 114.

97. Kane: 1856, II, 118.

98. Kroeber: 1899, 312.

99. Boas: 1888, 427.

100. Stefansson: 1914, 315.

101. Petroff: 1900, 220.

102. Rasmussen: 1929, I, 199 f.

103. Boas: 1907, 145.

104. Rasmussen: 1929, I, 199 f. Various other taboos are mentioned here, some of which last beyond four or five days.

105. Rasmussen: 1908, 113.

106. Kroeber: 1899, 315.
107. Lyon: 1824, 368.
108. Petroff: 1900, 214.
109. M. Smith in Kersting: 1902, 120.
110. Birket-Smith: 1929, I, 95. See also Rasmussen: 1927, 134.
111. Birket-Smith: 1929, I, 300.
112. Rasmussen: 1929, I, 199 f.; also Rasmussen: 1927, 134.
113. Boas: 1907, 486 ff.
114. Holm: 1887, 65 f.
115. See pp. 370 ff.
116. Bilby: 1923, 169.
117. Rasmussen: 1908, 113 f.; Rasmussen: 1921, 30.
118. Nelson: 1899, 314.
119. Klutschak: 1881, 210.
120. See pp. 318 f.
121. See pp. 372 f.
122. Nelson: 1899, 316.
123. Klutschak: 1881, 208.
124. Boas: 1907, 485; Boas: 1888, 611 f.
125. Holm: 1914, 76.
126. Boas: 1888, 590.
127. Hawkes: 1916, 136 f.
128. Boas: 1907, 131; also after the fourth night the soul is supposed to leave the house (Boas: 1907, 144).
129. Boas: 1907, 124. See also pp. 338 f.
130. Bilby: 1923, 168 f.
131. Nelson: 1899, 319.
132. Nelson: 1899, 314.
133. Turner: 1894, 193.
134. Crantz: 1767, I, 205.
135. Birket-Smith: 1924, 435.
136. Nelson: 1899, 311 f., 314 (Lower Yukon). Concerning grave offerings on Kodiak Island, see Petroff: 1900, 235; and on the Aleutian Islands, Weyer: 1929.
137. Weyer: Field Notes.
138. Nelson: 1899, 317 f.; and Hartmann in Jackson: 1886, 65 (illustration).
139. Rasmussen: 1927, 202 f.
140. Hantzsch: 1930, 181.
141. Weyer: Field Notes.
142. Stefansson: 1914, 317.
143. Stefansson: 1914, 193.
144. Klutschak: 1881, 153.
145. Birket-Smith: 1929, I, 303.
146. Mathiassen: 1928, I, 229.

147. Comer: 1910, 89.
148. Boas: 1907, 493.
149. Turner: 1887, 101.
150. Crantz: 1767, I, 237.
151. Hawkes: 1916, 136 f. See also Hawkes: 1916, 120; Kroeber: 1899, 311; and Hantzsch: 1930, 180.
152. Holm: 1914, 75.
153. Dall: 1878, 28.
154. Weyer: Field Notes.
155. Jenness: 1922, 176.
156. Rasmussen: 1929, I, 199.
157. Boas: 1888, 613.
158. Rasmussen: 1908, 115.
159. Birket-Smith: 1929, I, 303.
160. Hanbury: 1904, 67.
161. Sumner and Keller: 1927, II, 912 ff.
162. Nelson: 1899, 322.
163. Moore: 1923, 369.
164. Stefansson: 1914, 190. See also Murdoch: 1892, 424 f., and Ray: 1885, 43.
165. Stefansson: 1914, 193.
166. Hawkes: 1916, 120, also 90.
167. Jenness: 1922, 174.
168. Sarychev: 1806–7, II, 77.
169. Sauer: 1802, 177; and Petroff: 1900, 227, citing Shelikof.
170. Boas: 1907, 117 (Repulse Bay); Rasmussen: 1929, I, 159 (Iglulik Eskimos); Hawkes: 1916, 139 (Labrador); Peary; 1898, I, 506 (Polar Eskimos); Crantz: 1767, I, 238 (West Greenland); Birket-Smith: 1924, 410 (West Greenland); Holm: 1914, 62 (Angmagsalik). See also pp. 132.
171. Weyer: Field Notes.
172. Rasmussen: 1908, 113; Peary: 1898, I, 506.
173. Fries: 1872, 121; Crantz: 1767, I, 237.
174. See pp. 314 ff.
175. Thalbitzer: 1914, 636 ff.
176. Nelson: 1899, 318 f.
177. Dall: 1878, 5, 29 f.
178. Rasmussen: 1927, 350 f.
179. Rasmussen: 1929, I, 198 f.
180. Petroff: 1900, 219, citing Zagoskin.
181. Nelson: 1899, 358; Petroff: 1900, 214.
182. Nelson: 1899, 363 ff., 318;

Petroff: 1900, 219 f. Concerning feast for dead on Kodiak Island, see Petroff: 1900, 235 f., and Holmberg: 1855, 122.

183. See pp. 294 f.

184. Condensed from Nelson: 1899, 365 ff.

185. Ray: 1885, 43.

186. Turner: 1894, 193; Turner: 1887, 108.

187. Hall: 1865, 426.

188. Hall: 1864, 197, see also 321.

189. Boas: 1907, 145.

190. Hantzsch: 1930, 181.

191. Stefansson: 1914, 315.

192. Stefansson: 1914, 317.

CHAPTER XVII

ANIMISM

U NDER the subject of animism we shall discuss some broad, basic concepts of the Eskimos regarding souls or spirits inherent in persons, animals, objects, and places. Strictly speaking, this topic will embrace only such spirits as are associated with their original bodies. On the other hand, spirits which may be implanted in bodies or objects that are not their original abodes, will be discussed later, under the subject "Fetishism." This arrangement will separate animism from fetishism, two subjects that are, however, closely allied.

The natural starting point for a discussion of animism is in the beliefs regarding the souls of human beings.

§1. HUMAN SOULS

Each Person Possesses More than One Soul

IN general, the Eskimos distinguish three sorts of human souls. One of them is the immortal spirit which leaves a person's body at death and goes to live in the future world; a second, which is conceived as the vital breath and warmth of the body, ceases to exist at death; and a third sort of soul is thought to abide in the person's name. Though the name-soul is not exactly a soul in the usual connotation of the word, it is thought to possess abstract traits of the person to whom it refers and to persist after his death. It will be shown later how the name-soul is chiefly a thing of this world, perpetuated, however, through the custom of naming children after relatives who have recently died.[1]

The Eskimos of the Bering Sea region regard the spirit of life which departs when one dies as being distinct from the soul which continues to live after death. In form both are exactly like the body. One of them (*po-klĭhm′tā-ghûn′-u-g'ă*) is the life-giving warmth which is without sense and takes flight into the air when the person dies. The other (*tă-ghûn′-û-g'âk*) is the invisible shade that is sentient and destined for a future life. This latter spiritual essence sometimes appears as a visible ghost, when it is called *ä-lhi-ukh′-tok*. In addition it is thought that still another shade which is able to cause evil, in a limited degree, remains with the body.[2] The Copper Eskimos believe that one soul, *nappan,* which is the mainspring of a man's vital strength, ceases to exist altogether with death; but another shade, *tarrak,* lingers for a time around the place where the body was laid. The word *tarrak,* in addition to meaning the shade of a dead animal or human being, also means the shadow of any object cast by the sun or moon.[3]

The Iglulik Eskimos believe that every man and every animal has a soul (*tArniŋa* or *inuˑsia*), which is its miniature. The *inuˑsia* (meaning "appearance as a human being") is situated in a bubble of air in the groin; from it proceed appearance, thoughts, strength, and life. It is what makes a man a man, a dog a dog, etc. But in addition to the soul there is also the name, which typifies the strength and skill, and in a sense the physical qualities of the person bearing it.[4]

Rasmussen asked a native of the Great Fish River (Backs River), "What do you understand by the soul?" The native was plainly surprised that he could ask such a thing; nevertheless, he answered patiently, "It is something beyond understanding, that which makes me a human being."[5] The Baffin Islanders think that the *tarnak,* or soul of a man, has the shape of a man, but is only about one inch in length, and is to be discovered in the hand of a conjurer or in that of a newborn babe.[6] In addition to the soul that travels after death to the land of souls, the natives of Cumberland Sound believe that there is another soul which stays with the body and may enter temporarily the body of a child who is given the name of the departed.[7]

Likewise, in Labrador and throughout Greenland, a distinction is made between a person's body, his soul, and his name.[8] The immortal soul, according to the Labrador Eskimos, lingers around the village for three days before taking its final departure to the other world. But there is also the spirit which corresponds to the vitality of the body, as exemplified in its breath and warmth.[9] The name-soul is endowed with the qualities of the dead person who bore it previously.[10] The Polar Eskimos, like the other Greenland groups, consider that a man is divided into a soul, a body, and a name. The soul follows the body like a shadow, and as long as it remains near the person he lives. It is like the man himself, but it is immortal; when the soul departs the person dies. Animals also have souls. The name is not, properly speaking, a soul but a spirit to which is attached a certain store of vital power and skill.[11] Again it is said that the Polar Eskimos believe that every person has in addition to his body, breath or *aningnin,* which leaves the body when one dies. It is probably what becomes the *tornguang.*[12] Some of the West Greenlanders were of the opinion that aside from the name-soul there were two souls—breath and shadow.[13] "The Angmagsaliks believe that man consists of three parts, viz. body, soul, and name (*atekata*).

"The body is of course perishable. The soul is quite small, being no bigger than a finger or a hand, and lives in the man. When the soul falls ill, the man falls ill also, and when the soul dies, the man dies also. . . . After a man's death the soul comes to life again, either below the sea or up in the sky."[14] Hanserak's diary contains a statement of the Angmagsalik's conception of souls: "A man has many souls. The biggest of them live in the larynx and in a man's left side, and are tiny manikins about the size of sparrows. The other souls live in all the other members of the body and are about the size of a finger joint."[15] According to Eskimo notions, ". . . in every part of the human body (particularly in every joint, as for instance, in each finger joint) there resides a little soul. . . ."[16]

The Eskimos' beliefs about souls show some unusual features, especially regarding the name-soul; but the concept of a plurality of souls is, of course, held by many other peoples of the world.[17]

The Chukchi, for instance, Siberian neighbors of the Eskimos, distinguish five or six souls.[18] These people believe that "the soul resides in the heart or the liver, and animals and plants, as well as men possess it. One hears, however, more about other 'souls'—those which belong to various parts of the body: e.g., there is a limb-soul, nose-soul, etc. And so a man whose nose is easily frost-bitten is said to be 'short of souls.' "[19]

The identification of the breath as the spirit of life is a concept which the Eskimos hold along with many other peoples.[20] It might be mentioned that this concept and the association of the idea of the soul with bodily warmth might naturally be reinforced in a region where the climate is cold most of the time.

The Name-Soul

PERSONAL names, according to the Eskimo belief, are endowed with intangible attributes such as wisdom, skill, and power, and so in one sense must be regarded as souls. They are not to be confused, however, with the souls that journey at death to a future world, there to enter upon the after life. For name-souls are almost entirely of this earth, though, strangely, they are immortal in the sense that they do not perish with death, but are perpetuated through the custom of naming children after persons who have recently died. The implications of this naming custom differ widely among the various groups of Eskimos. In some the practice carries very little suggestion of a transfer of the soul, while in others this idea is so strong that the namesake is treated as though he were actually the dead person, living again on earth. With various shades of meaning, however, the custom of passing personal names on from the dead to the living is practiced generally by all groups of Eskimos.[21]

Slight local variations appear in the manner of applying names to children. In the region of Point Barrow the name of a deceased person uttered when the child happens to stop crying is the one given.[22] The Copper Eskimos name their children two or three days after birth, customarily after a near kinsman who has recently died, but in later life a nickname may supersede the deceased relative's.[23] Among the Iglulik Eskimos a child is usually named after the last relative to die on the mother's side.[24] In Davis Strait, Baffin Island, children are named after persons who have died since the last birth; and if a relative dies while the child is younger than four years his name becomes its proper name.[25] In Cumberland Sound the soul of the person after whom a child is named enters the body of the child, where it stays for about four months and may return.[26] In Labrador a child often receives several names of deceased relatives, the correct name being left to a future decision; and a widower names his first child after his deceased wife.[27] The West Greenlanders prefer to name a babe after a lately deceased relative, except when the latter came to an untimely death.[28] At Niaqornârssuk, Greenland, a child should be placed on the grave of the person after whom it was named: for then it will live long.[29] The Angmagsalik Eskimos believe that "the 'name' (atekata) is of the same size as a man and enters the child at the moment when a finger dipped in water is passed over the child's mouth, the names of the dead ancestors being simultaneously pronounced. . . . When a man dies the 'name' remains with the body in the water or earth where it has been buried, until a child is called after it. It then enters the child and continues its existence there."[30]

Generally, there is no differentiation in Eskimo names with regard to sex.[31] In view of this the child can be, and sometimes is, named before it is born.

It is reported from Smith Sound, however, that men's names differ from women's;[32] and from Labrador and the Mackenzie Delta that certain names are apt to be applied only to persons of one sex or the other.[33]

Stefansson's curiosity was roused by the odd custom he noted, chiefly among Eskimos of the Mackenzie region, of one native's calling another "mother" or "father," etc. when such a relation-

ship did not actually exist and even sounded ridiculous in view of
age relation. Questioning two grown women as to why they called
a child of eight "mother" he received the answer, "Simply because
she is our mother." Thus, he was led to discover the true import
of the name-soul among these people.

"When a Mackenzie Eskimo dies, the body is taken out the same
day as death occurs to the top of some neighboring hill and covered
with a pile of drift logs, but the soul (nappan) remains in the house
where death occurred for four days if it is a man, and for five days if
it is a woman. At the end of that time a ceremony is performed by
means of which the spirit is induced to leave the house and go up to the
grave, where it remains with the body waiting for the next child in the
community to be born.

"When a child is born, it comes into the world with a soul of its own
(nappan), but this soul is as inexperienced, foolish, and feeble as a
child looks. It is evident, therefore, that the child needs a more experienced and wiser soul than its own to do the thinking for it and
take care of it. Accordingly the mother, so soon as she can after the
birth of the child, pronounces a magic formula to summon from the
grave the waiting soul of the dead to become the guardian soul of the
new-born child, or its *atka,* as they express it."[34] The name thus applied endows the child with the wisdom of the dead person who formerly bore it.[35] Indeed, the child becomes in a sense the living representative of the dead person. There was, for instance, a couple whom
Stefansson knew ". . . who had for a child a boy of seven years,
whose father called him stepmother and whose mother called him aunt,
for those were the respective relationships to the woman whose soul
was the boy's guardian, or *atka.* . . . A person may continue through
his entire lifetime to address certain individuals by the terms of relationship required by their position with regard to his guardian spirit,
but as a usual thing the older a man gets the more this wears off and
the more the real blood relationship begins to come forward."[36] "It
appears from the foregoing that every man has two souls, the one
with which he was born and the one he acquired immediately after
birth. He may, in fact, have more souls than that. If three people, or
thirteen, have just died before the child was born, then he gets three
guardian spirits, or thirteen, according to the circumstances. But when
he dies it is none of these acquired souls, but the soul he was born with,
which in turn remains for four or five days in the house after death,
which is then ceremonially driven out to the grave, and which waits
there until it is summoned to become the second soul of a new-born
child. . . . No one knows what becomes of the guardian souls after
the death of the person whose guardians they have been."[37] "It hap-

pens sometimes that between the occurrence of one death and the occurrence of the next, several children are born. Each of them can and does receive the soul of the dead man as his guardian."[38] The name-soul, or *atka*, ". . . is sometimes in a child, sometimes near it, sometimes it goes quite away. When a child's atka gets farther from it than a fathom or so the child will begin to cry and will not cease until the atka returns. Sometimes a shamanistic performance is resorted to, to get the atka to return."[39] "If a child is scolded, it is not only the baby that one scolds, but also the soul of the one whose name it bears; this will make the 'name' (soul-nappan) angry and it will make the child sick or cause it to die. If habitually scolded, the soul or souls received by name (the child's names) will (one, some or all of them) leave the child and go to a child that is not scolded. This will be to that child's advantage, and will not much hurt the child that loses them. Yet to lose the soul thus seems to be considered a misfortune. But if the souls have no child to which they can flee, they will make the child sick through their discontent at having to stay in a child so badly treated."[40] "As the child grows up the soul with which he was born (the *nappan*) gradually develops in strength, experience, and wisdom, so that after the age of ten or twelve years it is fairly competent to look after the child and begins to do so; at that age it therefore becomes of less vital moment to please the guardian spirit (*atka*), and accordingly it is customary to begin forbidding children and punishing them when they come to the age of eleven or twelve years. People say about them then: 'I think the nappan is competent now to take care of him and it will be safe to begin teaching him things.' "[41]

The concept of the name-soul, as described above, does not exactly apply to all groups of Eskimos; nevertheless, there is everywhere some indication at least of the same idea. Undoubtedly, the notion that since the name-soul has been implanted more or less artificially by the bestowal of the name it may very easily be dislodged, influences the attitude of the Eskimo parent toward his child.[42] Thus, it is commonly noted that children are never spanked or even scolded.[43] The precept of sparing the rod, it might be mentioned, does not seem in this instance to spoil the child. As a rule the Eskimo child is very well behaved, according to Eskimo standards. Hawkes's statement that the child is never punished but is never seen to disobey[44] (while somewhat hyperbolical) is in agreement with the observations expressed by others.

At Norton Sound, Alaska, the festivals that are held in honor of the dead are characterized by a practice of making offerings to the dead vicariously by giving gifts to their namesakes.[45]

The namesakes are overwhelmed with presents, and clothed anew from head to foot with the most expensive clothing.[46] Petroff mentions[47] that "men sometimes change their names several times during their lives by assuming a new one after every great memorial feast given in memory of a deceased relative." At Ikogmut, on the Yukon, during one of the ceremonies the namesakes of dead men are paired with the namesakes of their deceased wives, without regard to age; and the men and boys bring their temporary partners firewood, and the latter prepare food for them, thus symbolizing the former union of the dead.

With somewhat the same idea namesakes among the Iglulik Eskimos, upon meeting, must exchange gifts. This strengthens their souls and pleases all their dead name cousins.[48] This group and the Polar Eskimos are stated to believe that the namesake receives the strength and skill of the person for whom he is named.[49] The Diomede Islanders, although they seem to have no very well-defined ideas on the subject, at least suppose that the name-soul lives again in the namesake of the deceased.[50]

In Cumberland Sound the name-soul stays with the corpse until a child is named after the deceased, causing the soul to enter its body. It is said that the soul enters the body because it is in want of a drink. The belief is that its presence strengthens the child's soul, which is very light and apt to escape from the body. If the souls of children are not strengthened by those of a deceased friend, they are likely to fly away, or lie down, causing the child to die. But the name-soul is not supposed to remain in the child for more than about four months after naming; nevertheless, even after leaving it, this soul of the departed stays near by and may reënter the child in case of need. The name-soul seems also to retain some connection with the body of its former owner. A year after his death it leaves the grave temporarily and goes hunting, but returns frequently. When the body has entirely decayed, the soul may remain away for a long time. Evidently these ". . . Eskimos believe in the possibility of transmigration of souls. There is one tradition in which it is told how the soul of a woman passed through the bodies of a great many animals, until finally it was born again as an infant.[1] In another story it is told how a hunter caught a fox in a trap, and recognized in it the soul of his departed mother.[2] In still another tale, the soul of a woman, after her death, entered the body of a huge polar bear in order to avenge wrongs done to her during her lifetime.[3]"[51] Also on the west coast of Hudson Bay it is believed that the souls of the dead, if they choose, may return and be born again. "An old man who died in 1896 said at his death that he would be borne again by a certain woman. Sometime after this the woman gave birth to a girl, who was believed to be the old man returned. Another man, who died in 1885, said that he would be born again as the child of his own daughter. The latter had a son; and soon another son was born, who was looked upon as the dead one returned."[52]

The Pâdlimiut, inland Eskimos of the Barren Grounds, believe that all men are born again, the soul passing continually from one form of life to another. Good men return to earth as men, but evildoers are reborn as beasts.[53] Thus, although the Central Eskimos may not embrace a well-defined, invariable, and consistent concept of reincarnation through the name-soul,[54] they must be regarded as having the beginnings of this belief.

The same holds true throughout most of the Eskimo groups. An old shaman of Selawik (Kotzebue Sound) declared ". . . that once he himself had died and gone to the land of shades, remaining there until he became tired, when he returned to the earth and entering the body of an unborn child, was born again."[55] In West Greenland Crantz discovered a trace of the concept of reincarnation: "This sentiment is particularly propagated by the helpless widows, in order to allure the bounty of parents by imposing on their credulity; for instance, a widow will tell a father, that the soul of her deceased child is flown into his son, or the soul of his deceased child has taken up residence in one of her children. Accordingly the father (in the latter case) is studious to show kindliness to the supposed soul of his child, or (in the former case) believes himself to be very nearly related to the widow."[56]

The Copper Eskimos, on the other hand, seem to have no notion that the souls of the dead ancestors or relatives are reincarnated in the living, in spite of their custom of naming children after the dead.[57] Jenness even observed that one of these natives called his dog "grandfather" because it bore the same name as his grandfather; but children are never likewise called by the terms of relationship that would be applicable to the persons after whom they are named. A conspicuous difference is noticed in this regard, therefore, between these Eskimos and those of the Mackenzie region.[58]

"Name Modesty"

In the discussion of mourning customs attention was directed to the taboo observed, principally in Greenland, against speaking the name of a deceased person.[59] Clearly this restriction is best considered in the light of the general Eskimo custom of naming children after the dead and the belief that the name is a sort of soul.

There is also observed sometimes a reluctance on the part of Eskimos to mention their own names, or the names of other living persons, a reluctance which usually assumes more the aspect of self-conscious modesty than a rigid taboo.

For example, "some of the Malemut dislike very much to pronounce their own names, and if a man be asked his name he will appear confused and will generally turn to a bystander, asking him to give the desired information." And it is written that in this general region when one changes his name to obtain an extension of life it is considered improper to mention the former one.[60] At the opposite extreme of the Eskimo province, "the Angmagsaliks have a decided dread of pronouncing their own name. When asked what they are called they invariably turned to others to answer for them, and then assented the correctness of the answer given."[61]

A woman of the Mackenzie region ". . . should not tell, even if asked, the name of any relative if that relative be present; nor the name of parent, brother, sister, or husband whether they be present or absent. She should look away modestly and appeal to a bystander to give the information. . . . Men have somewhat greater liberties in telling names of relatives, but they differ according to their 'sense of modesty.' . . . A man will hospitably offer his wife for loan or exchange, but will be prevented by modesty from telling her name. No man should ask anyone the name of anyone present, but should wait till the subject of inquiry is out of sight and hearing. In general the 'modesty' prohibitions on a woman are stronger with those relatives older than she than those younger."[62] These taboos against speaking the name are, of course, quite in harmony with the great importance attached by this group to the name-soul. It is significant that the Copper Eskimos, who do not seem to embrace the concept of reincarnation through the name-soul, have no hesitancy whatever in telling their names.[63] The Copper Eskimos are not the only group, however, who are free from name shyness. Birket-Smith remarks, for instance, that the Caribou Eskimos, west of Hudson Bay, as well as the other central tribes he met do not exhibit name modesty, differing thus from the Greenlanders and Labrador Eskimos on the one side and from the Western Eskimos on the other. He comments, nevertheless, concerning the natives west of Hudson Bay, that ". . . it is only reasonable that the great importance of the name is reflected in another manner in religious matters. Thus, two bearing the same name must not marry. If two people named after the same person meet, one of them must for the time being relinquish his name after he has given the other a present, and in the meantime he is simply called 'his name fellow.' "[64] "In west Greenland and the Thule district there is a custom that two persons who call each other iliqi'k must not mention each other's name or speak to each other. It may be that originally there was some religious idea behind this, but now it is only a sort of fun. Some Caribou

Eskimo averred that they knew nothing whatever of anything of the kind, whereas others believed that they had heard that two must not mention each other's names, but otherwise might very well talk together. In this case, too, it was done only for fun."[65]

Sickness and the Soul

SINCE death is characterized by the absence of the soul, sickness is sometimes interpreted as its temporary departure. Therefore, any tendency for the soul to take leave is regarded anxiously. Thus, when an Eskimo sneezes, he may exhort the soul to "come back,"[66] or may utter some magic word to the dead person for whom he has been named.[67] The Eskimos of Bering Strait sometimes change their names when old, hoping to gain an extension of life.[68] And in Ponds Inlet and Davis Strait sickness is treated by changing the patient's name.[69]

Further information concerning the influence of the Eskimos' ideas of the soul upon their method of treating disease is contained in chapter xix. It should be understood here, however, that sickness is not-attributed exclusively to impairment or departure of the person's soul; sometimes it is ascribed to the intrusion of an evil spirit.

Miscellaneous Folkways Pertaining to the Name

"THE name among the Mackenzie people while as yet little influenced by the Westerners, was dropped by men and women at the birth of their first child as our women drop theirs at marriage." Thereafter they are known by the name of their oldest child. If an only child died before the age of eight or ten, the parents would cease being known as his father and mother and would go back to their original names. The sex of the child was immaterial. If their oldest child were a daughter, hers would be the name by which the parents would be designated, regardless of how prominent a slightly younger son might become.[70]

It is reported that the Kaniagmiut Eskimos of Kodiak Island name the newborn babe after the first object in view, be it animal, bird, or anything else.[71] Similarly, Nelson, writing of the Eskimos of Bering Sea, states:[72] "In case the child is born away from the village, at a camp or on the tundra, it is commonly given the name of the first object that catches its mother's eyes, such as a bush or other plant, a mountain, lake, or other natural object." For that matter, Eskimo names irrespective of how they are chosen frequently mean something.[73]

On Kodiak Island the bridegroom takes the name of the father-in-law.[74]

§2. SOULS OF ANIMALS, OBJECTS, AND PLACES

The Inua

ACCORDING to Eskimo belief, souls reside not only in human beings but in animals and even lifeless things. In view of the haziness of the notions regarding human souls we cannot expect the concept of other souls to be definite and consistent. At the outset, however, we see that the key to the subject lies in the nature of the human soul; for even the word *inua*, which is used to designate the soul of an inanimate object, means "its man." *Inua* is simply the possessive of *inuk* meaning "man," or "person," the nominative plural of which, *inuit*, is the term by which Eskimos refer to themselves as a people. The *inua* of anything, therefore, which is the agency that causes the thing to be mysterious and not completely understood, is literally "its man" or "its person." The fact that the Eskimos think even of souls of inanimate objects in terms of themselves offers a nice illustration of the anthropomorphic or human-like character of a very primitive religious concept.

In the region of Bering Strait the word for the soul in the broad sense is *yu-ă*, a variant of *inua*. The *yu-it* are the spirits of the elements, of places, and of inanimate things in general.[75] Hunters at sea and elsewhere in lonely places cast down food and water as offerings to the *yu-ă* of the place before eating or drinking, often adding propitiatory words.[76] The *nûn'-wûm yu'-ă* is the essence or mystery which is believed to be present in or near a lake, whose occasional departure from the place is manifested in the drying up of the lake.[77] *Yu-it* are believed to have the forms of men and women but their faces are curiously distorted and grotesque.[78] Indeed, shamans, who claim sometimes to see these creatures, fashion fantastic masks after their likenesses.[79] Furthermore, Alaskan Eskimo dance masks representing animals are often made double, with the outer portion, which shows the animal form, so hinged that the inner mask, representing the *inua*, can be revealed at will. Alaskan mythology contains the correlative idea that animals are able to change from their own shapes to those of men by the simple expedient of pushing up their beaks or muzzles.[80]

The everyday connotation of the word *inua*, however, is not to be taken too strictly from its literal meaning. Perhaps the root word might better be translated "individual," rather than "man" or "person." The soul of an animal or an object is not always envisaged as a homunculus. Sometimes it is imagined as a miniature of the thing itself. Thus, among the Iglulik Eskimos, while the word for soul, *inu'sia*, means literally "appearance as a human being," the souls of animals are miniatures of themselves.[81]

Some idea of the Labrador Eskimo's conception of the souls of in-animate objects is gained from their custom, when making long trips, of sometimes wearing a pair of tiny boots on the back of the *a"'tige* so that the owner's boots will not wear out. Similarly, in making a soapstone lamp or kettle, they believe that if a small model is made, the large lamp or kettle will last until the little model is cracked or broken.[82] A diametrically opposite, though related, custom is observed on the west coast of Hudson Bay in the practice of men who are work-ing up steatite into lamps and kettles of making a small model of the object as well and then smashing it to prevent the large utensil from accidentally breaking.[83]

In Greenland the *inua* of an animal is not exactly its soul but rather its vitality; and, in spite of the literal meaning of the word, it re-sembles the animal itself.[84] That the literal meaning "its human being" is not accidental, however, is suggested by the fact that in southeast Greenland, where a human being is called *tâq*, the angakok's familiar spirit is called *târtâ*, which again means "its human being."[85]

There are many kinds of spirits, of course, known to the Eskimos by a variety of names; nevertheless, it seems well to hold fairly closely to the connotation of *inua*, "human," for this term is basically rooted in the animistic notions of the people. At a loss to imagine any being en-dowed with more powers than a man in spirit form, or capable of exer-cising them with greater independent will, the Eskimos attribute any inexplicable phenomena displayed by an animal or object to "its man."

The Koksoagmiut, of Ungava Bay, believe that every prominent rock, bay, island, or other local feature is possessed of a spirit, all of which are of the malignant type and are to be propitiated only by ac-ceptable offerings.[86] In Baffin Island every object is believed to have its *inua*, or its owner; and the angakok acquires such an *inua* as his fa-miliar spirit.[87] The soul of a bear is like a bear, that of a walrus, like a walrus; but the soul of a deer resembles a spider, and that of a salmon, a man. Animals' souls are black and hairless, but those of inanimate objects are clothed in deerskin.[88] Essentially the same conception was reported from West Greenland, by Glahn many years ago: ". . . The Greenlanders believe that all things are souled, and also that the small-est implement possesses its soul. Thus, an arrow, a boot, a shoe sole, a key, a drill has each for itself a soul. This soul is separated from the coarse stuff and is constituted out of something finer, imperceptible to our sight, touch and other senses; nevertheless of similar form as the bodies from which they go forth, so that the soul of a man resembles a man, the soul of a dog a dog, an arrow an arrow."[89]

There is a belief that the trees along the shores of certain lakes in the Barren Grounds are living beings; and the Eskimos rarely visit these forests, due to an ancient tradition that the tree folk would not suffer any human being among them for more than ten nights.[90] Again, it is written that there is a haunted island in Baker Lake (Barren Grounds) where none dares live even for a night.[91]

Propitiation of Animistic Spirits

SOMETIMES the Eskimos endeavor to propitiate the animistic spirits, especially those that are supposed to affect the security of life. Control over the most critical circumstances is more often vested in individual divinities, the conciliation of which constitutes the main body of religious observance;[92] but even nature spirits require their share of attention.

In the Egedesminde District, West Greenland, a sacrifice of some sort is required, for instance, at each of several rapids.[93] In another case the Eskimos show deference to supernatural power simply by maintaining reverent silence: during the long passage across the west end of Hudson Strait they do not utter a single word, through fear of a gale.[94] In Bering Strait the somewhat uncertain voyage from the Diomede Islands to the mainland, about twenty-three miles distant, occasions certain observances with the same purpose. If a storm arises the boatmen invoke the spirits; and upon arriving safely at the opposite shore they throw a piece of meat into the air as a thank offering.[95]

It is more characteristic of the Eskimos to elicit good fortune from the spirits ahead of time and to pay for supernatural aid in advance. As soon as they have been favored by good fortune they are apt to forget their gratitude.

Ray remarks that at Point Barrow ". . . we never knew them to offer thanks or to be grateful for any benefits. . . . Everything they received was taken as a matter of course, and as the result of some particular incantation."[96] In the spring of the year these natives implore the southeast wind to drive off the pack ice and open the water lanes, so that whales can pass up near the coast. "During the ceremony the men sit in a semi-circle facing the ocean, the middle man or magician beating a drum and singing a monotonous chant addressed to a spirit. . . . In the fall of the year they howl for the large ice to come from the north and bring with it nan-nuk' (bears). . . . When the steam whaling ship 'North Star' . . . was nipped abreast of Point

Barrow, the Eskimo doctors kept up a continuous howl for her to be crushed [so they could enrich themselves on her canvas and cargo]. For three weeks they encamped upon the ice near the ship, waiting for the crisis to come."[97]

As almost the only instance of a real offering made by the Eskimos of Baffin Island, Boas mentions the presentation of dried sealskins to the three sisters, Kadlu, who produce thunder and lightning. These sisters are supposed to live far inland, where it is their function to cause these phenomena by rubbing skins.[98] Among the Iglulik Eskimos during a thunder storm ". . . a small piece of white-bleached skin and a firestone and a small kamik sole are laid out as an amulet. . . ."[99]

Nature is believed to abound with spirits, whom the Eskimos must deal with on occasion just as they would with human beings. Even when breaking steatite from a quarry, the people of Cumberland Sound deposit a trifling present at the place, believing that otherwise the stone would become hard.[100]

The natives do not always spontaneously and without reason ascribe a spirit to a certain object or location. Generally, some inexplicable peculiarity in it leads to the belief that it is possessed of a spirit or a soul. Where, for instance, there are inordinately bountiful food resources, supernatural forces must reside; furthermore, where many living creatures are killed many souls are apt to accumulate. Thus, Amitsoq (King William Island) is regarded as a sacred spot because the fishing there often provides those reserves of food that may be indispensable in winter should the caribou hunting fail; and in the same way certain spots are held sacred because they are particularly haunted by caribou.[101]

The souls of animals are far more important in the religion of the Eskimos than the souls of inanimate objects. Solicitude for the souls of slain animals seems at times to be even more intense than solicitude for the souls of deceased tribesmen. A member of the Iglulik group is recorded as asserting, for instance, that the greatest peril of life lies in the fact that human food consists entirely of souls.[102] The far-reaching implications of this statement are made plain in a later chapter.[103]

Kinship between Man and the Animals

IN various forms the concept is common among the Eskimos that people are closely related to animals. This idea of kinship is developed perhaps most fully among the Alaskan Eskimos, particularly in the region of Bering Sea and Bering Strait, where it bears some rudimentary affinities to totemism. Nelson imputes to certain marks used by these people the function of defining totemic groupings.[104] Rasmussen, on the other hand, came to the conclusion that the marks found on implements in northwestern Alaska which have been adduced as evidence of incipient totemism, were purely personal symbols, a means whereby the owner could readily identify his property, as we might use initials or a crest.[105] But even though totemism in its true form is absent, nevertheless in former times totemic groups may have existed among Alaskan Eskimos.

The Eskimos of Alaska believe that in early days all animate beings had a dual existence, becoming at will either like men or taking on the animal forms they now wear. In those early days there were but few people; if an animal wished to assume its human form, the forearm, wing, or other limb was raised, the muzzle or beak was pushed out as if it were a mask, and the creature became manlike in form and features. It is believed that many animals still possess this power. The manlike form thus appearing is called the *inua* and is supposed to represent the thinking part of the creature, and at death becomes its shade.[106] This concept suggests the similar belief, lycanthropy, observed in other parts of the world, wherein a person is supposed to change himself into a wolf. The belief that the white whale can change into the reindeer, it might be mentioned, is held by all the Eskimos along the shore of Bering Sea.[107]

Illustrative of the notion of kinship between human beings and animals is the myth told by the Iglulik Eskimos of how a woman gave birth prematurely to an offspring, which was eaten by a dog and reborn as a dog, and how, after passing through a series of phases as various animals, its soul finally passed into a woman who bore the same being in the form of a child.[108] A tale from Angmagsalik also tells how the "name," in the period between its existence in two human beings, wanders through a number of animals.[109] Eskimo mythology is, indeed, replete with instances of transformation from man to animal and vice versa.[110] Additional basis for the bond of kinship between men and animals lies in the fact that the familiar spirit of the Eskimo medicine man is often the shade of an animal.[111]

NOTES

1. See pp. 291 ff.
2. Nelson: 1899, 422.
3. Jenness: 1922, 177.
4. Rasmussen: 1929, I, 58 f.
5. Rasmussen: 1927, 198.
6. Bilby: 1923, 205.
7. Boas: 1907, 130.
8. Hawkes: 1916, 136 f., 112 f. (Labrador); Rasmussen: 1908, 106, 116 (Polar Eskimos); Rasmussen: 1921, 31 f. (Polar Eskimos); Birket-Smith: 1924, 443, citing Crantz: 1765, I, 257, and P. Egede: 1788, 92, 126 (West Greenland); Holm: 1914, 80 (East Greenland).
9. Hawkes: 1916, 136 f.
10. Hawkes: 1916, 112 f.
11. Rasmussen: 1908, 106, 116; Rasmussen: 1921, 31 f.
12. Kroeber: 1899, 308. Thalbitzer comments in a communication to the writer that linguistically these forms are open to question.
13. Birket-Smith: 1924, 443, citing Crantz: 1765, I, 257, and P. Egede: 1788, 92, 126.
14. Holm: 1914, 80.
15. Holm: 1914, 81.
16. Thalbitzer: In Kroeber and Waterman: 1931, 430 f.
17. Sumner and Keller: 1927, II, 819 ff.; IV, 310, 325, 329.
18. Bogoras: 1901, 98.
19. Czaplicka: 1914, 260. See pp. 321 ff.
20. Sumner and Keller: 1927, II, 783, 798 ff., 815 ff.; IV, 308 ff., 325 ff. E. B. Tylor has collected a number of cases in which the term for breath is that for soul (*Primitive Culture*, I, 388 ff.).
21. Nelson: 1899, 376 f. (Yukon Delta); Nelson: 1899, 219, 289 (Bering Sea and Bering Strait); Weyer: Field Notes (Diomede Islands and Cape Prince of Wales); Nelson: 1899, 433 (Kotzebue Sound); Stefansson: 1914, 161 (Colville Eskimos and Kogmollik Eskimos); Stefansson: 1914, 202 (near Point Barrow); Stefansson: 1914, 158, 364 f. (Mackenzie Delta region); Stefansson: 1913,

395 ff. (Mackenzie Delta region); Jenness: 1922, 167 f. (Copper Eskimos); Birket-Smith: 1929, I, 282 (Caribou Eskimos); Rasmussen: 1929, I, 58 f. (Iglulik Eskimos); Rasmussen: 1927, 130 (Iglulik Eskimos); Mathiassen: 1928, I, 212 (Iglulik Eskimos); Boas: 1888, 612 (Davis Strait, Baffin Island); Boas: 1907, 130, 132 f., 145 (Cumberland Sound); Bilby: 1923, 144 (Baffin Island. "The children are named after some place or object, and many of the names descend from father to son."); Hawkes: 1916, 112 f. (Labrador); Rasmussen: 1908, 116 (Polar Eskimos); Rasmussen: 1921, 32 (Polar Eskimos); Kroeber: 1899, 309 (Polar Eskimos); Birket-Smith: 1924, 412 f. (West Greenland); Crantz: 1767, I, 161 (West Greenland); Holm: 1914, 81 (East Greenland); Thalbitzer: 1923, 184 (No. 1), 188 (No. 5), 191 (No. 6), and 500 (No. 244) (East Greenland).
22. Stefansson: 1914, 202.
23. Jenness: 1922, 167.
24. Mathiassen: 1928, I, 212.
25. Boas: 1888, 612.
26. Boas: 1907, 130.
27. Hawkes: 1916, 112.
28. Crantz: 1767, I, 161.
29. Birket-Smith: 1924, 412.
30. Holm: 1914, 80 f.
31. Weyer: Field Notes (Bering Strait); Stefansson: 1914, 161 (Colville Eskimos and Kogmollik Eskimos); Jenness: 1922, 167 (Copper Eskimos); Birket-Smith: 1929, I, 282 (Caribou Eskimos); Rasmussen: 1929, I, 47 (Iglulik Eskimos); Mathiassen: 1928, I, 212 (Iglulik Eskimos); Lyon: 1824, 268 (Iglulik Eskimos); Boas: 1907, 480 (Baffin Islanders); Boas: 1888, 612 (Baffin Islanders); Turner: 1894, 190 (Ungava District); Turner: 1887, 108 (Ungava District).
32. Kroeber: 1899, 268.
33. Hawkes: 1916, 112; Stefansson: 1914, 364.
34. Stefansson: 1913, 395 ff.
35. Stefansson: 1913, 398 f.

36. Stefansson: 1913, 401.

37. Stefansson: 1913, 401 f. See pp. 249 f.

38. Stefansson: 1913, 402.

39. Stefansson: 1914, 363 f.

40. Stefansson: 1914, 358; Stefansson: 1930, 46 f.

41. Stefansson: 1913, 399 f.

42. Hawkes: 1916, 112 f.

43. MacAdam: 1928, 417 ff. (Western Canada); Turquetil: 1926, 423; Birket-Smith: 1929, I, 288 (Caribou Eskimos). Other references testify to the leniency toward children without mentioning that it may be due to the significance of the name soul: Jenness: 1922, 169 (Copper Eskimos); Lyon: 1824, 258 (Iglulik Eskimos); Bartlett: 1916, 247; Hall: 1864, 314 (southeastern Baffin Island); Turner: 1894, 191 (Ungava, Labrador); Turner: 1887, 103 (western end of Hudson Strait); MacKeevor: 1819, 35 (Hudson Strait); Birket-Smith: 1928, 204. At variance with the usual restraint from corporal punishment is Mathiassen's testimony that the Iglulik Eskimos harshly reprimand their children (Mathiassen: 1928, I, 214 f.).

44. Hawkes: 1916, 114. See also Murdoch: 1892, 417.

45. See p. 281.

46. Nelson: 1899, 289, 219.

47. Petroff: 1900, 214.

48. Rasmussen: 1929, I, 183.

49. Rasmussen: 1929, I, 58 f.; Rasmussen: 1921, 32; Rasmussen: 1908, 116.

50. Weyer: Field Notes.

51. Boas: 1907, 132 f., (1) 232, (2) 234, (3) 252.

52. Boas: 1907, 146.

53. Rasmussen: 1927, 86.

54. Turquetil: 1929, 57 ff.

55. Nelson: 1899, 433.

56. Crantz: 1767, I, 200 f.

57. Jenness: 1922, 168, 177.

58. Jenness: 1922, 239.

59. See p. 271.

60. Nelson: 1899, 289.

61. Holm: 1914, 81.

62. Stefansson: 1914, 365 f. See also 326, 234.

63. Jenness: 1922, 168; Stefansson: 1914, 234.

64. Birket-Smith: 1929, I, 286; also Boas: 1907, 466, 117. .

65. Birket-Smith: 1929, I, 286.

66. Boas: 1907, 506 (west coast of Hudson Bay).

67. Stefansson: 1914, 339.

68. Nelson: 1899, 289.

69. Boas: 1907, 239, 494 f.; Boas: 1888, 612; also Hawkes: 1916, 113.

70. Stefansson: 1914, 365.

71. Petroff: 1900, 227, quoting Shelikof.

72. Nelson: 1899, 289.

73. Birket-Smith: 1929, I, 282; Turner: 1887, 108.

74. Holmberg: 1855, 119.

75. Nelson: 1899, 394.

76. Nelson: 1899, 437 f.

77. Nelson: 1899, 443.

78. Nelson: 1899, 443.

79. Nelson: 1899, 394.

80. Hawkes: 1916, 127. See also pp. 302 f.

81. Rasmussen: 1929, I, 58.

82. Hawkes: 1916, 135.

83. Boas: 1907, 503.

84. Birket-Smith: 1924, 439; also Schultz-Lorentzen: 1928, 232 f.

85. Birket-Smith: 1924, 441.

86. Turner: 1894, 194; and Turner: 1887, 107.

87. Boas: 1887, 37; also Bilby: 1923, 170. See also pp. 425 ff.

88. Bilby: 1923, 205.

89. Glahn: 1771, 347, cited by Thalbitzer: 1928, 388.

90. Rasmussen: 1927, 77. For parallel cases of tree fetishism, see Sumner and Keller: 1927, II, 989 ff.

91. Birket-Smith: 1929, I, 73.

92. See chapters xxi and xxiii.

93. Birket-Smith: 1924, 220.

94. Boas: 1888, 463.

95. Weyer: Field Notes.

96. Ray: 1885, 43.

97. Smith, in Kersting: 1902, 126.

98. Boas: 1887, 37.

99. Rasmussen: 1929, I, 182 f.

100. Boas: 1907, 138.

101. Rasmussen: 1927, 207.

102. Rasmussen: 1929, I, 56 f.

103. Chapter xx.

104. Nelson: 1899, 322 ff.

105. Rasmussen: 1927, 320. See also pp. 264, 179 ff., and 371.

106. Nelson: 1899, 394; also Rasmussen: 1927, 323 ff.

107. Nelson: 1899, 444.

108. Rasmussen: 1929, I, 59 ff. See also Boas: 1907, 321.

109. Holm: 1914, 272 ff.

110. For typical examples, see Boas: 1907, 251 ff., 303; Jenness: 1924a; Holm: 1914, 272 ff. The Copper Eskimos (Jenness: 1922, 167; see also Stefansson: 1914, 284) and the Caribou Eskimos (Birket-Smith: 1929, I, 172), it might be mentioned, not uncommonly name dogs after deceased persons; but from the evidence at hand it seems that, although this is exactly the procedure followed by these groups in naming their children, they do not attach so much spiritual importance to the name as do some other Eskimos.

111. See pp. 425 ff.

CHAPTER XVIII

FETISHISM

THE discussion of fetishism follows naturally after animism. Fetishism is, in fact, a phase of animism, specifically that phase which deals with spirits associated with inanimate objects, especially those spirits that have not been original tenants of the objects but have been induced into them. Fetishism involves the application of the theories of animism; yet the origin of the soul or spirit in fetishism cannot always be determined.

An amulet or fetish does not in itself bring good fortune to the owner; it is the spirit within that makes it valuable.[1] Thus, when Rasmussen sought by barter to obtain amulets from the natives in the vicinity of the Magnetic Pole he found that they readily agreed that the owner of an amulet would still enjoy its protection even in the event of his losing the amulet itself.[2] Even so, it is often exceedingly expensive to collect amulets. A native will place a fantastic value on a charm if he is convinced of its power. When an Eskimo girl saw Captain Lyon looking at an old broken spearhead hanging around her neck she tried to hide it in her hair; and when the white man tried to buy it she refused to part with it for fear that if she returned home without it her father would kill her mother and herself.[3]

Where danger of bad luck is especially grave so much the greater weight is apt to be attached to amulets. We read that the terrible uncertainty of life in the region of the Netsilingmiut of King William Island

". . . accounts to some extent for the prevalence of more or less superstitious rites and the use of amulets. The Netsilingmiut hold the same views on the subject of amulets as the Igdlulingmiut, but use them wholesale. One little lad of seven years old went about with no fewer than eighty sewn up in various parts of his clothing, which sadly hampered him in his play."[4]

§1. THE EXUVIAL FETISH

To approach the subject of fetishism from its most easily grasped aspect, let us consider those fetishes that are derived directly from living bodies possessing souls. Even though the soul is believed to quit the body at death it is thought that some measure of spiritual essence remains inherent in the corpse. Hence, any portion of a body, living or dead, may by its very nature be a fetish. Fetishes of this sort are called exuvial fetishes, from the word *exuviae*, meaning "strippings."

Typical of this class is the navel cord. Among the Iglulik Eskimos a boy must keep as amulets the umbilical stump and the flint knife used to cut it with;[5] sometimes the dried navel string is sewn into the inner jacket.[6] The custom is mentioned also on Baillie Island of a girl wearing her own navel string.[7] Likewise, in West Greenland, the navel strand was valued as an amulet.[8]

On Diomede Island the umbilical cord is tied with sinew and one hair from the mother; and the discarded section, together with the afterbirth, is hidden away in the rocks on the hillside.[9] The Caribou Eskimos lay the afterbirth where the dogs cannot get it;[10] also the natives of Cumberland Sound place the placenta in a crack between rocks, where the dogs cannot touch it.[11] The inland Eskimos of the Colville River region of northwestern Alaska are known to hang the afterbirth high in a tree.[12] Of the Labrador Eskimos Hawkes writes that "the placenta is carefully wrapped up and buried on the beach. The Eskimos are very careful that no dogs get hold of it. Probably their care is due to the same idea that impels them to preserve their hair and nail parings, a feeling that it is a part of themselves, which may be used for purposes of witchcraft."[13]

With reference to the natives of East Greenland it is stated that the afterbirth from a mother bearing a stillborn child is used as a fetish to injure other persons;[14] but the nail of a dead man's great toe tied on the great toe of a child serves as a good amulet, and the nail of the fourth finger of a dead man is thought to prevent disease.[15] These natives of Angmagsalik did not cut their hair for fear lest losing this important exuvial fetish would result in the loss of their lives.[16] And it is by no means improbable, as Holm points out, that the custom of casting the dead into the sea is traceable to a fear that the flesh of corpses might otherwise be put to evil uses.[17]

The author, while collecting anthropometric data in the region of Bering Strait, encountered no natives who refused to relinquish hair samples except a few who would not be measured either; but in justice it should be said that most of the hair samples were snipped off before the subject knew what was happening. The Iglulik Eskimos believe that whoever cuts his hair cuts away part of his soul; therefore, hair cut off must never be thrown away, but burned in the house or tent.[18] Rasmussen, after trading with the natives in the neighborhood of the

Magnetic Pole for amulets, was asked to give to each of the Eskimos a lock of his hair as an amulet.[19]

An extracted tooth is sometimes fed to a dog on the west coast of Hudson Bay[20] and in the Mackenzie Delta.[21] Teeth of old men were worn, at Cape Smyth, as wrist charms or pendants around the neck.[22] The custom has been observed in Greenland of smearing an old man's spittle around a child's mouth and of putting some of his lice into the child's head, so that the vital force of the old one may enter into the young.[23] It is mentioned with reference to the Cumberland Sound natives[24] and the Iglulik Eskimos[25] that a mother feeding her child will sometimes cut off a morsel of meat and, after rubbing it on the infant's mouth, deposit it in a small bag as a sort of sacrifice to the spirits but also with the idea that it will serve the child as a fetish.

Nelson reports from St. Michael that: "Men who are not shamans, but who understand some of these things, will sometimes cause the death of a new-born child for the purpose of having the services of its shade to secure success in hunting. The child must be killed secretly and its body stolen, so that no one knows of it; after the body is dried, it is placed in a bag and worn on the person or carried in a kaiak when at sea. One of the best hunters of St. Michael had such a body, which he carried, wrapped in a little bag, in his kaiak."[26]

On Kodiak Island, corpse fetishes were employed in a startling fashion. "On the occasion of the death of a whaler his fellows would cut the body into pieces, each man taking one of them for the purpose of rubbing his spear heads therewith. These pieces were dried or otherwise preserved, and were frequently taken into the canoes as talismans." It is also stated that these people preserved the bodies of brave or distinguished men in secluded caves; and before proceeding on a whale hunt they would carry these dead bodies into a stream and then drink the water thus tainted.[27] Information secured by Frederica de Laguna from Athabascan Indian informants at Kenai, Cook Inlet, concerning the use to which the Kodiak Eskimos put dead human bodies is confirmatory but somewhat perplexing. The statement of these natives that the Kodiak Islanders killed whales with poison extracted from corpses by means of boiling may not mean that it was actually poison but only a fetish substance. The stuff was smeared on their weapon points, and was kept in the prows of their bidarkas. When they had lanced a whale, they used to paddle in a circle around it, and then paddle to the shore, dropping poison in the water behind them; the whale was supposed to wash up on the shore where they landed. The flesh around the wound had to be cut out before the whale could be eaten. No one was allowed to touch the bidarka of a whale killer or even look into it, and these boats were drawn up on the beach with the bows facing toward the water, not toward the land, as was customary. The poison was so powerful that if a duck flew over a group of whale killers' bidarkas lined up on the beach, it would fall dead.

§2. CEREMONIAL CANNIBALISM

ANOTHER custom with deep animistic significance is observed occasionally among the Eskimos when a murderer eats a morsel of his victim's body, usually the heart or liver, to safeguard himself against the dead man's shade. This is a solemn rite, and as such must of course be considered in a different light from the eating of human flesh under pressure of starvation.[28]

In West Greenland a slain man is thought ". . . to have power to avenge himself upon the murderer by 'rushing into him,' which can only be prevented by eating a piece of his liver."[29] Kane mentions the practice specifically at Upernivik, where, after an evil magician was put to death ". . . small portions of his heart were eaten, so as to make it secure that he could not come back to earth unchanged. All this in accordance with venerated custom."[30] A related observance is reported from Hamilton Inlet, Labrador. "When a man was 'made' an angakok, the 'old fellow' [initiating angakok] would come to him with a knife like a cheese cutter's knife, and try to kill him. The angakok would try to elude him. If the 'old fellow' killed him he cut out his liver, and ate it. Both the 'old fellow' and the angakok possessed the power to 'go right through' the side or the roof of the house where there was no door or other opening, so that the chase was a lively one. The angakok often escaped, but sometimes he was caught, and the 'old fellow' feasted on his liver."[31]

When some missionaries were murdered at the hands of the Copper Eskimos just southwest of Coronation Gulf in 1913 the ceremony of eating the murdered men's livers was observed in order to render their spirits harmless.[32] The Eskimos of the Mackenzie region generally ". . . did not eat any of the flesh of a murdered man, but the murderer should lick his knife off at once."[33] Stefansson records an instance, however, wherein the medicine man told an Eskimo who had murdered an Indian to eat a little piece of his victim.[34] It is interesting that the people in the region of the Eskimo Lakes, just west of the mouth of the Mackenzie, are said to receive their name, Inúktuyut, from an occurrence of cannibalism following murder. It is supposed that long ago a man shot a kayak paddler as he was about to land. Thereupon the murderer's older brother scolded him, saying, ". . . were you so hungry you wanted to eat a man?" Angered by this chiding, the murderer cut himself a piece of flesh and ate it.[35] In the Unalit group, of Alaska, in former days each young warrior, in order to become brave, ate a small piece of the heart of the first enemy he killed on a hostile raid.[36]

§3. ANIMAL FETISHES

FETISHES and amulets derived from animals are used extensively by the Eskimos. Belief in their potency is based, of course, on the idea that animals, like men, have souls. A very common motive behind the use of this sort of amulet is the acquisition of the admirable qualities possessed by the animals.

Illustrative of this purpose is Rasmussen's report from the region of the Magnetic Pole of the use of amulets made from a tern for skill in fishing, the foot of a loon for skill in handling a kayak, head and claw of a raven for a good share of meat in all hunting (the raven always being on the spot when any animal is killed). A fly makes a person invulnerable; for the fly is difficult to hit. "One of the few amulets worn by women on their own account is a strip from the skin of a salmon, with the scales along the lateral line; this is supposed to give fine strong stitches in all needlework."[37]

The Copper Eskimo babe will wear on one shoulder a bone from the fore flipper of a rough seal, or on its wrist the penis bone of a seal, so that it will grow up to be a good sealer; scraps of caribou skin on the other shoulder will make it a good caribou hunter. One of these natives once wrapped a live bumble bee in a shred of cloth and tied it around a pup's neck to make the animal fierce and bold like a bee.[38]

Living animals are sometimes thought to be possessed with spirits other than their own souls. Those that are thus endowed, like the sacred animals of other parts of the world, may be regarded as living fetishes. Certain dogs, for instance, among the Eskimos of Kotzebue Sound and the Kittegaryumiut group (Mackenzie region), are fed charms; thus imbued with supernatural power, they can drive away evil spirits.[39] In a sense they partake of the ability of the angakok, who, it should be mentioned, is in a sense the most important of all fetishes, a fetish man, with the soul of an animal or a man as his helping spirit.

On the Diomede Islands a curious fetish bird figures in the whale-boat-launching ceremony. When an umiak is launched for the first whale hunting of the season this mummified bird is produced, and its inclosing mantle, fashioned from a walrus' stomach, is discarded and renewed. A young boy of the Diomede Islands will commonly preserve as a fetish the first bird he kills. One instance was mentioned (Cape Prince of Wales) of a bereaved father destroying this trophy when his son died.[40] Similarly, a boy of the Iglulik group uses his first catch as a fetish in one way or another.[41]

A hunter of the Diomede Islands informed the author that a snarl of wolverine hair that he wore inside his clothes between his shoulders was to bring him success in seal hunting. Another amulet consisting of two weasel tails and some beads might well be worn any time about the head, the same Eskimo affirmed, with assurance of good luck. These fetishes were valued very highly, their superior efficacy being due to the fact that they were very old.

One form of amulet that is known throughout the whole of Canada, as well as Greenland and Alaska, is the skin and skull of the strong little ermine, or a lemming; the dried skin is worn inside the hood. The wearer of such an amulet can, when attacked by any superior force, breathe life into it, and the ermine or lemming, small and inconsiderable though it is in outward seeming, will dash in unnoticed among the hostile party with such force as to drive right through the bodies of the enemies.[42]

Rasmussen tells of a young girl at Cape Adelaide who possessed a swan's beak amulet. Upon being asked what it was for, she very sweetly and shyly cast down her eyes and answered: "That I may have a man-child for my first born." "The Eskimo idea is that it is the man and not the woman who has to fight the battle of life, and consequently, one finds little girls of five and six years old wearing amulets for the protection of the sons they hope to bear—for the longer an amulet has been worn, the greater is its power."[43]

§4. INANIMATE OBJECTS AS FETISHES

Even inanimate objects are capable of having souls. The most obvious manner in which an article can become endowed with a spirit is by being associated with a dying person. In this way it is thought to retain some portion of the departing soul, which is generally regarded as malicious. Therefore, the house of death is abandoned, the clothing and implements of the deceased are destroyed, and the grave itself, a fetish spot of the first order, is shunned or visited only with the observance of proper ritual.[44] On the other hand, articles that have belonged to or been in contact with a fortunate hunter may be prized after his death as possessing supernatural power.[45]

Sometimes a spirit is induced into an object; sometimes it is assumed that there must naturally be a spirit there because of the peculiar appearance or behavior of the object. Small fragments of quartz crystal are accounted for by certain Eskimos of Alaska as being the centers of masses of ice that have frozen so hard that they become stone; hence they are prized as amulets.[46] Iron is often believed to be a fetish substance, and its use is restricted on various occasions by taboos. This is to be explained by the fact that iron is peculiar in that it will take a very keen edge and that it is a strange material by reason of its fairly recent introduction among practically all Eskimos.[47] It is mentioned also that the natives of Cumberland Sound impute to pyrites the power to drive away spirits.[48]

The Diomede Islanders carve wooden boxes, often bearing the likeness of some marine animal, to contain their harpoon heads and other hunting accessories. Aside from their utility these boxes are believed to impart mysterious potency to the weapons; the hunter will put his weapons into one of them, to give the articles the proper spiritual benefit, with all the confidence of a surgeon putting his operating tools into a sterilizing cabinet.[49]

A common practice among many Eskimos is to construct a fetish in the form of a doll or miniature animal. The so-called Doll-Festival is held by the Eskimos of the Yukon and also by the Tinneh as far at least as Anvik, and is believed by the Eskimos to be of local origin. At this festival a wooden doll or image of a human being is placed in the ceremonial chamber and is made the center of various ceremonies. After these it is wrapped in birch bark and hung in a tree in some retired spot until the following year. Only the shamans know where it is; and they pretend to be able to foretell the future by consulting it.[50] The Copper Eskimo angakok sometimes calls his familiar spirit into a rude human image made from the bark of a cottonwood tree, and then asks it questions.[51] In Labrador the Eskimos commonly have personal fetishes in the form of dolls, which represent in a way their guardian spirits. If the spirit possessing the doll does not bring good fortune, the owner sometimes strips the doll of its clothing and shakes and beats it into submission. Finally, if the fetish proves unmistakably false, its owner will surreptitiously foist it off on another person by concealing it in some of his belongings.[52]

Tupileks

In Greenland a variety of fetishes known as *tupileks* play an important part in native beliefs. In the region of Angmagsalik, for instance, the most important operation of an inferior order of shamans (*ilisitsut*), who work in secret,[53] is the creating of these *tupileks*, which will kill persons against whom they are sent. "They are made from certain animals, such as bear, foxes, ptarmigan, and seal. The tupilek must also contain a piece of the anorak [clothing], or the hunting spoil, or something else of the man against whom it is to be sent. It is then animated by chanting a magic charm over it."[54] With the same purpose in view an evil-working magician (*ilisîtsoq*) in northwestern Greenland constructs a *tupilak*, usually in the form of a seal. It appears before the man against whom the sorcerer bears a grudge and can either upset the unfortunate man's kayak without allowing itself to be taken or it can let itself be harpooned and killed. In the latter event the hunter who kills the *tupilak* seal loses all his bodily strength and becomes a cripple.[55] In other groups of Eskimos the word *tupilek* is applied to spiritual entities of somewhat different sort.[56]

Masks

THE belief that spiritual powers are implanted in inanimate objects and can be enlisted to serve men, gains expression also in the use of masks. When a person wears a mask he appropriates the spirit which it represents. In Alaska this cultic usage has advanced far, and it represents at the same time one of the finest artistic attainments of the Eskimos. Doubtless, the development of the art has been favored by the common custom of destroying the masks at the termination of each ceremony, necessitating the frequent making of new ones. Great care is exercised in the fashioning of these ceremonial appurtenances, and the results are in some cases exceedingly impressive. The most grotesque and fiendish creations of the imagination here take form.

Masks are used widely throughout the world,[57] more commonly, it seems, in the Americas than in Asia.[58] They are utilized chiefly in two ways: in actual ceremonies, and as funeral properties. Their utilization in ceremonies is the more important purpose, both among the Eskimos and their Indian neighbors. Petitot mentions the use of masks by the Tinneh Indians both in games and at the interment of the dead.[59] In the Aleutian Islands and thence eastward[60] masks have figured prominently in ceremonial observances and have sometimes been employed for funeral purposes. The characteristic Aleut mask has a crosspiece on the inside that is clenched between the teeth.

Among the Eskimos of Bering Sea, masks do not figure prominently in the cult of the dead, though occasionally maskoids are used on grave markers.[61] In ceremonial, however, they have an important function. Though used along the whole Eskimo coast of Alaska, even to Point Barrow,[62] they manifest the highest attainment south of Bering Strait and especially in the Yukon-Kuskokwim region.[63]

"A study of the available collections brings out so strikingly the great abundance of masks and carvings in the extreme south, and a rapid decrease in their number northward, that the character of their geographical distribution must be considered proof that these carvings are due to contact with the elaborate art of the Indians of the North Pacific coast. In fact, the forms of the masks would hardly be intelligible without a knowledge of the masks of the Tlingit. Although the masks are found in many parts of the world, such complex forms as occur among the Eskimo and Indians of Alaska are rare. Here we see, among both Indian and Eskimos, animals attached to parts of the face, parts of the body attached to the mask, in order to bring together in the compass of the mask the whole individual to be represented. Notwithstanding the difference in style, these features are so striking that they appeal to me as proof of common origin."[64]

The Bering Sea Eskimos ". . . believe that everything, animate or inanimate, is possessed of a shade, having semi-human form and features, enjoying more or less freedom of motion; the shamans give form to their ideas of them in masks, as well as of others which they claim inhabit the moon and sky-land." Some of the masks of the Yukon-Kuskokwim region ". . . are made with double faces. This is done by having the muzzle of the animal fitted over and concealing the face of the *inua* below, the outer mask being held in place by pegs so arranged that it can be removed quickly at a certain time in the ceremony, thus symbolizing the transformation.

"Another style of mask of the lower Kuskokwim has the under face concealed by a small hinged door on each side, which opens out at the proper time in the ceremony, indicating the metamorphosis."[65]

In the Inviting-in Festival on the coast of Bering Sea, the ceremonial performer who wears a mask aims to honor the spirit whom it represents and whom he temporarily personifies.[66]

During certain religious festivals the female dancers wear finger masks, ". . . small, round flat pieces of wood with a projection below, through which are one or two holes for admitting the first or first and second fingers; they are carved to represent a human face or a face supposed to belong to some animal, an *inua*, or some supernatural being. They are generally painted and surrounded by a halo-like fringe, formed by the upstanding hair on a narrow band of skin, usually of the reindeer or wolf. They are also tipped with down."[67]

Again in the center of the Eskimo region the ceremonial use of masks appears, in a much less elaborate phase.

In Baffin Island wooden or leather false-faces are employed in the religious festivals held in autumn and winter in honor of the Sea Goddess Sedna;[68] and their utilization is also reported from the natives north and west of Hudson Bay.[69] Among the Caribou Eskimos, however, Birket-Smith heard only one man, in the Pâdlimiut group, acknowledge using masks in the manner that they are used by the Iglulik and Netsilik Eskimos. Others denied their existence.[70]

In the eastern extremity of the Eskimo region, at Angmagsalik, masks were formerly used to represent the spirits of the angakoks, though they were not employed by the angakoks themselves in the ceremonies. In recent times, however, they have been used only as toys to frighten children, as such remaining as remnants of a past cult.[71]

Amulets in General

AMULETS are used by the Eskimos specifically to ward off every conceivable adversity and to bring good fortune in every sort of undertaking. In West Greenland the *ârnuaq*, or personal amulet, was given a child in its earliest years and used as long as it contained magical power.[72]

The Polar Eskimos even give amulets to dogs; and the *ârnuaq* was used more extensively by men than women.[73] Characteristic of East Greenland is a harness-like arrangement with rawhide pieces across the chest and back for the attachment of amulets.[74] Straps for amulets, probably similar, were used in West Greenland;[75] and Nelson describes amulet straps from Sledge Island that were exactly the same.[76] On Little Diomede Island [77] and St. Lawrence Island[78] and possibly in Dolphin and Union Strait[79] amulet straps are worn obliquely across the chest and over one shoulder. A hunter of Diomede Island wore on his chest, hung from a thong passed around his neck and under his left armpit, an amulet consisting of about five tiny bits of some curious mineral sewn to a leather tab; and for this "medicine," which he guaranteed would bring its owner good luck in sealing, he asked the author twelve dollars or its equivalent.

The Iglulik and Aivilik Eskimos have been known to deposit amulets in the inflated floats used in hunting marine mammals.[80]

Even tattooing is sometimes regarded as an amulet.[81] A Diomede Islander who had a mark tattooed at each corner of his mouth explained

it as a preventive stipulated by his mother against the fate that had be-
fallen his father—death by drowning.[82]

§5. FETISH WORDS AND PHRASES

CERTAIN words and phrases believed to exercise supernatural
power might be included in the category of fetishes on the ground
that their utterance is thought to set into operation spiritual influences. The speaking of these words may produce either good or
evil results. The taboo against mentioning the name of a dead
person, for instance, indicates fear of a malicious spirit.[83] Good
fetish words, on the other hand, are a cherished possession of the
angakok. The great value placed upon these charms is evinced by
the agreement which an Eskimo has been known to make to furnish another with food and clothing for the rest of her life in exchange for a few magic phrases that have been handed down for
generations.[84] Certain magic formulas are inherited as personal
property in the Iglulik group; and none save him who is to use
them must hear them, or they will lose their potency. They can be
uttered only with the face covered with the hood (in the case of a
woman) or the head covered with the hood (in the case of a
man).[85]

This custom of covering the head when pronouncing a charm implies
the presence of a spirit, for it is also a common mourning observance.[86]
It is not to be supposed, however, that magic formulas are spoken as
prayers to specific spirits. Thalbitzer is of the opinion that, at least in
Greenland, they owe their efficacy to a potency inherent in themselves.[87]
It is reported from Angmagsalik, for instance, that "the natives do not
conceive of any spirit connection with the charms, and are ignorant as
to how they work; it is only the words themselves, they declare, which
have 'power.' " In this locality charm formulas are used during sickness and famine in order to ward off dangers. They can also be used as
a defense against foes, having the power to inflict disease, injury, or
death upon them. The charms are of great antiquity, and are as a general rule handed down from one generation to another by sale. They
are most effective the first time they are used, and little by little they
lose their power; hence, they must not be used except in times of danger, or when they are transferred to another. When the transference
takes place, none but the buyer and seller may be present, and in order
that they may have effect, the purchaser must pay for them immediately, and pay dearly, too. "The charms are recited slowly in a low
mystic tone, but the words are unintelligible. As far as our experience

goes, they all begin with '*ija—ija*.' "[88] Thalbitzer has compiled a large assortment of these spoken charms from East Greenland, showing that certain ones are to be employed specifically against sickness, others for success in hunting, while special formulas are required during mourning, for the purpose of counteracting an enemy's spiteful thoughts, and for safety in traveling.[89]

The Polar Eskimos believe that these fetish phrases must be spoken softly and that after a man has spoken one he must not take a knife in his hand for five days.[90]

Longer incantations and choruses also have an implication of magical potency. An example of this sort is the invitation sung by the Alaskan Eskimos to the shades of their dead to join them at the festival, which in part is as follows:

> "Dead ones, come here; Ä-la'-ai-ya'.
> Sealskins for a tent you will get; Ä-la'-ai-ya'.
> Come here, do; reindeer skins for a bed you will get.
> Ä-la'-ai-ya'; Come here, do."[91]

When long usage conventionalizes an invocation to the point of its becoming a rigid ritual it is apt to take on the nature of a fetish. The Copper Eskimos say that their various incantations, *akeutit,* to appease or drive away the malignant spirits, have been handed down from "men of the first times." Many of them have lost their original meaning, but this does not impair their potency. Jenness tells of an Eskimo, who, in order to drive away evil spirits causing a storm, chanted an incantation over and over again for an hour:

> "I come again, I, again.
> I come again, I again. Do you not know?
> I come again, I again."

A spirit was supposed to be speaking all through the incantation, but no one had a clear idea of what it meant.[92]

The number four seems to possess some mystic virtue, especially in Alaska. Thus, "in the creation legend the Raven waved his wing four times over the clay images to endow them with life. The first man in the same legend slept four years at the bottom of the sea. The Raven was absent four days in the sky inland when he went to bring berries to the earth. The whale in which the Raven entered, in another tale, was four days in dying. In the tale of the Strange Boy, from the Yukon, the hero slept in the kashim every fourth night. The woman in the tale of the Land of Darkness, from Sledge Island, was told to take four steps, and these transported her to her home from a great distance. In the Bladder festival, witnessed south of the Yukon mouth, four men, representing four gentes, took a prominent part."[93] Attention is called also to the fact that the duration of mourning is generally set at four or five days.[94] It is to be noted also that the Indians of North America regard four as a sacred number. Nearly all of the tribes who were conscious of any preferential custom exalted this number; and the remaining groups, those of the North Pacific coast, were addicted to five.[95]

The various aspects of fetishism described in this section reveal the great breadth of the concept. The space devoted here to the subject of amulets is small in proportion to the emphasis placed upon them by the people themselves.[96] The belief that souls or spirits reside in human beings, animals, and inanimate objects permeates the entire structure of the religion of the Eskimos and furnishes a key to much of their spiritual expression.

NOTES

1. Rasmussen: 1929, I, 150, 153; Sumner and Keller: 1927, II, 984, 1011.
2. Rasmussen: 1927, 183.
3. Lyon: 1824, 122.
4. Rasmussen: 1927, 224 f.
5. Rasmussen: 1929, I, 171.
6. Rasmussen: 1929, I, 155.
7. Stefansson: 1914, 379 f.
8. Birket-Smith: 1924, 408 f.
9. Weyer: Field Notes.
10. Birket-Smith: 1929, I, 281.
11. Boas: 1907, 484.
12. Stefansson: 1914, 254.
13. Hawkes: 1916, 112.
14. Thalbitzer: 1914, 642 f.
15. Thalbitzer: 1914, 625 ff.
16. Holm: 1914, 86.
17. Holm: 1914, 101.
18. Rasmussen: 1929, I, 182.
19. Rasmussen: 1927, 186.
20. Boas: 1907, 514.
21. Stefansson: 1914, 196.
22. Stefansson: 1914, 395.
23. Rasmussen: 1921, 31; Rasmussen: 1908, 145.
24. Boas: 1907, 484; Boas: 1888, 611.
25. Rasmussen: 1929, I, 173.
26. Nelson: 1899, 429.
27. Petroff: 1900, 234; also Dall: 1878, 26 f.

28. See pp. 117 ff.
29. Rink: 1875, 45. See also Birket-Smith: 1924, 139, citing other authors.
30. Kane: 1856, II, 127.
31. Smith: 1894, 213.
32. Jenness: 1928, 79.
33. Stefansson: 1914, 378.
34. Stefansson: 1914, 323.
35. Stefansson: 1914, 378.
36. Nelson: 1899, 328; Ratzel: 1896–98, II, 212 (Chukchi).
37. Rasmussen: 1927, 185 f. It is likewise mentioned (Murdoch: 1892, 436) that at Point Barrow parts of animals are worn to impart to the wearer the qualities of these animals.
38. Jenness: 1922, 169.
39. Stefansson: 1914, 342.
40. Weyer: Field Notes.
41. Rasmussen: 1929, I, 178.
42. Rasmussen: 1929, I, 150 f.
43. Rasmussen: 1927, 184.
44. See pp. 254 ff.
45. Murdoch: 1892, 434 ff.
46. Nelson: 1899, 446.
47. See pp. 105 and 370 f.
48. Boas: 1907, 138.
49. Weyer: Field Notes.
50. Nelson: 1899, 494 ff.
51. Jenness: 1922, 197.
52. Turner: 1894, 193 f.; Turner: 1887, 107; Hawkes: 1916, 135 f.

53. See pp. 442 f.

54. Holm: 1914, 100 ff.

55. Rasmussen: 1908, 155.

56. In the Hudson Bay district a *tupilak* is simply an evil spirit (Rasmussen: 1929, I, 143), sometimes in the form of an animal (Boas: 1907, 506 ff.). The Central Eskimos, moreover, call the soul of a dead person a *tupilaq* during its stay in Sedna's house. The *tupilaq* is a malevolent spirit: to see it foretokens bad luck, and to be touched by it causes instant death (Boas: 1887, 36; Boas: 1888, 591). The Copper Eskimos sometimes call a familiar spirit *tupilek,* a designation which may be borrowed with them, though probably not (Jenness: 1922, 191). Stefansson states that the word *tupilak* was introduced in the Mackenzie region by missionaries. There it refers to a spirit causing a disease, without holding a prominent position, however, in popular beliefs (Stefansson: 1914, 333, 371 ff., 377).

57. Birket-Smith: 1929, II, 118; Wissler: 1928.

58. Birket-Smith: 1929, II, 201 f., and Table 62B.

59. Thalbitzer: 1914, 640, after Petitot: 1876, xxvi.

60. Dall: 1878, 4 f. (Aleutian Islands); Sauer: 1802, 160, 272 f. (Aleutian Islands); Coxe: 1787, 258 (Aleutian Islands); Weyer: 1930, 260 (Alaska Peninsula); Dall: 1878, 32 (Chugach of Prince William Sound); Dall: 1884.

61. Weyer: Field Notes. See also p. 279.

62. Murdoch: 1892, 365 ff.

63. Weyer: Field Notes; Nelson: 1899, 393.

64. Boas: 1907, 368.

65. Nelson: 1899, 394 f., also 356.

66. See pp. 343 ff.

67. Nelson: 1899, 353.

68. Boas: 1888, 605 ff.

69. Mathiassen: 1928, I, 227 f. (Iglulik Eskimos); Rasmussen: 1929, I, 241 (Iglulik Eskimos); Hall: 1879, 219 (west coast of Hudson Bay); Boas: 1887, 37 (west coast of Hudson Bay).

70. Birket-Smith: 1929, I, 268.

71. Thalbitzer: 1914, 636. See also Trebitsch: 1910, 130.

72. Birket-Smith: 1924, 446 ff.

73. Rasmussen: 1908, 138.

74. Holm: 1914, 32.

75. Thalbitzer: 1914, 635 f., citing Dalager: 1752, 79.

76. Nelson: 1899, 435.

77. Weyer: Field Notes.

78. Moore: 1923, 344 f.

79. Stefansson: 1914, 243.

80. Rasmussen: 1929, I, 188; Boas: 1907, 152, 364.

81. Holm: 1914, 85 f.

82. Weyer: Field Notes.

83. See p. 271.

84. Rasmussen: 1929, I, 165 f. See also p. 234.

85. Rasmussen: 1929, I, 157 ff.

86. See p. 270.

87. Thalbitzer: 1928, 386.

88. Holm: 1914, 87 f.

89. Thalbitzer: 1923, 248 ff. See also Thalbitzer: 1923, 248 f.

90. Rasmussen: 1908, 140 ff. When an Iglulik woman sneezes or breaks wind she must say $qA^{\bullet\, ?}q$, and men who have committed a murder must do the same (Rasmussen: 1929, I, 182). "The Caribou Eskimos, when anyone breaks wind, say [$morA^{\bullet}q$], 'good luck!' or 'through the heart.' That gives good luck on the hunt" (Birket-Smith: 1929, I, 266).

91. Nelson: 1899, 364.

92. Jenness: 1922, 187.

93. Nelson: 1899, 427, also 465.

94. See pp. 275 f.

95. Kroeber: 1923, 253. See also Mooney: 1900, 431.

96. For further information regarding amulets see Murdoch: 1892, 275 (Point Barrow); Birket-Smith: 1929, I, 194 ff. (Caribou Eskimos); Boas: 1907, 151, 505 ff. (west coast of Hudson Bay); Rasmussen: 1929, I, 149 ff. (Iglulik Eskimos and Netsilingmiut); Rasmussen: 1929, I, 177 (Iglulik Eskimos); Boas: 1888, 592; Turner: 1894, 201 (Koksoagmiut, Ungava District); Hawkes: 1916, 136 (Labrador); Crantz: 1767, I, 216 f. (West Greenland); Holm: 1914, 61 (East Greenland).

CHAPTER XIX

TREATMENT OF DISEASE

§1. ANIMISM AND DISEASE

THE Eskimo attributes sickness, as he does other inexplicable misfortunes, to supernatural agency, and believes it to be avoidable or remediable through the use of magic. He commonly supposes that a bodily affliction comes as a punishment for some offense which has angered the spirits. When pinned down as to the exact manner in which disease is produced he will usually explain a disorder as due either to the departure of the soul from the body or to the intrusion of an evil spirit.

Disorders of the Soul

ACCORDING to Eskimo belief it is quite possible to get a new soul when the original is lost; the angakok can provide one or exchange the sick soul for a well one which he can get out of an animal or a child. Furthermore, fragments of the soul may go astray and the angakok can collect them and piece them together.[1]

"The soul," as the Copper Eskimos conceive of it, "is the mainspring of a man's vital strength. A dead man, or more accurately his shade, *tarrak,* may steal the soul of a living man, who will then pine away and die."[2] One method of healing applied by these people consists of salving the afflicted part with the saliva of a healthy person to augment the vitality of the ailing person.[3] It is stated that among the Polar Eskimos a person's illness and death are always attributed to the loss of the soul, and that a stolen soul may be reacquired by a magician.[4] These natives describe a birdlike creature, *angiyang,* which causes sickness and informs the angakok when someone has disobeyed his orders.[5]

Likewise, in East Greenland, the angakok attempts to cure sickness by bringing back the soul of the ailing man.[6] "For, according to Eskimo notions, all disease is nothing but loss of a soul; in every part of the human body (particularly in every joint, as for instance, in each finger joint) there resides a little soul, and if a part of the man's body is sick, it is because the little soul has abandoned that part. In most cases the loss of the soul is regarded as due to one of the following causes: either that evilly disposed persons have driven it out by means of magic, or that higher powers, the moon for instance, have removed it as a punishment for men's sins (some sacrilege, breach of tabu, or other)."[7] When an angakok removes one of a person's souls, ". . . that part of the man which has lost the soul falls ill. If another angakok, finding on examination that the soul has been removed, fetches it back and replaces it, the man becomes well again; but if it is found impossible to get the soul back, the man dies and the soul wanders about to the dismay and terror of all around."[8]

The Siberian neighbors of the Eskimos, the Chukchi, have a belief in a plurality of souls which resembles that of the East Greenlanders.[9] They believe that a man may lose one or two of his five or six souls without becoming sick, but no more. Their medicine men likewise attempt to cure by replacing losses in souls.[10]

It will be recalled that some groups of Eskimos believe that the name-soul is very easily provoked and sometimes dislodged by scolding or striking the person.[11] And in accordance with the belief that the name-soul possesses vitalizing energy, the name of an invalid is sometimes changed as a means of curing him, and in the case of an old person, simply as a means of gaining an extension of life.[12]

Among the Eskimos of Alaska, when a child is sick the medicine man will sometimes extract its soul from its body and place it for safekeeping in an amulet, which for further security he deposits in his own medicine bag.[13] And the Iglulik Eskimos believe that a special protection is given to a man if at birth the shaman takes the soul out of its body and lays it under the mother's lamp, where it stays as long as the boy lives.[14]

A state of unconsciousness is most naturally accepted as indicating that something has happened to the soul: it has been spirited away, or at least impaired, by an evil spirit. It follows that if the soul has not gone too far and can be restored the patient will recover, even from death itself. The conviction of the Eskimo that the dead can be brought back to life is clinched by cases wherein patients regain consciousness after being in a state of coma.

Jenness cites a number of stories from the Copper Eskimos of people dying and coming back to life, and he finds such cases ". . . so common among these Eskimos that one is almost tempted to believe that catalepsy may not be at all infrequent. . . . Strangest of all is the tale of Akarak, a Kilusiktok Eskimo: A spirit or the malignant shade of a dead man struck him on the nape of the neck while he was hunting south of Bathurst Inlet. He fell dead into a swamp and his face was buried in the water. There at sunset his son found him; his face was blue, his hands were frozen stiff and his body was cold and dead. The son caught hold of his ring finger with one hand and extended the arm, then laid his other hand on Akarak's shoulder. Forthwith the latter's soul returned to his body and he was restored to life again. . . . As soon as they arrived in camp the shamans invoked their magic powers and restored the hunter to health again. Akarak had been a fairly powerful shaman before his adventure, the natives said, but afterwards his prestige was greatly augmented."[15]

"Is it true," an Eskimo asked Stefansson, "that Christ was the only white man who could raise people from the dead?" "Yes," Stefansson told him, "He was the only one; and some of my countrymen doubt that even He could." Said Tannaumirk: "I can understand how that might easily be so with your countrymen. If Christ was the only white man who could do it, and if you never knew of any one else who could, I can see why you should doubt His being able to do it. You naturally would not understand how it was done. But we Eskimos do not doubt it, because we understand it. We ourselves can raise people from the dead. You know that some years before you first came to the Mackenzie district Taiakpanna died. He died in the morning, and Alualuk, the great shaman, arrived in the afternoon. The body of Taiakpanna was still lying there in the house; Alualuk immediately summoned his familiar spirits, performed the appropriate ceremonies, and woke Taiakpanna from the dead, and, as you know, he is still living. If Alualuk could do it, why should we doubt that Christ could do it, too?"[16]

Sickness Sometimes Attributed to Evil Spirits

IN the Mackenzie District an illness marked by chills, shivering, and general lassitude is diagnosed according to the principles we have been discussing: the inference is that the person's soul has been stolen. The treatment is simple: the shaman merely summons his familiar spirits and sends them in search. A disease may be caused, on the other hand, by an alien spirit, in which case the ailment may take any form at all. The evil spirit is called a *tupīla^rk*,[17] and the treatment takes the form of exorcism.[18] Similarly, the Copper Eskimos conceive of a malady ". . . as something concrete implanted in the body by an offended soul. The shaman then has to extract the object, which he does by the aid of his familiar spirits. To prove his success he displays to his audience pieces of bone, or worms, or similar things that he has secreted on his person beforehand."[19] On the Diomede Islands and elsewhere in the region of Bering Strait the angakok, or medicine man, employs this method of curative exorcism, extracting with his mouth from the patient's body an object, commonly a small piece of bone or ivory.[20] In Labrador the angakok would thump the patient on the diseased part, or blister it by sucking out the trouble through a tube.[21]

Infected wounds lend themselves readily to the explanation that they are inflamed by evil spirits, whose embodiment is seen in the pus that forms. The treatment adopted by the Copper Eskimo follows rationally from this theory as to their cause: he puts the pus on a piece of meat and feeds it to a dog.[22] A similar instance of the use of this sort of scapegoat in casting off disease is reported from the Egedesminde District, West Greenland. The expectoration of a patient is fed to a dog, and when it shows signs of illness it is killed. In the Julianehaab District a dog belonging to the patient is hung on the house post.[23]

One of the commonest of Eskimo remedies is to bleed the patient. Reliance on this expedient might seem to have grown out of the impression that the expulsion of the evil spirit would be facilitated through the escaping stream of blood; but Thalbitzer, for one, insists that "bleeding," as the Eskimo practices it, has nothing to do with exorcism.

The angakok of the Diomede Islands in practicing this favorite treatment would sometimes eat, or pretend to eat, what came out. The knife he used was commonly made from the bone of a sea gull's wing, but it might be of iron. Sleight of hand enhances the angakok's art as a doctor. The natives described seeing him open up a person's abdomen and take out the parts and clean them in front of everybody's eyes. He rubbed them thoroughly, put them back into the body cavity, and then beat his drum. In five minutes his patient was whole again. One native informed the author of what he had witnessed after a man's wrist had been hurt by a shell which exploded while he was loading his gun: "Angutkok put the wrist to his mouth," declared the Eskimo, "five minutes, all well, all well."

A civilized doctor who was acquainted with the Eskimos on the American side of Bering Strait told the author that he had seen one of these angakoks bleed a man on the top of his head to cure nosebleed; quite naturally the patient became very weak. At Selawik they use a sharpened bear's claw as a lancet, applying it to the forehead, scalp, and even to the body. Referring to the Eskimos about Bering Strait, Nelson writes: ". . . Blood letting is commonly practiced to relieve inflamed or aching parts of the body. For the purpose small lancets of stone or iron are used. In one instance I saw a man lancing the scalp of his little girl's head, the long, thin iron point of the instrument being thrust twelve or fifteen times between the scalp and the skull."[24]

Bloodletting was practiced on Kodiak Island[25] and in the Aleutian Islands.[26] It is reported also in the northern extremity of Alaska at Point Barrow,[27] and far to the east in the Mackenzie region,[28] and on Coronation Gulf.[29] Birket-Smith concludes that in West Greenland the idea that insanity is due to possession by an evil spirit is a result of the influence of Christianity.[30] However, the practice of bleeding and sucking to cure disease[31] leads us to believe that prior to Christian influence these natives probably held the theory that illnesses are sometimes caused by the intrusion of an evil spirit.

The same author states that the Caribou Eskimos do not put forth this explanation, but instead attribute disease to less definite supernatural causes.[32] When an Eskimo of the Pâdlimiut branch of the Caribou group is sick and undertakes to be cured, ". . . he must give away all his possessions, and is then carried out and laid on the earth far from any dwelling: for whoever would invoke the Great Spirit must have no possessions save his breath."[33] The natives of southeastern Baffin Island also seem to attribute sickness to supernatural agency without specifically imagining the malady to be embodied as an evil spirit. It is hazardous, however, to deny categorically the existence of the notion of possession.

Sickness Believed To Be Punishment for Wrongdoing

THE natives of southeastern Baffin Island explain disease as a punishment for breaking taboos; as such it is a penalty of the same nature as poor luck in hunting, which is sent by the deity Sedna when she is enraged. The guilt of transgression adheres to the offender in the form of a dark vapor, which is avoided by the animals. The stigma of wrongdoing also affects the soul of the transgressor:

"It becomes attached to it and makes him sick. The angakok is able to see these attachments with the help of his guardian spirit, and is able to free the soul from them. If this is not done, the person must die. In many cases the transgressions become also fastened to persons who come in contact with the evil-doer. This is especially true of children, to whose souls the sins of their parents, and particularly of their mothers, become readily attached. Therefore, when a child is sick, the angakok, first of all, asks its mother if she has transgressed any taboos. The attachment seems to have a different appearance according to the taboo that has been violated. . . . As soon as the mother acknowledges the transgression of a taboo, the attachment leaves the child's soul, and the child recovers."[34]

Sometimes in the face of some misfortune the confession of taboo breaking prompts the angakok to issue a command which must be carried out in atonement for the misdeed. "Exchange of wives between two men or adoption of a sick child by another family in order to save its life are frequently demanded."[35]

It is stated with regard to the Baffin Islanders: "Bodily ills and death, to them, admit of only one explanation. The sufferer has in some way or another in some particular transgressed the communal law. The disorders of women are considered as a punishment for the infringement of some of the meticulous regulations laid for their observance at certain times. Hence, the first business of the conjurer on being summoned to a sick bed, is to scare or worry the invalid into remembrance and acknowledgment of whatever he or she may have done contrary to the general well-being of the village. He does this after his usual fashion, by crawling into the *igloo* in some particularly horrid guise, and sitting down in a darkened place with his face to the wall and his features well concealed by his hood, giving vent to the most horrific howls, mutterings, ventriloquisms and unhuman-sounding noises, at his ingenious command. Then he proceeds to interrogate the sick person, and of course wrings some acknowledgment from him or her. Treatment—of sorts—may ensue; but as a rule the issue of commands as to atonement or compensation is the wind-up of what the Americans would aptly describe as the whole 'stunt.' Occasionally a piece of flaming moss wick from one of the lamps is laid on the painful part of the sufferer's body and fanned with the conjuror's breath, or merely blown up into the air."[36]

The Copper Eskimo shaman usually discovers ". . . that some taboo has been broken, or that the patient has committed some action which offended a certain dead person's shade. . . . In most cases of sickness the diagnosis alone is considered sufficient to arrest the evil, especially if it is reinforced by an abstinence from such articles of food as the shaman may ordain."[37]

With reference to the Eskimos of East Greenland, Thalbitzer writes that in most cases the loss of the soul (to which all disease is attributed)

". . . is regarded as due to one of the following causes: either that evilly disposed persons have driven it out by means of magic, or that higher powers, the moon for instance, have removed it as a punishment for men's sins (some sacrilege, breach of tabu, or other). The sick man's relatives send for the angakok, who passes a night summoning his spirits, finding by their aid the spot of the earth, or in the sky or in the sea, where the lost fragment of the soul is, in order afterwards to have it fetched and returned to its place in the sick man's body, who is thereby healed. . . .

"[It is the spirit known as] . . . Aperqit 'the consulted one, the oracle,' which sits down by the edge of the sea below the hut and helps the angakok who has been summoned to cure the disease, by answering questions as to the nature of the disease. . . ."[38]

The Medicine Man as a Healer

THE routine technique of the shaman lends itself well to his operations as a healer. His convulsive seizure, ventriloquism, and legerdemain create the conviction that he can enlist the assistance of powerful spirits to treat with the mysterious agents of disease. The patient has a far clearer understanding of how the shaman is coping with the ailment than does the civilized invalid in the hands of a specializing physician, for unlike the procedure of a scientific practitioner, which is worked out from an intricate knowledge of physiology and chemistry, the ministrations of the native medicine man are so simple that anyone may understand the basic principles simply by observing his technique.

Witness a cure performed on the coast of Bering Sea: "In one of the dwellings sits the patient suffering from fever and rheumatic pains; before him are placed two lighted oil lamps, and a parkee is drawn over his head, while two shamans or tungaks, one standing on each side, alternately sing and beat the drum. Behind them faintly visible in the semi-darkness, is the head of an old woman, who, while imitating the croaking of a raven, rubs and pounds the back of the patient. If the pain does not cease the old woman changes her tactics and also her voice, imitating successively the chattering of magpies, the barking of dogs, and the howling of wolves; and if all this be in vain she throws herself upon the sufferer, cuffing and beating him until she makes him forget one pain in another, while the tungaks sing louder and louder and the drums give forth a deafening noise. At last she snatches the parkee from the patient's head, yells repeatedly, and points to the roof; the cover of the smoke-hole is removed and the evil spirit which has caused the sickness escapes amid the beating of drums and the triumphant cry, 'He is gone! Ugh! Ugh!' and the old woman, her task accomplished, collapses into a mass of rags on the floor. It is the third spirit driven out of this patient—how many more dwell within him nobody can tell; if it was the last he will soon mend, but on the other hand, if not the last, there will be more chanting, more drumming, more cuffing, and more payments to the cunning tungaks, until the sick man either dies or can pay no more. The tungaks claim that their science and skill consist in discovering what spirit infests the sick man, and to drive it out they do not consider difficult at all."[39]

It is said that in this region the spirit of life (*iltkhluaghúm*) is involved on all occasions, but principally in cases of sickness. This spirit is believed to appear in five distinct forms.[40]

§2. THE PRACTICAL ASPECT OF THE TREATMENT OF AILMENTS

THE modern art of healing doubtless owes some of its really efficacious methods to the old practice of magic. Whether a disease is caused by spirits or by bacteria matters little if one hits upon a specific treatment that will actually combat the condition. Primitive man generally assigns supernatural causes to illness, but this does not preclude his sometimes finding an effective remedy for it. We are prompted to consider, therefore, in how far the Eskimo has achieved a truly curative art.

Over and above the psychical benefits accruing from implicit confidence in the skill of a doctor, improvement is probably effected in some cases by the osteopathic treatment of the Eskimo shaman. Accustomed to dissecting animals as a consequence of hunting them, he is likely to have a practical knowledge of anatomy. His aptitude in treating aches and pains is favored by his familiarity with the bodily structure. The angakok ". . . knows the positions of joints, muscles, ligaments, veins and arteries, and can find any one of them."[41]

Fortified by a dulling materialistic outlook on life, the Eskimo submits to an operation with startling complacency. The author assisted in the amputating of two fingers of a boy whose hand had been mashed. Without so much as a local anesthetic, the lad calmly allowed his fingers to be cut off. The surgery was no finer than the technique of a reasonably accomplished butcher. Thanks to the boy's strong resistance and the slightness of danger of infection in the Arctic, the damaged hand healed promptly.

A native operation which Bilby witnessed will illustrate the rough and ready angakok in action as family physician. A young woman developed a large mysterious swelling in the groin. There was acute inflammation, pointing to deep-seated accumulation of pus. A native "doctor" decided to lance. His lancet was a rough, dirty piece of steel inserted in an ivory handle. He wiped off an oilstone with a soiled piece of birdskin previously used for scouring out cooking pots, spat upon it and whetted the blade. Then he wet his fingers in his mouth and moistened and cleansed the skin over the inflamed part. Sawing the blade back and forth on the swelling he reached the pus and expelled it by repeated pressure, wiping it away from time to time with a little bit of dirty mouse or lemming skin. When this was finished, the wound was covered with a piece of lemming skin, licked by the surgeon's tongue and stuck over the spot. Two days later the patient was walking about, as well and jolly as she had ever been in her life.[42]

The Eskimo's surgery is crude but often effective. The Caribou Eskimos are known to place broken limbs between wooden splints;[43] and the same expedient is practiced by the Copper Eskimos, who furthermore amputate frozen members. The latter people sometimes use a counterirritant in treating snow blindness: a louse tied to a thread is allowed to scratch the cornea.[44] In West Greenland it is said that even operations for cataract are undertaken, consisting of removal of the membrane with a needle and knife.[45] "If they have newly wounded their hand or foot, they thrust it into the urine tub to staunch the blood. . . . But if the wound is large, they sew it up first."[46] Wounds are treated in East Greenland with blubber.[47]

The Eskimos have scarcely developed any sort of pharmacopeia, and herbs believed to be curative are rarely prescribed. The Caribou Eskimos, for instance, have no remedies for such simple complaints as diarrhea, constipation, snow blindness, toothache, and earache. Shamanistic methods prevail, and these are not medicinal.[48] Likewise, the Copper Eskimos possess no knowledge of medicine;[49] and at Angmagsalik internal maladies are treated only by the angakok.[50] Commenting upon the lack of medicines among the natives of Baffin Island, Bilby says that the Eskimos are probably far behind other uncivilized folk for the simple reason that their homeland, being very poor in vegetation, affords nothing with which to experiment by way of herbs and simples. "An absolutely barren land, covered for the most part of the year with snow, provides no material for the empirical pharmacist."[51] Furthermore, the Eskimo in his native state seems relatively free from disease. Death is more apt to result from accident or famine or old age than in some other parts of the world.

The normal diet of the Eskimo protects him ordinarily from scurvy, but when he is stricken with this malady, as occasionally happens, he sometimes employs expedients for curing it; since scurvy is a lingering disorder which readily responds to dietary adjustment, this is not surprising. According to Crantz, the early authority on West Greenland: "For the scurvy they eat some herbs and roots mentioned before, and also a kind of thin seaweed. . . . But they make no use at all of the noble scurvy grass."[52] We cannot be sure that this knowledge does not bear the imprint of European influence; but it is entirely reasonable to think that it may not. In West Greenland, more extensively than in some other sections, herbs are used as remedies.[53]

The Eskimo people considered as a whole, however, have scarcely made a beginning in the art of medicinal healing. Ingenious though they are in many ways, they cannot match the remarkable achievements of some other primitive peoples of the world in curative medicine. Nor, I may add in this connection, have they developed any processes for deriving poisons such as would aid them in hunting or fighting.

NOTES

1. Nansen: 1893, 225; Crantz: 1767, I, 200.
2. Jenness: 1922, 172.
3. Jenness: 1922, 171.
4. Rasmussen: 1908, 106 ff., 110.
5. Kroeber: 1899, 309.
6. Holm: 1914, 96.
7. Thalbitzer: in Kroeber and Waterman: 1931, 430 f. See also pp. 325 f.
8. Hanserak's diary, quoted by Holm: 1914, 81.
9. See p. 291.
10. Bogoras: 1901, 98.
11. See p. 294.
12. See p. 298.
13. Frazer: *Golden Bough,* 1 vol. ed. (1924), 679 f.
14. Rasmussen: 1929, I, 172.
15. Jenness: 1922, 173 f.
16. Stefansson: 1913*a,* 679. See pp. 429 ff. and 439 f.
17. See pp. 313, 427, 443.
18. Stefansson: 1913, 394; Stefansson: 1914, 371. See also Stefansson: 1908*a.*
Thalbitzer, on the contrary, is of the opinion that exorcism to cure disease is not practiced by the Western Eskimos. "The sucking curing has certainly nothing to do with evil spirits," he asserts. "The idea of sickness as possession by evil spirits is foreign to Eskimo manner of thinking." (From a communication to the writer.)
19. Jenness: 1922, 173.

20. Weyer: Field Notes. See p. 434.
21. Hawkes: 1916, 131.
22. Jenness: 1922, 173.
23. Birket-Smith: 1924, 423 f.
24. Nelson: 1899, 309.
25. Petroff: 1900, 236.
26. Coxe: 1787, 246.
27. Murdoch: 1892, 423; Smith in Kersting: 1902, 125.
28. Stefansson: 1914, 163, 169.
29. Jenness: 1922, 171.
30. Birket-Smith: 1929, I, 299.
31. Birket-Smith: 1924, 423.
32. Birket-Smith: 1929, I, 299.
33. Rasmussen: 1927, 82.
34. Boas: 1907, 124 ff. (Cumberland Sound).
35. Boas: 1888, 592 f. Concerning wife exchanging with religious significance, see pp. 358 and 384; and Sumner and Keller: 1927, II, 1158.
36. Bilby: 1923, 225.
37. Jenness: 1922, 171.
38. Thalbitzer: in Kroeber and Waterman: 1931, 430 f. and 436.
39. Petroff: 1900, 222; compare Nelson: 1899, 432; Turner: 1887, 107 (Ungava District); and Stefansson: 1914, 374 f.
40. Petroff: 1900, 218. See also Bell: 1886, for general information.
41. Bilby: 1923, 226.
42. Bilby: 1923, 226.
43. Birket-Smith: 1929, I, 299.
44. Jenness: 1922, 171.
45. Birket-Smith: 1924, 425, citing other authors.

46. Crantz: 1767, I, 235.
47. Holm: 1914, 74.
48. Birket-Smith: 1929, I, 55, 299.
49. Jenness: 1922, 171.
50. Holm: 1914, 74.
51. Bilby: 1923, 224.
52. Crantz: 1767, I, 234.
53. Birket-Smith: 1924, 425 f.

CHAPTER XX

ANIMISM AND THE FOOD QUEST

§1. CONCILIATION OF ANIMALS' SOULS

A FLUCTUATING game supply is one of the most pressing circumstances in the Eskimo's life. The inexplicable variations in the returns from hunting are just the sort of thing the nature man is ready to attribute to supernatural causes. It follows that the spirits controlling the supply of game must be propitiated in order to secure their good graces. And since food, clothing, and fuel—the basic essentials of life—are secured through hunting, observances for the purpose of causing success in this pursuit preponderate in the religion of the Eskimos.

The belief that all animals possess souls[1] strongly influences those observances pertaining to self-maintenance. As a native of the Iglulik group expresses it, the greatest peril in life lies in the fact that human food consists entirely of souls.[2] Whether he wishes to or not, the Eskimo must reckon with the spirits of the animals he kills. When a seal or a bear, for instance, is slain its soul returns to a vague spiritual realm. In this realm, beyond normal human ken, dwell also the souls of animals not yet liberated to earthly existence. This concept, though it is never very clearly defined, provides for an other world of animals whence come the creatures that are hunted on earth and whither constantly fly the souls of the ones that are slain. The returning souls are able to keep the other world of animals well apprised of the conduct of men on earth. As a consequence the people are constantly striving to avoid antagonizing the source of the food supply. The Eskimo exhibits little or no tendency toward the preservation of game. He may conserve the food that he has in his stores; but he does not consider that the supply of game in nature is diminished even by unrestricted slaughter. Religious rules rather than economic laws govern him in this respect. The spirits of the animals cannot be destroyed simply by killing the animals;[3] their earthly forms represent only a transitory phase of the creatures. But failure to observe traditional rites will certainly occasion dearth of game. A slain animal must be properly treated, lest his soul return to the other world bearing a grudge.

In addition there is the belief, of relatively minor concern here, that the shades of the dead also are capable of sending misfortune to the hunters. And over and above both the shades of the dead and the souls of the animals, there are specific divinities. These divinities, of which there is generally only one very powerful one in a single tribe, elicit deep respect and occasion some of the most important religious observances of the Eskimos. Deferring the discussion, however, of these superior deities, we shall first direct our attention toward the more rudimentary phase of the Eskimo religion, which concerns the belief that animals have souls.

The Eskimo feels it always incumbent upon him to ingratiate himself with the souls of the animals and to avoid their retaliation. Toward this end, he must govern himself by a formalized system of observances, lest the dreaded punishment of food shortage follow upon his noncompliance. Motivated by the pressing need for the primary requisites of life, the Eskimo's reactions reveal the basic, unadorned impulses of primitive religion.

The treatment accorded slain animals bears many analogies to the funeral and mourning observances for human beings. In both cases the primary aim is toward conciliation of the departed soul. Indeed, both cults fit into the same general pattern. But in the practices regarding animals, any sentiment of personal attachment, which to be sure is sometimes weak even in the mourning observances, is, of course, lacking. The cult pertaining to dead animals, therefore, displays simply the fundamental religious motive, apprehension of the unpredictable.

Slain Animal Is Given Drink

A PRACTICE that is reported from most of the groups of Eskimos from the extreme west to the extreme east is that of giving a sea mammal a drink of water after it has been killed.

The Diomede Islanders pour a drink of fresh water into the mouth of a seal (but not a walrus) so that the spirit will carry a favorable report to the realm of the seal spirits.[4] Nordenskjöld reports an instance from the Asiatic neighbors of the Eskimos, the Chukchi: "When . . . they succeeded at last in catching a number of seals, they threw water in their mouths before they were carried into the tents. This was done, they said, in order that the open 'leads' in the ice should not close too soon."[5] At Point Barrow, before a whale is cut up a few drops of water must be sprinkled on its head and some magic words spoken to insure future luck. On whaling expeditions the necessary water for this purpose is contained in bags made from seal flippers which, to prevent freezing, are carried near the small of the back between the outer and inner jackets. Similarly, every seal taken on the ice, whether by spearing, shooting, or netting, must be sprinkled with fresh water before it is taken to the land. When a wife catches sight of her husband dragging home a seal over the ice she will immediately run to him with a cup of fresh water to pour on the seal's nose.[6] Also with reference to Point Barrow, Ray states that besides pouring a few drops of fresh water into the mouth of each seal before taking it to the land, the natives generally go through the same ceremony with ducks that have been killed at sea, but never with those that have been killed over the land.[7] Stefansson states that at Cape Smyth caribou as well as sea mammals were given a drink.[8] At Cape Bathurst dead seals are given a drink because it is believed that otherwise they would not allow themselves to be caught and that a seal thus refreshed will return in the form of another seal for another drink.[9] The Copper Eskimo is said to believe simply that seals have an intense desire for water and that a person who does not administer to their wants will have bad luck.[10] Every seal that a man drags ". . . inside his hut must have a little water poured into its mouth, or a little lamp oil instead, for seals are thirsty animals and have a great craving for water (or blubber). Caribou would be given the same, the natives say, only they have not the same strong desire. Geese and other water-fowl, and ptarmigan, all have a longing for oil, so before an Eskimo skins or plucks such a bird he rubs a little fat or blubber on the head, the wing-joints and the feet; but birds of other species have no desire of this kind."[11]

The Caribou Eskimos pour a little fresh water over the nose and belly of a fiord seal.[12] On the west coast of Hudson Bay every new moon the boys run out to a spot where the snow is clean, and, taking a lump of it, call up to the moon, "Give me luck in hunting!" Then they run into the house and put the snow into a water vessel. Or, as Captain Comer reports from the same general region, they allow the melting snow to drip into the seal's mouth, since these animals, which live in salt water, are always thirsty.[13] The rite is intended to please Nuliayoq, the guardian deity of the seals. After the animal has been cut up and put away, a handful of snow is put where the seal was carved, and stamped down in place.[14] Among the Iglulik and Aivilik Eskimos, "when a seal is brought into a snow hut, a lump of snow is dipped into the water bucket and allowed to drip into the seal's mouth. . . . In summer, it does not require water."[15] Also in Baffin Island a few drops of water are sprinkled on the seal,[16] and Clavering states that the Eskimos of the northeast coast of Greenland sprinkled seals and walruses before flensing.[17] Again it is said that at Angmagsalik "a hunter who brought a seal home dipped his fingers in the urine tub, and smeared the head of the captured animal with urine."[18]

Observances Accorded Animals Analogous to Mourning Customs

THE analogy between the cult pertaining to dead animals and the funeral observances for a dead relative becomes very striking in some cases. Thus, a hunter of the Iglulik group is subject to the same taboo, in the event of his bringing down a white caribou or killing a caribou of any description at Taserssuaq, a lake near the base of Melville Peninsula, as would be imposed if he had lost his sister.[19] And when a man catches a seal in a great lake at Pingerqalik (northeastern Melville Peninsula) the propitiatory observances are the same as if he were in mourning for his brother. This is due to the fact that the seal was in fresh water.[20]

At Repulse Bay no man's or woman's work is permitted for three days after the capture of a whale.[21] At Tununeriseq (Admiralty Inlet, northern Baffin Island) no work must be done for three days after a caribou or bearded seal, narwhal, walrus, or bear has been caught.[22] And a hunter of the Unalit group of Bering Sea who has killed a white whale observes taboos very similar to those enforced upon mourners. Even if he simply aids in taking the animal from the net, he is not permitted to do any work for four days, this being the time the shade remains with the body. The hunter takes the bones of the white whale to some secluded spot and leaves them there with some broken spear shafts. "No one in the village must use any sharp instrument at this time for fear of wounding the whale's shade, which is supposed to be in the vicinity but invisible; nor must any loud noise be made for fear of frightening and offending it. Whoever cuts a white whale's body with an iron ax will die. The use of iron instruments in the village is also forbidden during the four days, and wood must not be cut with an iron ax during the entire season for hunting these animals."[23]

At Kigiktauik, after skinning a red fox, a hunter carefully severed the tendons of the fore and hind legs and cut a hole in the navel. "Carrying the carcass outside he took it to the roof and, opening the smoke hole, held the body over it. The men sitting in the kashim at once united in shouting, 'Än-ok'! (he goes) Än-ok'! Än-ok'!' at the top of their voices. . . . If this should not be done it [the shade] might remain with the body and go about in that shape, doing evil to the hunters or others in the village."[24]

The inland Eskimos of northwestern Alaska observe an exceedingly intricate ritual for the soul of a slain wolf. On returning home with the skin of the animal, the hunter must first walk around his own house following the sun. For a male wolf, he strikes his heel four times against the wall of the house, five times for a female, symbolic of the four and five days' mourning taboo. At the same time the women inside must bow their faces away from the entrance, while a man runs out to inform all the other men of the kill. Then all go out with their knives, in the hope that the soul of the wolf may "like" their knives and let itself be caught the next time. The killer of the wolf strips, and standing naked in the snow rubs himself all over with a piece of caribou skin; then he further cleanses himself in the smoke of a fire. His knives, bows, and arrows are hung up beside the wolf's skin and all present cry aloud, "Now it sleeps with us"—"it" being the wolf's soul. The hut is decked out with all sorts of valuable possessions that are calculated to please the wolf. With all the male visitors present, stories are told by the hunter for the amusement not of the guests but of the soul of the wolf. It is strictly forbidden to laugh or smile, for the wolf might mistake it for gritting the teeth. On the following morning the soul of the wolf has to be sent on its way. The hunter falls on one knee by the fireplace with a white stone hammer in his hand, and sings a magic song; and then he howls, "Uhu!," four times for a male wolf, five times for a female, and raps four or five times on the floor of the hut. In all other houses this rite is repeated with variations and finally at the place where the skin is hung up, all crying out, "Leave us now as a good soul, as a strong soul!" Thereupon a great banquet is held at the hunter's house, the feast symbolizing the dead wolf's provision for the journey. Every guest brings his knife, but none must use it, the food having been cut up beforehand. The food must be entirely consumed or fed to the dogs. No hunter may kill more than five wolves and five foxes in a season. Transgression exposes one either to the loss of the animal already caught or the risk of being bitten to death.[25]

The Alaskan Eskimos have a taboo that walruses must always be hauled up on the ice to be cut up and that this must not be done in the boat.

"As the whale (bowhead) is too heavy to be thus disposed of, it is cut up in the water, but its eye (the one appearing out of the water) is slit, so that it may not see the operation. Probably there is the idea involved here that it is distasteful to the inua (genius) of the animal to have its body disposed of out of its native element or amid strange surroundings."[26]

In Labrador it is believed that in killing seals if the eyeball is cut other seals will be blinded and therefore easily captured.[26]

Exceptionally strict observances are required when a bear is killed, for the shade of this animal is believed to be especially powerful.

At the Horton River, just east of the Mackenzie Delta, the skin of a female bear was hung up by the nose for four days with an offering of needles near it, that of a male bear for one day, with a bowdrill near it.[27] At Kotzebue Sound one who had killed a polar bear must not grind or file iron, but was bound by no other taboos.[28] The custom of the Copper Eskimos is to lay a miniature bow and arrow beside a male bear or wolf, and beside a female a strip of deerskin or sealskin, which she can use as a needle holder. These animals are like human beings and have need of the same things: a male his hunting weapons, a female her needlecase.[29] On the west coast of Hudson Bay, "after a polar bear has been killed, it is cut up on the spot, the intestines are thrown to the dogs, and the rest of the body is taken home. A piece of the tongue and other small parts are hung up in the hut; and knives, saws, drills, and other small objects, are attached to them as presents to the bear's soul. It is believed that then the soul will go to the other bears and tell them how well it has been treated, so that the others may be willing to be caught. At the end of three days, the man who killed the bear takes down the objects, carries them out into the passage-way, and then throws them into the house, where the boys stand ready to get what they can. This symbolizes the bear-spirit presenting these objects to the people. The boys must return the objects to their owners. During these three days, the women are not allowed to comb their hair."[30] The Iglulik and Aivilik Eskimos observe a taboo likewise for three days after a whale has been killed or a bearded seal or a bear: during the time, there must be no man's or woman's work, and no turf must be cut or fuel gathered from the earth; clothing may be mended but not made.[31] Regarding southeastern Baffin Island it is written that "a bear's soul remains for three days near the place where it left the body. Among the Nugumiut it is customary, when a male bear has been killed, to take its bladder, milt, sweetbreads, and gall, and some man's tools such as drill, knife, spear-point, and file, and hang all on a pole. There they remain for three nights. When a female bear has been killed, the same parts of the body are hung up, together with some woman's tools, such as knife, needle, scraper, and brass fillet for the head,—an ornament which was used very frequently in former times. They are very careful not to transgress any taboos during the three days after a bear's death, because it is believed that such transgressions will be punished very speedily, much more so than in the case of animals going to Sedna's abode."[32] The Polar Eskimos regard the soul of a bear as the most dangerous of all animals' souls, and the taboos and observances are the most elaborate. For five days some skin and meat are hung up over the snout of a female bear, and a harpoon point and harpoon are added if it is a male.[33]

Behind many of the practices mentioned above is the intention to provide for the soul of the animal after it has been killed. The food and weapons offered suggest the very similar grave deposits and other presentations to the ghosts of dead persons. The Eskimos attach more importance to the propitiation of animals' souls than do many other peoples, especially those who are not so dependent upon hunting. Their cult pertaining to slain animals has the aim of encouraging other animals to be caught in the future. In this respect the purpose of the observances differs from those paid to the souls of deceased persons; and, too, the animal cult is dissociated from any sentiment of personal attachment; otherwise, the practices with respect to animals and men show marked similarities. These similarities suggest that the funeral measures, apart from a sense of bereavement, which incidentally must not be overestimated through implication, are the response to a deep apprehension of the disastrous vengeance of incensed spirits.

Sacrificing a Part for the Whole

OFFERINGS made to slain animals frequently differ from the usual human grave offerings in that they are a part of the body of the dead animal. The Eskimo has a vague idea that such offerings will benefit and placate other animals of the same species, or possibly the spirits of the dead. A reasonable interpretation is that the part sacrificed represents the soul or essence of the animal which must not be appropriated to use on earth lest the realm of spirit animals become depleted.

The Copper Eskimo cuts off a small piece of the meat and blubber and throws it away before dragging home the animal.[34] Similarly, he propitiates the spirit of the slain caribou by throwing away a part of its liver.[35] When an Iglulik hunter has cut up a caribou killed with an arrow he places a small piece of meat or suet under a stone.[36] Similarly, when the natives of southeastern Baffin Island ". . . kill a reindeer, and have skinned it, they cut off bits from different parts of the animal, and bury them under a sod, or some moss, or a stone at the exact spot where the animal was killed."[37]

Crantz observed in West Greenland that the heads of seals must not be fractured or thrown into the sea but piled in a heap before the door, that the souls of the seals might not be enraged.[38] In the region of the

Bukland River, Alaska, when the whaling is completed the natives collect the bones and burn them; those who can afford it burn the clothes worn while whaling, the poorer natives paying tribute to the "God of the White Whale," by cutting off and burning a small piece of some garment.[39] At Point Barrow ". . . the bones of seals are carefully preserved unbroken and returned to the sea, if possible. . . ."[40]

When an Iglulik boy catches his first seal all its bones are dropped into a blowhole in the conviction that they will become seals which the boy is to catch in later life. His first catch prompts also another ceremony: he must lie down and let his father drag the dying animal across his bare back, so that the seals will not be afraid of him.[41] In Labrador, when a seal is cut up, if the tip of the heart and liver are thrown back into the water it is thought that more seals will come in the future to the hunter.[42]

The Bladder Festival

IT is in Alaska that the concept of sacrificing a portion of the carcass of the slain animal in order to maintain a balanced relationship with the animal spirits is observed in its most advanced development. Here, in the region of Bering Sea, the Eskimos exemplify their beliefs concerning the souls of animals in an elaborate ceremony of a sacrificial nature known as the Bladder Festival. The salient feature of this festival is the offering of a year's accumulated bladders of slain animals in expiation and in appeal for future success in hunting. This cult practice is not directed toward a specific guardian deity of the animals, as are usually the ceremonies of the central region, but toward the spirits of the animals themselves or toward unnamed supernatural forces controlling their propagation. One sees in this observance the earnest purpose of these hunting people to solve the mystery of the luck element and to lessen the uncertainty of their food quest.

At St. Michael, near the mouth of the Yukon, the Bladder Festival is generally held during the December moon and it sometimes extends into January. It lasts five days, with a subsequent taboo period of four days during which no work is to be done. During the festival the men keep rigidly apart from the women. No females are allowed to go near the bladders except those who have not reached puberty.

On the first day of the festival the ceremonial chamber and its fire pit are cleaned out; and a song is sung to the wild parsnip plant (Archangelica), *i-ki'-tûk* as the natives call it, which figures prominently in the ceremony. The resinous smoke of flares made of it is deemed efficacious as a purifying or fumigating agent and is thought to be very pleasing to the shades of the animals. On the second day the stalks of the wild parsnips are gathered, dried, and stacked into a large sheaf. On the following day this sheaf is opened and a smaller sheaf made out of its contents, which is placed in front of a lamp. Each hunter brings the bladders of all the seals, walruses, whales, and polar bears that he has killed during the year and they are hung up in the kashim, or ceremonial room. Small fragments of food are thrown before the bladders and a libation of water is made at the same place. Then all partake of food. The bladders represent the inuas, or souls, of the animals, and the Eskimos think that by making offerings to them they will prove their good will.

On the fourth day the hunters paint the bladders with bands and dots, using oil mixed with charcoal, generally from wild parsnip stalks. Sometimes they paint their faces in stripes with the same pigment used on the bladders. They cavort about the chamber waving firebrands of parsnip stalks; now they bathe the suspended bladders in the smoke of resinous flames, now they wave the torches in the faces of the men sitting about. Possessed with intense fervor they prance and shriek wildly, making a scene of mad pandemonium.

On the fifth day the ceremony reaches its climax. The hunters, running out of the ceremonial room pell-mell with inflated bladders tied to their spears, go to a hole in the ice. There the bladders are burst with the seal claws of ice scratchers, and after several strands of seal sinew are tied to each they are thrust down under the ice. Thus, the shades are returned to their proper element; they are believed to swim far out to sea and enter the bodies of unborn animals, rendering game more plentiful. Every man puts his personal sign on his bladders; and the confidence in reincarnation is strengthened in this region by the story that one man killed a seal whose bladder bore the same mark with which he had labeled his bladders a previous year. To culminate the festival they build a fire of parsnip stalks on the sea ice and all jump through its cleansing smoke. The festival is concluded with various dances.[43]

The whole performance may be regarded as a belated funeral ceremony for the slain animals. The object is to conciliate their souls, which are feared because of their power to cause hardship by diminishing the food supply.

One group of people (Chifukhlugumut, near the Yukon) who, because they lived far from the coast, had killed no seals or walruses and therefore had no bladders, simply placed the wild parsnip stalks unburned upon the ice of a small river as an offering. The use of iron axes was tabooed here as elsewhere in this region during the festival period.[44]

On Nunivak Island, not far from the scene of the ceremony described above, a great festival is held every autumn in honor of the ribbon seal, which is an important factor in the lives of these natives. The preparations for the festival begin in November and last a whole month. During this time the men must live apart from the women; for the latter are regarded as unclean with respect to all animals hunted. Every festival begins with new songs composed by the men, which are sacred and must be conceived in the darkness and silence of the dance house. As soon as one has been made, it must be learned by the women, who sing and dance in company with the men. During the daytime, all are busy with other things, the women sewing, the men carving selected pieces of driftwood into various utensils for the winter. When the men and women have finished their respective tasks, the angakok, or medicine man, is invited to call upon his helping spirits. He appears in new winter boots and crackling waterproof skins, and sits down in the middle of the floor. A line is brought out and a noose laid around his neck. Four men haul at each end of the rope; yet in spite of the fact that he is apparently being strangled, he utters warnings and prophesies in a clear voice. Almost hanging by the neck from the rope, he invokes the various animals and informs the company when the winter hunting can begin. A further preliminary to the feast consists in a sweat bath, performed by the men in the dance room, terminated by a wash in cold water. The purpose is to purify themselves. On the same occasion all the vessels, marked with the owner's respective marks, must be exposed to the heat of the fire.

The feast itself lasts eight days. During the previous year the bladders of all ribbon seals caught have been carefully preserved, and these are now brought into the dance house and hung up with bundles of herbs under the roof, where a harpoon and line are also fixed, with a small lamp burning beneath them. Then, with great solemnity, the new clothes are put on and the new utensils are handed around to their respective owners. The women are called in, and feasts are held every day, ending with song and dance. At last, the seal bladders are dropped into the sea through a hole in the ice, while the medicine men implore the animals to be generous to men. On the eighth evening men and women exchange gifts, and promise to try their best in the coming winter to be better in conduct and in their respective tasks. The festival ends, as it began, in deep silence—the silence of good wishes and resolutions. And then the winter hunting can begin.[45]

At Kushunuk, northeast of Nunivak Island, the bladders are kept in the ceremonial chamber for seventeen days, with a different set of ceremonies each day. Reindeer bladders, also, are used, but they are not hung up with those of the sea animals. Bird images and pantomimes of birds, also female genital symbols, figure in the ceremony. Offerings of food and water are made to the bladders, which in the end are deflated by a spear point and ceremonially put through a hole in the ice. The shaman is tied securely under the floor of the ceremonial room in the exit passage, with a long cord leading up into the kashim. He is supposed to travel to the land of the seal bladders, and upon returning he recounts the reactions of the shades of the bladders to the festival in their honor. At the conclusion all bathe in urine to cleanse themselves of evil influences, and no work must be done until this has been completed.[46]

The Bladder Festival is characteristic only of Bering Sea, but Eskimos elsewhere know of the basic idea. As far east as the Horton River, about 250 miles east of the Mackenzie Delta, the bladders and noses of all seals were saved and after the season they were put into a crack in the ice or thrown away.[47] Not far beyond, the Copper Eskimos do not keep the bladders and nose skins of the seals.[48]

§2. THE "INVITING–IN" FEAST[49]

EQUALED in importance only by the Great Feast of the Dead[50] in the Yukon-Kuskokwim regions is the so-called "Inviting-in" Feast (Aithu′kāgûk, or I-thû′-ka-gûk according to Nelson). This ceremonial differs from the Bladder Festival, in that while the latter placates the spirits of animals already slain, the "Inviting-in" Feast is an appeal to the totemic guardians of the performers, who wear masks representing these spirits, for future success in hunting. It takes place in January, after the completion of the Asking Festival[51] and of the Bladder Feast, which are held in November and December.

The maker of the feast saves for years; for he has to feed the entire tribe of visitors during the first day of the ceremonial. He often beggars himself, but he gains great fame among the Eskimos and lays his guests under lasting obligation.[52] A messenger is chosen to carry the invitation to another tribe desired as visitors. To gain the privilege of performing this errand there is considerable rivalry among the young men; for the envoy is newly clothed from head to foot in fine apparel. He bears a curious "asking stick" as a symbol of invitation, a wand, from the end of which dangle three spheres made of bent strips of wood. Acceptance of the invitation is almost a sacred duty. The visiting people are expected to bring gifts of exchange.

Weeks are consumed in learning songs for the occasion. Nightly the participants practice them in the ceremonial chamber (kaz′-gee) which is darkened so that any spirits attracted by the sound of music will not be frightened away.

The ceremonial proper, as witnessed by Ernest Hawkes, probably for the first time by any scientific observer, began with humorous dances. If in the course of the first day's program the home tribe could make the visitors laugh they were privileged to ask of them anything they wished. As each man entered he threw down a small gift before the maker of the feast. As soon as everyone was seated, the dances began. Strange noises were heard in the entrance tunnel, gradually approaching the room. Then a horrible-looking wooden face was thrust up through the floor, worn by the chief comic dancer of the Unalit. He gazed around the audience in silence a full minute, throwing the children into fits of mingled terror and delight. Then the leader commenced the dance invitation and the pantomime began. The Malemiut visitors, although their eyes twinkled, never cracked a smile throughout his crazy performance. Then he disappeared through the hole and returned wearing a hideous green mask, with a long nose, and a big red streak for a mouth. His second act was even funnier than his first, but the cautious visitors sat through it as solemn as owls. Thereupon the home tribe trotted out their champion, a little old fellow, wonderfully impressive in his movements. He took his place in the center of the floor amid perfect silence. The mask he was wearing was adorned with feathers and had an enormous nose. It purported to caricature the Yukon Indians, whom the Eskimos derisively call *ingkilik'*, or "those having lice."[53] With head on breast and hands at rest on his lap the old man seemed sunk in some deep reverie. Then he raised his hand to his head and cracked a louse audibly. This was too much for the visitors. They howled with laughter. And the old man performed his dance. Immediately after, food was brought in and the feasting began.

The second day was characterized by competition in dancing between the givers and the guests.

On the third day the contest reached its climax. The best dancers of each party in full regalia of armlets, fillets, and handlets were put forth; and the interest became intense. First, there were dances by the women, imitative of their daily occupations of curing skins, sewing, and so forth. Then one of the guests took the floor, disguised behind an appropriate mask, and depicted the maneuvers of a walrus being hunted. Other dances followed in succession, representing various phases of animal life.

Finally, the shaman donned an *inua* mask. This mask serves a different purpose from the humorous ones which excite merriment; it is intended to honor the *inua* or spirit it represents, which is the totemic guardian of the performer who wears it. The shaman had daubed soot from the *kaz'-gee* walls on his breast, as a means of putting himself *en rapport* with the spirit guests. He began his part by running around the entrance hole in ever lessening circles. Then at last he tumbled over and lay in a trance. While in this state he accomplished his confabulation with the spirit guests in the fireplace below. Thus, the culminating feature of the festival is a shamanistic séance, suggesting that the ultimate purpose is the propitiation through entertainment of the invited spirits. After a time the shaman came to and informed the hunters that the *inuas* had been pleased with the dances and promised future protection for a successful season. With appropriate offerings of meat and drink and tobacco, which were transmitted to the spirits through cracks in the floor, the celebration terminated.

The masks are burned in the end, and should a man sell his he must replace it with an equal amount of wood for the sacrificial fire which takes place subsequent to the ceremony.

§3. OBSERVANCES APPLYING TO WHALE HUNTING

HUNTING whales is an activity which, of course, requires the co-operation of many men. When it is successful the Eskimos are rewarded with a bounty of food and other useful materials, but like other types of hunting it is an uncertain pursuit and at times a dangerous one. Observances to insure the good will of the spirits, therefore, attend the preparation for the hunt, the chase itself, and the feasting at its termination.

On the Diomede Islands, for instance, a rather elaborate ceremony accompanies the launching of a whaleboat. When a new boat is constructed it is simply given a drink of water for good luck in hunting; but when an umiak is relaunched at the beginning of the season in the spring a time-honored ceremonial is held. The villagers sing all during the morning. A strange sort of bird mummy is brought out and the walrus-stomach mantle which envelops this strange fetish, leaving the beak protruding, is discarded and a new one put on. All the paddles and oars are scraped and cleaned. The boat is washed on the outside with urine while it is on the rack; and then, still inverted, it is fumigated with a driftwood fire built underneath. Three persons, especially, must have new clothing: the woman who leads the umiak to the edge of the ice, the helmsman, and the best harpooner. The woman goes ahead of the boat as it is carried down. She is wearing a long string of beads made from crab shells which she removes when she reaches the edge of the ice and does not put on again until a whale has been caught. Near the water's edge she dances. Here occurs a practice that suggests imitative magic in its similarity to the custom followed after the harpooning of a whale, when all the other boats race to the spot to share the catch according to the order of their arrival.[54] In the present analogous ceremony two or more boys race to where the woman waits at the edge of the ice; and there the runners receive from her many good things to eat as reward.[55]

At Cape Smyth the master of an umiak, before going to the edge of the ice to begin looking for whales would stand astride the trapdoor in his dwelling and throw pieces of whale meat between his legs into the trapdoor.[56] In West Greenland, preparatory to a whaling expedition both men and women made a very careful toilet and all the lamps in the house were extinguished.[57]

At Point Barrow the umiak must be launched from the ice bow first; otherwise it would be impossible to capture a whale during the entire season. "After the umiaks are ready, all the natives are restricted from pounding on iron, chopping wood, or digging in the earth, and all their movements must be made in a quiet manner."[58] "During the months the whaling lasted, all the men lived uninterruptedly out at the edge of the ice. . . . Tents were forbidden, and they had therefore to be content with storm-shelters made of skins, or seek some protection from the elements under the boats. It was also forbidden to dry clothes, and raw food was tabu; all meat had to be boiled. Meantime, the women and children spent an anxious time up in the winter houses."[59] The women were tabooed during the whaling season.[60]

It is reported from the Kaniagmiut that during the whaling season the whalemen were considered unclean and did not mingle with the rest.[61] A Kodiak Islander's wife was expected to lie in the hut without eating while he was out whale hunting, in order that his luck would be good.[62] Similarly, in Labrador, during the whale hunt the women and children must remain indoors, silent and motionless, while the men are out.[63] The natives of Repulse Bay will not bail out a boat or urinate or spit while out whaling; and when a whale is on the line all the women, except the old ones, must lie relaxed with their clothing loosened. As for the old women and also the boys, as soon as a whale is on the line they have their legs tied in pairs and run a three-legged race inland out of sight of the sea.[64]

At Point Barrow "whaling implements were only allowed to be used for one season; this applies to the skins of the boats, and all gear and equipment. In earlier times, all the harpoons were burned with the other implements in a great bonfire during the festival held at the conclusion of the season; later, it became the custom simply to hang up the harpoon heads on a frame, where they were left until the chieftain died, when they were placed with him in his grave."[65]

On Nunivak Island, also, it is considered unpropitious to enter the hunting grounds with any old gear, and generally a new kayak is constructed each year. The man who is building a kayak must not enter a woman's house. Eating is allowed only at night after the day's work. The small boat is consecrated the first calm day. The ceremony takes place at dawn, with the whole family dressed in new clothing. The man walks ahead of the kayak bearing a lighted lamp, the idea being that the flame frightens away evil spirits.[66]

At Point Hope, Alaska, the most important of all the seasonal feasts is the Great Thanksgiving Festival to the souls of dead whales. "This is held in the qagsse, which serves ordinarily as a place of assembly for all the men of the place, but on special occasions as a temple or banqueting hall. The upper part of the interior at the back is painted to represent a starlit sky, much trouble being taken to secure colored stones to serve for pigments. A carved wooden image of a bird hangs from the roof, its wings being made to move and beat four drums placed around it. On the floor is a spinning top stuck about with feathers, close by is a doll, or rather the upper half of one, and on a frame some distance from the floor is a model skin boat, complete with crew and requisites for whaling.

"The proceedings open with the singing of a hymn; then a man springs forward and commences to dance; this, however, is merely the signal for mechanical marvels to begin. The bird flaps its wings and beats its drums with a steady rhythmic beat. The top is set spinning, throwing out the feathers in all directions as it goes; the crew of the boat get to work with their paddles; the doll without legs nods and bows in all directions; and most wonderful of all, a little ermine sticks out its head from its hole in the wall, pops back again and then looks out, and finally runs across to the other side to vanish into another hole, snapping up a rattle with a bladder attached as it goes. All hold their breath, for should the creature fail to enter the hole with the rattle and the bladder behind it, one of those present must die within a year. But all goes well, and the company gasp in relief. Then follows a general distribution of gifts, edible delicacies mostly, to all present, and the guests depart."[67]

NOTES

1. See pp. 299 ff.
2. Rasmussen: 1929, I, 56 f.
3. Turner: 1894, 200.
4. Weyer: Field Notes.
5. Nordenskjöld: 1881a, II, 130.
6. Smith in Kersting: 1902, 120 f.; see also Murdoch: 1892, 270.
7. Ray: 1885, 40.
8. Stefansson: 1914, 389.
9. Stefansson: 1914, 351.
10. Jenness: 1922, 114.
11. Jenness: 1922, 181.
12. Birket-Smith: 1929, I, 95.
13. Rasmussen: 1929, I, 75.

14. Boas: 1907, 147 f.
15. Rasmussen: 1929, I, 184; also 186.
16. Hall: 1866, 575; Hall: 1864, 332; Boas: 1907, 489. Giving a seal a drink is mentioned from West Greenland (Birket-Smith: 1924, 283, after Elgström: 1916, 94).
17. Birket-Smith: 1924, 283.
18. Holm: 1914, 49.
19. Rasmussen: 1929, I, 194. Boas mentions a prohibition on the west coast of Hudson Bay against killing albino caribou (Boas: 1907, 501).

20. Rasmussen: 1929, I, 185.
21. Rasmussen: 1929, I, 188.
22. Rasmussen: 1929, I, 195.
23. Nelson: 1899, 438 f.
24. Nelson: 1899, 423.
25. Rasmussen: 1927, 321 ff.
26. Hawkes: 1916, 84 f., 134.
27. Stefansson: 1914, 353.
28. Stefansson: 1914, 347.
29. Jenness: 1922, 181.
30. Boas: 1907, 501, also 147, and Rasmussen: 1929, I, 188 f.
31. Rasmussen: 1929, I, 184 f., 188 f.
32. Boas: 1907, 124; Boas: 1888, 596; also Hall: 1864, 331.
33. Rasmussen: 1908, 111 f.; Steensby: 1910, 376.
34. Jenness: 1922, 113.
35. Jenness: 1928, 103.
36. Rasmussen: 1929, I, 194.
37. Hall: 1864, 321.
38. Crantz: 1767, I, 216.
39. Hooper: 1881, 24.
40. Ray: 1885, 40. See also p. 370.
41. Rasmussen: 1929, I, 178; Boas: 1907, 161.
42. Hawkes: 1916, 134.
43. Nelson: 1899, 380 ff., 392 f. See also Petroff: 1900, 218 ff.; Jacobsen: 1884, 289 ff. (Adnek, Norton Sound region); Nelson: 1899, 391 (Kaialigamiut).
44. Nelson: 1899, 392.

45. Rasmussen: 1927, 352 ff.
46. Nelson: 1899, 382 ff.
47. Stefansson: 1914, 351 f.
48. Jenness: 1922, 114, n. 3.
49. The description of this feast is taken from Hawkes (Hawkes: 1913), who witnessed it among the Unaligmiut, of Norton Sound, and from Nelson (Nelson: 1899, 358 f.).
50. See p. 281.
51. See p. 197.
52. See pp. 196 ff.
53. See p. 152.
54. See p. 176.
55. Weyer: Field Notes.
56. Stefansson: 1914, 286.
57. Birket-Smith: 1924, 337, citing a number of authorities.
58. Smith in Kersting: 1902, 120. See also Murdoch: 1892, 274.
59. Rasmussen: 1927, 310.
60. Ray: 1885, 39.
61. Dall: 1878, 26.
62. Holmberg: 1855, 112; Petroff: 1900, 234.
63. Hawkes: 1916, 134.
64. Rasmussen: 1929, I, 187. Boas also mentions the latter two customs as applying to the west coast of Hudson Bay (Boas: 1907, 499 ff.).
65. Rasmussen: 1927, 312.
66. Rasmussen: 1927, 351.
67. Rasmussen: 1927, 332 f.

CHAPTER XXI

THE DEITY OF THE SEA

THE rites performed with the purpose of making game bountiful are by no means directed simply to the souls of the animals. Specific divinities, whose chief function is the control of the animals, are besought to this end. In the central region, and to less extent in Greenland, ceremonies are devoted to the Sea Woman, who is believed to be the protectress of sea animals and to dwell at the bottom of the deep. It is wholly natural that people who live in close contact with the sea and are dependent largely upon the fruits of sea hunting should embrace such a concept. Inasmuch as the observances constituting the cult of the Sea Goddess are the highest religious expression of some Eskimo groups, it is well to consider the root ideas in the concept.

§1. MYTHOLOGY AND THE SEA GODDESS

THE belief in the Sea Goddess centers about a myth which is known in one version or another over a large section of the Eskimo realm. In Cumberland Sound, Baffin Island, a type locality, the myth is as follows:

A girl named Avilayoq married a dog, who had transformed himself from a speckled stone. She had many offspring, who were Eskimos, white men, and various fantastic creatures. These children were so noisy that the family moved to an island so as not to annoy the girl's father. Every day Avilayoq sent her dog-husband to her father for food, which he would put in a pair of boots tied around the dog's neck. One day while her husband was thus absent a man came to the island and induced the girl to go away with him. She lived for some days in the village of her new husband, who turned out to be a petrel instead of a man. Meanwhile, her father set out alone to find her, and succeeding, started back with her hidden in some skins in a boat. Her second husband pursued in his kayak. Upon overtaking them he asked the young woman to show her hand, as he was very anxious to see at least a part of her body. But she did not move. Then he asked her to show her mitten; but still she did not respond. With that he began to cry and so fell far behind. The father proceeded, with his daughter concealed, through calm water. After a time they saw a strange object overhauling them. Sometimes it looked like a man in a kayak, sometimes like a petrel. It flew up and down, then skimmed over the water. Finally, it came up to their boat and circled around it several times, then disappeared again. Suddenly ripples appeared, the waters began to rise, and in a short time a gale was raging. The boat was quite a distance from shore. The old man, fearing that they might be drowned, and dreading his son-in-law's revenge, *threw his daughter overboard. She held on to the gunwales; but her father took his hatchet and chopped off the first joints of her fingers. When they fell into the water they were transformed into whales, the nails becoming the whalebone. Still she clung to the boat. Again he swung his hatchet and he chopped off the last joints of her fingers, which became seals. Now she clung to the boat with only the stumps of her hands; and her father finally wielded his steering oar and knocked out her left eye. Whereupon she fell backward into the sea,* and he paddled ashore. Then he filled with stones the boots in which the first husband, the dog, had been accustomed to carry meat to his family. The dog started to swim across, but when he was halfway the heavy stones dragged him down and he was drowned. The father also became a victim of the sea. *The woman became Sedna, who lives in the lower world,* in her house built of stone and whale ribs. She has but one eye, and she cannot walk, but slides along, one leg bent under, the other stretched out. Her father dwells with her in her house, and the dog lives at the door.[1]

This myth is recorded, with slight variations, from the east coast of Melville Peninsula.[2] The Island where the girl lived with her dog-husband, according to this version, was Qiqertârjuk, close to Iglulik at the eastern end of Fury and Hecla Strait. Her finger tips became seals, the second joints bearded seals, and the third joints walruses; and the girl is called Takánâluk arnâluk, "the woman down there."

Consequent upon these and other related myths which derive the sea mammals from the severed finger joints of a woman holding onto the gunwale of a boat, the Central Eskimos fear that whenever they kill these animals the deity will be enraged as by the murder of her own offspring.[3] It is well to note that she is, indeed, the foremost figure in the religion of these groups, and most of their religious observances are for the purpose of retaining her good will and propitiating her if she has been offended.[4] These observances will be discussed later, together with similar ones from other Eskimo tribes.[5]

In different parts of Greenland variants of the Sedna myth are told, and the protectress of the creatures of the deep is customarily respected as a powerful spiritual being.

The Polar Eskimos designate her as Nerrivik, "the food dish" or "the place of food."[6] Their myth depicts her as having lived on earth with a petrel for a husband, and explains that her grandfather cut her hand off and that she sank into the depths of the sea, where she rules over all the sea creatures.[7] Some of the dead go to her, and so do dogs when they die. Elsewhere in Greenland the Sea Woman whose fingers were changed into seals and whales has the names Arnakuagsak, Arnarquagssaq, etc.[8] In a myth from South Greenland set down by C. Lytzen[9] the girl is called the parentless Nivikkaa, "the woman thrown backward over the edge."[10] She was thrown out of her umiak by a man as she sat rowing in it. She held fast to the gunwale and the man chopped off her fingers with his ax; and when she sank back he threw in her dog and her lamp. Scorned in life, in death she became the ruler of all the animals of the sea, which she collects in the drip shell under her lamp. The dog guards over her house. If there is a good catch of sea animals or birds, it is because Nivikkaa has put aside her lamp and let the animals swim out. But she is offended if, for example, a man uses the kayak or clothing of a dead man out on the sea and thereby profanes her territory. Then she sends the bad southwest wind and fog, and shuts up all the sea animals and causes poor hunting.

P. Egede,[11] the early observer in West Greenland, writes that at the lowest part of the earth a very bad woman, the arch-mother of Tornarsuk, lives in an enormous house over which one cannot shoot an arrow. This woman has command over all the sea animals. In the oil basin under her lamp swim all kinds of sea birds.[12] The name Arnarquáshaaq, known only from the west coast, is specified for the first time in Rink,[13] and is never used as a proper name for a divinity, but only as an epithet. Egede's "Old Mother" is possibly a free interpretation of this name. The translation given in the early dictionary[14] of "Old Woman" or "Old Hag" probably implies an undeserved measure of disparagement. The derivation of the word would seem to warrant our calling her even "The Majestic Woman" or "The Mighty Woman." An East Greenland shaman characterized the spirit of the deep as being above all friendly and beautiful.[15]

A striking feature of this cycle of myths is the wide variety of names used by different groups in referring to the Woman of the Sea.

Thus we note the East Greenland designation *Sättuma eeva* "Spirit of the Sea depths," corresponding to *Säsvsuma inua* in West Greenland; and the name Nerrivik, meaning "the food dish" or "the place of food," used by the northernmost Eskimos of Greenland. The Baffin Islanders call this deity Sedna, a word perhaps coming from *Sänvna* "the one down on the sea bottom";[16] but they also refer to the girl in the myth who became Sedna as Avilayoq. The natives of Iglulik also refer sometimes to the protectress of the sea mammals as Aywilliayoo. In addition they call her Anavigak. The myth relates her marriage to a red dog, who was the father of the white people (the Ijiqan), the dwarfs, and the Eskimos. Ordinarily, when speaking of her she is called Kunna[17] or Katuma. The names Uiniyumissuitoq and Unaviga are also used.[18] In the region northwest of Hudson Bay the Sea Goddess is frequently designated by the name Nuliayok, "the ever copulating one" or rather "the one who was (is) always in a sexual desire or state."[19] Lyon reported the form Nooliayoo from Iglulik.[20] Also the Aivilik Eskimos speak of Nuliayok, saying that she is particularly sensitive to transgressions of taboos made near Wager River, and that as punishment she will wait at the entrance to the inlet and upset boats and kayaks.[21] The immigrant Netsilingmiut employ the appellation Nuliajuk, supposedly the name she bore when she lived among men in the days before she became a spirit.[22] A Netsilik Eskimo is reported as saying: "And most of all we fear Nuliajuk. . . . Nuliajuk is the name we give to the Mother of Beasts. All the game we hunt comes from her; from her come all the caribou, all the foxes, the birds and fishes."[23] It has already been stated that the Iglulik Eskimos dwelling on the east coast of Melville Peninsula call her Takánáluk arnâluk, "the woman down there." In this group she is also called Takánakapsâluk, "the bad one" or "the terrible one down there," almost contemptuously.

Many of the names applied to the guardian of the sea creatures imply that she lives beneath the ocean. The location of her abode is, indeed, one of the characteristic features of the concept. But it should be noticed that the groups of Eskimos whose concepts of a guardian of animals we have been considering are essentially coastal people and that there are other Eskimos who pass their lives inland, out of contact with the sea. Such people would not be expected to have the concept of a submarine deity. Among the Caribou Eskimos, for instance, there are groups who never see the sea; and in view of the fact that their territory lies near the type locality of the Sedna cult, it is of interest to compare their religion on this point. We find that the Pâdlimiut of this group do believe in a deity that corresponds to Sedna in some ways. This spirit, Pinga, is feared as the omnipresent deity who keeps watch on all the doings of men, especially as regards their dealings with the animals killed. One of her principal commandments appears to be that daily food should be treated with respect, care being taken that nothing be wasted. The creation of animals and mankind is not attributed to her; nor does she dwell in the sea, but somewhere out in space.[24] She is, indeed, a specialized Air Spirit and is to be associated with the spirit known to most Eskimos as Sila rather than with the Sea Woman.[25]

Passing westward to the Copper Eskimos we again encounter a typical coastal group; and here the cult of the sea deity reappears, embodied in Kannakapfaluk. This greatest of all spirits in the religion of the Copper Eskimos is clearly to be linked with Takánakapsâluk of the Iglulik Eskimos, who in turn appears as a local personification of Sedna.

Kannakapfaluk, who controls the supply of seals, dwells with a dwarf, Unga, at the bottom of the sea in a hut like the Eskimo's. Besides hoarding the seals she can send bad weather in winter, thereby keeping the natives indoors till they starve; and she can break up the ice and drown them. Failure to observe various taboos prompts her to send bad luck.[26] The Copper Eskimos of Bathurst Inlet conceive of the undersea goddess, whom they call Arnakapfaluk, as dwelling with another woman, possibly her daughter, and two men.[27]

The mythology of these people, which seems far less elaborate than that of other groups, contains the story of a woman who married a dog and bore strange progeny. This theme is to be linked with various related myths, including the first part of the Sedna story from Cumberland Sound, which relates that a girl with a dog as husband gave birth to Eskimos, white men, and various fantastic creatures. The Copper Eskimo story does not ascribe to the woman the creation of sea animals, but simply states that she finally went into the water to live. Yet she holds a prominent position in the religious beliefs of these Eskimos. When the Eskimos are plagued with bad weather, their shamans call upon this woman to relieve them. Sometimes she is kind and helps people, but sometimes she is angry and tries to kill them by sending bad weather and breaking up the ice.[28]

The Copper Eskimos represent the westernmost extent of the cult of the Sea Woman in Arctic America. In Alaska, nevertheless, there is evidence of the existence of this myth although the woman may not figure as a supernatural power. From Port Clarence, near Bering Strait, comes the story of a girl who was thrown overboard by her father. As she clung to the side of the boat her father cut off the joints of her hands and fingers, one after another; the first joints were transformed into salmon, the second into seals, the third into walruses, and the metacarpal bones into whales.[29]

In the arctic province west of Alaska the deification of a woman
of the sea reappears. The Eskimos of Indian Point, Siberia, sacrifice to the old woman living at the bottom of the sea, Nuli'ṛahak
("big woman") as they call her. One of the sea spirits of the
neighboring Chukchi is the "Walrus Mother," an old wife who
lives on the seabottom and rules over the animals of the deep. As
in the case of Sedna, there is a mythological explanation of this
woman's earthly origin, but apparently it is unrelated to the
Sedna myth. Some Chukchi do tell tales, however, of a young
girl who was thrown overboard by her father. When she tried to
catch the bow of the boat, her fingers were chopped off with an
adz. After that she turned into a walrus and upset the boat. This
walrus girl, however, has never been identified with the Mother of
Walrus, as far as Bogoras could find out. The chief "Beings of
the Sea" of the Chukchi are Kere'tkun and his wife. Kere'tkun
owns all the sea game, especially walruses.[30] The Koryaks, too,
seem to embrace the concept of the Sea Goddess; and far to the
west, at the mouth of the Ob River, the Samoyeds believe in a female divinity whose servant is the spirit of the water.[31]

Among the Eskimos of Bering Sea, however, the Moon Spirit
takes the place of the Sea Goddess of the Central Eskimos as the
divinity to whom the shamans make their journeys of conciliation.
This spirit is envisaged as a great manlike being who controls all
the game animals.[32]

The Labrador Eskimos believe that the animals of the sea are
in the charge of a male divinity, but he does not reside in the moon
as does the primary spirit of the Eskimos south of Bering Strait,
and generally his protection does not extend to include the land
animals. It is to this foremost divinity, Tornga'rsoak, that the
Labrador Eskimos appeal when in search of whales and seals.

The natives of the east coast visualize him as a huge white bear who
lives in a cave in the great black mountains at the northern extremity
of the peninsula. These mountains, incidentally, which are wild and
impressive, are called Torngat, or "Spirit Mountains." In the dialect
of the natives of southern Labrador this bear-divinity is called Tunga'rsuk. According to Turner the Eskimos of Ungava Bay, Hudson
Strait, likewise personify Tornga'rsoak as a huge white bear dwelling
in a great cavern near the end of Cape Chidley, but they empower him
with the control of the caribou.[33]

Tornga'rsoak's wife, Supergu'ksoak, is the other of the two main
deities of the Labrador Eskimos. She seems to preside over the land

animals; and the shamans, through their relation with her, are able to draw the reindeer.[34] She is conceived in mythology as creating the walrus from her boots and the caribou from her breeches.[35] This mythical feat is also recounted on the west coast of Hudson Bay and in southeastern Baffin Island. In the latter locality the supernatural woman *Tuktut ikviat* is supposed to have transformed her breeches into caribou which wore tusks, and then she transformed the tusks into antlers.[36] Among the Akudnirmiut of Baffin Island the version is somewhat different: "During a famine a woman . . . carried her boots to the hills and transformed them by magic into deer which spread all over the country. Then she carried her breeches to the sea, where they were changed into walrus. The first deer, however, had large tusks and no horns, while the walrus had horns but no tusks. . . . Therefore, an old man transferred the horns to the deer and the tusks to the walrus." Though Boas could not learn whether the woman in this story was identified with Sedna, he is of the opinion that she probably was.[37]

That the Labrador Eskimos are not utterly outside of the culture area of the Sedna Goddess is shown by the fact that they know the myth of the woman who was thrown out of a boat and had her fingers chopped off. But it seems that the story is told in a curtailed form and without the deep religious significance that it contains for the Baffin Islanders. "There was a woman who married a dog," according to the version that Hawkes sets down in his report *The Labrador Eskimos*.[38] "Her father was ashamed of her and took her in his umiak to a lonely island. When out at sea he threw her overboard. She seized hold of the boat, but he cut off her fingers with his knife. The thumb became the walrus, the first finger the seal, and the middle finger the white bear."

The closest approach to the cult of the Sea Goddess among the Labrador Eskimos seems to be found in the northern part of the country. At Cape Chidley an old woman living at the bottom of the sea is spoken of. She controls everything that swims in the sea: the fish, the seals, and especially the polar bears. The natives here used to cast offerings into the deep for her, old hunting implements, etc. But they did not fear the old woman of the sea as much as Tornga'rsoak, the male protector of animals.[39]

§2. THE CULT OF THE SEA GODDESS

ALL groups of Eskimos dwelling on the Arctic coast between Coronation Gulf and East Greenland perform ceremonies that characterize their religion in one way or another as belonging to the cult of the Sea Goddess. In most of the groups this divinity is the predominant figure among the supernatural beings. As protectress of the marine animals she must be approached and propitiated so that hunting will be successful and the people will have the necessaries of life—food, materials for clothing, and blubber for fuel. Broadly, the most characteristic practice of the cult is the séance of the angakok, or medicine man, in which he seeks to effect the liberation of the sea animals from this guardian deity. Generally, he makes a journey to her abode for this purpose; but occasionally she is harpooned and brought into communication beneath the floor of the ceremonial room.

The Iglulik Eskimos consider that one of the greatest feats of their shaman is his journey to Takánakapsâluk's abode at the bottom of the sea and his taming and conciliating her so that men may live untroubled. Some natives assert that it is his soul or spirit that makes the flight, others that it is the shaman in the flesh. When he wishes to visit Takánakapsâluk he sits on the inner part of the sleeping place behind a curtain and must wear nothing but boots and mittens. There he remains for a while in silence, breathing deeply, and then after some time he begins to call upon his helping spirits, repeating over and over, "The way is made ready for me; the way opens before me." Whereat all present must answer in chorus, "Let it be so."

When the helping spirits have arrived, the earth opens under the shaman, but often only to close up again so that he has to struggle for a long time with hidden forces, before he can cry at last, "Now the way is open." Presently one hears, "Halala—he—he—he, halala—he —he—he!" at first from under the sleeping place, and afterward under the passage below the ground; and the sound can be perceived to recede farther and farther until it is lost altogether. Then all know that the angakok is on his way to the ruler of the sea beasts.

Meanwhile, the members of the household pass the time by singing spirit songs in chorus, and here it may happen that the clothes that the shaman has discarded come alive and fly about the room, above the heads of the singers, who are sitting with closed eyes. One may hear deep sighs and the breathing of persons long since dead. These are the souls of the angakok's namesakes, who have come to help. But as soon as one calls them by name, the sighs cease, and all is silent in the house until another dead person begins to sigh. The sighing and puffing of the departed who have lived many generations earlier sound as if the spirits were marine animals in the sea; and in between all the noises one hears the blowing and splashing of the creatures coming up to breathe.

The angakok encounters perils in his submarine journey before he at last reaches the house of Takánakapsâluk, situated on a broad plain at the sea bottom. Her house is built of stone, with a short passageway, just like the houses of the Tunit.[40] In the passage lies Takánakapsâluk's dog, taking up all the room, but the shaman steps right over the animal who then knows that he is a great angakok and does him no harm. Should a great shelter wall be built outside the house it means that she is very angry, and the angakok must fling himself upon the wall, kick it down, and level it to the ground. Some declare that her house is without a roof, so that she can better watch the doings of mankind. All the different kinds of sea animals are collected in a great pool at the right side of her lamp—seal, bearded seal, walrus, and whale; they lie there puffing and blowing. The angakok finds Takánakapsâluk sitting defiantly with her back to the pool of animals. Her hair hangs down loose all over one side of her face, a tangled untidy mass hiding her eyes. It is the thought that the misdeeds and offenses committed by mortals gather in dirt and impurity over her body. All the foul emanations from the sins of mankind nearly suffocate her. As the angakok moves toward her, her father, Isarrataitsoq, tries to restrain him, thinking he is a dead person come to expiate offenses before passing on to the Land of the Dead. The shaman must then cry out, "I am flesh and blood," and he will not be hurt. And he must now grasp Takánakapsâluk by one shoulder and turn her face toward the lamp and toward the animals, and stroke her hair which she has been unable to comb out herself because she has no fingers; and he must smooth it and comb it, and as soon as she is calmer, he must say, "Those up above can no longer help the seals by grasping their fore flippers."

Then Takánakapsâluk answers in the spirit language: "The secret miscarriages of the women and breaches of taboo in eating boiled meat bar the way for the animals."

The shaman must now use all his efforts to appease her anger, and at last, when she is in a kindlier mood, she takes the animals one by one and drops them on the floor, and then it is as if a whirlpool arose in the passage, the water pours out from the pool and the animals disappear in the sea. This means rich hunting and abundance for mankind.

It is then time for the angakok to return to his fellows on earth. They hear him a long way off, and then with a mighty "Plu-plu!" as though some creature of the sea were shooting up from the deep to take breath, he shoots up into his place behind the curtain.

There follows a wholesale confessing of breaches of taboos. Under terrific emotional stress all are eager to make a clean breast of their transgressions, especially the women, whose offenses are regarded as the more serious. In the end there may almost be a feeling of thankfulness toward the offenders; for thus at last the cause of Takánakapsâluk's anger is explained and all are filled with joy at having escaped disaster. They are now assured that there will be abundance of game on the following day.

Thus it is that the shamans go down and propitiate the Great Spirit of the Sea.[41] She is a mighty deity, in whose hands are the very lives of the earth folk. Deference is shown to her in trivial observances as well. As soon as the sealing begins after the close of the caribou season, a narrow strip of caribou skin and a piece of sinew thread are set out as offering to Takánakapsâluk.[42] On the same occasion, on the west coast of Hudson Bay, the offering is left on the ice for the Sea Woman (Nuliayok).[43] But her jurisdiction does not extend to all animals, only to those of the sea. When the Iglulik Eskimos are hunting caribou, for instance, in kayaks on a river or a lake, they must lay out a piece of sealskin under a stone as a sacrifice to Tugtut Igfianut, the Mother of the Caribou.[44]

On Baffin Island the great Sedna ceremonial is performed in the autumn. At the end of the arctic summer, before the new shore ice begins to form, the weather is characteristically tempestuous. As a consequence sealing increases in risk and difficulty, and food is apt to become scarce. The Goddess Sedna is supposed to cause storms to prevent her animals from being killed. And so, to induce her to liberate the seals, a conjuration has to be performed.

The whole ceremony reveals the angakok, or medicine man, in his typical rôle as intermediary between his fellow men and the supernatural forces, as performer of miracles, and as a sort of father confessor of taboo breaches. Several conjurors or understudies for the profession take part in the first episode, in which they pair the natives off unconventionally as husbands and wives. The conjurors, dressed in strange, bulging clothing, half men's, half women's, and wearing grotesque leather masks, determine who shall be partners; although sometimes preliminary conniving influences the allotting. This practice of exchanging wives for a period of about twenty-four hours has a religious significance: it is thought to please the Sea Goddess.[45]

The next feature of the ceremonial program is an extraordinary trick performed by the angakok. He is speared, or spears himself, through the jacket, deep into the breast. When the whole performance is not merely a spectacular trick, it seems to be quite genuinely done. Attached to the deeply imbedded, barbed spearhead is a line, and the people catch hold of this and haul the man about, to prove that he is fairly caught, as a hunter's victim might be. The angakok is streaming blood. At length he is let go, and makes his wounded way alone to the seashore. Here his *tongak* (familiar spirit), which is the shade of a walrus or bear, releases him from the spear, and he returns to the festival whole and well as ever, with no sign except his torn clothing to indicate the rough handling he has undergone.

"After this the principal Angakok prepares to give battle to Sedna. The goddess can be killed; but as she subsequently comes to life again, this killing has to take place every year. The whole performance is a representation of seal-spearing on the ice. The conjuror coils a rope on the floor of a large hut, and leaves a little opening at the top to represent the blow hole. Two assistants stand at either side, armed respectively with harpoon and spear. A third chants incantations at the back of the dwelling. Sedna is supposed to be lured from the underworld, and when she comes to the hole, is transfixed at once. She sinks away again, dragging the harpoon with her, wounded and incensed. The conjurors haul on the line for all they are worth, and recover the weapon.

"Then the chief Angakok squats on the floor, with his arms and legs bound by a length of light hide line. The lamps are pressed down to burn so dimly that it is all but dark. The rest of the folk also sit about the floor with their heads bowed, so that none may stare at the conjuror's face. He begins his incantations, rocking to and fro and uttering sounds that it seems incredible for a human throat to compass. He works himself into a state of insensibility (but not before his familiar spirit has undone the knots and released him from his bonds). It is this trance which makes such an impression on the tribesfolk." They believe that the disembodied spirit of the angakok has flown to the supernatural sphere where Sedna dwells, and that he kills her and thus liberates the seals. When in the near future the advancing season brings weather that is more favorable to seal hunting the Eskimos readily attribute the good fortune to these machinations of the angakok. And he, too, probably believes it, though he has done nothing but hypnotize himself and strike awe thereby into the others.

Additional features of the ceremonial are the confessing of transgressions of taboos to the angakok, and a tug of war between the people who were born in summer and those born in winter; if the winter ones win there will be plenty of food, but otherwise there will be bad weather.[46]

There seems to be no counterpart of the Sedna ceremony among the Caribou Eskimos, inland dwellers of the Barren Grounds. They have no regular ceremonials and festivals, although there is a religious implication in the songs they sing, which generally are self-derogatory and concern poor skill in hunting, etc.[47]

It is instructive to compare the Sedna rites just described with a ceremony performed by the Copper Eskimos of Coronation Gulf.

It will be remembered that Kannakapfaluk, the greatest of all spirits to these Eskimos, is the deity corresponding to Sedna. She lives at the bottom of the sea in a snow hut like those used by the living people. A dwarf dwells with her, called Unga because of the cry he utters when the shamans drag him up to the surface. Thalbitzer points out that this creature suggests the gruesome spirit *Ongaa* at Angmagsalik, which serves the angakok as one of his minor, terror-inspiring helpers.[48]

If the Copper Eskimos ". . . sew too much on the ice, or break any of the taboos in reference to either sewing or cooking, Unga gathers all the seals inside the hut, and the Eskimos in consequence have no success in their sealing. The shamans then hold a séance in the dance-house and lower a long rope through the floor with a noose at the end of it. All the people gather round the rope and sing the following incantation, which is known from one end of the Copper Eskimo country to the other:

> The woman down there she wants to go away.
> Some of the young sea-gulls I can't lay my hands on.
> That man he can't mend matters by himself.
> That man he can't mend matters by himself.
> Over there where no people dwell I go myself and right matters.
> He can't right matters by himself.
> Over there where no people dwell, thither I go and right matters myself."

One native said that when Kannakapfaluk cannot shut up the seals she shuts up sea gulls instead. More probably "sea gulls" is the shamanistic expression for "seals." "That man" refers to the shaman in the dance house, but whether another shaman is supposed to be speaking or not is uncertain.

As soon as the song is ended the shamans are supposed to slip a noose over Kannakapfaluk's wrists and haul her up until her head is just below the level of the floor. They must not draw her any higher because she would be very angry if the people in the dance house saw her. The shamans talk to her, telling her that the people are starving for want of seals and asking her to release them again. Unga in the meantime remains below guarding the seals. Kannakapfaluk is now lowered again; and at once orders Unga to release some of the seals. Then the Eskimo hunters are successful once more and the community prospers.[49]

Close similarities are seen between this performance among the Copper Eskimos and the Sedna ceremony on Baffin Island, although the deity is known by different names in the two regions. In both cases the Sea Woman is harpooned and besought to be generous with her seals.

West of the Copper Eskimos the cult of the female Sea Divinity does not exist in Arctic America. In the region of Bering Sea the Moon Spirit, a masculine divinity, takes her place.[50] At the opposite end of the Eskimo realm the Goddess of the Sea figures in the religion of the Greenlanders but, as among the Copper Eskimos, without the elaborate festivals which characterize the cult among the natives of Baffin Island and Hudson Bay. In Greenland as elsewhere, however, the shaman's mysterious journey to the depths of the sea stands out as a prominent feature of the religion.

Among the Polar Eskimos the angakok who travels to the abode of Nerrivik combs and braids her tangled hair to induce her to release the animals under her protection.[51] South of this group on the west coast Poul Egede portrays the journey of the angakok to the woman of the deep as it was described in early times.[52] The wizard must have his tornak, or guardian spirit with him when he visits her; for at her door one can see whole herds of seals which stand upright and bite anyone who wishes to go near her. When the angakok makes this journey he must pass the souls of the dead, which appear as though still living. Then appears a great gulf leading into the depths of the earth, which he must cross by a great wheel as smooth as ice and constantly revolving rapidly. Over this the guardian spirit leads the angakok. They come next to a great kettle in which living seals are being cooked; and eventually they arrive at the abode of the archmother of the devil (Tornarsuk). The guardian spirit grasps the angakok by the hand and leads him through the strong guard of seals. The entrance is broad, but beyond it the angakok goes over an abyss by a path no wider than a cord with nothing to hold on to. Within sits the horrible woman. She makes all kinds of convulsive gestures and tears out her hair over the newly arrived guests. Suddenly she seizes the wing of a bird, lights it, and holds it under their noses, whereupon they become faint from the odor and are her captives. But the angakok, who has been instructed by his tornak, quickly grasps her by the hair, and, aided by his tornak, tumbles her about until she is utterly powerless. In her hair, which hangs about her face like the snaky locks of Medusa, are parasites (*Aglerutit*).[53] Some believe that these parasites—"unanimals" as Poul Egede terms them—originate from the failure of women to confess miscarriages; they are the guilt that caused the creatures of the sea to leave the earth and go to Sedna. The angakok and his helper must tear them out of her head. When this has been done the whales and the seals fare forth into the water with a great commotion and betake themselves to the coast where the Greenlanders can catch them. His mission achieved, the angakok departs with his tornak on the homeward way, which, contrary to the dangerous outward journey, is smooth and easy.

Certain parts of this description are a bit questionable, as, for example, the statement about the relationship between the "devil" Tornarsuk and the Sea Woman as his archmother, and the spinning wheel over which the angakok must pass. The latter idea does not sound as if it had originated in the Eskimo mind. But otherwise this description from early Greenland portrays the angakok in his customary rôle as mystic envoy to the Protectress of Sea Animals. As usual, it is the duty of the angakok to make right with her the violations of taboos. The notion recurs that breaches of rules somehow defile the Sea Woman by lodging in her hair. Transgressions of taboo revert directly upon the deity, so that she becomes angry and withholds the animals in her charge. Here in West Greenland the angakok is supposed to tear loose from the Sea Goddess these attachments in order that she will mete out the animals. That he combs out her tangled hair is frequently mentioned among different groups,—for instance among the Polar Eskimos, the Iglulik Eskimos, the East Greenlanders,[54] and the Eskimos of Labrador.[55] This idea may well arise from the belief that the goddess lost her fingers in the creation of sea creatures and so is unable to comb her own hair.[56]

Wherever the cult of the Sea Woman is followed among the Eskimos it conforms at least in some features to the general basic concept. Most fully developed in the central regions, it becomes less pronounced in the west and east.[57] The Greenlanders seem not to have paid much regard to the deity of the sea, as Crantz writes,[58] ". . . because there is so much rage and malevolence in her, and she so often occasions them scarcity of provisions, trouble and expense." It must be said, however, that she is preeminent in her sphere. The spirit Tornarsuk[59] cannot be compared with her in status; for he belongs to a different order of spirits. The religion of the Greenlanders is not unified; nor is it signalized by periodical cultic festivals. We know of no seasonal ceremonials connected with the honoring of the Sea Woman or any other divinity, though in times unchronicled such observances may have been held.[60]

NOTES

1. Boas: 1907, 163 ff. See also Bilby: 1923, chapter xiii, for Sedna myth in Baffin Island.
2. Rasmussen: 1929, I, 62 ff.; also Rasmussen: 1927, 27 ff.
3. Boas: 1888, 562.
4. Boas: 1900, 624 and 626; and Boas: 1907, 138 f.
5. See pp. 355 ff.
6. Rasmussen: 1908, 142; Kroeber: 1899, 317.
7. Rasmussen: 1908, 151 f.
8. Kroeber: 1899, 317.
9. Lytzen: 1874, 209 ff., quoted by Thalbitzer: 1928, 393 f.
10. Thalbitzer: 1928, 401.
11. Egede, Poul: 1790, 103 ff., cited by Thalbitzer: 1928, 394 f.
12. See p. 399. It is very difficult to decide what the relation of this deity is to Tornarsuk (Thalbitzer: 1928, 395).
13. Rink: 1868, 204, cited by Thalbitzer: 1928, 401.
14. Egede, Poul: 1750, cited by Thalbitzer: 1928, 401.
15. Thalbitzer: 1928, 395 f., 401.
16. Thalbitzer: 1928, 401.
17. *"Kanna(?)"* (Thalbitzer: in a communication).
18. Boas: 1907, 492.
19. Thalbitzer: 1928*a*, 378.
20. Lyon: 1824, 262 f.
21. Boas: 1907, 145 f., also 496.
22. Rasmussen: 1929, I, 62.
23. Rasmussen: 1927, 195.
24. Rasmussen: 1927, 81 f.
25. See pp. 389 ff.
26. For further information about Kannakapfaluk, see the next section in this chapter.
27. Jenness: 1922, 188 f.
28. Jenness: 1924*a*, 80*a*–81*a*.
29. Boas: 1894, 205. See also Smith, H. I.: 1894, 209 (Nachvak, Labrador); Turner: 1894, 262 (Ungava, Labrador); Kroeber: 1899*a*, 179 (Polar Eskimos); and Lytzen: 1874, 209 ff. (South Greenland).
30. Bogoras: 1904, II, 316 ff. See also Bogoras: 1902, 627 (Chukchi).
31. Thalbitzer: 1928, 403 f.

32. See pp. 381 ff.
33. Hawkes: 1916, 125, and 14 (footnote). See also p. 400.
34. Hawkes: 1916, 124.
35. Hawkes: 1916, 160.
36. Rasmussen: 1929, I, 67 f.
37. Boas: 1888, 588.
38. Hawkes: 1916, 152.
39. Hawkes: 1916, 126.
40. See pp. 409 ff.
41. Rasmussen: 1929, I, 123 ff.
42. Rasmussen: 1929, I, 193.
43. Boas: 1907, 502.
44. Rasmussen: 1929, I, 195.
45. Regarding wife exchanging with religious significance, see Sumner and Keller: 1927, II, 1158.
46. Bilby: 1923, 210 ff.; and Boas: 1907, 138 ff. See also Boas: 1907, 119 ff. (Cumberland Sound); Boas: 1888, 587 ff. (Akuliarmiut); Boas: 1888, 608 (Akudnirn, eastern Baffin Island north of Cumberland Sound); Boas: 1887, 36 f. (northeastern Baffin Island).
47. Birket-Smith: 1929, I, 268 ff.
48. Thalbitzer: 1928, 402, 380.
49. Jenness: 1922, 188, also 206 f.
50. See pp. 381 ff.
51. Kroeber: 1899, 306.
52. P. Egede: 1790, 103 ff. The present description is taken from Thalbitzer's critical rendering of Egede (Thalbitzer: 1928, 395).
53. Thalbitzer: 1928, 397 ff. Thalbitzer points out (1928*a*, 379 f.) that Rink referred to the *aglerutit* as "certain impurities," and explained them (in agreement with the earlier description) as a kind of parasite, due to secret crimes, especially women's abortions or ill treatment of a prematurely born fetus (*agdlerutit*, in his spelling, phonet. *dlhlerutit*). "This explanation," states Thalbitzer, "may be due to a misinterpretation of the word as derived from the verb *agdlerpoq* (I) 'she bears a still-born child.' The word (seemingly the same) also means (II) 'is abstinent from cultic reason' and *agdlerutit* might just as well be derived from

this word and explained as meaning something like 'the cause of being abstinent,' or perhaps the state of abstinence, the forbidden fruit or the prohibition." See also pp. 372 f.

54. Holm: 1914, 83.

55. Smith, H. I.: 1894, 209.
56. Thalbitzer: 1928, 401.
57. See Wardle: 1900.
58. Crantz: 1767, I, 206.
59. See pp. 399 ff.
60. Thalbitzer: 1928, 401 f.

REFERENCES PERTAINING TO CHART
OF TABOOS

I-1. Murdoch: 1892, 270.

I-4. Ray: 1885, 39; also Murdoch: 1892, 274, and Simpson: 1875, 261. Also, Stefansson states (1914, 182) that at Point Hope, the wives of men who are engaged in whaling must not work skins in their own houses.

I-10. Smith: in Kersting: 1902, 120.

I-12. Smith: in Kersting: 1902, 120.

II-1. Rasmussen: 1927, 320.

II-6. Rasmussen: 1927, 320.

II-18. Rasmussen: 1927, 320.

III-4. Stefansson: 1914, 322 f.

III-8. Stefansson: 1914, 322 f.

III-27. Stefansson: 1914, 329.

IV-1. Jenness: 1922, 111, 184, 189; Jenness: 1928, 35 f.

IV-6. Jenness: 1922, 183.

IV-8. Jenness: 1922, 182 f. Seal and caribou are eaten at the same meal by the Nagyuktogmiut, Kogluktogmiut, Pallirmiut, Puiplirmiut, Noahonirmiut, Akuliakattagmiut, and Kanhiryuarmiut, although some families had a mild taboo against cooking them in the same pot. (Stefansson: 1914, 48.)

IV-9. Jenness: 1922, 182, 111; Jenness: 1928, 48.

IV-10. Jenness: 1922, 182 f.; also Stefansson: 1914, 48.

IV-11. Jenness: 1922, 183.

IV-18. Jenness: 1922, 183.

IV-20. Jenness: 1922, 183, and 111.

IV-25. Jenness: 1922, 98, 184.

IV-27. Jenness: 1922, 98.

IV-28. Jenness: 1922, 184.

V-3. Rasmussen: 1927, 207, 220.

V-19. Rasmussen: 1929, I, 190.

V-20. Klutschak: 1881, 158.

VI-1. Birket-Smith: 1929, I, 126, 236.

VI-2. Birket-Smith: 1929, I, 126.

VI-3. Birket-Smith: 1929, I, 96.

VI-5. Birket-Smith: 1929, I, 126.

VI-20. Birket-Smith: 1929, I, 119.

VI-27. Birket-Smith: 1929, I, 96, 234.

VI-28. Birket-Smith: 1929, I, 89.

VII-1. Boas: 1907, 148, 502.

VII-2. Boas: 1907, 148.

VII-3. Boas: 1907, 502.

VII-3. Boas: 1907, 503.

VII-5. Boas: 1907, 149.

VII-6. Boas: 1907, 148.

VII-6. Boas: 1907, 501.

VII-7. Boas: 1907, 149.

VII-10. Boas: 1907, 148.

VII-11. Boas: 1907, 500.

VII-14. Boas: 1907, 148.

VII-28. Boas: 1907, 149.

VIII-1. Rasmussen: 1929, I, 191.

VIII-2. Rasmussen: 1929, I, 186.

VIII-2. Rasmussen: 1929, I, 192.

VIII-3. Rasmussen: 1929, I, 191.

VIII-5. Rasmussen: 1929, I, 191.

VIII-6. Rasmussen: 1929, I, 186; Rasmussen: 1927, 133.

VIII-7. Rasmussen: 1927, 133.

VIII-10. Rasmussen: 1929, I, 193.

VIII-12. Rasmussen: 1929, I, 188.

VIII-13. Rasmussen: 1927, 133.

VIII-14. Rasmussen: 1927, 133.

VIII-19. Rasmussen: 1929, I, 190, 193; Rasmussen: 1927, 133.

VIII-20. Rasmussen: 1929, I, 190.

VIII-22. Rasmussen: 1929, I, 190, 193; Rasmussen: 1927, 133.

VIII-23. Rasmussen: 1929, I, 190.

VIII-24. Rasmussen: 1929, I, 186; and Boas: 1907, 503 (Iglulik).

VIII-25. Rasmussen: 1929, I, 182.

VIII-26. Rasmussen: 1929, I, 188; also Hall: *Narrative of Second Expedition . . .*, 364.

VIII-27. Rasmussen: 1929, I, 183.

VIII-28. Rasmussen: 1929, I, 184.

IX-1. Boas: 1907, 492 f.

IX-2. Boas: 1887, 36.

IX-4. Boas: 1907, 492 f.

IX-7. Boas: 1887, 36.

IX-27. Boas: 1907, 493.

X-2. Boas: 1907, 122 (Cumberland Sound); Boas: 1907, 478 (70° W., on the south coast).

X-8. Boas: 1907, 123.

X-9. Boas: 1907, 489.

X-10. Boas: 1907, 123.

X-14. Boas: 1907, 122.

X-15. Boas: 1907, 123.
X-16. Boas: 1907, 123.
X-19. Boas: 1907, 123.
X-20. Boas: 1907, 123.
X-21. Boas: 1907, 123.
X-22. Boas: 1907, 123.

X-23. Boas: 1907, 123.
XI-7. Hawkes: 1916, 133.
XI-9. Hawkes: 1916, 133.
XI-12. Hawkes: 1916, 134.
XI-12. Hawkes: 1916, 85.
XI-16. Hawkes: 1916, 133.

CHAPTER XXII

TABOO

§1. TABOOS PERTAINING TO GAME ANIMALS

THE hazards and uncertainties attending the Eskimo in his struggle to obtain the necessaries of life have given rise to an elaborate system of taboos. He labors under the constant hindrance of intricate, standardized restrictions which are believed to elicit the favor of the spiritual forces presiding over his food supply. Practically all his material needs are satisfied through hunting, and consequently most of the taboos are directed toward the spirits of the game animals themselves or toward their protecting deities.

Almost every detail of hunting and utilizing the catch is regulated in some respect by taboo. The outstanding feature of the system is the rule that land animals and sea animals must be kept separate. Seals, walruses, and whales must not be defiled by caribou and other creatures of the land. From this basic differentiation the system ramifies to many less obvious restrictions. For example, certain groups prohibit the working-up of soapstone, a product of the land, during the time they are living on the ice; and in some sections it is forbidden to work on wood back from the coast while the hunters are catching seal in the sea. All such taboos are based on the theory that to associate the products of these two realms will offend either the souls of the animals or the spirit who controls them.

The principal observances of this nature are assembled in the tables represented in Figures 18a, 18b. Here the taboos are classified under several headings. Parallel taboos observed by different tribes are aligned on the chart and connected by arrows, whereas dotted lines connect such as are of opposing natures. The source of information for each case is recorded on pages 365–366, and can be found by reference to the vertical and horizontal scales at the edge of the chart, to be read as though they were coördinates on a map.

Inasmuch as the hunting and other activities of the Eskimos are to a great extent differentiated seasonally,[1] the taboo system does not impose as narrow a constraint as might at first be imagined. Thus, the prohibitions in force among some Eskimos during winter, restricting the utilization of products of the land, merely tend to differentiate more sharply the seasonal program; for during this part of the year these natives have little or no contact with the land, but habitually live on the sea ice hunting seals.

To mention some of the basic taboos, a common one prohibits the sewing of caribou skins while the people are living on the sea ice or when hunting walrus; another stipulates that caribou and seal meat must not be eaten on the same day; again, fish caught in fresh water must not be treated in association with sea mammals. Beneath the details, a fundamental principle is apparent: the differentiation of the marine realm from the terrestrial.

Occasionally, further restrictions within this principle lead to more specific discriminations, as the taboo of southeastern Baffin Island and Labrador against eating on the same day seal and walrus, both of which come from the sea. The broadly dominant tone of the taboos is, nevertheless, quite consonant with the general premise that care must be exercised lest the products of the land contaminate those of the sea, and *vice versa*. An even closer uniformity than is represented by the chart might appear if our sources of information were more specific. While the chart well represents the information already collected by investigators, observances as yet unreported might amplify it considerably. However that may be, liberties have not been taken in venturesome generalizing.

Taboos differentiating the land and the sea are most intricately developed among the groups of the central area, from Coronation Gulf to Baffin Island, exclusive of the inland Eskimos of the Barren Grounds. Occasionally we observe widely separated groups enforcing some of the same taboos. For example, the natives of Point Barrow cleanse themselves after the winter sealing before engaging in the caribou chase, and the Baffin Islanders discard their winter clothing when the caribou season sets in. Again, the Point Barrow Eskimos and those of Labrador observe similar restrictions to prevent contamination between caribou and whales. In general, however, the basic system of the central groups does not extend in its typical form to the extreme eastern and western limits of the territory.

The system of taboo which differentiates the products of the land from those of the sea has been interpreted as evidence of the adjustment of a people who formerly lived inland to a new and unfamiliar coastal life. The fact that those bands of the Caribou

Eskimos who at present live inland do not embrace these observances can, however, scarcely be argued in support of this theory. The very fact that they do live inland and consequently have no equivalent to the sea hunting pursued by the coastal groups precludes the possibility of differential taboos. If a coastal tribe following the dual mode of life should move to a permanent residence inland we should expect that in time they would lose the differential taboo system. And the existing taboo system of the Eskimos might well have been developed by a people who had lived primarily at the coast from time immemorial. That the coastal tribes of the Central Eskimos may formerly have dwelt inland is not denied; it is merely suggested that the taboo system offers very insubstantial evidence either for the theory or against it.

In Greenland the differential system is almost or entirely lacking; and the same is true of some coastal sections in Alaska. It would seem that this phase of the religious folkways originated in the heart of the Eskimo region, after the dispersal of the Eskimos from their earliest stem; for if these taboos were very old there is no very binding reason why they should have been winnowed out of the peripheral coastal groups, eastward and westward.

While the differential taboos are absent from some of the Eskimos in the extreme east and west, all of the groups observe hunting taboos of one sort or another. In East Greenland, if a man takes his first crested seal in the spring, and he is living in a house and not a tent, the seal must not be eaten until three days have passed, even if the people are hungering; and if a tent is not provided with a new skin covering in spring, crested seals and Greenland seals may not be taken into it until after a lapse of some days.[2]

Very generally the Eskimos observe a taboo of one kind or another restricting dogs from gnawing bones. This rule applies sometimes to the bones of land animals, sometimes to those of sea animals, and so it cannot be included as a feature of the broad system of observances differentiating the two realms. The dog would not readily fit into this basic system, for he is employed both on the land and on the sea ice in hunting and traveling. As the only domesticated animal of the Eskimos and one not customarily utilized for food, the dog occupies an inconspicuous position in their animal cult.[3] The restriction against allowing dogs to gnaw bones is, indeed, one of a very few general taboos applying to them.

At Point Barrow, no matter how hungry the dogs may be, after a seal is cut up and eaten its bones must all be returned to the sea, or ill luck will surely follow.[4] Along the northern coast of Bering Sea great care is exercised that no dog shall have the opportunity to touch the bones of white whales.[5] And at Kigiktauik, on the Alaskan mainland just east of St. Michael, no dog must be allowed to touch or defile the body of a red fox.[6] During the fall migration of caribou, the Copper Eskimos do not permit their dogs to gnaw marrowbones of the caribou near the spot where the animal is killed.[7] At Simpson Strait dogs are kept from gnawing seal bones during the sealing; and none of the bones of the caribou must be broken while it is being cut up. The bones are either buried or weighted with great stones and thrown into a deep river so that the dogs will not get them.[8] Also, the Iglulik Eskimos do not allow dogs to gnaw the bones of caribou during the hunting season.[9] At Cumberland Sound dogs must not be given seal bones, which at times are put into the sea to be out of their reach. Caribou bones must not be broken until after the caribou-hunting season.[10]

Among the Koksoagmiut of Hudson Strait dogs are prevented from eating the flesh of the reindeer and from gnawing the leg bones unless an abundance has been obtained. If by some mistake a dog gets at the meat, a piece of the offending animal's tail is cut off or his ear is cropped to allow a flow of blood.[11] The natives of Hamilton Inlet, too, are very careful not to let their dogs eat certain parts of the bones of the deer.[12]

§2. TABOOS AGAINST THE USE OF IRON

FARTHER removed from the general taboo system are the various restrictions against the use of iron on particular occasions and for certain purposes. It seems that these taboos are most frequently mentioned as relating to the Eskimos of Alaska and Greenland. This is perhaps to be explained partly by the fact that in these regions the Eskimos have been familiar with iron a longer time and have consequently evolved more intricate rules regarding it.

There is a widespread taboo in Alaska against using anything but the traditional stone-pointed weapons under certain circumstances in the hunting of sea mammals.[13] Especially in the hunting of the white whale the taboo against iron prevails. The restriction forbids even the chopping of wood with an iron ax after a white whale has been beached, for fear of death. The same danger impends if one cuts wood with an iron ax near where salmon are being dressed.[14] The use of iron is taboo also during the Bladder Festival, which is held to propitiate the souls of animals.[15]

On the upper Noatak not many years ago it was the rule that ". . . caribou caught in snares must be skinned with stone knives only (anmark). . . . Deer shot with guns might be skinned with iron knives and cooked in metal pots." The native giving this information ". . . thinks deer shot with bows in the open might be cooked in metal pots, but those shot with bows in 'kañirkat' in enclosures must, he thinks, be cooked in pottery pots."[16] Among the Iglulik Eskimos men are not allowed to work on iron during the time when caribou are hunted with bows and arrows; if arrowheads have to be sharpened, the women must do it for them.[17]

Taboos against the use of iron are common in East Greenland, where the natives met white men for the first time at Angmagsalik in 1884. Those who have clothed a dead man must refrain from working iron. This precaution, it seems, must be observed for several years, lest some bad luck come to the family. When they begin again, a spell must first be employed.[18] Neither will these natives let iron come in contact with their hair, which they cut with the jawbone of a shark, if at all.[19]

Perhaps these taboos against the use of iron express a reluctance to employ something new and strange. The attitude may be likened to the hesitancy one feels about eating a sort of food that one has never tried. Walrus meat had never been seen by the inland Eskimos at Lake Yathkied when the members of the Fifth Thule Expedition brought some of it from the coast, and the natives at once strictly tabooed it and insisted that the white men use their own knives in cutting it up.[20] The people of this region also have a taboo against using iron when hunting musk ox.[21] Musk-ox hunting was a pursuit of long standing among them; iron had been introduced relatively recently.

Before the coming of white men iron was used by very few Eskimos.[22] Then it was introduced in West Greenland, Labrador, and Alaska, and ultimately in the central area. Parallel taboos concerning it could easily grow up independently in widely separated groups. Its newness and its peculiarity in taking a very keen edge would naturally create the feeling that it must not be treated as other materials. Many peoples of the world, indeed, have formulated taboos applying to iron.[23]

Traditional ways of doing things are always favored, especially in religious matters. People are reluctant to use anything strange or newfangled where there is risk of offending the spirits, with the result that old-fashioned methods are employed, in some cases long after they have been superseded in other phases of life by more practical methods.

§3. TABOOS AFFECTING WOMEN

The women of an Eskimo household must guard their actions according to traditional regulations to a greater extent than men. Many of their taboos are grounded in the belief that members of the female sex are at times unclean, hence capable of offending certain spirits, of contaminating other persons, and of bringing them bad luck. Another expression of this unfortunate trait of women is apparent in the funeral customs of the Eskimos, for the mourning restrictions in the case of a woman's death are often observed for a day longer than in the case of a man.[24]

Punishment for transgression of the taboos governing women does not descend solely upon their own sex; all are in danger of the consequences. The inconveniences involve the men when they pertain to activities which bear upon the general domestic life, such as cooking, sewing, etc.

Menstruation as the Occasion for Special Observances

Eskimos believe widely, as, indeed, do many other peoples in the world at large,[25] that women should observe certain taboos during menstruation. These restrictions usually manifest a belief that at this period a woman emanates an evil influence; and the measures taken to avoid contamination remotely resemble the rules of quarantine against disease among civilized people.

At Norton Sound, Alaska, hunters avoid women who are menstruating lest they fail to secure game.[26] Near the southern periphery of the Western Eskimos, on Kodiak Island, ". . . each woman must quit the yurt at the outset of each menstruation and occupy a little shed without daring to leave it, whither her food is brought."[27] In the same case a Caribou Eskimo woman must cook her food in a separate pot and must not eat raw or rotten meat.[28] Similarly, the Aivilingmiut near Repulse Bay have taboos against a woman's cutting raw meat or eating it, against her using any but a special cooking pot, beating out blubber, or even going outdoors unless she washes herself in the urine of a child. The Iglulik Eskimos believe that a woman in this condition is especially dangerous to young men who have not killed one of each sort of animal, and she is especially unclean to the spirits of all animals. On Southampton Island a menstruating woman must not use the customary doorway, but must lift up the bottom of the tent to crawl in and out.[29] The natives of Cumberland Sound believe that the spirits of animals ". . . can see the effect of flowing human blood, from which a vapor rises that surrounds the bleeding person and is communicated to everyone and everything that comes in contact with such a person. . . . The hunter must therefore avoid contact with . . . those who are bleeding, more particularly with menstruating women or with those who have recently given birth. . . . Women must make known when they are menstruating, or when they have had a miscarriage. If they do not do so they will bring ill luck to all the hunters."[30] Hall also remarks that women at certain times have separate huts and observe food taboos.[31] Among the Koksoagmiut of the Ungava District, "a menstruating woman must not wear the garments she does at other times, the hind flap of her coat must be turned up and stitched to the back of her garment. . . . She must not touch skins and food which at that particular season are in use."[32] During her menstrual period the Eskimo woman of Labrador must never step over a kayak, but always go around. The evil influence believed to emanate from her would cause game to avoid the kayak. Her left hand must remain ungloved, and the first joints of her right hand (representing the cut-off joints of Sedna's hand) must also be bared. She must not touch certain foods and skins.[33] Among the Polar Eskimos a menstruating woman is ". . . under the same restrictions as after a death,—she must wear a hood outdoors, may not carry water, may not eat the prescribed kinds of food. She also eats from her own plate."[34] In West Greenland a woman must be cleansed after menstruation.[35]

Rites at Puberty

At the time of a girl's first menstruation more exacting requirements are sometimes imposed. Generally, they are merely an elaboration of the customary monthly taboos, without the added social significance that is implied in the rites observed commonly among the peoples of the world denoting transition from one age group to another. Notably among the Western Eskimos, however, we find instances of special observance upon a girl's attainment of maturity.

"Among the *Malemute,* and southward in the lower Yukon and adjacent districts, when a girl reaches the age of puberty she is considered unclean for forty days; she must therefore live by herself in a corner of the house with her face to the wall, and always keep her hood over her head, with her hair hanging dishevelled over her eyes. During this time she must not go out by day but once each night when everyone is asleep, but if it is summer the girl customarily lives in a rough shelter outside the house. At the end of the period she bathes and is clothed in new garments, after which she may be taken in marriage. The same custom formerly prevailed among the Unalit, but at present the girl is secluded behind a grass mat in one corner of the room for a period of only four days, during which time she is said to be ă'-gû-lĭn-g'a'-gŭk, meaning she becomes a woman, and is considered unclean. A peculiar atmosphere is supposed to surround her at this time, and if a young man should come near enough for it to touch him it would render him visible to every animal he might hunt, so that his success as a hunter would be gone."[36] In the Yukon-Kuskokwim region, in the case of an early marriage, ". . . when the girl reaches puberty both she and her husband are considered unclean, and neither of them is permitted to take part in any work for a month. . . ."[37]

On Kodiak Island the girl at puberty ". . . was led into a hut, in which she was compelled to remain for six months in a stooping position upon her knees. After that the hut was enlarged sufficiently to enable the captive to straighten her back, but in this position she had to remain another half year, and was considered unclean and an outcast with whom nobody was allowed to communicate during all this period."[38]

An old native of Selawik, near Kotzebue Sound, described a strange custom observed among those natives. When a girl became a woman they sent her abroad for a long time with a big hood that hid her face. She had a staff in her hand, shaped like the letter "T" with twelve different beads hanging from the crosspiece. When one bead fell off she left it where it lay, and so on until all the beads had dropped. Then she washed and returned home, but remained away from the village a whole year, living separately in a snow hut in the winter and in a hut in summer, getting food freely from her parents and therefore not suffering much.[39]

The Caribou Eskimos have no ceremonial initiation at puberty. Certain taboo rules come into force when a young girl has had her first menstruation; but it is not because she has passed from one female age class to another.[40] At this time she assumes the long frock-hood; and she must then eat with a man who is under taboo, owing to a death, for instance; his taboo is thereby removed.[41]

Taboos Relating to Propagation

OCCASIONALLY, the customs entail a strict separation of men and women,[42] even for a considerable length of time. But restrictions of this nature, together with taboos upon women such as the ones mentioned above, probably do not deeply influence the sexual life of the Eskimos.

Childbearing also occasions taboos similar to those applying to maturity and menstruation. At Point Hope, Alaska, ". . . pregnant women could not work at whaling, because they must not urinate on the ice, and the whaling is done some miles from shore."[43] Menstruating women were under the same restriction.

In almost all Eskimo tribes, when a woman gives birth to a child a period is set during which she must remain secluded. In some cases the mother is confined simply to her dwelling for a certain time, as though she were unclean; but the more significant requirement is that she inhabit a special small tent or hut in solitude.

Seclusion taboos practised with greater and less strictness, have been reported among the Unalit of Alaska (in case of a woman's first child),[44] from the Nunatama;[45] from the Point Barrow natives (until the child is one moon old);[46] among the Qaernermiut of the Caribou Eskimos (for two months if it is a boy, three months if it is a girl);[47] among the Iglulik Eskimos;[48] in southeastern Baffin Island (except generally in the case of a first child);[49] and among the Polar Eskimos.[50] The Polar Eskimos and at least some of the Iglulik enforce strict segregation only until the child is born. It is stated concerning certain Eskimos of the central region, that if a birth takes place unexpectedly the tent or snow hut must be abandoned.[51] At Cumberland Sound, the mother must not enter any hut but her own for two months.[52]

The Eskimos see in childbirth, as in death, a marvelous phenomenon taking place, to a large degree irrespective of human intervention. Since the function of reproduction is beyond understanding, it naturally gives rise to the idea that certain taboos should be observed. It is significant that the measures taken to avoid a woman in childbirth are similar to those that apply to a dead person: in both cases the intention is to prevent contamination.

Some groups do not practice strict isolation at childbirth. The Mackenzie Eskimo mother, for instance, goes out as soon as she is able after delivery;[53] the Copper Eskimos observe no sort of seclusion either before or after childbirth;[54] and the Pâdlimiut woman does not live alone, although she must not go outside for a month after her child is born.[55]

Certain groups in Alaska, however, are notably strict in their isolation requirements. At Selawik when a woman was about to have a child, she was sent far out from the dwellings and made to live in a small hut built in the snow and not warmed by any fire. There she lived during all her illness, having only one robe for a blanket, suffering from thirst, and receiving no food save what was thrown to her by her grandmother or other friends. When past her sickness she washed herself in snow, no matter how cold and stormy the weather. All the clothes that she had worn were burned and she dressed in new garments. Food taboos were continued after she returned home.[56]

One case came to the knowledge of Nelson in which a young Malemiut woman on the lower Yukon was put outside in midwinter in a small brush hut covered with snow and kept there for about four months.[57] Petroff states concerning Alaskan Eskimos that during twenty days after childbirth the mother refrained from fresh food and stayed within the house, generally sitting in some dark corner with the infant; and that every five days during this period she was required to bathe.[58]

The Diomede Islanders[59] and, at least in Lyon's time, the Iglulik Eskimos,[60] made it a practice to bathe the infant in urine. Among the Koksoagmiut of Hudson Strait a newborn babe must not be washed until six or eight hours have elapsed.[61]

Among the Qaernermiut[62] and the Polar Eskimos[63] after a woman has borne a child she must wash herself and discard her clothing. Clothing must be discarded also in southeastern Baffin Island.[64] It is stated that on the west coast of Hudson Bay the clothes worn by a woman during confinement are given to an old woman, who takes them apart at the seams and makes them over for herself in such a way that the top of the garments becomes the lower part.[65] At Angmagsalik, after a birth all furs, etc., are washed, and the gutskin window removed.[66]

From various localities comes the information that a woman at the time of childbirth must use her own cooking utensils or cook her own food.[67] In some groups the mother of a newborn babe must as a rule eat only animals killed by her husband;[68] moreover she must not eat animals which have been killed suddenly.[69] Eating raw meat is tabooed for the Iglulik mother for a year after the birth of her child; and if the infant is a boy she must not drink cold water for two or three months.[70] Similarly, the Diomede mother will refrain from drinking any water for some time after the birth of a boy, so that he will get fat.[71] Women in the Mackenzie Delta drink only snow water at the time of childbirth.[72] The Caribou Eskimo mother must not fetch water for one month after delivery.[73]

In West Greenland childbirth taboos extend even to the husband, who for several weeks must neither work nor carry on any dealings, except the necessary fishing, lest the child die.[74] Here is the closest approach, perhaps, to the couvade, which is absent from the folkways of the Eskimos in its typical form, wherein the father goes to bed on the occasion of his wife's giving birth to a child.

An outstanding belief among Central Eskimos and natives of Greenland is that a premature birth is sure to incur the grave disfavor of certain spiritual powers. A still more serious offense is for a woman to have a miscarriage and to keep it secret, thereby escaping the special taboos it entails.[75] Among the Polar Eskimos, for instance, a wife who has a miscarriage is forbidden to mention by name animals that are used for food, and her husband must not speak of them except by using special names for them. At Cumberland Sound, cases of premature birth require particularly careful treatment. The event must be announced publicly, else dire results will follow. If a woman should conceal from the other people that she has had a premature birth, they might innocently come near her, or even eat in her hut of the seals procured by her husband. The vapor arising from her would thus affect them, and they would be avoided by the seals. The transgression would also become attached to the soul of the seal, which would take it down to Sedna.[76]

§4. THE COMPELLING POWER OF TABOO RULES

THE belief that one who has transgressed taboo is a menace to others engenders the conviction that a solemn duty rests on every member of an Eskimo community to confess his offenses.[77] The Eskimos of Cumberland Sound believe that the failure of anyone to observe religious rules causes a sort of vapor to surround him, which repels the sea mammals.[78]

"A number of customs may be explained by the endeavors of the natives to keep the sea-mammals free from contamination." Taboos of mourning, as well as of the sort discussed above, are sometimes directed toward this end. "All clothing of a dead person, the tent in which he died, and the skins he obtained, must be discarded; for if a hunter should wear clothing made of skins that had been in contact with the deceased, these would appear dark, and the seal would avoid him. . . .

"A woman who has a new-born child, and who has not quite recovered, must eat only of seals caught by her husband, by a boy, or by an aged man; else the vapor arising from her body would become attached to the souls of other seals, which would take the transgressions down to Sedna, thus making her hands sore."[79]

Violation of taboo incurs social disapproval, but not for the same reason as do such crimes as murder and theft. These latter offenses have very little significance in the Eskimo religion.[80] The acts that are to be avoided for fear of divine judgment are, on the other hand, very trivial from our point of view. A girl in northern Labrador persisted in eating caribou and seal together, and she was banished from her village in the dead of winter.[81] She was regarded as a menace to society, not because she directly offended her people by jeopardizing their rights to life and property, but because she had repeatedly transgressed a time-honored taboo and thereby exposed the community to punishment from the supernatural powers. Divine retribution following disregard of taboos falls upon the community as well as upon the offender. The spirits are supposed to express their disfavor through each and every misfortune that visits the people—sickness, stormy weather, disappearance of game, and death from any cause. These calamities are taken as ample evidence of the vigilance of the spirits over human affairs.

Preoccupied with material problems and harassed by the tribulations of his hand-to-mouth existence, the Eskimo does not project his imagination beyond this present life in search of punishment for his misdeeds. He has very little notion, if any, that compliance with, or violation of, taboo will effect reward or punishment *after death*. Manner of dying has more influence than moral conduct upon the destiny of the soul.[82]

We see in the Eskimo's religion only the thinnest roots of the abstract concept of a divine justice above worldly morality. The restrictions and requirements are for the most part unrefined, and they pertain to material things rather than to ethical ideals. Beset by immediate trials, the native does not ponder much over abstract philosophy. Comfort and security as known to us are not his heritage; and the idea of deferred judgment upon sins does not occur in his religious outlook. Punishment for noncompliance with taboos does not take the abstract form of indemnity; it comes in the most direct form imaginable, through depletion of the very necessaries of life. All supplies, such as food, furs, and fuel, are supposed to be dispensed by the spirits. Privation and ultimately death may be inflicted upon the living at any time as punishment for some, to us, trivial offense.

NOTES

1. See pp. 79 ff.
2. Holm: 1914, 49.
3. See pp. 100 ff.
4. Smith, in Kersting: 1902, 121.
5. Nelson: 1899, 438.
6. Nelson: 1899, 423.
7. Jenness: 1922, 185.
8. Klutschak: 1881, 123 f.
9. Rasmussen: 1929, I, 194; Rasmussen: 1927, 133.
10. Boas: 1907, 123.
11. Turner: 1894, 201.
12. H. I. Smith: 1894, 216.
13. Petroff: 1900, 215; Nelson: 1899, 145, 392; Hooper: 1881, 59; and Smith, in Kersting: 1902, 117.
14. Nelson: 1899, 440.
15. Nelson: 1899, 392. See pp. 340 ff.
16. Stefansson: 1914, 320.
17. Rasmussen: 1929, I, 194.
18. Holm: 1887, 65 f.
19. Nansen: 1893, 174.
20. Rasmussen: 1927, 64; and Birket-Smith: 1929, I, 126.
21. Birket-Smith: 1929, I, 234.
22. See p. 105.
23. Sumner and Keller: 1927, II, 1433 ff.
24. See p. 275.
25. Sumner, Keller and Davie: 1927, IV, 995 ff.
26. Nelson: 1899, 440.
27. Holmberg: 1855, 122.
28. Birket-Smith: 1929, I, 292, also 138 f.
29. Boas: 1907, 478. See p. 260.
30. Boas: 1907, 120 f.
31. Hall: 1864, 315.
32. Turner: 1894, 208.
33. Hawkes: 1916, 134.
34. Kroeber: 1899, 313.
35. Birket-Smith: 1924, 422.
36. Nelson: 1899, 290 f.
37. Nelson: 1899, 292.
38. Petroff: 1900, 235; and Holmberg: 1855, 121.

39. Weyer: Field Notes.
40. Birket-Smith: 1929, I, 258.
41. Birket-Smith: 1929, I, 292.
42. See pp. 140 f.
43. Stefansson: 1914, 182.
44. Nelson: 1899, 289.
45. Stefansson: 1914, 161 f.
46. Ray: 1885, 46; Murdoch: 1892, 414 f.; and Smith, in Kersting: 1902, 118 f.
47. Birket-Smith: 1929, I, 279 ff. See also Klutschak: 1881, 233.
48. Rasmussen: 1929, I, 170 ff., 48 f.; Rasmussen: 1927, 134; and Mathiassen: 1928, I, 211 f.
49. Hall: 1864, 313. See Kumlien: 1879, 28.
50. Rasmussen: 1908, 119.
51. Turquetil: 1926, 420.
52. Boas: 1888, 611.
53. Stefansson: 1914, 161.
54. Jenness: 1922, 164.
55. Birket-Smith: 1929, I, 279 ff.
56. Weyer: Field Notes.
57. Nelson: 1899, 289.
58. Petroff: 1900, 214.
59. Weyer: Field Notes.
60. Lyon: 1824, 268. Rasmussen states that the infant must not be washed in water but simply wiped with the skin of a small snipe. (Rasmussen: 1929, I, 171.)
61. Turner: 1894, 190.
62. Birket-Smith: 1929, I, 279 ff.
63. Rasmussen: 1908, 120 f.
64. Boas: 1907, 484; Boas: 1888, 610 f.
65. Boas: 1907, 514.
66. Holm: 1914, 62.
67. Murdoch: 1892, 415 (Point Barrow); Ray: 1885, 46 (Point Barrow); Rasmussen: 1929, I, 172 f. (Iglulik Eskimos); Mathiassen: 1928, I, 211 f. (Iglulik Eskimos); Boas: 1907, 484 (Cumberland Sound); Birket-Smith: 1929, I, 279 ff. (Qaernermiut, of the

Caribou Eskimos); Holm: 1914, 61 f. (Angmagsalik).

68. Rasmussen: 1929, I, 172 f. (Iglulik Eskimos); Boas: 1888, 611, and Boas: 1907, 125 (Cumberland Sound; there she may also eat animals killed by a boy on his first hunting expedition); Crantz: 1767, I, 215 (West Greenland).

69. Rasmussen: 1929, I, 172 f., 169 f. (Iglulik); Boas: 1907, 159, and Boas: 1888, 611 (west coast of Hudson Bay).

70. Rasmussen: 1929, I, 172 f.

71. Weyer: Field Notes.

72. Stefansson: 1914, 133.

73. Birket-Smith: 1929, I, 133.

74. Crantz: 1767, I, 215; also Birket-Smith: 1924, 409.

75. Rasmussen: 1929, I, 179, 98 (Iglulik Eskimos); Boas: 1907, 150 (Iglulik Eskimos); Rasmussen: 1908, 120 f. (Polar Eskimos); Birket-Smith: 1924, 409 (West Greenland).

76. Boas: 1907, 124 ff.

77. Thalbitzer: 1928, 399 f.; Rink: 1875, 40; Stefansson: 1914, 128 (Copper Eskimos); Boas: 1907, 512 (west coast of Hudson Bay); Rasmussen: 1929, I, 169 (Iglulik Eskimos); Bilby: 1923, 210 ff., 222 (Baffin Island); Boas: 1900, 627, and Boas: 1907, 121 (the Central Eskimos); Rasmussen: 1908, 127 f. (Polar Eskimos). See pp. 231, 326, 357.

78. See *Aglerutit*.

79. Boas: 1907, 124 ff.

80. See pp. 228 ff.

81. Hawkes: 1916, 133.

82. See pp. 249 ff.

CHAPTER XXIII

ESKIMO DIVINITIES AND SECONDARY SPIRITUAL CREATURES

§1. THE MOON SPIRIT

AT the western extremity of the Eskimo province the natives of Bering Strait impute to the Moon Spirit, who is a male divinity, the control of all animals. This spirit holds a position that is correlative in some ways to that of Tornga'rsoak in Labrador and the Sea Goddess in the central regions and Greenland.[1] In times of scarcity the shamans of Bering Strait perform their mysterious journeys to the moon and make offerings to him. Their familiar spirits lead them on this errand; and almost ·invariably two shamans go together, in order to aid and encourage each other. The great manlike Spirit of the Moon is wont to grow disagreeable upon their arrival; but if they succeed in pleasing him he gives them one of the kind of animal that has become scarce, whereupon the shamans return to the earth with it and turn it loose, so that the species may become plentiful again. "On the lower Yukon and southward they say that there are other ways of getting to the moon, one of which is for a man to put a slip noose about his neck and have the people drag him about the interior of the kashim until he is dead."[2]

The old headman at the village of St. Michael was seen on one occasion at the beginning of the fall seal hunting to go out secretly and make food offerings to the new moon while he sang a song of propitiation to the Spirit of the Moon.[3]

Occasionally, outside of Alaska, the Moon Spirit is thought to influence the success of hunting.

It is recorded that a native of Cumberland Sound asserted, "Takaq gives us what we want, seals and deer."[4] On the west coast of Hudson Bay at the time of the new moon the boys run out to a spot where the snow is clean and from there take up a lump of snow and call up to the moon, "Give me luck in hunting!" Then they run into the house and put the snow into a water vessel. This is done because of the perpetual thirst of the seals.[5] In this region the Moon Spirit is called *Aningâp inua* or *Tarqiup inua,* the word for moon being *tarqeq.*[6] He is regarded as a good and well-intentioned spirit, as he is also by the Iglu-

lik Eskimos immediately to the north, who call him *Tāt-kuk*.[7] The East
Greenlanders, on the contrary, personify the moon as a terrible being.
They are frightened by an eclipse, for it is interpreted as a visitation
of the moon among them, in a dangerous, vengeful mood. He will steal
the souls of people who have sinned. When he descends to earth the
men utter charms against him, carry snow in, and throw it into the
water containers. The children give voice to the wish that the moon
may cause good whale hunting, and bring walruses and polar bears;
but they must hurriedly crawl under the bed covers to hide themselves.[8]

The offering of water or snow to the Moon Spirit is a common observance among the Eskimos. It has been mentioned as occurring on the
west coast of Hudson Bay and in East Greenland. The Kittegaryumiut
of the Mackenzie region spill a cup of water at the time of the new
moon for the *"Tatkin inua."*[9] Again, in Greenland, it is reported that
when there was an eclipse, an old woman who wished to mollify the
Moon Spirit held up melting snow to him. The water disappeared as
the eclipse ceased; he had drunk it.[10]

In the region of Bering Strait:

"Nearly all epidemic diseases are supposed to come from the moon,
but occasionally they descend from the sun. An eclipse of the moon is
said to foretell an epidemic, and the shamans immediately proceed to
learn the cause in order to appease the being living there and, by di-
verting his anger, save the people. Among the inhabitants along the
lower Yukon it is believed that a subtle essence or unclean influence
descends to the earth during an eclipse, and if any of it is caught in
utensils of any kind it will produce sickness. As a result, immediately
on the commencement of an eclipse, every woman turns bottomside-up
all her pots, wooden buckets, and dishes."[11]

Besides portending epidemic disease, an eclipse of the moon may
presage an attack of the Indians living inland in Alaska.[12] On
Little Diomede Island we find the Moon Spirit figuring as a sort
of war god. Just before setting out to fight a neighboring people,
these natives would throw eggs into the air as a success offering to
Tah'kuk; and after the raid was over, they would sacrifice to this
spirit a small portion of every plundered article, for example a
little corner cut off each piece of fur clothing. The Moon Spirit
ranks high in the religious scheme of these Eskimos.[13]

Sometimes the abode of the Moon Spirit is described in detail.

From Greenland come the most graphic conceptions of the moon
land. The Polar Eskimos have the idea that the moon (Aningaan) and his

sister the sun (Seqineq) live in a double house with a single entrance. In one house lives the moon with his wife (Akoq or Aqong); and in the other, the sun. In front of the house stands the sled of the moon piled full of sealskins, and he possesses a team of spotted dogs with which he often drives down to the earth. Besides his wife and sister, the moon has a cousin, also a woman, Irdlirvirisissong, the "Disemboweler."[14] She cuts open people who laugh, and gives their entrails to the dogs.[15]

On the central portion of the west coast of Greenland the natives describe the Moon Spirit as living in a small house with one window and two lamps burning before his bed. The benches of his house are covered with the pelts of young polar bears, on which the souls of the dead rest when they travel to heaven. The sun has a little chamber alone on one side of the house. The moon has a sled drawn by four great black-headed dogs; and, unlike the sun, he still has to seek his livelihood on earth or in the sea. There he catches seals, his customary food, and takes them home on his sled. This is happening when the moon is not to be seen in the sky.[16] Similarly, in East Greenland, when there is no moon at the time of new moon, the spirit is supposed to be out hunting on the moon sea in his kayak. He hunts only white whales, narwhals, and bears, and possesses neither tent nor umiak, but travels with his kayak or sled.[17] Thalbitzer, writing of East Greenland, states that the Eskimo Moon Spirit, Aningáhk, ". . . is regarded as a man, a hunter, who catches sea-animals, who has his house, his hunting grounds and his implements of the chase in the sky. . . ."[18]

The Utkuhikhalingmiut of Backs River believe that when they die, they are carried by the moon up to the land of heaven. In former times their angakoks are supposed to have been able to visit the moon.[19] This magic journey to the moon is also believed possible by the natives of the west coast of Hudson Bay.[20] On Baffin Island the man in the moon is considered the protector of orphans, and is supposed to descend from heaven to assist them against their abusers. In his storehouse roam enormous herds of deer and seals, and in a small annex to his hut lives his sister, the sun.[21]

Beneath the local variations in the native concept of the moon can be detected a broad, basic uniformity. This uniformity is partly sustained by a myth explaining the origin of the moon and sun, which in one version or another has been reported from almost all groups of Eskimos and from among the Indians as well.[22] The moon and sun are represented as a brother and sister who once lived on earth. The boy is supposed to have chased the girl, who fled away from the earth into the heavens with her brother behind her. She became the sun and he the moon; and ever since he has followed her.[23] The almost continuous distribution of this myth in one version or another over a wide area suggests that it has not been invented independently here and there but passed from tribe to tribe. And the spiritual beliefs about the moon, in turn, have not simply grown up sporadically in response to an astronomical phenomenon familiar to all peoples, but have been shaped by the basic mythological concept.

In his earthly form the moon wooed his sister in the dark without her recognizing him for her brother. When she learned who he was, which she did, according to one version, by smearing lampblack on her lover and later identifying him, she was ashamed of having committed incest. Her shame caused her to take flight into the heavens. That the Moon Spirit is constantly pursuing the object of his desire is in accord with the common Eskimo belief that the moon can cause women to become pregnant. The supposed influence of the moon upon the sexual functions of women, furthermore, is of course a natural deduction from the similarity between the phases of the moon and the monthly period of women.

It is reported that in East Greenland a childless woman will have the medicine man fly to the moon to get her a child, and will allow him to sleep with her.[24] In the same region the Moon Spirit was thought to take it very ungraciously when two men exchanged wives.[25] On the west coast of Hudson Bay the Moon is regarded as the maintainer of fertility and thought to make barren women pregnant.[26] In West Greenland a girl is warned against standing outdoors and gazing at the moon lest he may be able to cohabit with her;[27] and if the full moon shines on water, a maiden must not drink it lest she become pregnant.[28] Crantz mentions that taboos are "prescribed to a single woman, in case the sun or moon (though we should rather call it a bird flying by) should let any uncleanness drop upon her. . . ."[29] The belief is common to both coasts of Greenland that the moon shining on a sleeping woman causes menstruation.[30]

The Eskimos almost invariably personify the moon as a man and the sun as a woman, and the opinion prevails that each is ill disposed toward the opposite sex. Because of the lustful intentions ascribed to the Moon Spirit in mythology, the natives of the Mackenzie region regard him as the enemy of women, who consequently dare not venture out in moonlight.[31] In early Greenland, when the phenomenon of parhelion occurred—the appearance of three suns in the sky—a maiden explained to the inquirer that her people called the mock suns the forehead locks or earrings worn by the sun because of happiness over the death of a male or the birth of a girl, a sentiment which remains from her old hatred of her brother, the moon. When, on the contrary, a ring appeared around the moon, it was said to be a hood worn by the moon in grief over the same occurrences.[32] The opposite inference could be drawn, however, from another statement by the same author, to the effect that no woman dared go out during an eclipse of the sun, nor man during an eclipse of the moon, because the sun and moon hate members of their *own* sex.[33]

In any case, however, the fact is plain that the Moon Spirit of the Eskimos is conspicuously masculine, and is believed to control fertility among women. The Moon Spirit is a mighty power that demonstrates his strength through his phases, and through other natural phenomena, especially ebb and flow of the tide. He is not a divinity primarily associated with the food quest, although in the region of Bering Strait, where his importance is greatest, he does control the animals. His influence reaches farther, to the functions of human reproduction; he is particularly to be placated to the end that boy children will be born. With power to regulate menstruation, fertility, and pregnancy, the moon enjoins and enforces the taboos concerning reproduction and childbirth.[34]

For example, the Angmagsalik Eskimos are said often to recall a frightful occasion when the moon descended to punish a woman who had broken taboo, and the angakoks had great difficulty in driving him away. The rocks shook and the dogs of the moon barked. The helping spirit was able to snatch the weapon out of the moon's hand and drag him out through the house entrance. But the moon was heard to threaten that there should be no more tides and that the seals should beget no more young.[35]

§2. THE SUN, A LESS IMPORTANT SPIRIT THAN THE MOON

In Eskimo mythology and religion the sun, personified, occupies a minor rôle, chiefly as sister of the moon. The Eskimo reveres the sun neither as a controlling force in nature nor in the affairs of man. She does not put out any mysterious influence beyond her mere presence as a heavenly body, and even as such she does not seem to be accorded due respect.

Actually, as science tells us, the sun influences human daily life in very direct and far-reaching manner. Even to primitive observers the deviations in its path must seem less erratic than the phases of the moon, and it shows itself to be unmistakably the primary factor in the changing seasons. In autumn the gradually sinking sun day by day foretells the approach of winter, with its cold and gloom. In a variety of ways, darkness adds to the perils and uncertainties of life. Hunting becomes difficult, traveling dangerous. In short, darkness augments the insecurity that lurks in the unknown, and it allows the imagination of primitive man full play to create a host of evil-working spirits. The reappearance of the sun, in turn, heralds the warmer summer season of long daylight.

It is quite reasonable to suppose that the prolonged darkness and monotony of winter contribute to the prevalence of a peculiar mental disorder, arctic hysteria, among the people around the polar basin.[36] And since hysterical manifestations are common in religious ceremonies, we have further reason to study the relation of the sun to the religious expression of these people. We would have thought it only natural if the Eskimos had elevated the Sun Spirit to a dominant position as master dispeller of the forces of darkness; we would think it reasonable that the sun should be honored as the supreme counterforce to the misery of dearth, cold, and gloom. Actually, however, the Eskimos rarely, if ever, venerate the sun as a divinity. And only indirectly does the religion stress seasonal phases. Remote from the present issue, it is rather the cycle of hunting activities to which the program of ceremonies and taboos conforms.

There is occasional mention of an annual ceremony performed in recognition of the return of the sun.

Among the Iglulik Eskimos when the sun reappears for the first time after a season of darkness ". . . children must run into the snow huts and put out the lamps. . . . The new sun must be attended by new light in the lamps."[37] Similarly, in southeastern Baffin Island, ". . . at the time which answers to our New Year's day, two men start out, one of them being dressed to represent a woman, and go to every igloo in the village, blowing out the light in each. The lights are afterwards rekindled from a fresh fire."[38] Crantz's early report from West Greenland mentions that at the winter solstice a feast and dance were held to rejoice at the return of the sun.[39] But the Moon Spirit is accorded greater importance than the Sun Spirit in West Greenland both in legend[40] and in the living religion.

At Point Barrow a ceremony is held at the time of the return of the sun, which differs from the aforementioned observances in that it is not directed toward the spirit of the sun but against the evil forces of darkness. The supernatural being, Tuña, is hunted out of each igloo ". . . by incantations that would daunt the boldest spirit. A fire is built in front of the council-house, and at the entrance to each iglu is posted an old woman wise in ghost lore; the men gather around the council-house while the young women and girls drive the spirits out of the iglu with their knives, thrusting them under the bunk and deerskins in a vicious manner, calling upon Tuña to leave the iglu; after they think he has been driven out of every nook and corner, they drive him down through a hole in the floor and chase him out into the open air with loud shouts and frantic gestures. While this is going on the old woman at the entrance, who was armed with a long knife used for cutting snow, made passes over the air with it to keep him from returning. Each party drove the spirit towards the fire and invoked him to go into it; all were by this time drawn up in a half circle around the fire, when several of the leading men made specific charges against the spirit; and each, after his speech, brushed his clothing violently, calling upon the spirit to leave him and go into the fire; two men now stepped forward with rifles loaded with blank charges while a third came with a vessel of urine, which was thrown upon the fire, at the same time one fired a shot into it; and, as the cloud of steam rose, it received the shot, which was supposed to have finished him for the time being."[41]

A curious reaction to the seasonal movements of the sun is to be noted in the taboos of certain Eskimo groups regulating the pastime of making "cat's cradles" with string. It is only during the dark days in the absence of the sun that the Copper Eskimos are allowed to make these string figures.[42] Likewise, the Iglulik Eskimos forbid the making of string figures except when the sun cannot be seen; at other times the ring-and-pin game must be adopted instead.[43] On the west coast of Hudson Bay it is stipulated that the natives play the game of "cat's cradle" while the sun is going south in the fall in order to prevent its disappearance; whereas when the sun is coming back, the game of cup-and-ball is played to hasten its return.[44]

To sum up: the religious observances pertaining to the sun indicate the relatively slight importance attached to it as a supernatural power. Much deeper veneration might be expected by reason of its intimate and direct influence upon physical and mental life. The moon, on the other hand, whose actual influence is distinctly subordinate, is seen to command a relatively high position in the religious scheme. The rôles of these two heavenly bodies seem inconsistent, therefore, with their comparative significance as conditioning agents.

One might suppose, hypothetically, that it would make little difference to the Eskimos if there were no moon in the arctic heavens, whereas the light and warmth of the sun are so vital in the Far North that their lack in winter must be very obvious. Can it be that the very failure of the sun to furnish light in the depth of winter lends added significance to the moon, which shines sometimes even when the sun is absent? In the gloom of winter the prolonged moonlight of high latitudes aids the hunter and sledge traveler. When the sun hides below the skyline, giving the land at best only a dim twilight, even the pale light of the moon is a great boon. Where most of the Eskimos dwell, however, it is only for a comparatively brief season that the moon reigns supreme in the heavens; and, of course, it never affords more than an imperfect relief.

Aside from ameliorating the protracted darkness, the moon need be considered only in one other respect, namely, in its influence upon the tides. Tides have a bearing, occasionally, on the food quest of the Eskimos. Where they cause strong currents, thereby breaking up the ice, they may produce conditions favorable for hunting sea mammals.[45] And where broad mud flats are exposed at ebb the Eskimos sometimes supplement their food resources by gathering shellfish; but this pursuit is not of much consequence. Throughout a large section of the Eskimo habitat the influence of the tides is almost negligible. As a general proposition, therefore, the agency of the moon in causing ebb and flow is not of great practical importance. And, for that matter, the information at hand points only to certain Eskimos of Greenland as having derived the inference that the moon affects the tides.[46]

Yet the Eskimos attach considerable importance to the moon as a supernatural agent, commonly assigning to it the power over fertility in women, and in Alaska ascribing to it the important function of controlling all game animals. The guesses of the Eskimo as to the influence of the moon are not always correct. The complex lunar phases provide ready explanations for happenings with which the moon has no real connection; it is supposed to perform a variety of mysterious functions. The sun, on the contrary, in spite of its profound influence upon life-conditions, is accorded very little significance in religion. Doubtless, the very fact that its influence is so obvious partly accounts for its inferior rank as a spirit. In contrast with the waxing and waning of the moon, the apparent path of the sun through the heavens is fairly simple and regular, and less mysterious. Since the effects of the sun are obvious, less remains inexplicable, and the primitive curiosity is given a narrower scope for assigning to it supernatural functions.

§3. THE SPIRIT OF THE AIR: *SILAP INUA*

THE belief is widely held among the Eskimos that a mysterious force resides in the air, which manifests itself in changes of weather and other natural phenomena beyond their understanding. Less fixed and definite are the traits and functions ascribed to this spirit, Sila, than to other supernatural entities. Unlike many spiritual members of the Eskimo pantheon, Sila cannot easily be envisaged as a corporeal being. Sometimes spoken of as masculine, sometimes as feminine,[47] Sila pervades the natural world, as Ruler of the Elements. In its nonmaterial aspects this concept resembles the *mana* of the Melanesians, a spiritual force or virtue, and giver of good luck. A second usage of the word *sila* has an abstract connotation: *silaqartoŋa* (Greenland) and *slangchaqtoa* (Alaska) mean "I think" or "I consider"; and *sla'ka* (Alaska) means "my mind."[48] Yet Sila does not correspond exactly to *mana*, for it is not merely a power or virtue, or the force that is manifested in any and every sort of good luck. Sila works with evil purposes as well as with good, and is at times thought of to some degree as a personality. The full appellation, *Silap inua*, literally "the person of the air," suggests that the spirit is not simply an essence or an abstract power, but the personification of these characters. The purpose and will ascribed to certain natural phenomena are imagined as the attributes of Sila. The wind that blows and the blizzard that rages are regarded as manifestations of supernatural design, and in this as in other religious concepts the spirit is supposed to deliberate as a person deliberates and to be susceptible to persuasion as is a human being. It does not follow that the spirit is always imagined as having substance; much less is an earthly origin presupposed. In these respects we notice a departure, indeed, from other religious concepts of the Eskimos, for example from that of the Sea Woman. There is no cycle of myths accounting for the origin of this Air Spirit. As a spiritual personification of the elements, or as a world intellect, Sila works through natural phenomena, generally having slight bearing, however, on those phases of spiritual influence that concern the souls of men and animals or that conform to strictly material aspects of the element of luck. High-sounding interpretations of the name of this spirit are apt to convey the mistaken impression that it has supreme power and an all-pervasive influence. Sila is neither a dictator among the more clearly defined anthropomorphic divinities, nor their agent.

In southern Alaska, the most marginal group of Eskimos, the so-called Kaniagmiut of the region of Kodiak Island, know of the Air Spirit under a name that is related in derivation and meaning to the general terms even though their language departs widely from the typical Eskimo. In the event of stormy weather at sea they call him *hlam-choua* or *shljam-shoa*,[49] which is of the same derivation as *Silap inua. Hlam* is the genitive of *hlak*, "the light" "pure air"; *choua* is a form of *choŭk*, "man." North of this region, in the Yukon section, these words recur as *sla* and *yua*, which show closer resemblance to the *sila* and *inua* used eastward even to Greenland.[50]

The Diomede Islanders declared that they used to invoke Sila before setting forth on the raiding expeditions they perpetrated in the old days.[51] Jenness describes Sila according to the belief of the Copper Eskimos: "Sila, the being who lives in the sky and makes the sun go down when he walks along, also holds a high place in the Eskimo cosmology. Sila is often hostile to human beings and carries one off; but sometimes he is gracious and will cure a sick man by imparting to him some of his own vitality." This spirit typifying the weather is spoken of as a man and is conceived as a mighty power.[52] Among the Netsilingmiut and in the region of Repulse Bay, it is called Nârtsuk, or Nârshuk.[53] The Iglulingmiut and the Aivilingmiut regard Sila chiefly as the weather, hence they call it *persɔq* ("snowstorm") or *anɔre* ("wind"). Originally, it may have been a great spiritual world power; now, however, it plays a surprisingly small part independently, acting instead only as an agent.[54]

The Pâdlimiut, inland Eskimos of the Barren Grounds, conceive of Sila, in the religious sense, as a power that can be invoked and applied by mankind, the medicine man serving as interpreter. Sila's leading qualities are those of healing sickness and of guarding one against the ill will of others. All the rules of taboo are connected with Sila and are designed to maintain a balance of amicable relations with this power. Transgressions of the obligations imposed by Sila are severely punished with bad weather, dearth of game, sickness, in short, with all that is most feared.

Often the term "Pinga" is used to denote a spirit in the form of a woman who is understood to dwell somewhere in space and manifests herself only when specially needed. All fear her as a stern mistress of the household, keeping watch on all the doings of men, especially their dealings with animals killed. Though to Pinga is not attributed the creation of living creatures of the earth, she looks after the souls of animals and does not like too many of them to be killed. Nothing should be wasted; the blood and entrails must be covered up after a caribou has been killed.[55] Thus, the powers and duties of Pinga resemble in some measure those of the Sea Woman. However, these natives who never see the sea say that Pinga lives in the air, which is the abode ascribed elsewhere to Sila.

Curiously, the Eskimos of Ponds Bay, Baffin Island, link the idea of Sila with the (imaginary) eggs from which albino animals are hatched.[56]

To the Polar Eskimos "Sila" means weather, the universe, or the whole.[57] Similarly in West Greenland the word, while difficult to translate, means roughly "power," "weather," "world," or "understanding."[58] The Greenland dictionary[59] defines *sila* as "the personified air . . . on the basis of its arbitrary changes thought to possess a soul or life in itself. . . . A sort of half-god or independent spirit: air-spirit, the cause or source of the wind-changes." The West Greenlanders sometimes use the longer word "Sillagiksartok" to designate the spirit causing good weather.[60] Their general attitude toward Sila is one of fear, however, toward a powerful and dangerous spirit which grows angry if certain rules of conduct are disregarded. Thus, it is said that on one occasion the air became malevolent because an angakok had neglected his duty of performing a great invocation, and desecrated the day by visiting a neighbor. Thereupon the wind stirred up a frightful storm. On days after a death the air demands silence: there must be no hammering, no stone throwing, no contact with metals.[61] This reminds us of the belief on Diomede Island, far distant from Greenland, that bad weather will surely ensue if people who are in mourning hang clothes or other property out of doors.[62] Again, in West Greenland, it is believed that a pregnant woman who has transgressed taboo will be punished by having her infant changed from a boy into a girl at the instant of birth. And when in a certain region a protracted storm occurred in the year 1738 it was attributed to the fact that a whip had accidentally come into contact with a corpse; Sila had seen the whip and heard it snap and was angered. But the air can create clement weather when it wishes. On one occasion an old man put a banner on the grave of his mother to please the east wind; it became obedient.

From East Greenland we learn that the angakok travels to the Lord of the Wind in order to make the wind blow or to make a bad wind subside. One can also compel the wind to accommodate one by sticking it with a knife or by whipping it.[63]

All these beliefs imply that the air is possessed of the moods and responses of a living creature. This spirit also manifests powers similar to those of the more personal daimons such as the Sea Woman and the Moon Man, but without occupying a comparable position in mythology. Nor is it supposed like them, according to folklore, to have been a human being who had actually lived on earth at some definite time. We must regard the concept of the Air Spirit as relatively old in the religion of the Eskimos, both because it is so widely current and because the direct implication of supernatural force in natural phenomena, or, as it might be stated, the personification of Nature, is an elemental and presumably primitive deduction.

Finally, it should be noted that Sila does not motivate each and every atmospheric phenomenon. Thunder, we recall, is supposed to be caused by certain other spirits rubbing skins, and the aurora borealis is produced when the shades of the dead play ball.[64] The Greenlanders even have a special rain spirit, Asiaq. Our first wonder at the belief in a spirit of this nature among an Arctic people is dispelled when we realize that even in Greenland rain may sometimes be greatly desired. If the snow has fallen in great abundance the people cannot go on the hunt. So, with the aim of facilitating travel, the angakok makes a spiritual journey to Asiaq to beseech her to send rainy weather.[65] Thus, the people of Angmagsalik, in addition to the Moon Spirit and the old nameless woman of the sea, ". . . speak of a third power of the sky, an old woman of the name of *Asiak*, who procures rain by shaking a skin drenched in urine down upon the earth so that a shower of drops is sprinkled upon it."[66]

§4. MINOR SUPERNATURAL ENTITIES

ONE of the most grotesque creatures that the fancy of the Eskimo has created is a horrible woman who disembowels anyone whom she can make laugh. Her grim purpose in this, to get food for her dogs, contrasts strongly with her ludicrous and outlandish bearing. She is commonly supposed to live near or in the house of the moon. The souls of the dead encounter her on their journey to the other world, and so may the angakok on his visit to the house of the moon. If any stranger breaks into laughter over her crazy antics she will slit open his body and throw his entrails to the dogs or eat them herself.

In South Greenland the Disemboweller is called *Erhlaveersisoq*;[67] and in northwestern Greenland, *Irdlirvirisissong*. In the latter locality, the Polar Eskimos believe that she is a cousin of the Moon Spirit, and that she presents one of the dangers which the angakok must encounter when he visits the moon. He must turn his face away to keep from laughing, for that would incite her to cut out his entrails.[68] In the central regions the natives conceive of her as a frightful menace to those who travel the eerie spaces of the other world. In Baffin Island it seems that she (here called *Ululiernang*) is one and the same person as the mistress of the moon, whereas in Smith Sound and East Greenland the two are conceived of as separate individuals.[69] On the west coast of Hudson Bay the Disemboweller is called *Ululiarnâq*,[70] and among the immigrant Netsilingmiut, *Aukjûk*.[71]

Many a spiritual being in the Eskimo religion appears in mythology over a broad area, but under differing local designations. This diversity of names may have resulted from a tendency of the native to refer to awesome supernatural objects by circumlocution. In regard to the secondary spirits the problem becomes involved, for we are plunged into a maze of trivial details. Bilby has recorded over fifty minor spiritual entities garnered from the cultural complex of a small division of the race. Many of the subordinate spirits are mere hobgoblins, sprites, and gnomes. Strictly local supernatural characters rarely figure prominently in the folkways of any particular tribe; those that find wider acceptance are more likely to be the ones, naturally, which command serious respect. The spirit Nigsillik, for instance, which is known among widely separated groups, possesses considerable local importance among the secondary spirits. The Copper Eskimos believe that he lives in the sky, and ascribe to him dreadful powers. They ". . . are very much afraid of him, for he carries a great hook, *nigsik*, which he stabs into his enemies. . . . Now and again the Eskimos hear him break up the passage of a hut; then they frighten him away by driving a knife through the snow wall at the edge of the window, or by pouring water through a hole in the wall or throwing it out into the passage."[72] In Baffin Island, Niksiglo is a *tongâk* of evil intent. He lives under the earth, and is a being in the form of a walrus tusk who possesses a hook with line attached. This he uses to steal hunters' caribou and seals.[73]

Similarities in the designations for specific spirits over wide areas do not always imply that the spirits are everywhere the same. For instance, the Copper Eskimos believe that there are numerous *inyuor-ligat,* dwarfs who are exceedingly strong in spite of the fact that they are so short that their bows trail behind them on the ground.[74] The Iglulik Eskimos, in turn, conceive of the *iη nEriugjät* as spirits of both land and sea.[75] In West Greenland, the *Innuarolit* are spirits of the mountains, pigmies only a foot tall who, nevertheless, are very expert creatures and have taught the Europeans their arts; and the *Ingnersoit* are described as ". . . ignipotent or salamandrine spirits, that inhabit the clefts of the rocks by the sea-side. . . ."[76] At Angmagsalik, the *inersuaks* are spirits living in the sea.[77] Thus, even though these classes of spirits might seem to be related in name, they are diverse, and do not represent an important phase of Eskimo religion.[78]

It is interesting to note that a possible connection has been pointed out between certain words commonly used by the Western Eskimos to designate Indians, "Ingalik" and "Irkréléït,"[79] and forms such as *Ingaliliks* and *Erkileks* from the East Greenland speech, which signify certain kinds of mythical creatures.[80] On this point Thalbitzer states: "While there is no doubt but that the *Erqihlit* and *Tornit* of the Greenlanders are to be found in the Eskimo names of foreign tribes (Indian neighbors) as far off as the northern part of the Northwest Territory, the case is different with the parallel E. Gr. *Ingalilik* [*Iηalilik*]—Al. *Ingalik* (=*Inkalik*), for in spite of the great similarity in the spelling of these names, they have probably no connection with each other. . . . The Greenlandic *Iηalilik* means . . . 'having a cooking utensil,' thus designating an inland-dweller who carries a pot or lamp on his person when on a journey ('a pot-troll')."[81]

We have mentioned but a few of the host of awesome creatures that haunt the imagination of the Eskimo. Some of them are harmless, some even benevolent; others strike fear into the primitive heart by their dreadful capacity to cause misfortune. The Eskimos envisage these many fantastic forms as the agents of bad luck, not confining their worries to actual hazards but creating imaginary terrors.[82]

§5. SPIRITS CALLED *TORNAIT*

THE Eskimos conceive of yet another order of spirits, namely the *tornait*. These spirits comprise a *group* in which specific members are not distinguished, except that some tribes acknowledge the existence of a chief spirit among them. In many sections the *tornait* command very serious respect. Quite generally it is from the *tor-*

nait that the angakok recruits his helping spirits, through the medium of which he comes into relation with the superior powers. Sometimes the *tornait* resemble more closely nature spirits; again they are directly associated with the dead. Their manifold diversity will be apparent from a discussion of the concept among various groups of Eskimos.

The name applied to these spirits varies locally but retains traces of its etymological origin. The differences in spelling and sound are, indeed, a bit confusing. We are obliged, nevertheless, to include variant forms of the word here, in view of an interesting question concerning the derivation of *tornait* and the origin of the concept implied. At the outset the reader is asked to notice that the variant designations used in different localities are allied, and so also are the ideas contained in them.

A study of the religious notions of the Central Eskimos led Boas to the opinion that ". . . the tornait, the invisible rulers of every object, are the most remarkable beings next to Sedna [the Sea Woman]." It is from this class of spirits, in the form of men, stones, and bears, that the medicine man enlists his familiar spirit, or *tornaq*.[83] According to Bilby the familiar spirit of the Baffin Island medicine man is called *tongak,* and *tarnuk* is the word for a person's soul.[84] Among the Iglulik Eskimos, *tɔ•ʳŋʳa•luit* are evil spirits and *tɔ•ʳŋʳait* are helping spirits.[85] Guardian spirits of an angakok are called *tɔ•ʳŋʳät* (sing., *tɔ•ʳŋʳAq*), or *apErʃät* (sing., *apErʃAq*), which are sometimes the spirits of animals.[86] Captain Lyon, who encountered this group of Eskimos over a century ago, recorded their use of the word *Torngak* or *Tornga* as applying to a guardian spirit.[87] Also in the parlance of the Caribou Eskimos, a *to•nrAq* is a spirit.[88] Thus, Tûnraqtalik is the name given to a haunted island in Baker Lake where none dares to live even for a night;[89] and *to•nrawiarneq* is the name of a game played by the Caribou Eskimos in which one of the players is a spirit.[90] A neighboring people, the Netsilingmiut of King William Island, refer to a somewhat similar "spirit game" by the designation *tunangussartut*.[91]

To the Eskimos in Labrador the *tornait* (sing., *torngak* [northern Labrador], *tungak* [Ungava and southern Labrador]) are a class of malignant spirits, sometimes disembodied, sometimes having strange and terrifying forms. They are more or less under the control of the shamans, who do not seem to aspire, however, to more than one *to'rngak* each.[92]

In West Greenland the word *tornak* (northern dialect) and *torngak* (southern dialect) correspond to the Labrador form *torngak,* and are used to denote a helping spirit.[93] An angakok has a number of *tôrnat,* which are the spirits of animals or objects, or the souls of dead persons.[94] The soul is called *tarngek.*[95]

The Polar Eskimos ascribe tornarssuit ". . . to all localities—house-floor, space behind the skin-walls, the lamp, house-entrance, refuse-heap in front of the entrance, the fells, the sea—from which they have special opportunities of receiving impressions and moods, or in other words, to nearly everything for which they have names. In earlier days they were afraid of these spirits and believed that they had no good-will towards men. Now they are somewhat more superior in these matters, though the belief in spirits is by no means extinct."[96] Kroeber writes regarding the beliefs of the Polar Eskimos: "The breath of soul after death becomes a tornguang. The *tornat,* accordingly, live in the air between heaven and earth. . . . The angakok uses his tornguang as an instrument for almost every purpose, and it is in possessing a tornguang that all his angakok power seems directly or indirectly, to lie." If a person sees a *torngang* he dies immediately.[97]

In East Greenland the word *torngat* has been tabooed and replaced by *taartat.*[98]

Passing far to the westward in Canada we learn that the Copper Eskimos believe in supernatural beings known as *tornrait,* which are not identified as souls of dead persons although they bear close affinities to them. While the *tornrait* are semihuman in form they are supposed never to have had a normal life like human beings. In a sense they are of a different order from the shades of men and animals, which are called *tarrait.* The *tornrait* ". . . live in isolation as a rule, though divided into male and female. . . . At times some little peculiarity in their appearance distinguishes them from human beings, for example, extraordinarily long hair; but they can change their forms and appear or disappear at will. Some have definite homes in hillocks or in tide-cracks or in old stone houses, but they are not altogether confined to these places. . . . They are especially dangerous in solitary places, and to natives wandering alone in the dark. A woman who had to take the usual portion of food one evening over to a house some thirty yards away ran the whole distance for fear of spirits." In Bathurst Inlet the opening of the sealing season is marked by a pitched battle between the shamans and the many little *tornrait* that live on the ice. The shamans pursue the spirits with their snow dusters, fighting them as if they were dogs, so that often both the mouths of the men and the ends of the snow dusters are covered with blood. Unless they were got rid of in this manner they would drive away all the seals and the Eskimos would starve during the winter.[99] Among the Copper Eskimos the shaman's familiar spirit is usually called *tornrak,* and is the shade of a dead person or animal. It should be remarked that "the Copper

SPIRITUAL BEINGS	GHOSTS OF THE DEAD	ANIMALS' SOULS	SEA GODDESS	TORNAIT	TORNARSUK (Chief of the Tornait)	MOON AND SUN	SILA	MISCELLANEOUS NATURE-SPIRITS; TUPILEKS; and VARIOUS FANTASTIC CREATURES
THEIR POSITION IN FOLKLORE	*Memory and Tradition*		*The girl who was thrown overboard and had her fingers chopped off.*	*? The legendary Tunit tribe*	*The bereaved father (Labrador)*	*The brother and sister who fled into the sky*		*Sometimes depicted in folklore*
THEIR ACTUAL EARTHLY ANTECEDENTS	*Tribesmen*	*Animals hunted*	*?*	*The people of the Thule culture*	*?*			

DIAGRAM ILLUSTRATING THE MAJOR SPIRITUAL CONCEPTS OF THE ESKIMOS IN RELATION TO MYTHOLOGY AND EARTHLY LIFE

FIGURE 19

Eskimo Divinities and Lesser Spirits

Eskimo makes no sharp and definite distinction between the shades of the dead, the spirits that have never been men or animals, and the spirits that the shamans control; there are separate names for both the first and the last; but all alike may be, and usually are, called *torn-rait.*[100] The shades of the dead, *inyuin tarrait,* and the spirits, *torn-rait,*[101] are very closely allied: some of the shades of the dead, for instance, "change to *tornrait,* and are identified more or less closely with those malignant spirits that never had a normal human existence, though they sometimes assume human form."[102]

West of the Copper Eskimos the designation for this group of spirits takes variant forms. In the Mackenzie region the word *turn-ñrat* is used to signify spirits possessing human characteristics.[103] At Point Barrow an evil spirit causing a sickness is sometimes called a *turn'gak.*[104] Just south of Bering Strait, at Port Clarence, the usual word for spirit is *turngnaq.*[105] And among the westernmost group of Eskimos, in Siberia, the corresponding word is *to'rnaṛak.*[106] Nelson writing on the Eskimos about Bering Strait gives the form *tun'ghâk,* singular; *tun'ghûk,* dual; and *tun'-ghät,* plural. The spirits thus referred to are personifications of various objects and natural forces or the wandering shades of men and animals. They are often of evil character, bringing sickness and misfortune among the people from mere wantonness or for some fancied injury.[107] Inasmuch as these spirits serve the shaman as his familiars he is known here as a *tun'gha-lik* or *tungra'lik,* a person possessing a *tun'ghâk.*[108]

The Point Barrow natives apply the name "Tuña" to an important supernatural being, visible at times, resembling in form the upper part of a man with very large head and long fangs. Tuña has no fixed abode; he seems to abide in the earth, the sea, and the air. Destroyer as well as creator, he is ever to be feared; and when men and women are out at night they usually carry a large knife to defend themselves in the event of meeting him. An old native devised an interesting contrivance to keep Tuña from entering an igloo. He suspended the handle of a seal drag in the trapdoor of the hut by means of a thong spiked to the wall with a large knife. The theory was that if Tuña tried to enter he would catch hold of the handle to help himself and would pull down the knife on his head and so be frightened away.[109] Another instance also illustrates the native attitude toward this spirit: an Eskimo was observed to break off very small pieces of tobacco and throw them into the air, crying out: "Tuǝna, tuǝna, I give you tobacco! Give me plenty of fish."[110]

An interesting example of divergence in word meaning is seen in the application of the word *tûña* as the name for rum.[111] The inference is, of course, that the alcoholic liquor is possessed of a spirit; so the Eskimos, in coining this name for rum, are merely paralleling the English usage of "spirits" and "spirituous liquors."

The similar word, *Tû'n-nyin*, strangely, is applied by the Point Barrow natives to white men. Perhaps the connotation here is "strangers," from the implication conveyed by the root word of "strange" or "mysterious" in the supernatural sense. Although these Eskimos usually spoke of white men as Kablu'na, a word known by practically all groups, they were observed to employ this other word, *Tû'n-nyin,* when they saw a ship.[112]

Some groups embrace the idea that there is a chief spirit among the *tornait*. This concept of a master *tornak* is most prominent in Greenland, but it exists in other sections as well.

In West Greenland, Tornarsuk, as this particular spirit is called, was misrepresented by the early missionaries as the highest divinity of the natives. The misconception was due partly to the restricted religious ideas of these observers and partly to the impulse of the native informants to endow this being with powers correlative with those of the Christian God. Tornarsuk is not a supreme dictator of the universe or a spirit that holds sway over all other supernatural beings.[113] He rules only over the *tornaks* as their master,[114] being a "special" or "particular" *tornak,* as his name implies.[115] As such he may be characterized as a very important oracle.

Anthropological investigations among the Eskimos of East Greenland at the time of their first contact with white people elucidate the Greenland conception of this supernatural being. The personal familiars of the angakok, which are called *taartaat,* are identical with the spirits called by other Eskimos *tornat* (*torngat*) ; he acquires them by rubbing the stone during his novitiate.[116] They belong to a sphere into which only the initiated have insight. A full-fledged angakok has a host of familiars: five, ten, fifteen, or more. But within the circle of helping spirits of each angakok there are three or four which have greater significance than the rest. Tornarsuk, or Tornartik as he is called in East Greenland, is among these, and perhaps the most prominent.[117] He functions as a supernatural intelligence, capable of telling the cause of sickness, famine, and similar troubles. The East Greenland Tornartik acts specifically as the angakok's guide through the depths of the sea or underworld, and helps him to come into alliance with the mighty woman of the sea.[118] As these people of Angmagsalik believe, Tornartik is an animal-like creature in the sea; and, it appears, there are at least two of them. It was described to Thalbitzer as three yards long, one yard broad across the chest, with the upper part like a man, with arms and legs, but the lower parts looking like a seal.

"It is not related to the woman of the sea and has nothing to do with her. Nor is it counted among the angakok's taartaat tornat; it is an independent creature which lives in the sea and can be used by the angakok for different purposes."[119]

The Polar Eskimos conceive of a somewhat similar being, called Torngaxssung. "The same person once spoke of several Torngaxssut, once called him the oldest tornguang, at another time called him an old angakok. He has power over the tornat, but does not seem radically distinguished from them. . . . He is also described as a dead person, who is often heard whistling . . . when persons are alone, who are then much afraid. . . ."[120]

The Labrador Eskimos assign supreme control of all the *tornait* to Tornga'rsoak, "The Great Tórngak"[121] who, as the husband of the Sea Goddess Supergu'ksoak, is one of the two main deities, and presides over the sea animals.[122] The Eskimos of the east coast visualize Tornga'rsoak (or Tunga'rsuk in southern Labrador dialect) as a huge white bear who lives in a cave in the great black mountains at the northern extremity of the peninsula. These mountains, which are wild and impressive in appearance, are called Torngat, or "Spirit Mountains." Also, according to Turner, the Ungava Eskimos personify Tornga'rsoak as a huge white bear dwelling in a great cavern near the end of Cape Chidley and controlling the reindeer.[123] These Eskimos believe that the minor nature spirits are under the control of the great spirit, whose name is Tung ak. This one great spirit is more powerful than all the rest together. The lesser spirits are under his immediate control. The shaman alone is supposed to be able to deal with Tung ak.[124] The mythology of these people represents Tung ak as a father who, ever since he lost his beloved children and became embittered thereby, has sent famine, disease, and death to harry the living.[125]

Among the Baffin Island groups the concept of Tornarsuk seems to be less prominent than in Greenland or Labrador; indeed, in parts, it seems to be wholly lacking.[126] Hawkes states, however, that "the supreme control of all the Tornait is assigned to Tornarsuq in Baffin Island. . . ."[127]

Far to the west, the Copper Eskimos consider the greatest of all the *tornrait* to be Kannakapfaluk, whom we identify with that widely respected Eskimo deity, the controller of the sea animals.[128] Therefore, these Eskimos and the natives of Labrador agree in holding that it is the chief of the *tornait* who presides over the sea animals. Again, in Alaska, we observe the tendency to single out one spirit as the master of associated spirits. At the Russian mission at Ikogmut, on the Lower Yukon, the Eskimos used the word *Tun'rûñ-ai'-yuk*, or "chief *tunghâk*," to denote the Christian God.[129] And an incantation is sung by the Nunivagmut, which, as Thalbitzer points out,[130] may show an affinity in the concepts of the Tornarsuk as it prevails among these Alaskan Eskimos and those of the east.

> "Toŋraŋajak's song
> The tungralik (angakok) always sings it
> My whole body is covered with eyes:
> Behold it! be without fear!
> I see all around."[131]

According to Barnum's vocabulary, *toŋraŋajak* is the word of the Yukon Eskimos for the same spirit that on the island of Tununa is called *toŋraŋazak,* and this was translated "devil" by the American missionaries.

Thalbitzer suggests that a certain spirit which a Netsilik Eskimo, in the central region, depicted in a drawing as having long arms, short legs, and many eyes should be linked with Tornarsuk in Greenland and Alaska. The name of this spirit is *ijitooq,* "the many eyed," which, while it does not definitely identify it as Tornarsuk, suggests the all-seeing attribute that has occasionally been ascribed to the latter elsewhere. The general appearance of the spirit as depicted, moreover, reminds one of certain Tornarsuk figures in East Greenland.[132]

NOTES

1. See chapter xxi.

2. Nelson: 1899, 430.

3. Nelson: 1899, 430 f., 515 (Selawik, Kotzebue Sound).

4. Boas: 1888, 583, quoting Warmow's *Journal:* 1859, I, 19.

5. Rasmussen: 1929, I, 74 f.

6. Rasmussen: 1929, I, 62.

7. Lyon: 1824, 270 (Iglulik Eskimos).

8. Thalbitzer: 1928, 407 f.

9. Stefansson: 1914, 327.

10. Thalbitzer: 1928, 407, citing Funch: 1840 (German ed.), 74.

11. Nelson: 1899, 431.

12. Thalbitzer: 1928, 410 f., citing Nelson: 1899, 431.

13. Weyer: Field Notes.

14. See pp. 392 f.

15. Kroeber: 1899, 318.

16. Thalbitzer: 1928, 406 f., after P. Egede.

17. Thalbitzer: 1928, 407.

18. Thalbitzer: in Kroeber and Waterman: 1931, 430.

19. Rasmussen: 1927, 196 f.

20. Rasmussen: 1929, I, 76.

21. Boas: 1887, 37. See also Boas: 1888, 598 f.

22. See pp. 241 f.

23. Boas: 1887, 37; Nelson: 1899, 482 (lower Yukon); Rink: 1875, 236 f. (Point Barrow and Greenland); Stefansson: 1914, 327 (Mackenzie Delta); Birket-Smith: 1929, I, 157 (Caribou Eskimos); Rae: 1850, 79 (Aivillirmiut of Repulse Bay); Boas: 1907, 306 f. (west coast of Hudson Bay); Rasmussen: 1927, 125; Rasmussen: 1929, I, 77 ff. (Repulse Bay); Boas: 1888, 597 ff. (Akudnirnmiut and Oqomiut, Baffin Island); Boas: 1907, 173 (Cumberland Sound); Turner: 1894, 266 (Hudson Strait); Kroeber: 1899, 318 (Polar Eskimos); Kroeber: 1899a, 179 f. (Polar Eskimos); Rasmussen: 1908, 173 (Polar Eskimos); Crantz: 1767, I, 232 (West Greenland); Saabye: 1818, 245 f. (West Greenland); Birket-Smith:

1924, 437 (West Greenland), with numerous references; Holm: 1888*b*, 34 (East Greenland). Occasionally it is believed that the brother became the sun instead of the moon, and the sister the moon (Hawkes: 1916, 156 [Labrador]; Nelson: 1899, 481 [St. Michael, Alaska]).

24. Holm: 1914, 97.

25. Thalbitzer: 1928, 408, citing Holm: 1888, 309 f.

26. Rasmussen: 1929, I, 74 f.

27. Thalbitzer: 1928, 407, citing P. Egede: 1790, 101.

28. Thalbitzer: 1928, 407, citing Saabye: 1816, 108.

29. Crantz: 1767, I, 216.

30. Thalbitzer: 1928, 410, citing Holm: 1888, N4, 34, 314 (East Greenland); and Birket-Smith: 1924, 437 (West Greenland).

31. Petitot: 1886, 5.

32. Thalbitzer: 1928, 407, citing P. Egede: 1790, 247.

33. Thalbitzer: 1928, 407, citing P. Egede: 1790, 150.

34. Thalbitzer: 1928, 410.

35. Thalbitzer: 1928, 408.

36. See Novakovsky: 1924; and Jenness: 1928, 52. It is said that among the Polar Eskimos, arctic hysteria is strikingly common late in the autumn, when the winter darkness is just coming on. Women are more subject to it than men; and the attacks last from some minutes to about a half hour (Steensby: 1910, 377).

37. Rasmussen: 1929, I, 183.

38. Hall: 1864, 323.

39. Crantz: 1767, I, 176.

40. Birket-Smith: 1924, 437.

41. Ray: 1885, 42 f.; compare Murdoch: 1892, 432 f. (Point Barrow), and Smith, in Kersting: 1902, 125.

42. Jenness: 1922, 184.

43. Rasmussen: 1929, I, 183; also Frazer: *The Golden Bough,* 1 vol. ed. (1924), 79 f. Here, in addition, boys who have not yet caught a bearded seal or walrus must not play "cat's cradle," for it will make them awkward with the harpoon line.

44. Boas: 1907, 151.

45. See pp. 111 f.

46. Holm: 1914, 106. See also Crantz: 1767, I, 231.

47. "The Greenlanders seem to consider him as a man, as most other Eskimos do, but the inland Innuit west of Hudson Bay conceive of this person as a woman (Hila)." (Thalbitzer: 1928*a*, 375, citing Rasmussen.)

48. Thalbitzer: 1928, I, 392. See also Thalbitzer: 1928*a*, 375 ff.

49. Petroff: 1900, 237 f.

50. Thalbitzer: 1928, 392 f.; also Birket-Smith: 1924, 433 f.

51. Weyer: Field Notes.

52. Jenness: 1922, 189, 179.

53. Rasmussen: 1929, I, 71 f.

54. Rasmussen: 1929, I, 62 ff.

55. Rasmussen: 1927, 80 ff.

56. Boas: 1907, 493.

57. Rasmussen: 1908, 124.

58. Birket-Smith: 1924, 433 f.

59. Kleinschmidt: 1871.

60. Crantz: 1767, I, 208.

61. Thalbitzer: 1928, 266 f.

62. Weyer: Field Notes.

63. Thalbitzer: 1928, 390 f.

64. See pp. 242 and 239 f.

65. Thalbitzer: 1928, 414 f.

66. Thalbitzer, in Kroeber and Waterman: 1931, 430.

67. Thalbitzer: 1928, 406.

68. Kroeber: 1899, 318. See also Kroeber: 1899*a*, 180 f.

69. Thalbitzer: 1928, 406, also 416.

70. Rasmussen: 1929, I, 76.

71. Rasmussen: 1929, I, 81.

72. Jenness: 1922, 189.

73. Bilby: 1923, 269 f.

74. Jenness: 1922, 180.

75. Rasmussen: 1929, I, 208.

76. Crantz: 1767, I, 208.

77. Holm: 1914, 83.

78. Other local concepts which show relationship with one another are mentioned in Rasmussen: 1929, I, 204, 208.

79. See p. 152.

80. Holm: 1914, 83 f.; Schultz-Lorentzen: 1928, 231.

81. Thalbitzer: 1923, 384.

82. For detailed information regarding secondary spiritual beings see Nelson: 1899, 442 ff., 459 (Alaska); Petroff: 1900, 238 (Kodiak Island);

Birket-Smith: 1929, I, 156 (Caribou Eskimos); Bilby: 1923, 265 ff. (Baffin Island); Kroeber: 1899, 320 (Polar Eskimos); Birket-Smith: 1924, 221, 439 (West Greenland).

83. Boas: 1888, 591. See also Boas: 1907, 236 ff. (Tales of Spirits [tornait] from Cumberland Sound).

84. Bilby: 1923, 203, 205.

85. Rasmussen: 1929, I, 144.

86. Rasmussen: 1929, I, 113.

87. Lyon: 1824, 260 ff., 125.

88. Birket-Smith: 1929, I, 291.

89. Birket-Smith: 1929, I, 73.

90. Birket-Smith: 1929, I, 291.

91. Rasmussen: 1927, 208.

92. Hawkes: 1916, 127, 131.

93. Thalbitzer: 1928, 371.

94. Birket-Smith: 1924, 453.

95. Crantz: 1767, I, 206.

96. Steensby: 1910, 370 f., citing Rasmussen: Nye Mennesker, 148. See also Rasmussen: 1908, 134; 1921, 30.

97. Kroeber: 1899, 303 ff. Cf. p. 290.

98. Thalbitzer: 1928a, 368. See pp. 300, 399, and 426.

99. Jenness: 1922, 186 f.

100. Jenness: 1922, 191.

101. Jenness: 1922, 185.

102. Jenness: 1922, 178, also 186.

103. Stefansson: 1914, 321 f.; see also 221 ff. (Langdon Bay), 325 (Horton River), 256, 378 f., 267, 273, 284.

104. Murdoch: 1892, 422, after Simpson: 1875, 275.

105. Boas: 1894, 208.

106. Bogoras: 1913.

107. Nelson: 1899, 428 f., 394.

108. Nelson: 1899, 428.

109. Ray: 1885, 42 f.; also Murdoch: 1892, 432.

110. Murdoch: 1892, 433.

111. Ray: 1885, 41.

112. Murdoch: 1892, 53.

113. Thalbitzer: 1928, 385 ff.

114. Thalbitzer: 1928, 379.

115. Thalbitzer: 1928, 371.

116. Thalbitzer, in Kroeber and Waterman: 1931, 435. See p. 396.

117. Thalbitzer: 1928, 374 f.

118. Thalbitzer: 1928, 382.

119. Thalbitzer, in Kroeber and Waterman: 1931, 436. Cf. Thalbitzer: 1928a, 371 f.

120. Kroeber: 1899, 304 f. Cf. Steensby: 1910, 370 f.

121. Hawkes: 1916, 128.

122. Hawkes: 1916, 124.

123. Hawkes: 1916, 125, 14 (footnote).

124. Turner (1894, 194), contrary to Hawkes (1916, 128), considers that "Tung ak is nothing more or less than Death, which ever seeks to torment and harass the lives of people that their spirits may go to dwell with him."

125. Turner: 1894, 195.

126. Boas: 1887, 37; Thalbitzer: 1928, 370 f.

127. Hawkes: 1916, 128.

128. Jenness: 1922, 188 f. See also pp. 353 and 360.

129. Nelson: 1899, 427.

130. Thalbitzer: 1928, 382 f.; 1928a, 373 f. Cf. Thalbitzer: 1928a, 373 f.

131. Barnum: 1901, sec. 841, p. 311.

132. Thalbitzer: 1928, 382 f.; 1928a, 373 f.

CHAPTER XXIV

ROOTS OF ESKIMO SPIRITUAL CONCEPTS

THE religion of the Eskimos has been found to revolve about several sorts of supernatural beings. Of these the shades of the dead stand in the most intimate relation to the people. The folkways pertaining to the phenomena of death imply a conviction that the human soul continues to exist after the expiration of life, as a supernatural entity capable of taking part in the affairs of the living. All manner of earthly misfortunes are ascribed to the shades of the departed. The spirits of slain animals persist in a mysterious realm, to favor or frustrate men according to their whims. Moreover, the Eskimo is constrained to heed nature spirits that inhabit natural features such as lakes, trees, rocks, and islands.

Most important of all the spirits, however, are the major individual divinities. These are usually envisaged in personal form and endowed with specific powers: e.g., the Sea Deity is a woman believed to control the creatures of the sea; the moon is a manlike being capable of causing (among other things) fertility in women; and Sila, the Air Spirit, is the power that effects changes in the weather.

The Eskimos propound no explicit origin for some of their spiritual beings. The existence of the Air Spirit, for instance, seems scarcely to demand explanation; Sila simply exists as a dissociated entity manifesting power through certain natural phenomena. For like reasons most of the minor nature spirits demand no explanation for their being. Animistic spirits in lake, rock, and tree seem not to arouse the curiosity of the native as to how they got there. They are taken for granted, because they seem to manifest their presence in mysterious displays of power for good or evil. Beyond these effects, their origin does not deeply concern the native.

As a rule, however, the Eskimos have myths to account for the origin of their higher spiritual beings. The stories recounted commonly ascribe earthly origin to them and explain how they rose from earthly forms to the rank of dominant spirits. The Sea Goddess, for instance, once lived among men as a girl; she was thrown out of a boat and her fingers were chopped off, whereupon they changed into animals of the sea. The Moon Man is supposed to have lived on earth as the brother of the Sun Girl, but when the latter fled from his wooing he chased her out into the heavens where they became the moon and sun. Tornga'rsoak is described by the Labrador Eskimos as having been a father who lost his beloved children, became embittered thereby, and ever since has sent misfortune to the living.

The interesting question arises whether the mythological explanations regarding these divinities have any actual basis in fact. Is there a mundane foundation in the evolution of these religious concepts? The fantastic character of some myths—especially those relating to natural phenomena and those which account for astronomical bodies—precludes the possibility of any such basis. The alternative to a factual interpretation is the supposition that they simply show man's predilection to create spiritual beings after his own image and to endow them with human characteristics, even to the point of ascribing an earthly origin to them. Other deity myths, however, sound plausible as narratives. Many of the events related in them might easily have actually occurred. And they are sometimes narrated so realistically that it is almost as if the incidents were actually remembered by the living. A tribe imparts to its particular version of a myth an individuality that sometimes makes the tale sound as though it were possessed exclusively by them. Hearing only a single version of a myth, one might take it for granted that it had arisen out of a local incident and had developed into a culture-hero tradition of one particular tribe. Comprehensive investigation, however, generally reveals the same myth told over a wide area, in slightly varying forms. And the spiritual characters described in it are accepted so widely and accorded so much importance that they cannot reasonably be thought of as the ghosts of the remembered dead. It does not weigh either for or against there being a basis of fact, when a story of wide distribution is adopted by each of several tribes as its own. The various versions can, of course, ramify from a common source, whether true or false. And it is not unreasonable to think that occasionally an event may have occurred that was so significant to the people that in being told and retold it became embodied in mythology.

Regardless of their authenticity, however, the deity myths indicate that the Eskimos commonly presuppose earthly antecedents for their divinities. In fancy, if not in fact, the divinities are derived from ancestral ghosts. True, they hold an especially high rank by virtue of their extraordinary attributes, which in some cases they are supposed to have possessed even while they lived on earth. Generally, some incident associated with their reputed death furnishes the acceptable reason for their authority as divinities. Thus, in a sense, they were predestined to higher rank. Nevertheless, their passing into the beyond is essentially similar to the passage of an ordinary human soul into the after life. The myths accounting for the origins of deities imply, in other words, that these higher beings are of the same order as the shades of the dead. Even the spiritual entities who have attained high supernatural authority are, therefore, identified by the Eskimos as spirits of individuals once on earth.

The natives assume that a transition occurs, by which living personalities pass through the ghost stage to divinities. The religious myths suggest what to the Eskimo is a plausible method by which deification can take place. Thus, the living folklore persistently suggests the trend of religious thought. And the earthly origin which the Eskimos ascribe to deities may, indeed, contain a true hint of the actual evolution of these ideas. But theorizing on this question is unsafe. It is futile to search for facts in the folklore of a people who do not record history in writing. Obviously, it cannot be taken for granted that true-to-life incidents recorded in folklore once actually happened whereas fantastic features are certainly born of the imagination. Therefore, the living Eskimo culture offers us only unverifiable hypotheses as to the evolution of deities.

Archaeology, on the other hand, while it fails to trace the origins of specific personalities, nevertheless can reveal the history of the Eskimo race, piecing the story together from the excavated relics of bygone tribes. In the present case the purely material findings of the archaeologist may shed light upon the development of abstract religious concepts. This is difficult, to be sure, in a culture which has no altars or idols, no temples or other adjuncts of higher cultures. But knowledge unfolds itself sometimes where least expected; here a hypothesis suggests itself in a roundabout way.

Eskimos over a wide area narrate incidents which involve a tribe of people called Tunit or Tornit, who once lived in close proximity to them. Investigations have satisfied the leading archaeologists in this field that these people actually existed. The unearthed relics of the Thule culture, as it is known to excavators, are now accepted as the imperishable evidence of this earlier people. Thus, while archaeology is not able to authenticate myths concerning specific personalities, it has established the actual existence in past time of a tribe *such as is described in the mythology.*

We do not suggest for a moment that on these grounds the deity myths, too, must be true. The significance of the present evidence reaches into a sphere of its own, for the Tunit people seem to have their spiritual counterparts in the so-called *tornait*, which were described in the preceding chapter as supernatural beings envisaged in semihuman form and enlisted by the medicine men as helping spirits.

Common sense as well as anthropological theory rouses our curiosity as to whether the similarity between the designation *tornait* and Tunit or Tornit, the name of the vanished tribe, may not indicate a connection. We may accept it as fairly certain that the legendary Tunit were a real people; and it is principally the very groups of Eskimos who relate the Tunit myths that have introduced the *tornait* spirits into their religion. The parallelism in the names and the ideas is so striking that we are prompted to make detailed investigation, in the hope of learning something more of the development of certain religious concepts. The *tornait* seem not to have been fabricated out of the imagination, but to have evolved out of a previous concept wherein they were identified as the shades of a former people. If this be true we have here a demonstration of the growth of religious ideas hitherto unexampled so far as the author is aware.

We recall that the *tornait* spirits occupy a place of greater or lesser prominence in the religion of all Eskimo groups. Among the central tribes they constitute the most important *class* of spirits; elsewhere some divergence from the type concept is encountered. In the east and west, we encounter the belief in a chief *tornak*, Tornarsuk and Toŋraŋazak. Quite generally, the most conspicuous rôle of the *tornait* is that of familiar spirits to the medicine men.[1] Usually endowed with human attributes, they nevertheless are sometimes identified as the shades of animals. At times they seem to be animistic genii. They do not always occupy fixed abodes, nor can they as a rule be classed as nature spirits. The *tornait* show very definite resemblance to human souls. Not uncommonly they suggest more than anything else the ghosts of dead people, wanting only identification with specific earthly precursors. One can easily suppose them to have been identified formerly as the shades of certain dead people, though they have now lost practically all identification with earthly forms. The grotesque and terrifying forms in which they are envisaged quite naturally depart from human semblance where manlike features would fail to symbolize their frightful attributes. According to the belief of the present Eskimos, the *tornait* wander about like lost souls, sometimes intruding maliciously into the affairs of men, sometimes abetting the angakok as his guardian spirits.

From the Copper Eskimos eastward to Baffin Island and Labrador the *tornait* are known by approximately the same name and endowed with practically the same characteristics, although in the peripheral areas of the Eskimo province the concept undergoes slight changes of form. Most typical in the central area and gradually shading off in the east and west, the distribution corresponds very closely with the distribution of the Tunit legends.

The Eskimos themselves do not associate the *tornait* spirits with the Tunit people, a fact which renders the possible connection only the more interesting as a scientific problem. The Tunit people do not command the moral respect of the natives; and they now belong to the realm of legend rather than to religion. One recorded instance in which a certain shaman of the Iglulik group claims as one of his familiar spirits the shade of a member of the vanished Tunit tribe, is perhaps unique.[2] An Eskimo might scoff at the suggestion were he told that all the spirits which he knows as *tornait* are really the shades of the Tunit and that his ancestors recognized them as such. The native would, on the other hand, freely follow the deduction of the archaeologist who would argue that the relics which he unearths prove the actual existence at one time of the people known to legend as the Tunit.

It is the traditions of the Central Eskimos that contain the most complete and matter-of-fact description of the old Tunit tribe. The culture possessed by this former people doubtless resembled that of the modern Eskimos; but no living group regards them as their direct ancestors. They seem to have constituted a contiguous group, generally standing in the relation of an "outgroup." The accounts agree in that the Tunit disappeared either through extermination or migration. Mathiassen, the authority on Eskimo archaeology, writes:

"An Aivilik Eskimo told me that once his people lived in the interior of the country; they went out to the coast where they met the Tunit, big, strong people, who lived in permanent winter houses [not snow huts like the present natives] and hunted the whale and walrus; their men wore bearskin trousers and their women long boots. When the Aiviliks settled down at the coast, the Tunit left their settlements and went away to the north; only on Southampton Island did they remain; these were the Sadlermiut who died off in 1902 and whose most important settlement is still called Tunirmiut. We met the same beliefs everywhere among the Igluliks. House ruins and strong tent rings were ascribed to the Tunit; at Ponds Inlet an Eskimo whom I asked as to the use of certain objects from Qilalukan, said that an Eskimo could not be expected to know, as these things had belonged to the Tunit. . . . Apart from the admixture of fantastic embellishment which of course is to be found in all Eskimo legends, these Tunit legends agree surprisingly well with the archaeological conditions; that the Tunit are the Eskimos of the Thule culture is beyond doubt."[3]

From the country of the Netsilingmiut archaeological material corroborates similar traditions. The present inhabitants believe that at some distant date their land was occupied by the Tunit. The immigrant ancestors of the Netsilingmiut drove them out and took possession of the country.[4] The following tradition of the Tunit was related to Knud Rasmussen by the Netsilingmiut Eskimos of King William Island:

"It was the Tunit who made our country inhabitable, who discovered where the caribou crossed the water and made hunting grounds there, found the fish in the rivers and built salmon dams, built fences here and there and forced the caribou to follow certain paths. They were strong but timid and were easily put to flight and it was seldom heard that they killed others. They caught caribou (where they crossed the water) and rowed the kayak on the sea; at Avertoq, Bellot Strait, one can see the remains of animals caught, whales, walruses, and narwhals; they were also skilful hunters of the musk ox and the bear. Once they held land at Netsilik, Willersted Lake; then they killed an Eskimo's dog at his request, by throwing a spear at it with the foot, but became frightened and fled. By Lake Qipkiaq, at Netsilik, ruins can still be seen of their stone houses with the doorways surrounded by large, yellow, sappy flowers with thick stalks.

"Once the Tunit lived at Qingmertoq (Adelaide Peninsula); there the land was taken from them by the Ugjulingmiut. The Tunit fled eastwards to Saitoq, but when they reached Naparutalik, they threw off all their clothes and swam over Kingarsuit. On the little Island Pagdlagfik they reached land, but they were so exhausted that they fell forward and died.

"They also lived at Itivnarsuk, Back's River, and wept when they were driven away from this good hunting ground.

"The ruins of the strong tent rings at Malerualik, too, were built by the Tunit, who fled from there in the direction of Victoria Land. At Malerualik there was good caribou hunting in the fall. Once, while the men were hunting at breathing holes, the women and children were attacked by the Tunit and killed; the Eskimos therefore went on an avenging expedition to the dwelling places of the Tunit and killed the inhabitants, who tried to hide behind the skin curtains. They brought the boys away with them and, when they became tired, bored an awl into their foreheads until they died. When the Tornit fled from Qingmertoq they left behind them an old woman, whom they buried in a stone grave of big stones although she was not dead; the caribou hunters of the present day still make offerings to her."[5]

Amundsen also recounts Tunit legend from the Netsilik Eskimos: "There was in this tribe an ancient tradition as to a race of giants who had once lived in this land before they themselves came here. These were called 'Tungi,' and were always spoken of with the greatest respect. They were said to have been considerably taller than the Eskimo and much stronger. Bearskin was their clothing. Some ruins of ancient stone huts which we found in the neighborhood of Ogchoktu were supposed by the Eskimo to have been Tungi huts. Old Aleingan, among all his other rigmaroles, would also relate that he had slain the last of the Tungi."[6]

Birket-Smith gives his opinion that there is undoubtedly a historical basis for the Tunit legends.[7] The coastal Caribou Eskimos believe that the now obsolete permanent winter houses within their region were built by the Tun'it, whom they describe as giants who used kayaks and umiaks and caught seals, walruses, and whales. But the Caribou Eskimos of the interior, where there are no such ruins, know nothing of the Tun'it.[8] The Eskimos of the west coast of Hudson Bay have the tradition that "in early times the Tornit, a race of very large people, inhabited the country. They quarrelled with the Eskimo because the latter intruded upon their land. This made the Tornit angry, who broke the ground with their lances and spears, and split the rocks into pieces." "It is said that in the Iglulik country the land still shows how the Tornit tore it up with their harpoon-shafts when they were about to leave, in fear of the Eskimo." The mythological Tornit, giants, are believed to inhabit the interior.[9]

At Cumberland Sound the natives believe that a long time ago their country was inhabited by these people, who were a tall, strange race. "They lived in large stone houses. They did not know how to dress skins. After a caribou had been killed, they would wet its skin and wrap it around their bare bodies in order to dry it. Their beds were

made of skins that had neither been cleaned nor stretched. They kept
seal-meat next to their bare bodies, under their jackets, until it became
strong and rancid. Then they would eat it. When one of their number
had a severe headache, they would drill a hole through his skull, from
which blood and matter oozed out. This operation cured the headache."[10] As described by Bilby[11] the "Tooneet" were a legendary race
of dwarfish people who were pushed farther and farther north and
were finally completely exterminated.

According to tradition among Labrador Eskimos the "Tunnit," a
gigantic race, formerly inhabited the northeastern coast, Hudson
Strait, and southern Baffin Island.

"Ruins of old stone houses and graves which are ascribed to them
by the present Eskimos, are found throughout this entire section, penetrating only slightly, however, into Ungava Bay. Briefly we may say
that there is evidence, archaeological as well as traditional, that the
Tunnit formerly inhabited both sides of Hudson Strait. The oldest
Eskimo of northern Labrador still point out these ruins, and relate
traditions of their having lived together until the Tunnit were finally
exterminated or driven out by the present Eskimos.

"According to an account given by an old Nachvak Eskimo, the
Tunnit in ancient times had two villages in Nachvak Bay. . . . They
had little knowledge of the use of boats. When they wanted boats, they
stole them from the Eskimo. From this thieving of kayaks the original
quarrel is said to have begun.

"For all their bigness and strength, the Tunnit were a stupid slow-
going race (according to the Eskimo version) and fell an easy prey to
the Eskimo, who used to stalk them and hunt them down like game.
They [the Eskimos] did not dare attack them openly, so cut them off,
one by one, by following them, and attacking and killing them when
asleep. Their favorite method was to bore holes in the foreheads of the
Tunnit with an awl (a drill in the Greenland story in Rink). Two
brothers especially distinguished themselves in this warfare, and did
not desist until the last of the Tunnit was exterminated. The Tunnit
built their houses of heavy rocks, which no Eskimo could lift. They
used the rocks for walls, and whale ribs and shoulder blades for the
roof. At the entrance of the house two whale jaw-bones were placed.
Ruins of these houses can still be seen, overgrown with grass, with the
roofs fallen in. They may be distinguished from old Eskimo iglus by
the small, square space they occupy."

The Tunnit did not use the bow and arrow, nor understand the dressing of skins. They were accustomed to carry pieces of meat between
their clothing and their bodies, until it was putrid, when they ate it.
They were powerful men, skilful with the lance, which they sometimes
hurled with the throwing stick. But the weapons they made, while

large, were cruder than the Eskimos'. The Tunnit were gradually exterminated by the Eskimos, until only a scattered few remained here and there in their villages. Legend relates that the last of their race, the giant at Hebron, was outwitted and put to death. He is described as being so heavy that he could not walk on the ice unless it was very thick. For this reason, and also because he was somewhat lazy, he would not hunt seal with the others; but being a powerful bully he took what he wanted of what was caught. Once he expressed the wish to go out with the hunters. Perceiving a good opportunity to get the better of him they allowed him to accompany them on condition that he would do exactly as he was told. Bivouacked in a snow hut, they informed him that it was their custom to be lashed and left alone in the igloo all night. So he let them tie him up, and lay down to sleep. When they returned they fell upon him, and after a struggle killed him.[12] A version of this tale is told in Cumberland Sound[13] but seemingly not in explanation of the final extermination of the Tornit and with less pretense to historical truth.

The Tunit legends are known as far west as the Copper Eskimos from whom Jenness reports the story that "long ago there lived in the ground a people named Tunektan. The women were very beautiful, and the men, although only about four feet high, were exceedingly strong. One day an Eskimo attempted to carry off one of the women, but her husband seized him by the wrists and snapped them. Unable to hunt or help himself in any way the Eskimo starved to death."[14]

Again, according to the Copper Eskimo mythology, it was the Tornrin who built the curious stone structures that can be seen here and there; and one may pick up an occasional arrow point that the Tornrin have dropped. Thus, the Tornrin remind us of the Tunit, who are supposed everywhere to have built the obsolete stone dwellings. And it is significant that in the category of purely spiritual beings, the *tornrait* of the Copper Eskimos, which are thought never to have had a normal life as human beings, are, nevertheless, believed to haunt abandoned stone houses. The Tornrin, on the other hand, are a race that lived in the days when Eskimos were few, and hunted caribou but not seals. Eventually, they were driven underground by the shamans.[15] Again, Stefansson states that it was said concerning a tower trap on Victoria Island that "it was built by the turnrat long before the time of their forebears."[16] The use of the word "turnrat" here, strongly suggesting the Tunit, conveys a significant hint; for in the Mackenzie region the designation *turnñrat* refers to spirits of the *tornait* description without definitely delineating a local counterpart of the legendary Tunit. Farther west, near Bering Strait in Alaska, the word becomes *tun'-ghät*, referring to spirits for which no counterpart can be discovered in mythology. Nowhere in Alaska, indeed, does there seem to be a version of the Tunit legend.[17] Perhaps in the region of Bering Strait we have a last remnant of evidence of the Tunit or Tornit, as a traditional people. There the word for "man" in the special language used only by shamans is tō'rnak.[18] It is quite possible that this language of the shamans represents an archaic dialect no longer retained save for ceremonial and ritual, in a way somewhat analogous to the use of Latin in the Catholic church.[19] If this be so, the word tō'rnak may be a survival from the time when there lived a group of people similarly designated by the Eskimos. We are reminded in this connection of the derivation of the more explicit English word "vandal," from the Latin Vandalus, of Teutonic origin, which was the name of a tribe that lived in the northern part of Germany. The concept of tornait spirits persists in the region southeast of Bering Strait in the tun'-ghät, which are personifications of various objects or of natural forces or the wandering shades of men and animals. Like the tornait elsewhere, they regularly serve the medicine man as his familiar spirits. At Point Barrow, to repeat a striking end-development, the connotation has departed so far from the root word that tuñ-a is used as the name for the spirituous liquor rum; and Tû'n-nyin is a designation applied to white men.

At the opposite extreme of the Eskimo province the Greenland Tornit legends preserve a distant memory of the former Tunit tribe. They ". . . tell the same tales transplanted to a foreign soil and there altered to these new conditions in such a manner that their original form can hardly be distinguished."[20] These myths have acquired another, more imaginary version: the "Tunnersuit" have become an inland people conceived as having more or less fantastic and mysterious qualities.[21] Distant from the probable center of diffusion of the Tunit legends, the Greenlanders quite understandably have come to endow these beings more markedly with supernatural characteristics. Here and there, nevertheless, we recognize affinities with the old Tunit concept. The Polar Eskimos, for instance, describe the Tornit as large beings, who live in the ground, where they have houses (igluling). They are afraid of dogs; and sometimes they hold intercourse with men.[22]

Reviewing our findings, we are aware that the Tunit legends of the central area carry a conviction of reality, and in conjunction with archaeological discoveries they reveal the existence of a former race of people who lived in permanent winter houses and made strong tent rings and stone-set graves. Even one who is inclined to place a minimum of reliance upon legend, as is the author, sees in the present case a strong hint of dependable tradition. Many of the features which are ascribed to the Tunit people are apparently fantastic embellishments; but in others, such as their dress and their unskilful skin curing, we recognize features which are known to have existed among the Sadlermiut who persisted on Southampton Island until 1902.

"There is hardly any doubt that the Tornit are the people who had the Thule culture and there is thus a certain amount of historic foundation for these legends. They continually speak of the Tornit having fled to the north; in this we have, perhaps, a memory of the time when the Arctic Archipelago, and possibly Greenland as well, received their first inhabitants or at any rate a contribution of newly immigrated elements of a race."[23]

Such is the inference from archaeology. What bearing, then, has it upon the evolution of religion? The similarities are too striking between the variants of Tunit and *tornait* and between the two concepts implied in them reasonably to deny the existence of a relationship. It is scarcely conceivable that these two designations could have originated independently and later converged toward similarity. The transitional link words indicate growth from a single root. Likenesses between the two concepts appear in the fact that both the Tunit and the *tornait* are associated with permanent stone houses, and that both are conceived in human form, but with grotesque peculiarities. The preëminent rôle of the *tornait* is that of familiar spirit of the shaman; and a plausible explanation of how they have assumed this function is intimated in the specific instance from the Iglulik group of a certain shaman claiming as his familiar spirit the shade of a member of the former Tunit tribe. A remotely analogous derivation suggests itself even from civilized culture: in spiritualistic practices in America it is especially common for operators to have "Indian" controls, calling the ladies "squaws" and the men "braves," the house a "wigwam," etc.[24]

Signs of relationship between the Tunit and *tornait* such as those stated demand attention regardless of the question of the authenticity of the Tunit legends. Even if we were obliged to regard the legends as having no demonstrable foundation in history we should at least have to admit a connection between them and the *tornait* spirits. It is clear that one of the concepts has influenced the other. Now the archaeological evidence that the Tunit actually lived at one time adds great significance to this relationship. Convinced that the Tunit were a people whom the ancestors of the present Central Eskimos saw exterminated or expelled, we are prompted to inquire what specific relationship should be assigned between them and the *tornait*. We are limited to two hypotheses hinging upon whether the *tornait* concept is older or younger than the Tunit people. Either the word "*tornait*" was used first to designate spirits and later applied in a variant form to a legendary people, or *vice versa*.

The hypothesis that the *tornait* spirits preceded the Tunit is perhaps strengthened by a seeming relationship with similar words used widely in northern Asia to designate various spirits. For, while the Tunit tribe is obviously fairly recent, a broad, circumpolar distribution for words of the *tornait* order would indicate considerable antiquity. With the aim of finding a possible Asiatic origin for the latter through the Alaskan forms *tungra(k)* and *tunera*,[25] Thalbitzer has collected a striking series of similar words.[26] Among these is the term *Tanara*, used by the Yakuts, meaning the "divine protector," also the "protecting spirits of the house," and taken over in modern times as the designation for the Christian heaven and God. Another example is the word *Tärn* of the Ostyaks, which means "spirit of fire." In drawing attention to a number of such cases, Thalbitzer points to the well-known name for the god of thunder of the Icelanders, Thórr, which in Old English is called *Thunar,* in Old High German *Thonar,* and Old Celtic *Tanarus.*

While even these remote forms resemble certain of the Eskimo words pertaining to the present discussion they carry us far afield from the immediate subject. The important point is that, if there is a linguistic relation between the *tun'-ghät* of Alaska and the Asiatic terms applied to various sorts of spirits, it would seem that we must be dealing with a concept that is very old— older, indeed, than that of the Tunit tribe.

But there are certain things which render this hypothesis obviously weak. In view of the individuality of the Eskimo language it seems more reasonable to consider the evidence of an Asiatic derivation for words of the *tun'-ghät* order as being merely founded on coincidence. Furthermore, it is not very likely that the tribal name "Tunit" would be improvised from a designation previously employed to denote a class of spiritual beings. The verisimilitude of the legends of the Central Eskimos, even in minute details, implies a completeness of record which makes it highly improbable that such a fundamental thing as the original name of the tribe should have been superseded by an artificial appellation.

Clearly, the alternative hypothesis is more likely: that "Tunit" or a similar word was first applied as the name for this tribe and that in time the shades of this tribe came to be designated by the variant, divergent forms, *tornait, tornrait, turnñrat, tun'-ghät,* etc.

In perfect accord with the Eskimo concept regarding souls is the hypothesis that after the disappearance of the tribe their shades persisted as awesome spirits. We are merely postulating the same general explanation by which the Eskimos themselves account for the origin of their deities, and the same transition that we witness in the ghost cult, where, however, it is constantly being curtailed by the disappearance of the dead from memory. People are prone to call to mind those who have recently died and to recollect their whims and aversions. Although death has excluded them from direct participation in the doings of men, they are thought still to take a hand in earthly affairs, and to have acquired in the realm of the supernatural a power to cause mysterious evils. With the passage of time the memory of the departed becomes less vivid, until all recollection of personalities is lost. Even in parts of Alaska where the memorial festival is carried out most fully,[27] the Eskimos consider that all duties to the dead terminate, after six or eight years, with the Great Festival. Though the identity of the individual ghost is short-lived, it is, however, reasonable to suppose that the ghosts of a whole tribe might collectively persist longer, being sustained by a rich folklore recounting their exploits on earth. Gone but not forgotten, the Tunit tribe would take their place among the shades of the dead. Originally an enemy people, and subsequently conceived as supernatural beings, they would be endowed with a power for evil more potent than that of the ghosts of friendly ancestors. According to a common version, the Tunit were actually killed off by the forebears of the Eskimos. The enemies of the natural world become vengeful beings in the supernatural sphere. Gradually, they attain the status of spirits in their own right. The *tornait*-cult diverges from its parent concept, which, however, lingers on in tradition; so that, today, the Eskimos no longer consciously associate the two things.

We do not go so far as to suggest that the chief spirit, variously known as Tornarsuk, Toŋraŋazak, etc., who is supposed by some Eskimos to control all the *tornait*, must have originated as an actual individual among the Tunit. A Labrador legend relates, to be sure, how the last survivor of the Tunnit was killed; and another story from the same region depicts Tornga'rsoak as having been a father who lost his beloved children and as a consequence ever since has sent misfortunes upon the living. But here we are blocked by that lack of verification which is generally encountered in deity myths. Opinions are bound to differ as to the probability of the concept of the chief *tornak* having its root in a specific person among the Tunit. Regarding this question as it pertains to religion in general, Wundt states that "the contention, for example, that a Zeus or a Jahve was a human ancestor elevated into a deity is a completely arbitrary supposition, lacking the confirmation of empirical facts."[28] Sumner and Keller, on the other hand, hold more strongly to the belief that deities of the culture-hero type may easily have evolved from actual persons.[29] In the present instance it must be said that even if there were originally no chief *tornak* the idea of one might develop spontaneously.

The question of the possible derivation of this specific spirit from a particular person is decidedly subordinate and is far less certain than the derivation of the whole class of spirits from the tribe. The hypothesis that the *tornait* have evolved from the Tunit presents a case that is in some respects unique among the religions of the world. In the mythology of India, to be sure, we find something similar in the case of spirits known as asuras, for these semihuman creatures seem to have their origin, like the *tornait*, in an aboriginal people who actually lived at one time. In the oldest parts of the Rig-Veda, the word "asura" is applied to a god or spirit; later, in a reverse sense, it signifies an evil spirit or demon, and enemy of the gods. Used collectively as in the Mahābhārata, the term "asuras" applies to a class of spirits, which, although they exhibit a variety of traits, nevertheless constitute a definite group. And it is fairly probable that their existence in mythology has a factual basis in the history of the aboriginal peoples of India. Thus, it is likely that the wars, which, according to mythology, were fought between the asuras and the suras, actually were waged between two early tribes, though they now have become the symbols of the eternal strife between good and evil.[30]

In the case of the *tornait* of the Eskimos, the noteworthy feature is the linguistic and archaeological evidence sustaining the present hypothesis. This evidence leads through a train of reasoning that is both singular and convincing. Viewed broadly, the parallelism of the existing concepts of the Tunit tribe and the *tornait* spirits strongly suggests that the latter has developed out of the former. It implies that the Tunit and the *tornait* are distinct from one another only as the physical, earthly body is distinct from the soul.

In the central region, which seems to have been the former home of the Tunit people, the myths possess the greatest verisimilitude, while the *tornait* in this section are as purely spiritual beings as elsewhere. Hence, it is here that the two concepts stand most distinctly apart from one another. Moving toward the periphery of the dispersal area the Tunit legends have taken on a more fantastic aspect, which obscures the factual basis. Among the Copper Eskimos we find that most of the specific detail has been lost. Here the fabulous people (*tunektan* or *Tornrin*) are endowed with prominent supernatural features and seem very unreal. At the same time they retain just those characteristics which hint of a relationship with the *tornait* spirits. More striking similarity than ever between the names adds emphasis to the fact that both the fabulous people and the spirits are associated with old stone ruins, and makes the two ideas seem more intimately related. But the fabulous people have lost all semblance of reality; and west of there they vanish from mythology.

If our reasoning be correct, this case from the Eskimo religion affords a remarkable illustration of the evolution of a certain form of spiritual concept. It seems to exemplify the transition from ghosts that are identified with earthly counterparts to spirits dissociated from any human antecedents.

NOTES

1. See pp. 425 ff.
2. Rasmussen: 1929, I, 38.
3. Mathiassen: 1927, II, 186.
4. Rasmussen: 1927, 221 f.
5. Mathiassen: 1927, II, 186 ff.
6. Amundsen: 1908, I, 321.
7. Birket-Smith: 1929, I, 155 f.
8. Birket-Smith: 1929, II, 7.
9. Boas: 1907, 315 f.
10. Boas: 1907, 209 f. See also Boas: 1888, 634 ff., 640; Boas: 1887, 38 (Baffin Island). Rink (1875, 469 f.) states that the Labrador Eskimos believe that their ancestors used to live with the *tunneks,* but that the *tunneks* fled from fear of the others, who used to drill holes in their foreheads while yet alive.
11. Bilby: 1923, 64 ff.
12. Hawkes: 1916, 143 ff.
13. Boas: 1907, 292 f.
14. Jenness: 1924a, 84a.
15. Jenness: 1922, 180, 58. Elsewhere the *toynyit,* singular *toynyeq,* are referred to as a semimythological people (Jenness: 1928b, 121).
16. Stefansson: 1914, 297 f.
17. Mathiassen: 1927, II, 189.
18. Boas: 1894, 208.
19. See pp. 435 f.
20. Mathiassen: 1927, II, 190.
21. Mathiassen: 1927, II, 189, citing

Polar Eskimos—Communication by Rasmussen.

West Greenland—Glahn's diaries published in 1924, 222; and Thalbitzer: 1913, 39, who collects everything regarding the Tornit legends but without arriving at a final settlement of the question.

Angmagsalik—Holm: 1924, 26.

See also Kroeber: 1899, 320 (*tornit*) (Polar Eskimos); Birket-Smith: 1924, 221 ff. (West Greenland); Holm: 1888*b*, 52 (East Greenland); and Boas: 1887, 38 (Greenland).

22. Kroeber: 1899, 320.

23. Mathiassen: 1927, II, 189.

24. James: 1910, I, 394.

25. See Nelson: 1899, 428; and Barnum: 1901, 370.

26. Thalbitzer: 1928, 422 f. (footnote).

27. See pp. 279 ff.

28. Wundt: 1916, 361.

29. Sumner and Keller: 1927, II, 946 ff., 970 ff.

30. Fausbøll: 41 f. *Encyclopaedia Britannica:* 1910, XXIV, 168; XXVIII, 1041; and XIV, 395.

CHAPTER XXV

THE ANGAKOK, OR MEDICINE MAN

THE elaborate system of ritual and belief revolves about a central figure, the angakok. He is primitive priest, prophet, and practitioner of magic or "medicine," the intermediary between the living and the dead, between the natural world and the supernatural. He is a strange soul, the Eskimo medicine man, a compelling and absorbing personality, both to his people and to the investigator, who sees in him the embodiment *par excellence* of primitive religious expression.

What powerful force galvanizes him when he is in the throes of an ecstatic trance, and whence come his oracular pronouncements? Is it really a supernatural manifestation, the promptings of his familiar spirit; or is it the natural impulse of self-expression? Call it what you will, when he enters into a state of trance he becomes as a man possessed. At times he seems the very personification of sincerity; but again we must suspect him of acting on the maxim that the end will justify the means, as though hocus-pocus, ventriloquism, and sleight of hand were the legitimate artifices of a spiritual genius. Now we see him transported in his fanatical ardor into an inspired trance; but shortly, in a different mood, he may shamelessly bamboozle whomsoever he can, performing sideshow miracles to gain profit or prestige.

In how far does he honestly believe himself to be a supernatural agent when he holds conference with the spirits, or when he kills a man simply by commanding him to die,[1] or when he asserts his extramarital privilege with barren wives? He certainly employs trickery, knowing full well that delusive magic enhances certain of his operations. But on psychological grounds it must be insisted that the angakok cannot be denounced as an utter charlatan. Beneath his superficial artifices there stirs a tremendous spiritual force that is incontestably real.

Eskimo women are not debarred from the spiritual calling.

In the region of Point Barrow, ". . . in each village there are a number of old women who are treated with the greatest consideration by all, they being credited with wonderful powers of divination, and are consulted in all important affairs."[2] Stefansson asserts[3] that some of the greatest shamans known to him have been women. It is stated that shamans may be of either sex among the Copper Eskimos;[4] among the Pâdlimiut;[5] the Iglulik Eskimos;[6] in eastern Baffin Island;[7] and in West Greenland.[8] Among the Polar Eskimos, too, both men and women are "angakut," but women "angakut" are said rarely to be dangerous.[9] It seems that in Greenland as a whole, men more often perform the rôle.[10] The same was observed to hold among the natives of Bering Strait.[11]

It is probable, indeed, that, speaking generally, among the Eskimos shamanism is predominantly man's function; the women, on the other hand, more commonly practice a sort of sorcery, which may represent an older cult now somewhat eclipsed by the arts of angakoks.[12]

§1. DUTIES AND PREREQUISITES OF THE ANGAKOK

THE angakok takes a hand in all the affairs of life in which the element of luck figures prominently. His practices apply to the many issues that are unpredictable and inexplicable on natural grounds, such as sickness, death, fluctuations of game supply, and the vagaries of the weather. In part, his prestige may be based on superior knowledge: he is likely to be a skilful hunter, wise in the habits of animals, or a practical weather prophet. Such proficiency as is to be gained through experience, valuable to any Eskimo, naturally adds to the reputation of the angakok. It is remarked, for instance, that the Polar Eskimos lay stress upon his qualities as a hunter.[13]

But the Eskimo shaman's imputed powers transcend these mundane abilities; and it is the occult that distinguishes him preeminently as an active factor in the mysteries of life. It is significant, for example, that in East Greenland he is not esteemed for being a skilful hunter, and that he does not play any part in strictly social life.[14] The fact that women frequently rise to prominence in the profession proves that actual competence in the food quest, for instance, is not a prerequisite. The prestige of an angakok rests upon his demonstrated possession of supernatural powers. He takes it upon himself, for example, as one of his most important functions, to control the weather.[15] Unfavorable weather goes hand in hand with hardship and famine; hence, great importance is attached to the shaman's power to avert it. Thus, the very important Sedna ceremony in Baffin Island, performed in the autumn, is designed to drive away the boisterous weather usual at that season and to secure better hunting.[16]

Aside from the technique of the angakok and the traditional wisdom which he employs, singularities of personality sometimes enhance the effect of his art. Certain tendencies toward mental abnormality or the possession of physical peculiarities, favor the prospective angakok. A case is mentioned of an inordinately skinny man who became a powerful angakok at Point Barrow.

"By virtue of his paper thinness he was reckoned a good doctor, for he could get into places where larger men could not go, so that the 'evil spirit' had a hard time to conceal himself from this doctor. He was very successful in driving out the devil from the innermost recesses of the Eskimo heart, soul, and body."[17]

Mental abnormality, either inherent or induced, plays an important part in the character of the angakok. This fact will become evident when we discuss the training for the office and the angakok's most important demonstration, the séance.

The mysteries of life lie beyond intelligence; practical abilities fall short of solving them. Skill and knowledge in everyday matters may come to the assistance of the medicine man, but the strength of his reputation rests upon nothing so obvious. For at best there remains a vast gulf of unfathomable problems whose solution cannot be sought through natural, demonstrable means. Only with the assistance of supernatural agencies can mischance and disaster be averted. The supreme authority of the angakok is based upon his supposed alliance with the spirits. His cultic operations are grounded on the assumption that he is the representative of spiritual forces among men; he must establish the conviction that he can exert a mysterious influence over natural events.

The line of thought that prompts the people to accept their angakok is not critical. It differs from the empirical reasoning which convinces them of the dependability of a skilful hunter, namely, that since his skill has been repeatedly proved by results, he may be relied upon to bring in a good catch. Rather they reason that inasmuch as the angakok professes a knowledge of mysterious things and can perform tricks which in their eyes are miracles, he must possess a widely applicable supernatural control. Scarcely any limit is set, indeed, upon what he may be able to do.

But over and above all reason, critical or uncritical, there is the powerful emotional impress of the inspired trance, upon both the onlookers and the performer himself. Group phenomena of this nature, utterly fantastic and foreign to the usual experiences of everyday life, move people to accept the angakok's capacity for supernatural machinations. They believe what they do not actually see; and they see what is not actually there. When such a combination of circumstances reduces people to a state of stupefied credulity, very little actual demonstration is necessary to establish the angakok as a worker of all manner of miracles. Shamanism therefore defies cold reason.

Thus, the medicine man's practice extends to all phases of life where the element of chance is supposed to operate. His most important functions touch upon the fundamental activities of life. The getting of food is subject to hazard or mischance through bad weather, accident, or scarcity of game; consequently, there is built up around the food quest a complex of rites and observances, which are largely under the domination of the angakok. Sickness and even accident are attributed to spiritual agency; hence, it usually devolves upon the angakok to discover the cause and to effect a recovery. In funeral rites, on the contrary, he does not seem to figure so conspicuously; and the institution of marriage among the Eskimos, being unsanctified by religion, does not require his participation. Wedding formalities are so simple that there is no place for an officiating functionary at all. Thus, the angakok is not called upon to give his sanction to a contract which so capriciously results in either happiness or misery that among some peoples every expedient is employed to secure its success. The Eskimo shaman does, however, sometimes perform specialized functions in connection with marital relations other than the marriage. Among the Koksoagmiut (Ungava District) he often decides the course to be pursued by man and wife in their relations and often decrees that they shall separate.[18]

At Angmagsalik a childless wife will have the angakok supposedly go to the moon to get her a child, and will allow him to sleep with her.[19] Also, in West Greenland, childless wives have intercourse with the angakok.[20] And it is reported that in Baffin Island the childless woman will permit him to cohabit with her, and that no woman in the community is safe from him.[21] It seems that in the Mackenzie region, however, a different measure is adopted by a woman who has no children or wants more than she has. She or her husband pays an "añatkok" to perform a ceremony to make her fruitful, but this is merely an ordinary conjuring performance, such as he would perform to cure disease, bring good weather, or make the hunting season successful.[22]

"There are four main occasions in which the services of an angakok at Ammassalik will be called in request, and when he must summon his spirits to a meeting under the floor of the huts: dearth of sea animals in the sea; snow masses blocking the ways to the hunting-places (on the land or on the fjord-ice); a man's loss of soul (illness); a married woman's barrenness."[23]

The duties of the angakok will become clearer after a discussion, later in this chapter, of the ceremonies and feats that he performs. It will be well first, however, to account more fully for his prestige, his possession of a familiar spirit, and the origin of his supernatural powers.

§2. FAMILIAR SPIRITS

THE underlying ground for the angakok's magical influence over the fortunes of the living is his supposed alliance with one or more familiar spirits. This idea is common to many other peoples of the world, and we find its counterpart even in advanced cultures in the "control" of the spiritualistic medium. The Eskimo shaman is believed to be leagued with a spirit which during his moments of inspiration takes possession of his being.

In various ways he may acquire this guardian spirit or familiar. A practice reported from Alaska indicates the human origin of some familiar spirits: "Along the coast of Norton Sound and the lower Yukon shamans sometimes cause the death of new-born infants and afterwards steal the body and dry it carefully, in order to keep it and have control of its shade as a specially strong influence."[24] But while the familiar spirit is often the soul of a dead person, animals or even inanimate objects can perform the part. In Cumberland Sound, for instance, "the angakok may have for his helpers walrus, bear, man, wolf, raven, owl, or any other animal, even inanimate things like a kayak, which, although not persons, are equal to them. These helping spirits may wander about, but as soon as the angakok needs them, they return to him. They are with him as soon as the wish has been formed."[25] Among the Unalit and adjacent people of Bering Sea coast the shaman is known as the Tun'-gha-lĭk, or "possessor of tun-ghät (wandering shades of men and animals)," and he controls these spirits and impersonates them by assuming the masks which represent them.[26]

The Eskimo shaman as a rule possesses several helping spirits, but the Labrador angakok is an exception in seeming not to acquire more than one *to'rngak*.[27] "The ordinary Mackenzie River shaman," writes Stefansson,[28] "has about a dozen familiar spirits, any one of which will do his bidding." Again, in West Greenland, it is stated that the angakok may have a number of spirits (*tornât*), each of which is the *inua* of some animal or object or the soul of a dead person.[29]

In East Greenland a helping spirit is called *taarteq* or *târtâ*, which may be translated "its human being," from *tâq*, meaning "human being."[30] As Thalbitzer explains it, the word *taartat* ". . . seems to mean 'their (the angakkut's) appurtenant shadows or substitutes' i.e. the souls of the spirits as substitutes of the angakkut when they are absent (i.e. in trance, their souls travelling in the world beyond)."[31] These *taartat* are nature spirits, sometimes the helping spirits of dead angakoks or animal souls which have changed into "men." Most frequently they are creatures which live unnoticed in the neighborhood of the settlements under the earth, under the beach rocks, or inland. Only the angakoks can see them and speak to them, using the sacred language of the spirits. A full-fledged angakok has a whole host of familiars: five, ten, fifteen, or more.[32]

"These attendant spirits have peculiar names and shadows, houses and hunting implements. . . . They all belong to the 'other world' (asia), which is only visible to the angakoks. Otherwise they have their being in the same visible world as men—the Eskimo do not see anything self-contradictory in this—and they belong to three kinds of people; each of which have their own special dwelling places and peculiarities: *Timerseet,* who live in the interior of the country, *Eajuätsaat* (= *Taarajuätsaat*), 'semi-men' who live under the ground close to men's huts, and *Innertiwin,* 'the fire-people,' who live on the beach under the rocks of the coast, where the water is shallow. The latter are said to have houses with windows and they can, as distinct from the others, make long journeys in umiaks over to the west coast of Greenland where they buy metal and European clothes. *Timerseet* follow the course of the rivers out to sea when they want to hunt seal. All these beings have the language of men but speak it more or less awry, for instance with distorted mouths, or lispingly, or merely indistinctly on account of obsolete or foreign words.

"This last feature applies also to the beings which come from the sea to serve the angakok during the sacred rites. One of these is called Aperqit 'the consulted one, the oracle,' which sits down by the edge of the sea below the hut and helps the angakok who has been summoned to cure the disease. . . .

"Aperqit is only an intermediary, a messenger between Toornartik and the heathen priest. From the hut the angakok addresses his questions to Aperqit, the attendant spirit who listens at the water's edge and thence passes on the questions out to the sea."[33]

The Greenlanders of both the east and west coasts entertain the notion of certain especially important familiar spirits that may be enlisted as aids by any angakok, unlike the minor ones, which are purely personal helpers. Thus, in Angmagsalik every angakok has his Tornarsuk and Aperketek, who act as his spirits.[34] The first of these, perhaps more properly called Tornartik in East Greenland, escorts the shaman on his magical journey through the depths of the sea or to the underworld and helps him come into alliance with the mighty Woman of the Sea.[35] On the west coast, Tornarsuk rules over the *tornaks* as their master,[36] being a "special" or "particular" *tornak,* as his name implies. Endowed with supernatural intelligence, he is regarded as a very important oracle.[37]

The ministering spirits of the angakok among the Polar Eskimos are called *tornarssuit* and are spoken of as invisible beings attached to localities or objects and exercising powers for evil. Also the word "tornguang" is applied to an angakok's guardian spirit, to which are ascribed directly or indirectly all his powers.[38] Among the Iglulik Eskimos guardian spirits, which are sometimes the spirits of animals, sometimes of men, are called $t\mathfrak{z}^{\cdot r}\eta^r Aq$, plural $t\mathfrak{z}^{\cdot r}\eta^r \ddot{a}t$, or $apErf Aq$, plural $apErf\ddot{a}t$, the latter signifying "one that exists to be questioned," an answering spirit.[39]

In the region of Coronation Gulf "a shaman's powers are due to the control he presumably exercises over certain spirits, which are either the spirits (the shades?) of certain animals or the shades of the Eskimo dead. One or two shamans were reputed to control also certain white men, but whether it was their shades or their living powers was never stated; in any case they were remote enough to count as dead. The familiar spirit is called either *tornrak* or *tupilek,* usually the former; the word *keyugak,* which is the usual term in the Mackenzie delta, seems to be unknown, and even *tupilek* may be a borrowed word. . . . Control over any familiar may be obtained by purchase. . . . This statement, however, is only partly true, for all that the owner can impart is his good-will, and a knowledge of how to approach and summon the particular spirit that he has sold; the rest depends on the spirit itself."[40] The angakok of the Mackenzie Delta, similarly, can sell one of his several familiars; and one man paid the equivalent of $200 or $150 for one.[41]

The manner in which the familiar spirit appears to enter the body of the shaman is vividly described by Jenness as he witnessed it in the Colville Hills (Victoria Island). A séance was held to determine the advisability of his traveling to Lake Tahiryuak. Higilak, the female angakok, began by delivering a long speech, presenting the whole issue.

Suddenly, she uttered cries of pain and buried her face in her hands. Dead silence ensued for a few minutes, broken only by an occasional muttered remark from one in the audience. Presently, the angakok began to howl and growl like a wolf, then as suddenly she ceased and raised her head, when, behold, two canine teeth, evidently a wolf's, were protruding one from each corner of her mouth. She leaned over to Avranna and pretended to gnaw his head, then began to utter broken remarks which her audience caught up and discussed, though very little of them could be interpreted. (Now and again she had to put her hand to her mouth to keep the teeth from falling out.) After about a quarter of an hour she suddenly broke out again into cries of pain and once more concealed her face. Evidently, she slipped the teeth into her boot; for a moment later her face reappeared without them. At this moment the wolf's spirit inside her body gave answer to the question at issue. A few broken words came from her, uttered in a feeble falsetto voice almost inaudible. In about two minutes more it was all over, and Higilak, after a few more cries of pain (the familiar was leaving her), followed by two or three gasps, resumed her normal bearing. In speaking of this séance sometime afterward the natives stated as an incontestable fact that Higilak had been transformed into a wolf.[42]

§3. PREPARATION OF THE ANGAKOK

BOTH inherent proclivity and prescribed training are prerequisites to the office of angakok. Physical or mental abnormality is accepted as a sign that one is suited to the calling; and strange dreams or visions may prompt one to aspire to it. There is a current belief that certain persons are born with supernatural abilities; generally, however, some strange experience signalizes the acquisition of a familiar spirit. And over and above all these things, instruction from past masters is necessary. The Eskimos regard such training as of minor importance, however, the essential factor being not any earth-taught art, but the mysterious endowment of a supernatural gift.

At Smith Sound, for instance, where there is generally an angakok in every family,[43] or at least one in every village,[44] the Eskimos say that persons are born *angakut*. Here the aspirant goes alone at night to a cavernous cliff and walks straight toward it in the dark. If he is predestined to become an angakok he will walk into a hole or cave in the hill; if not, he will strike the face of the cliff. Upon his entering the cavern it closes after him; and when it reopens he must go out, else he will be shut in forever. He is now an angakok, but he has not yet learned to use his powers. To this end he must go to another place, at the edge of the permanent ice cap. Here abides the spirit Torngaxssung, the oldest of the tornguang, who will instruct him in his mysterious art.[45] In this account we have the idea of inherent supernatural endowment, predestined appointment, and guidance from a powerful tutelary spirit.

The natives seem reluctant to explain just how the novice acquires the technique of his office, which, of course, is taught him by an older magician. On the Diomede Islands the art was frequently passed on from father to son, but not always.[46] In any case the people tend to overlook the routine instruction, preferring to regard the power as acquired in a purely supernatural manner. This attitude applies even to the most obviously artificial aspects of the calling. One gets the impression that the natives are eager to convince anybody in the least degree skeptical that all the performances of the angakok are part and parcel of the same supernatural gift, even when they themselves must realize that he employs a goodly amount of pure trickery. It is the tenacity of the zealot to his ideal that causes the Eskimo to hold fast to the most absurd features of his faith, seeming to fear lest an incredulous person will throw out the baby with the bath. No line of demarcation exists here between miracle and magic.

In the preparatory training of the angakok it is commonly supposed that the novice at some time quits his earthly life and is miraculously "reborn."

In Labrador, for instance, the aspirant retires to a lonely place for a period of prayer and fasting; whereupon the Great Spirit, Tornga'rsoak, appears in the form of a great white bear and devours him limb by limb. Other tornait figure in the proceedings in different but no less terrible forms. Having passed through the ordeal, the novice possesses a portion of his power and the promise of future assistance from his familiar spirit. Full power and knowledge of the spirit world are attained only after long and arduous apprenticeship. The beginner customarily attaches himself to an older angakok for several years.[47]

Likewise, in West Greenland, the familiar spirit is acquired in solitude. One method is for the novice to sit on a great stone, the embodiment of Torngarsuk, and to tell this spirit his wish. Thereupon the spirit appears and the neophyte dies and remains dead for three days. He then comes to life and gets his torngak.[48] Also, in East Greenland, the neophyte is supposed to die and then come back to life. In some solitary spot he remains for three consecutive days rubbing constantly on a rock with a small stone. The lonely monotony at length induces an exalted state that is thought to signalize possession by a spirit. This probational practice is repeated for three or four years, and the novitiate may last even as long as ten years. Moreover, the neophyte must observe certain taboos on foods; and he must learn a special language.[49] On the west coast of Hudson Bay, "A young angakok must not whip his dogs for a whole year. . . . He must not drink out of a cup that anyone else has used."[50] Again, it is reported that among the Iglulik Eskimos for one year after men and women become shamans they must observe taboos against eating certain foods and against sewing.[51] All these observances and experiences are conducive to the notion that the angakok is unlike other persons, a strange individual, in league with the spirits and therefore not subject to earthly laws. If the East Greenland neophyte falls ill he cannot work as an angakok in the future.[52]

Every angakok in East Greenland ". . . has, as a rule, had several paid teachers and has received instruction in different branches. . . . At the early age of seven or eight the future angakok begins to receive instruction from an older angakok, who is willing and eager to confide his secret knowledge to him. He teaches him first how he is to go in perfect secrecy and fetch a special kind of sea-weed from the beach when the tide is low, and wash himself with it over his whole body; how then he is to go into the depths of the land among the high mountains to the place where he has selected his grindstone, a large stone with a flat upper surface, often found lying near a lake, a river, a high declivity or a cave. I have seen one lying at the end of an old Eskimo grave. Proceeding according to fixed rules the novice seeks for a little stone to be used for grinding against the flat surface of the larger one. Not seldom a little crustacean from the sea or river is laid between the two stones which are rubbed together.

"There sits the disciple hour after hour rubbing the little stone in a circle against the large one, in anxious expectation of what is to appear. According to the tradition quite a definite event is to take place. The bear of the lake will rise up, go towards him and eat him, whereby he 'dies' i.e. loses his consciousness. It will spit him out again and then leave him. After the lapse of an hour he returns to consciousness, his skeleton clothes itself in flesh again, and his garments come rushing up to him one by one until at last he emerges fully dressed. Every summer of this and the following years he keeps on rubbing the stone and thereby on different occasions acquires his attendant spirits, who are said to be his very own, and whose names he alone knows, and he alone may use. During this time he is rubbing the stone, he must fast i.e. he may not eat the entrails of animals. Similarly he may not work in metals or engage in any noisy occupation whatsoever.

"It should be observed, that it is not the disciple himself who announces himself as a candidate for discipleship; it is the older angakok who exhorts the young one, the boy, whom he thinks well adapted for initiation in the religious mysteries, to receive training, in order that a knowledge of the highest powers in existence may be preserved for the coming generation. . . .

"During the whole course of his discipleship the angakok novice carefully conceals the fact, that he is receiving instruction, rubbing the stone and having meetings with his spirits. But when—after a novitiate of from five to ten years—he finally grows into a fullfledged angakok, his house-mates begin to have an inkling about it and to pass their comments on the fact. One fine evening he at last goes and proclaims himself to the world: angakittuppoa, 'I am an angakok,' and admonishes the others to extinguish the lamps, in order that he may for the first time give them proof of his prowess."[53]

Supernatural powers are sometimes conveyed by a laying on of hands: thus, on the west coast of Hudson Bay, an old angakok transmits power to another person by putting his hands upon the other's head. Another way was for the aspirant to place a worm on his forearm and allow it to eat the flesh; when the wound healed over, the person would have become a great angakok.[54]

Among the Iglulik Eskimos the main period of tutelage for an angakok is only about five days,[55] but the training entails further study and meditation. The personal account of one of these natives, explaining how he became an angakok, shows that the calling requires more than the mere learning of a few set formulas from others. This angakok, Aua by name, living in the vicinity of Lyon Inlet, asserted that everything was made ready for him to be an angakok, even before he was born; and though he tried to become one through the help of others, he did not succeed in this way. He visited many famous shamans and gave them great gifts which they at once gave away to others; for if they had kept the things for themselves they or their children would have died. This they believed because Aua himself had been threatened from birth. Indeed, he had been born dead, according to his own statement, but had been predestined to live and so came to life. Despairing of instruction from other shamans, he sought solitude, "and here," he relates, "I soon became very melancholy. I would sometimes fall to weeping, and feel unhappy without knowing why. Then for no reason, all would suddenly be changed, and I felt a great, inexplicable joy, a joy so powerful that I could not restrain it, but had to break into song, a mighty song, with only room for one word: joy, joy! And I had to use the full strength of my voice. And then in the midst of such a fit of mysterious and overwhelming delight I became a shaman, not knowing myself how it came about. But I was a shaman. I could see and hear in a totally different way. I had gained my *qaumanEq*, my enlightenment, the shaman-light of brain and body, and this in such a manner that it was not only I who could see through the darkness of life, but the same light also shone out from me, imperceptible to human beings, but visible to all the spirits of earth and sky and sea, and these now came to me to become my helping spirits.

"My first helping spirit was my namesake, a little *aua*. . . . An *aua* is a little spirit, a woman, that lives down by the sea shore. . . . There are many of these shore spirits. . . . My second helping spirit was a shark. One day when I was out in my kayak, it came swimming up to me, lay alongside quite silently and whispered my name. . . . These two, the shore spirit and the shark, were my principal helpers, and they could aid me in everything I wished."[56]

Another shaman, Igjugarjuk, also underwent interesting experiences while becoming an angakok.[57] He is a member of the Pâdlimiut, inland Eskimos of the Barren Grounds. As a young man he was constantly visited by dreams which he could not understand, in which strange beings spoke to him. It became evident to all that he was destined to become an angakok. An old man was appointed his instructor, and in the depth of winter, when the cold was most severe, he was carried far away on a small sledge and put in a tiny snow hut, with barely room for him to sit cross-legged. No food or drink was given him. He was exhorted to think only of the Great Spirit and of the helping spirit that should presently appear. Thus, he was left to his meditations. After five days his instructor brought him a drink of lukewarm water and departed. He fasted then for fifteen days, after which he was given another drink of water and a very small piece of meat, which had to last him a further ten days. During all that time he thought only of the Great Spirit. Toward the end of the thirty days there came to him a helping spirit in the shape of a woman. She came while he was asleep and seemed to hover in the air above him. After that he dreamed no more of her, but she became his helping spirit. He declared that the strain of those thirty days of cold and fasting was so severe that he "sometimes died a little." At the end of this period his instructor came and fetched him home. But for five months thereafter he was kept on the strictest diet and was required to abstain from all intercourse with women. The fasting was then repeated; for such fasts at frequent intervals are the best means of attaining to the knowledge of hidden things. As a matter of fact the mortification of the flesh is limited only by how much the subject is willing to suffer and how anxious he is to learn.

This Igjugarjuk later initiated his sister-in-law in a severe manner. She was hung up to some tent poles planted in the snow and left there for five days. It was midwinter, with intense cold and frequent blizzards, but she did not feel the cold, for the spirit protected her. At the end of the five days she was taken down and her brother-in-law shot her with a gun loaded with real powder but with a stone instead of a leaden bullet, in order that she might retain connection with the earth. She fell to the ground unconscious. On the following morning, just as her initiator was about to bring her to life again, she awakened from the swoon unaided.

A third aspirant in this group was subjected to ordeal by water. He was lashed to a long pole and thrust down through a hole in the ice, in such a manner that he actually stood on the bottom of the lake with his head under water. For five days he was left in this position, and when they hauled him up his clothes showed no sign of having been in the water at all. Having thus overcome death he became a great wizard. No explanation is given for this miracle.

Sometimes the instructor, having initiated a novice into the mysteries of the angakok's art and having helped him to obtain a familiar spirit, receives recompense for his service. At Iglulik it was customary for the beginner to give a tent pole to his instructor, wood being scarce in these regions. A gull's wing was attached to the pole, symbolic of the novice's wish to learn to fly.[58] Other instances will be recalled in which a familiar spirit is actually bought, sometimes for a very high price.[59]

A certain angakok of East Greenland ". . . was so young when he underwent his first training that he had nothing to pay his first teacher with. On the other hand he paid all his later teachers, partly with bear and seal skins, partly with implements. One of them received from him a sledge and a dog. When the angakok *Takiwnalikitseq* had taught him iliseetsoq lore (iliseenilisaat), i.e. such magic means by the aid of which the attempts of the enemy can be warded off, or even pain or disaster brought upon them as a vengeance, he gave him in payment a large fine bearskin, a sealing bladder and a skin thong in return for the wisdom imparted to him."[60]

§4. PRACTICE OF THE ANGAKOK

Fees for Services

THE angakok does not undergo the trials of his preparation simply for the spiritual satisfaction of approaching closer than ordinary mortals to the mysteries of the supernatural. It is to his economic advantage to learn the art of curing disease and bestowing good luck in hunting. The angakok's specialized ability commands a price. Often it is not the medicine man himself, however, but his helping spirit that is rewarded.

Stefansson writes that if the shaman stipulates that a pair of mittens be given for curing a sick person, the mittens may be made of miniature size, and when they are put under the sick person's bedding or hung over his bed or given to the shaman, they are supposed to benefit the angakok's familiar. "Recompense is made to the spirit in another way also: the añatkok, representing the spirit, has as a bed partner for one or more nights a relative of the sick person or the sick person herself after she has been cured. Beside this payment, which is considered to be made directly to the spirit, there was a far more substantial fee paid the shaman himself. For one performance this often went as high as an umiak with equipment. It was well known that unless one paid the shaman well he could not get cured. The Alaskans had the same belief."[61] Holm reports from East Greenland: "When an angakok has performed his arts in order to heal a sick person, an indispensable condition for the success of the cure is that it shall be paid for. It is the *tartok,* however, and not the angakok that is paid for its trouble. . . . The payment is, of course, proportioned to the circumstances of the sick person."[62] The Iglulik Eskimo medicine man very strictly exacts his reward whether good or ill betide the patient.[63] Similarly, Jenness writes with reference to the Copper Eskimos that if someone is ill and a shaman is called in, he must be paid for his services whether he be successful or not.[64] In southeastern Baffin Island the angakok ". . . before proceeding to his peculiar work, demands payment for his services, stating his price, usually some article to which he has taken a liking. Whatever he demands must be given at once, otherwise the expected good results of the ministering would not follow." The Eskimos ". . . considered that in proportion to the value of what they give for the angako's services, so are the benefits conferred upon the sick."[65] Bilby writes that the angakok ". . . earns a fat livelihood. He exacts payment, of course,—a dog, a sled, a skin, a length of line, and the favors of the patient's wife. . . ."[66]

The Diomede *angutkok* is suspected even of causing a person to become sick in order that he can exact his fee. When he needs worldly goods or desires some particular object he resorts to this evil magic. The instrument of his sorcery is an ivory rod, spindle-shaped and about four inches long. He informs this fetish that he wants tobacco, skins, etc., and flings it out into the night. Soon, if the charm works, some one becomes sick. To cure the patient, the *angutkok* extracts the evil spirit by sucking the rod of ivory out of the inflicted part. For thus restoring health he demands payment in the articles specified.[67]

Aside from his actual services, it will be recalled that he sets a price, sometimes very high, upon the secret magic formulas which he possesses, and also upon his familiar spirit. For his benefits to the community, however, as distinct from private services, he receives no reward directly. Causing good weather, for instance, or summoning the game animals to the hunting sites, does not bring any specific recompense from the community. The shamans of the Copper Eskimos, as Jenness expresses it, ". . . resemble doctors rather than priests, doctors who give their services free in any public cause, but are paid for treating private individuals. Thus the shaman receives no reward when he placates the spirits that cause the blizzard, or induces Kannakapfaluk to send the Eskimos plenty of seals."[68] Possibly, such services accrue to the angakok's advantage indirectly through added prestige in society. Preferential rights are doubtless accorded him simply out of respect for his powers.

Angakok's Language

POSSESSED of a familiar spirit and a knowledge of mysterious rites and spoken charms, the angakok personifies the supernatural; he is the embodiment of unknowable powers. His inspired trance, adept voice control, and, in some instances, grotesque masks, contribute to the awesomeness of his performances. These adjuncts are, of course, common to shamanistic art in many parts of the world. Their effectiveness in creating an atmosphere of mystery is well known. The angakok employs, furthermore, a strange dialect in his incantations, not spoken in everyday life. This quaint and peculiar tongue in which he appropriately speaks when confabulating with the spirits enhances his repute and distinguishes him more certainly as a person who transcends earthly existence and belongs to the supernatural sphere.

An angakok of East Greenland declared that no special teaching was necessary in order to learn the sacred or mystic language.

"As, however, it is identical for all angakoks and even, as it seems, more or less the same for angakoks from all quarters, it must be a really stereotyped language preserved through many centuries. Presumably every angakok learns a great part of it by attending the angakoks' colloquies with their spirits, when they conjure them up in their huts; those that are training to become angakoks impress these words on their memory with particular care. The words are not sheer abracadabra, but obsolete or metaphorically used Eskimo words, a kind of inherited art language, which contributes in a high degree to the solemn and mystical character of the spiritual gathering. The religious

forms or expressions themselves are made no secret of: only the way
in which the disciple receives his training is wrapped in mystery."[69]

Here in East Greenland the angakok is supposed to learn this jargon from supernatural creatures known as Inersuaks.[70]

Among the Polar Eskimos the "angakoq language" which the shaman uses in ceremonies consists of fifty or a hundred metaphorical, descriptive, obsolete, or mutilated terms. There is no secret connected
with them; sometimes they must be used by people who are not shamans, as, for example, by mourners.[71]

The Copper Eskimo angakok employs, besides archaic expressions,
semipoetical circumlocutions, sometimes difficult to understand. A seal,
for example, may be referred to as "the thing that has blubber."[72]

Boas remarks that a great number of the words of the angakok's language ". . . have been lost from common usage in the
lapse of time. These archaic words are very interesting from a
linguistic point of view. Indeed, some are found [in the language
of the Central Eskimo angakok] which are still in use in Greenland, though lost in other dialects, and others are only used in
Alaska."[73] The same authority comments on the ceremonial language at Port Clarence, Alaska: "It is worth remarking that,
generally speaking, the angakok word is found in the dialects of
Greenland and Labrador, while the ordinary word may be unknown in these countries. This corroborates the view that the
angakok word represents an older form of speech."[74]

This is reasonable in view of the conservatism shown toward
sacred things, for the retention of obsolete phraseology in ritual is
found in many other parts of the world. The Semites in ancient
times, for instance, when they moved into the land of the Sumerians, adopted and retained the Sumerian as a sacred language,
for which, as time went on, they were compelled to compile dictionaries.[75] Christian liturgy also presents examples of this in the
retention of archaic inflection, and more strikingly in the employment of Latin in the Roman Catholic church.

The Eskimo angakok will even make shift to speak to the spirits
in a foreign tongue, in the supposition that foreign spirits possess
greater virtue. Hawkes once heard an Alaskan shaman, for instance, whose *tungak* was supposed to be talking a dialect of
Asiatic Eskimo; but an Eskimo friend in the audience who came
from that district, afterward stated that the spirit talked it very
badly.[76]

Angakok's Manifestations

ONLY the most characteristic acts of the angakok will here be discussed, otherwise we should unfairly rob other topics in religion of what belongs to them. Scattered references already made supplement the present description of this conspicuous and interesting phase of the primitive cult.

The angakok generally knows a few tricks of magic, involving very elementary sleight of hand; and when he performs these under proper circumstances they always enhance the psychic effect. But purely illusory hocus-pocus in itself does not establish him in his community as a mystery man. If he performs his prestidigitation without pretense of supernatural power, the tricks are apt to lose their religious import in the eyes of the people. The working of mechanical magic could never win for the angakok deep respect as a spiritual genius His fame rests rather upon his inspired trance, which very forcibly convinces his audience that he is under the control of a powerful spirit. This psychical exhibition, at least in part genuinely induced, is contagious inasmuch as the awestruck natives are thrown into a similar state of ecstasy; and they unite in the conviction that the angakok is, indeed, able to summon the spirits into their very midst and to compel them to accomplish his own mysterious purposes. His art as a magician is but accessory to his acknowledged alliance with the spirits. We must not be too critical, therefore, lest perceiving nothing but palpable sham in the magic art of the angakok we fail to grasp the more important phase of his operations.

A widely practiced and conspicuous feat of the Eskimo shaman is his trick of being tied up, and then making a "spirit flight" to the supernatural regions. This feat is performed on the Diomede Islands as follows: the angakok is bound with strong rawhide lines, with his neck secured to his knees and his hands lashed behind his back, wrists tied to elbows. A pair of bearskin pants as wings for him to fly with are hung from the ceiling, but out of his reach. Then the seal-oil lamps are all extinguished. Soon there is a flapping noise as of wings, and a swishing and whirring while the audience feel the rush of wind pass their faces. The angakok's voice seems to soar off into distant space; and he holds conference with the spirits. Upon his return to earth the lamps are relighted and the angakok is seen doubled up on the floor and bound in his original position *but with the bearskin pants on his arms and his arms still bound behind his back.*[77]

With slight variations this feat is performed by angakoks in almost all groups of Eskimos. Far distant from Bering Strait essentially the same trick is performed in East Greenland. The angakok's ". . . arms are tightly bound behind his back, being lashed from the hands to the elbows with a long thong which is tied in knots. It is a part of his art to free his hands in the dark and afterwards, before the lamps are lit, to stick them back again in the still fastened thongs. The angakok is supposed to fly through the air (towards the interior of the country) in his doubled-up posture with the hands bound behind him."[78]

In Hamilton Inlet, Labrador, during the initiation ceremony for an angakok, a similar rite was performed. They took the man and doubled him up with his knees to his chin and bound him as if about to kill him. Thereupon they put out the lights and sang an ancient song. Then the man would groan, and as he groaned the bonds would be loosened, as the natives believed, by a spirit, though in reality accomplices untied him. The seal lines used in tying would whip around the room. This ceremony of being unloosed by the spirit made the neophyte an angakok.[79]

Time was when the Polar Eskimos' angakoks had the power to fly up to heaven or down to the bottom of the sea; but this art is now dead.[80]

At Cumberland Sound the feat is performed as follows: The angakok, dressed in trousers and shirt, seats himself on a piece of skin. His assistants take a thong of white-whale or ground-seal hide and fasten the angakok's hands behind his back. His neck is pulled down toward his legs with another piece of thong so that he is unable to move. Then his jacket is hung over his head. As soon as he is covered his head begins to shake, and continues to do so all through the performance. He calls upon his familiar spirits, which are believed to be the souls of living persons whom he can command, and they undo the knots of the thongs. It is supposed that while the angakok is tied up his soul journeys to the land of the souls above. As soon as his soul returns, the thongs are found to be unfastened. This performance is held only during the winter months, at full moon.[81]

As recounted by an angakok just north of Lyon Inlet, ". . . the man who travels to the Land of Day must be bound before he is laid down behind the curtain; his hands must be fastened behind his back, and his head lashed firmly to his knees; he also must wear only breeches, leaving legs and the upper part of his body naked.[82] When this is done, the men who have bound him must take an ember from the lamp on the point of a knife, and pass it over his head, drawing rings in the air, and say: '. . . Let him who is now going a-visiting be fetched away.' . . . Up in the land of Day, the thong with which the shaman was bound falls away of itself, and now the dead ones, who are always in high spirits, begin playing ball with it."[83]

At Cape Vancouver, Alaska, the Bladder Festival is the occasion for a trick in which the shaman is tied under the floor of the ceremonial chamber, in the exit passage, with a long line leading into the room. He is supposed to visit the land of the seal spirits, and as he travels to this distant realm the long line is pulled out of the ceremonial room (by an accomplice) for a length of ten or fifteen yards, as though no more slack than that were necessary for the wizard to reach his destination.[84]

Curiously, among the Copper Eskimos Jenness never saw or heard of the so-called spirit flights for which the shaman is bound with thongs.[85] These natives perform a ceremony, however, wherein the angakok, instead of journeying to the land of seal spirits, supposedly slips a noose around the wrists of the guardian deity of the seals and hauls her up until her head is just below the level of the floor.[86]

As already mentioned, a common feature of the training through which a person goes to become an angakok is an apparent dying and coming back to life. A full-fledged angakok also performs feats in which he deceives his fellows into believing that he is killed and then returns to life. In connection with Sedna ceremonies on Baffin Island a variant of this trick has already been described, wherein the angakok is harpooned in the chest and dragged around, apparently bleeding profusely.[87] In the more complete example, however, the sorcerer is supposed actually to die. The miraculous return to life, of course, suggests the acquisition of a new and more powerful soul, enhancing the atmosphere of mystery surrounding the medicine man.

On Diomede Island the angakok will stick a long knife into the side of his abdomen. Blood spurts out and blood also issues from his mouth, pouring down his neck. The spectacle is highly realistic; but here as elsewhere the trick lies in small bladders filled with blood concealed about the person.[88] A Diomede Islander recounted to the author one of these miraculous suicides in which a rifle was used instead of a knife. Old Took'tok, an angakok famed for his powers, returned from a hunting trip with his mind made up that he would be better off dead. So he took his gun and fired it directly at his heart. Blood spattered out all over his parka. All his strength ebbed from his body and he gradually slumped to the floor, an inert mass. After ten minutes, however, slight twitchings indicated the return of life, and in a short time he was on his feet again. There was a hole through his parka over his heart and another in the back of the jacket; but the skin of his chest showed only powder marks to indicate where the discharge had struck him. On another occasion this same angakok of Diomede Islands had himself hanged. Three men and one woman tied a noose around his neck and hoisted him to the roof beams. For ten minutes he emitted gruntings and barkings like a walrus till, finally, his strangled gasps died away and he became limp. The Eskimos cut the body down and it dropped to the floor like a dead weight, leaving the parka caught at the ceiling. After lying there for about an hour his body became quite cold. But the Eskimos could interpret this only as a temporary departure of the life-giving spirit, for soon the miraculous man was seized with awful convulsions, as though some powerful spirit had taken possession of him. He danced and capered about with wild, waving gesticulations of his arms; and it was known that a new vital force, a new soul, had entered his body.

Just south of the mouth of the Yukon another feat of the same order is described. The shaman is placed in a waist-high funeral pyre, with a mask concealing that portion of his body which would project above the crib of wood. The spectators believe that the shaman remains behind the mask, but, of course, he does not. Nevertheless, at Norton Sound there is a grave of a shaman who failed in this trick. One who successfully returns to life after the burning is believed to be able to assume, or to cast off, any bodily form at will.[89]

In a less startling trick commonly performed in the region of Bering Sea, a bead is broken up and then returned to its original form.[90] On Little Diomede Island this feat of prestidigitation was performed as part of a curing ceremony. A girl had a severe pain; so the medicine man took the finest bead from her necklace and put it into a glove. Before the eyes of the distressed girl, who may have been more concerned about her bead than her bodily complaint, he pounded the bead up and shook the powder out of the door. Then, with the empty glove, he slapped the aching spot and in the end produced from inside the glove the restored bead. Miraculously, all the girl's pain vanished.[91]

Another minor trick of the Diomede angakok is the cutting in two of a rawhide line, apparently by using the edge of the open hand as a knife, and then joining the severed ends by chewing them together. Also, the conjuror will wrap a long whetstone in skin and then work it between his hands until it becomes soft like meat, but of such consistency that when wrapped about a person's wrist it seems to clutch the member tightly. Another stunt is to whirl a sharp knife on the end of a line in a room filled with people, who must not open their eyes under punishment of being slapped across the face with a glove.[92]

A séance in which Sir Hubert Wilkins participated discloses the angakok in his characteristic rôle. It was held near Bernard Harbor, Dolphin and Union Strait, with the purpose of increasing the catch of fish. Very few fish had been secured for some days. The natives had waited all day and there was not a sign of any fish making the run. About nine o'clock they decided to hold a séance. A shaman of great repute, named Iglulik, had arrived that evening. Wilkins was asked to help in the séance and was given a seat beside the shaman. For about thirty minutes there was conversation, mostly about fishing but not pertinent to the immediate issue. At length the angakok broke into a kind of singsong, and the audience whispered to each other or nodded across the tent. At intervals the shaman would address someone in the crowd in his unintelligible jargon. When the audience were thoroughly puzzled by his several fruitless attempts to communicate, the old man gave a shout and clapped his hands to his forehead. Shutting his eyes, he started swaying backward and forward. After about an hour of the monotonous singsong he shouted and uttered some comprehensible sounds, and Mr. Wilkins was asked to hold on to his hand. While he was held thus and by the shoulder on the other side, a woman gave him a smart tap on the left side of the head with a lump of copper. Thereupon he took away his hand from his forehead and opened his eyes. Huge drops of perspiration stood out all over his face and his eyes were wild and bloodshot. Now released, he kept up his backward and forward swaying motion, with renewed vigor. He was talking intelligible language but so fast that most of the people in the audience could not understand him. Taking no notice of their shouted questions he soon began to point to one or another of the audience and, fluttering his fingers to indicate that the fish were swarming in the river, would prophesy that such and such a person would catch a number of fish. For about half an hour he kept this up, pointing mostly to two or three persons who were, incidentally, always successful in the contests when there were any fish to be caught. The whole performance had now lasted about three hours, and during that time no one had been keeping a lookout at the creek for fish, except perhaps the children who had been playing about outside. Finally, when the angakok's utterances from his still frothing mouth became less frequent and his movements indicated a return to normality, the old woman gave him a smart tap on the right side of the head with a copper spearhead, and he looked around in a dazed sort of way as if he had just come out of a hypnotic trance. Instantly, the men bolted toward the creek, not stopping to prepare in the ordinary way for fishing. It was apparent at first sight that there were a number of fish in the trap; and within a few minutes they had caught sixty, a big haul in ordinary times and an extraordinary one now, for it seems that the fish had stopped running the day before. The Eskimos fully believed, needless to say, that the séance had done the trick. Mr. Wilkins is inclined to attribute the success to the fact that during the ceremony they were not outside making a noise and frightening the fish from coming into the trap, and that during the three hours' séance a number of stragglers had collected in the trap. The particular Eskimos that the shaman had pointed out had surely caught the most fish, but for that matter they always did. The shaman had prophesied that a certain boy would catch three fish and another only two; and in both cases he prophesied correctly.[93] The man who caught the most cut out a section from between the ventral fins of the largest fish and gave it to the shaman and cut a similar section from the next largest for Mr. Wilkins, who followed the shaman's example of swallowing it, to the evident satisfaction of the people.

§5. SORCERY AS DISTINGUISHED FROM SHAMANISM

APART from the shamanism of the angakoks, magic arts are practiced by a lesser order of sorcerers. Strictly regarded, the practices of these sorcerers do not include the rites performed for the deities of the sea, the air, the moon, etc. They operate with more obscure spiritual forces, which seem to stand on a lower plane and to represent a cruder stage of religious thought. This voodooism is especially common among the Eastern Eskimos. In both East and West Greenland there is a fairly defined cult, independent of the usual shamanism and secondary to it.

At Angmagsalik the sorcerers, *ilisitsut* as they are called, serve a term of discipleship under an older *ilisitsok,* in much the same way as does the neophyte for the office of angakok. It is not impossible, indeed, for an *ilisitsok* to be also an angakok. "There are many ways in which the ilisitsuk believe themselves to have the power of harming people, for instance, by making snares of dead men's sinews, and fastening one round a knee-cap, and sticking a small human rib on either side of the knee-cap. *Pitiga* took the gall of a dead man and cast it on the spot where a girl had made water, as a punishment for her refusal to lie with him. The girl died a short time afterward."[94]

With reference to Upernivik, on the west coast, Kane writes: "Besides the angekoks, who are looked up to as the heirophants or dispensers of good, they have issiutok [*ilisitsok?*], or evil men, who work injurious spells, enchantments, metamorphoses."[95] South of here Crantz refers to these witch doctors as *illiseesok*.[96] The Polar Eskimos similarly designate as an *ilisîtsoq* an angakok who can call down misfortune upon his fellows. One of these sorcerers can kill a person with a *tupilak,* without showing himself to his victim. The *tupilak* is a malicious fetish which is made by the operator himself.[97]

Among the Baffin Islanders witchcraft is said not to be so prominent as it is in Greenland.[98] From the Iglulik Eskimos, however, it is reported that certain men and women known as *ilise'cut* practice witchcraft.[99]

Sorcerers suspected of causing death through evil practices are liable to be killed by other members of the community.[100]

One kind of divination performed among virtually all Eskimos should perhaps be considered as pertaining to the art of the witchdoctor rather than to that of the acknowledged angakok. To carry out this practice, which we shall call "head-weighing," the operator ties a thong around the head of the subject, who is reclining on his back, and attaches a stick to the thong. He then lifts the weight of the head with the purpose of determining the answer to questions asked. Sometimes, instead of the subject's head, one of his feet is lifted. Depending upon whether the part of the body feels heavy or light the answer "yes" or "no" is signified.[101] Divination by this method is commonly called *qilaneq,* from which the title *qilalik* is given to the operator who practices it. A *qilalik* is a person, often a woman, who has a *qila* (a spirit in the earth). The services of the *qilalik* are sought to obtain enlightenment, usually on questions which relate to the healing of an invalid.[102]

In West Greenland, the rule is that if the head feels light, the patient will get well, if heavy he will die.[103] Polar Eskimos believe that the spirit is present when the head grows heavy.[104] The Baffin Islanders attempt to discover taboo transgressions by "head weighing": if the head feels heavy it signifies guilt; if light, innocence.[105] As practiced at Ponds Bay[106] and Cumberland Sound[107] an affirmative answer is indicated when the head feels heavy and negative when light. The natives of Iglulik[108] and those on the west coast of Hudson Bay[109] employ "head weighing" in the usual way, to determine which of the taboos has been violated and has caused sickness, giving the customary interpretation of an affirmative answer when the head seems heavy. In Labrador, where it is said that a corpse is used instead of a living subject, an answer is obtained by the same signs.

Another practice seemingly with the same purpose as "head weighing," is called *kilu'xin* by the natives of Sandwich Bay, Labrador. The magician raps three times on the ground with a stick, and on the third rap the spirit is supposed to come. Thereupon it is questioned; and finally it is sent back. Old men and women, not regular angakoks, engage in this practice.[110]

The Copper Eskimos practise divination by weighing, using in place of the head a coat bundled up, which they call *kila*. The spirit has entered the bundle when it grows heavy, and thereafter heaviness and lightness indicate "yes" and "no," respectively. One purpose to which the practice is put is the detection of attempted murder by witchcraft.[111] In the Mackenzie region the variant method which involves lifting a foot or a mitten seems to have been employed.[112]

In Kotzebue Sound "head weighing" again occurs in typical form, except that here if the head feels heavy a negative answer is indicated.[113] Among the Chukchi, with whom this is one of the chief methods of divination, the answer "no" is likewise signified when the head is difficult to raise.[114]

Lifting tests with the purpose of divination are used widely, not only among the Eskimos,[115] but also among other arctic peoples. Instances occur among many groups in Siberia and as far west as the Laplanders. Aside from being used in cases of sickness, divination of this sort is applied with the aim of recovering objects that have gone astray or been stolen.[116]

§6. ORIGIN OF ESKIMO SHAMANISM

A THEORY suggested by Rink and supported by Thalbitzer and others, is that the Eskimo religion consists of two strata, one being the residue of a pre-shamanistic cult, and the other a form of shamanism of Asiatic origin. Thus, the mysteries of the sorcerers which we have just discussed are considered as a relic of a former cult. The theory gains support from analogous cases found in the history of religions in other parts of the world, wherein an earlier form of worship becomes reduced to the status of black magic under an ascendant cult.

It is difficult, however, in the Eskimo religion to determine which elements are the older and which the younger. The wide distribution of the elements of both sorcery and shamanism throughout Arctic America and Asia seems to show that both branches are very old. We must differentiate where possible the specific ceremonies from the general technique of the officiating operatives. Broadly similar shamanistic arts are practiced in many tribes of the world, whereas the specific cultic significance differs considerably. The cult of the Sea Goddess as embraced by the Eskimos, for example, seems to be uniquely their own development, not extending even to the western groups. The spirit flight of the shaman, on the other hand, is widely prevalent among Eskimos, and in Asia as well. Far from the Eskimo province and in a different geographic setting the shamans of central Asia are known sometimes to make mysterious flights into the supernatural sphere. It must be realized that in the two cases there are differences in the details of spiritual belief, as well as in the physical features conditioned by environment. The manner in which the spiritual flight of the shaman is performed is, however, much the same in the two separate regions. Forming his opinion chiefly upon evidence of this nature, Thalbitzer concludes that: "No doubt can exist that it is the central Asiatic world of ideas, with the connecting cult, which has . . . formed the religious life of the Eskimos."[117] Caution must be exercised, nevertheless, in deciding to what degree the resemblance denotes actual relationship between the two cults and not merely parallelism.

The word "angakok" seems to be purely an Eskimo term. A very thorough search led Thalbitzer to the discovery of no roots in northern Asia whence it could have been derived. Far and wide among the Eskimos this term, with minor variants, designates the shaman; only rarely does some other word take its place, as for instance south of Bering Strait where the term *tungra'lik* is employed.[118]

The derivation of the word "angakok" in the Eskimo language hints, nevertheless, at a western rather than eastern origin for it, and by inference, possibly also for the institution itself. "As a hypothetical conclusion," writes Thalbitzer, "I will explain the word angakkoq as: mother's brother of the family, perhaps, the most powerful brother of the mother, or perhaps, inheritor of the brother of the mother." On this evidence he suggests that the shamanism which is connected with the institution of the angakok may have arisen among a people who connected priesthood with chieftainship and who recognized inheritance from the brother of the mother to the sister's son. These traits do not characterize the folkways of the Eskimos themselves; among them the office of the angakok is neither joined to the chieftainship nor inherited. Likewise among the Chukchi, adjacent to the Eskimos in Asia, shamanism is a special calling. But in the immediate vicinity of the *western* tribes of the Eskimos we find people embracing the system of inheritance that is suggested in the word "angakok." Among the Thlinkets, dwelling near the Eskimos on the Pacific coast, the office of shaman regularly passes on from father to son, while chieftainship, independent of this, is inherited from uncle to nephew. Closer to the Eskimos lives the northern branch of the same Indians on the Kenai Peninsula, who recognize in the sister's son the nearest heir. Also among Siberian peoples there are instances of inherited shamanism. Finally, in regard to the Eskimos themselves, the only examples we find of the inheritance of shamanism are from the westernmost natives. There is a definite case of this on St. Lawrence Island;[119] and nearby on the Diomede Islands an *ahng-ut-kok* frequently, though not invariably, transmits his art to his son. A fact perhaps pertinent to this custom of inheritance is that the Diomede words for "father" and "uncle" are almost indistinguishable: *ahng-ah'-gah* and *ahng-uh-gah*, respectively, the latter being pronounced slightly more rapidly.[120]

Thalbitzer also suggests that Eskimo shamanism may have been influenced by a prominent feature of Alaskan Eskimo mythology, namely, the personification of the Great Raven as creator of the world and of man and as the bringer of culture. Among the Eskimos this idea is confined virtually to those of Alaska, though it occurs as far east as the Mackenzie region. But it extends beyond the Eskimos to the neighboring folk in Asia and America. This element in the mythology forms a bond of cultural relation between the Indians of the North Pacific (Kolosh and Thlinket) and the northeastern Siberians, particularly the Koryaks and the Kamchadals. And there are indications that point toward an Asiatic rather than an American origin for the Great Raven as an important creature.[121] The idea is strongly entrenched in the religion of the Koryaks, where the Great Raven plays a rôle in their festivals and is regarded as the creator. He is supposed to have been the first man, a reorganizer and a mighty shaman. In fact, Asiatic shamanism culminates in the raven mythology and the cult connected with it. Thalbitzer goes so far as to say, "I could imagine—hypothetically—a center of a cult in which the shaman called himself once 'Great Raven' or represented him in a rôle in cultic practices." "The Alaskan myths concerning the first appearance of the Great Raven on earth, his meeting with men and the founding of human relations, contain perhaps, latently and symbolically, a description of the genesis of angakokism." This and other evidence convinces Thalbitzer that Eskimo shamanism came from Asia.[122]

Shamanism, moreover, constitutes the highest phase of Eskimo religious expression. The cult of the *illiseetsok*, or evil sorcerer, on the other hand, appears less highly developed as a rule, and is everywhere obscured by the major religious practices of the angakoks, especially in the western groups. These facts suggest that the cult followed by the sorcerers is a relic of a more primitive institution, whose growth was arrested by the intervention of a stronger system of belief, the ascendant shamanism, which overshadows it.

NOTES

1. See pp. 459 ff.
2. Ray: 1885, 43.
3. Stefansson: 1913, 392.
4. Jenness: 1922, 194.
5. Birket-Smith: 1929, I, 218.
6. Rasmussen: 1929, I, 114.
7. Bilby: 1923, 196.
8. Birket-Smith: 1924, 452.
9. Rasmussen: 1908, 155; also Kroeber: 1899, 303.
10. Schultz-Lorentzen: 1928, 235; Nansen: 1893, 284 (footnote).
11. Weyer: Field Notes.
12. See pp. 442 ff.
13. Steensby: 1910, 282.
14. Holm: 1914, 58.
15. See Nelson: 1899, 431 f., for three examples from northwestern Alaska of the angakok changing the weather.

16. See pp. 358 f.; also Boas: 1887, 36 f.
17. Smith, in Kersting: 1902, 126.
18. Turner: 1894, 199.
19. Holm: 1914, 97.
20. Birket-Smith: 1924, 407.
21. Bilby: 1923, 203. Klutschak's assertion is perhaps open to question, that among the Kinipetu Eskimos, in the central area, the *jus primae noctis* is accorded the shaman (Klutschak: 1881, 234).
22. Stefansson: 1914, 370.
23. Thalbitzer, in Kroeber and Waterman: 1931, 433.
24. Nelson: 1899, 429. Hawkes writes that he never heard of this practice among the Labrador Eskimos (Hawkes: 1916, 131).

25. Boas: 1907, 489. See also Boas: 1888, 591.

26. Nelson: 1899, 427 f.

27. Hawkes: 1916, 131.

28. Stefansson: 1913, 392.

29. Birket-Smith: 1924, 453.

30. Birket-Smith: 1924, 441.

31. Thalbitzer: 1928a, 368. In Kroeber and Waterman (1931, 435), Thalbitzer interprets *taartat* as meaning "successors."

32. Thalbitzer: 1928, 374.

33. Thalbitzer, in Kroeber and Waterman: 1931, 435 f. Cf. Thalbitzer: 1928a, 369.

34. Holm: 1914, 88.

35. Thalbitzer: 1928, 382; Thalbitzer, in Kroeber and Waterman: 1931, 436. See pp. 351 and 361 f.

36. Thalbitzer: 1928, 379.

37. Thalbitzer: 1928, 371. See also p. 399.

38. Rasmussen: 1908, 134; Rasmussen: 1921, 30; Steensby: 1910, 370; Kroeber: 1899, 303 ff.

39. Rasmussen: 1929, I, 113. Regarding the angakok's familiar spirit among the Central Eskimos, see Boas: 1888, 592 f.; in Baffin Island, Bilby: 1923, 203; and, in general, Nansen: 1893, 239.

40. Jenness: 1922, 191, also 92 f.

41. Stefansson: 1914, 368 ff. See also Stefansson: 1913, 392 ff.

42. Jenness: 1922, 194.

43. Kroeber: 1899, 303.

44. Rasmussen: 1908, 146.

45. Kroeber: 1899, 307.

46. Weyer: Field Notes.

47. Hawkes: 1916, 128 ff. See also Smith: 1894, 213 ff.; and Turner: 1894, 195 f. (Ungava).

48. Crantz: 1767, I, 210; also Birket-Smith: 1924, 452, citing H. Egede, P. Egede, and Rink. Schultz-Lorentzen describes how one becomes an angakok (1928, 236).

49. Holm: 1914, 88. See pp. 435 f.

50. Boas: 1907, 510.

51. Rasmussen: 1929, I, 114.

52. Holm: 1887, 72, 85, 90, 93, 94, cited by Sumner and Keller: 1927, II, 1364; Thalbitzer, in Kroeber and Waterman: 1931, 433.

53. Thalbitzer, in Kroeber and Waterman: 1931, 431 f.

54. Boas: 1907, 153 f.

55. Rasmussen: 1929, I, 111.

56. Rasmussen: 1929, I, 115 ff.

57. Rasmussen: 1927, 82 ff.

58. Rasmussen: 1927, 126.

59. See p. 427. Concerning the angakok's training, see also Stefansson: 1914, 367 ff. (Mackenzie region); Boas: 1888, 591 f. (Central Eskimos); and Bilby: 1923, 196 ff. (Baffin Island).

60. Thalbitzer, in Kroeber and Waterman: 1931, 432.

61. Stefansson: 1914, 374 f.; also 170.

62. Holm: 1914, 97. See also Nansen: 1893, 283.

63. Lyon: 1824, 266.

64. Jenness: 1922, 195.

65. Hall: 1864, 318 f.; also Boas: 1888, 594.

66. Bilby: 1923, 233 f.

67. Weyer: Field Notes.

68. Jenness: 1922, 195.

69. Thalbitzer, in Kroeber and Waterman: 1931, 432 f.

70. Holm: 1914, 86.

71. Kroeber: 1899, 307, 313. See also Kane: 1856, II, 126, on this subject in the northern section of the west coast of Greenland; Rasmussen: 1929, I, 114 (Iglulik Eskimos); short vocabularies of angakok words are to be found in Boas: 1894a, 46 ff.; Boas: 1894, 207 ff.; Boas: 1907, 350 ff.; Bilby: 1923, 167; and Rasmussen: 1908, 153.

72. Jenness: 1922, 211.

73. Boas: 1888, 594.

74. Boas: 1894, 207.

75. Kroeber: 1923, 449.

76. Hawkes: 1916, 131.

77. Weyer: Field Notes. Stefansson (1913, 403 ff.) describes the feat as it is performed in the Mackenzie Delta.

78. Thalbitzer, in Kroeber and Waterman: 1931, 433 ff. Holm gives a very complete description of the performance he witnessed (Holm: 1914, 91 ff.). See also Holm: 1914, 96 ff.; P. Egede: 1790, 103 ff. (West Green-

land); and Crantz: 1767, I, 210 ff. (West Greenland).

79. Smith, H. I.: 1894, 213.

80. Rasmussen: 1908, 149.

81. Boas: 1907, 490 f., from a description by Captain Mutch. See also Boas: 1888, 594.

82. Boas (1907, 511) gives an illustration, probably from the west coast of Hudson Bay.

83. Rasmussen: 1929, I, 129 f.; also Rasmussen: 1927, 28 ff.

84. Nelson: 1899, 382 ff.

85. Jenness: 1922, 198.

86. Jenness: 1922, 188. This ceremony is fully described, p. 360.

87. Bilby: 1923, 202, also 230 f.

88. Weyer: Field Notes. Bladders filled with seal's blood are mentioned also in connection with a ceremonial on the Nushegak River (Bristol Bay) wherein combats occur between men and between men and animals (Petroff: 1900, 225).

89. Nelson: 1899, 434.

90. Schwatka: 1900, 356; and Schwatka: 1885a, 340; also Hawkes: 1916, 131 f.

91. Weyer: Field Notes. Curing sickness is, of course, one of the chief duties of the angakok; but the discussion of this art is left to a separate chapter.

92. Weyer: Field Notes. See Jenness: 1922, chaps. xv and xvi, for further information concerning the angakok among the Copper Eskimos.

93. Jenness: 1922, 201 f.

94. Holm: 1914, 89, 100 ff.

95. Kane: 1856, II, 127.

96. Crantz: 1767, I, 214. See also Birket-Smith: 1924, 456.

97. Rasmussen: 1908, 155. See pp. 313 f. Kroeber states, contrary to the above given evidence, that these Eskimos seem not to have a cult of black magic in contradistinction to the true shamanism of the angakoks (Kroeber: 1899, 307 f.).

98. Boas: 1888, 595.

99. Rasmussen: 1929, I, 143.

100. See pp. 226 and 451 f.

101. An illustration is given in Boas: 1907, 511.

102. Thalbitzer: 1928, 420. Other references by Thalbitzer: 1923, 464 ff., and 450 f., 453.

103. Crantz: 1767, I, 214. See also Birket-Smith: 1924, 449, citing H. Egede, Olearius, and N. Egede. Thalbitzer: 1924, 285 f.

104. Rasmussen: 1908, 154 ff. See also Kroeber: 1899, 302; and Bessels: 1879, 367 f.

105. Bilby: 1923, 232 f.

106. Boas: 1907, 495.

107. Boas: 1907, 135.

108. Rasmussen: 1929, I, 141.

109. Boas: 1907, 158 f.

110. Hawkes: 1916, 119, 132 f., 137 f.

111. Jenness: 1922, 212 ff., 217.

112. Stefansson: 1914, 359 ff.

113. Healy: 1887, 51 (by Cantwell). Nelson mentions "head weighing" in the region of Bering Strait (1899, 433).

114. Bogoras: 1901, 95; and Bogoras: 1902, 635.

115. See also Rink: 1875, 269, 467; and Reclus: 1891, 39.

116. Thalbitzer: 1928, 420.

117. Thalbitzer: 1928, 426 ff.

118. See p. 398.

119. Thalbitzer: 1928, 420 ff., especially 424, citing Bogoras: 1904, 420.

120. Weyer: Field Notes.

121. Thalbitzer: 1928, 411 ff.

122. Thalbitzer: 1928, 419 f. See also Thalbitzer: 1928a, 386 ff.

CHAPTER XXVI

RELIGION AS A SOCIAL FORCE

§1. HAZARDS IN THE ANGAKOK'S PRESTIGE

ONE is naturally curious to know how strong is the faith of the Eskimo in his religion and in his spiritual leader, the angakok. To what extent can the angakok's prestige survive unfortunate reverses? His duties lie almost wholly in the field of chance; hence, he is certain to experience failures as well as successes. He does not enjoy the more defensible authority of a chief who concerns himself with purely practical matters. The angakok undertakes to delve into the mysteries of life, to predict its uncertainties, even to modify the immutable laws controlling natural events. Attempting to operate with forces which, for the most part, he does not really understand, he cannot always even appear to succeed. Experience may have taught him roughly to forecast the weather and the movements of game animals, but he cannot maintain his prestige simply by predicting. He is expected to produce good luck in the face of impending misfortune. When faced with obviously unpropitious circumstances, there is naturally a limit beyond which he cannot delay his operations. The supposedly miraculous efficacy of his ministrations does not allow him to procrastinate. In practice, therefore, he is bound to fail some of the time. When protracted bad luck obliges him to perform a succession of ineffectual incantations or hold unsuccessful séances, he may easily earn the reputation of causing calamity instead of good fortune. How, then, do his followers reconcile his failures with their faith in the limitless power of shamanism?

As a rule the people hold to their deep-seated trust in shamanism, preferring rather to impute evil intent to the individual angakok than to ridicule his entire art as so much fraud. A medicine man whose operations seem to bring bad luck is likely to gain a reputation for working with definitely malicious spirits. Thus, he may come to be classed with the sorcerers, whose black magic is not to be confused with the recognized shamanism.[1] It is generally regarded as a very grave offense to employ magic with evil design, and sorcerers are liable to suffer severe retaliation. When one is suspected of having caused a death by witchcraft, which is by no means uncommon, he is in danger of being killed.[2] This offense offers one of the indeed few occasions for capital punishment among the Eskimos.

"Magicians are sometimes soul-stealers," writes Rasmussen concerning the Polar Eskimos; "the people affected then fall ill and die. Some little time before our arrival at Cape York a man named Kajorapaluk had been murdered 'because he stole souls.' "[3] In Labrador, if the shaman discovers, after a person has died, that someone bewitched the deceased and thus caused his death, the offender is killed by the relatives.[4] In West Greenland, witchcraft was an offense against the group, punished by death;[5] and among the Caribou Eskimos, black magic is classed with murder as one of the two really serious crimes.[6] Near Bering Strait, if a shaman is suspected of using his powers to work evil upon his fellow villagers, he is in danger of being killed by the common consent of the community. Nelson heard of such men being killed in the region lying between the mouths of the Yukon and the Kuskokwim for failing to fulfil their predictions and for suspected witchcraft. In the fall of 1879 the Malemiut Eskimos of Kotzebue Sound killed a shaman, saying in explanation that he told too many lies.[7]

Cases such as these show that the medicine man is held accountable for actions that incur the disapproval of his people. It is not without misgiving, however, that the Eskimos put to death a medicine man. It is a matter which often entails the performance of special rites. Kane reports such a happening at Upernivik, West Greenland, in 1828. The evil magician (*issiutok*) was first harpooned, then eviscerated, and a flap was let down from his forehead "to cover his eyes and prevent his seeing again." (He had the evil eye, it would seem.) Finally, small portions of his heart were eaten, to make sure that he could not come back to earth unchanged.[8] With regard to this last measure, the evidence[9] seems to indicate that ceremonial cannibalism following murder takes place chiefly when the victim is supposed to have possessed supernatural powers.

On the Diomede Islands, if a person killed an angakok, the traditional instructions were that he should cut off the first joints of the victim's little fingers and little toes and put them in the dead man's mouth;[10] also he must make a bonnet of the medicine man's bladder and put it on the latter's head.[11]

Only as an extreme measure is killing resorted to in case someone is suspected of witchcraft. A failure of the angakok to cause good luck is apt to be slurred over with a trivial excuse. Repeated

unsuccessful attempts by the medicine men of Point Barrow to
drive the ice off shore and to open the sea for favorable whale
hunting, were explained as balked by some offense that had been
given the spirits.[12]

"Quite often a serious illness is attributed to the machinations of a
neighboring angekok," asserts Hawkes.[13] "There is nothing to do in
such cases except to fight him with local magic. Such a case came to
my attention in Bering strait. An Eskimo girl who was sick could keep
nothing on her stomach. The cause was attributed to a spirit (tungak)
sent by another shaman to inhabit her stomach. As fast as she swallowed her food it was pushed up by this 'devil.' Five local shamans
could not overcome the spell of the stranger."

§2. STABILITY OF RELIGION

It is significant that the excuses usually given for failure do not as
a rule put the blame on the cultic practices themselves; some extraneous cause is generally assigned, such as the influence of counter magic or the transgression of a taboo by someone in the community. Faith in the ceremonies themselves is unshaken; they have
served generations of ancestors, and it is not for ordinary mortals
to criticize them. The same ceremonial procedure may enhance the
renown of one angakok while it brings discredit on another, yet it
continues to be followed and approved as a method. Thus the
time-honored custom is a more stable thing than the prestige of
those who practice it.

The probability that the religious observances of the Eskimos
have persisted through generations virtually unmodified is supported by their present uniformity over wide areas. The ceremony
of "head weighing," for example, is a method of divination employed by the Eskimos from Alaska to Greenland.[14] In actual
practice, it must often yield predictions which later prove incor-
rect, yet it continues to be relied upon. Out of nine references at
hand to this rite, ranging from the Chukchi in northeastern Siberia through the Eskimos to Labrador, it is specifically stated in
seven of them that when the head feels heavy an affirmative answer
to the question is indicated, while in only two of the instances is
the opposite interpretation accepted. The latter exceptions may
have come about when failures in prediction prompted a reversal
of the original rule. So close an approach toward absolute uniformity, however, as is indicated by but two departures from the

general rule can only suggest that faith in the method has remained unshaken through many failures in prediction. If the rule were continually checked by trial and error it would be altered repeatedly, with the result that at any one time we should expect to find about an equal number of cases for each of the two opposite interpretations. Actually, however, there is a preponderance of one of them, in the ratio of seven to two. To be sure, the divination is not always of such a sort that the answer can later be verified. It seems certain, nevertheless, that the practice of "head weighing" holds its ground in defiance of empirical observations.

Instances of diametrically opposite meanings being assigned to the same cultic practice are rare but not wholly lacking. In Labrador, for example, there is a taboo against cooking caribou and seal together,[15] while not far distant, in southeastern Baffin Island, the natives believe that cooking caribou and seal in the same kettle will create friendship between the souls of these animals.[16]

Stefansson relates how certain inland Eskimos in northwestern Alaska were deeply impressed by the efficacy of a Christian prayer as an aid in caribou hunting. But the second year it did not work so well, and they decided that white men's prayers, like their rifles and other things, deteriorate with age. When this particular prayer had lost its power they wanted to secure a new and more effective one.[17] These natives had an eye open, therefore, for possible improvements in the sacred ritual. By and large, however, the conspicuous feature of the Eskimo cult is its persistence, unaltered through generations in spite of adverse results. Deep-rooted conservatism, rather than progressive variation, is characteristic of the religious beliefs.

§3. INEXPEDIENT FOLKWAYS

THE stability of the Eskimo religious folkways is emphasized in the fact that many of their ideas and customs persist in defiance of practical considerations. The custom of destroying the property of those who have died and of depositing implements and food at their graves entails considerable economic sacrifice. Restrictions during mourning sometimes constitute an additional handicap. Among the Central Eskimos, for instance, "in winter a long spell of bad weather occasions privation, since the hunters are then prevented from leaving the huts. If by chance some one should happen to die during this time, famine is inevitable, for a strict law forbids the performance of any kind of work during the days of mourning."[18]

The shades of the dead are only one class of spirits to whom the Eskimo must show deference. The higher deities require ceremonies, which at times handicap the native in his purely practical occupations. Moreover, a host of nature spirits claim their share of consideration. The inhabitants of Cumberland Sound believe that stone for pots must be *bought* from the rock; consequently, when they take a piece they leave ivory carvings, beads, food, or the like.[19] Though the economic sacrifice in cases of this sort may seem small, it is not negligible considering the poverty of the people.

The Eskimo disciplines himself in many ways which, so far as his immediate physical welfare is concerned, seem to render his struggle for existence the more arduous. The natives of Point Barrow forbid themselves during the whaling season to dry out wet clothing; and they will not use the coverings of the boats or any of the implements for more than one season.[20] Witness, also, the stern taboo which forbade the Netsilik Eskimos of Boothia Isthmus ". . . to make themselves new clothes or warmer sleeping rugs until they had shivered their way through the first of the snow right on into November."[21] The Copper Eskimos have a taboo against burning driftwood to cook caribou or fish caught inland.[22] And it was observed that most of the Mackenzie people of all ages and both sexes were forbidden to eat eggs of any sort in the springtime.[23]

In building a snow house the Iglulik Eskimos encumber themselves by curious rules which have no bearing upon the strength or convenience of the finished dwelling. And while living in such a house if it stands on the sea ice they believe that only melted snow should be used for drinking; old sea ice yields fresh water, but to use it is supposed to cause the young ice to break up and thus to expose the people to the danger of being carried out to sea.[24]

It may almost be said that the basic spiritual beliefs of the Eskimo regarding hunting run counter to the preservation of game. The natives believe that if only the proper propitiatory rites are observed, the souls of the animals that they kill will not perish but will return to earth in new bodies. Consequently, no amount of slaughtering will jeopardize the supply of game if only the traditional precautions are taken. Here, the system of religious regulations works against the practical wisdom of conservation.[25]

§4. HAS RELIGION A SURVIVAL VALUE?

THESE and many other beliefs seem to militate against the economic interests of the Eskimos. The question arises whether the survival of the race has occurred in part *because* of its religion or altogether *in spite* of it. May we see in the survival of the Eskimo people a hidden and marvelous vindication of these seemingly inexpedient folkways? or is their religion to be deplored as a stupidly self-imposed encumbrance?

It is undeniable that a religion must either benefit or handicap a people in their struggle to survive. To imagine an extreme example, suppose that the Eskimos were to carry their religious requirements to the extreme of sacrificing half their material resources to the spirits. Other things being equal, those groups that otherwise could barely subsist would then die out. Perhaps, if we could penetrate deeply enough into the history of the Eskimo people, we might discover instances where an increasing emphasis upon the exactions of religion actually brought about the extinction of certain groups. At any rate, the problem of the survival value of religion has a distinct bearing upon the life of a people situated at the border of the habitable world.[26]

Various authorities on the history of social institutions[27] have developed the idea that morals and customs contend for survival in their natural environments, the "more fit" triumphing for reasons analogous to those that operate in organic evolution. It is argued by some that the selection of expedient social adjustments and the elimination of inexpedient ones can even take place without the conscious discrimination of the people. Everyone will agree at least that sometimes a religious practice exerts an effect, favorable or unfavorable, upon the group without their being fully aware of its real significance; and the reasons for which people retain or reject customs are sometimes extraneous to the vital issue. Instances occur in the religious ideas of races other than Eskimo, for instance, in which a custom, quite apart from the motives for which it is preserved, justifies its existence by its hygienic value.

To generalize here, however, may be unwarranted; practical utility does not support every custom. One must be wary, since if he sets about the task, he can usually find some utilitarian aspect of a practice that will supply him with a practical justification of it. The Eskimos, like many other peoples of the world, customarily avoid having contact with a dead body. One might conclude off-hand that this regulation owes its acceptance to the fact that it prevents contagion among them. But, in the case of the Eskimos, their freedom from contagious diseases in their native state[28] lends little weight to such an explanation.

In the search for a plausible justification of a custom, rite, or practice of any kind, it is all too easy to overlook some aspect the effect of which is unqualifiedly detrimental. A custom may work to the disadvantage of society yet continue to be practiced. In very rare instances, to be sure, the harm may be so serious as to cause the extinction of the people, in which case the custom will, of course, die out. By and large, however, cultural evolution progresses with far less drastic strides. Troublesome customs persist long, in some cases even after the resulting harm has become so marked that the people are very definitely aware of it.

Our training is calculated to engender the feeling that a religion must be the repository of ultimate truth; but primitive religions fail to substantiate any such assumption. In many cases we seek in vain to discover any connection of religious practice with morality or even with physical well-being. This fact sometimes distresses not only the moralist but also the hard-headed thinker who approaches the subject with somewhat the attitude of the efficiency expert. The mind that is satisfied only with obvious, practical explanations cannot comprehend the full significance of spiritual beliefs.

It cannot be argued that religion is infallible on the grounds that it transcends the intellect of the individual or is shaped by inexorable laws comparable to those of organic evolution. Even progressive evolution implies some disadvantageous adjustments in the course of improvement. The fact that a custom has been continually followed for a long time does not necessarily imply, therefore, that it has proved its utility.

The advance of religion, like that of other forms of knowledge, proceeds through a process of trial and error. But it is not fair to regard religion simply as a sort of blind science. To do so is to accord it meager dignity.

Thus, if we confine our attention to the narrowly pragmatic aspects of religion, its seemingly unsuccessful blunderings appear conspicuous. We are not able to assign a tangible reason to each and every custom, and there is a temptation to condemn religion as a discredit to human rationality because it preserves misguided beliefs. Its cumbrous conservatism looms up as a drawback to progress, without ameliorating qualities.

We must not, however, "fail to see the wood for the trees." Actually, the characteristic conservatism of religion can be defended as performing an essential function in social development. If the folkways were not balanced by any conservating tendency, society would be a chaos of transitory fads. The good and the bad alike would perish after brief duration. Religion serves somewhat the same purpose among human institutions that a heavy keel does in a sailboat: it adds equilibrium. While at times religion impedes social progress, it furnishes a stability that enables the social organization to weather storms that otherwise would upset it. Concerted compliance with the folkways, even in matters of trivial practical importance, promotes coöperation in the vital affairs of life. Religion lends a very necessary stability when it imparts its sanction to a principle of social conduct that has been proved useful through long experimentation. With its tremendous emotional force, religion can exert a more powerful regulative compulsion than the dictates of cold reason. Sometimes, to be sure, rationality, practicality, and shrewdness go down before it. But if religion leans heavily on emotion and seems at times a weakness in our human nature, it is in the long pull a source of strength and therefore an asset worth holding in spite of the occasional sacrifice of rationality.

§5. THE POWER OF BELIEF

In the face of numerous failures and of handicaps involved in its regulations, the faith of the Eskimo in his religion seems to lose nothing of its stability and strength. Much of the time-honored ritual seems inconsistent and contrary to rational considerations, while its meaningless duties impose burdens wholly needless if judged upon practical grounds. Yet unswerving trust remains, which, to us, is a miracle as hard to explain as the miracles of the angakoks must be to the Eskimos. One hesitates to suggest any mystical solution or to pass over the remarkable permanence of the Eskimo's beliefs simply by explaining it as due to the power of faith. The faith that supports these religious phenomena which seem so inconsistent with reasonable thinking is not to be regarded as a divinely bestowed quality which sprouts up in the soul, independent of tradition, of cultic demonstrations, and of the emotional experiences accompanying them. At the same time, the Eskimo's emotional fervor is an expression of something inherent in the religious constitution of man. A mysterious power is felt, indeed, by the civilized onlooker when present at certain of the protracted ceremonies, and this impression must fall far short of what it is to the naïve and uncritical savage mind.

Unless facts are drawn in from the outside, the religious system of the Eskimo appears not at variance with reason. Furthermore, it is very closely connected with the affairs of everyday life, such as hunting, cooking, eating, and curing disease. Unlike the highly metaphysical beliefs of more advanced peoples, the Eskimo's spiritual notions are concerned largely with actual, concrete things. To him, religion is not merely a diaphanous plexus of fanciful beliefs. It follows that the abstract premises which form the logical core of the Eskimo's religion do not stand out so prominently. The solid background of his known world so substantially supports his faith that only here and there is there a hollow brick. With a mass of knowledge proved true by experience, and only a few suppositions that must be accepted on the word of the angakok or on tradition, his religious system appears to him to be wholly consistent.

Learning much of his really reliable information through tradition, the Eskimo is not apt to single out occasional teachings that are false. The beliefs that are untrue do not betray their weakness, for they bolster one another up and fit very snugly into the whole scheme. Confidence in tradition is tremendous. Thus, when the medicine man, who is far better qualified to know than the ordinary person, accepts a few hypotheses as incontestably true, the keystone of the system is inserted. The Eskimos believe implicitly in the angakoks, as Hawkes states,[29] ". . . and balk at no marvel which is attributed to them. They say that they have no knowledge of the spirit world and must believe those who possess it."

Sometimes at the very moment when the angakok finds his influence over the minds of his following ebbing away, he can strengthen it by charging some member of the community with a misdemeanor that has offended the spirits.

"Apropos of the extraordinary command the conjurors universally exercise over the people, and of the paramount psychic influence they establish in the community," writes Bilby, "it is not too much to say that they hold every man's life in their hands. We know how the fatalistic-minded Asiatic can die by auto-suggestion. The Eskimo, too, dies by suggestion, even when strongly against his will.

"A fully qualified practitioner, well known for a sensual and indulgent man, was particularly tenacious of his purposes and able to bide his time. He had long desired the good-looking half-breed wife of a certain hunter, and had frequently approached the man on the question. Contrary to the general rule, in this instance he was consistently refused. Now, Moneapik, the hunter, was a skilful fellow, well able to provide himself and his wife with food and clothing. He was careful, too, and rather exclusive, not liking to squander his gains upon the lazy folk of the village, after the generally accepted fashion. For this reason he was unpopular. He had his own circle of friends, however, and was content not to enlarge it. The conjuror had nothing to work upon so far as Moneapik was concerned, except the latter's superstition. The man was neither poor, nor feckless, nor friendless.

"At length a long spell of bad weather set in, bringing in its train a season of sickness and semi-starvation. The conjuror was expected to set matters right by his arts and incantations; but on this occasion he had only a signal failure to register. He loudly excused himself for it on the ground that the spirits were profoundly offended by the unsociable practices of Moneapik. He had committed the heinous offence of keeping largely to himself; he had not given freely to the tribesfolk. Only by his death could the powers be propitiated and the famine ended. The majority of the villagers were prone enough to agree with this, for over and over again the hunter had set their greed at nought. Whereupon the conjuror boldly faced the man, stated the incontrovertible facts, pronounced his death sentence, and departed saying: 'I command you to die!'

"Moneapik was a strong, healthy man, in the prime of life and the pink of condition. Normally, he should have lived to a ripe old age. But so ingrained was his belief in the conjuror, in his power to get into communication with the spirit world, that this command was virtually fatal. He said: 'I am commanded to die.' He gave up his active occupations, withdrew into his tent, ate and drank very sparingly, and within four days was dead. They sewed up the body in skin blankets and left it on the rocks of a neighboring island, to be devoured by the foxes. The writer visited the spot a few days later—but only bones remained.

"Friends had indeed visited Moneapik in his tent before the end, and argued with him, laughed at him, tried by every possible means to disabuse the man's mind of its obsession. But all in vain. The victim's sole response was, 'I am commanded to die!' And die he did, although it was by no means death from starvation. It was death by suggestion.

"The conjuror, of course, obtained his own ends."[30]

When the natives participate in the séance of the angakok they are transported into an emotional state of high tension. Concerted singing and dancing preliminary to the shaman's mysteries are designed to draw everyone into accord; so that when finally he falls into convulsive seizure and his voice becomes not his own, they are susceptible to almost incredible delusions. But group phenomena under stress of religious fervor are encountered the world over. Among ourselves the familiar revival meeting exhibits features which are almost identical with the happenings at primitive ceremonials. Inspired dancing, uncontrollable ecstasy upon "getting religion" or confessing of wrongdoing are common throughout the human race.

Primitive religions are often characterized by elaborate paraphernalia, including symbolic costumes, masks, and other ceremonial accouterments. The Eskimos in general do not make extensive use of these things, with the exception of certain groups living in Alaska. Secret societies have not developed among Eskimo peoples.[31] The size of their communities is small, their social organization simple.[32] But the force of their spiritual ardor is tremendous. Among them one realizes that spectacular display is not necessary in order to make ceremony impressive, and that the welling up of the primitive spirit can raise religious expression to dramatic heights.

Whether it be a solemn and important ceremonial or merely an incidental séance, the procedure is remarkably effective. Drumming, dancing, and singing afford the necessary concerted activity that serves to unite all in a fervent enthusiasm. Under the influence of the primitive rhythm one is drawn into accord almost without knowing it.

Preliminary to a performance the drummers may pass half an hour in preparatory operations, humming random bits of song and adjusting their drums to the proper resonance by applying water to them. All this seems idle at first; but suddenly one senses it as a call to the primitive instincts and an awakening to something immanent, strange, and full of portent. Then a slight irregularity in the beating of the drums, or perhaps a signal from the leader, and the dancing begins. There is no longer anything trivial about the affair. It is intensely serious. The dancers move in perfect unison, their rhythm almost like that of a machine; yet it gives no sense of the mechanical, so perfectly graceful and artistic is each individual movement. As the performance proceeds, the enthusiasm grows wilder. Now and again there is an intermission, when the drummers moisten their drumheads as well as their own strained vocal cords, for they have been singing lustily like the other participants. Each pause is broken suddenly: at once the air is vibrant with the thumping of the drums beating in strange, irregular tempo, and with the weird harmony of the voices.

A sort of hypnosis comes over the gathering. The dancers assume strange fixed expressions; their necks bulge with the volume of their voices and the arteries of their throats swell to cords. Their sleek bodies move in graceful perfect unison. Now their eyes are momentarily cast down as in dreamy trance, again they are thrown up in open, steady gaze, while the drummers beat out a pulsing undercurrent, intermittent yet rhythmic. The marvelous uniformity of movement and the nerve-shattering clamor of all the voices, straining in elemental harmony, combine to throw the group into fervid excitement. At the very climax the music breaks off abruptly, as though the finishing chords were left unsung.

As a preliminary to the mysteries of the angakok, such a performance creates the proper emotional state. The people are not behaving at all as they would if in their normal minds. The strangeness of the spectacle, producing in all the appearance of concentrated attention, reacts upon the individuals. They are ready for anything; their minds are hyper-receptive to any manifestation of the supernatural. And forthwith the angakok demonstrates his alliance with unearthly powers. Under normal circumstances the people may be well able to make fun of the angakoks and their tricks; yet ". . . when the hour of ecstasy arrives, both parties are equally serious. For the ecstatic state has power over the mind of man; it carries away, acts as an infection and is contagious."[33]

The angakok who has worked himself into this mental fervor is able to believe his own flimflam.

"Long practice in self-hypnosis, combined at times with organic weakness and an inclination toward hallucinations," writes Jenness concerning the Copper Eskimo shaman, "help to induce the condition more readily. So intense is the strain that the man nearly faints with exhaustion at the close of the performance. The insertion of the teeth of the animal familiar, or the wearing of garments made from its fur, serve, like stage scenery, to increase the illusion. The shaman is not conscious of acting a part; he becomes in his own mind the animal or the shade of the dead man that is deemed to possess him. To his audience, too, this strange figure, with its wild and frenzied appearance, its ventriloquistic cries and its unearthly falsetto gabble, with only a broken word here and there of intelligible speech, is no longer a human being, but the thing it personifies. Their minds become receptive of the wildest imaginings, and they see the strangest and most fantastic happenings. If the shaman ejaculates that he is no longer a man but a bear, forthwith it is a bear that they behold, not a human being; if he says that the dance-house is full of spirits they will see them in every corner. It is in this way, apparently, that most of the tales arise of shamans cutting off their limbs, or flying through the air, or changing to bears and wolves. . . . Even if a shaman begins by consciously deceiving his audience, the constant repetition of the action, combined with auto-suggestion and a belief that others have done what he is pretending to do, must inevitably lead in most cases to his deceiving himself. He will accept as true the wildest tales that are told about him by his audiences, tales that are magnified as they pass from mouth to mouth."[34]

Occasionally, shamans confess fraudulence to outsiders. An ill-famed angakok of East Greenland, Avgo by name, came to the anthropologist Holm and told him of his own accord that although he certainly performed angakok arts in his younger days he could no longer cause the drum to dance by itself and was, therefore, no real angakok. Sanimuinak, on the other hand, he said, was able to make the drum dance, and was a far greater angakok. Avgo admitted that he could not cure people, much less travel to the moon and fetch down children for barren women. When people declared that he could steal souls, they lied; for he was just as powerless in this respect as in the other things. Holm believed that Avgo made these confessions with the aim of currying favor with the white men. The explorer mentions the venerable old Ilinguaki as an angakok who, unlike many of the others, did not perform his arts simply with his own private ends in view. When asked whether he had cured a certain sick man, he returned an evasive answer and seemed rather embarrassed, as if he were ashamed to admit that people under his ministrations sometimes died. He had also the reputation of being able to go to the Lord of the Winds and procure any wind that might be desired. As to this, he simply said that it might happen that the desired wind came after the performance of the arts.

"It is, however, quite possible that both *Ilinguaki's* and *Avgo's* confession of their own incapacity as angakut to do good or evil respectively is merely an instance of the extreme diffidence which the Eskimo always showed in speaking of themselves, a diffidence which though it often comes under the guise of modesty, must nevertheless rather be ascribed to a superstitious fear of speaking of anything which affected themselves, just like their fear of naming their own name. It is therefore quite possible that the angakut really do believe after all in their own power of communing with the spirit world, yet without having any clear notion of the way in which it takes place."[35]

The typical Eskimo shaman is by no means a charlatan who simply perpetrates his mysteries opportunely and without believing them to exert any influence. Boas writes of the Central Eskimos that ". . . most of the angakut themselves believe in their performance, as by continued shouting and invoking they fall into an ecstasy and really imagine they accomplish the flights and see the spirits."[36] On the northern portion of the west coast of Greenland, Kane asserts that ". . . the angekoks believe firmly in their own powers. I have known several of them personally, after my skill in pow-wow had given me a sort of correlative rank among them, and can speak with confidence on this point. I could not detect them in any resort to jugglery or natural magic: their deceptions are simply vocal, a change of voice, or perhaps a limited profession of ventriloquism, made more imposing by darkness."[37] Referring to the Polar Eskimos, Rasmussen states as his opinion that "the magicians themselves are undoubtedly self-deceived in the conduct of their incantations; I do not believe that they consciously lie."[38]

A salient feature of the séance is its power to dispel any tendency either on the part of the operator or of the spectators to be critical or skeptical. Tense emotion crowds out rationality. What is left to the imagination is likely to be as vividly experienced as what is actually seen or heard. Remembering afterward but vaguely the details of the séance, the participant is apt to visualize more, rather than less, than that which occurred.

The religion of the Eskimos outlined in words may appear to a civilized person as the fantasy of a childish imagination. One must not, however, call this or that belief a superstition, without acknowledging that other religions contain many beliefs that similarly owe their acceptance to blind faith. The word "superstition," indeed, does not possess sufficient dignity and force to justify its application to the Eskimo religion. The Eskimo himself believes the teachings of his faith not merely because it is just as well to be on the safe side: the far more powerful conviction that spiritual forces dynamically influence his life makes him deeply religious. In his groping efforts to secure favorable relations with the spirits, he may sometimes doubt whether he is on the right track, but his faith in the fundamental principles remains unshaken. He implicitly believes what a civilized person would unhesitatingly refute as untrue; yet does not also the civilized person often accept things on blind faith? The Eskimo, like other people of the world, relegates what he cannot explain on natural grounds to the realm of the supernatural. Because his mental horizon is far more narrowly circumscribed than that of highly advanced peoples, the outside world is no more real to him than are his own fantastic myths. "Natural laws," since they lie beyond his knowledge, do not serve to curb his fancy. In place of them he holds a theory of spiritual causation in which no boundary divides the possible from the impossible.

NOTES

1. See pp. 442 ff.
2. See p. 443.
3. Rasmussen: 1908, 156.
4. Hawkes: 1916, 138.
5. Birket-Smith: 1924, 139, citing H. Egede and Saabye. See also Saabye: 1818, 238 ff.
6. Birket-Smith: 1929, I, 265.
7. Nelson: 1899, 429 f., also 301.
8. Kane: 1856, II, 127.
9. See pp. 310 f.
10. It would be more consistent with Eskimo custom if, contrary to what the informant seemed to mean, the murderer were to eat these parts himself.
11. Weyer: Field Notes.
12. Ray: 1885, 39.
13. Hawkes: 1916, 138.
14. See pp. 443 f.
15. Hawkes: 1916, 133.
16. Boas: 1907, 489.
17. Stefansson: 1913, 81 ff.

18. Boas: 1888, 427.
19. Boas: 1888, 596.
20. Rasmussen: 1927, 310, 312.
21. Rasmussen: 1927, 207.
22. Jenness: 1922, 98.
23. Stefansson: 1914, 136.
24. Rasmussen: 1929, I, 180 ff.
25. See chapters xx, xxi, and xxii.
26. See chapter vii.
27. Alexander: 1889; and Keller: 1922.
28. See pp. 51 f.
29. Hawkes: 1916, 139.
30. Bilby: 1923, 228 ff.
31. Birket-Smith: 1924, 140 f.
32. See chapter xii.
33. Schultz-Lorentzen: 1928, 235 f.
34. Jenness: 1922, 216 f.
35. Holm: 1914, 98 ff.
36. Boas: 1888, 594.
37. Kane: 1856, II, 126.
38. Rasmussen: 1908, 156.

BIBLIOGRAPHY

ACLAND, F. A. Canada's arctic islands. 1927.

ALEXANDER, SAMUEL. Moral order and progress. 1889.

ALLEN, JOEL ASAPH. History of the North American Pinnipeds. 1880.

—— "The muskoxen of arctic America and Greenland," *Bulletin of the American museum of natural history*, XIV. (1901.)

—— "Ontogenetic and other variations in the muskoxen with a systematic review of the muskox group, recent and extinct," *Memoirs of the American museum of natural history*, n.s., I (1913), Pt. 4.

AMUNDSEN, ROALD. The northwest passage. 1908.

ANDERSON, M. B. A. The crossing of Baffin island to Foxe basin by Bernhard A. Hantzsch in 1910. 1930. Appendix in MILLWARD, A. E. 1930.

ANDREE, R. Ethnographische Parallelen und Vergleiche. Leipsic, Veit and comp. 1889.

"ARKTIS." A periodical.

ARMSTRONG, ALEXANDER. A personal narrative of the discovery of the northwest passage. 1857.

ASTRUP, EIVIND. With Peary near the pole. Philadelphia, n.d.

—— Blandt Nordpolen's Naboer. Christiania, 1895.

BANCROFT, H. H. The native races of the Pacific states of North America. 1875.

—— History of Alaska, 1730–1885. 1886.

BARNUM, FRANCIS. Grammatical fundamentals of the Innuit language . . . in Alaska. Boston, 1901.

BARTHOLOMEW'S ATLAS. Vol. V, "Zoogeography" (1911).

BARTLETT, CAPT. ROBERT A. The last voyage of the Karluk. 1916.

—— "The Putnam Baffin Island expedition" (joint authors: PUTNAM, G. P., and GOULD, L.), *Geographical review*, XVIII (1928).

BEECHEY, FREDERICK WILLIAM. Narrative of a voyage to the Pacific and Beerings Strait, to co-operate with the polar expeditions . . . 1825, 26, 27, 28. 1831.

BELL, ROBERT. The "medicine-man"; or, Indian and Eskimo notions of medicine. 1886.

BELLOT, LIEUT. JOSEPH RENÉ. Memoirs of Lieutenant Joseph René Bellot, with his journal of a voyage in the polar seas, in search of Sir John Franklin. London, 1855. 2 vols.

BESSELS, EMIL. Einige Worte über die Innuit (Eskimo) des Smith-Sundes nebst Bemerkungen über Innuit Schädel. *Archiv für Anthropologie*, Band 8, 1875.

—— Die amerikanische Nordpol-Expedition. Leipsic, 1878.

—— Die amerikanische Nordpol-Expedition. 1879.

—— "The northernmost inhabitants of the earth." An ethnographic sketch. *American naturalist*, XVIII (1884), 861–882.

BILBY, J. W. Among unknown Eskimos. 1923. Twelve years in Baffin Island.

BIRKET-SMITH, KAJ. "The country of Egedesminde and its inhabitants." *Meddelelser om Grønland*, LXVI (1924).

—— "The Greenlanders of the present day," *Greenland*, a compilation of various authors, II (1928), 1–207.

—— "Physiography of West Greenland," *Greenland*, a compilation of various authors, I (1928a), 423–490.

—— "The Caribou Eskimos," *Fifth Thule expedition*, V (1929), Pts. I and II.

BOAS, FRANZ. "The Eskimo," *Proceedings and transactions of the royal society of Canada*, V (1887), sec. 2, p. 35.

—— The Central Eskimos, Sixth annual report of the bureau of American ethnology, pp. 399–669. 1888.

—— "Notes on the Eskimo of Port Clarence, Alaska," *Journal of American folklore*, VII (1894), 205–208.

—— "Eskimo tales and songs," *Journal of American folklore*, VII (1894a), 45–50.

—— "Zur Anthropologie der nordamerikanischen Indianer," *Zeitschrift für Ethnologie*, XXVII (Berlin, 1895), 366–411.

—— "Property marks of Alaskan Eskimo," *American anthropologist*, n.s., I (1899), 601–613.

—— "Religious beliefs of the Central Eskimo," *Popular science*, LVII (Oct., 1900), 624–631.

—— "A. J. Stone's measurements of natives of the northwest territories," *Bulletin American museum of natural history*, vol. XIV, art. 6. New York (1901).

—— "The Eskimo of Baffin Land and Hudson Bay," *Bulletin American museum of natural history*, XV (1907).

BOGORAS, WALDEMAR. "The Chukchi of northeastern Asia," *American anthropologist*, n.s., III (1901), 80–108.

—— "The folklore of northeastern Asia, as compared with that of northwestern America," *American anthropologist*, IV (Oct.–Dec., 1902), 577–683.

—— "The Chukchee," Jesup North Pacific expedition, Bd. VII, Pt. 1, *Memoirs of the American museum of natural history*, XI (1904).

—— "The Eskimo of Siberia," Jesup North Pacific expedition, Bd. VIII, Pt. 3 (1913).

BROOKS, A. H. The geology and geography of Alaska, United States geological survey, professional paper 45, 327 pp. 1906.

BROWN, GEORGE MAXWELL. "Menstruation and its disorders," *Journ. M.S.M.S.*, January, 1924.

BROWN, ROBERT N. R. The polar regions; a physical and economic geography of the arctic and the antarctic. 1927.

BURWASH, MAJOR L. T. "Canada's western arctic," Report on investigations in 1925–26, 1928–29, and 1930. Ottawa, 1931.

BYHAN, U. Die Polarvölker. 1909.

CADZOW, D. A. "Native copper objects of the Copper Eskimo," Indian notes and monographs, museum of the American Indian, Heye foundation. 1920.

—— "Clean and honest Eskimos," *Scientific American,* CXL, 105–107 (Feb., 1929).

CAMERON, JOHN. "Osteology of the western and central Eskimos," *Report of the Canadian arctic expedition,* 1913–18, XII (1923), Pt. C.

—— "The nasal (nasion-akanthion) height as a criterion of race" (Craniometric studies, No. 25). "A study of the width of the nasal aperture of the skull in representative types of modern man" (Craniometric studies, No. 26). "A study of the nasal index in representative types of man" (Craniometric studies, No. 27); *American journal of physical anthropology,* XIV, No. 2 (Apr.–June, 1930), 273–304.

CANTWELL, J. C. Report of the cruise of the revenue marine steamer *Corwin* in the Arctic Ocean in the year 1884, by Capt. M. A. Healy, commander. Washington, 1889. Containing section entitled "Exploration of the Kowak River, Alaska. Ethnological notes," by Third Lieut. J. C. Cantwell. Washington, 1889.

CARR-SAUNDERS, A. M. The population problem. 1922.

CHIPMAN, KENNETH G., and Cox, JOHN R. "Maps and geographical notes on the arctic coast of Canada," *Report of the Canadian arctic expedition, 1913–18,* XI (1924), Pt. B.

CLARK, JANET H. "Ultraviolet light and scurvy," *Science,* Jan. 9, 1925.

CLAVERING, DOUGLAS CHARLES. "Journal of a voyage to Spitzbergen and the east coast of Greenland," *Edinburgh new philosophical journal,* IX (1830).

COATS, CAPTAIN W. The geography of Hudson's Bay: being the remarks of Captain W. Coats, in many voyages to that locality, between the years 1727 and 1751. Ed. by John Barrow. Hakluyt society, London, 1852.

COLEMAN, A. P. The northeastern part of Labrador and New Quebec. Canada, Department of mines, Memoir 124. 1921.

COMER, GEORGE. "A geographical description of Southampton island and notes on the Eskimo," *Bulletin of the American geographical society,* XLII (1910), 84–90.

Cox, JOHN R. *See* Chipman, Kenneth.

COXE, WILLIAM. Account of Russian discoveries between Asia and America. 1787.

CRANTZ, DAVID. Historie von Grönland. 1765. 3 vols.

—— The History of Greenland. 1767. 2 vols.

CZAPLICKA, M. A. Aboriginal Siberia. A study in social anthropology. Oxford, 1914.

DALAGER, LARS. Grønlandske relationer, indeholdende Grønlaendernes Liv og Levnet deres Skikke og Vedtaegter, etc. 1752.

DALL, WILLIAM HEALY. Alaska and its resources. 1870.

—— "Tribes of the extreme northwest," United States Geographical and Geological Survey, I (1877), Pt. 1, 1–156.

—— "On the remains of later prehistoric man obtained from caves in the Catherina Archipelago, Alaska territory, and especially from the caves of the Aleutian islands," Smithsonian contributions to knowledge, 1878.

—— "On masks, labrets, and certain aboriginal customs, with an inquiry into the bearing of their geographical distribution." Bureau of American ethnology, Third annual report, 1884.

DAVIS, J. The Voyages and Works of . . . Ed. by A. H. Markham. Hakluyt society, London, 1880.

DAY, P. C. Summary of the climatological data for Alaska, by sections. To 1921, incl. United States department of agriculture, weather bureau. 1921.

DENIKER, J. The races of man. London, 1900.

DUGMORE, A. A. R. The romance of the Newfoundland caribou. 1913.

EGEDE, HANS. Det gamle Grønlands nye Perlustration. 1729.

—— Det gamle Grønlands nye Perlustration eller Naturel-Historie, etc. Kiöbenhavn, 1741.

—— A Description of Greenland. Translated from the Danish, London, 1745.

—— A Description of Greenland. London, 1818. 2d. ed.

EGEDE, POUL. Continuation af Relationerne betreffende den Grønlandske Missions Tilstad og Beskaffenhed. (i Form af en Journal fra Anno 1734 til 1740. Do do til 1744.) 1741a.

—— Dictionarium Grönlandico-Danico-Latinum. Hafniae, 1750.

—— Efterretninger om Grønland uddragne af en Journal holden fra 1721 til 1788. 1788.

—— Nachrichten von Grönland, aus einem Tagebuch. Kopenhagen, 1790.

EKBLAW, W. E. "Material responses of the polar Eskimo to their far arctic environment," Annals of the association of American geographers, XVIII, No. 1 (1928).

ELGSTRÖM, OSSIAN. Noderna Eskimåer. 1916.

ELLIS, HENRY. Voyage to Hudson's-Bay, by the Dobbs Galley and California, in the years 1746 and 1747, for discovering a north west passage; with an accurate survey of the coast, and a short natural history of the country, together with a fair view of the facts and arguments from which the future finding of such a passage is rendered probable. London, 1748.

ELLIS, JOHN. Reise nach Hudsons Meerbusen. 1750.

ENCYCLOPAEDIA BRITANNICA. 1910. 11th ed.

—— 1929. 14th ed.

FABRICIUS, O. "Nøiagtig Beskrivelse over Grønlaendernes Landdyr-, Fugle- og Fiskefangst med dertil . . .," Det Kgl. danske Videnskabernes-Selskabs Skrivter, VI (1818), 181.

FAUSBØLL, V. "Indian mythology according to the Mahābhārata." Luzac's oriental religions series.

FEILDEN, H. W. "Distribution of the muskox in Greenland," Zoologist, ser. 3, XIX (Feb., 1895).

FRANKLIN, SIR JOHN. Narrative of a second expedition to the shores of the polar sea in the years 1825, 1826, and 1827. 1828.

FRAZER, J. G. The Golden Bough. 2 vol. ed., 1922.

FREUCHEN, P. and MATHIASSEN, TH. "Contributions to the physical geography of the regions north of Hudson bay," Geographical review, XV (Oct., 1925), 549–561.

FRIES, T. M. Grönland dess Natur och Innevanåre. 1872.

FROBISHER, M. The three voyages of Martin Frobisher in search of a passage to Cathia and India by the north west, 1576–78. Ed. by R. Collinson. Hakluyt society, London, 1867.

FUNCH, J. C. W. Syv Aar i Nord Grønland. German ed., 1840.

GILDER, WILLIAM H. Schwatka's Search. Sledging in the Arctic in quest of the Franklin records, 1878–80. 1881.

GLAHN, H. C. Anmaerkninger over de tre første Boger af Hr. David Crantzes Historie om Grønland. 1771.

—— "Om Grønlaendernes Skikke ved Hvalfiskeriet." Norske Videnskabernes Selskabs Skrivter. 1784.

—— Glahn's diaries. 1924.

GREELY, ADOLPHUS W. Three years of arctic service. New York, 1886.

GREENLAND. A compilation of various authors, published by a commission for the purpose. 1928.

HALL, CHARLES FRANCIS. Life with the Esquimaux. . . . 1864.

—— Arctic researches and life among the Esquimaux: being the narrative of an expedition in search of Sir John Franklin, in the years 1860, 1861, and 1862. New York, 1865.

—— Arctic researches, and life among the Esquimaux. . . . 1860, 61, 62. 1866.

—— Narrative of the second arctic expedition made by Charles F. Hall. Ed. by J. E. Nourse. Senate documents, 45th Cong., 3d sess. Washington, 1879.

—— Narrative of the second arctic expedition made by Charles F.

Hall: his voyage to Repulse bay, sledge journey to the straits of Fury and Hecla and to King William's land, and residence among the Eskimos during the years 1864–69.

HANBURY, D. T. "Through the barren ground of northeast Canada to the Arctic coast," *Geographical journal*, XXII (1903), 178–191.

—— Sport and travel in the northland of Canada. 1904.

HANDBOOK OF AMERICAN INDIANS. Bulletin 30 of the bureau of American ethnology. Ed. by Frederick W. Hodge. Washington, 1907. 2 vols.

HANSEN, JOHANNES (HANSÊRAK). "List of the inhabitants of the east coast of Greenland," *Meddelelser om Grønland*, XXXIX (1914a), 181–202.

HANSEN, SØREN (joint author: HOLM, G.) "Contributions to the anthropology of East Greenland," *Meddelelser om Grønland*, XXXIX (1914), 149–189.

HANTZSCH, BERNHARD. "Eskimo stone graves in north-eastern Labrador and the collection of anthropological material from them," tr. by M. B. A. Anderson, *Canadian field-naturalist*, XLIV (Nov., 1930).

—— "Contributions to the knowledge of extreme north-eastern Labrador," tr. by M. B. A. Anderson, *Canadian field-naturalist*, XLV (Apr., 1931).

HARRINGTON, GEORGE L. Mineral resources of Goodnews Bay region, Alaska. United States geological survey, Bulletin 714, 207–228. 1919.

HARRISON, ALFRED H. In Search of a Polar Continent, 1905–1907. London, 1908.

HATT, GUDMUND. "Moccasins and their relation to arctic footwear," *Memoirs of American anthropol. association*, vol. III, No. 3 (1916).

—— "Notes on reindeer nomadism," *Memoirs of American anthropol. association*, vol. VI, No. 2 (1919).

HAWKES, ERNEST W. The "inviting-in" feast of the Alaskan Eskimo. 1913.

—— The Labrador Eskimo. Memoir 91 of the Geological survey of Canada, Anthropological series No. 14. Ottawa, 1916.

HAYES, ISAAC I. The Open Polar Sea. A narrative of the voyage toward the pole in the *United States,* 1860–61. 1867.

—— An arctic boat journey in the autumn of 1854. Boston, 1867a.

HEALY, M. A. Report of the cruise of the revenue marine steamer *Corwin* in the Arctic ocean in the year 1885. 1887.

HEINBECKER, PETER, and IRVINE-JONES, EDITH M. "Susceptibility of the Eskimos to the common cold and a study of their natural immunity to diphtheria, scarlet fever and bacterial filtrates," *Journal of immunology*, XV, No. 5 (Sept., 1928).

HEINBECKER, PETER. "Studies on the metabolism of Eskimos," *Journal of biological chemistry*, LXXX, No. 2 (Dec., 1928).

—— and PAULI, RUTH H. "Blood groupings of Baffin Island Eskimos," *Journal of immunology*, XV, No. 5 (Sept., 1928).

HESS, ALFRED F. Scurvy, past and present. 1920.

HOARE, W. H. B. Conserving Canada's musk-oxen. Department of the interior, Canada, Northwest territories and Yukon branch. Ottawa, 1930.

HOFFMAN, W. J. "The Graphic Art of the Eskimo," Annual report of the United States national museum, 1895, 739–968. Washington, 1897.

HOLM, G. "Bidrag til Kendskabet om Eskimoernes Herkomst," *Geografisk Tidsskrift*, 1886.

—— "Ethnologisk Skizze af Angmagsalikerne," *Meddelelser om Grønland*, 1887.

—— and GARDE, T. V. Den danske Konebaads-Expedition til Grønlands Østkyst. Kbhavn., 1887.

—— "Sagn og Fortaellinger fra Angmagsalik, samlede af G. Holm," *Meddelelser om Grønland*, X (F. Dreyer). Kjøbenhavn, 1888.

—— "Ethnological sketch of the Angmagssalik Eskimos," *Meddelelser om Grønland*, XXXIX (1914).

—— "Small additions to the Vinland problem," *Meddelelser om Grønland*, LIX (1924).

HOLMBERG, H. J. Ethnographische Skizzen über die Völker des russischen Amerika. 1855.

HOOPER, C. L. Report of the cruise of the United States revenue steamer *Corwin* in the Arctic ocean. Treasury document No. 118. 1881.

—— Report of the cruise of the U.S. revenue steamer *Thomas Corwin* in the Arctic ocean, 1881. Washington, 1884.

HOOPER, WILLIAM H. Ten months among the tents of the Tuski. 1848–51. London, 1853.

HOUGH, WALTER. The Lamp of the Eskimo. Report of the United States national museum. 1896.

—— "The origin and range of the Eskimo lamp," *American anthropologist*, XI (1898), 116–122.

HRDLIČKA, ALEŠ. Contributions to the anthropology of the central and Smith Sound Eskimo. Anthropological papers of the American museum of natural history, V, Pt. 2. 1910.

—— Anthropological survey of Alaska. 46th annual report, Bureau of American ethnology. Washington, 1930.

HUTCHISON, ISOBEL W. "Flowers and farming in Greenland," *Scottish geographical magazine*, XLVI, No. 4 (July 15, 1930), 214–230.

HUTTON, SAMUEL K. Among the Eskimos of Labrador. 1912.

—— Health conditions and disease incidence among the Eskimo of Labrador.

JACKSON, SHELDON. Alaska, and missions on the north Pacific coast. 1880.

—— Report on education in Alaska, with maps and illustrations (1886). United States bureau of education. 1886.

—— Report on education. 1886–88.

JACOBSEN, J. A. Reise an der Nordwestküste Amerikas, 1881–83. 1884.

JAMES, WILLIAM. Psychology. New York: Henry Holt and Company, 1910. 2 vols.

JENNESS, DIAMOND. Life of the Copper Eskimos. Report of the Canadian arctic expedition, 1913–18, XII (1922).

—— Physical characteristics of the Copper Eskimos. Report of the Canadian arctic expedition, 1913–18, XII (1923), Pt. B.

—— "The origin of the Copper Eskimos and their copper culture," Geographical review, XIII, No. 4 (Oct., 1923a), 540–551.

—— Eskimo string figures. Report of the Canadian arctic expedition, XIII (1924), Pt. B.

—— Myths and traditions from northern Alaska, the Mackenzie delta and Coronation gulf. Report of the Canadian arctic expedition, 1913–18, XIII (1924a), Pt. A.

—— "A new Eskimo culture in Hudson bay," Geographical review, XV (1925), 428–437.

—— The People of the Twilight. 1928.

—— Comparative vocabulary of the western Eskimo dialects. Report of the Canadian arctic Expedition, 1913–18, XV (1928b), Pt. A.

—— "Little Diomede island, Bering strait," Geographical review, XIX (1929), 78.

JENSEN, A. S. "The fauna of Greenland," Greenland, I (1928), 319–355.

JOCHELSON, WALDEMAR. The Koryak. Jesup North Pacific expedition, VI (1908).

—— The Aleut language and its relation to the Eskimo dialects. International congress of Americanists, 28th sess., London, 1912. London, 1913.

—— Archaeology of the Aleutian islands. Carnegie institute, Publication No. 367. 1925.

KANE, ELISHA KENT. Arctic explorations in the years 1853, 1854, 1855. The second Grinnell expedition. 1856.

KAYSER, OLAF. "The inland ice," Greenland, I (1928), 357–422.

KELLER, ALBERT GALLOWAY. Societal evolution. Yale university press, 1922.

—— See Sumner, W. G., and Keller, A. G. 1927.

KELLY, H. A. Medical gynecology. London, 1912.

KELLY, JOHN W. Bureau of education, Circular of information No. 2, 1890. English-Eskimo and Eskimo-English vocabularies. Compiled by Ensign Robert Wells, Jr., U.S.N., and Interpreter John W. Kelly. Preceded by Ethnographical memoranda concerning the arctic Eskimos in Alaska and Siberia, by John W. Kelly. Washington, 1890.

KERSTING, RUDOLPH. The white world. A compilation of various authors, ed. by Rudolph Kersting. 1902.

KITTO, F. H. The Northwest Territories. Department of the interior, Canada, Northwest territories and Yukon branch. Ottawa, 1930.

KLEINSCHMIDT, S. Den Grønlandske Ordbog. 1871.

KLUTSCHAK, HEINRICH W. Als Eskimo unter den Eskimo. 1881.

KOCH, LAUGE. "The physiography of North Greenland," *Greenland*, I (1928), 491–518.

KÖNIG, HERBERT. "Der Rechtsbruch und sein Ausgleich bie den Eskimo," *Anthropos*, XX (1925), 273–315.

—— "Das Recht der Polar Völker," *Anthropos*, XXII (Sept.–Dec., 1927), 5–6.

KRAUSE, AUREL, and ARTHUR. "Die Expedition der Bremer Geographischen Gesellschaft nach der Tschuktscher-Halbinsel," *Deutsche Geographische Blätter*, V (1882), 1–35, 111–133.

KROEBER, A. L. "The Eskimo of Smith Sound," *Bulletin of the American museum of natural history*, XII (1899).

—— "Tales of the Smith Sound Eskimos," *Journal of American folklore*, XII (Cambridge, 1899a), 166–182.

—— Anthropology. New York: Harcourt, Brace & Co., 1923.

—— and WATERMAN, Y. Y. Source book in anthropology, pp. 430–436. New York, 1931. An extract of Thalbitzer's "The heathen priests of East Greenland," from *Verhandlungen des XVI Amerikanisten-Kongresses, Wien, 1908*, pp. 447–464. 1910.

KROGH, A., and M. "The dietary habits of the Eskimos of South Greenland," *Meddelelser om Grønland*, LI (1915).

KRUUSE, C. "Angmagsalikerne," *Geografisk Tidsskrift*, XVI (1902).

—— "Rejser og botaniske Undersøgelser i øst-Grønland mellem 65° 30′ og 67°20′ (1898–1902) samt Angmagsalik-Egnens Vegetation," *Meddelelser om Grønland*, XLIX (1912).

KUMLIEN, L. Contributions to the natural history of arctic America. The Howgate Expedition, 1877–78. Bulletin No. 15 of the United States national museum. 1879.

LEDEN, CHRISTIAN. Uber Kiwatins Eisfelder; drei Jahre unter kanadischen Eskimos. 1927.

LEFFINGWELL, E. DE K. The Canning River region, Northern Alaska. United States geological survey, Professional paper 109. 1919.

Letourneau, Ch. Property: its origin and development. New York, 1892.

Lewis, Rev. Arthur. The life and work of the Rev. E. J. Peck among the Eskimos. New York, 1904.

Light, William. The last voyage of Captn. Sir John Ross, R.N., for the discovery of a north west passage, performed in the years 1829–30–31–32–33. From the original documents transmitted by William Light, purser's steward to the expedition. London, 1835.

Lindow, H. "Blandt Eskimoerne i Labrador," Grønl. Selsk. Aarsskr., 1923–24. 1924.

Low, A. P. Report on the explorations in the Labrador peninsula. Annual report of the geological survey of Canada, VIII (1895).

—— Report on the Dominion government expedition to Hudson bay and the arctic islands on board the D.G.S. Neptune, 1903–04, by A. P. Low, officer in charge. 1906.

Lyon, George Fr. The private journal of Captain G. F. Lyon of H.M.S. Hecla, during the recent voyage of discovery under Captain Parry. London, 1824. Also Boston, 1824.

Lytzen, C. "Grönlandske Sagn," Fra alle Lande, Bd. XIX. Köbh., 1874.

MacAdam, George. "Where white men travel alone and few return to tell the story," World's work, LVI, No. 4 (August, 1928), 417–425.

M'Clintock, F. L. The voyage of the Fox in the arctic seas. A narrative of the discovery of the fate of Sir John Franklin and his companions. London, 1859.

MacKeevor, Thomas. A voyage to Hudson's bay, during the summer of 1812. 1819.

MacMillan, Donald B. Four years in the white north. 1918.

—— Etah and beyond. Boston, 1927.

Markham, C. R. "The arctic highlanders," Transactions ethn. soc., n.s., IV (1866), 125–137.

Mathiassen, Th., and Freuchen, P. "Contributions to the physical geography of the regions north of Hudson bay," Geographical review, XV (Oct., 1925), 549–561.

Mathiassen, Therkel. Archaeology of the central Eskimos. Report of the fifth Thule expedition, IV (1927). 2 vols.

—— Material culture of the Iglulik Eskimos. Report of the fifth Thule expedition, 1921–24, VI, No. 1 (1928).

Mauss, M., and Beuchat, M. H. "Essai sur les variations saisonnières des sociétés Eskimos," Étude de morphologie sociale, l'Année sociologique, 9me année, (1904–5).

Mecking, Ludwig (joint author: Nordenskjöld, Otto). The geography of the polar regions. American geographical society, No. 8 (1928).

MEDDELELSER OM GRØNLAND. (Abbreviated M.o.G.) Kommissionen for
   Ledelsen af de geologiske og geografiske Udersøgelser i Gronland.
MERRIL, G. P. "Jade: supposed crude jade from Alaska," *Science*, V
   (1885), 209.
MIKKELSEN, EJNAR. Conquering the arctic ice. Philadelphia, n.d.
—— Lost in the arctic. New York, 1913.
MILLWARD, A. E., B.Com., B.A. Southern Baffin island. An account of
   exploration, investigation, and settlement during the past fifty years;
   with an appendix: "The crossing of Baffin island to Foxe basin by
   Bernhard A. Hantzsch in 1910." Collated and edited by A. E. Mill-
   ward. Appendix translated by M. B. A. Anderson. 1930.
MOLTKE, H. (joint author: MYLIUS-ERICHSEN, L.) *Grønland*. 1906.
MOONEY, J. Myths of the Cherokee. Bureau of American ethnology,
   19th annual report (1900), 3–548.
MOORE, RILEY. "Social life of the Eskimos of St. Lawrence island,"
   American anthropologist, n.s., XXV, No. 3 (July–Sept., 1923), 339–
   375.
MUIR, JOHN. The cruise of the *Corwin*. Expedition of 1881 in search
   of De Long and the *Jeanette*. 279 pp. 1917.
MUNN, H. T. "The Eskimo of arctic Canada," *Geographical journal*,
   May, 1926.
MURDOCH, JOHN. International polar expeditions, 1882–3. 1885.
—— The Point Barrow expedition. Ethnological results of the Point
   Barrow expedition. Bureau of American ethnology, 9th annual re-
   port. Washington, 1892.
MUTCH, J. S. Whaling in Ponds Bay. Boas anniversary volume. New
   York, 1906.
MYLIUS-ERICHSEN, L. (joint author: MOLTKE, H.) *Grønland*. 1906.
NANSEN, FR. The first crossing of Greenland. London, 1890.
—— Eskimo life. 1893.
—— In northern mists. London and New York, 1911.
—— Hunting and adventure in the arctic. 1925.
NATHORST, A. G. Två-Somrar i Norra Ishafvet. Stockholm, 1900.
NATURAL RESOURCES. A periodical. Canada.
NELSON, E. W. The Eskimo about Bering strait. Bureau of American
   ethnology, 18th annual report. Washington, 1899.
NORDENSKJÖLD, ADOLF E. Vega's färd kring Asien och Europa. Stock-
   holm, 1880–81. 2 vols.
—— The voyage of the *Vega* round Asia and Europe. Trans. by Alex-
   ander Leslie. London, 1881. 2 vols.
NORDENSKJÖLD, OTTO (joint author: MECKING, LUDWIG). The geogra-
   phy of the polar regions. American geographical society, No. 8
   (1928).
NOVAKOVSKY, STANISLAUS. "Arctic or Siberian hysteria as a reflex of

the geographical environment," *Ecology*, V, No. 2 (Apr., 1924), 113–127.

O'Neill, J. J. The geology of the arctic coast of Canada, west of Kent peninsula. Report of the Canadian arctic expedition, 1913–18, XI (1924), Pt. A.

Osborn, Capt. Sherard. Remarks upon the amount of light experienced in high northern latitudes during the absence of the sun. Read before the Royal geographical society of London, June 14, 1858.

Ostenfeld, C. H. "The flora of Greenland," *Greenland*, I (1928), 277–290.

Packard, Alpheus Spring. The Labrador coast, a journal of two summer cruises to that region. With notes on its early discovery, on the Eskimo, on its physical geography, geology, and natural history. New York, 1891.

Parry, Capt. William Edward. Journal of a voyage for the discovery of a north-west passage, 1819–20. London, 1821.

—— Journal of a second voyage for the discovery of a north west passage from the Atlantic to the Pacific; performed in the years 1821–'22–'23, in His Majesty's ships *Fury* and *Hecla*. London, 1824.

Peary, Josephine Diebitsch. My arctic journal. New York, 1893.

—— The snow baby, a true story with true pictures. New York, 1901.

Peary, R. E. Northward over the "great ice." 1898.

Petersen, Helge. "The Climate of Greenland," *Greenland*, I (1928), 257–276.

Petitot, Emile. "Vocabulaire Français-Esquimaux, dialecte des Tchiglit des bouches du Mackenzie et de l'Anderson, précédé d'une monographie de cette tribu et de notes grammaticales," Pinart's *Bibliothèque de linguistique et d'ethnographie Américaines*, III (1876).

—— Traditions indiennes du Canada nordouest. Paris, 1886.

—— Les grands Esquimaux. Paris, 1887.

Petroff, Ivan. Alaska: its population, industries, and resources. Tenth census of the United States, VIII (1884).

—— Compilation of narratives of explorers in Alaska. Reprint of Petroff's report in the Tenth census of the United States, VIII (1900).

Phillips, Sir R. Voyage of discovery in the South seas, and to Behring straits, in search of a north east passage, 1815, 1816, 1817, and 1818. 1819.

Pittard, Eugène. "Contribution à l'étude anthropologique des Esquimaux du Labrador et de la baie d'Hudson," *Bulletin de la Société Neuchateloise de géographie*, XIII, 158–176. Neuchâtel, 1901.

Ploss, Heinrich (joint authors: Bartels, Max and Paul). Das Weib in der Natur- und Völkerkunde. 1927. 3 vols.

Poincy, Louis de. Histoire naturelle et morale des Îles Antilles de l'Amérique. Rotterdam, 1658.

PORSILD, M. P. "Studies on the material culture of the Eskimos in West Greenland," *Meddelelser om Grønland,* LI (1915).

—— "On 'Savssats': a crowding of arctic animals at holes in the sea ice," *Geographical review,* VI (1918).

RAE, JOHN. Narrative of an expedition to the shores of the Arctic sea in 1846 and 1847. London, 1850.

RASMUSSEN, KNUD. The people of the polar north. 1908.

—— Grønland langs Polhavet. København, 1919.

—— Greenland by the polar sea. 1921.

—— Fra Grønland til Stille havet. Bd. I–II. København, 1925–26.

—— Across arctic America. 1927.

—— Intellectual culture of the Iglulik Eskimos. Report of the fifth Thule expedition, 1921–24, VII, No. 1 (1929).

RATZEL, FRIEDERICH. Anthropo-geographie. Stuttgart, 1882–91. 2 bde.

—— The history of mankind. Trans. from the 2d German ed. by J. Butler. London and New York: Macmillan & Co., 1896–98.

RAY, P. H. Report of the international polar expedition to Point Barrow, Alaska. Washington, 1885.

—— In Compilation of narratives of explorers in Alaska. 1900. (See Petroff.)

RICHARDSON, SIR JOHN. Arctic searching expedition: a journal of a boat-voyage through Rupert's land and the Arctic sea. London, 1851.

—— "Eskimos, their geographical distribution," *Edinburgh new philosophical journal,* LII (1852), 322–323.

—— The polar regions. Edinburgh, 1861.

RICHET, E. Les Eskimaux de l'Alaska. Bulletin Soc. R. Géogr. d'Anvers. Tomes XLI–XLIII. Anvers, 1921–23.

RINK, H. Om Aarsagen til Grønlaendernes og lignende, af Jagt levende, Nationers materielle Tilbagegang ved Berøringen med Europaeerne. Dansk Maanedsskrift. 1862.

—— Om Grønlaendernes gamle Tro og hvad der af samme er bevaret under Kristendommen. Aarbøger for nordisk oldkyndighed og Historie. Copenhagen, 1868.

—— Eskimoiske Eventyr og Sagn med Supplement Indeholdenende et Tillaeg om Eskimoerne, Deres Kulturtrin og Ovrige Eiendommeligheder Samt Formodede Herkomst 1866, 1871. København, 1871.

—— Tales and traditions of the Eskimo. London, 1875.

—— Danish Greenland, its people and its products. London, 1877.

—— "The Eskimo tribes." Their distribution and characteristics, especially in regard to language; with a comparative vocabulary. *Meddelelser om Grønland,* XI (1887).

RITCHIE, S. G. (joint author: BAGNALL, J. STANLEY) The dentition of the western and central Eskimos. Report of the Canadian arctic expedition, 1913–18, XII, Pt. C (1923).

Ross, John. A voyage of discovery, made under the orders of the admiralty in His Majesty's ships *Isabella* and *Alexander,* for the purpose of exploring Baffin's bay, and inquiring into the probability of a northwest passage. London, 1819.

—— Narrative of a second voyage in search of a northwest passage, and of a residence in the arctic regions during the years 1829,–30,–31,–32,–33. London, 1835. (Also Paris, 1835, and Philadelphia, 1835.)

Ruttel, F. C. P. Ti Aar blandt østgrønlands Hedninger. Copenhagen and Christiania, 1816.

Saabye, Hans Egede. Brudstykker af en Dagbog, holden i Grønland 1770–'78. Odense, 1816.

—— Greenland: being extracts from a journal kept in that country in the years 1770–1778. Trans. from the German. New York: A. S. Boosey & Sons; London, 1818.

Sarychev, G. *See* Sarytschew, G., 1806–7.

Sarytschew, G. Account of a voyage of discovery to the northeast of Siberia, the frozen ocean and the northeast sea. Trans. from the Russian. 1806–7.

Sauer, Martin. An account of the geographical and astronomical expedition to the northern part of Russia. . . . Performed by Captain Billings in the years 1785–94. Publ. 1802.

Schultz-Lorentzen, C. W. "Intellectual culture of the Greenlanders," *Greenland,* II (1928), 209–270.

Schwatka, Frederick. "The Netschilluk Innuit," *Science,* IV, 543–545. New York, 1884.

—— Nimrod in the north. Hunting and fishing adventures in the arctic regions. New York, 1885.

—— Along Alaska's great river . . . 1883. 1885*a.*

—— In Compilation of narratives of explorers in Alaska. U.S. Cong. Senate. Committee on military affairs. 1900. (See Petroff.)

Seemann, Berthold. Narrative of the voyage of H.M.S. *Herald* during the years 1845–51. London, 1853.

Shapiro, H. A. The Alaskan Eskimo. A study of the relationship between the Eskimo and the Chipewyan Indians of Central Canada. Anthropological papers of the American museum of natural history, Vol. XXXI, Pt. VI (1931).

Simpson, J. Observations on the western Eskimo and the country they inhabit. . . . London, 1855. Reprinted in Further papers relative to the recent arctic expeditions. 1875.

Simpson, T. Narrative of the discoveries on the north coast of America effected by the officers of the Hudson's bay company during the years 1836–39. 1843.

SMITH, HARLAN I. "Notes on Eskimo traditions," *Journal of American folklore,* VII (1894), 209–216.

SMITH, MIDDLETON. In The white world, ed. by Kersting, Rudolph, pp. 113–130. 1902.

SMITH, RUSSEL GORDON. Fugitive papers. New York: Columbia university press, 1930.

STEENSBY, H. P. Om Eskimokulturens Oprindelse. 1905.

—— "Contributions to the ethnology and anthropo-geography of the polar Eskimos," *Meddelelser om Grønland,* XXXIV (1910).

—— "An anthropogeographical study of the origin of the Eskimo culture," *Meddelelser om Grønland,* LIII (1917).

STEFANSSON, V. "Notes on the theory and treatment of disease among the Mackenzie river Eskimo," *Journal of American folklore,* XXL (1908), 43–45.

—— My life with the Eskimos. 1913.

—— "On Christianizing the Eskimos," *Harper's magazine,* Oct., 1913*a,* 672–682.

—— The Stefansson-Anderson arctic expedition of the American museum: preliminary ethnological report. Anthropological papers of the American museum of natural history, XIV, Pt. 1 (1914).

—— "Original observations on scurvy and my opinion of the medical profession," *Med. Rev. of Rev.,* XXIV, 257–264. New York, 1918.

—— "Temperature as a factor in determining the age of maturity among Eskimos," *Journal of the American medical association.* Sept. 4, 1920.

—— The friendly arctic. 1921.

—— "Some erroneous ideas of arctic geography," *Geographical review,* XII, 264–277. Apr., 1922.

—— "Savages are pleasant people," *Redbook magazine.* Mar., 1930.

STEIN, ROBT. "Geographische Nomenklatur bie den Eskimos des Smith-Sundes," *Petermann's Mittheilungen,* XLVIII (1902).

STORGAARD, EINAR. "The physiography of East Greenland," *Greenland,* I (1928), 519–575.

SUMNER, W. G., and KELLER, A. G. The science of society. Vols. I, II, III. Yale university press, 1927.

—— and DAVIE, M. The science of society. Vol. IV (casebook). Yale university press, 1927.

TARR. "Rapidity of weathering and stream erosion in the arctic latitudes," *American geologist,* XIX (1897), 2, 131–136.

THALBITZER, WILLIAM. "The heathen priests of East Greenland," *Verhandlungen des XVI Internationalen Amerikanisten-Kongresses, Wien, 1908,* pp. 447–464. 1910. An extract of this work is contained in Kroeber and Waterman, pp. 430–436. 1931.

—— Grønlandske Sagn om Eskimoernes fortid. Stockholm, 1913.

—— Four Skraeling words from Markland (Newfoundland) in the saga of Erik the Red. Bulletin, 18th Congress of Americanists. London (1912), 1913a.

—— "The Ammassalik Eskimo," Substantially a translation of Ethnologisk Skizze af Angmagsalikerne. *Meddelelser om Grønland,* XXXIX. Copenhagen, 1914.

—— "The Ammassalik Eskimo." Contributions to the ethnology of the East Greenland natives. Pt. II, *Meddelelser om Grønland,* Vol. XL. Copenhagen, 1923.

—— "The Aleutian language compared with Greenlandic," *International journal of American linguistics* (ed. F. Boas), Vol. II. New York, 1923a.

—— Parallels within the culture of the arctic peoples. XX Congresso internacional de Americanistas, pp. 283–287. Rio de Janeiro, 1924.

—— Cultic games and festivals in Greenland. XXI Congress of Americanists. Göteborg (1924), 1925.

—— "Die Kultischen Gottheiten der Eskimos," *Archiv für Religionswissenschaft,* XXVI (1928), 364–430.

—— Cultic deities of the Inuit (Eskimo). XXII Congress of Americanists, II, 367–391. Rome, 1928a.

THOMPSON, ARTHUR, and BUXTON, L. H. DUDLEY. "Man's nasal index in relation to certain climatic conditions," *Journal of the royal anthropological institute,* LIII (1923), 92–122.

TOCHER, J. F. "Notes on some measurements of Eskimo of Southampton island," *Man,* II, No. 115. London, 1902.

TOLENTINO, MARIANO. "A study of menstruation in young girls," *Journ. P.I.M.A.,* VII, No. 10 (Oct., 1927).

TREBITSCH, R. Bei den Eskimos in Westgrönland. Berlin, 1910.

TURNER, LUCIEN M. "On the Indians and Eskimos of the Ungava district, Labrador," *Transactions of the Royal society of Canada,* V, sec. 2 (1887), 99–119.

—— "The physical and zoological character of the Ungava district, Labrador," *Transactions of the Royal society of Canada,* V, sec. 4 (1887a), 79–83.

—— Ethnology of the Ungava district, Hudson bay territory. Bureau of American ethnology, 11th annual report, 1889–90. 1894.

TURQUETIL, A. "Notes sur les Esquimaux de Baie Hudson," *Anthropos,* XXI (1926), 419–434.

—— "The religion of the Central Eskimo," *Primitive man,* 1929, pp. 2, 57–64.

TYLOR, E. B. Primitive culture. London, 1903.

UNITED STATES CENSUS. Tenth report, 1884. *See* Petroff, 1884.

—— Fourteenth report. 1920.

VIRCHOW, R. "Eskimos von Labrador," *Zeitschrift für Ethnologie,* XII, 253–274. Berlin, 1880.

WALDMANN. "Les Esquimaux du Nord du Labrador," *Bulletin de la Société Neuchateloise de géographie,* Tome XX (1909–10).

WALLACE, D. The long Labrador trail. New York, 1907.

WARDLE, H. NEWELL. "The Sedna cycle: a study in myth evolution," *American anthropologist,* n.s., II (1900), 568.

WARMOW. (His journal.) Missionsblatt aus der Brüdergemeinde. 1859.

WELLS, R., and KELLY, J. W. Eskimo vocabularies. United States bureau of education. Washington, 1890.

WESTERMARCK, EDWARD. The origin and development of the moral ideas. London: Macmillan & Co., Ltd., 1906. 2 vols.

WEYER, EDWARD MOFFAT, JR. An Aleutian burial. Anthropological papers of the American museum of natural history, XXXI, Pt. 3 (1929), 219–237.

—— Archaeological material from the village site at Hot Springs, Port Möller, Alaska. Anthropological papers of the American museum of natural history, XXXI, Pt. 4 (1930), 239–279.

WISSLER, CLARK. Harpoons and darts in the Stefansson collection. Anthropological papers of the American museum of natural history, XIV, Pt. 2 (1916).

—— Archaeology of the polar Eskimo. Anthropological papers of the American museum of natural history, XXII, Pt. 3 (1918).

—— "The lore of the demon mask," *Natural history,* XXVIII, No. 4 (1928), 339–352.

WUNDT, WILHELM. Elements of folk psychology. (Trans. by E. L. Schaub) 1916.

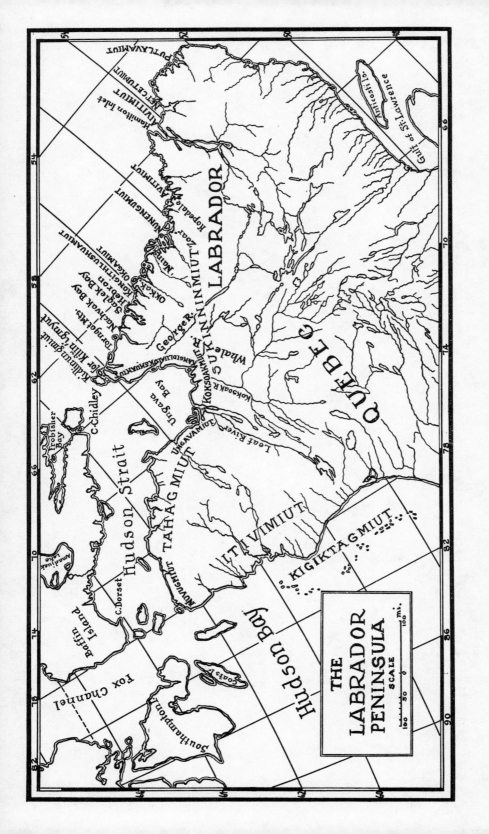

THE
LABRADOR
PENINSULA

SCALE   mi.
100 50   0   100

INDEX

Abortion, 132

Adoption, 133, 145 f., 208, 325

Adultery, 230 ff.

Amaut, Babies carried in, 67 ff.

Amputation, 329

Amulets, 194, 234, 302, 307 ff., 309, 314, 316 ff.

Amulet straps, 316

Angakok (medicine man), demonstrations and tricks of, 437, 439; duties of, 422 ff.; hazards of the profession of, 451 ff.; his *aperqit,* 426; his fees, 430; his grindstone, 430; his *inersuak,* 436; his journeys, 251, to Asiaq, 392, to the Moon, 381, to Sedna, 356 ff., 359, 361, to Sila, 391; his *tupilek,* 427, 443; initiation of, 310, 317, 438; language of, 414, 426, 435 ff.; origin of term, 445; prestige of, 451 ff., 460; psychology of, 421; séances of, 441, 461; sincerity of, 462, 463; technique of, as healer, 321 ff., 327, 433; training of, 429 ff.; trances or spirit flights of, 359, 437, 445; in various tribes, 212 ff., 226, 230, 236 ff., 258 ff.; women as angakoks, 421

Animal life, *see* Fauna

Animals slain, 302; given a drink, 334 ff.; treatment of, 334, 336

Animism, 289 ff.

Aperqit (spirit messenger or oracle), 426

Asiaq (rain spirit), 392

"Asking" Festival, 197; "asking stick," 343

Association units, 141, 203 ff., 217; varies with the seasons, 207

Atonement for breaking taboos, 325

Aurora borealis, 239, 252, 392

Authority, 208

Awl, 411

Babies, method of carrying, 67 ff.

Bags, tongued, 164

Baleen, 70, 71, 73, 166

"Barren Grounds," 12, 89, 90

Barter, 156–160, 166 ff.

Bear, *see* Polar bear

Beluga, *see* White whale

Berries, 53, 54, 57, 85, 116

Bird catching, 73, 85

Birds, 28, 30, 73

Birth rate, 124 ff.; seasonal, 127; West Greenland, 125 ff.

Black magic, *see* Sorcery

Bladder-buoy, 179; -dart, 179, 181

Bladder Festival, 140, 319, 340 ff., 342

Bleeding, 324

Block and tackle, 68

Blood revenge, 219 ff.; tribal, 154 f., 161 f.

"Bloody knife" method of killing wolves, 73

Blubber, as fuel, 102, 116

Boats, 87; ownership of, 210. *See* Kayak

Bodily adjustment to life-conditions, 47 ff.

Bone, 71

Breastplates, 156

Breathing holes of seals, 31, 100, 112, 175

Burial, alive, 255; binding corpse, 260, 268; disposal of body, 263; grave escort, 278; preparation for burial, 257; rites of, 258. *See also* Grave

Caching places, 184

Calendar, 86

Cannibalism, 117 ff.; antiquity of, 122; aversion to, 120; ceremonial, 119, 229, 310, 452

Caplin, 116

Captives, 208

Caribou, 38 ff., 85, 86, 90, 143, 182; white, 336

Casting out evil spirits, 254

Cat's cradles, *see* Games

Cephalic index, 4, 8 f.

Chieftainship, 156, 209 ff.

Childbearing, age of, 51, 375; out of wedlock, 139

Children, adoption of, 133, 145; affection toward, 132; communalism in, 145; discrimination against female, 133 ff.; preponderance of males, 134 ff.; treatment of, 135

Civilization, influence of on Eskimos, 5